90571

General Aviation
Marketing
and
Management

Second Edition

General Aviation Marketing and Management

Second Edition

by

Alexander T. Wells, Ed.D.

and

Bruce D. Chadbourne, Ed.D.

Embry-Riddle Aeronautical University

KRIEGER PUBLISHING COMPANY
MALABAR, FLORIDA
2003

Original Edition 1994
Second Edition 2003
Based on General Aviation Marketing

Printed and Published by
KRIEGER PUBLISHING COMPANY
KRIEGER DRIVE
MALABAR, FLORIDA, 32950

Library of Congress Cataloging-In-Publication Data

Wells, Alexander T.
    General aviation marketing and management / by Alexander T. Wells
and Bruce D. Chadbourne. — 2nd ed.
        p.   cm.
    Includes bibliographical references and index.
    ISBN 1-57524-192-7 (hc : alk. paper)
    1. Airplanes — Marketing.   2. Aircraft industry — Management.
  I. Chadbourne, Bruce D.   II. Title
  HD9711.A2 W45   2002
  629.133′340422′0688 — dc20   2002022838

10   9   8   7   6   5   4   3   2

*To our students
past and present
who have been
our inspiration*

Contents

Preface

It has been an exciting time to prepare the second edition of *General Aviation Marketing and Management*. The General Aviation Revitalization Act of 1994 reversed the downward spiral of general aviation and set the stage for the industry's remarkable resurgence. Unit shipments and billings of general aviation aircraft recorded their seventh consecutive year of increase in 2001. Industry-wide programs designed to attract new pilots to general aviation have resulted in growth in the pilot population that had been declining for years. The total number of corporate flight departments continues to increase along with fractional ownership programs that represent a significant factor in the growth of the general aviation industry. Another positive trend has been the decline in general aviation accidents.

Unfortunately, the unprecedented growth and exuberance in the industry during the late 1990s was somewhat abated during the early 2000s when the overheated economy began to slow down and then was further jolted into a downturn by the tragedy of September 11, 2001.

However, most analysts felt that the economy was long overdue for a correction and the positive trends in the general aviation industry would continue once the economy began to turn upward.

The text has been critically reviewed, updated, and revised where appropriate. Clear and interesting communication has been a priority—as it was in the first edition. Smooth structure and flow of the material, coupled with careful explanations and a focus on the principles, continue to be our major objective. Statistics appearing in tables and charts have been drawn from accessible sources, such as GAMA Statistical Databook, GAMA Annual Industry Review, NBAA Business Aviation Factbook, FAA Statistical Handbook, and FAA Aerospace Forecasts.

Students are encouraged to explore and keep abreast of current periodicals such as *Aviation Week and Space Technology, Aviation International News, Business and Commercial Aviation, Flight International, HAI Helicopter Annual, Professional Pilot,* and *Rotor and Wing.*

It is anticipated that professors will supplement the basic material covered with current applications drawn from their own experiences and timely articles and reports.

The text retains its major objective: to enable a student with little or no background in general aviation marketing and management to proceed through the material in a step-by-step manner beginning with a historical perspective and scope of the industry and followed by the management, financial planning, and marketing processes applied to general aviation.

Students should find the book readable and understandable. The approach taken is practical; it emphasizes the application of management, financial, and marketing knowledge through the many illustrations, exercises, and appendixes so that the reader will gain a useful understanding of the subject.

MAJOR CHANGES IN THE SECOND EDITION

The theory and practice of general aviation marketing and management are dynamic, and as new developments occur, they should be incorporated into a textbook such as this one. Also, we are constantly on the lookout for ways to improve the book in terms of clarity and understanding. As a result, we have made several important changes in this edition, including the following:

1. All tables, figures, statistics, key terms, review questions, and study guide have been updated.
2. Chapter 1 includes a historical perspective that has been thoroughly reviewed and updated through the year 2000. New sections have been added, including factors causing the decline in GA sales from the late 1970s through the mid-1990s. Major initiatives taken by government and the GA industry that revitalized the industry during the 1990s are thoroughly discussed.
3. The uses of general aircraft covered in Chapter 2 have been rewritten and greatly expanded, with a new section on the economic role of general aviation airports. A complete listing of over 500 general aviation websites has been added to this edition.
4. The opening part of Chapter 3 describing FBO services has been rewritten to clarify the multifaceted role played by this important segment of general aviation.
5. A new section has been added to the financial planning and control chapter entitled "Determining the Value of an Aviation Business."
6. Portions of Chapter 6 covering the role of marketing have been rewritten and enlarged upon to clarify the readability.
7. Chapters 8 and 9 have been completely rewritten, expanding upon existing sections and introducing new examples into the transportation needs assessment and costs/benefits analysis.
8. Chapter 10 has been expanded with revised sections encompassing company-owned aircraft operated by management companies and fractional ownership programs.
9. Prospecting, the first step in the sales process, has been removed from Chapter 7, which now focuses entirely on marketing research, and added to Chapter 11, which covers promotion and sales.

The aim of all this revising, refining, editing, and illustrating was to make sure that each student really does get a good feel for *General Aviation Marketing and Management.* General aviation marketing and management is an important and fascinating career field. We hope that every student who reads the text and trade publications will share our enthusiasm for the field.

LEARNING TOOLS

This text employs a number of features that are designed to facilitate student learning. The main ones are:

1. *Chapter outlines.* Each chapter opens with an outline of the major topics to be covered.
2. *Chapter objectives.* After the outline, each chapter includes a list of objectives that the student should be able to accomplish upon completing the chapter.
3. *Relevance.* Most of the examples, applications, and extensions of the basic material are drawn from and apply to the environment of general aviation at the turn of century.
4. *Staying power.* The text is designed to have staying power over the years. It emphasizes the structure of the industry, marketing and management functions that will not change appreciably over time. It is recognized that professors will supplement the material covered with current applications based on their own experiences and from articles appearing in the aviation trade publications.
5. *Logical organization and frequent headings.* The material covered here has been put in a systematic framework so that students know where they have been, where they are, and where they are going in the text.
6. *Key terms.* Each chapter concludes with a list of key terms used in the text.
7. *Review questions.* Review questions at the end of each chapter cover all of the important points.
8. *Appendixes.* Four appendixes present objective self-test questions, a sample aircraft marketing proposal, case studies and a sample training program.

9. *Complete index.* The book includes a complete index to help the student find needed information.

ORGANIZATION OF THE TEXT

The following is an outline of *General Aviation Marketing and Management.*

PART ONE INTRODUCTION

Chapter 1   General Aviation: A Historical Perspective. Chapter 1 provides a historical sketch of the general aviation industry from its early roots in the barnstorming period of the 1920s to the tremendous growth years of the 1960s and the period of retrenchment starting in the early 1980s. The factors causing the decline in aircraft sales are thoroughly explored. Major initiatives taken by government and the GA industry that revitalized the industry during the 1990s are thoroughly discussed.

Chapter 2   The Scope of General Aviation. This chapter defines general aviation and discusses the variety of uses of general aviation aircraft including the statistics which describe the various segments of the industry. Other components of the industry including general aviation airports, pilots, FAA services to pilots, and airframe manufacturers are covered in detail. A discussion of the significance of pilots to aircraft manufacturing follows this section. The chapter concludes with a comprehensive listing of over 500 general aviation web sites.

PART TWO FBO MANAGEMENT

Chapter 3   The Fixed Base Operator: Backbone of General Aviation. Chapter 3 explains the important role and functions provided by the FBO, truly the backbone of general aviation. The size and scope of the FBO industry is covered along with current trends in the business and future outlook. The critical decisions in establishing an FBO are explored, including the advantages and disadvantages of remaining independent or joining a chain. A comprehensive customer services checklist covering all areas of an FBO's operation is included at the end of the chapter.

Chapter 4   Managing a Fixed Base Operation. FBOs expecting to survive in the competitive and challenging years ahead must be managed well. The chapter begins with a description of the characteristics of successful FBOs. This is followed by an in-depth analysis of the five functions of management as applied to an FBO. They are planning, organizing, staffing, directing, and controlling. Drawn from a number of sources, the flow of material is comprehensive, yet concise, as the student is introduced to each of the functional areas.

Chapter 5   Financial Planning and Control. Financial planning affects how and on what terms an FBO will be able to attract the funding required to establish, maintain, and expand the business. Chapter 5 first presents information on financial management including the primary tools: the balance sheet and the statement of income. The next section covers financial ratio analysis in which students are introduced to methods of using the financial statements to detect and analyze trends. Forecasting and budgeting naturally follow with an emphasis on planning for profit. The chapter concludes with an in-depth discussion of types, uses, and sources of capital including long-term planning and determining the value of an aviation business.

PART THREE THE MARKETING PROCESS

Chapter 6   The Role of Marketing. This chapter investigates the role of marketing in a firm and demonstrates how essential marketing is to the firm's long-term survival. The chapter begins with a definition of marketing and then discusses marketing management as a three-phase process of planning, implementing, and controlling marketing plans. Marketing activities described are determining objectives, segmenting the market, selecting target markets, and establishing unique market mixes (product, price, promotion, and place) for each market. The chapter concludes with a discussion of the major uncontrollable influences which the marketing manager must recognize and understand their influence on decision making.

Chapter 7   Marketing Research. Unquestionably, one of the most critical and yet most difficult tasks facing marketing management is that of research activities and the search for new customers. The scope of marketing research is investigated and steps to carry out research are suggested. Special emphasis is given to the collection of primary and secondary data by means of sampling techniques. The chapter concludes with a discussion of methods of collecting data and presenting the findings.

Chapter 8.   Transportation Needs Assessment. The major marketing tool used by FBOs and aircraft manufacturers to help potential customers uncover the need for their own air transportation in called a travel analysis. This chapter covers some of the key characteristics of business-to-business marketing and includes all of the components in a travel analysis for a hypothetical company, Champions Stores, is used to completely illustrate the process of aircraft selection and the tax and financial implications of acquiring an aircraft.

Chapter 9   Value Analysis: Costs versus Benefits. One of the most powerful tools used in an aircraft sales presentation is a value analysis. This comparison of a commercial airline trip versus the same trip on the recommended aircraft vividly illustrates time savings and productivity. The chapter concludes with a discussion of the many intangible benefits derived from the use of business aircraft.

Chapter 10   Methods of Acquiring a Business Aircraft. The decision to acquire a business aircraft is certainly one on which management expends a great deal of time and effort. Chapter 10 reviews the methods of acquiring a company aircraft including company owned and operated aircraft, company owned, management company operated, leasing, fractional ownership and charter. Because of the continued importance of the used aircraft market, a whole section is devoted to buying and selling used aircraft listing the major items to be considered in evaluating a used aircraft. The chapter concludes with a discussion comparing the various methods of acquiring a business aircraft.

Chapter 11   Promotion and Sales. Promotion is the communication with identified target markets with the objective of either informing, persuading, or reminding them about products or the firm. This chapter discusses the components of the promotion mix which involve advertising, sales promotion activities, publicity, and personal sales. Since personal sales is the major activity in aircraft sales, the seven steps in the personal selling process are covered in detail.

Chapter 12   Sales Management. This final chapter rounds out coverage of general aviation marketing and management by adding the dimension of sales management. Sales management is the management of the personal selling component of the FBO's marketing program. The responsibilities include the following three functional areas: establishment of a strategic sales program; implementation of the program; and then evaluating and controlling the program.

Finally, feedback—from both students and instructors—is encouraged. It is our intention to prepare the best teaching materials available. Learning should not only be enjoyable, but should accomplish specific objectives. Any suggestions for improving the learning process in the field of general aviation marketing and management will be greatly appreciated.

Acknowledgments

Although the textbook has been written by two authors, it owes it existence to many people who have worked in and written about general aviation marketing and management. Source material for this book was obtained from numerous trade associations such as the General Aviation Manufacturers Association and the National Business Aircraft Association. Information from the individual general aviation aircraft manufacturers was also used in structuring this textbook. We are deeply indebted to these and many other sources for their marketing related materials and photographs used in the text.

To the many students at Embry-Riddle Aeronautical University and other University Aviation Association member colleges and universities who reacted to material in the first edition, we owe a special thanks, because they represent the true constituency of any textbook authors. This text is dedicated to our students past and present who have been our inspiration.

A special thanks to Gary Kiteley, retiring Executive Director of the University Aviation Association, who shared his General Aviation Operations course syllabus with me 30 years ago when he was a professor at Auburn University and I was putting together my first general aviation course at Embry-Riddle.

We would like to give special thanks to Robert Krieger for his foresight in agreeing to publish the first textbook in this specialized field. Thanks are also due the other members of the Krieger Publishing team. This text has benefited greatly from the comprehensive review of the manuscript by Elaine Rudd, whose copyediting expertise smoothed out many rough edges.

Alexander T. Wells, Ed.D.
Bruce D. Chadbourne, Ed.D.
Embry-Riddle Aeronautical University
Daytona Beach, Florida

PART ONE
INTRODUCTION

Chapter 1

General Aviation: A Historical Perspective

OUTLINE

OBJECTIVES

At the end of the chapter, you should be able to:

Discuss some of the major developments in aviation that took place up to the outbreak of World War I.

Describe the role of the barnstormers in the development of general aviation.

Explain how Wichita became the home for many general aviation aircraft manufacturers.

Describe how Beech, Cessna, and Piper got started and some of their early successes in aircraft development.

Highlight the general feeling of the light aircraft manufacturers regarding market potential in the immediate postwar period.

Discuss the change in market orientation which took place in the 1950s.

Explain why it can be said that general aviation reached maturity in the 1960s.

Discuss the factors that led to record sales of general aviation aircraft during the 1970s.

List the primary factors leading to the decline in general aviation aircraft sales during the 1980s.

Describe the challenges faced by the industry during the 1980s and early 1990s.

Identify some of the initiatives taken by government, manufacturers, and the GA industry.

Discuss some of the factors causing a revitalization of the industry during the 1990s.

GENERAL AVIATION'S ROOTS

It can be said that general aviation was born on December 17, 1903, when Orville Wright completed the first sustained powered flight in a heavier-than-air aircraft. However, it was not until 1908 that the U.S. Army purchased its first Wright Flyer and not until 1911 that it received five more. Consequently, most of the early Wright models were used to instruct new pilots and for pleasure flying. Others became attractions for special events such as fairs, and some were used to take paying passengers aloft.

As early as 1909, the Wright brothers encountered their first competition from the Curtiss Aeroplane and Motor Corporation as well as from several foreign models shipped to the United States to take part in flying contests and exhibitions. On June 26, 1909, the first commercial sale of an airplane took place. An improved version of the 1908 Curtiss "June-Bug" was sold to the Aeronautic Society of New York for $7,500.

Like the Wright brothers, Glenn Curtiss was a bicycle maker. By 1902 he had graduated to motorcycles, both building and racing them, and his company had grown by 1908 to over 100 employees, working round-the-clock to meet demand. Part of the demand came from budding aviators who were charged a premium for Curtiss's coveted air-cooled engines. In 1905 the famed Alexander Graham Bell, inventor of the telephone, hired Curtiss to head up a group of aviation experimenters known as the Aerial Experimental Association. On July 4, 1908, Curtiss's June Bug won the *Scientific American* prize of a silver trophy for the first officially observed flight in the United States exceeding one kilometer.

In August 1909 Curtiss traveled to Reims, France, to enter the first Gordon Bennett Speed Trophy race. He won the $10,000 prize money with an average speed of 47.4 miles per hour, which captured the public's imagination on both sides of the Atlantic. Aviation activity experienced a sharp increase between 1909 and 1911 partly as a result of fierce competition among newspapers for aviation news. Another reason was the public's sudden interest in flying. In October 1910 the first international air meet was held in the United States at Belmont Park, New York. Britisher Claude Graham-White won the second Gordon Bennett Speed Trophy with a speed of 60 miles per hour.

More and more people were entering the general aviation picture, and by 1911 several manufacturers were building airplanes as "professional" devices. Many amateur airplane builders were also involved with aviation projects; some were killed or injured trying to fly their home-built machines. At the close of 1911, there were 82 pilots in the United States licensed to fly in air meets and exhibitions. In addition to the licensed pilots, about 50 more individuals had flown solo. The licensing authority at that time was the Aero Club of New York.

When war broke out in Europe in 1914, the United States had as many as 12 aircraft manufacturers including some companies that were producing only three or four airplanes per year. Fewer than 200 flying machines had been commercially produced since 1903 and about one-half had gone to the U.S. Army and Navy. The Curtiss Aeroplane and Motor Company, successor to the Aerial Experimental Association, was the largest company in America producing airplanes.

During World War I, Curtiss produced about 6,000 JN-4 Jenny trainers for the army (along with the navy version of the Jenny, the N-9). The Jenny was first built in 1914 to meet U.S. Army requirements for a training aircraft. Over 95 percent of the 10,000 American pilots trained during the war years flew this aircraft. Thousands of Curtiss OX-5, water-cooled 90 hp V-8 engines were built. So durable were Jennies that they stayed around for many years after the war, becoming the standard barnstorming plane during the 1920s and continuing in use by the Air Corps until 1927. These aircraft — which had cost the government in the neighborhood of $17,000 new depending upon how they were equipped — became surplus after the war and were sold for as high as $750 new, and as low as $50 used.

The Barnstormers

Many of the early barnstormers were ex-World War I pilots who could not get aviation out of their systems. Flying war surplus aircraft such as the Curtiss Jenny, they toured the country putting on aerial shows and giving rides to curious townspeople. Teams of pilots working together as a "flying circus" put on thrilling exhibitions, including wing walking and plane changes, in which a stunt man would transfer between planes in the air.

The biggest and best known of the circuses was developed by an ex-automobile racer and salesman, Ivan R. Gates. The Gates Flying Circus attracted some of the best stunters and wing-walkers ever to thrill a crowd. Pilots like Clyde Pangborn and Ormer Locklear would fly inverted over a field and perform loops to an astonished audience. These two individuals were as popular as movie stars of the day. The barnstormers kept aviation alive during the early 1920s when most people looked upon the airplane as good for only two things: war and exhibitions.

By 1925 crashes and neglect had diminished the surplus warplanes and the barnstormers needed new and better performing airplanes. Federal legislation also had its effect in shaping the industry. The Kelly Air Mail Act of 1925 turned the transport of mail over to private carriers. The newly formed airlines and airmail service lured the barnstormers into more settled work. The Air Commerce Act of 1926 created the first Aeronautics Branch and provided the establishment of airports, airways, and navaids, as well as the first licensing of planes and pilots. It also made stunting difficult, if not illegal in many instances.

The gypsy pilots, as they were called, became more of an oddity and the flying circuses came to be looked upon as bad for aviation. More and more bad days curtailed their barnstorming seasons. In December 1928 the Gates Flying Circus broke up. In its career it had appeared in 2,500 towns and cities and carried more than 1.5 million passengers.

Commercial and general aviation truly began to go their separate ways around this time. The government asked the budding manufacturers to build aircraft for airmail service, and companies like Boeing, Ryan, Douglas, and Lockheed chose to develop mail and passenger planes. Others, including Wright, Laird, Bellanca, and Aeronca concentrated on smaller planes for racing and sport flying.

Another significant civil market, the corporate user, was also developing. In 1927, 34 non-aviation companies were operating business aircraft; by 1930 that number had grown to 300, and manufacturers such as Stinson, Travel Air, Waco, and Fokker were actively cultivating the market. Even private flying, largely the province of the wealthy, was being eyed as a possible market.

Wichita: Home of General Aviation

Jake Moellendick was a wealthy oilman who resided in Wichita, Kansas. He was also a gambler. The gamble of aviation appealed to him, and in 1919 he agreed to put up $15,000 to back several barnstormers who needed three new planes to replace their worn-out Curtiss Jennies. Billy Burke was sent to the 1919 Chicago Air Show to find the new aircraft. He approached an aircraft builder by the name of Matty Laird who had recently formed the E. M. Laird Company and was developing plans for a new three-place biplane. Burke realized that Laird's aircraft could easily become the country's first successfull commercially sold private plane. Burke wired Jake about the new plane and suggested that instead of forming the flying circus, they get into the airplane building business. The idea appealed to Jake with the one stipulation that the company be moved from Chicago to Wichita.

The Burke-Moellendick-Laird partnership began work, and in April 1920 the first Laird Swallow rolled out of the hangar. It was everything Billy Burke had hoped for in a barnstorming aircraft: a sturdy, well-built and easy-to-fly craft that set the standard for all subsequent private biplanes of the 1920s. Production went from two planes a month to four, and Jake Moellendick went on a hiring spree to keep the plant meeting its orders. He assembled a group of unknowns, mostly ex-barnstormers like Buck Weaver, who later organized the Weaver Aircraft Company (subsequently shortened to "WACO"). Others included Lloyd Stearman and his brother, Waverly, and Walter Beech. The company should have prospered, but Jake was impossible to work for and one by one his fine team quit. After 43 Laird Swallows had been sold, Matty Laird went back to his own company in Chicago, which built high-quality private aircraft until World War II. Jake renamed his plant the Swallow Airplane Manufacturing Company, but the next year, 1924, the

Stearman brothers and Beech also left Moellendick. In partnership with another barnstormer named Clyde V. Cessna, they formed the Travel Air Manufacturing Company in Wichita. Beech, Cessna, and Stearman eventually went their separate ways, each establishing his own company. By now, Wichita had come to house the greatest concentration of aircraft-building talent in the country and to this day remains the heart of the American general aviation industry.

Beech Aircraft Corporation

In 1905 at the age of 14, Walter H. Beech made his first flight in a homemade glider in Pulaski, Tennessee. He later went on the barnstorming circuit, where he developed the experience and piloting skill that helped Travel Air Manufacturing Company to become the country's number one planemaker by 1928.

In 1929 Travel Air merged with Curtiss-Wright and Beech went to New York as vice president of sales and chief pilot. He quit in 1930 and headed back to Wichita. In the depth of the depression in April 1932, he established the Beech Aircraft Corporation, with his wife Olive Ann as director and secretary/treasurer, and rented part of an inactive factory. With chief engineer T. A. Wells, he got the first Model 17—a luxurious, five-place, 200 mph cabin biplane called the Staggerwing—into the air on November 4, 1932. It could fly almost 1,000 miles, and in January 1933 it won the Texaco Trophy at the Miami races. The prototype was bought by the Ethyl Corporation, and the money helped the young company to keep producing. By 1934 the Model 17, already famous, had begun to sell, and by the end of 1935, 54 had been sold. The company moved into a new plant to rival those (also in Wichita) of Stearman and Cessna. The Staggerwing Beech continued to sell (up to 781 in 1948) and its distinctive shape had no rival.

In 1937 the Model 18 Twin Beech was born. An eight-place monoplane, it was as fast as the Model 17; but instead of being priced at $12,000 to $24,000, it sold for $35,000 with two Jacobs engines, or $38,000 with more powerful 350 hp Wright radials.

Employment peaked during World War II when the U.S. Army and Navy needed transports and trainers for bombardiers and gunners. The Twin Beech remained in production until November 1969, a 32-year history during which 7,091 were built, almost all with neither of the original engines but with the 450 hp Pratt & Whitney Wasp Junior instead.

In 1946, Beech again hit the market exactly right with the V-tail Bonanza. It featured seating for four people (including the pilot), full flight and navigation instruments necessary for day or night VFR cross-country flights, and even a two-way radio as standard equipment. It had fully retractable tricycle landing gear and a 165 hp Continental engine. The price tag was set at $7,500 and Beech had over 500 orders from eager customers before publicity was released about performance. By 1950 the Bonanza represented 53 percent of the aviation industry's deliveries of high-performance, single-engine airplanes. It was Walter Beech's last classic. He died of a heart attack in 1950, and Mrs. Beech was elected president and chairman of the board.

The number of production models tripled, and three additional plants were established. The company supplied the popular T-34 military trainer and, in conjunction with other major firms, produced transports, fighters, and helicopters. Eventually, Beech had contracts for the Gemini, Apollo, and lunar-module projects.

Cessna Aircraft Company

Clyde V. Cessna was one of the original barnstorming pioneers. He bought a French-built Bleriot monoplane in 1911, and until the war years, Cessna improved and refined the basic design. Barnstorming was profitable and more fun than building aircraft at that time. On July 5, 1917, Cessna set a notable speed record of 125 mph on a cross-country flight from Blackwell, Oklahoma, to Wichita—an event prophetic of many more racing and competition triumphs to be scored by Cessna airplanes.

In 1924 with a total of six successful airplane designs to his credit, which he personally built and flew, Cessna joined Walter Beech and Lloyd Stearman in establishing the Travel Air Manufacturing Company at Wichita and became its president. He sold out his interest in

Travel Air to Beech in 1927. Part of the trouble at Travel Air had been Cessna's lack of interest in biplanes. If anything he was ahead of his time, for he believed the monoplane did not have to be covered with wires and struts in order to be strong and efficient.

Cessna's first independent production-model airplane, built in 1927, was the four-place, full cantilever high-wing "Comet" monoplane. His 1928 Model A, an expensive four-seater, won the New York–Los Angeles Air Derby and also flew to Siberia and back. Developments followed, but the depression almost brought business to a stop. Despite a $398 glider and a $975 powered version, the new plant closed in 1931. Not until January 1934 did the directors agree to restart the business. Cessna installed his nephew, Dwayne Wallace, as plant manager. A recent aeronautical engineering graduate from Wichita University, he went to work with no salary, but with the opportunity to design, build, test, sell, and even race new Cessnas.

Wallace's first creation was the C-34, a high-wing, four-place cabin monoplane with a 145 hp Warner Super-Scarab engine. The airplane refined the fully cantilevered wing of earlier Cessnas but added flaps. In 1935 the C-34 won the Detroit News trophy race, part of the prestigious National Air races which put Cessna in the first rank of aircraft builders. The company's reputation as a builder of fast, efficient aircraft was assured and Cessna retired the following year. The C-34 was developed into various Airmaster models, but Wallace was looking for a light twin-engine aircraft, easy to fly and not too sophisticated to build. By 1939, the T-50 was flying; by 1940 it was in production and ready for buyers. War came and the military bought 5,401 as the AT-17 Bobcat (RCAF Crane) advanced trainer and UC-78 light transport.

After the war Cessna built the 120/140 series followed by the 190/195 series. These airplanes were strong and simple single-engine aircraft that helped Cessna survive the postwar shakeout and launched it into the 1950s. Modern twins began with the 310, flown in January 1953, and the 318 in 1954 which led to the T-37 twin-jet trainer. The Fanjet 500 (later renamed Citation) began a family of business jets in 1968, and the low-wing Ag aircraft entered the market in 1971. The first turboprop was the highly efficient Conquest announced in 1974. Wallace retired in 1975 and was succeeded by Russ Meyer. By 1979 the Pawnee factory, where single-engine aircraft are made, had toped 120,000, and Cessna had become the number one builder of general aviation aircraft.

Piper Aircraft Corporation

William T. Piper entered aviation at a relatively older age than most of the pioneers. When he was 48 years old and a successful oilman in Bradford, Pennsylvania, Piper invested in a local company, the Taylor Brothers Aircraft Corporation, which had designed several light planes. Serving as treasurer, he ended up acquiring the company for $761 when it fell into bankruptcy in 1931. Piper reorganized the assets into Taylor Aircraft Company, giving C. Gilbert Taylor half interest in the new enterprise as an inducement to stay with the company. The new company's formula was simple: build easy-to-fly machines and price them low enough to attract buyers.

After an unsuccessful attempt to design a glider, the Taylor Aircraft Company developed the E-2 Cub, an excellent example of Piper's idea of the simple airplane. By 1934, the Taylor Cub was making money for the company; it was priced at $1,425 with a 38 hp Continental engine. Throughout many years of refining the design, Piper resisted changing the Cub's airfoil or flight characteristics, even though to do so would have increased its speed. He also resisted building fancier, more costly aircraft.

In 1936, Taylor resigned and set up his own company, which eventually went bankrupt in 1946. Piper hired a new chief engineer by the name of Walter Jamouneau and changed the name to the Piper Aircraft Corporation.

Following Piper's penchant for simple aircraft, the company did well. In recognition of Jamouneau's contribution to enhancing the E-2, subsequent models were called the J-2 and J-3. The PA-11 followed next in the Cub line and finally the PA-18 Super Cub. From its first flight in September 1930, through widespread wartime service and with various improvements and derivations thereafter, the Cub formula provided business for Piper up to the 1950s and for a total of more than 40,000 aircraft. Eighty percent of the U.S. World War II pilots received their initial training in the Cub.

Piper Aircraft Corporation boomed and then nearly busted during the difficult period that hit general aviation following World War II. The company rebounded to produce the popular Pacer and Tri-Pacer series and to introduce light twin-engine aircraft to buyers who previous had considered nothing but single-engine planes. The model line expanded, as did the Piper facilities, when a major development center was built in Vero Beach, Florida.

Active in the business well into his eighties, William T. Piper died in 1970. Walter Jamouneau retired in 1977.

THE IMMEDIATE POSTWAR PERIOD

Even during the darkest days of World War II, the general aviation aircraft manufacturers were aware of the ordinary citizen's desire to fly and were preparing for the postwar period. In 1943, Cessna advertised in *Flying Magazine* that "Texas won't be much larger than Rhode Island when you are driving your Cessna Car-of-the-Air, the airplane that everyone can fly." Piper called for "Wings for all America." Other advertisements featured pretty girls in bathing suits, fishermen in remote trout streams, flying couples basking under the Florida sun while their nonflying friends faced winter winds up north.

Surveys, polls, questionnaires, and other marketing studies conducted for and by the industry and the government were the basis for highly optimistic predictions of a staggering potential requirement for light aircraft after the war. The Department of Commerce, which administered civil aviation at that time, informed the Congress that there would be a demand for as many as 200,000 light aircraft a year for the civilian market. With an eye on the 12 million veterans who would be taking advantage of the educational benefits under the newly legislated GI Bill, industry experts concurred that there would be at least 1.3 million private pilots within five years after the war and as many as 400,000 privately owned aircraft by 1950.

Many leading magazines in 1943 and 1944, including journals with such diverse audiences as *Business Week* and *Better Homes and Gardens,* regularly carried major articles featuring postwar airplanes for the common man and woman. *Time* reported that there were 5,750,000 people "conditioned to flying." These included army and navy pilots who at the time numbered 350,000; civilian pilots and students, 150,000; skilled aviation men in the war (other than pilots), 2,500,000; students taking aviation courses, 250,000; and employees during the war in aircraft factories listing 2,500,000 men and women. A *Woman's Home Companion* survey showed that 39 percent of the women interviewed were interested in flying themselves and 88 percent had no objection to anyone in their family owning a plane.

The aviation industry acted as quickly as it could to meet the anticipated avalanche of new student pilots and returning veterans who would be the first buyers of postwar civilian aircraft. Surveys indicated that prices should be about $2,000 for a two-place aircraft and $4,000 for a four-place plane. All the wartime light aircraft manufacturers wanted to be in on the market with new models within a few months.

Piper, which had delivered 5,000 Cubs to the armed services, announced that it would soon come out with a two-place, low-wing, tricycle-gear, all-metal plane to be called the Skycycle. Beech and Cessna reorganized their production lines to roll out all-metal planes. Some of the manufacturers of combat aircraft entered the market. Republic Aircraft, which had produced thousands of P-47 fighters, geared up to offer a four-place single-engine amphibian called the Seabee for sportsman pilots at an announced price of $3,995. North American Aviation, developer of the P-51 fighters and B-25 bombers, designed a bulky, four-place retractable-gear "family car of the air" called the Navion for a price of $5,000.

Despite all the design activity, the first airplanes to appear on the civilian market were the prewar models: Aeronca's Champion, Piper's Cubs, Taylor's Taylorcraft, Stinson's Voyager, and Luscombe's Silvaires. Cessna came out with the 120/140 series and Globe produced the Swift. Production increased and by the end of 1945, when the war was over, there were 37,789 aircraft of all categories (including airline equipment) in the U.S. civil aircraft fleet.

During 1946 hundreds of civilian flight training schools blossomed all over the country as recently discharged veterans took advantage of the new VA flight training legislation. It was apparent that the ordinary citizen did want to fly; the dream of a mass market was coming true. In 1946, the first full year of peace, 33,254 light aircraft were built and sold.

No one was concerned that the demand for 200,000 airplanes did not materialize in the first year; everything with wings that was made was sold. It would be better to have the market develop slowly to the 200,000 level. More important, the sales volume was 455 percent higher than it had ever been before the war.

Airline services expanded rapidly after the war and it was not long before the airlines were demanding that the government regulate small airplanes out of "their" airspace and keep them out of "their" airports. The government refused and the light aircraft manufacturers seemed to be receiving good news on all fronts. The year 1946 had been a record-setting period: Piper–7,780; Aeronca–7,555; Cessna–3,959; Taylorcraft–3,151. The non-spinnable Ercoupe sold a surprising 2,503, and Globe and Stinson both went over the 1,000 mark.

Beech introduced the Bonanza for $7,435, and a small acrobatic biplane called the Pitts Special came on the market. Twenty manufacturers were engaged in making planes for the general aviation community. However, there were clouds on the horizon. The all-around utility of the automobile far surpassed that of the light airplane for the simple reason that there were not enough ground-support facilities where people could land which were close to resort and vacation areas. The airplanes also cost a lot more than people had been led to believe they would, particularly when compared with automobiles. The $3,995 Seabee of 1945 had been more realistically priced at $6,000 by the end of 1946. The Bonanza was up to $8,945, and Navion to $4,750, and the Swift to $3,750, and the Cessna 170 to $5,475 — all a long way from the $2,000 price tag advertised during the war.

As for the less expensive models, there were complaints that most were basically prewar models and not very good for cross-country transportation. They were noisy, drafty, cramped, uncomfortable, and not at all reliable for taking carefully planned vacation trips to the mountains or the beach.

The industry also experienced a high percentage of VA students dropping out of flying soon after receiving their private pilot licenses and an increasing number quitting immediately after soloing. Once airport circling had lost its charm, many ex-GIs began to take a hard look at the practicalities versus expenses, particularly when they learned how easily low ceilings or fog could ground them.

Army and navy veterans who had been flying high-performance airplanes were simply not satisfied to poke along at 95 or 100 miles an hour, especially after a long cross-country flight against a headwind when they could see automobiles making better time on the highways below.

Another problem faced by the light aircraft manufacturers was the availability of war surplus aircraft at bargain prices. In 1946, the Reconstruction Finance Corporation sold more than 31,000 aircraft ranging from Cessna T-50 "Bamboo Bombers" to P-51s. Many ex-military C-47s and Twin Beeches, as well as bombers, went into the corporate market to be modified as executive transports.

The manufacturers began to realize that the general public might have been oversold on lightplane flying, and that they could not hope to have a mass-production industry comparable to the automobile industry. In 1947, a year before Cessna introduced its 170 — which would eventually be developed into the 172, the world's most successful lightplane — the industry was beginning to flounder.

Manufacturing companies with delivery ramps clogged with unsold airplanes began to feel the pinch. Globe was in bankruptcy. Republic had discontinued the Seabee. North American had sold the Navion design to Ryan. Stinson was in deep financial trouble. Taylorcraft was looking for new capital. By the end of 1947, the severity of the problem was evident. Sales were down 44 percent from the previous year, to 15,617 units. Things got worse in 1948. Sales again dropped by more than 40 percent when only 7,302 airplanes were manufactured.

The public's reluctance to spend money on private flying was understandable. A cold war had developed with the Russians, culminating in the blockade of Berlin in the summer of 1948. The United States countered by mounting the Berlin Airlift, and the possibility of another major conflict was on the horizon. GI flight training was restricted to vocational pursuits and tougher regulations were enacted to restrict private flying.

The downward trend followed the deteriorating international situation resulting in an even more dismal year in 1949, when 3,545 aircraft were built. New aircraft designs appeared on the scene, only to disappear from sight forever as light aircraft manufacturers ran out of operating capital.

THE 1950s—A PERIOD OF INTROSPECTION

The 1950s began a period of introspection and review by the general aviation aircraft manufacturers. Executives began to look at the future from a different angle. Mass-producing airplanes for everyone at low prices was not the answer to growth. The future lay in developing a fleet of airplanes that would provide solid, comfortable, reliable business transportation. Aircraft that could operate in instrument conditions with speed and range would be the wave of the future. A certain number of training airplanes would have to be built to get new people started, but a utility airplane that businessmen could afford was the target design for the future. Some such airplanes were already available, but the business community doubted their utility. The Twin-Bonanza and the Twin Beech were well thought of, but there was a lingering doubt in the public's mind about single-engine aircraft. One event that helped to change that attitude was a flight by William P. Odom in January 1949 from Hawaii to Oakland, California, in a Beech Bonanza. Three months later he flew the same Bonanza from Hawaii to Teterboro, New Jersey, 5,273 miles, nonstop.

Cross-country navigation was being made simpler and more efficient by the new very-high-frequency omnidirectional radio ranges—the VORs. Spotted around the country, the pilot merely had to follow a needle on the instrument panel. No longer did pilots have to keep sectional charts on their legs hour after hour to check their position, or to keep working with their calculators to dead reckon their way under instrument conditions.

In June 1950 the Korean War broke out and once again the public's attention was focused on the international scene. General aviation continued to limp along, although the ranks of the manufacturers were thinning. Beech, Bellanca, Cessna, Piper, and Ryan were still producing airplanes, but not all of these companies were sure that they could hang on much longer. Production in 1950 was only 3,520 units.

On the positive side, more and more omni stations were commissioned; VHF radios—static free and easy to navigate by—became factory options on more and more airplanes. In 1950 general aviation airplanes were awarded their own frequency, 122.8, called "unicom." Bill Lear developed the first lightplane three-axis autopilot in 1950, which made cross-country flying easier and more relaxing. Toward the end of the year, Ryan stopped production of the Navion, but a new company, Aero Design and Engineering, was ready with its five-place Aero Commander. Mooney also unveiled its single-place, $1,000 Mooney Mite. Piper put a nosewheel on its little Pacer, renamed it the Tri-Pacer, and created a new surge of interest in light aircraft for pleasure as well as for business.

Aircraft production hit bottom in 1951 with only 2,477 units produced all year, just half the number produced in the month of August 1946. The situation began to look brighter in 1952. Max Conrad flew a Piper Tri-Pacer to Europe and back, which again demonstrated the capability and reliability of light aircraft. In 1952, 3,509 airplanes were delivered, an increase of 1,032 over the previous year. Things were beginning to move. Cessna discontinued the 195 in 1953 and produced the four-place 180, a more powerful aircraft than the 170. Piper stayed with the Tri-Pacer and the Super Cub; Beech was backlogged with orders for the Bonanza, the Twin Bonanza, and the Super-18. Total production hit 3,788 units in 1953, up 279 from the previous year. Growth was solid as the industry emerged from a period of readjustment.

In 1954 Cessna and Piper introduced their four-place light twins — the 310 and the Apache, which would start a long line of descendents. Max Conrad ferried an Apache to Europe and started the transatlantic ferry business. No longer would general aviation aircraft be crated and shipped to Europe for reassembly.

By the mid-1950s aircraft production hovered around the 4,500 per year mark and the need for IFR capability increased. Companies like ARC, Bendix, Collins, Lear, Mitchell, and Wilcox entered the avionics business. By the end of the decade, Cessna introduced the Skylane as a package airplane — one with basic avionics already installed.

THE SOARING SIXTIES

As the 1950s turned into the 1960s, general aviation was developing an unmistakable stability and purpose. Though pleasure flying was far from extinct, it was clear that the general aviation airplane was developing into a viable means of business transportation. In 10 years, the general aviation fleet had more than doubled to 60,000 aircraft, more than half of which were equipped for instrument flying. General aviation had become a major part of the nation's transportation system, with an inventory of light aircraft that were fully capable of flying people in comfort 1,500 miles in one day to thousands of places not served by the commercial air carriers. Expansion, modernization, and increasing complexity characterized the aviation world of the 1960s. A decade that began with radial-engine transports ended with the Concorde and landing a man on the moon.

Beech brought out the Travel Air, to be followed by the Baron, the Queen Air, and the King Air. Cessna put tricycle landing gear on their 170s and 180s in developing the 172 and 182 series, which became the best selling airplanes in history. Piper terminated the Tri-Pacer and entered the Cherokee, Comanche, and Twin Comanche in the market. Many of the old names such as Bellanca, Mooney, Navion, and North American would come back.

By 1965 the general aviation aircraft fleet had grown to 95,000 airplanes, and production totaled 11,852 new aircraft. The following year, 1966, saw a record 15,768 units produced. General aviation growth during the late 1960s paralleled growth in the economy and all segments of aviation at that time.

Three airplanes in particular that were introduced in the 1960s — the Piper Cherokee, the Beech King Air 90, and the Lear 23 — proved to be bellwether designs for years to come.

The Cherokee was the first Piper model to be produced at the company's new Vero Beach, Florida, manufacturing plant. Vero Beach and the Cherokee were Piper's solutions to the high cost of building airplanes in Lock Haven, Pennsylvania. The production line was designed for speed and volume.

Piper dedicated the Vero Beach plant, rolled out the first Cherokee, and celebrated William Piper's eightieth birthday, all on January 8, 1960. The Cherokee was certified in 1961. Two versions were offered. The PA-28-150 sold for $9,795. An additional $200 bought 10 more horsepower.

The Cherokee marked Piper's break with its traditional tube-and-fabric, high-wing design approach to light singles. It became the template for all of the piston-powered models Piper would develop over the next 20 years, with the exception of the Tomahawk and Navajo.

Beech entered the 1960s with a pair of piston-powered, cabin-class executive transports in the Model 18 and the Queen Air. But the company had been studying turboprops for several years. Beech had a technical agreement with a French firm, Société Francaise d'Entretien et du Réparation de Matériel Aéronautique, to test Turbomeca turboprop engines on a Travel Air, the new Baron, and a Beech 18.

In December 1962, Beech unveiled a mock-up of a turboprop-powered, pressurized Model 120, an all-new design. The goal was to test the marketing waters before committing to an expensive development program. At the same time, Beech was working on a new pressurized version of the Queen Air 80.

As the potential costs and time to develop a new top-of-the-line turboprop began to mount, Beech executives opted to take a less risky road and adapt turbine power to the Queen Air.

Details of the forthcoming King Air were revealed in August 1963. Two 500-shaft-horsepower Pratt & Whitney turboprop engines would provide the power to cruise at 270 mph at 16,500 feet, with the cabin pressurized to an altitude of 8,000 feet. The price was projected at about $300,000. In a press release announcing rollout of the first production prototype in November 1963, Beech said it had received $11 million in orders for King Airs. The potential market was estimated to be at least 200 airplanes over the next few years.

The King Air 90 was certified in May 1964, five months after its first flight. Contrary to Beech's modest expectations, the King Air 90 proved to be the tip of a product-line iceberg. A through F model 90s would be introduced, along with larger and more powerful King Air 100s, 200s, and the 300.

Beech has dominated the turboprop market from the beginning. Other designs have a considerable performance edge, but the King Air's combination of roomy cabin, docile handling, and commanding presence have made it the passenger-carrying choice for thousands of companies, government agencies, and individuals. Over 4,000 have been built, including 500 for the U.S. Army, Air Force, Navy, and Marines. No other airplane is in service with all four branches of the military.

Just as the King Air 90 started Beech on a new product line that was to define the executive turboprop, Lear Jet Corporation's Lear 23 launched corporate aviation into the jet age.

The Learjet has its roots in a European private-venture military jet that never went into full production. The P-16 was a ground-attack warrior that a Swiss firm hoped to sell to the Swiss air force. Four were built, but two crashed during test flights. The accidents saddled the airplane with a suspect reputation, and as a consequence, the military could not be sold on it.

One person who was sold was William P. Lear. The prolific inventor, showman, marketer, and chairman of Lear, Incorporated, flew in it several times and was very impressed.

It was to be the first jet designed specifically for general aviation. The Lockheed JetStar and North American Sabreliner already were in service, but they were originally designed to ferry military VIPs and were much larger, heavier, and costlier than the airplane Lear envisioned.

Speed and style were a large part of that vision. The Model 23, with its two small but powerful military derivative General Electric CJ610 turbojet engines, would cruise at 458 knots and look every bit as fast. Today the Learjet still is regarded by many as the finest example of what a civilian jet should be: fast and easy to handle.

Learjet passengers would ride comfortably above the weather in a cocoon-like office. Bill Lear professed disdain for walk-around airplane cabins with lavatories—at least until he designed the Learstar, which eventually became the widebody Canadair Challenger.

The prototype Lear 23 was built in seven months by the new Lear Jet Corporation in Wichita. It flew for the first time on October 7, 1963. Eight months later the second prototype (the first was destroyed a few days earlier in a nonfatal off-airport landing) was flown to the Reading Air Show for a dramatic first public appearance. Certification took just 10 months, a remarkable achievement considering that the Model 23 was the first under-12,500-pound jet the FAA had been asked to certify. It went on the market for $595,000.

The Lear 23 and Lear Jet Corporation would suffer a series of unexplained accidents and a financial recession soon after deliveries began. The airplane survived; the company did not. Bill Lear, who had been forced to sell his shares in Lear, Incorporated, in order to finance development and certification of the 23 and its immediate successor, the 24, had to sell Lear Jet Corporation to avoid financial collapse.

Gates Rubber bought it in 1967 and, before the decade ended, certified the Model 25, a longer version of the 23/24. Later, the turbofan-powered Lear 35 and 55, an enlarged, stand-up cabin version, would be certified.

THE 1970s—INFLATION, REGULATION, AND RECORD SALES

The 1970s can be briefly summarized as the decade of the Terminal Control Area (TCA), the Airport and Airways Development Act, and fuel crises.

In 1970 the manufacturers of light aircraft established a strong and effective lobbying and public relations organization in Washington, the General Aviation Manufacturers Association (GAMA). The National Business Aircraft Association (NBAA) blossomed into a highly professional Washington-based service organization for business users. The Aircraft Owners and Pilots Association (AOPA) and other special-aircraft-use organizations developed into effective lobbying groups. The Federal Aviation Administration (FAA), under administrator Jack Shaffer, appointed a deputy administrator for general aviation.

Despite an economic recession during the first two years of the 1970s and an oil embargo in 1973, general aviation continued to grow, reaching a high-point in 1978 with 17,808 units produced. Personal aviation's production heyday came at a most unusual time. While the post-World War II airplane manufacturing spree held production records for decades (the sales crash that followed in 1947 also set records), the record sales days came, surprisingly, in a decade of sky-rocketing inflation, fuel shortages, and increasingly more restrictive airspace. Despite those factors, more aircraft were sold in the 1970s than before or since.

While the number of aircraft sold was a departure, the aircraft themselves largely were not. Aircraft based on existing models—some dating back to the 1940s and 1950s—formed the bread-and-butter models of this decade of record sales.

In the meantime, the industry saw upstarts like the fast Grumman-American singles mature, and the Rockwell Commanders reached full bloom in the 1970s, even though their production numbers could not touch those of the recycled Cessnas and Pipers. Beech also worked to refine the Aero Club airplanes—the Sierra and Sundowner singles, to name two—but continuing reluctance on the part of the sales staff and buying public ultimately was cited for the closing of that line.

Mooney saw its fortunes change in the 1970s. Finally with stable financial ground under it, the company performed a thorough remake of the M-20-series airplanes. The short- and long-fuselage M-20 line, which for a time included both 180- and 200-hp power plant options, was condensed into the quick and far more refined 201.

Cessna gambled on improving its product and market image for the 1970s. Although the venerable Skyhawk was selling in unprecedented numbers, Cessna felt the competition from the newer Cherokee line and wanted to respond with something new, bold, and exciting. Their answer was the Cardinal but it was never a complete success. Sales of the popular 172 continued to grow.

Cessna tried another tack in 1978 by adding new features to a well-known airframe and, in the process, brought pressurization to the piston single. The idea was not new— Mooney tried it with the Mustang, but fewer than 30 were sold before it was terminated in 1970. Cessna introduced the pressurized 210 with weather radar, known-icing equipment and more radios at a base price of $40,000. A total of 874 were built before the line was shut down in 1986.

While Cessna gambled that the market was there for the P210, Piper took no such risks with its new trainer. Although the Cherokee 140 had been the maker's primary trainer, it was more expensive to buy, maintain, and refuel than the Cessna 150 it competed against; Piper wanted a model to once and for all capture the trainer market from Cessna's 150. Piper queried thousands of flight instructors and fixed base operators; they asked for an airplane with low maintenance requirements, an engine that would tolerate 100LL fuel, good visibility, and flight characteristics that would make the student respect what a real stall could do, unlike those of the nearly stallproof Cherokees.

Piper went to work and produced the Tomahawk, which, when it debuted in 1978, appeared to be the answer to every instructor's dream.

In nine months, Piper churned out nearly 1,000 of the PA-38s, about eight per day, according to the company. With that substantial production rate came quality problems, which severely hurt sales in its second year. Also, some feel that Piper went too far in giving the Tomahawk very noticeable stall characteristics. The 150 and 152 were much easier to handle.

Nearly 1,500 of the Piper trainers had been made by production's end in 1982. Interestingly, Beech's nearly identical Skipper suffered an equally truncated life: Only 312 were made from 1979 to 1981.

A new market segment opened up in the late 1970s that Piper turned to its advantage. With the price of fuel higher than it had been since the 1973–74 fuel crunch, the manufacturers perceived a demand for relatively inexpensive, efficient twins — aircraft that could provide low-cost multiengine training; the light-light twin was born. Piper stepped up with the Seminole, Beech with the Duchess, and Grumman-American with the Cougar.

Of the three, the Seminole sold the best. Piper sold three quarters as many Seminoles the first year, 1979, as Beech made Duchesses in that airplane's entire five-year life span. When the bottom fell out of the light-light twin market, the Seminole fell too, and the total run of PA-44s, ending in 1982, numbered just 468 units (including 86 turbocharged models, produced in the last two years), a handful more than the quantity of Duchesses produced.

While not as noteworthy for being a technological hotbed of activity as the 1940s and 1950s, the 1970s was a decade of immense production, providing harsh lessons for the marketing departments of both Cessna and Piper — lessons learned that ultimately helped shape the kinds of airplanes kept alive (or brought back to life) during the lean times of the 1980s.

By the late 1970s both manufacturer and user began to experience a confidence that general aviation had seldom enjoyed before. Perhaps for the first time, the general aviation community perceived that its potential problems of government controls, charges, fees, and taxes, as well as restrictive legislation, were manageable. Unfortunately, the 1980s brought on a new round of challenges for the industry.

Soaring interest rates and a depressed economy during the early 1980s had an effect on sales. Aircraft shipments dropped from 11,877 in 1980 to 9,457 in 1981 and 4,266 in 1982. By 1985 the number had reached a record low, 2,032 units.

THE 1980s—A DECADE OF RETRENCHMENT

The first five years of the decade had been rough for the general aviation community. The air traffic controllers went on strike in August, 1981, and by October, the General Aviation Reservation (GAR) system was put into effect for two years. This program put quotas on the number of IFR general aviation flights in each of the nation's ATC centers. Changes also took place in ownership of the three leading airframe manufacturers. At the turn of the decade, only Piper Aircraft was owned by a conglomerate. All that had changed by the end of 1985. Ironically, at the end of the decade, Piper was the only independently owned company of the big four. Beech and Raytheon Corporation signed a merger deal in 1980. Cessna was acquired by General Dynamics in 1985. France's Euralair — an air charter, executive jet, and cargo operator — bought Mooney in 1984.

Piper's owner, Bangor Punta Company, was bought by Lear Siegler, which was bought by Forstmann Little & Company. Finally, in 1987 a businessman by the name of M. Stuart Millar purchased the company.

In the mid-1980s, the problems posed by growing costs of insuring newly manufactured airplanes against product liability claims threatened to choke off the nation's supply of new airplanes. The general aviation fleet at large was—and still is—rapidly aging. With $1-million-plus accident settlements now commonplace, each new airplane had to bear the insurance premium burden for all other airplanes. Cessna Aircraft Company's chairman, Russell W. Meyer, Jr., reported in 1985 that 20 to 30 percent of the cost of a new airplane reflected the cost of escalating product liability insurance.

Other financial pressures working against aircraft ownership were also taking place at the same time. The Internal Revenue Service announced a proposal to do away with the 10-percent investment tax credit (ITC) on December 31, 1985, denying prospective owners of aircraft used in business a considerable tax incentive. In a later congressional action (the Tax Reform Act of 1986), the ITC was extended for one year, as long as aircraft purchased by the end of 1986 were put in service before July 1987.

During the 1980s the manufacturers focused their efforts on turboprops and jets. Among the variety of twin turboprops offered was the 425 Corsair, later to become the Conquest I. The 425 is a turboprop version of the 421 Golden Eagle. For operators who preferred to stick to piston engines, Cessna offered a lower cost version of the pressurized 340A in the Model 335. About the only difference between the two was the lack of pressurization in the 335.

Cessna also offered its line of Citation business jets. The Citation III was certified in 1982 with a new airframe and supercritical swept wing and Cessna's only medium-sized jet. Cessna announced a further fuselage stretch in the Citation V.

The booming small-package delivery industry in the 1980s was a benefit to Cessna and the Caravan I, the single engine turboprop it designed to replace and supplement the workhorse Otters, Beavers, and even smaller Cessna 180s and 206s of earlier decades. Certification was granted in 1984 and a stretched model was certified in 1986.

While production of the larger business aircraft had remained steady for Cessna, sales of single-engine piston aircraft and even the twin turboprops continued to decline in the first half of the decade. In 1986 Cessna announced that it was stopping production of all but the Caravan and Citation models.

Similarly, because of the product liability situation Beech stopped producing its Sundowner and Sierra light aircraft in the mid-1980s. One single-engine piston aircraft that has withstood the test of time is the F33 Bonanza. For a number of years, the Bonanza has been the best-selling single-engine aircraft, though the 1980s saw the last of new V-tail V35 Bonanzas. The twin-engine Baron also remained a steady seller.

Like Cessna, Beech felt it needed a machine for its turboprop operators to step up to. In late 1985, it acquired the Mitsubishi Diamond II business jet design from its Japanese builder. While Diamond sales did not live up to expectations for Mitsubishi, Beech turned the Beechjet 400 into a success. Early in 1988 Beech certified the 1300, a 13-seat commuter airliner version of the King Air B200. Another big hit in the airline industry has been the Beech 1900, a 19-seat commuter aircraft certified in 1983. The Super King Air 300, also a derivative of the B200, was certified in January 1984.

In 1983 Beech contracted with Rutan's Scaled Composites, Incorporated, to build an 85-percent scale model of the airplane, called Starship 1. The aviation community watched intently as Beech moved from scaled model to prototype to certification and finally in June, 1988, the first aircraft was delivered at the Paris Air Show.

The Starship not only looked different from other aircraft—with no tail, giant winglets called tipsails, a movable canard, and pusher engines—it is also built differently of different material. The airframe was mostly composite. The whole thing went together like a plastic model, and then it was baked in a high-pressure autoclave.

Mooney Aircraft also tried new things. Most notable is the Mooney PFM. The PFM stands for Porsche Flugmotor, a 217-hp derivative of the engine in the Porsche 911 automobile. The engine is housed in a stretched version of the Mooney 252 fuselage with interior appointments given the Porsche touch of class. The panel, too, with many electronic instruments, is different from those of all other Mooneys. The PFM was certified in May 1988, joining the 201, 205, and 252, also introduced in the 1980s. In 1987 Mooney joined French builder Aerospatiale to develop the TBM 700, a single-engine, pressurized turboprop. The first delivery was made in 1990.

The TBM 700 competed for customers in the same class as Piper's most innovative 1980s airplane — the Malibu. Of the general aviation manufacturers, none was the subject of more industry gossip during the 1980s than Piper Aircraft. The rumors of its demise were rampant in the 1980s when it abandoned its Lock Haven, Pennsylvania, plant, which had become synonymous with Piper, and production slowed to a trickle. But within months of his purchase of the company in 1987, Millar announced that he was putting the venerable Super Cub back into production and that he would also offer the airplane for sale in kit form. At the same time, he announced the Piper Cadet, a stripped-down training version of the Warrior. By the end of 1989, Piper was producing a full line of aircraft from the Cub to the Cheyenne 400 twin turboprop, with the Cheyenne IIIA rapidly becoming the trainer of choice for foreign airlines.

The six-seat Malibu, claimed to be the first cabin-class, pressurized single-engine aircraft, was certified in 1983 with a 310-hp turbocharged Continental engine. The marriage between engine and fuselage was a difficult one, and in 1988 the Continental was replaced with a 350-hp Lycoming engine resulting in the Malibu Mirage.

While the builders of small aircraft had to seek new niches and markets in order to survive the 1980s, others simply made the big and fast bigger and faster. An example is Gulfstream Aerospace. While it too was acquired by a conglomerate in the 1980s (Chrysler Corporation), it steadily continued to produce and sell large business jets. The Gulfstream IV, a bigger and faster version of the G-III, was certified in 1987.

Learjet, too, took the same basic fuselage it developed in the 1960s and continued refining it to produce airplanes that appealed to the 1980s buyer. The Learjet 60 was the latest larger variant, while the Learjet 31A has been called an "entry-level jet." The 31, certified in 1988, combines the usual Lear good looks and speed with good handling characteristics.

Factors Causing the Decline in General Aviation Sales

Historically, the general aviation industry has paralleled the economic cycle of the national economy. The 1980s proved to be an exception to that analysis. In the early 1980s, general aviation followed the rest of the economy into recession. Interest rates were at an all-time high when the new administration took office in 1980. Everything from housing starts to durable goods sales, including autos and general aviation aircraft sales, plummeted. The economy began to recover in 1983, but general aviation did not. In fact, the number of general aviation aircraft delivered fell from a high of 17,811 in 1978 to 928 in 1994 (see Table 1–1).

A number of factors have been cited:

1. **Costs.** No doubt the high interest rates of the late 1970s and early 1980s had an effect at the beginning of the slide. Acquisition costs, including avionics equipment, rose sharply during the early to mid-1980s despite very little change in design of features in the typical single-engine aircraft. Used aircraft were available, and prospective buyers were reluctant to purchase new equipment at considerably higher prices. Total operating expenses — including fuel, maintenance, hangaring charges, insurance — all steadily increased during the 1980s, making it more expensive for the occasional flier.

Table 1-1 General Aviation Manufacturers Association (GAMA) Aircraft Shipments by Type of Aircraft, 1962–2000

Year	Total	Single Engine	Multi-Engine	Total Piston	Turbo-prop	Jet	Total Turbine	Companies Reporting	Factory Net Billings (Millions)
1962	6,697	5,690	1,007	6,697	0	0	0	7	136.8
1963	7,569	6,248	1,321	7,569	0	0	0	7	153.4
1964	9,336	7,718	1,606	9,324	9	3	12	8	198.8
1965	11,852	9,873	1,780	11,653	87	112	199	8	318.2
1966	15,768	13,250	2,192	15,442	165	161	326	10	444.9
1967	13,577	11,557	1,773	13,330	149	98	247	14	359.6
1968	13,698	11,398	1,959	13,357	248	93	341	14	425.7
1969	12,457	10,054	2,078	12,132	214	111	325	14	584.5
1970	7,292	5,942	1,159	7,101	135	56	191	13	337.0
1971	7,466	6,287	1,043	7,330	89	47	136	11	321.5
1972	9,774	7,913	1,548	9,446	179	134	313	12	557.6
1973	13,646	10,788	2,413	13,193	247	198	445	12	828.1
1974	14,166	11,579	2,135	13,697	250	202	452	12	909.4
1975	14,056	11,441	2,116	13,555	305	194	499	12	1,032.9
1976	15,451	12,785	2,120	14,905	359	187	546	12	1,225.5
1977	16,904	14,054	2,195	16,249	428	227	655	12	1,488.1
1978	17,811	14,398	2,634	17,032	548	231	779	12	1,781.2
1979	17,048	13,286	2,843	16,129	639	282	921	12	2,165.0
1980	11,877	8,640	2,116	10,756	778	326	1104	12	2,486.2
1981	9,457	6,608	1,542	8,150	918	389	1307	12	2,919.9
1982	4,266	2,871	678	3,549	458	259	717	11	1,999.5
1983	2,691	1,811	417	2,228	321	142	463	10	1,469.5
1984	2,431	1,620	371	1,991	271	169	440	9	1,680.7
1985	2,029	1,370	193	1,563	321	145	466	9	1,430.6
1986	1,495	985	138	1,123	250	122	372	9	1,261.9
1987	1,085	613	87	700	263	122	385	9	1,363.5
1988	1,143	628	67	695	291	157	448	9	1,918.4
1989	1,535	1,023	87	1,110	268	157	425	11	1,803.9
1990	1,144	608	87	695	281	168	449	14	2,007.5
1991	1,021	564	49	613	222	186	408	14	1,968.3
1992	941	552	41	593	177	171	348	16	1,839.6
1993	964	516	39	555	211	198	409	16	2,143.8
1994	928	444	55	499	207	222	429	13	2,357.1
1995	1,077	515	61	576	255	246	501	13	2,841.9
1996	1,115	524	67	591	290	233	523	13	3,047.5
1997	1,549	898	86	984	223	342	565	12	4,592.9
1998	2,200	1,434	94	1,528	259	413	672	12	5,761.2
1999	2,504	1,634	114	1,748	239	517	756	13	7,843.0
2000	2,816	1,810	103	1,913	315	588	903	15	8,558.4

Source: General Aviation Manufacturers Association (GAMA), "General Aviation Statistical Databook," 2001.

2. **Airline Deregulation.** Deregulation of the U.S. commercial airline industry in 1978 affected general aviation. Increased service combined with better connections and lower fares by the air carriers, including regional/commuters reduced the desirability of using general aviation aircraft when planning business as pleasure trips. Business aircraft were harder to justify.

3. **Product Liability Claims.** Another major factor mentioned earlier is the product liability claims causing the light aircraft manufacturers to concentrate on their higher-priced line of turbine equipment. During the 1980s, annual claims paid by the manufacturers increased from $24 million to over $210 million despite an improved safety record. In 1985, the annual premiums for the manufacturers totaled about $135 million, and based on unit shipments that year of 2,029, the price almost approached $70,000 per airplane. This was more than the selling price of many basic two and four place aircraft. Dropping its piston aircraft production in 1986, Cessna self-insured up to $100 million. Piper decided to operate without the benefit of product liability coverage, and Beech insured the first $50 million annual aggregate exposure with their own captive insurance company.

4. **Taxes.** Passage of the Tax Reform Act in 1986 eliminated the 10 percent investment tax credit (ITC) on aircraft purchases. This was followed by a luxury tax on boats and planes, which only exacerbated the problem of declining new aircraft sales.

5. **Foreign Aircraft Manufacturers.** In 1980, there were 29 U.S. and 15 foreign manufacturers of piston aircraft. By 1994, there were 29 foreign and only nine U.S. manufacturers. In 1980, 100 percent of the single-engine pistons sold in the United States were manufactured in the United States. In 1994, less than 70 percent was manufactured in the United States. Many foreign governments have supported their fledgling aviation industries by subsidizing research, development, production, and financing. Foreign manufacturers continue to gain an ever-increasing foothold in the U.S. market. By the early 1990s, aircraft made abroad accounted for more than 50 percent delivered to U.S. customers. Even in the high-end market, sales of foreign manufactured business jets were close to 40 percent of all business jets sold here in the early 1990s.

6. **Other Factors.** Other factors have had an effect on general aviation, especially the personal and business use of aircraft. In 1979, Congress repealed the GI Bill of Rights, which provided dollars for thousands of ex-service personnel to take flying lessons. Changes in redundant, discretionary income; increases in air space; restrictions applied to VFR aircraft; reductions in leisure time; and shift in personal preferences as to how free time is spent all had their effect on the decline in the 1980s. Interest in sports cars and boats by the traditional aircraft customer, which require less training and recurrence, seemed to have peaked during the 1980s. Finally, the Clean Air Act of 1991 threatened the availability of aviation gasoline because it required the phase-out of leaded gasoline after December 1995. Initially, it was feared that the ban would include piston aircraft, as well as automobiles. EPA clarified that the ban on lead-fuel-burning engines would not apply to general aviation. Though this was good news, the possibility still exists that market forces could lead refiners to stop production of 100-octane low-lead aviation gasoline, or alternatively, lead to very high prices for leaded fuel.

The Downturn in Pilot Numbers

From the late 1970s through the early 1990s, student starts were in a virtual free fall, as equally dramatic as the downward slide in light plane production. In 1978, there were 137,032 new student pilot certificates issued. By 1996, this number had reached 56,653, almost a 60 percent decline. Similarly, newly rated private pilots went from 58,064 in 1978 to 24,714 in 1996 and the total number of private pilots fell from 357,479 to 247,604 during the same period.

Although this disappearance of pilots and prospective pilots at airports may seem mysterious, it really is not. The onset of the phenomenon simply coincided with the end of the chain of great economic programs and the beginning of a natural life cycle. Beginning in 1939, the United States Government provided virtually free flight training for approximately the next 40 years, until the late 1970s. The Civil Pilot Training Program, the war training service after Pearl Harbor, trained an amazing 435,165 pilots between 1939 and

1944. The World War II GI Bill and its subsequent extension, the Korean War GI Bill continued this trend of providing free flight instruction and flight training for those who only had to claim that they were interested in using it as "career development." But the government subsidy finally ran out in the late 1970s. The effect of the civil pilot training, the GI Bill, and other training programs was enormous. They were responsible for the majority of flight training students for many years; they were responsible for general aviation's infrastructure being larger than it would have been without these programs; and they were responsible for the sale of more airplanes, particularly trainers, than ever before.

Military pilots and others who had received their training during the war and immediate postwar periods, when they were in their twenties and early thirties, were reaching their sixties in the 1980s. They were beginning to retire from flying. Fundamentally, what we were seeing in the 1980s was our general aviation community seeking its natural level — shrinking back to the size it might have been had there never been civil pilot training, war training service, and the GI Bill.

There were other elements at work. In the 1980s, by the time prospective new pilots were typically age forty-plus and were established in their careers and could meet their financial obligations, time and attitudes had changed dramatically. These were people who were in their twenties in the 1960s, the era of the cold war, the race to the moon, The Beatles, the Great Society, the Vietnam War, hippies, and the antiwar protests. For them, flying was no longer the highest aspiration a young person could have, as it had been in the 1930s; there was no patriotic memory of World War II and the dramatic air battles that were trumpeted every evening on the radio news.

Having come of age in an era when the very foundations of our political and social systems were challenged, they were far less tolerant than previous generations of the hassle factor imposed through militaristic regulation and enforcement by government agencies like the FAA. Economically, they had higher expectations for ownership of consumer goods and services. At a time when their real income, adjusted for inflation, was decreasing, so was competition for their disposable income. General aviation, which was complacently mired in the attitudes and technology of the 1940s, was simply not able to compete in the marketplace of the 1980s and beyond. By the end of the 1980s, the top sellers in the personal airplane field were no longer the decades-old designs offered by the few light plane manufacturers still in the business but, rather, sleek homebuilts that were more attuned to the times.

Industry Challenges

The long-term decline in the number of manufacturers, combined with the precipitous decline in the shipments of single engine piston aircraft and the number of pilots during the 1980s and early 1990s was a major concern for the general aviation industry. The single engine piston aircraft is the base on which general aviation had to build its future. Historically, new pilots are trained in single-engine piston aircraft and work their way up through retractable landing gear and multiengine piston and turbine aircraft. When the single-engine piston market is in decline, it signals a slowing of expansion in the general aviation fleet and, consequently, a slowing in the rate of growth of general aviation activity.

In addition to the long-term decline in the production of single-engine piston aircraft, there was an accompanying deterioration in the flight instructor and flight training infra-structure in this country. Over the years, the number of flight schools declined. In addition, there were fewer FBOs offering flight training and fewer formal flight training programs offered at other facilities.

The physical facilities of many of the FBOs and flight schools deteriorated. This was partially due to the economic strain experienced by a large number of FBOs. The FBO problems were further compounded by the fact that there were no new training aircraft built in the United States during this period. Only a small number of imported aircraft were available.

For the long term, there were a number of challenges faced by the general aviation industry. In order to stimulate growth in the student and private pilot populations, as well as generate demand for new single-engine piston aircraft, the industry had to make fundamental improvements in both its infrastructure and how it promoted itself.

In the post "product liability reform environment," manufacturers realized that they must develop and incorporate new production processes, new materials, and new technologies in the production of single-engine piston aircraft. Their overall aim was to improve the quality and safety of their product while at the same time reducing the perceived cost of their product to the consumer.

On the pilot side, the industry had to develop programs or incentives which would entice or attract greater numbers of individuals to want to fly. The industry had to develop incentives which would reduce the number of people who drop out of aviation due to time and cost factors. There was nothing more fundamental to increasing the number of new aircraft purchases than a growing pilot population.

However, there were proportionally fewer young people during the late 1980s and early 1990s than in the past, and most of them had less disposable income than in previous generations at a comparable point in time. This posed the greatest single threat to the future growth in the number of new pilots and successful resumption of demand for single-engine piston aircraft.

To counter this threat, the general aviation industry had to make every effort to make it easier to access general aviation flying and improve student starts, and adding to the number of FBOs. Training costs had to be reduced, while still improving safety. The industry also needed to develop new innovative and alternative training methods that would reduce the time and cost of learning to fly in order to attract and retain new pilots.

Government/General Aviation Initiatives

During the 1990s, there was a growing climate of partnership between the FAA and the general aviation community. The FAA streamlined its certification process for new entry-level aircraft (Primary Category Rule), and this could also increase production of new light, affordable aircraft.

Another example of cooperation was the formation of the General Aviation Action Plan Coalition by eleven general aviation organizations to support implementation of the FAA's General Aviation Action Plan.

The General Aviation Action Plan was based on four principles associated with President Clinton's "reinventing government" program. These principles included cutting red tape, putting the customer first, empowering employees, and getting back to basics. Within this framework, the plan set forth three goals relating to general aviation safety, provision of FAA services to general aviation, general aviation product innovation and competitiveness, system access and capacity, and affordability.

The goals of the plan sought to provide for:

- Regulatory relief and reduced user costs achieved through reduced rules and processes and implementation of a general aviation parts policy that was consistent with maintaining or increasing safety.
- Improved delivery of FAA services achieved by reducing excess layers of management, decentralization of the decision-making process, and giving the general aviation customers a voice in the development of FAA programs and how services are delivered.
- Lastly, the elimination of unneeded programs and processes, and investment of FAA resources in those programs that provide the greatest government productivity and responsiveness to its customers' needs.

The FAA continued its efforts to develop common aviation standards. The FAA and the European Joint Aviation Authority (JAA) established a program in 1991 with the goal of making FAA Federal Aviation Regulations (FARs) and the JAA's Joint Aviation Regulations compatible for smaller aircraft (under 12,500 pounds) seeking type certification. In February 1996, the two organizations developed a new set of "common harmonization patterns" for both U.S. and European small aircraft.

These standards apply to new types of aircraft. They are intended to expedite certification and increase safety standards. Under these rules, U.S. manufacturers can use the same standard aircraft design to comply with U.S. regulations, as well as those in each JAA member country.

In addition, the FAA continued to expend considerable effort cooperating with aviation authorities in Russia, China, and elsewhere to develop common aviation standards. It was felt that these initiatives, combined with efforts by industry, could tap vast new markets for general aviation products in places where general aviation does not currently exist.

There was also a growing effort to unlock general aviation's transportation potential through product innovation. The FAA and the National Aeronautics and Space Administration (NASA) collaborated with the general aviation community to implement a research program aimed at fostering new technologies in general aviation. This program, the Advanced General Aviation Transport Experiments (AGATE) Consortium, provided a unique partnership between government, industry, and academia that was established to help revive the general aviation industry. The goal of AGATE was to utilize new technology to produce aircraft that are safer, easier to operate, and affordable to today's pilot. The purpose is to make learning to fly less time consuming and less costly. This goal will be accomplished through employing improved avionics, and more crashworthy airframes.

NASA and the FAA also started sponsoring a General Aviation Design Competition for students at U.S. aeronautical and engineering universities in 1994. This competition allowed students to participate in the monumental rebuilding effort of this country's general aviation aircraft sector by attempting to design their own general aviation aircraft in a manner that focuses on current design challenges.

Another example of the programs involving new technology are two contracts signed in September 1996 between NASA and several industry leaders to develop technologies for new intermittent and turbine engines. Under the support of NASA's General Aviation Propulsion (GAP) program, two companies were selected to begin three-year design projects for new, smoother, quieter, and more affordable engines. The hope was for NASA, aircraft manufacturers, and supplier industries to work together and share their technical expertise, financial resources, and facilities to demonstrate new general aviation propulsion systems.

Teledyne Continental Motors was selected to work with NASA to design a revolutionary intermittent combustion aircraft engine, the CSD-283. The new engine will be used in the development of an entry-level, single-engine general aviation aircraft with four seats and a cruising airspeed of 200 knots or less. The engine will be more fuel efficient and have lower acquisition and maintenance cost.

Williams International also is working with NASA to design an ultraquiet, more efficient turbofan engine with low exhaust emissions, the FJX-2. The new design is expected to improve the cruise speed and range of general aviation aircraft at costs competitive with piston engines.

The Aviation Weather Information (AWIN) program was another effort started in the 1990s to put real-time weather information in the cockpit. The FAA Safer Skies Initiative is another effort to improve weather, airspace, and other critical information in graphic and text form for pilots.

The FAA is committed to improving navigation through satellite-based systems such as Global Positioning System (GPS) for airport precision approach. FAA is also pursuing Wide Area Augmentation System (WAAS) and Local Area Augmentation System (LAAS). WAAS is an augmentation to GPS that supports navigation in all phases of flight, improving positional accuracy with a series of ground reference stations monitoring

GPS signals. The initial 25 WAAS stations were installed in 1998. Most IFR aircraft are expected to have GPS/WAAS by 2007.

LAAS provides signal-corrected information, like WAAS, except that it is for use in aircraft and other vehicles on the airport surface. FAA began prototype testing LAAS in 1998. Because of concern about the possible jamming of GPS signals, the Department of Transportation decided not to discontinue LORAN C, the current positioning system, but rather to upgrade that system.

Manufacturer/General Aviation Initiatives

The general aviation industry launched a series of programs and initiatives during the early 1990s to promote growth. These included the "No Plane, No Gain" campaign sponsored jointly by GAMA and the National Business Aviation Association (NBAA); "Project Pilot," sponsored by AOPA; and the "Learn to Fly" campaign sponsored by the National Air Transportation Association (NATA).

The "No Plane, No Gain" program was directed at the business community and designed to promote the use of general aviation aircraft as an essential tool of business. The thrust of the effort was to show that companies that use GA aircraft in the performance of their day-to-day business are well managed, more efficient, and more profitable than those that do not. The program uses videos, speaker's kits, slide shows, and advocacy materials for distribution among the business community to highlight the benefits of general aviation to business and to the bottom line of the company's balance sheet.

"Project Pilot" and "Learn to Fly" were programs directed at individuals and were designed to promote the growth in the number of new student starts and general aviation flying.

AOPA's "Project Pilot" encouraged its members to identify individuals who would benefit from special encouragement and assistance in the pursuit of becoming a private pilot. The sponsoring AOPA member then served as a mentor to the student, offering support and assistance to the student during his or her training. AOPA members/mentors were provided with materials designed to help them identify students who would benefit from the program. The participating students were also introduced to the program through a special program kit that included such items as a video on the joy of flying, decals, a special issue of *Pilot Magazine,* and AOPA membership information. By year-end 1999, AOPA claimed that, over the course of the program, more than 22,910 members had identified and mentored nearly 33,240 students.

The purpose of NATA's "Learn to Fly" campaign was to increase the number of active GA pilots by increasing the number of student starts and by motivating inactive pilots to return to active flying. The program was designed to promote the benefits of learning to fly. It stimulated the interest of a targeted audience through advertising and promotional efforts. In addition, it provided interested prospects with fast and easy access to information on how to go about learning to fly. This was accomplished through the use of a toll free telephone number—1-800-I-CAN-FLY—information packets provided through direct mail response resulting from telephone inquiries, and follow-up calls by participating flight schools in the interested caller's ZIP code area.

Beyond the goal of bringing new pilots into general aviation, both "Project Pilot" and "Learn to Fly" programs were interested in rekindling the desire to fly of students who have abandoned their training by encouraging them to complete their certification, as well as to convince licensed pilots who stopped flying to return to active status.

Another program started in the mid-1990s to stimulate new interest in learning to fly was the "Young Eagles" program sponsored by the Experimental Aircraft Association (EAA). This program involved taking young people ages 12 to 14 on their first flight in a small aircraft and could spark an interest in their learning to fly.

On July 3, 1996, Cessna dedicated its new 500,000-square-foot final assembly plant in Independence, Kansas. Cessna committed to resume production of selected single-engine piston aircraft models—the 172, the 182, and the 206. It would be the first new single-engine piston Cessna produced since 1986.

Another important industry program called the Piston Engine Aircraft Revitalization Committee (PEARC) completed its work in 1996. The committee included senior managers and directors from GAMA member companies, aviation organizations, academic institutions, and the FAA. The committee's goal was to find new methods of expansion and growth for the general aviation industry and to review the efforts already undertaken by the industry in order to adopt the best practices. The committee estimated that there were approximately 1.2 million individuals—900,000 men and 300,000 women—interested in flying. According to the committee's findings, 57 percent of the potential pilots were between the ages of 25 and 40. In addition, committee findings indicated that many potential pilots generally overestimate both the time and the cost of learning to fly.

"GA Team 2000" was a direct result of the work performed by PEARC. This program, started in 1996, was sponsored jointly by AOPA and GAMA, and supported by more than 100 industry organizations. The goals of GA Team 2000 were multifaceted:

- To revitalize the influx of new pilots.
- To generate flight training leads.
- To encourage improvement in flight school marketing and training infrastructure.
- To secure additional funding to expand the GA Team 2000 effort.

The program encouraged people of all ages to "Stop Dreaming and Start Flying." Renamed the "Be A Pilot" program, it began issuing introductory flight certificates to interested respondents in May 1997. The certificates can be redeemed for a first flight lesson at a cost of $35.

In the four years since the program started, over 110,000 certificates have been requested. In 2000, there were more than 35,000 requests for certificates. The program has over 1,600 participating flight schools and attracts new market entrants via the Internet and cable television advertising.

Contributions for 2000 were close to $2 million and the program was planning to move to a higher level in 2001 by hiring a full-time president and chief executive. As a result, the program was expected to include new initiatives in media exposure on the benefits of being a pilot for personal, business, and career interests.

During the 1990s, the light aircraft manufacturers launched programs to make aircraft ownership easier. The New Piper Aircraft Company created Piper Financial Services (PFS), which offers competitive interest rates for the purchase and/or leasing of Piper aircraft. Cessna accepted refundable deposits for nontransferable position reservations for its new aircraft. The Experimental Aircraft Association entered into an agreement with TFC Textron (formerly Green Tree Aircraft) to finance kit-built planes. The general aviation industry also sought to increase the number of lending institutions that offered special low, competitive rates for aircraft financing.

The number of fractional ownership programs for general aviation aircraft continued to grow. Executive Jet Aviation (NetJets) became the dominant name in fractional ownership; however, manufacturers also joined the movement. They formed their own programs or allied themselves with ongoing programs. Boeing Business Jets and Gulfstream started working relationships with Executive Jet. Raytheon established Raytheon Travel Air. Bombardier Aerospace (Flexjet) also entered the competition, along with Dassault Falcon Jets. Fractional ownership also arrived in the rotorcraft market with the entry of the Lynton Group. These programs have greatly increased the accessibility to aircraft ownership for many who could not otherwise afford it.

Finally, several industry organizations are also targeting young people through the Internet to pique their interest in the world of aviation. The NBAA sponsors "AvKids," a program designed to educate elementary school students about the benefits of business aviation to the community and career opportunities available to them in business aviation. Even the National Agricultural Aviation Association developed a webpage with information on careers in aerial application. GAMA offers publications, awards, and scholarships to bring education into the nation's classrooms. AOPA's "Apple Program" brings aviation into the classroom, targeting middle and high school students.

THE 1990S— REVITALIZATION OF AN INDUSTRY

General aviation continued its downward slide into the 1990s, reaching a low of 928 shipments in 1994 (see Table 1–1). However, there were a number of reasons for guarded optimism in the industry. Several ongoing events suggested that general aviation may experience a renaissance. There was a growing realization in the aviation community that general aviation must reinvent itself and create a new demand growth curve, much as it did in the 1950s.

The main reason for this optimism was the industry perception that product liability legislation had a better chance of being enacted by Congress. The industry felt that passage of this legislation would not only lower its insurance costs, but would enable manufacturers to begin to design and produce new technology and cheaper general aviation aircraft.

Additionally, the amateur-built aircraft market showed steady growth during the early 1990s. Almost 1,000 new amateur-built experimental aircraft received airworthiness certificates, and 2,000 kits were sold by 14 major kit manufacturers in 1992. By 1995, it was estimated that 23,000 experimental aircraft were included in the general aviation fleet. This represented an increase of roughly 20,900 over the estimated 2,100 in 1970. The popularity of amateur-built aircraft resulted from several factors, including:

- **Affordability.** Amateur-built aircraft are substantially less expensive than new production aircraft (aircraft produced under a type and production certificate) because of the large amount of labor that the builder provides.
- **Performance.** Many amateur-built aircraft have superior speed, maneuverability, fuel economy, and/or handling characteristics compared to light production aircraft. In many cases, the performance benefits are due to features and technologies not available on used or even most new production aircraft. These benefits include (1) new technology engines, (2) low-drag, natural laminar flow wings and carefully contoured fuselage aerodynamics, and (3) very smooth surfaces held to high tolerances and crafted from advanced composite technologies.

These aircraft represented the test-bed for new technologies, which eventually are introduced in the development and manufacture of the next generation of light general aviation production aircraft.

Some kit builders became production companies at the entry level. Cirrus Airframe Parachute System (CAPS), a device designed to lower the entire aircraft to the ground in case of a catastrophic event eliminates opportunities for control of the aircraft.

The used aircraft market also remained strong during the early 1990s with almost 36,000 aircraft changing hands in 1992. Additionally, prices for piston aircraft also remained strong, thus reflecting some pent-up demand for these aircraft. The success of the kits and the strength of the used aircraft market showed the creativity and resilience that still existed in the market.

The international use of general aviation aircraft increased. Based on sample flight-strip data obtained from the North Atlantic oceanic centers, weekly operations of general aviation aircraft increased from 119 in 1983 to 338 in 1991, 293 in 1992, and 396 in 1993. Some of this increase resulted from concerns of business for the safety and security of its traveling employees. However, a large part of it was the result of business adapting to meet expanding global markets and opportunities. The corporate flying market antici-pated the new Gulfstream V, capable of flying 7,500 miles nonstop.

Passage of the General Aviation Revitalization Act (GARA) of 1994 ushered in a new wave of optimism in the general aviation industry. With some exceptions, GARA im-posed an 18-year statute of repose, limiting product liability suits for aircraft having fewer than 20 passenger seats not engaged in scheduled passenger-carrying operations. Cessna immediately announced that it would resume production of single-engine aircraft in 1996. The New Piper Aircraft Corporation was formed, and, in 1995, general aviation aircraft shipments finally increased after a 17-year decline.

In 1997, the optimism so prevalent in the industry since the passage of GARA was evidenced by the release of new products and services; expansion of production facilities; increased student starts; increased aircraft shipments, and record-setting gains in aircraft billings. These conditions suggested continued improvement in the general aviation indus-try in 1998 and beyond. According to a poll of Aircraft Owners and Pilots Association (AOPA) members conducted in March 1992, only 41 percent said that they were optimis-tic about the future of general aviation. In response to a similar poll in January 1997, 61 percent responded optimistically, and, by April 1998, the poll of certificated pilots re-ported that 74.5 percent of its members thought the state of aviation was the same or better than it had been. This renewed optimism among the pilot community, aircraft manufacturers, and the industry as a whole could be directly attributed to the strong economy and the passage of GARA in 1994.

In January 1997, Cessna delivered its first new single-engine piston aircraft since 1986. In addition, Lancair International, Diamond Aircraft, and Mooney also produced new piston models. Galaxy Aerospace rolled out its new business jet in the fall of 1996. Aerospatiale and Renault announced plans to join forces to produce light aircraft piston engines for certification in 1999. Piper announced plans to manufacture the Meridian, a single-engine turboprop scheduled for its first flight in 1999 with delivery in 2000.

New manufacturing facilities opened to support expanded production. Cirrus broke ground on two facilities to support production of the SR 20. Also, Sabreliner started a large expansion program at their Missouri facility.

In 1999, Cessna announced plans and orders for the new Citation models — the CJ1, CJ2, Sovereign, and Ultra Encore. Raytheon announced that it would begin deliveries of its Premier I, an entry-level jet that features a composite fuselage with metal wings, in 2000. Mooney delivered its first Eagle in 1999.

Boeing Business Jets announced its plan to build a larger version of its long-range corporate jet, the BBJ-2. Boeing Business Jets, a joint enterprise of Boeing and General Electric, entered the market in 1998 with the long-range BBJ based on a hybrid of the 737-700/800 aircraft. Twenty-eight aircraft were delivered in 1999. Airbus and Fairchild are also marketing business jets that are based on aircraft originally designed for commercial operations.

During the 1990s, fractional ownership programs offered by Executive Jets' NetJets, Bombardier's Flexjet, Raytheon's Travel Air, Flight Options, and TAG Aviation grew at a rapid pace. From 1993 through the end of 1999, these five major fractional ownership providers increased their fleet size and shareholders at average annual rates above 65 percent. According to AvData, Inc., as of December 1999, the fractional ownership fleet numbered 329 and shareholders totaled 1,567. Despite this record growth, it is believed, only a small percentage of this market has been developed.

Fractional ownership programs are filling the niche for corporations, celebrities, and business people that do not generate enough flying to warrant a flight department. Frac-tional ownership providers offer the customer a more efficient use of time by providing a faster point-to-point travel time and the ability to conduct business while flying. In addi-tion, shareholders of fractional ownership find the minimum startup concerns and easier exiting options of great benefit.

The business aviation community was initially concerned that the success of fractional ownership programs would result in a shutdown of corporate flight departments. These concerns were unfounded. Fractional ownership providers have generally found their business base to be first-time users of corporate aircraft services, users that traditionally utilized commercial air transportation. Once introduced to the benefits of corporate flying, some users of fractional programs found it more cost effective to start their own flight departments, instead of incurring the costs of a larger share in a fractional ownership program. As a result, the fractional ownership community may be partially responsible for the increase in traditional flight departments since 1993.

The 1990s truly represented a revitalization of the industry. Total billings in 1999 soared 35.1 percent over 1998, reaching $7.9 billion, and units shipped increased from 2,200 to 2,504, or 12.6 percent. Put into perspective, general aviation sales in 1999 were quadrupled those of 1991. The last year of the decade also marked the first time in GAMA's history that both billings and shipments increased for five consecutive years. It marked the first full year of deliveries of the Cessna 206H Stationair and T206H Turbo Stationair. Deliveries of the composite-construction Cirrus Design SR 20 began, and Mooney Aircraft Corporation began production of the Ovation 2, a faster and more fuel-efficient version of the firm's best-selling model, the Ovation.

The biggest jump in 1999 sales revenue, similar to 1998, was in the turbofan aircraft segment. Sales rose 23.9 percent, in large part due to strong incremental growth and fractional ownership programs. Gulfstream Aerospace, for example, racked up almost $2.4 billion of sales, with 70 deliveries. Cessna's revenues topped $1.8 billion, most of which were Citation sales. Bombardier delivered the first 34 Global Express aircraft into completion. Sales of the 4000-nm range Challenger 604 remained strong, with 40 deliveries in 1999. The Learjet division also delivered 43 Learjet 45 aircraft. At the end of Bombardier's January 31 fiscal year, its order backlog had climbed to $18.9 million.

According to AvData, the number of corporate flight departments in the United States grew by 6.6 percent in 1999, from 8,236 to 8,778. The National Air Transportation Association reported that charter activity was up by over 20 percent in 1999.

The decade closed with across-the-board growth in general aviation activity, corporate flight departments, fractional programs, and charter flights.

THE NEW MILLENNIUM

General aviation is an important component of both the aviation industry and our national economy. It provides aviation services that commercial aviation cannot or will not provide. In addition, the production and sale of general aviation aircraft, avionics, and other equipment, along with the provision of support services such as flight schools, fixed base operators, finance, and insurance, make the general aviation industry an important contributor to the nation's economy.

As we head into the new millennium, the future of general aviation looks bright as evidenced by the industry's actions to stimulate the development and production of new general aviation products and services. New manufacturing facilities are being built and old facilities are being expanded. Sales of general aviation aircraft are setting new records for value of aircraft shipped. Much of this record sales value is for aircraft at the higher priced end of the general aviation fleet — turbine powered aircraft — and is likely due in part to the increase in fractional ownership. More than 900 turbine aircraft were delivered in 2000 (see Table 1–1) as production capacity soared to keep up with record backlogs in manufacturers' order books. Cessna, for example, doubled the number of Excels it delivered and increased Bravo production by 50 percent. Dassault Falcon Jet deliveries reached 73, five more than in 1999, while its backlog of orders increased. Learjet 45 deliveries were up from 43 in 1999 to 71 in 2000. Even deliveries of the venerable Raytheon Hawker 800 XP increased by 22 percent.

Piston aircraft shipments grew by almost 11 percent, buoyed by an infusion of new technology from Lancair and Cirrus Design, as well as increased piston deliveries from

Cessna's Independence, Kansas, plant. The year 2000 saw the first deliveries of Lancair's Columbia 300. Cirrus delivered 95 new four-seat SR 20 models. Cessna piston singles deliveries increased to 912 units.

In 2001, Cirrus Design's 310-hp SR 22, capable of flying faster than a Raytheon Bonanza A36 at less than half the price, joins the piston-engine singles market. Cessna's Turbo Skylane went back into production, this time with a fuel-injected Lycoming 540 engine.

The business jet section, though, is where major changes are occurring. The Sino Swearingen SJ30-2, having made its first test flight in production configuration in 2000, made its debut as the second least-expensive entry-level fanjet. While having the smallest cabin cross section of any business jet in production, the SJ30-2 offers mid-size jet speed and range.

Embraer's Legacy, a derivative of its best-selling EMB-145 regional jet fitted with winglets, made its introduction in two forms—a 19-passenger corporate shuttle and a 12-passenger executive transport. The Legacy Executive, fitted with auxiliary fuel tanks, has the most cabin volume of any mid-size business jet and virtually the same tanks—full range as a Dassault Falcon Jet 50EX.

Boeing Business Jets offered its BBJ2 in 2001, a $60 million version of its next generation 737-800 fitted with auxiliary fuel tanks, winglets, and upgraded engines, enabling it to fly 22 passengers from Los Angeles to London.

Dollars spent on research and development are advancing avionics and computer technology; advances that are not only expected to increase aviation safety, but are expected to make it easier to learn how to fly. Of course, without pilots to fly the planes, there would be no industry. To stimulate growth in the pilot population, the industry is promoting flying with "learn to fly" programs. The industry is also developing programs to assist schoolteachers in bringing aviation into the classroom with the hope of encouraging students to pursue careers in the field of aviation.

Overall, these trends bode well for general aviation industry in the foreseeable future. However, unexpected events such as the tragedy on September 11, 2001 and the economic slowdown during the first two years of the new millennium vividly demonstrate that the future, as in the past, will bring new challenges to this ever-changing industry.

REVIEW QUESTIONS

1. How did Glenn Curtiss get started in manufacturing aircraft? What was the military trainer Curtiss developed that became the most popular aircraft with the barnstormers? Did the barnstormers make any contribution to the development of general aviation? How?

2. How did Wichita become the home for many of the light aircraft manufacturers? What successful aircraft was developed in 1932 that brought the Beech name into prominence? Cessna gained prominence in 1935 with the development of which aircraft? What were some other successful aircraft developed by Cessna during and immediately after World War II? Piper's Cub developed out of which aircraft?

3. Why did the manufacturers have such a feeling of optimism concerning market potential during the postwar period? What were some of the reasons why sales did not live up to expectations?

4. What was the new direction that the manufacturers took for light aircraft starting in the early 1950s? What were some of the developments that took place during the 1950s that helped general aviation grow?

5. Why can it be said that general aviation really arrived at a level of maturity during the 1960s? Describe some of the new aircraft that were developed during the 1960s. What was the first jet designed specifically for the general aviation market?

6. Describe some of the major events during the 1970s that impacted general aviation.

What are some of the reasons for the decline in general aviation aircraft sales during the 1980s? Why did Cessna stop production of single-engine training aircraft? Specifically, why did the light aircraft manufacturers concentrated on turbine aircraft?

7. Discuss the reasons for the downturn in the number of pilots from the late 1970s through the early 1990s. Describe the challenges faced by the industry in light of the decline in all segments of the general aviation community. How did the government agencies, manufacturers, and the general aviation community respond to these challenges?

8. How was the general aviation industry revitalized during the 1990s? What was the purpose of the General Aviation Revitalization Act (GARA) of 1994? Describe the role that fractional ownership has played in revitalizing the industry.

REFERENCES

Cessna Aircraft Company. *An Eye to the Sky—Cessna—First Fifty Years 1991–1961.* Wichita, KN: Cessna Aircraft Company, 1961.

Chant, Christopher. *Aviation An Illustrated History.* New York: Crescent Books, 1978.

Christy, Joe. *High Adventure—The First 75 Years of Civil Aviation.* Blue Ridge Summit, PA: TAB Books, Inc., 1985.

Department of Transportation, Federal Aviation Administration, FAA Aerospace Forecasts, various years, FAA, APO-110, Washington, D.C: U.S. Government Printing Office.

Hedrick, Frank E. *Pageantry of Flight—The Story of Beech Aircraft Corporation.* Wichita, KN: Beech Aircraft Corporation, 1967.

Piper—The New Piper Aircraft, Inc.: A History of the Legendary Company. Vero Beach, FL: The New Piper Aircraft, Inc., 2000.

Chapter 2

The Scope of General Aviation

OUTLINE

What Is General Aviation?
The Uses of General Aviation Aircraft
   Public Use
   Business Flying
   Personal Flying
   Instructional Flying
   Aerial Application, Aerial Observation, and Aerial Other
   Sightseeing, Air Tours and Air Taxi
   External Load and Medical
   Other Flying
General Aviation Airports
   Economic Role of General Aviation Airports
      Attracting Industry
      Stimulating Economic Growth
Pilots
FAA Services to Pilots
Airframe Manufacturers
   Significance of Pilots to Aircraft Manufacturing
Industry Outlook
General Aviation on the Web
   Airframe Manufacturers
   Aircraft Sales
   Business Aviation Services
   Flight Planning and Weather
   Charter Reservations
   Avionics
   Parts Suppliers
   Training
   Publications
   Associations

OBJECTIVES

At the end of this chapter, you should be able to:
Define "general aviation."
Identify the FAA primary use categories.
Describe the purpose of public use flying.
Distinguish between executive/corporate transportation and business transportation.
Discuss the importance of personal flying.
Give several examples of general aviation aircraft used for aerial application and aerial observation.
Describe the size and scope of general aviation airports in the United States.
Discuss the economic role of general aviation airports.
Identify the primary FAA services provided to pilots.
Discuss the changing size and scope of the airframe manufacturers.
Understand the importance e-commerce in the marketing and sales process.

WHAT IS GENERAL AVIATION?

In 1848 the English historian Thomas Babington Macaulay postulated that "of all the inventions, the alphabet and the printing press excepted, those which bridge distance have done the most for civilization of our species." The role aviation has played in helping America achieve its position of world preeminence can hardly be overstated. In fact, the growth and success of our nation during its 200-year existence have always been closely related to the innovative abilities of its various forms of transportation.

Land, water, and air transportation systems historically have provided the lines of communication and distribution required to unite the nation and foster the development of its commerce. Throughout history, progress has depended upon developing a better transportation system.

Air transportation is a purely 20th century phenomenon. It has developed with almost incredible swiftness from scarcely noted experiments on the hills of Kitty Hawk in 1903 to its role today as a vital public necessity that touches the lives of everyone.

Today, transportation as an industry, in its many public and private forms, accounts for fully 20 percent of the total gross national product of the United States. Air transportation makes a significant contribution to this total economic impact.

The term *general aviation* refers to all civil aviation activity except that of the certificated airlines. Together, general aviation and the airlines make up America's balanced air transportation system, which is the safest and most efficient aviation network in the world.

Air service in America is available to almost everyone because the airlines and general aviation fulfill separate but compatible transportation roles. The general aviation fleet of some 220,000 business, commercial, and personal planes serves all of the nation's 19,000 airports, bringing the benefits and mobility of air transportation to virtually everyone, including millions of people who live outside of the metropolitan areas that the airlines serve through some 600 airports.

General aviation is air transportation on demand. It moves millions of passengers a year and tons of cargo and mail faster and farther than any earthbound mode of transportation—and with almost unlimited flexibility. Statistically, the general aviation fleet represents 96 percent of all civil aircraft registered in the United States.

- General aviation aircraft range from two-seat training aircraft to international business jets.
- General aviation is estimated to be an $18 billion industry, generating more than $64 billion annually in economic activity.
- General aviation exports nearly one-quarter of its production and leads the world in development of new technology aircraft.
- General aviation aircraft fly over 32 million hours (nearly two times the airline flight hours) and carry 166 million passengers annually.
- Approximately 70 percent of all the hours flown by general aviation aircraft are for business and commercial purposes.
- Most people learn to fly in a general aviation aircraft.

Before general aviation became a factor in the nation's transportation system, most factories and distribution centers were located in or near large metropolitan areas. Today, industrial decentralization is locating facilities away from major population centers to smaller communities—those that have a general aviation airport.

General aviation is a major reason why the map of United States industry is changing perceptibly and constantly. As a result, business flying is one of the largest categories in general aviation. General aviation aircraft are also used for instruction, to fight fires, carry medical patients, perform aerial mapping and pipeline patrol, fertilize crops, enhance law enforcement, and many other functions.

Today's general aviation airplane, because of advances in technology that provide better speed, range, fuel efficiency, and flexibility, has become an integral business tool.

THE USES OF GENERAL AVIATION AIRCRAFT

The size and diversification of general aviation create difficulty when attempting to categorize it for statistical purposes. General aviation has no reporting requirements comparable to those of the certificated air carrier industry. Aircraft flown for business during the week may be used for personal transportation on weekends, as a family car is used. Instructional aircraft may be used for charter (air taxi) service or rented to customers for business or personal use. An air taxi airplane may be used for advanced flight instruction, for rental to business or personal use customers, and so on.

Even though aircraft have multiple purposes, the Federal Aviation Administration's Statistics and Forecast Branch conducts an annual survey of owners requesting the number of flight hours for the previous year by *primary use category.*

Based on the results of the latest GA survey, there were an estimated 219,464 active general aviation aircraft in 1999. An active aircraft is an aircraft flown at least one hour during the survey calendar year (see Table 2–1). By the turn of the century, the active fleet had increased for five consecutive years, up 26.9 percent over this five-year period.

Single-engine piston aircraft continue to dominate the fleet during this period, accounting for approximately 70 percent of the total active fleet. The next largest groups are multiengine piston and experimental aircraft, which make up close to 9 percent each. Turboprops, turbojets, rotorcraft, and all others represent small shares of the active fleet, accounting for roughly three percent each. The number of active experimental aircraft increased by close to 70 percent during this five-year period.

While turboprops, turbojets, and rotorcraft represented less than 10 percent of the active fleet in 1999, they accounted for nearly 23 percent of total hours flown (see Table 2–2). The number of hours flown by general aviation aircraft increased for five consecutive years, showing an increase of 32 percent for the five-year period.

Public Use

The *public use category* includes owned or leased aircraft for fulfilling a federal, state, or local government function. Government aircraft are an essential part of our national air transportation system. These 4,000 plus aircraft, most of which were designed for civilian use, are flown thousands of hours a year on government business, from firefighting and pest control to operations requiring high levels of security, such as prisoner transportation. Public use aircraft also play a critical role in fast responses to disasters and emergencies, such as use by the National Transportation Safety Board (NTSB) and FAA (see Table 2–3).

Many areas of our country are inaccessible to ground transportation, so people and

Table 2–1 General Aviation Active Aircraft by Aircraft Type (in Thousands)

Aircraft Type	Year					
	1999	1998	1997	1996	1995	1994
Piston—Total	171.9	163.0	156.1	153.6	152.8	142.2
Single-Engine	150.9	144.2	140.0	137.4	137.0	127.4
Multi-Engine	21.0	18.8	16.0	16.2	15.7	14.9
Turboprop—Total	5.7	6.2	5.6	5.7	5.0	4.1
Turbojet—Total	7.1	6.1	5.2	4.4	4.6	3.9
Rotorcraft—Total	7.4	7.4	6.8	6.6	5.8	4.7
Other—Total	6.8	5.6	4.1	4.2	4.7	5.9
Experimental—Total	20.5	16.5	14.7	16.6	15.2	12.1
Total All Aircraft	**219.4**	**204.7**	**192.4**	**191.1**	**188.1**	**172.9**

Source: 1994–1999 General Aviation Activity Surveys.
Note: Columns may not add to totals due to rounding and estimation procedures.

Table 2–2 General Aviation Hours Flown by Aircraft Type (in Thousands)

Aircraft Type	Year					
	1999	1998	1997	1996	1995	1994
Piston—Total	22,895	20,402	20,743	20,091	20,251	18,823
Single-Engine	19,325	16,823	18,345	17,606	17,831	16,404
Multi-Engine	3,569	3,578	2,399	2,485	2,420	2,419
Turboprop—Total	1,812	1,765	1,655	1,768	1,490	1,142
Turbojet—Total	2,738	2,226	1,713	1,543	1,455	1,238
Rotorcraft—Total	2,744	2,342	2,084	2,122	1,961	1,777
Other—Total	319	295	192	227	261	388
Experimental—Total	1,247	1,071	1,327	1,158	1,194	724
Total All Aircraft	**31,756**	**28,100**	**27,713**	**26,909**	**26,612**	**24,092**

Source: 1994–1999 General Aviation Activity Surveys.
Note: Columns may not add to totals due to rounding and estimation procedures.

equipment must be airlifted. With lives, property, or national security often at stake, many government missions cannot wait for the next airline departure. For security reasons, air transport of key personnel on government aircraft is often the only choice.

Government aircraft are often configured for unique jobs. Some are fitted with firefighting apparatus; others are stripped of all furnishings to accommodate heavy equipment and cargo; still others are equipped with communications equipment and modified so that cameras, radar, and other equipment can be installed.

Fifty-one percent of the public use aircraft in 1999 are powered by piston engines. An additional 39 percent are helicopters. Eight percent of the fleet are turbine-engine powered aircraft. Many of these aircraft are used for research or in-flight checking of navigational aids. Only a small number of government operated jets are configured for passenger travel.

Government missions include:

- Firefighting. The air dropping of water, chemicals, and fire retardant slurry by aircraft is a major weapon in the control of forest and brush fires, from the pine woods of New Jersey to the Florida Everglades, from the forests of the Big Sky country to the hills of Southern California.
- Law Enforcement. Several government agencies use aircraft to patrol borders, spot, chase, and apprehend crime suspects, transport prisoners, and play a major role in drug interdiction.
- Scientific Research and Development. Atmospheric research, especially severe weather prediction such as hurricanes, represents a major share of air operations in this category.
- Flight Inspection. Flight checking hundreds of navigational aids across the country to ensure safe and accurate readings is accomplished by government aircraft.
- Surveying. Aircraft operated by the Department of the Interior agencies, such as Fish and Wildlife and Park Service, help to conduct geological surveys such as wetlands

Table 2-3 Number of Active General Aviation Aircraft and Hours Flown by Aircraft Type and Primary Use—1999

| | Aircraft Type | | | | | | | | | | | | | | | |
| Use Category | Piston | | Turboprop | | Turbojet | | Rotorcraft | | Gliders | | Lighter-Than-Air | | Experimental | | Total | |
	Aircraft	Hours (000)	Aircraft	Hours (000)	Aircraft	Hours (000)	Aircraft	Hours (000)	Aircraft	Hours (000)	Aircraft	Hours (000)	Aircraft	Hours (000)	Aircraft	Hours (000)
Public Use	2,104	459	242	61	79	30	1,622	541	0	0	0	0	91	20	4,138	1,111
Corporate	2,635	601	2,368	702	5,170	2,061	482	208	0	0	30	3	119	41	10,804	3,616
Business	21,794	3,096	1,061	184	676	167	368	76	0	0	19	2	625	74	24,543	3,598
Personal	120,678	9,806	516	120	430	108	1,206	106	1,707	96	3,751	104	18,797	954	147,085	11,294
Instructional	14,458	5,370	46	30	36	24	836	378	256	48	205	8	244	35	16,081	5,893
Aerial Application	3,146	985	337	173	106	57	603	184	0	0	0	0	63	16	4,254	1,415
Aerial Observation	2,491	981	7	2	15	10	617	231	0	0	6	0	104	19	3,240	1,243
Aerial Other	207	49	20	12	18	15	102	38	0	0	0	0	20	5	366	120
Sightseeing	150	105	7	4	0	0	145	77	63	10	445	22	22	2	832	220
External Load	5	7	0	0	0	0	166	118	0	0	0	0	19	3	190	128
Air Tours	37	17	0	0	0	1	138	125	0	0	102	3	12	0	290	146
Air Taxi	2,223	883	935	447	496	235	608	324	0	0	0	0	18	8	4,279	1,897
Medical	255	71	82	49	16	12	435	392	0	0	0	0	46	27	834	461
Other	1,582	465	60	27	79	20	119	38	15	1	166	21	343	43	2,363	613
Total	171,923	22,895	5,679	1,812	7,120	2,738	7,448	2,744	2,041	155	4,725	164	20,528	1,248	219,464	31,756

Source: FAA

Note: Row and column summation may differ from printed totals due to estimation procedures, or because some active aircraft did not report use.

mapping and volcano monitoring. Pilots conduct regular and annual wildlife surveys for certain mammals and waterfowl, such as migratory bird surveys.

- Search and Rescue. U.S. Coast Guard and other government agencies save many lives every year through search and rescue.
- Drug Interdiction. To a great degree, the war on drugs is fought in the skies through the work of government pilots. These government pilots, flying air patrol, aircraft escort, and aerial spotting of suspect fields and plantings, help stop the flow of drugs into the U.S.
- Transport of Government Personnel. Because of security, timeliness, remote locations, and other reasons, government aircraft are often the only viable transportation choice. Safe and efficient transport of government officials is an important and legitimate use of public use aircraft.

Business Flying

Business flying includes two primary use categories. They are:

Executive/Corporate Transportation. Any use of an aircraft by a corporation, company, or other organization for the purposes of transporting its employees and/or property not for compensation or hire, and employing professional pilots for the operation of the aircraft.

Business Transportation. Any use of an aircraft not for compensation or hire by individuals for the purposes of transportation required by business in which they are engaged.

The Corporate Business fleet included 35,347 aircraft in 1999, which represented 16 percent of the total active, general aviation aircraft and 23 percent of the estimated total hours flown (see Table 2–3).

Business aircraft complement airline services in satisfying the nation's business transportation requirements. Although airlines offer transportation to the largest cities and business centers, business aviation specializes in many areas where major airlines cannot satisfy demand. These aircraft provided quick, safe, and reliable transportation whenever and wherever business needs required them.

Business aviation operators use all types of aircraft from single- and twin-engine, piston powered airplanes, helicopters and turboprops to the fastest jets to ensure maximum business effectiveness. Over two-thirds of the *Fortune 500* companies operate business aircraft, and virtually all of these aircraft operators are members of the National Business Aviation Association (NBAA). NBAA is the principal representative of business aviation before Congress, the administration, and its regulatory agencies such as the Federal Aviation Administration. It represents over 6,000 companies that operate over 8,000 aircraft. Turbojets are the most widely used type of aircraft. Some two-thirds of NBAA members have turbojets, approximately one-third have turboprops, and about one-eighth use multiengine piston powered aircraft. While most of these aircraft are operated domestically, an increasing number are utilized to expand markets overseas.

Numerous examples of typical traveling schedules purport to demonstrate the advantages of business aircraft over use of the commercial airlines. Because of the proliferation of airline hub and spoke systems since deregulation, flying business aircraft directly between airports has become a big advantage. The monetary-equivalent savings in terms of executives' time which would otherwise be spent in traveling to and from air carrier airports and in waiting for scheduled air carrier flights, plus hotel expenses, meals, and rental car expenses, loom large on the benefit side of such calculations. Normally unquantified are the advantages of flexibility and prestige (which may or may not bring about pecuniary benefits) and of the fact that business meetings may be held in privately owned aircraft.

The same is also generally true of smaller businesses that have discovered the benefits of their own aircraft. Keeping business appointments in several cities hundreds of miles apart—on the same day—is not unusual for general aviation aircraft operators.

Today's business aircraft are quieter, more efficient, and safer than ever before. Much like the computer, business aircraft are powerful business tools that make a company more profitable by making better use of a company's most valuable assets—time and personnel.

Personal Flying

Personal flying includes any use of an aircraft for personal purposes not associated with a business or profession, and not for hire. This includes maintenance of pilot proficiency. A personal plane is like a personal car. When the owner (or renter) uses a car or plane for a business trip, it becomes a business automobile or a business aircraft. It does not change its appearance. There is no way for anyone to tell whether a car or an airplane is being used for business or pleasure just by looking at it. A multimillionaire may own a large airplane as a purely private conveyance, with no business use. However, since the majority of privately owned (as distinguished from company-owned or corporate-owned) aircraft are of the light single or light twin-engine variety, it is appropriate to discuss this important segment of the general aviation industry.

Just as automobiles and boats are used for personal transportation and recreation, personal flying is a legitimate use of the sky. Flying is an efficient and effective business tool, but it is also a pleasant recreational vehicle. Thousands of private pilots use their aircraft to visit friends and relatives, attend special events, and reach distant vacation spots.

These aircraft are also flown by doctors, lawyers, accountants, engineers, farmers, and small business owners in the course of conducting their business. Typically, such persons use their aircraft partly for business and partly for pleasure. They differ primarily from the purely business flier with respect to the type of aircraft flown. A much higher proportion of the 147,085 aircraft they fly are single-engined piston aircraft (see Table 2–3).

Aircraft flown primarily for personal purposes represented two-thirds of the general aviation fleet and 36 percent of the total flying hours in 1999 (see Table 2–3).

A number of organizations represent the interests of the business and pleasure flier; by far the most important is the Aircraft Owners and Pilots Association (AOPA). This organization, headquartered in the Washington area, includes over 360,000 members, which represents over one-half of the pilots in the United States. In addition to its function of congressional liaison, the AOPA provides a variety of services for its members, many of which are designed to enhance air safety.

Instructional Flying

Instructional flying accounted for 16,081 aircraft or 7 percent of the total in 1999 (see Table 2–3). This category includes any use of an aircraft for formal instruction, either with the instructor aboard or when the student is flying solo but is carrying out maneuvers according to the instructor's specifications excluding proficiency flying. It is dominated by instruction leading to the private pilot's license, and close to 90 percent of the aircraft used for instruction are single-engine.

Obtaining a private pilot's license for business or personal reasons is the primary goal for some students. Others use it as a stepping stone to an airline or military aviation career. Most people learn to fly through a local *fixed base operator* (*FBO*). FBOs provide fuel and service, and they also rent and sell airplanes. They usually have a professional flight instructor on staff who provides ground and flight instruction. Many individuals also learn to fly through a local flying club that offers flight training. Such clubs are groups of individuals who own aircraft and rent them to members. They usually offer flight instruction and other flying-related activities to their members. Many vocational and technical schools, colleges, and universities offer aviation programs that include flight training.

Aerial Application, Aerial Observation, and Aerial Other

Aerial application includes any use of an aircraft for work that concerns the production of foods, fibers, and timber production and protection. This category primarily includes aircraft that distribute chemicals or seeds in agriculture and reforestation.

The use of aircraft in agriculture is a major factor in the production of food and fiber all over the world. Japanese, Russians, and Chinese are spending huge amounts of money to develop aerial application of fertilizers to spread seeds in inaccessible locations, to control pests, and to harvest crops.

Although the public image of crop dusters is that they are flying daredevils who operate flimsy crates and pollute the environment, the fact is that the industry is a major factor in the production of cotton, vegetables, and beef (by seeding and fertilizing grazing lands) and in the eradication of pests, such as the fire ant, the screw worm, and the gypsy moth.

It is an expensive business. These specially designed Ag aircraft can cost in excess of several hundred thousand dollars each. Needless to say, the operators, many of whom have fleets of as many as 50 aircraft, are involved in big business, requiring bank loans for equipment renewal, which in turn requires insurance coverage. If the business were as hazardous as the common impression, no banker or insurance company would deal with it.

Aerial observation includes any aircraft engaged in aerial mapping/photography, surveillance, fish spotting, search and rescue, hunting, highway traffic advisory, ranching, oil and mineral exploration, and criminal pursuit.

Land-use planners, real estate developers, beach erosion engineers, businessmen seeking new industrial sites, as well as city officials and highway designers, are relying on photographs taken from aircraft more and more in their deliberations. For years now, general aviation aircraft have been used to inspect pipelines and powerlines. These inspections must be made every couple of weeks. The locations of most pipelines and powerlines are remote and hard to reach by land, but general aviation aircraft can take care of this vital need economically and efficiently, saving thousands of gallons of fuel and power outages if undetected leaks or damage to pipelines or powerlines were not discovered.

Geophysical survey pilots search for new sources of energy using general aviation aircraft. With sophisticated instruments in the aircraft, a general aviation aircraft can locate and identify oil and gas deposits, coal, diamonds, and even water below the earth's surface.

Commercial fishing fleets on both coasts have found that their operations are more productive and profitable when they can be directed to concentrations of fish schooling far from the shore. Hence light aircraft for that purpose have evolved into making a major contribution to the industry.

The Fish and Wildlife Service retains commercial operators to survey herd and flock movements and to count the size of herds, as well as to air-drop food when natural forage is unavailable. Ranchers also use general aviation aircraft to inspect fences, round up strays, and check cattle for possible injuries. Because of the versatility of these aircraft, they can land and make necessary repairs or take care of cattle that may need treatment.

Major metropolitan police departments have found that road patrols by aircraft are highly effective for keeping watch over the flow of traffic during morning and evening rush hours and as an aid in apprehension of lawbreakers. Most police air patrols are performed in aircraft leased from general aviation operators.

Another specialized service usually performed on a contract basis is flying at very low levels along public utility rights-of-way to inspect the integrity of energy lines and check for transformer failures, broken insulators, short circuits, or line breaks. Inspection by air is frequently the only economical means of performing such service.

Aerial other includes the use of aircraft for weather modification, firefighting, and insect control. The creation of irrigating rain in arid regions and of snow for ski resorts would fall into this category. Air-dropping chemicals and fire retardant slurry by aircraft is a major weapon in the control of forest and brush fires.

Resort operators have found that spraying light oils and suspensions by aircraft (as distinguished from agricultural use of similar aircraft) has enhanced their business by eliminating the irritations of small flying insects. In addition to the elimination of a nuisance, aerial application of pesticides has been highly effective in controlling and, in many cases, eliminating diseases transmitted by insects, such as malaria.

These three primary use categories included 7,860 aircraft, or 4 percent of the total fleet in 1999 (see Table 2–3). There is no way to put a specific figure on the value of these commercial aviation operations, but we would not have the crops, the fibers, and the meat available at reasonable prices without it. The protection of natural resources, land planning, and disease and pest control are valuable, but their worth is difficult to compute in dollars.

Sightseeing, Air Tours, and Air Taxi

Aircraft flown for the purpose of *sightseeing* and *air tours* totaled 1,122 in 1999, or less than 1 percent of the active fleet. Sightseeing includes commercial sightseeing conducted under FAR Part 91, whereas air tours are conducted under FAR Part 135 (see Table 2–3). More than one-half of the sightseeing flights are made in lighter-than-air aircraft. The majority of air tours are conducted in rotorcraft and lighter-than-air aircraft.

Air taxi or charter firms serve as on-demand passenger and all-cargo operators. This category covers all types of aircraft, including single- and multiengine piston, turbine, and rotorcraft operating under FAR Part 135. The great advantage of the on-call air taxi or charter operator is its flexibility.

Chartering an airplane is similar to hiring a taxi for a single trip. The charter company or air taxi operator provides the aircraft, flight crew, fuel, and all other services for each trip. The charterer pays a fee, usually based on mileage or time, plus extras such as waiting time and crew expenses. An air taxi is particularly attractive for a firm that does not frequently require an airplane or does not often need a supplement to its aircraft. Firms will also charter when they need a special-purpose aircraft, such as a helicopter.

As commercial operators, air taxi firms must conform to more stringent operating and maintenance requirements called for in Federal Aviation Regulations. In addition, each air taxi or charter operator, regardless of the types of airplanes used, must have an air taxi certificate on file with the FAA. This certificate is issued by the FAA after proper application and local inspection. It also evidences certain minimum insurance coverage and limits. In 1999, the FAA listed 4,279 air taxi aircraft, which represented 2 percent of the general aviation fleet (see Table 2–3).

External Load and Medical

External load includes aircraft under FAR Part 133. The majority of aircraft under this category are rotorcraft used for external load operations, such as hoisting heavy loads and hauling logs from remote locations. If it were not for general aviation aircraft, primarily helicopters that transport heavy, expensive drilling equipment, as well as people, day and night, good weather and bad, America's dependence on foreign oil would be far greater and would surely impact negatively on the American consumer.

The *medical* category is also dominated by helicopters, which present more than 50 percent of the aircraft flown to carry people or donor organs for transplant. There are times when the American Red Cross needs to transport emergency supplies to disaster victims or blood of rare types or in large quantities. The entire medical emergency evacuation process was changed when state and local governments began establishing "MEDE-VAC" units to respond to critically injured persons such as those involved in auto accidents. The survival rate in life-threatening injuries has been greatly enhanced when a person can be transported quickly to nearby hospitals. The 1,024 aircraft in these two categories represent less than one percent of the active fleet (see Table 2–3).

Other

The FAA defines *other flying* as any other use of an aircraft not included under the other categories. Examples include aircraft for research and development, testing, air shows, air racing, parachuting, towing gliders, and aerial advertising. Aerial advertising is a highly specialized—but very lucrative—part of commercial aviation. On the basis of "cost per thousand," key words in the advertising business, a towed banner or a message written in smoke over a city will draw a larger audience for less cost than any other form of advertising. A banner towed over a sports stadium or along a hundred miles of crowded beach is seen by more eyes than a similar message carried for the same price in any other communications medium. A message sky-written over Manhattan on a clear day can be seen by 10 million people at one time.

In 1999 2,363 aircraft fell into this category which represented 1 percent of the total active fleet.

Generl aviation aircraft save time, lives, and money and provides efficient energy-saving transportation for people in all walks of life who are involved in all different kinds of activities. But the ultimate value of general aviation, which contrasts it to the air carriers, is the flexibility and utility of the aircraft and the pilots. General aviation operates when the air carriers do not, and it goes to locations not served by air carriers.

GENERAL AVIATION AIRPORTS

In a broad sense, all airports are general aviation airports because they can be used by general aviation aircraft, including those used by the certificated air carriers, which are sometimes referred to as Commercial Service airports. At the end of 1999, the gross figure of aircraft landing facilities reported by the FAA was 19,119 (see Table 2–4). However, this figure is not restricted to airports but includes other forms of landing facilities not used by conventional aircraft. It includes heliports, stolports (short takeoff and landing airports), and seaplane bases. It also includes airports located on American Samoa, Guam, Puerto Rico, the Virgin Islands, and U.S. Trust Territories in the South Pacific.

There are 5,145 *publicly owned airports* in the United States, ranging in size from the enormous Dallas/Ft. Worth and JFK layouts to the small grass fields owned by local communities. All of these may be used by light general aviation aircraft. Fliers intending to use any airport have publications from which they can ascertain its capacity and equipment.

An airport owned by a government body can usually be regarded as permanent and stable, particularly if federal funding has been obtained for improving the facilities. In addition, there are 13,974 *private use airports* that are not open to the general public, but are restricted to the use of their owners and the invited guests of the owners on an exclusive-use basis. Such airports are comparable to private roads or private driveways.

Table 2–4 U.S. Civil and Joint-Use Airports, Heliports, Stolports, and Seaplane Bases on Record by Type of Ownership— January 2000

| FAA Region | Total Facilities | Total Facilities By Ownership | | Airports Open to the Public | | | | Total Airports |
| | | Public | Private | Paved Airports | | Unpaved Airports | | |
				Lighted	Unlighted	Lighted	Unlighted	
Grand Total	19,119	5,145	13,974	3,634	256	402	763	4,934
United States*	19,058	5,110	13,948	3,616	254	402	762	4,913
Alaskan	559	386	173	49	4	105	144	302
Central	1,551	497	1,054	382	16	39	52	479
Eastern	2,514	357	2,157	335	23	50	81	489
Great Lakes	4,405	912	3,493	746	23	136	157	1,062
New England	733	141	592	117	16	5	25	163
Northwest	1,992	688	1,304	414	43	20	145	622
Southern	2,833	944	1,989	637	36	28	46	636
Southwest	3,115	821	2,294	643	41	13	71	768
Western	1,417	499	918	311	54	6	42	413

Source: FAA
Note: *Excludes Puerto Rico, Virgin Islands, and South Pacific.

Economic Role of General Aviation Airports

General aviation airports play an important role in the transportation network, but this fact is not publicized well. The United States has the finest scheduled air transportation system in the world. The service points, the equipment, the personnel, and the schedules are as excellent and as much in the public interest as it is humanly, mechanically, and economically possible to make them. This does not alter another fact: that unless the traveler is flying among the major metropolitan areas, many gaps in airline service still exist, including infrequent schedules requiring roundabout routes, time-consuming layovers, and frequent changes.

Since deregulation, many smaller cities have lost airline service from the major and national carriers, who simply find it uneconomical to serve these points with their jet equipment. Regional air carriers are now serving many of the smaller cities, but voids in service throughout the nation are apparent.

In scheduling, it is economically sound for the air carrier to place more flights at the most popular times in service between pairs of cities that have the highest passenger loads. This factor also leads to very sparse service during off-peak hours.

Thousands of smaller cities, towns, and villages also need air transportation service. There are close to 20,000 incorporated communities in the 48 contiguous states and an additional 15,000 unincorporated communities. Because the scheduled airlines serve less than 4 percent of the nation's 19,000 landing facilities with approximately 7,000 aircraft, many communities are without immediate access to the fine airline system.

The role of general aviation airports serving 220,000 aircraft, or 96 percent of the total active aircraft in the United States, in providing air access is increasing. By having air access to all the nation's airports, general aviation aircraft can bring the benefits and values of air transportation to the entire country.

Attracting Industry

Cities and towns that years ago decided not to build an airport have learned that lack of an airport jeopardizes community progress. Time and again, the lack of an airport has proved to be the chief reason that a community has been bypassed as a location for a new plant or a new industry.

Although scheduled air service is concentrated in major metropolitan areas, business and industry are moving to less populated areas. Shifts in population, lower taxes, room for expansion, less congestion, and better access to highways are some of the factors causing this trend. With branch plants, the source of production is nearer the distribution points, but management is farther away from its responsibilities. Without flexible transportation, industry faces the dangers of absentee management both in the widely spread branches and in the home office (because of extended trips).

The general aviation airport has become vital to the growth of business and industry in a community by providing access for companies that must meet the demands of supply, competition, and expanding marketing areas. Communities without general aviation airports place limitations on their capacity for economic growth.

Flexibility is the key word in business flying—flexibility to go whenever and wherever necessary. The key to flexibility is airport facilities. The shorter the time between desk chair and pilot's seat, the greater the benefits of the business airplane. This flexibility in reaching destinations serves not only in direct point-to-point travel but also is a factor that has made business aviation one of the biggest suppliers of passengers to the airlines. Business and private airplanes feed passengers into major terminals. Charter and air taxi services let passengers step from a long-distance jet liner into a single-engine or twin-engine air taxi for swift completion of their trips to cities and towns hundreds of miles from airline hubs.

Time equals dollars to business people who cannot afford the luxury of a long wait between business appointments or who arrange their travel work schedules to fit the rigid timetables of public transportation. Between cities with frequent service, this is not a problem. It is easy to go from New York City to Chicago or Atlanta, but considerably more difficult to go with equal speed between Peoria, Illinois, and Rochester, Minnesota, or between Decatur, Illinois, and El Dorado, Arkansas.

The competitive nature of today's business and the value of an individual's time prohibits unproductive or uneconomical periods. A person who saves only 30 minutes a day in one year will accumulate 125 hours of productive time—more than three weeks' additional time on the job rather than on the go.

In most large metropolitan areas, business fliers can choose among several general aviation airports that are not available to the scheduled airlines. For example, Atlanta has 12 general aviation airports within a 30-mile radius of the city. One or more of these alternative airports are commonly used by the majority of business aircraft operators in the region and, in most instances, are chosen for their more convenient location to the user's office. Such airports typically offer closer and more available parking, more rapid boarding, better security and much shorter walking distances than a major airline terminal.

Stimulating Economic Growth

Airports and related aviation and nonaviation businesses located on the airport represent a major source of employment for many communities around the country. The wages and salaries paid by airport-related businesses can have a significant effect on the local economy by providing the means to purchase goods and services while generating tax revenues, as well. But local payrolls are not the only measure of an airport's economic benefit to the community. Indirectly, the employee expenditures generate successive waves of additional employment and purchases, which are more difficult to measure but nevertheless substantial.

In addition to the local economic activity generated by the regular expenditures of resident employees, the airport also stimulates the economy through the use of local services for all cargo, food catering, aircraft maintenance, and ground transportation on and around the airport. Regular purchases of fuel, supplies, equipment, and other services from local distributors inject additional income into the local community. The airport retail shops, hotels, and restaurants further act to recycle money within the local community as dollars pass from one person to another, supporting many people and businesses. This so-called multiplier effect operates in all cities as aviation-related dollars are channeled throughout the community.

Airports provide an additional asset to the general economy by generating billions of dollars per year in state and local taxes. These taxes increase the revenues available for projects and services to benefit the residents of each state and community. Whether the extra tax dollars improve the state highway system, beautify state parks, or help prevent a tax increase, airport-generated tax dollars work for everyone.

Cities with good airport facilities also profit from tourist and convention business. This can represent substantial revenues for hotels, restaurants, retail stores, sports clubs, nightclubs, sightseeing, rental cars, and local transportation, among others. The amount of convention business varies with the size of the city, but even smaller communities show a sizable income from this source.

Beyond the benefits that an airport brings to the community as a transportation facility and as a local industry, the airport has become a significant factor in the determination of real estate values in adjacent areas. Land located near airports almost always increases in value as the local economy begins to benefit from the presence of the airport. Land developers consistently seek land near airports, and it follows inexorably that a new airport will inspire extensive construction around it.

PILOTS

At the end of 1999, the FAA reported 635,472 active pilots in the United States, including 97,359 student pilots and 258,749 private pilots (see Table 2–5). Many of these individuals own, rent, borrow, and lease small aircraft for business and pleasure purposes.

It is easy to become caught up in the business and economic aspects of general aviation and the contribution it makes to a locality's economy and to overlook another important

Table 2–5　Active U.S. Pilot Certificates Held 1980–1999

Category	Year					
	1980	**1985**	**1990**	**1995**	**1998**	**1999**
Student	199,833	146,652	128,663	101,279	97,736	97,359
Private[1]	357,479	311,086	299,111	261,399	247,226	258,749
Commercial[1]	183,442	151,632	149,666	133,980	122,053	124,261
Airline Transport[1]	69,569	82,740	107,732	123,877	134,612	137,642
Helicopter (only)	6,030	8,123	9,567	7,183	6,964	7,728
Other[2]	10,718	9,307	7,920	11,466	9,707	9,733
Pilot Total	**827,071**	**709,540**	**702,659**	**639,184**	**618,298**	**635,472**
Instrument Rating[3]	260,461	258,559	297,073	298,301	300,183	308,951
Flight Instructor Certificate[3]	60,440	58,940	63,775	77,613	79,171	79,694

Source: FAA
Note:
[1]Includes pilots with an airplane certificate
[2]Includes Glider (only), Lighter-Than-Air, and Recreational.
Lighter-Than-Air ratings no longer issued after 1989.
[3]Not included in Pilot total.

part of the general aviation's contribution—personal flying. There is a widely held attitude that commercial airlines are a business and are therefore important and that personal flying is just an unimportant frivolity. However, one must keep in mind that the certificated airlines carry just about as many people for vacation travel and visiting friends and relatives as they do for business purposes. On special charters, virtually all the passengers are on pleasure trips on every flight.

The flexibility of transportation offered by general aviation is not restricted to business use. By light plane, it is possible for a citizen of the middle-Atlantic states or the Midwest to visit the warm climate of Florida for the weekend or to fly from Montgomery, Alabama, to Canadian lakes in a few hours. Air transportation for vacationing is unabashedly advertised by the air carriers. It should not be overlooked as an aspect of general aviation.

Many pilots who start off as weekend pilots upgrade into high-performance equipment and obtain higher ratings and pilot privileges and eventually become business as well as pleasure air travelers in light aircraft. Others start out to obtain their Commercial and Airline Transport certificates with the intention of making a career in aviation. Many pilots now flying for the airlines, corporate aviation, or the military got their start in general aviation. Because of the downsizing of the military during the 1990s, it is anticipated that an ever-increasing number of individuals who started their careers in general aviation will be called to fill the needs of the air carriers and corporate aviation in the future.

The decline in the number of active student pilots and student starts began in 1980 following the repeal of the GI Bill of Rights in 1979. As discussed in Chapter 1, the effect of the Civil Pilot Training Program, the GI Bill, and other training programs was enormous. They were responsible for the majority of flight training students for many years. They were responsible for general aviation's infrastructure being larger than it would have been without these programs. Things began to stabilize in the late 1990s, and after reaching a low point in 1995, student starts increased for the remainder of the decade. This has been the result of a concerted effort on the part of the general aviation community and government to increase the number of general aviation pilots.

FAA SERVICES TO PILOTS

Today's sophisticated air navigation network has its roots in the 1920s, when pilots relied on scattered radio stations and rotating light beacons to hop from one landing field to the next. During periods of poor visibility, however, the usefulness of light beacons was severely limited. By the end of the decade, the federal government had introduced the first of many navigational aids that could serve the pilot day or night, fair weather or foul. This was the four-course radio range, a device that transmitted radio signals in four directions. The government installed a network of these facilities to guide pilots to their destinations.

As aviation grew, more than four paths were needed to handle the navigational needs of air traffic, and the original radio range was replaced by the *very-high-frequency omnidirectional range (VOR)*, a device developed during World War II. VORs were deployed on the airways in large numbers after the war and are still the chief air navigation aids on the U.S. airways. In 1999 there were 1,044 VORs, including 71 nonfederal and 37 military locations (see Table 2–6).

Today's VOR has sophisticated electronics but operates on the same principle as its predecessors. It emits signals in the pattern of a huge wheel, with the station at the center and 360 spokes radiating from the hub. Each radial represents a radio course that a pilot can use to guide an airplane accurately along a desired track.

Navigational facilities also help a pilot descend from cruising altitude to land on an airport runway, even under poor weather conditions. The *Instrument Landing System (ILS)* is the most widely used equipment in the world for making safe runway approaches in difficult weather. The FAA deployed 1,327 of these systems at airports across the United States by the end of 1999 (see Table 2–6).

An ILS sends out two radio beams to approaching aircraft. One beam, the localizer, gives the pilot left-right guidance; the other, the glide slope, gives the pilot the correct angle of descent to the runway. Even when visibility from the approach end of the runway is only a few hundred feet, properly instrumented aircraft can now land with pinpoint accuracy.

The air traffic control system is crucial to civil aviation, keeping airplanes safely separated from each other and regulating their flow into and out of airport terminal areas.

Under instrument flight rules, standard separation between two airplanes depends on a number of factors, including the size of the airplanes being separated and the kind of airspace they occupy. Generally, airplanes close to an airport are kept apart by at least three miles horizontally and 1,000 feet vertically. When airplanes are flying between

Table 2–6   FAA Air Route Facilities and Services—1999

VOR VORTAC[1]	1,041
Non-Directional Beacons[1]	1,320
Air Route Traffic Control Centers	24
Airport Traffic Control Towers[1]	680
Flight Service Stations[2]	75
International Flight Service Stations	3
Instrument Landing Systems	1,327
Airport Surveillance Radar	295

Source: FAA
Note:
[1]Includes nonfederal and military
[2]Includes Automated Flight Service Stations (AFSS)

major terminal areas, standard separation is never less than five horizontal miles and 1,000 vertical feet.

Making this system work are the personnel who staff air traffic control towers, terminal-area radar facilities, air route traffic control centers, and automated flight service stations. Each type of facility performs a different task. Tower and terminal-area controllers handle airplanes that are landing and taking off, taxiing on the ground, and flying in the vicinity of the airport. There were 680 airports in the United States with control towers in 1999 (see Table 2–6). With the exception of the major hubs that serve large metropolitan areas, general aviation is the primary user of the tower-controlled airports.

The busier tower-controlled airports have an additional facility for the safe and expeditious movement of air traffic: radar. Many civil airports have Airport Surveillance Radar which is also available to general aviation pilots who operate in the areas of their coverage. In 1999 there were 295 airports with surveillance radar (see Table 2–6). When using airports with such equipment, the majority of general aviation pilots use radar assistance because it is available and in some cases required.

Another service available to all fliers is the en route air traffic control complex, which consists of 24 *air route traffic control centers* (*ARTCCs*). These centers provide radar air traffic separation service to aircraft operating on instrument flight plan within controlled airspace. No aircraft may be operated when the visibility or ceiling falls below prescribed limits unless they are operated on instrument flight plan under instrument flight rules (IFR). Air carrier category aircraft, particularly those operated by certificated air carriers, operate under instrument flight rules all the time, no matter how good the actual weather may be, an a matter of course. General aviation pilots who are instrument qualified, or instrument "rated," tend to file instrument flight plans only when it is necessary to make a flight in adverse weather.

The most widely used service provided by the FAA to general aviation pilots is the *Flight Service Station* (*FSS*) network of 75 facilities for collecting and disseminating weather information, filing flight plans, and providing in-flight assistance and aviation advisory services. Air carriers have their own meteorological service, and their instrument flight plans are prefiled by computer. (These are called "canned" flight plans.) General aviation flight plans are filed individually via FSS facilities.

Flight service stations are the sole means of general aviation's filing flight plans, which are required under actual instrument conditions and are optional in good weather. They are the sole source from which to obtain official weather information, either in person (face-to-face briefings) or by telephone, or, when airborne, by air/ground radio communications.

The FSS system is vitally important to general aviation operations, and it is used by pilots of every level, from student pilots to air transport-rated pilots of large business jets. Flight service stations are indispensable to all general aviation flight operations.

Airframe Manufacturers

The period from 1980 through the mid 1990s was one of considerable restructuring, downsizing, and consolidation for the general aviation aircraft manufacturers. The large-scale manufacturing of single-engine aircraft virtually ceased. The emphasis of major U.S. manufacturers shifted almost entirely to turbine business aircraft. With the maturation of the U.S. market being hastened by a lack of growth being supplied from smaller aircraft markets, the foreign manufacturers of piston and turbine aircraft made inroads into the market. In 1992, for the first time ever, a foreign manufacturer, Aerospatiale, sold more single-engine airplanes than any U.S. manufacturer.

Between 1994 and 2000, general aviation shipments and billings more than tripled (see Table 1–1). The General Aviation Manufacturers Association (GAMA) estimated that more than 25,000 manufacturing jobs were created during that time period. GAMA also reported increases in general aviation exports and new products as a result of increases in research and development.

Table 2-7   GAMA Airplane Shipments 1999–2000

Manufacturer & Model	Total 1999	Total 2000	Manufacturer & Model	Total 1999	Total 2000
American Champion			**Maule Aircraft**		
Adventurer 7GCAA	19	23	M6-235	1	1
Aurora 7ECA	9	3	MX-7-180C Millennium	2	2
Citabria Explorer 7GCBC	31	22	MXT-7-180 Star Rocket	1	7
Scout 8GCBC	5	23	MXT-7-180A Comet	18	6
Super Decathlon 8KCAB	27	25	M-7-235B Super Rocket	8	7
Total	**91**	**96**	M-7-235C Orion	16	17
Aviat Aircraft			MT-7-235 Super Rocket	4	5
Husky A-1A	23	4	M-7-260	6	1
Husky A-1B	44	76	MT-7-260	2	2
Pitts S-2C	16	11	M-7-260C	10	9
Total	**83**	**91**	M-7-260	1	0
Bellanca Aircraft			**Total**	**69**	**57**
Super Viking 17-30A	1	1	**Micco Aircraft**		
Boeing Business Jets			SP20	N/A	5
BBJ	29	14	SP26	N/A	1
Cessna Aircraft			**Total**	**N/A**	**6**
172 Skyhawk	452	490	**Mooney Aircraft**		
182 Skylane	248	267	Bravo M20M	25	26
206 Stationair	79	53	Ovation M20R	24	55
T206 Stationair	120	122	Ovation 2 M20R	10	0
208 Caravan I	20	16	Eagle M20S	38	19
208B Caravan 1B	67	76	**Total**	**97**	**100**
Citation CJ1 525	59	56	**New Piper Aircraft**		
Citation CJ2 525A	0	8	Warrior III PA-28-161	20	43
Citation Bravo 550	36	54	Archer III PA-28-181	107	102
Citation Encore 560	0	6	Arrow PA-28-R-201	6	18
Citation Excel 560XL	39	79	Saratoga II HP PA-32R-301	28	28
Citation Ultra 560	32	0	Saratoga II TC PA-32R-301	52	70
Citation VII 650	14	12	Malibu Meridian PA-46-500TP	0	18
Citation X 750	36	37	Malibu Mirage PA-46-350P	63	63
Total	**1,202**	**1,256**	Seminole PA-44-180	8	11
Cirrus Design			Seneca V PA-34-220T	57	42
SR20	**9**	**95**	**Total**	**341**	**395**
Commander Aircraft			**Raytheon Aircraft**		
Commander 114B	8	0	Bonanza A36	74	85
Commander 114TC	5	1	Bonanza B36TC	22	18
Commander 115	0	11	Baron 58	49	50
Commander 115TC	0	8	King Air C90B	41	46
Total	**13**	**20**	King Air B200	44	59
Gulfstream Aerospace			King Air 350	43	46
Gulfstream IV-SP	39	37	Beechjet 400A	48	51
Gulfstream V	31	34	Hawker 800XP	55	67
Total	**70**	**71**	Beech 1900D Airliner	24	54
Lancair			**Total**	**400**	**476**
Columbia 300	**N/A**	**5**			
Learjet					
Learjet 31A	24	27			
Learjet 45	43	71	**Grand Total**	**2,504**	**2,816**
Learjet 60	32	35			
Total	**99**	**133**			

Source: General Aviation Manufacturers Association (GAMA)

Table 2–8 Worldwide Business Turbine Airplane Shipments 1999–2000

Manufacturer & Model	Total 1999	Total 2000	Manufacturer & Model	Total 1999	Total 2000
Airbus			**Galaxy (IAI)**		
ACJ	2	6	Astra SPX	9	11
Boeing			Galaxy	1	6
BBJ	29	14	**Total**	**10**	**17**
Bombardier			**Gulfstream**		
Learjet 31A	24	27	GIV-SP	39	37
Learjet 45	43	71	GV	31	34
Learjet 60	32	35	**Total**	**70**	**71**
Challenger 604	42	39	**Piaggio**		
Global Express	32	35	P-180 Avanti	0	6
Total	**173**	**207**	**Pilatus**		
Cessna			PC-12	55	69
Citation Jet[1]	59	4	**Piper**		
CJ1	0	52	Meridian[3]	0	18
CJ2	0	8	**Raytheon**		
Citation Bravo	36	54	King Air C90B	41	46
Citation Encore[2]	0	6	King Air B200	44	59
Citation Excel	39	79	King Air 350	43	46
Citation Ultra[1]	32	0	Beechjet 400A	48	51
Citation VII	14	12	Hawker 800XP	55	67
Citation X	36	37	**Total**	**231**	**269**
Total	**216**	**252**	**Socata**		
Dassault			TBM 700	21	23
Falcon 50EX	11	18			
Falcon 2000	34	26			
Falcon 900C	8	6			
Falcon 900EX	16	23	**GRAND TOTAL**	**876**	**1,025**
Total	**69**	**73**			

Source: Aviation International News, March 2001.
(1) Production ended in 2000. (2) Deliveries started in 3Q00. (3) Deliveries started in 4Q00.

Tables 2–7 and 2–8 show the general aviation aircraft in production and usually available in the United States. While there is enough momentum in the form of back orders to propel airframe manufacturers through a successful 2001, there are clouds on the horizon. Inventories of used aircraft have climbed dramatically and the economy slowed in 2000 and continued into 2001, along with a precipitous decline in the stock market. There is no question that the new decade will bring new challenges to the industry; but this is nothing new if we reflect on the history of general aviation.

Significance of Pilots to Aircraft Manufacturing

The significance of pilots to the growth in airframe manufacturing cannot be overstated. Traditionally, the industry has looked at pilots in two ways. First of all, as people who would learn to fly, and in some form or fashion, then buy an airplane. They might buy a new or used aircraft, or join a flying club or rent from an FBO, but in essence, they were purchasing the aircraft, either in total, or by the hour. The manufacturers also looked at pilots as those who would fly their products for a living with the air carriers, military, corporate, utility, agricultural, air ambulance, state, local or federal government, or other operations.

The overwhelming majority of business aircraft sales are by companies that already own and operate an aircraft and are acquiring more capable, new equipment. The awareness of aviation — the influences that go into creating the potential for a company to use aircraft as a business tool — comes significantly from pilots. Over the years, manufacturers have recognized that one of the key indicators of aircraft usage or acquisition by a company is the presence of a pilot, even a noncurrent pilot, in the senior management ranks of a company. These advocates inside the company are often much more influential in the sales process than the manufacturers' sales and marketing staffs.

Industry Outlook

For a thorough discussion and statistical analysis of the industry see *FAA Aerospace Forecasts* and *FAA Statistical Handbook of Aviation* which are published annually and may be obtained by phone: (202) 267-3355, or by writing Federal Aviation Administration, Office of Aviation Policy and Plans, Statistics and Forecast Branch (APO-110), 800 Independence Avenue, S.W., Washington, DC 20591. The *FAA Aerospace Forecasts* covers a ten-year period and covers all segments of the industry. APO Websites which includes annual conference proceedings, statistical publications, and latest data are: Forecasts/Statistical Publications: http://api.hq.faa.gov/apo_pubs.htm

APO Data System: http:///www.apo.data.faa.gov

Another excellent source for current and forecasted statistics is the "General Aviation Statistical Databook" which may be obtained by phone: (202) 393-1500, or by writing General Aviation Manufacturers Association, 1400 K Street, N.W., Suite 801, Washington, DC 20005.

GENERAL AVIATION ON THE WEB

The aviation industry, like most industries, has been affected dramatically by the dawning of the Information Age. For example, the challenges confronting dealers of pre-owned business airplanes have become particularly acute. In the past, a handful of experts possessed an advantage simply because they had access to information that others did not. Being the first (and preferably the only) person to know where a certain aircraft type was available meant a competitive advantage, and it was to be protected at all costs. But now, with immediate access to information about pre-owned aircraft available at the click of a mouse, the monopoly on such information has been broken. The Information Age has irreversibly democratized the industry. Information flows so freely, in fact, that many buyers and sellers today work without any broker or dealer representative.

Widespread use of fax machines meant offers could be transmitted and agreed upon the same day. Overnight delivery of packages redefined the time schedule of not only gathering but also disseminating information, and, soon, this timing became nearly as important as the information itself. Then, as if things were not changing rapidly enough, along came the Internet and World Wide Web.

The Internet has brought about the convergence of information gathering and purchasing decisions. Customers are armed with data before they ever get in touch with the company and, hence, are more empowered than ever before. Similarly, to be successful on the Web, one must give a lot to get a lot. A business must learn to grapple with large amounts of fast-changing data and use that information to help its clients. An effective website can then be used to bridge time and distance to create new levels of customer intimacy and a higher level of dealer/broker availability.

Those who adopted the Internet early have already taken the risks and made mistakes from which others can learn. There is now less risk than ever in applying resources to a strong Web presence. In some ways, the risks are higher for those companies who have not implemented an Internet strategy.

Customers are struggling with the deluge of information they face in making decisions. Unfortunately, the Internet has developed a lot of useless, redundant, and even wrong information. It is the company's responsibility to help clients gain access to the right data and interpret and apply that data intelligently. This is where the true value of the Information Age lies, and smart customers are willing to pay to have access to it.

Gaining an edge in the Information Age, therefore, will depend on leveraging Internet technology to create niches based on a company's particular areas of expertise and service delivery. For example, each dealer and broker must stake out a unique place in the new marketplace and stream critical information out to the audience most interested in it. In so doing, the company will become a consultative resource for its clients and will realize tangible benefits through the unique networking opportunities made possible by a connected aviation community.

Included at the end of this chapter is a listing of general aviation websites chosen for their relevance and usefulness to the general aviation community. Space constraints do not permit listing every beneficial aviation site, but it should provide an excellent starting point. Another excellent source of aviation-related organizations is the World Aviation Directory.

Airframe Manufacturers

Airframe manufacturers face a dilemma when developing websites. On the one hand, the site can be tremendously useful in disseminating information to operators; but it can also generate a flood of casual queries from the general public, as well as sales leads from dubious sources.

Each manufacturer with a website has attacked the problem differently, choosing either to deliver some information along with password-limited access to customer service areas or simply to use the Web as a brochure-like publishing and distribution medium.

The Web has a tremendous potential for saving manufacturers money by allowing them to distribute the kind of information their operators need. Sites can provide basic product information, as well as links to sales and support personnel, including contact phone numbers and e-mail addresses. They can also be used to order parts or download technical information such as service bulletins. Customers who have clicked through online parts catalogs and updated their maintenance manuals over the Web recognize that it can be a tremendous time saver. Not only does it save the customer time, but it also allows the manufacturer to devote its resources to other areas.

The greatest potential for aviation Web utility is with customer-oriented aircraft manufacturers. Aircraft manufacturing does not stop after the product is delivered. There is a constant need for two-way communication between manufacturers and aircraft owners and operators, and the Web is the perfect way to enable that type of dialogue.

Aircraft Sales

In the world of Web classifieds, Trade-A-Plane is the dominant source. For an annual fee (free to print subscribers), Web users can access TAP's entire content, which includes more than 5,000 aircraft and other aviation products. Access to display advertisers' material is free.

Searches can be done for aircraft by manufacturer or model, location (by state), price, model year, total time, engine time, and keywords. To finish a search request, the user selects either to browse listings or to see the complete ads. For aircraft, browsing works better because it delivers a list of all the aircraft that fall close to the search constraints, depending on a 1 to 5 order of importance that the user assigned to each search category.

Another excellent site is Aircraft Shopper Online, a Web-only directory of aircraft for sale, accessible free of charge. Using ASO's PowerSearch, visitors can look for airplanes and helicopters by manufacturer, price range, year built, and time on airframe. Links are provided to contact the seller by e-mail and telephone, and many listings have photos showing the exterior and interior of aircraft for sale.

Sales of pre-owned aircraft over the Web may not be threatening traditional aircraft selling, but dealers and brokers are using it extensively to help develop leads. And for the buyer, the Internet is a great place to comparison-shop for pre-owned aircraft.

Business Aviation Services

Service companies such as maintenance shops, training organizations, and FBOs face a special challenge when publishing on the Web: What content can they deliver on a website that will bring in new customers and serve the needs of existing customers?

Much of the information that an aviation service company publishes is brochure-like and does not need frequent updating. But without timely updating, material on a website does not change often enough to attract repeat visitors.

Although some aviation sites have attacked the repeat visitor problem in unique ways, such as offering discount coupons, some companies simply feel it is good enough to have a website with descriptions of services, photos, and no dynamic information.

Flight Planning and Weather

There are excellent resources for professional online assistance for every facet of trip planning. Retrieval of weather information online has become the most popular use of the Web among pilots, either through commercial vendors or no-fee government and university-sponsored sites. Beyond that, flight plans can be filed, locating bargains on fuel, ordering parts, accessing federal regulations and safety-related information, scheduling trips and finding hotels, rental cars, and restaurants.

Charter Reservations

Because the Web can provide a high level of interaction between buyer and seller, it is fast becoming the preferred tool for an array of online charter reservations services. For example, Skyjet, which was acquired by Bombardier in 2000, allows visitors to check fares and book flights on any of over 1,300 aircraft in its charter network.

Avionics

For a glimpse into aviation's future, the avionics manufacturers provide excellent sites for emerging airspace issues from RVSM and ADS-B to Free Flight and WAAS/LAAS. Some of the best sites for taking a look into the future are those maintained by Honeywell, Rockwell Collins, and UPS Aviation Technologies. All three update their sites regularly with interesting and useful information.

Parts Suppliers

There are sites that provide huge parts databases for technicians. One of the best known parts distributors, Aviall, provides its customers with full access to its entire inventory online. Users can search by part number and find out if the part is available, how much it costs, including discount, and whether any parts are on back order or have been shipped. Once parts are found, users can order them online.

Training

Flight training organizations are mainly using their websites to list course schedules and locations. SimuFlite allows customers to sign up for courses over its website, although confirmation does not come until an account representative contacts the customer. All of SimuFlite's simulators are listed, along with detailed specs for each aircraft type in which training is offered. The company offers a number of interactive sections, such as its "Ground Chatter" page and live broadcasts between ATC and pilots flying in the Dallas/Fort Worth area.

Publications

Because the Web is such an inexpensive communications medium, accessible by anyone with a computer, modem, and Internet connection, hundreds of electronic only (no print counterpart) publications have appeared online. In their wake, nearly all the nation's major newspapers and magazines have launched sites of their own, with the result being that a seemingly unending source of news and information is available online, 24 hours a day.

Aviation print publications have approached the Web in similar fashion, but most are still grappling with issues such as how much content to provide for free, how to serve existing readers and attract new readers online, and how much manpower to devote to the Web.

Associations

The Web provides a means by which association members and interested visitors can learn about the latest developments regarding the association. One of the most comprehensive sites is offered by the National Business Aviation Association (NBAA). Launched in 1995, it has seen a dramatic increase in member use. It offers an online discussion forum where members can chat with each other via e-mail and on the site itself. Users can subscribe to any or all categories, which include sections for flight department managers, pilots, schedulers and dispatchers, maintenance personnel, and flight attendants, as well as topical sections on taxes, jobs, and even fractional ownership.

The main reason for conducting business online is to increase revenues and reduce transaction costs. E-commerce, used correctly, can strengthen the relationship between a company and its customers. Consumers benefit from being able to use their computers to enhance the overall buying experience. For example, customers can track the status of orders they have placed, get quick answers to technical questions, swiftly compare prices between multiple vendors, search online catalogs with ease, and solve product warranty issues. In short, the onus is on the seller to create a business environment that makes the buyer's job simple. With the right interactive programming, an aviation website can be transformed into a sophisticated marketing and sales tool that offers every visitor a highly personalized and responsive experience.

And someday, e-commerce will live up to that lofty expectation. In the meantime, today's sellers, buyers, and producers must be pioneers, enduring the same setbacks encountered by the vanguard in any endeavor.

GENERAL AVIATION WEBSITES

The following listing of general aviation websites contains nearly 500 entries, which are broken down into 20 categories for quick reference by company or organization. It provides a fairly comprehensive listing of firms and organizations that fall within the scope of the GA industry. However, no attempt was made to make it all-inclusive.

Airframe Manufacturers

AASI: www.aasiaircraft.com
Adam Aircraft Industries: www.adamaircraft.com
Agusta: www.agusta.it
Airbus: www.airbus.com
Alliance Aerospace: www.allianceaero.com
American Utilicraft: www.utilicraft.com
Ayres: www.ayrescorp.com
BAE Systems: www.baesystems.com
Bell/Agusta Aerospace: www.bellagustaaerospace.com
Bell Helicopter Textron: www.bellhelicopter.textron.com
Boeing Business Jets: www.boeing.com/bbj
Bombardier: www.aero.bombardier.com
Britten-Norman: www.britten-norman.com
Century Aerospace: www.centuryaero.com
Cessna: www.cessna.com
Cirrus: www.cirrusdesign.com
Commander: www.commanderair.com
Dassault Falcon Jet: www.falconjet.com
Derringer: www.derringeraircraft.com
EADS: www.eads-nv.com
Eclipse: www.eclipseaviation.com
Embraer: www.embraer.com
Enstrom: www.enstromhelicopter.com
Eurocopter: www.eurocopter.com
Explorer Aircraft: www.exploreraircraft.com
Fairchild Dornier: www.fairchilddornier.com
Farnborough Aircraft: www.farnborough-aircraft.com
Galaxy Aerospace: www.galaxyaerospace.com
Groen Brothers Aircraft: www.gbagyros.com
Gulfstream: www.gulfstream.com

Ibis Aerospace: www.ibisaerospace.com
IPTN: www.iptn.co.id
Kaman: www.kamanaero.com
Lancair: www.lancair.com
Learjet: www.learjet.com
MD Helicopters: www.mdhelicopters.com
Mooney: www.mooney.com
Piaggio: www.piaggioamerica.com
Pilatus: www.pilatus-aircraft.com
Piper: www.newpiper.com
Raytheon: www.raytheon.com/rac
Robinson: www.robinsonheli.com
Saab: www.saabaircraftleasing.com
Safire: www.safireaircraft.com
Scaled Composites: www.scaled.com
Sikorsky: www.sikorsky.com
Sino Swearingen: www.sj30jet.com
Socata: www.socata.com
Soloy: www.soloy.com
Twin Commander: www.twincommander.com
VisionAire: www.visionaire.com

Aircraft Sales

Aeroprice: www.aeroprice.com
Aero Trader: wwww.traderonline.com/aero
Aero Toy Store: www.aerotoy.com
Aircraft Auctioneers: www.aircraftauctioneers.com
Aircraftbuyer: www.aircraftbuyer.com
Aircraft Dealer Online: wwww.aircraftdealer.com
Aircraft Dealers Network: www.aircraftdealers.net
Aircraft Sales Corp.: www.aircraftsalescorp.com
Aircraft Services Group: www.yourjet.com
Aircraft Shopper Online: www.aso.com
Air Partner: www.airpartner.com
AviaBid: www.aviabid.com
Bidjet.com: www.bidjet.com
Bizjet: www.bizjet.ch
BusinessJets.com: www.businessjets.com
Executive Aircraft: www.execaircorp.com
Executive Controller: www.aircraft.com
The Hangar Floor: www.thehangarfloor.com
HelicopterBuyer.com: www.helicopterbuyer.com
Helivalues: www.helivalues.com
JB&A Aviation: www.jbaaviation.com
Jetplane: www.jetplane.com
Mesinger Corporate Jet Sales: www.jetsales.com
MyPlane.com: www.myplane.com
National Aircraft Resale Association: www.nara-dealers.com
Par Avion: www.paravionltd.com
Peregrine Aviation: www.peregrineaviation.com
PlanBid: www.planebid.com
Trade-A-Plane: www.trade-a-plane.com
Tyler Jet: www.tylerjet.com
Universal Jet Trading: www.ujt.com

Vance & Engles: www.vanceengles.com
Welsch Aviation: www.welschaviation.com

Associations

Aerospace Industries Association: www.aia-aerospace.org
Aircraft Electronics Association: www.aea.net
Aircraft Owners and Pilots Assn.: www.aopa.org
Air Line Pilots Association: www.alpa.org
Air Transport Association: www.air-transport.org
Allied Pilots Association: www.alliedpilots.org
American Assn. Of Airport Execs.: www.airportnet.org
American Helicopter Society: www.vtol.org
Aviation Insurance Association: www.AIAweb.org
Canadian Business Aircraft Association: www.cbaa.ca
Corporate Aircraft Association: www.corpaa.org
Corporate Angel Network: www.corpangelnetwork.org
European Business Aviation Assn.: www.ebaa.org
European Regions Airline Association: www.eraa.org
Flight Safety Foundation: www.flightsafety.org
General Aviation Manufacturers Association: www.generalaviation.org
Helicopter Association International: www.rotor.com
International Business Aviation Council: www.ibac.org
Make It Fly Foundation: www.makeitfly.com
National Aeronautic Association: www.naa-usa.org
National Air Traffic Controllers Assn.: www.natca.org
National Air Transportation Assn.: www.nata-online.org
National Association of Air Traffic Specialists: www.naats.org
National Business Aviation Association: www.nbaa.org
The Ninety-Nines: www.ninety-nines.org
Prof. Aviation Maintenance Assn.: www.pama.org
Regional Airline Association: www.raa.org
Royal Aeronautical Society: www.raes.org.uk
Society of Automotive Engineers: www.sae.org
University Aviation Association: uaa.auburn.edu
Women in Aviation, International: www.wiai.org
Women in Corporate Aviation: www.wca-intl.org

Avionics

AirCell: www.aircell.com
Airshow: www.airshowinc.com
Ametek Aerospace: www.amtek.com/aerospace
Archangel: www.archangel.com
Arinc: www.arinc.com
Arnav Systems: www.arnav.com
Avidyne: www.avidyne.com
Avionics Zone (Honeywell): www.avionicszone.com
AvroTec: www.avrotec.com
BAE Systems: www.baesystems.com
BAE Systems Canada: www.baesystems-canada.com
Baker Electronics: www.be-inc.com
Ball Aerospace: www.ballaerospace.com
Becker Avionics: www.becker-avionics.com
Bendix/King: www.bendixking.com
BF Goodrich Aerospace: www.bfgavionics.com
Century Flight Systems: www.centuryflight.com

David Clark Co.: www.davidclark.com
EMS Technologies: www.ems-t.com
Eventide: www.eventide.com
Flight Visions: www.flightvisions.com
Garmin: www.garmin.com
Honeywell: www.honeywell.com
Icarus Instruments: www.icarusinstruments.com
ICOM America: www.icomamerica.com
IEC International: www.iecinternational.com
Innovative Solutions & Support: www.innovative-ss.com
Intheairnet: www.intheairnet.com
Kollsman: www.kollsman.com
Litton: www.littonapd.com
L3 Communications: www.l-3com.com
Meggitt: www.meggitt.com
Narco: www.narco-avionics.com
Northstar Technologies: www.northstarcmc.com
Pentar Avionics: www.pentar.com
Racal Avionics: www.ravl.co.uk
Rockwell Collins: www.collins.rockwell.com
Rockwell Collins Flight Dynamics: www.fltdyn.com
Rosen Products: www.rosenproducts.com
Ryan International: www.ryan-tcad.com
Safe Flight: www.safeflight.com
Sandel Avionics: www.sandelavionics.com
Securaplane Technologies: www.securaplane.com
Sextant Avionique: see Thales Avionics
Sierra Flight Systems: www.sierraflightsystems.com
Sigma Tek: www.sigmatek.com
Smiths Industries: www.smithsind-aerospace.com
S-Tec/Meggitt: www.s-tec.com
Teledyne Controls: www.teledyne-controls.com
Thales Avionics (formerly Sextant Avionique): www.sextant.thomson-csf.com
Thrane & Thrane: www.tt.dk
Trimble: www.trimble.com
Universal Avionics: www.uasc.com
UPS Aviation Technologies: www.upsat.com
Wulfsberg Electronics: www.wulfsberg.com

**Charter Reservations/
Price Quotes**

Aircharter.com: www.aircharter.com
Air Charter Guide: www.aircharterguide.com
Air Charter Guide e-Services: www.aircharterguide.com/industry
Air Charter Online: www.aircharteronline.com
AirCharter World: www.acworld.com
BidjetCharter: www.bidjetcharter.com
Charter Alliance: www.charteralliance.com
CharterX: www.charterx.com
Corporate Jet Link: www.corporatejetlink.com
Daimler Chrysler Automotive Air Charter: www.automotiveair.com
EBizJets: www.ebizjets.com
Ejets.com: www.ejets.com
EmptyLeg Charter.com: www.emptylegcharter.com
FlightServ.com: www.flightserv.com

FlightTime: www.flighttime.com
Jet Aviation Charter: www.jetaviation.com/charter
Skyjet: www.skyjet.com
Transjet: www.transjet.com

Completion Centers

AAR Aircraft Services: www.aarcorp.com
ADI Interiors: www.flyadi.com
Air Methods: www.airmethods.com
Associated Air Center: www.associatedaircenter.com
Atlantic Aviation: www.atlanticaviation.com
Aviation Concepts: www.aviationconcepts.net
Avmats: www.avmats.com
B/E Aerospace: www.beaerospace.com
Bizjet International: www.bizjetinternational.com
Bombardier Completions: www.aero.bombardier.com
Byerly Aviation: www.byerlyaviation.com
Capital Aviation: www.capitalaviation.com
Cheyenne Airmotive: www.cheyenneairmotive.com
Commuter Air Technology: www.commuterair.com
Dassault Falcon Service: www.dassault-falcon.com
DeCrane Aircraft: www.decraneaircraft.com
Downtown Airpark: www.downtownairpark.com
Duncan Aviation: www.duncanaviation.com
Eagle Aviation: www.eagle-aviation.com
Elliott Aviation: www.elliottaviation.com
Executive Aircraft: www.execaircorp.com
Flying Colours: www.flyingcolourscorp.com
Garrett Aviation Services: www.garrettaviation.com
Gulfstream Aerospace: www.gulfstream.com
H.A.S. Corp.: www.has-corp.com
Innotech-Execaire: www.innotech-execaire.com
International Jet Interiors: www.intljet.com
Jet Aviation: www.jetaviation.com
JetCorp.: www.jetcorp.com
Lufthansa Technik: www.lufthansa-technik.com
Mena Aircraft Interiors: www.aircraft-interiors.com
MidcoastAviation: www.midcoastaviation.com
Nordam Group: www.nordam.com
Ozark Aircraft Systems: www.ozarkaircraftsystems.com
Raytheon Aircraft Services: www.raytheonaircraftservices.com
Rose Aircraft Interiors: www.roseaircraft.com
The Servicenter: www.servicenterinc.com
Sierra Industries: www.sijet.com
Stevens Aviation: www.stevensaviation.com
Trace Aircraft Completions: www.traceww.com
Vee Neal Aviation: www.veeneal.com
West Star Aviation: www.weststaraviation.com

Engine Manufacturers

Agilis: www.agilis.com
CFM International: www.cfm56.com
GE Aircraft Engines: www.geae.com
Honeywell: www.honeywell.com
LHTEC: www.lhtec.com

Orenda Recip: www.orenda.com
Pratt & Whitney: www.pratt-whitney.com
Pratt & Whitney Canada: www.pwc.ca
Rolls-Royce: www.rolls-royce.com
Super 27 Re-engine Program (BF Goodrich): www.super27.com
Turbomeca: www.turbomeca.com
Williams International: www.williams-int.com

**FBO Chains/Fuels
Suppliers/Cards**

Air BP: www.airbp.com
Air Routing Card Services: www.airrouting-card.com
Amports: www.amport-aviation.com
Atlantic Aviation: www.atlanticaviation.com
Avcard: www.avcard.com
Avfuel: www.avfuel.com
Chevron: www.chevronaviation.com
Exxon Card Services: www.airworld.com
ExxonMobil: www.exxon.mobil.com/em_aviationfuels
Irving Aviation Service: www.irvingaviation.com
Jet Aviation: www.jetaviation.com
Mercury Air Centers: www.mercuryaircenters.com
Metro Business Aviation: www.metrofbo.com
Midcoast Aviation: www.midcoastaviation.com
Million Air: www.millionair.com
Multi Service: www.multiservice.com
Phillips 66: aviation.phillips66.com
Piedmont Hawthorne: www.flypiedmont.com
Raytheon Aircraft Services: www.raytheonaircraftservices.com
Shell Aviation: www.shell.com/aviation
Signature Flight Support: www.signatureflight.com
Skyservice: www.skyservice.com
Stevens Aviation: www.stevensaviation.com
TAC Air: www.tacair.com
TAG Aviation: www.tagaviation.com
Texaco: www.texaco.com
Uvair: www.uvair.com

Federal Government

Aviation Safety Reporting System: asrs.arc.nasa.gov
Bureau of Transportation Statistics: www.bts.gov
FAA Airport Delay Advisories: www.atcscc.faa.gov
FAA Capstone Program: www.alaska.faa.gov/capstone
FAA Flight Standards Information: av-info.faa.gov
Federal Aviation Administration: www.faa.gov
FedWorld Information Network: www.fedworld.gov/faasearch.html
Int'l Civil Aviation Organization: www.icao.org
NASA Agate: agate.larc.nasa.gov
National Transportation Safety Board: www.ntsb.gov
U.S. Dept. of Transportation: www.dot.gov

Financial Services

AirFleet Capital: www.airfleetcapital.com
Boeing Capital: www.boeing.com/special/capitalcorp
Bombardier Capital: www.bcgroup.com
Cessna Finance: www.cfcloan.com
CIT Group: www.citgroup.com

DaimlerChrysler Capital Services: www.dcxcapital.com
Finova: www.finova.com
First Equity: www.firstequity.com
GE Capital Aviation Services: www.gecas.com
GE Capital Corporate Aircraft Group: www.gecorporateaircraft.com
Heller Financial: www.hellerfinancial.com
TFC Textron Business & Charter Aircraft: www.tfcaviation.textron.com
Textron Financial: www.flynancing.com

Fractional Aircraft Providers

Bombardier FlexJet: www.flexjet.com
Citation Shares: www.citationshares.com
Executive Jet NetJets: www.netjets.com
Flight Options: www.flightoptions.com
PlaneSense: www.planesense.org
Raytheon Travel Air: www.raytheon.com/rac/travelair

Flight Planning

AirNav: www.airnav.com
Airport Taxi Diagrams: www.aopa.org/asf/taxi
Air Routing International: www.argis.com
Air Routing's Flight Manager: www.flightmanager.com
Baseops International: www.baseops.com
FlightNeeds.com: www.flightneeds.com
FltPlan.com: www.fltplan.com
Jeppesen Corporate Flight Svcs: www.jeppesen.com
Logbook Organizer: www.logbookorganizer.cc
Ultra-Nav Aviation: www.ultranav.com
Universal Weather & Aviation: www.universalweather.com
Worldwide Airport Pathfinder: www.calle.com/aviation/airports.cgi

Information Resources

Ac-U-Kwik: www.acukwik.com
Aerolink Global Aviation Infosource: www.aerolink.com
Aeroseek: www.aeroseek.com
Aerospace Mall: www.aerospacemall.com
Aerospace Virtual Library: www.erau.edu/libraries/virtual/aerospace
Aircraft Technical Publishers: www.atp.com
Air Security's World Watch Online: worldwatch.airsecurity.com
Amstat: www.amstatcorp.com
ARG/US: www.aviationresearch.com
AvCrew: www.avcrew.com
Aviation Employee Placement Service: www.aeps.com
The Aviation Hub: www.theaviationhub.com
Aviation Information Resource Database: www.airbase1.com
Aviation Jobs Online: www.aviationjobsonline.com
The Aviation Search Engine: www.aviationsearchengine.com
Aviation Virtual Library: www.db.erau.edu/www_virtual_lib/aviation.html
Avjobs: www.avjobs.com
Best AeroNet: www.bestaero.com
BizjetPilot.com: www.bizjetpilot.com
Conklin & de Decker Associates: www.conklindd.com
Corporate Aviators, Inc.: www.corporateaviators.com
Corporate Jet Link: www.corporatejetlink.com
Corporate Pilot.com: www.corporatepilot.com
Embry-Riddle Aeronautical University: www.erau.edu

Executive Jet Aviation Pilot's Information Site: www.ejapilots.com
FBOweb.com: www.fboweb.com
Fillup Flyer Fuel Finder: www.fillupflyer.com
Find-a-Pilot Online Resume Service: www.findapilot.com
Global Aviation Navigator: www.globalair.com
JetLinks: www.jetlinks.com
JetNet: www.jetnetllc.com
Landings: www.landings.com
Professional Pilot's Wait Time Web site: www.pilotwait.com

Insurance

AIG Aviation: www.aig.com
Aircraft & Marine Insurance Group: www.aircraft-marine.com
Aircraft Insurance Group: www.aigltd.com
Aircraft Underwriters: www.aircraftund.com
Associated Aviation Underwriters: www.aau.com
Avemco: www.avemco.com
Aviation Insurance Network: www.aviationinsurnetwork.com
CS&A Aviation Insurance: www.aviationinsurance.com
Dorr Aviation: www.dorraviation.com
HCC Aviation Insurance Group: www.hccavn.com
LL Johns & Associates, Inc.: www.lljohns.com
Pilot Insurance Center: www.piclife.com
USAIG: www.usaig.com

Maintenance/Modifications

Aerial View Systems: www.aerialviewsystems.com
Aeromech: www.aeromechinc.com
Aerospace Lighting (B/E Aerospace): www.aerospacelighting.com
Aircraft Belts: www.aircraftbelts.com
Atlantic Aviation: www.atlanticaviation.com
Avcom Technologies: www.avcomtech.com
Aviation Fabricators: www.aviationfabricators.com
Aviation Partners: www.aviationpartners.com
Avmats: www.avmats.com
Avquotes: www.avquotes.com
Avtec: www.avtec-inc.com
Banyan Air Service: www.banyanair.com
BBA Aviation: www.bba-aviation.com
B/E Aerospace: www.beaerospace.com
Bizjet: www.bizjetinternational.com
CAMP: www.campsys.com
Dallas Airmotive: www.dallasairmotive.com
DeCrane Aircraft: www.decraneaircraft.com
DeVore Aviation: www.devoreaviation.com
Downtown Airpark: www.downtownairpark.com
Duncan Aviation: www.duncanav.com
Electrosonics: www.electrosonics.com
Elliott Aviation: www.elliottaviation.com
ERDA: www.erda-inc.com
EVAS Worldwide: www.evasworldwide.com
Flight Design: www.flightdesigninc.com
FR Aviation: www.fraviation.co.uk
Garrett Aviation: www.garrettaviation.com
Hartzell Propeller: www.hartzellprop.com

Innotech-Execaire: www.innotech-execaire.com
Jet Aviation: www.jetaviation.com
JetCorp: www.jetcorp.com
Kaiser Air: www.kaiserair.com
Keystone Helicopter: www.keystone-helicopter.com
King Aerospace: www.king-aerospace.com
Lufthansa Technik: www.king-aerospace.com
Magellan Aerospace: www.malaero.com
Messier-Buggati: www.messier-bugatti.com
Messier Services: www.messierservices.com
Midcoast Aviation: www.midcoastaviation.com
Nordam Group: www.nordam.com
Parker Hannifin Wheel & Brake: www.parker.com/airborne
Premier Turbines: www.premierturbines.com
Really Quiet: www.reallyquiet.com
Sabreliner: www.sabreliner.com
Securaplane: www.securaplane.com
Signature RMC: www.signatureflight.com
Southern Aviation: www.southernaviation.com
Standard Aero: www.standardaero.com
Stevens Aviation: www.stevensaviation.com
U.S. Paint: www.uspaint.com
West Star: www.weststaraviation.com

Online Publications

AIN Online: www.ainonline.com
AIN Reports: www.ainreports.com
AIN Weekly: www.ainweekly.com
Air Charter Guide: www.guides.com/acg
Air & Space Smithsonian: www.airspacemag.com
Aviation International News: www.ainonline.com
AviationNow: www.aviationnow.com
AvWeb: www.avweb.com
Business & Commercial Aviation: www.aviationnow.com/bca
European Business Air News: www.bizjet.com
FAA Aviation News: www.faa.gov/avr/news/newshome.htm
Flight International: www.flightinternational.com
Professional Pilot: www.propilotmag.com

Parts, Suppliers and Locators

Aerospace Products International: www.apiparts.com
Aerospan: www.aerospan.com
Aircraft Parts International: www.apiparts.com
Aircraft Parts Locator Service: www.apls.com
Avgroup: www.jetparts.com
Aviall: www.aviall.com
Aviation Online Network: www.airparts.com
Avolo: www.avolo.com
Avsupport Online: www.avsupport.com
Corporate Rotable & Supply: www.corporaterotable.com
Everything Aircraft: www.everythingaircraft.com
Inventory Locator Service: www.ilsmart.com
MyAircraft: www.cordiem.com
Parts Base: www.partsbase.com
Parts Logistics: www.partslogistics.com

TradeAir.com: www.tradeair.com
TRW Aeronautical Systems: www.lucas-aerospace.com

Pilots Only

Aviation Employee Placement Service: www.aeps.com
BizjetPilot.com: www.bizjetpilot.com
Fractional Operations Information: www.fracstats.com
IPilot: www.ipilot.com
Minority Pilots Assn./Academy: www.minoritypilot.org
PilotChat.net: www.pilotchat.net
Professional Pilot's Message Board: www.propilot.com
Professional Pilot's Rumour Network: www.pprune.org

Training

Aerolearn: www.aerolearn.com
Aviation Safety Training: www.airaces.com
CAE: www.cae.com
Embry-Riddle Aeronautical University: www.erau.com
Facts Training International: www.facts-aircare.com
FlightSafety Boeing: www.flightsafetyboeing.com
FlightSafety International: www.flightsafety.com
The International Aviation MBA Program: aviationmba.concordia.ca
Radar Training Systems: www.av-wx-rdr.com
SimuFlite Training International: www.simuflite.com

Weather Resources

Accuweather: www.accuweather.com
ASOS/AWOS: www.faa.gove/asos/asos.htm
Aviation Digital Weather Data Service: adds.awc-kc.noaa.gov
Aviation Weather Brief: www.aviationweatherbrief.com
FlightBrief: www.flightbrief.com
Flightneeds: www.flightneeds.com
GTE Duats: www.duat.com
National Weather Service (NWS): www.nws.noaa.gov
NOAA Aviation Weather Center: www.awc-kc.noaa.gov
NWS Interactive Weather Information Network: iwin.nws.noaa.gov
NWS Metar/TAF Information: www.nws.noaa.gov/oso/oso1/oso12/metar.htm
NWS Real-time Radar: weather.noaa.gov/radar/national.html
Pilotweather.com: www.pilotweather.com
Unisys: weather.unisys.com
Universal Weather & Aviation: www.universalweather.com
Weather Channel: www.weather.com/aviation
Weather Services International: www.pilotbrief.wsicorp.com
WeatherTap (Trade-a-Plane): www.weathertap.com
WSI's Intellicast: www.intellicast.com
Source: Aviation International News, 2001 Directory of Business Aviation Websites

KEY TERMS

General aviation	Aerial Application
Primary use category	Aerial Observation
Public use	Aerial Other
Executive/corporation transportation	Sightseeing
Business transportation	Air tours
Personal flying	Air taxi
Instructional flying	External load
Fixed Base Operator (FBO)	Medical

Other flying
Publicly owned airports
Private use airports
Very-high frequency omnidirectional
 range (VOR)

Instrument Landing System (ILS)
Air route traffic control centers
 (ARTCCs)
Flight Service Station (FSS)

REVIEW QUESTIONS

1. Define "general aviation." General aviation aircraft have traditionally represented what percent of the total active aircraft in the United States? What are the 14 FAA primary use categories? Approximately how many active general aviation aircraft were there in the United States in 1999? What is the dominant type aircraft?

2. Give some examples of public use aircraft. What is the preponderance of helicopters used for? What is the difference between executive/corporate transportation and business transportation? How many turbine aircraft are operated by business aircraft users? Give several reasons that businesses use their own aircraft.

3. Personal flying is primarily for wealthy individuals who want aircraft for recreation. Do you agree? Why? Discuss the importance of instructional flying. Distinguish between aerial application, aerial observation, and aerial other. Give several examples of each. Distinguish between sightseeing, air tours, and air taxi. What is the big advantage of chartering an aircraft? Describe several uses of aircraft for carrying external loads and medical flying. What is included in the other flying category?

4. Approximately how many publicly owned airports are in the United States? How many are reserved by the scheduled air carriers? Describe the important economic role played by general aviation airports. Why is the growth in the number of student and private pilots so important to the continued health of the general aviation industry?

5. Describe several services provided by the FAA for general aviation pilots. What is the purpose of flight service stations? What has been the trend in general aviation aircraft manufacturing since 1980? Identify some single- and multiengine aircraft available in the United States. What is the significance of pilots to aircraft manufacturing? Identify several sources for general aviation forecasts.

6. Describe the importance of the Internet and websites to marketing and sales of general aviation aircraft, components, and services. How are airframe manufacturers using their websites to service operators? How has the aircraft sales process been changed by the Internet? What is some of the information pilots can obtain online? How are flight training organizations using their websites? What is the main reason companies and their customers are conducting business online?

PART TWO
FBO MANAGEMENT

Chapter 3

The Fixed Base Operator: Backbone of General Aviation

OUTLINE

OBJECTIVES

At the end of this chapter you should be able to:

Describe the principal services provided by an FBO.

Explain the importance of nonincome services.

Describe the size and scope of the FBO industry, including the various categories.

Discuss several current trends in the FBO industry and the future outlook for the industry.

Identify and highlight the factors which go into the analysis of the market and selecting a location for an FBO.

List the basic facilities and equipment needed in establishing an FBO.

Discuss some of the advantages and disadvantages of joining an FBO chain.

Describe some of the important practices and procedures designed to improve service to customers in the following areas: ramp, ground personnel, aircraft, and flight personnel.

INTRODUCTION

In the early days of aviation, most individuals who made their living by flying went from field to field putting on air shows, giving rides, and providing maintenance services for other operators. These barnstormers, as they became known, did not have a fixed base of operation and were not highly regarded from the standpoint of dependability or business acumen. Some, however, became successful aviation business people and established airport facilities to base their aviation service operations. These respected, down-to-earth, here-to-stay stalwarts became know as *fixed base operators.*

Today, fixed base operators—or FBOs—are to the general aviation industry what service stations, repair garages, engine specialists, body and fender shops, paint shops, tire sales outlets, driver training schools, taxicabs, new and used automobile dealers, and auto supply stores are to the automobile industry. By the very nature of the aviation business, all of these services must be concentrated on or close to a designated airport, and usually at one or two locations on an airport, in many cases sharing the airport with air carrier operations and military operations.

FBO SERVICES

The principal business of fixed base operators is line service, which includes the retail sales of fuel and oil, minor repairs, emergency service, and other flight continuation services for general aviation aircraft. They also maintain storage facilities for private airplanes, provide continuing maintenance and overhaul services, and usually have small or medium-sized planes available for charter. Some of the larger FBOs are active in selling new and used airplanes, and some also operate flying schools. A few of the larger operators are equipped to offer complete flight service arrangements for business firms, including supplying both aircraft and crews.

Line Services

Line services include:
- Fueling
- Sale of lubricants
- Aircraft storage
   Bulk hangarage
   T-hangarage
   Outdoor tie-downs
- Aircraft preparation services
- Airline services

Line service is the main business of the fixed base operator. This service includes selling fuel and oil, providing storage and general services for aircraft regularly based at the airport, and also providing these for transient airplanes. An aircraft can land, be refueled, have its windshield cleaned, cabin vacuum-cleaned, oil checked, and minor engine and equipment adjustments made.

Fueling is the most common service offered at an FBO. In aviation there are two primary fuel types: AvGas, used in piston-powered aircraft, and Jet-A, used in turbine-powered aircraft. Most fuel sellers own and maintain storage facilities for both types. In some cases, the business may also maintain separate fuel storage tanks used to refuel aircraft operated by scheduled commercial air carriers. Additionally, some operators have government contracts to fuel military aircraft and have installed special storage tanks for this purpose. In other situations, fuel storage tanks may be owned and operated by the airport. The sale of fuel and lubricants is typically the leading revenue generator for an FBO.

Fixed base operators also have facilities for storing planes. Several storage options are usually available for both based and transient aircraft and they can be divided into two categories—hangar and tie-down. Hangars, offering protection from the elements, are often available for an individual to rent and can be found in a variety of sizes from those designed for a small single-engine airplane to large buildings that can house a corporate fleet. Also, many aviation businesses offer storage options in a general or community hangar. This is usually where any transient aircraft will be kept and can be less expensive than a single-user hangar. A tie-down space is generally less expensive than hangar storage. These are open areas on the airport ramp that allow an airplane to be secured to the ramp via ropes, chains, or other means.

Aircraft preparation services are also commonly provided. These include interior and exterior aircraft cleaning, aircraft lavatory servicing, and, during the winter in colder climates, aircraft de-icing and preheating services.

In recent years with the growth of the regional airlines, many FBOs have established contractual services with the air carriers, including fueling, exterior cleaning, interior cleaning, de-icing, turbine starting, minor maintenance, and even baggage handling and screening passengers and their baggage in some cases.

Maintenance

Maintenance includes:
- Aircraft maintenance
  - Major repairs
  - Minor repairs
  - Annual inspections/relicensing
- Engine maintenance
  - Minor
  - Major
  - Remanufacturers
- Avionics
  - Sales
  - Service
    - Maintenance
    - Recertification
- Parts sales and service
  - Tires, brakes and bearings
  - Batteries
  - Interiors

Maintenance and repair service is another basic part of the fixed base operator's business. All aircraft require periodic inspections and maintenance. Furthermore, regulations require all maintenance to be performed to specific standards by qualified personnel. Aircraft must be inspected and maintained by certificated technicians to assure their airworthiness. There are two primary organizations that can service aircraft: a repair station certificated under Federal Aviation Regulations (FAR) Part 145 or a company employing a technician certificated under FAR Part 65 as an airframe and powerplant (A&P) mechanic.

The basic requirements for performance of maintenance and alteration of airframes, powerplants, propellers, or appliances are constant regardless of the organization doing the work. A Part 145 Repair Station holds an FAA certificate and is limited to performing only the services the FAA has specifically authorized. Maintenance performed under the authority of an individual's FAA-issued A&P is limited only by the level of training and experience of the individual. Maintenance limitations and oversight are more general in nature for the A&P because the individual has been subject to extensive training and testing and enhanced specialized training on specific equipment and aircraft prior to issuance of the certificate. A repair facility wishing to do work for a certificated air carrier must hold a Part 145 certificate.

Nationwide, there are over 4,000 Part 145 certificated repair stations employing approximately 30,000 maintenance professionals. As with obtaining an air carrier certificate, repair station certification is a significant investment and requires more business overhead than an individual operating under Part 65 certification.

An additional specialized service that is routinely required concerns the avionics and instruments found in the aircraft. Often a shop and its employees will specialize in a specific area or even on specific equipment manufacturers. These services can only be performed under a Part 145 repair station certificate. Avionics include communication and navigational equipment, as well as radar and autopilot units installed in the aircraft. There are four general types of instruments in any aircraft: gyroscopic, pressure-based, electronic, and engine-status indicators.

Large, well-equipped repair stations include facilities for complete maintenance, overhaul and rebuilding airframes and powerplants, and a full complement of equipment for repairing, testing, calibrating, installing, and replacing avionics components.

Completion—design and installation of interiors on new airplanes delivered by airframe manufacturers without these facilities—is an important segment of business for some fixed base operators. A full line of completion work includes layout of the cockpit, placement of the avionics components and other systems, and design and installation of accommodations for the passenger cabins, as well as exterior custom painting. This work can also be performed for owners wishing to update or change the look of their aircraft. Compliance with continuing airworthiness requirements for older aircraft may require some amount of paint removal for airframe inspection. All services must be done in accordance with manufacturers' specifications and FAA regulations in addition to complying with strict environmental, health, and safety regulations due to the chemicals used in these processes.

Sale of parts and accessories is an important segment of business for most fixed base operators. The items carried by a well-stocked operator include engines, airframe parts, tires, and avionics components, as well as a wide variety of accessories. All parts are subject to strict FAA standards for tracking, storage, sale, and installation to prevent the introduction of fraudulent parts into the market.

Aircraft Sales

Aircraft sales includes:
• New aircraft
• Used aircraft

Larger FBOs often sell new aircraft, serving as dealers or distributors for aircraft manufacturers. They usually participate actively in the used-aircraft market as well, generally as a result of taking older models in trade on the sale of new aircraft. Some FBOs act as brokers, acting as a bridge between owners wishing to sell and buyers. They typically obtain exclusive listings authorizing them to market and sell a specific aircraft, but have no ownership interest in the aircraft. Sellers normally pay brokers a percentage of the purchase price.

Often, when other aviation services are provided, such as flight training or aircraft rental, the aircraft may be used to support these functions while awaiting sale.

Some of the larger FBOs are equipped to handle financing aircraft sales under an installment purchase arrangement. Long-term leases can also be arranged through these FBOs, though usually they do not retain the ownership of the planes themselves but serve as intermediary between the acquiring company and a professional leasing company.

Charter and Rental

Charter and rental consists of:
• Chartering aircraft
• Rental of aircraft

Most fixed based operators, even the relatively small ones, own at least a few planes that can be rented for short periods of time. Most facilities offer several single-engine piston aircraft with varying degrees of complexity, from the basic two-seat trainer to larger airplanes with retractable gear and adjustable propeller. Some businesses offer multi-engine aircraft as well. A rental agreement and inspection of the pilot's certificate and currency are always required. Many businesses also require a "check-out" before renting. In an aircraft check-out, one of the school's flight instructors reviews the performance aspects of the aircraft with the renter and then conducts a flight to evaluate the renter pilot's ability to operate the aircraft safely. Aircraft can be rented by the hour, day, or week, or for specific trips.

Other FBOs have a more complete line of aircraft available for chartering. These operators provide a variety of services to the public including personal aircraft charter, cargo transportation, emergency medical flights, and air tours. Accordingly, a wide range of aircraft is necessary to complete these missions and includes single-engine piston to large, turbine-powered, corporate aircraft to helicopters.

Many business firms, including quite a few that own their own planes, utilize chartering services regularly. Some companies prefer to own only one or perhaps two planes and to charter additional craft as necessary for special occasions or periods of peak load. Some firms chartering aircraft use only their own crews, but some of the fixed base operators provide crews, if desired.

Rates for chartered airplanes depend upon the length of time the plane is to be used, the size and type of plane, whether a pilot or flying crew is required, and whether other services are needed by the user.

There are over 3,000 on-demand air charter operators nationwide. All operators must hold an Air Carrier Operating Certificate, issued by the Federal Aviation Administration (FAA) and are regulated under Federal Aviation Regulation (FAR) Part 135 which sets forth operational, maintenance, training, and other safety requirements. Additionally, pilots and management personnel are subject to minimum qualification standards. A series of regular inspections, spot inspections, routine surveillance and in-depth inspections are all performed by the FAA to ensure compliance with applicable regulations.

Corporate Flight Service

Corporate flight service includes:
• Flight operations
• Maintenance
• Administrative services

Many of the larger fixed base operators offer a complete *corporate flight service* for business customers. Under such an arrangement, the owner or FBO supplies the aircraft and the FBO provides the flight, maintenance, and administrative personnel, and is responsible for conducting flight operations, performing maintenance, and handling administrative matters. Thus, the owner is relieved of the responsibilities of running an aviation department and all of the workload associated with it. The client company normally is billed monthly for the actual cost of the service, plus an agreed-upon management fee, which is usually a specified percentage of the cost of the service rendered.

The fixed base operator makes arrangements to acquire the plane or planes to be used by the company and supervises the installation of the appropriate avionics and passenger cabin accommodations. The FBO obtains the hull and liability insurance coverages on the aircraft, in accordance with minimums of liability coverage that are normally specified by the operator. The operator handles the assignment of pilots and copilots, either selecting crews from among its own personnel or hiring new personnel especially for the customer's operation. In either event, the flight crews are assigned to the customer company full time, though they remain the employees of the fixed base operator. The operator is responsible for checking out pilot and copilot qualifications, seeing that they receive the appropriate recurrent flight and ground school training, and arranging for the periodic medical examinations required.

The fixed base operator is completely responsible for flight operations, maintenance, and whatever administrative services and personnel are required to provide full service. His responsibility includes establishing safe operational standards for the aircraft and crews regarding such factors as aircraft performance, weather conditions, airport facilities, and crew duty times, as well as providing employees to handle scheduling, clerical, and secretarial duties. Office space is also provided, with furnishings and equipment for the use of the flight and administrative personnel and the customer company's passengers. Maintenance supervision is provided in the typical contract, though the supervisor usually does not work full time for a customer unless the size of the customer's fleet warrants such full-time assignment.

Flight Training

Flight training goes through the following steps:
- Primary
- Advanced
  Instrument
  Multiengine
- Recurrent

Another service provided by many fixed base operators is training new pilots and retraining experienced pilots.

Establishing a flight school, either stand-alone or as part of a larger aviation business, is quite common. However, flight schools are nearly always found at nonairline type and smaller airports due to the difficulties encountered in training when located at major airline-hub locations.

There are two types of flight training programs, FAR Part 61 and Part 141. The major difference between the two is the amount of structure present in training. Part 141 schools are certificated, as businesses, by the FAA and are periodically audited by the agency. These schools must have a detailed, FAA-approved course curriculum and their students must meet certain minimum performance standards. In contrast, Part 61 schools allow more flexibility to rearrange lesson content and sequence to meet the needs of the student. Depending on the student's overall goals, either type of training may be better and many flight schools offer training under both regulations. Regardless of the governing regulation, all flight training must be provided by FAA-certificated flight instructors (CFI), and, if advanced certificate training is offered, instrument (CFII) and/or multiengine (MEI) instructors are needed, as appropriate.

Other Specialized Commercial Flight Services

Some FBOs have arrangements with private and public organizations to provide various *specialized commercial flight services*. These include aerial advertising, aerial photography, fire fighting, fish spotting, mosquito control, pipeline and powerline surveillance, and wildlife conservation.

Not all fixed base operators perform all the functions set forth above; indeed, some aviation businessmen may elect to participate as specialists in only one or two categories. However, it is normal for FBOs to perform at least four of the services listed, either as part of their own business or by leasing space to specialists who perform the functions on their own (or leased) premises. A fixed base operator has been compared to a shopping mall manager who is charged with making a profit on each of the many widely diversified individual businesses within the orbit of the overall operation.

NONINCOME SERVICES

In addition to services for income, an FBO normally provides certain *nonincome services* for the convenience and well-being of its customers.

These services are not normally a stand-alone enterprise, but are frequently offered to enhance the customer-friendliness of the aviation business. Depending on location, market, and customer demands, any or all of these services may be available. One of the most rapidly emerging of these amenities is the provision of designated areas for business travelers. Many aviation businesses now offer private meeting rooms, phones, facsimile machines, photocopiers, and Internet access stations for their customers' use. Other commonly provided services are

- Clean rest rooms and showers.
- Pilot lounges and sleeping quarters.
- Preflight planning rooms.
- Pilot supplies.
- Recreational facilities.

- Vending machines and/or restaurant.
- Rental and/or courtesy cars.
- In-flight catering.
- Hotel accommodations.
- Tourist/visitor activities.

SIZE AND SCOPE OF THE FBO INDUSTRY

It has been estimated that there were as many as 10,000 FBOs during the late 1970s. *FBO* magazine conducted a study in 1992 and came up with a figure of 4,099. *FBO* magazine counted only those FBOs listed under an airport or FBOs not listed under an airport that sold fuel. In other words, the only facilities not counted were airports that did not sell fuel. Recent estimates by the National Air Transportation Association (NATA) indicate that the number is somewhere between 4,000 and 4,500. Of those, about 12 to 15 percent have the facilities and location to specialize in servicing turbine-powered business aircraft and their passengers. NATA defines an FBO as an organization that has a specific lease with an airport-owning entity and offers a minimum of two of the major services provided by FBOs.

At the start of 2000, there were 5,110 publicly owned airports in the United States, of which 773 were served by air carriers, as well as by general aviation. Of the remaining 4,337 airports, which might be called general aviation airports, plus several hundred privately owned airports open for public use, not all are attended or have service all the time; many are attended seasonally (summer resorts, for example), and many are attended only during daylight hours. On the other hand, many offer services 24 hours a day, and many large airports have several FBOs competing for aviation business.

FBOs fall into four categories:

1. *Major fixed base operators.* Major fixed base operators are located on major airports and are fully equipped to handle the servicing and maintenance of all types of aircraft from the large air carrier types used by the airlines and major corporations to the single engine aircraft that use the airport. Many of the major FBOs have multiplex operations as do some of the medium size FBOs, but most major operators have a single operations base. Their investments run into hundreds of millions of dollars, including leaseholds and equipment.

2. *Medium-sized fixed base operators.* The difference between major and medium-sized operations is chiefly the amount of investment, for most medium-sized operators are located at airports where air carriers are also served. FBOs must be able (by contract with the lessor) to remove and repair any aircraft that may be expected to use their facilities in the event that such aircraft becomes disabled on the ramps or runways. The investment in a medium-sized FBO may run as high as $50 million and sales volumes may run into the multimillion dollar figure annually, principally on aircraft sales, fuel sales, and maintenance.

3. *Small fixed base operators.* It is estimated that two-thirds of the FBOs fall into the

small category. Many are small firms doing business on a shoestring, using the cash-drawer system. At the beginning of the year there is so much money in the till; during the year some goes out and some comes in, and at the end of the year, whatever is left is "profit." The vulnerability of such operations in the modern business environment is too clear to require comment.

The vast majority of the small operators have no business training. A small FBO is started by a person who is an aeronautical specialist, a pilot or a mechanic, an artisan such as an engine rebuilder, a radio expert, or a sheet metal fabricator, because of love for aviation. Then the operation grows in size to meet the increasing demands of the aviation public.

Beginning with a flight instruction or repair facility, the small operator attracts a clientele, and as the flying public learns of the operation, expands services to include fueling, hangarage, and tie-downs. In a short time the specialist becomes a generalist and blossoms into a classic multiservice fixed base operation, with many employees and increased investments—an aviation shopping mall—which the specialist/generalist is often not educationally equipped to manage on a businesslike basis.

Recognizing that the fixed base operator is the major contact between the manufacturers and the general public for the sale of new aircraft and for flight instruction, it can be seen that there is a fragility in the general aviation industry that must be corrected if general aviation is to continue, not only to grow, but to exist as a transportation form of value to the nation.

4. *Special fixed base operators.* Some extremely *specialized aviation operations* found on public airports do not qualify as fixed base operations but are nevertheless totally involved with aviation. Engine manufacturers and remanufacturers, avionics specialists, propeller specialists, and certain flight training specialists who do nothing but recurrent flight training for professional or semiprofessional pilots of high performance aircraft. These operations are separate from and not competitive with true fixed base operators at the same airport, but fall within the category simply because they are located at the same airport.

General aviation air transportation cannot exist without a nationwide system of fixed base operators to support it. Not only is the FBO the interface between the manufacturing business and the public and the principal outlet for aircraft sales, it also provides the fueling, routine (and major) maintenance, inspection and relicensing facilities, storage, and general aviation buildings, in most cases. No one can plan a trip by general aviation aircraft unless such support facilities, at least fueling capabilities, are available at both ends of the trip. Fixed base operations are the sine qua non of general aviation transportation.

Trends in the FBO Industry

It was mentioned earlier that the FBO industry went through a transitional stage from the early 1980s through the mid-1990s wherein mergers and failures were the rule. By the mid-1990s, NATA statistics showed a drop in FBOs from a high of more than 10,000 to fewer than 5,000 with dire predictions of "2,000 in 2000," if something did not change. But something did change. The U.S. economy remained strong during the latter half of the 1990s. GARA was passed; Cessna resumed production of single-engine aircraft; new models entered the market; and fractional ownership all served to increase aircraft sales. These factors have led to a stabilization in the FBO industry with the number now between 4,000 and 4,500.

Historically, FBOs have been driven by the rate of new aircraft deliveries. The explosive growth in FBOs and other industry segments during the 1970s was led by new aircraft sales. The contraction in the number of FBOs in the 1980s and early 1990s again reflected the rate of new aircraft sales. Present, but not visible in new aircraft delivery statistics, was a growing trend on the part of airframe manufacturers to seek after-market work such as repair, overhaul, and maintenance including refurbishing, painting, interior, and avionics work. In the past, this work was almost entirely the province of independent FBOs, modification centers, and maintenance facilities. This trend began in the early 1980s as aircraft sales declined and manufacturers looked to other markets to supplement declining revenues and profits. Another trend is the move towards corporate self-fueling. Information collected by *FBO* magazine shows that close to 40 percent of the airports surveyed permit self-fueling and over 20 percent of the airports surveyed actually use self-fueling. Because most FBOs derive the highest percentage of their income from fuel service activities, this trend is very alarming.

Regulatory conformity creates yet another large cost for FBOs. This cost is difficult to assess as federal, state, county, city, and airport authorities each promulgate regulations. Additionally, FBOs are faced with increasing fees and charges from a number of regulatory authorities. These include, but are not limited to, leaking underground storage tank charges, fuel flowage fees, Superfund, and federal airways tax. Many FBOs also incur costs in order to conform to EPA underground storage tank regulations. Added to these fees and charges are the rising product costs, including large increases in av-jet and 100 low-lead fuels in recent years. Insurance premiums have also begun to rise since the fiercely competitive rates offered during the late 1980s to mid-1990s.

The entry of airframe manufacturers has impacted those FBOs that in the past had derived significant income from completions, modifications, maintenance, and parts. New aircraft completions were profitable business with significant margins available on material content and with somewhat lower margins on interior and paint. Now virtually all of the business jet manufacturers have in-house completion capability. At the same time, manufacturers have been able to extend warranty periods due to improved quality. Some manufacturers now offer inclusive long-term maintenance and parts packages with the purchase of the aircraft. This further erodes one of the FBO's traditional market opportunities.

Corporate self-fueling is justified by the corporate operator because their into-plane "cost" may be less than 50 percent of their neighboring FBO's retail fuel price. Ironically, that same corporate operator, when a transient, expects their destination FBO to have ground transportation, catering service, fuel trucks, line persons, lounges, telephones, and other services ready 24 hours a day. The host FBO now depends on retail fuel sales to pay for these services even if the transient purchases little or no fuel. These market forces will lead to a diversification of services on a pay-as-you-go basis. The purchase of fuel cannot remain the sole currency of the transient aircraft. Actually, this may be beneficial for both buyer and seller. A fairly priced menu of services allows the FBO to recognize and deal with the consequences of tankering, self-fueling, and fuel discounting. It also allows customers to buy what they need while not appearing to subsidize other transients.

Regulatory conformity, such as to the new FAA security requirements, will add such incremental costs to smaller or marginally profitable FBOs that they will fail. The larger FBOs, by their very nature, capital base and size, are better able to amortize these costs.

In conclusion, the increasing percentage of overseas aircraft sales, the entry of airframe manufacturers into the business, corporate self-fueling, and regulatory conformity all suggest that the FBO industry must look to nontraditional product/service areas and markets for future profits.

Future Outlook

Any factor which stimulates aircraft sales, in the long term, will help the FBO industry. An improving U.S. economy and growth in corporate net profits will contribute to an improved outlook.

The aging general aviation fleet creates opportunities for FBO growth in both the aircraft sales and the maintenance departments. When the upturn in aircraft sales began in 1995, the average single-engine, piston-powered aircraft in the U.S. fleet was over 27 years old and the average turbine-powered airplane, 15 years old. One-fourth of the aircraft in the single-engine, piston-powered fleet was more than 32 years old.

Despite an economic slowdown in the early 2000s, the U.S. economy is expected to rebound for the remainder of the decade which bodes well for new aircraft sales to replace the aging fleet.

Another positive sign is the heavy investment in research and development now underway by the aircraft manufacturers. Spurred on by aircraft sales and fractional ownership programs, turbine business jet manufacturers are making commitments in millions of dollars. FBO ramps are bustling and hangars are full. FBOs have enjoyed full flow volumes at the start of the new century that they never dreamed of in the early 1990s. While all of the foregoing elements portend a revitalization of the FBO industry, almost every one has been present in some form in the past, and, therefore, their effects are somewhat predictable. In the future, the FBO industry will need to look at itself in a completely new context as opposed to being a provider of its traditional products and services.

Analysts of the industry predict the following changes in the industry as we head into the twenty-first century.

1. Long-term contracts between the aircraft operator and the aircraft maintenance facility will provide over 50 percent of that facility's maintenance income. Such contracts will allow preplanned and guaranteed man-hours, thus allowing the provider to reduce his prices, knowing that he has exclusive access to a specific number of labor hours from a specific customer.
2. We may see the consolidation of individual and independent flight departments at a specific airport, thus allowing reductions in overhead, improved aircraft utilization, and reduced costs. These consolidated maintenance enterprises will in turn have increased negotiating power with their suppliers due to the size of their fleet.
3. Certain FBOs will become business centers. They will offer conference rooms, food service, video conferencing, reception of E-mail, fax services, voice mail, personal computers with modems, and other types of services which transient business aircraft passengers must now seek at an inconvenient downtown location.
4. Some FBO locations/operations may be acquired by or become partners with established hotel chains. Many top-flight American hotel chains now have locations just outside the airport fence. It is an easy migration to being on the airport and providing those services for transient business aircraft passengers. By capturing high-value passengers on the ramp, it allows vertical marketing within the hotel chains as these passengers seek other amenities and services.
5. Consolidation in the FBO industry will continue. Rather than two or three huge FBO chains, we may see ten or more FBO chains — that is five or more FBOs each. Rather than seeing top-tier markets building opulent FBOs, there will be a continual upgrading of second-tier markets. During the 1990s, the top 40 market airports have experienced improved FBOs. In the next few years, the next 100 market will have a similar improvement. With expanded travel because of spread-out demographics and the influx of fractional ownership, FBOs are facing a higher level of customer expectation.
6. Some FBOs will no longer directly dispense aircraft fuels. At airports which now offer multiple FBOs, it may simply become impractical to maintain multiple tank farms with their attendant capital costs, maintenance costs, and potential environmental liability. A single tank farm will serve FBOs, whereby the FBOs concentrate on the marketing of products and services and simply call upon the fuel provider as needed and charge commission or fee somewhat like the into-plane charges made by providers of fuel services at commercial airline airports.
7. It is expected that some FBOs will increase sales of nonaviation products. The traditional sale of aviation sunglasses and leather jackets will be vastly expanded and will be managed in partnership with established merchandising firms. Com-

puter terminals, catalogs, and the acceptance of video shopping networks will tend to break down existing barriers. Revenues from these concessions will constitute a large part of the FBOs' potential profits.

8. Local and regional charter services will market nationwide, being tied together through computer networks, whereby passengers can book services well in advance of their needs, while being assured of quality, safety, and dependability.

9. With relatively low unemployment levels in recent years, demand for talented people at all levels has raised the bar. Most FBOs find it difficult keeping pilots. Airline hiring has been at record levels in recent years. FBOs have also had difficulty retaining technicians, line-service, and customer service personnel. These problems must be addressed by higher pay, increased benefits, further education, and promotional opportunities.

10. There will be a move towards the flying club as a training device as opposed to individual instruction. The cost of obtaining a private license will drive the market in this direction. Colleges and universities offering aviation programs will assume a larger role in flight training.

11. Cities and counties which now are "landlords" for FBO tenants will become partners with these tenants and show an increased willingness to supply capital for the FBO if they perceive that it will create jobs. They will look less towards the per-square-foot rental income as a landlord and more towards the creation of jobs in a local community.

Present indications are that the new decade will bring many changes to the FBO industry including possible reductions in the number of smaller operators.

ESTABLISHING AN FBO

The simplist form of a fixed base operator is the flight instructor who owns an airplane who is in business independently. The only reason this person is in business at all is due to enthusiasm about flying. Then, take the single flight instructor operation, add satisfied customers, and let the business grow and expand. A second aircraft is added. The instructor has the start of a "fleet." While the instructor is flying one plane, the other is inoperative. At this point another pilot should be hired as a part-time instructor. Even with such simple acquisitions, business is suddenly becoming more complex. Now there is a payroll with tax deductions, additional insurance for the second plane, cost of maintenance of both planes, and hangar or tie-down charges.

The flying business, however, keeps both pilots and planes busy. The instructor begins to think further. By leasing a hangar and hiring a mechanic, the operation could handle its own maintenance, and then take in other work for additional income. Soon, in this oversimplification of FBO growth, the enterprise is generating more work for more people, and paying wages that directly or indirectly contribute to the economy of the community.

Another example is the FBO at a major airport with an executive aircraft terminal which is the base for general aviation aircraft as well as scheduled and charter air carriers. A personalized weather service is available at reasonable cost. There are direct phones to the U.S. Weather Bureau, airport control tower, and FAA communications for filing flight plans.

The firm has contracts with some scheduled airlines for fueling, cleaning, and supplying turbine-starting equipment to jet-powered aircraft. It operates a helicopter for charter/lease, and light aircraft for air taxi. Aircraft maintenance is offered by the same operator, as well as avionics services, and an aircraft interior shop. The owner-manager holds FAA repair station certificates for various categories of large and small aircraft.

The operation described here is obviously on a large scale. However, it was developed rather speedily at a time when the airport had decided to expand and upgrade its facilities.

Regardless of whether an FBO starts on a small or a large scale, its success will largely depend on how it plans for the future and responds to changing conditions. As the scope of services offered by the typical fixed base operator grows, technical aviation knowledge will continue to be important, but will become secondary to other qualifications needed to manage any successful enterprise. Management will have less direct contact with the aviation activities, and concern with running the FBO and problem-solving activities which accompany the growth of any business.

Analyzing the Market and Selecting a Location

Before deciding upon a location for a fixed base operation, a study of the potential market is needed. The process of studying the market is called *Market Analysis*. Information sought in a market analysis for a fixed base operator (or any kind of business) includes the number of potential customers, where they are located, and what kind and what quantity of business they are likely to bring to the firm.

In studying the potential market, it is necessary to recognize that the aviation industry as a whole has been undergoing tremendous and rapid change. The state of the art has been changing from year to year, and even from month to month. These changes have affected the kinds of products and services the flying public has come to expect.

One of the first questions in analyzing the potential market is what the firm has to offer the flying public in relation to the current state of the art. Next, the firm must consider how useful and how popular its offerings are going to be with the people in the community in which it plans to locate.

Other important market factors to be considered are population, weather conditions, income levels, the social and economic nature of the community, ground facilities to support efficient use of the aircraft, industrial developments and trends of the community, agricultural activities, survey or exploration activities, traffic problems, and other ground transportation problems in the area. For example, weather conditions are important to any flight-related business. Is the area subject to snow on the ground for several months during the year? Does it rain almost steadily for months at a time? Will fog close the airport for long periods? These are important questions which a prospective FBO must consider. A check with the FAA can determine the number of flying days in the past five years and would indicate the number of business days which can be expected during an average weather year.

The Community

The characteristics of the community will greatly affect an operation. Is general aviation an established fixture of the community, or is it still considered a rich man's pastime? Is the airport on established commercial routes? Will there be an opportunity for charter flights to neighboring communities? These and other questions concerning the community should be answered in any complete market analysis.

Activities such as agriculture, aerial survey, and aerial exploration are also covered in a market analysis. Occupations and activities such as these provide increased opportunities for charter operations. On the other hand, if such activities are not carried on to any extent, a firm must determine whether there is enough other business to compensate for this deficiency.

Industrial and business activities constitute another area to be examined in the market analysis. Many businesses use the airplane as a daily part of their operation, while other corporations fly personnel to and from conferences to conserve time. If these business practices do not exist in the location under consideration, it may be a sign that the firm will have to depend upon other sources of revenue.

The market for an FBO is not just one group, but many segments, and each requires a separate analysis. Major segments include, but are not limited to, the following list:

1. Business and corporate market
2. Private or pleasure market
3. Agricultural market
4. Government aircraft sales and service market

5. Transient potential
6. Other operations or airline markets

Each of these areas should be thoroughly explored before a location is selected, and regardless of the size of the FBO, possible sources of business must be considered regarding their potential. A large percentage of these possibilities should look promising or the chances for success will be slim.

Site Selection

The process of *site selection* should start with the choice of a geographical area. Having decided on a general area, the next step involves the selection of a specific airport. In making this choice, it is important to survey the competition of other FBOs and find out how well they are doing. A firm must also determine whether to locate on a private or publicly owned field.

In comparison with most other businesses, site selection for a fixed base operator can be a difficult process because suitable locations are limited. A firm must think in terms of the entire airport and its future development plans. Moving into an existing facility has good and bad points. Choosing an established facility is certainly beneficial, but if the airport master plan calls for relocation of the center of activities, leaving the FBO isolated, the result could be disastrous. The location on the airport has a significant effect on business both immediately and in the future. A few key factors include the distance to fueling facilities (if this service is not provided); distance to the main terminal area (especially if no restaurant is available); distance from the nearest competitor (to avoid customer confusion); and ease of access to and from public roads.

A firm often must consider whether to buy or rent the facility site. Do financial arrangements make it advisable to own the property, or is it more desirable to lease? The firm must consider whether or not the site is likely to be permanent. Being forced to vacate on short notice could be a great inconvenience.

Another consideration in deciding whether or not to buy an existing facility is the matter of who the predecessors were. If a similar fixed base operation existed, what was its reputation? A firm must consider whether its reputation will be favorably or unfavorably affected by the former tenant.

Getting Assistance

Individuals considering the establishment of an FBO can obtain assistance from a number of sources including chambers of commerce and local community aviation advisory committees. Various services can be rendered by the FAA, including those of the FAA District Airport Engineer. However, because of the small staff of the airport district offices, its services are usually limited to preliminary discussions and advice and do not include the solution of complex operational problems.

State aviation bureaus or similar bodies which exist in most states can be helpful. Frequently, it is necessary to obtain certification from the state bureau.

The airport manager or owner will, of course, have valuable information concerning the airport — statistics on aircraft movements, plans for future expansion of the facility, and much more information that will directly affect any proposed business.

Facilities

After considering all airport requirements, the firm can narrow its sights to specific facilities for its own operation. While the facilities chosen will largely depend upon the size of the FBO and services offered, there are three categories: aircraft storage areas, customer or public areas, and employee or work areas.

In a small operation, these facilities can easily be grouped together in one multipurpose structure. Often, a hangar can be converted, by a little simple carpentry, into office space, as well as storage and work areas. If the firm is planning a larger operation, it may have several large hangars, 20 or 30 smaller T-hangars, equipment and maintenance hangars, and a separate office building.

Aircraft Storage Areas

1. *Outdoor tie-down area.* Is the area adequate for the expected number of aircraft to be based at the airport as well as for transient aircraft? Are the tie-downs spaced properly? Are the parking spaces clearly marked? Can the area be policed and kept clean easily? These are just some of the questions which must be considered regarding this important category.
2. *T-hangars, design, and site.* There are literally hundreds of designs and types of T-hangars available to meet a particular FBO's needs. Consideration must also be given to having an adequate number, placed in good locations convenient for customers.
3. *Large hangar storage.* A large hangar is one which can hold many aircraft and can also be a combination hangar—both for storing aircraft and for maintenance work.

Customer (or Public) Facilities

These facilities are designed primarily for customer use and should always be kept neat and clean. The first requirement is the reception area, with a place for registration if necessary, and a pilots' service desk. Next is the pilot ready room, with maps, weather information, and FAA phones; which need not be a completely separate room, although such a room is always an attractive feature. It must be fully equipped and functional from the pilot's standpoint. The exact location of maps, forms, weather information, and assorted pilot aids should be carefully planned. Adequate space must be provided for pilots to spread out several maps.

Other facilities include:

1. *Pilot or crew sleeping quarters.* This may be considered a luxury facility, but is certainly important if the firm expects to attract corporate business.
2. *Rest rooms.* Clean and modern rest-room facilities including showers and a dressing area with lockers is a decided plus factor.
3. *Waiting lounge.* People are always waiting for other people at any transportation facility, and airports are no exception. Whether traveling by airline or business aircraft, individuals appreciate a comfortable waiting area or lounge.
4. *Classroom(s).* This facility should be neat and well equipped.
5. *Visitors' conference room.* The larger corporate aircraft are actually flying offices. Conferences and meetings are often held while the plane is en route. For firms using intermediate-size business aircraft or for those firms meeting customers, a conference room can be a real asset. This facility can also be used by the FBO for meetings with employees and customers when it is not scheduled to be used by corporate aircraft users.
6. *Recreational facilities.* Consideration should be given to whether outdoor or indoor recreational facilities would be appropriate for the kind of customer the FBO expects to attract.
7. *Display case or room.* Whether it is simply a display case or an entire room devoted to pilot supplies and accessories, this can be a highly profitable area for an FBO.

Employee (or Work) Facilities

The principal areas used by employees are as follows:

1. *Offices as required.*
2. *Line crew ready room.* This room should have a view of and be easily accessible to the transient aircraft ramp area.
3. *Maintenance shops.* This area should include at least one small office for mechanics to order parts, write up job tickets, and talk to customers.
4. *Parts and supply storage.* Parts and supplies require adequate shelves for access and inventory purposes. A separate storage area should be provided to place cartons, damaged parts, and other materials that can clutter up the main part of the hangar.
5. *Fueling facilities.* Normally, this is one of the easiest of all facilities to plan because of the readily available assistance from the oil companies. The major decision here is

whether to have trucks or a fixed fueling facility. Both have advantages but this decision largely depends upon the FBO's location on the airport.

Mobile equipment has the advantage of being more flexible in allowing the line personnel to reach aircraft at various locations on the ramp area. Generally mobile equipment enables an FBO to stock a greater variety of octanes or jet fuel, if these are required.

On the other hand, the initial cost and the maintenance cost of mobile equipment is higher than that of fixed fueling equipment. Moreover, with mobile equipment, there is always the possibility of accidents, for which insurance must be carried. Also, evaporation and stock losses are higher with mobile equipment.

For the average FBO, stationary facilities are dependable and economical to install and also require less manpower to operate.

6. *Wash ramp.* A specific site with good drainage should be provided for washing aircraft. The size of the area largely depends upon the expected size of the aircraft to be washed.

7. *Vehicle storage areas.* Gasoline trucks, courtesy station wagons, even scooters can get in the way and cause accidents unless they are parked in a designated area.

8. *Employee showers and locker room.* This may seem like a luxury facility but it is found at many successful FBOs and greatly enhances employee relations.

Equipment

The equipment needed is related to the services provided, but the following list gives an idea of the major items included.

1. *Fueling trucks.* The number of trucks and type of gasoline octanes or jet fuel required will depend entirely on the nature and volume of business expected.

2. *Other vehicles.* These include station wagons, utility trucks, scooters, and trailers or carts.

3. *Housekeeping needs.* Buckets, mops, brooms, carpentry tools, ladders, rags, and dust equipment fall into this category.

4. *Shop tools.* The type of aircraft to be worked on will determine the shop tooling needs. Appropriate cabinets and hanging devices for storing tools must also be considered.

5. *Supplies.* This area includes those items intended for resale and operating supplies used exclusively by the FBO.

6. *Office equipment.* Included are desks, chairs, word processors, file and storage cabinets, copying equipment, and desk supplies.

Inventory of Aircraft

Certainly one of the most important areas to consider is the type and quantity of aircraft to inventory, for sale or operation, or both. Operational inventory includes aircraft to be used for charter, flight training, and other commercial work.

CHAINS VERSUS INDEPENDENTS

To many FBOs, the question of remaining independent or becoming affiliated with a chain is an important decision to be made during the 2000s. Which of these choices can increase the odds for surviving in today's industry?

The best year for the general aviation industry from an aircraft sales standpoint was 1978, when 17,811 general aviation aircraft were sold. From an FBO-industry historical perspective, looking back at the very prosperous years of the FBO industry during the 1970s and early 1980s, any lack of attention or responsiveness to a specific problem area within the industry, or within an individual organization, would not necessarily be catastrophic. During this period, an FBO could easily compensate for oversights in any one problem area by increasing product or service margins, or increasing volume.

This all changed from the early 1980s through the mid 1990s. It was a different marketplace and operating environment in which there were dramatic declines in aircraft sales, fuel revenues, aircraft maintenance income, and revenues from the ancillary services provided by FBO organizations. During recent years, many FBOs have realized the importance of becoming part of a larger organization.

The most significant motivation for an FBO to become affiliated with a chain is the benefits and cost savings derived from marketing and identity and the resulting economies of scale inherent to such an organization. Belonging to a national or international chain is not for all FBOs. The chains are very selective, as are many independent owner-operators. The cost/benefit relationship may not be viable for some smaller FBOs. The approach of most chains is to support an individual operator as an independent business that has access to a well-financed and professionally developed marketing and identity program. This offers the best of both worlds as operators receive assistance from the chain in marketing, while making their own decisions regarding operation of FBOs.

The question of independence or affiliation can be a difficult decision for many FBO operators because of self-esteem issues that founders and/or operating management have developed from having survived and even prospered during the previous tenuous periods in the evolution of the industry. For the most part, the strength and determination of many FBOs have given them the feeling that they can go it alone; however, this approach may not always be the most prudent.

By examining some of the basic issues when evaluating the affiliation or independence question, readers can draw their own conclusions. Some considerations for remaining independent include the following:

1. A desire to continue to operate as a totally independent business, thereby ensuring control when making marketing, management, and operational decisions.
2. Operating an FBO that has a sound reputation for quality services and support, and a highly established and recognizable identity/image.
3. Established and profitable FBOs that would have little or no potential incremental revenue impact from increased marketing exposure or networking with affiliated organizations.
4. Operating an FBO in a strong geographical location, or established destination marketplace, which would not benefit from increased network exposure.

Conversely, the process for deciding if a program of affiliation would be desirable for an FBO would include the examination of these same issues from a slightly different perspective:

1. The desire to operate with the support of a larger organization and to have access to a variety of resources and expertise.
2. Limited advertising budget and the need to gain national exposure to increase market share and sales volumes.
3. Being located in an underexposed geographical area. Need for national marketing and networked transient clientele, with additional high cost/benefit exposure to the marketplace to develop a larger customer base.
4. Desire to work with other FBOs with similar interests and operating objectives who are also affiliated with the franchise organization through an advisory counsel approach.

Although they are not franchise organizations in the literal meaning of the word, several oil companies also offer marketing programs for their dealers to stress the advantages of their programs for promoting their brand products. Exxon/Mobil — with close to 50 locations in the U.S. and Canada — was the first to develop this concept over 20 years ago and continues to add new designated dealers each year. Phillips also has its "super dealer" program called Aviation Performance Center (APC). About 80 of the 900 Phillips dealers are APCs. Therefore, it stands to reason that FBOs seeking broader identity or deeper market penetration for their fuel products and services may be well served to consider the support available as an authorized franchisee or specialized dealer.

Million Air, one of the most successful chains with over 30 locations, identifies five primary benefits in joining a chain. They are (1) name recognition, (2) image enhancement, (3) value for advertising dollars spent (when cost of franchising is considered advertisement), (4) consistent service levels and product quality, and (5) standardized training and the potential to attract higher quality employees.

In any organized marketing program such as Million Air's or Exxon/Mobil's Avitat network, there is a large pool of ideas from which to draw, all within the same organization, all having the same objectives. There is no question that the chain concept has not only improved the outward appearance and perception of Million Air FBOs, but has markedly improved market share and sales volume for these operators as well.

The success enjoyed by Million Air franchisees is basically the same as that of any high-quality FBO. Operators are allowed maximum decision making in running their business. However, in order to maintain the integrity of the system, there are specific requirements for standardized identity signage and uniforms, and certain other operations and procedures are mandatory from a customer service standpoint.

By comparison, participants in the Avitat, APC, and other similar branding programs also have to meet the personnel and graphic identity standards required in the Million Air program — and all enjoy the benefit of cooperative advertising and network identity.

Regardless of an operator's decision concerning independence or affiliation, these challenging economic times mandate innovative and nontraditional approaches for increasing revenues in today's declining marketplace.

The theory of maximum competition within the FBO industry was once held as an indisputable dogma by the FAA and many airport management communities alike. However, this theory is being challenged everyday on the basis of pure economic survival. Competitors today may become partners tomorrow. The decision to remain independent or align with an external support program and identity (franchise) system may be clearer as dollar/value tradeoffs become more important.

In many business dilemmas, quick fix solutions, while appealing at first, may ultimately result in having to return to the basics of the business. Nevertheless, from a fundamental perspective, the decision of independence or affiliation may apply now more than ever.

An individual operator's choice to remain independent or align, with some form of franchise or other affiliation structure, is an important decision. However, one thing is clear — the once thriving dynamo of general aviation after-market sales has virtually ceased to produce the dramatic annual increases in sales volumes for products and services that the industry witnessed during the 1970s and early 1980s.

FBO CUSTOMER SERVICES CHECKLIST

Ramp Area

Exemplary service to customers is going to take on added significance for FBOs wishing to survive competition during the 2000s. Whether the customer is a prospective student pilot seeking flight instruction, a business requesting a charter flight, or a corporate operator looking for a maintenance or line service facility, service becomes an important element in distinguishing among competitors.

The following section provides a checklist of accepted practices and procedures designed to improve service to customers.

A well thought out ramp area will not only enhance the appearance of an FBO, it will reduce the possibility of ramp accidents and increase the utilization of equipment. Good ramp planning can also improve fuel service and tie-down business.

1. Training aircraft should be parked for easy access from the flight office. Parking should be arranged to place the most active aircraft in the most accessible spots. There should be adequate room for students to taxi safely in and out of parking areas.

2. When possible, one-way, flow-through taxi routes should be provided. Lead-in stripes for nosewheel guides into parking spots should be painted brightly. All obstructions close to taxi routes should be marked with high-visibility caution signs or symbols.

3. One-way, flow-through traffic paths to fuel islands should be used. A refueling parking spot for fuel truck operations should be designated so that it does not conflict with normal traffic flow.

4. If flood lighting is impractical or causes glare, a series of low (below wing level) ground illuminating lights should be considered. Warning lights on all obstructions close to taxi routes should be used. The refueling area should be well lit.

5. To attract transient aircraft, high visibility signs should be positioned to be seen from taxi-ways announcing transient fuel service. Lead-in signs and/or taxiway markings with lead-in stripes should indicate the route to refueling and parking areas.

6. The following items of ramp equipment should be provided in sufficient number, in good repair, and conveniently located:
   - tugs
   - tow bars
   - ladders and stands
   - power units
   - jacks
   - nitrogen, oxygen and air tanks
   - de-icing rigs
   - lavatory flush carts
   - survival gear (life rafts, radios, etc.) at ports of debarkation
   - avionics and component repair equipment to the extent that such service is offered or intended
   - windshield cleaner and cleaning cloths
   - oil wipe cloths
   - chocks numbered to tie-down spots
   - equipment lockers at strategic points on the flight line
   - covered trash containers

Ground Personnel

Dispatcher and/or receptionist personnel should be responsible for the following areas:

1. Complete understanding and be able to explain:
   - company rental policy and agreements
   - FAA pilot certificates, medical certificates, and Federal Communication Commission (FCC) radio license
   - Federal Aviation Regulations (FAR) currency requirements
   - company insurance policies
   - student enrollment procedures
   - Part 141 student record requirements
   - FAA, FCC, and Veterans Administration (VA) forms
   - flight training and services fee schedule
   - information regarding rental car service, hotel or motel facilities including rates, discounts, and distances
2. Familiar with all Unicom regulations, procedures, and responsibilities.
3. Rescheduling customers after each flight.
4. Calling customers who have become inactive.

5. Training in telephone sales techniques.
6. Use of an inquiry form to record the maximum amount of data from incoming phone inquiries.
7. Assume duties that relieve flight instructors from routine tasks and allow more time for training.
8. Monitor students progress (ground school and flight training).

Line personnel are not only in regular contact with customers but also have a high degree of responsibility for safe operations. They should be responsible for the following areas:

1. Thoroughly trained in the following:
   • the nature, coding, and handling of all aircraft servicing materials
   • all aircraft servicing procedures (including electrical, oxygen, and so forth)
   • aircraft towing and ground handling procedures
   • ramp safety procedures
   • aircraft spotting and parking techniques
   • all ramp signaling techniques
2. Be in uniform or dress that is immediately identifiable to transient pilots.
3. Develop a system of alert so that personnel are stationed where they can see incoming aircraft.
4. Train personnel to respond to customer service requests immediately. All employees should be instructed on the importance of a safe, prompt, efficient, dependable, and courteous service attitude to all customers. Some larger FBOs employ a customer service representative to meet all incoming business aircraft, their passengers and crews.

Aircraft

Aircraft must not only be airworthy, they must look airworthy. Nothing can add to the apprehension of a student or renter pilot more than an aircraft that looks unsafe to fly. The following list includes those items which demonstrate care and professionalism.

1. A clean and polished exterior finish
2. A clean engine compartment
3. Tires in good condition and properly inflated
4. Widows clean inside and out
5. A clean interior (trash removed, ash trays emptied, etc.)
6. All interior trim panels in good repair
7. Carpeting clean and in good repair
8. Instrument panel and anti-glare shield finish in good repair
9. Upholstery clean and in good repair
10. All knobs, levers, and switches in place and functioning
11. All unused instrument cutouts, avionics bays, etc. properly covered or blanked out
12. All loose equipment properly stowed and secured
13. All checklists, frequency reminders, etc. professionally printed and durable
14. All manuals and required paperwork on board and properly stowed or displayed

Flight Personnel

The demands on flight instructors should go far beyond pilot skills. The instructors must have ability in teaching, consulting, customer relations, and salesmanship. Flight instructors should be responsible for the following areas:

1. Maintaining a professional attitude about teaching.
2. Currency in the following:
   • all applicable FARs

- all FAA recommended flight procedures and techniques
- latest teaching techniques

Many FBOs require instructors to attend revalidation seminars. Regularly scheduled meetings with instructors to review recent changes and developments are also utilized. Information bulletins explaining recent changes and developments are distributed on a regular basis.

3. A system to standardize the following procedures and techniques used by instructors:
   - teaching methods
   - flight procedures and maneuvers
   - semantics
   - student evaluation
   - flight and ground curriculum

A program of standardization flights with the chief pilot can be established so that all instructors are teaching from the same syllabus.

4. A policy to eliminate conflict between student instruction and charter flights. Some FBOs schedule a specific day for each instructor to fly charter. The manager or chief pilot can fly all charters that conflict with an instructor's training schedule.
5. A plan for the continued upgrading of instructors' image and prestige. An area for student briefings and conferences (preferably including an office, cubicle or desk with nameplate). Some FBOs provide business cards for each instructor and instructor blazers with logo and name. If aircraft utilization permits, one aircraft could be assigned to each instructor with the individual's name on the door.
6. An incentive system to increase instructor remuneration. This might include incremental increases for such things as night instrument and multiengine training. A higher rate could be established for total hours after a preselected weekly minimum.
7. An understanding of sales and customer relations. Some FBOs pay bonuses to instructors whose students complete an entire course. Finders' fees are sometimes paid to instructors who recruit students. A small override fee is often established for a student's solo time.

The responsibilities of the chief pilot vary depending on the size and complexity of the fixed base operation and whether the chief pilot is also the manager. However, the following responsibilities should apply to most operations.

1. Maintaining a close liaison with local FAA personnel
2. Developing flight and ground school curricula
3. Conducting standardization flight for staff instructors
4. Conducting student phase check flights
5. Conducting regular instructor meetings to maintain standardization, review problem areas, and develop new methods
6. Providing written information for instructors and students on operational techniques and procedures
7. Maintaining student records and FAA reports
8. Monthly status reports to management
9. Maintaining a list of available local CFIs
10. Maintaining an open door policy to listen to student or instructor problems
11. Make regular checks on student attitudes
12. Conduct introductory flights and tours of the facility
13. Establish a program to recruit new students and improve attrition

KEY TERMS

Fixed base operators   Specialized commercial flight operations
Line service   Market Analysis
Maintenance and repair service   Site selection
Completion   Nonincome services
Corporate flight service

REVIEW QUESTIONS

1. How was the term "fixed base operator" coined? Why is line service considered the main business of an FBO? Describe some of the services provided under maintenance and repair. What are some of the services normally included under aircraft sales? How does charter and rental business differ from corporate flight service? Describe some of the services an FBO provides under a corporate flight service arrangement. Give several examples of specialized commercial flight services provided by FBOs.

2. What are "nonincome services?" Discuss their importance. Approximately how many FBOs are there in the United States? How are they categorized? Discuss some of the problems experienced by small fixed base operators. What are special fixed base operators? How is the FBO industry changed in the 1990s? Describe five specific changes that are forecast to change the way FBOs conduct their business.

3. In establishing an FBO, describe the importance of analyzing the market and selecting a location. What is market analysis? Discuss the importance of the community. Describe the factors which must be considered in selecting a site for an FBO. Where can a prospective FBO get assistance?

4. List the basic facilities found in the following areas: aircraft storage, customer (or public) facilities, and employee (or work) facilities. List the basic equipment needed to get started.

5. Why have many independent FBOs joined a chain? Why would an FBO choose to remain independent? Give some advantages and disadvantages of joining a chain.

6. What can an FBO do to improve efficiency and customer service in the ramp area? Describe some of the areas that ground personnel should be responsible for in carrying out their duties efficiently. Explain some of the little things that can be done to make aircraft look better. The demands of flight instructors should go far beyond pilot skills. Explain. Describe some of the responsibilities of the chief pilot.

REFERENCES

Cohen, David. *Fixed Base Operator's Management Handbook.* Basin, WY: Aviation Maintenance Publishers, Inc., 1980.

Richardson, J. D. *Essentials of Aviation Management* (4th ed.). Dubuque, IA: Kendall/Hunt Publishing Co., 1990.

Chapter 4

Managing a Fixed Base Operation

OUTLINE

OBJECTIVES

At the end of this chapter, you should be able to:

Summarize the characteristics of successful FBOs.

Discuss the importance of planning.

Describe the step-by-step approach to planning.

Distinguish between line and staff personnel.

Define unity of command and span of control.

Explain the purpose of the operations manual.

Describe the staffing process.

List the major items included in an employee handbook.

Discuss the role of leadership in directing a business plan.

Define personality and motives as they relate to understanding employees.

Compare and contrast Maslow's theory of human wants and needs with Herzberg's motivators and hygiene factors.

Describe the decision-making process.

Discuss the purpose of the controlling process.

In his book, *Thriving on Chaos,* Tom Peters argues that our national economy is in a volatile state. Rapid change is the order of the day. Those businesses that intend to survive must learn to love change. In turn, they must "thrive on chaos." Firms can only expect to successfully compete in the economy of the new century if they are willing to (1) quickly adapt to changing customer preferences, (2) pursue fast-paced innovation, and (3) achieve flexibility by empowering people to reach their full potential. What better an environment to thrive on chaos than the FBO industry? The important point here is not to just cope with chaos but to thrive on it. Chaos implies change and it is only through change — rapid change — that an FBO can stay ahead of competitive forces.

Owners and top managers have tremendous opportunities during the turbulent 2000s to influence (and even control) the future profit performance of their businesses. In order to do so, they need to objectively assess where they are now and where they need to be in terms of management expertise.

CHARACTERISTICS OF SUCCESSFUL FBOS

Successful FBOs have been good in developing strong organizational cultures that reflect the values and practices of their owners and managers. In fact, one of the primary roles of management is to shape and manage the values of the company. The outstanding FBOs have certain core values that are considered almost sacred throughout the organization. There is an espirit-de-corps among all employees. Firms with distinctive cultures furnish meaning for their employees. This provides a purpose in life that all humans are searching for, and as a result, morale and productivity are generally higher. In short, a strong culture is the binding agent that holds everything together.

Change is a given in the FBO business. When change occurs, it is generally fast with little notice or lead time. Hence, the well-managed FBO must be creative in structuring the organization to minimize reaction time.

Well-managed FBOs get quick action because they maintain organizational fluidity. They have developed successful techniques for informal communication. They use special methods and unorthodox approaches to attack difficult problems or affect sudden change. In short, they do not organize to promote bureaucracy and inflexibility. They have been successful in promoting the spirit of entrepreneurship and capitalism throughout the organization. In fact, it is part of their culture. All employees should understand the concept of risk and return and the link between productivity and profitability. FBOs that encourage the entrepreneurial concept the furthest in today's market are likely to be the most profitable in the future.

Certainly getting the job done on schedule and at a reasonable price is an FBO's continuing challenge. However, companies cannot become so production oriented that employees are treated like things. This approach can work in the short term, provided the company has enough supervisors to watch employees every minute of the day. Obviously this approach is not conducive to long-term productivity. Well-managed FBOs successfully balance the concern for people and production. They understand and practice the philosophy that people are their most important assets. There is genuine respect for the individual and an abiding faith that the source of productivity gain is through people.

Well-managed FBOs use positive reinforcement. It is specific and immediate. There are generally programs designed to enhance the employee's self-image. People are encouraged to achieve their full potential. Well-managed FBOs do not expect people to be motivated in a vacuum. They promote an environment of achievement. It is part of their culture. They expect extraordinary results from ordinary people and get it through positive reinforcement.

Quality conscientiousness is another important trait of well-managed FBOs. With some it is almost an obsession. They understand the only cost of quality is the expense of doing things wrong. Therefore, they encourage the attitude and reward the behavior of making quality certain. The result is more competitive pricing, a satisfied customer, and higher profits.

Well-managed FBOs strive to maintain an awareness of the industry's technological advancements, trends, and concepts. They are not timid about applying new technology — the integration of simulators into flight training and computers in record keeping, financial planning, and management. They attend trade shows and seminars to discover new approaches and methodology. They understand that such expenditures are an investment for the future. The end result is greater efficiency which leads to a competitive advantage and/ or higher long-term profits.

Well-managed FBOs are marketing oriented. They have a complete understanding of their markets and know their niche in those markets. They know their strengths and weaknesses and those of the competition. They have been successful in differentiating themselves from their competitors. Well-managed FBOs stress their technological and/or service orientation, focusing on quick turnaround time, quality, and reliability. In short, they compete as much as possible on anything other than price.

The well-managed FBOs have paid their dues in the community, to trade associations, and to customers. They listen and learn and use that valuable knowledge to prepare strategic and tactical plans. The bottom line is they are proactive rather than reactive in their marketing effort.

An important corollary to the marketing orientation is honesty in dealing with people. Customers, suppliers, and even employees have respect for an FBO's integrity. One's word is one's contract, and relationships are built on trust rather than suspicion. This philosophy builds long-term relationships that are extremely beneficial, particularly during tough times.

Finally, well-managed FBOs can literally manage by report. Their management information system provides timely and accurate reporting by profit and cost centers. Administration is viewed as a support function, not an end unto itself. Administrative people understand their service role and cooperate with operations people in solving problems. Reports are formatted in a manner that operations people can easily understand and use to better manage the business.

In short, whether it is job or equipment costing, purchasing and inventory control, or financial management, the system works and people know how to use the information provided. Moreover, direct costs and overhead expenses are budgeted, compared to actuals, and corrective strategies are taken when appropriate. Well-managed FBOs know how to evaluate their cost and capital structures and the analysis into their pricing strategies. This provides valuable information on how to be competitive yet profitable.

Although these concepts are simple, they are not necessarily easy to achieve; however, taken as a whole, they do provide a framework for a well-managed FBO. Excellence is, in fact, achievable but only in degrees. Few FBOs have completely mastered all of the attributes, which should not be surprising. Excellence is a journey, not a destination. These principles imply degrees of achievement and the need for constant striving to reach for higher levels of success.

PLANNING

Effective management begins with planning, which in turn implies setting goals. Planning is the most important function of all in establishing and maintaining a business. In essence, *planning* is problem solving and decision making: speculating on the future (both near and far), setting objectives (short and long term), considering alternatives, and making choices.

Planning for the future necessitates flexibility to cope with the unexpected, setting timetables, establishing priorities, and deciding on the methods to be used and the people who will be involved. A manager must analyze the existing situation, formulate targets, and apply both logic and creativity to all the details in between.

Owners and managers of small FBOs typically are so busy running their operations that they often put off planning. Yet, its importance cannot be overemphasized. As the owner or manager of a small FBO, planning takes on added significance because, unlike larger organizations with ample financial resources, poor or no planning can put a smaller firm out of business. Small FBOs have an aversion to business planning. Possibly the reason for this tendency lies in the fact that most owners and managers would prefer to be doing something physical like flying or overhauling an engine.

Some people are a bit suspicious about planning because they realize it has to do with the future, not the present, and the future is really unpredictable. Furthermore, many people have never been taught how to plan and do not have any idea how to proceed.

Maybe they resist the need for imposing self-discipline or do not have enough confidence in themselves. Perhaps they are reluctant to think on a conceptual level. Perhaps they have never mastered the art of establishing priorities.

Whatever the reasons, planning is often deferred to the future. Yet, planning gives purpose and direction to daily business activities. Without it, such activities are aimless and uncoordinated.

Types of Plans

Long-term plans are set up by top management to give overall direction to company efforts. Strategic in nature, long-term plans are needed to cope with an ever-changing environment. *Operational plans* design day-to-day work details. *Single-use plans* are formulated for specific situations. *Standing plans,* on the other hand, are set up for repeated use over a longer period of time.

Company policies are examples of standing plans. They serve as guidelines for management and employees, imparting solidarity and dependability to company operations. These policies exist in all areas of a well-managed business: in service, pricing, distribution, personnel, finance, and the like. To illustrate, consider these few examples of service policies:

- We shall inventory only those aircraft parts with a high turnover rate.
- We intend to add to the product line of our counter sale of up to three new items each year.
- We shall always have one single-engine aircraft available for short-notice charter flights.

Budgets are plans that have been translated into dollars-and-cents projections and that are the culmination of a great deal of careful analysis. In effect, they are both guides to follow and targets to shoot for. Materials budgets, sales budgets, labor budgets, and budgets for capital expenditures all become standards for management action. Good budgeting is needed to direct internal activity and to assign responsibility.

Step-by-Step Approach to Planning

The following outline will help to internalize the process of planning rapidly. Practice makes perfect, and it is often helpful to plan for something concrete the first time around, such as an open house in conjunction with the annual air show.

1. Assess the present state of affairs, external (the economy, competition, and so on) as well as internal.
2. Set target date for the activation of the plan.
3. Make a forecast of the future state of affairs (at the target date and, thereafter, for the duration of the plan-to-be).
4. List specific objectives that are both reasonable and attainable.
5. Develop methods for reaching the objectives.
6. Work out the details by using the "Five Ws" (Who? What? Where? When? Why?) — and How? Determine the resources available and structure of the plan with a time schedule.
7. Commit the details to paper.
8. Set up a control system to monitor the plan's operation and to make adjustments for deviations from planned outcomes.
9. As the plan unfolds, make the necessary changes to compensate for such deviations.

Planning is disciplined thinking, which is based on the present and oriented to the future. Plans begin with an analysis of the way things are and with a forecast of the way things will (or should) be. Of course, predicting future events based on an extrapolation of current — and incomplete — information can never by entirely accurate as discussed in Chapter 2.

ORGANIZATION

As a business grows and sales increase, additional duties and responsibilities follow. Additional personnel are required and the need for specialization and division of work becomes apparent. Each new employee must be placed in an appropriate niche and assigned specific duties. It is up to management to define those niches and then locate the right people to fill them.

Figure 4–1 depicts the organizational structure of a small FBO.

Over time, a company's management is increasingly challenged by the task of coordinating the activities of daily operations. Each business depends on the people who, interlocked and strategically deployed in some structural arrangement, perform all the functions necessary for the total system to accomplish its objectives. This framework or structure, called *organization,* represents the overall strategic design for operating the business.

Organization Theory

Organization is not and cannot be an exact science; theories of organization cannot specify wholly "right" answers. Nevertheless, the small FBO manager ought to be familiar with the dimensions that are most frequently discussed by organizational theorists. Some examples are conflicts between individual and organizational goals, departmentalization, line and staff positions, flat versus tall organizations, and unity of command.

Employee Goals Can Be at Odds with Company Goals. It should be recognized that people working in an organization are there primarily to satisfy their own needs. Perhaps they want security and income or the feeling that they have a place within a group, or they need to be recognized as somebody important, and so on. Although they will work willingly toward the firm's objectives, this will happen only if their personal aims remain attainable through employment with the company. Their goals and the goals of the com-

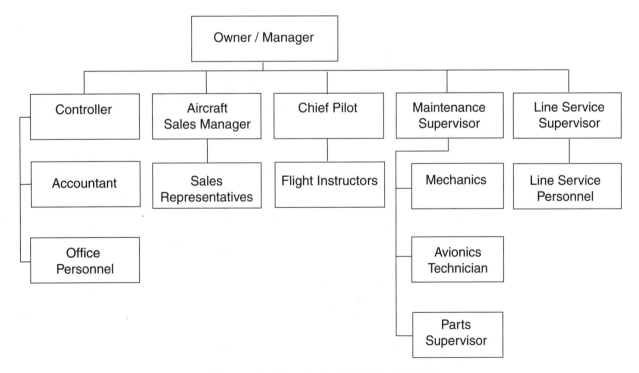

Figure 4–1. Organization Chart for a Small FBO

pany are not identical; at times, differences between individual and group goals will result in conflict. For the sake of internal harmony, a manager must concentrate on reconciling any differences that arise.

The Need for Departmentalization. As anyone in business knows, a wealth of activities must be performed by employees. Handling these myriad tasks is made easier by classifying the many work details into departments. *Departments* are segments of the business whose work functions are interrelated and so can be grouped together under the supervision of a single specialist. In addition to the line service, flight instruction, and maintenance departments, other departments commonly found at FBOs include aircraft sales, charter and rental, and corporate flight service.

Line and Staff Personnel. Most organizations have been arranged according to the *line-and-staff* concept. Line people both give and receive orders along the chain of command from the head of the company down to the lowest level worker. People in staff positions, on the other hand, are outside this chain of command. They are present to aid and support the line personnel. Examples of these staffers include administrative assistants, legal advisors, accountants, and other supportive service workers. These people possess a much more limited kind of authority. Within their own specialized areas of responsibility, of course, they direct their own department personnel.

Should the Organization Be Flat or Tall? As a business grows, the organizational structure shows layers of authority: top, middle, and lower (supervisory) management. Communication barriers tend to form between the layers. People at the top of the hierarchy usually have little contact with people at the bottom. In the traditional "tall" structure, people become relatively confined within their own specialized positions, and dissatisfaction begins to emerge from persons in middle and lower positions. Broadly interpreted, their feeling is that they are not really making a significant contribution to the business. This attitude spreads or deepens, and decisions are more and more likely to be made at the top and filtered down to the bottom levels.

Furthermore, management positions multiply. The organization gradually becomes laden with many chiefs and high salaries. A kind of rigidity sets in that mitigates against creative problem solving and results in an overabundance of red tape.

In the "flat" type of organization, on the other hand, there are only one or two levels of management. The supervisory leadership exercised by the executives is of a more personal nature, with more face-to-face contact. People in lower management niches take on more responsibility for their efforts and make more decisions. The fact that these individuals are closer to the action than higher management and are permitted to make decisions on the spot makes for increased initiative and higher morale.

One Manager or More? The *unity of command* principle is one policy that should seldom be violated. Most workers would agree that no employee, indeed no executive, should have to answer to more than one superior. Having more than one supervisor can cause confusion, as, for example, when an employee working within a partnership arrangement is given two opposing directives by the partners.

How Many Subordinates Can Be Supervised? The principle here is referred to as *span of management (or span of control)*. The average manager finds it relatively easy to oversee one to several workers on the job: to watch over them, train them, direct them, and guide them. As the number of subordinates increases, it becomes more and more difficult for the supervisor to devote enough attention to each person.

How many people a supervisor can oversee depends on several factors: the supervisor's capabilities, the abilities and characteristics of the subordinates, and the nature of the work being performed. The greater the span of management (that is, the number of individuals under one superior), the fewer the number of supervisors and departments necessary. A narrow span, however, enables supervisors to work more closely with their people.

The average small FBO owner can often manage up to six or eight subordinates before things become too unwieldy.

Decentralization. As a business grows, the mass of work details increases. Yet it is hard for the entrepreneurial personality to delegate, to let go of the responsibilities so far handled alone, and to assign them to people who he or she fears are less capable and less motivated!

Some managers keep a firm grasp on everything. They maintain control where power, authority, and tight supervisory controls are centralized. Others decentralize to the point where a capable group, to a large degree autonomous, manages each major division of the business. This concept of decentralization — organizing a firm around self-governing "profit centers" banded together in a loosely controlled federation — maximizes individual initiative, ensures localized decision making, and facilitates pinpointing responsibility.

Developing an Operations Manual

Operating a company without a formal set of rules and regulations would be similar to taking a cross-country flight without navigational charts. Rarely can objectives be reached without an *operations manual*. There are at least eight ways an operations manual can benefit a company. An operations manual

1. establishes a comprehensive source of company policies and procedures;
2. facilitates even-handed, consistent administration of personnel policies;
3. promotes continuity in management style throughout the organization;
4. helps identify problems before they arise, minimizing "crisis management";
5. reduces the number of emotional decisions, encouraging a businesslike climate of objectivity;
6. defines authority clearly and distributes responsibility;
7. becomes a training tool for employees; and
8. offers examples of standard forms, reducing the number and variety of forms used.

In any small FBO, generally no one has the time for an extra project such as creating an operations manual. Top management must personally endorse the project and provide leadership to keep it moving, establish deadlines, and designate a "doer" in the company to get the job done.

The manager must gather all existing procedures, systems, and forms. Ideas from all levels of management and staff must be put into the process. The manual must be discussed with all operations personnel to ensure that all actual day-to-day working needs will be covered. Input from former personnel can be helpful too. Concurrently, a checklist of points covered in the company's operations manual should be prepared. These 10 basic sections should be included:

1. Introduction: Purpose of the manual; how the company started; business objectives and philosophy; description of products and services; economics of the business.
2. Organization chart: Who reports to whom; job descriptions; addresses of company's facilities; importance of each department and division.
3. General employee information: Attitude toward customers, suppliers, and other employees; statement on how to handle telephone callers and visitors; housekeeping policies.
4. Personnel administration: Hiring practices; employment forms; when and how workers are paid; outside employment; reprimands; hours of operation; coffee breaks and lunch hours; dress code; personal behavior; frequency of salary reviews; advancement opportunities; benefits paid by the company; contributory benefits; explanation of payroll deductions; labor laws; use of time cards; scheduling; overtime; vacation entitlement and holidays.
5. Products and services: Customer relations; supplier relations; sales procedures; taking pride in what the company does.
6. Paperwork: Administrative procedures; ensuring accountability; billings; sample of

each form; purpose of each document; routing flow chart for paperwork; summary of deadlines and due dates.

7. Safety and security: Protection of physical premises; personal security; statement about protection of company assets; importance of safety to the employee and the company; handling of confidential information.

8. Emergencies: How to handle accidents; what to do in case of fire; emergency telephone numbers; power failures; robberies and thefts.

9. Maintenance and repair: Telephones; service people; repairs; who should authorize; trash removal; key control; handling of equipment; property damage or loss.

10. Legal: Compliance with local, state, and federal laws; handling of regulatory agencies; inspections; record keeping requirements; maintaining ethical standards.

The instructions should be presented in a logical order and be specific. Exceptions should be stated if those exceptions have occurred frequently in the past. Language and examples should be common to the company's employees. Finally, a qualified outsider (preferably an educator or a professional editor) should do the editing.

A loose-leaf, three-ring notebook format permits great flexibility in using, reviewing, and updating material. "Sections" should correspond to chapters of a book. Within each section, the material should be in outline form. There should be no "Miscellaneous" section because that would become a catchall, revealing less-than-thorough categorization.

Each page should contain the section title, the date the page was issued, and a page number. This simplifies both the task of keeping the manual updated and the distribution of new or revised material. To complete the manual, a thoroughly cross-referenced index to topics covered should be prepared.

A chain of command should be established to make revisions, and one person in top management should approve all proposals for change. Otherwise, duplication and overlap will create confusion. Finally, the operations manual should be reviewed at least once a year because a growing company is always changing.

STAFFING

Employees are the major resource of any firm. Hiring the right people and training them well can directly affect profitability of the business. Specific personnel policies should be included in the firm's operations manual. These become useful guides in all areas: recruitment and selection, compensation plan and employee benefits, training, promotions and terminations, and the like. All attendant systems and paperwork should be carefully designed and personnel files set up to hold application forms, testing and medical records, evaluation forms, changes in status, and so forth.

One practical activity that can be helpful in setting policy is preparation of job descriptions for all positions in the company. Each position should be analyzed and the details then set down on paper. It should include the specific job title, the duties and responsibilities assigned, the relationships with other segments of the business, and any other relevant details. This information will help in writing up job specifications for every opening that arises. In addition, special qualifications needed by the jobholder should be included, such as the levels of education and experience required, familiarity with special equipment, minimum physical requirements, and so on.

The *staffing* process includes all activities pertinent to the recruiting, selection, and training of employees. Outlining the details and correct procedures in advance can prevent errors later on that can cause trouble and expense.

Recruitment and Selection

The most common recruiting sources include the following:

1. Advertising through classified and display advertisements in newspapers, radio advertising, aviation trade publications and websites.

2. Advertising through posted announcements, window signs, and other "point-of-need" methods.
3. Recommendations (referrals) from others: friends, employees, acquaintances, and the like.
4. Schools and universities: vocational, academic, technical, business.
5. Employment agencies: public, private.
6. Agencies that provide temporary help.
7. People who just drop by or write in for positions.

Among the tools available to help in hiring and rejecting applicants are the employment application, the employment interview, the reference check, tests, and the probationary period for new employees.

Standard employment application forms are available at any local office supply store. They ask for the applicant's name, address, telephone number, work experience, education, health and financial information, and personal data. This form can also be adapted to meet any FBO's particular needs.

The employment interview is usually the next step and is one of the major tools in processing job applicants. Essentially, it has two aims: (1) to elicit information to supplement the facts submitted on the application form; and (2) to gain useful insights into the appearance, behavior, and personality of the prospective employee.

Because it is comparatively easy for an interviewer to be overly influenced by an outstanding characteristic of an applicant, it is wise to develop and use an interview rating form that touches on all important areas, which will help objectify the assessment of an individual. The art of interviewing comes with experience and any library has books on human resources administration and interviewing techniques.

Interviews can be patterned and directive. This means planning the approach in advance — that is, the kinds of questions to be asked, the order in which they will be asked, what in particular the FBO is looking for, and so forth. Interviews can also be nondirective: Here, the basic approach is to refrain from doing much talking and to encourage the interviewee to speak at length.

There are certain undesirable characteristics or symptoms that in themselves are generally sufficient cause for turning down an applicant. Among the more common factors are the following:

1. evidence of frequent job-hopping in the past,
2. excessive indebtedness,
3. poor communicative ability,
4. poor emotional control,
5. too high a standard of living, and
6. unexplained gaps in the employment record.

As a general rule, it is best for the owner/manager to check personally all references offered by job applicants. A simple form letter and questionnaire can be devised to cover the major points of concern. Or contacts with former employers and other references can be made by telephone. This method is often preferable, not only for quicker results but also because many people are reluctant to put negative comments down in writing. At times, telephone checking is useful in that any hesitancy about the person in question can be discerned quite readily and probed diplomatically during the conversation.

On the whole, most small FBOs do not test job applicants except when a position requires special skills. Measures of typing speed and accuracy, arithmetic and spelling tests for clerical employees, flight tests for instructors, and demonstrations of ability to run specialized equipment by line personnel all come under this classification.

Some FBOs make use of a variety of paper-and-pencil tests to aid in their selection processes. These range from intelligence tests and general knowledge measures to personality batteries, tests of selling ability, and so forth. These tests are expensive to use and are generally not recommended until a business has grown to a substantial size. Their most valuable contribution is probably in screening out applicants with personality defects or below-average intelligence.

Many managements shy away from testing, however, because of anxiety over conforming to the intent of equal employment opportunity laws. Tests used must be demonstrably both valid and reliable.

Medical exams can be helpful when a position requires frequent physical effort, but they can be quite expensive for the employer, especially if the number of employees is considerable.

Once the employee is hired, the first few days on the job are crucial for the newly hired person.

This period is when favorable or unfavorable work-related attitudes are formed and when the employee is either pleased or not. Of course, when an individual is given a schedule and assigned to a department, the person must receive some initial instruction — namely — about the company itself, the particular department, and the nature of the work. In addition, it is helpful to appoint an experienced member of the department to coach the new employee. In this same context, a well-prepared employee handbook can be extremely valuable. See the sample Table of Contents in Figure 4–2.

EMPLOYEE HANDBOOK
SAMPLE TABLE OF CONTENTS

1. Welcome Message
2. History of the Company
3. This Is Your Business
4. You and Your Future
5. What You Need to Know

Working Hours	Employment Record
Reporting to Work	Pay Period
Time Clock	Shift Premiums
Rest Periods	Safety and Accident Prevention
Absence from Work	Use of Telephones
Reporting Absences	How to Air Complaints

6. These Are Your Benefits

Vacations	Profit-sharing Plan
Holidays	Suggestion Awards
Group Insurance	Jury Duty
Hospitalization & Surgical Benefits	Military Leave
Training Program	U.S. Old Age Benefits
Christmas Bonus	Unemployment Compensation
Savings Plan	Equal Employment Opportunity

7. These Special Services Are for You

Credit Union	Flight Training & Aircraft Rental
Education Plans	Annual Outing
Medical Dispensary	Bowling League
Employee Purchases	Softball Team

8. Index

Figure 4–2. Sample Table of Contents for an Employee Handbook. Adapted from "Pointers on Preparing an Employee Handbook," Management Aid No. 197 (Washington, D.C.: Small Business Administration, 1989).

The final phase of the selection process should be a probationary or tryout period of a few weeks or months. This trial period is a valuable step; it will ensure that the FBO has not made an erroneous decision. During this time, the new worker should be observed and frequently rated. It is far more difficult to discharge a below-average performer after many months have elapsed, especially if the company is unionized.

Training

The training function is a vital, ongoing activity that requires the attention of the owner of a small FBO. Employees need and want training not only to perform their jobs satisfactorily but also as preparation for eventual promotion. Proper training alleviates many problems in the future.

Some of the advantages of well-trained employees are

1. better employee morale,
2. increased sales,
3. less waste,
4. lower turnover rate,
5. increased productivity,
6. reduced operational costs, and
7. speedier employee development.

Often a new employee receives adequate initial training but is thereafter expected to "go it alone." In a healthy business operation, training should be continuous. No worker attains 100 percent efficiency or output at his or her job; there is always room for improvement. Moreover, every worker should have the opportunity to move up the ladder; this implies training for a new and higher position.

In a small enterprise, most training occurs on the job; that is, the immediate supervisor is held responsible for training the worker. But as a business grows, the need for more thorough and professional training becomes evident. It's never too early to begin making plans for better training in the future, if only to fill additional niches as they open up in the organizational hierarchy. This is preferable to hiring supervisors and managers from the outside, usually at a higher cost.

A careful needs analysis of the organization and all the people in it should be the first step in coordinating training efforts.

The following steps are recommended in establishing a training program:

1. Make a needs assessment of the company on a departmental, section, and unit basis.
2. Set the objectives to be accomplished through the training efforts.
3. Determine the curriculum (subject matter). Make certain to include not only product, company, and customer knowledge but also skills development and personal adjustment training.
4. Select the types of training that best serve the purposes of the company.
5. Select the training methods to be used.
6. Set up a timetable and schedule for the program.
7. Select the instructor(s).
8. Watch costs.

A wide variety of training methods and techniques are available. Among the more frequently used approaches are lectures, small-group discussions, seminars, conferences, case analyses, programmed instruction, committee work, and role playing. Of course, the most commonly found method is on-the-job training; variations of this approach include apprenticeships and internships.

For employees pegged for eventual promotion to management levels, there are still other useful techniques: job rotation, special project assignments, management games, sensitivity training, outside training (at local colleges or by trade associations), and so on.

The Turnover Problem

One fact of life that any small business has to live with is employee turnover. Every business has it. Some firms lose people at a faster rate than others, but whatever the turnover rate, it always hurts to lose a good employee (financially, as well as psychologically).

There are initial costs involved in locating, interviewing, hiring, and training an employee to the point where he or she reaches full potential. Then there are intermediate costs of doing without that person until a replacement is found. Still more expenses are incurred in acquiring the replacement.

People leave their jobs for a variety of reasons. Some leave unexpectedly and for unavoidable reasons: ill health, death, marriage, relocation, return to school, a better paying position, and deliberate terminations for cause. Some losses are avoidable. They may be caused by poor supervisory practices on the part of owners or middle managers, by internal friction and personality clashes, by management's failure to provide proper incentives or an opportunity to move up the ladder.

When an employee leaves, an exit interview should be conducted and the results recorded. A review of the findings will be useful to management in taking corrective action to reduce the turnover rate. This step becomes more valuable as the company grows.

DIRECTING

Once the plan has been prepared and the firm has been organized and staffed to carry out its objectives, the next step is putting the plan into action and *directing* it. Up to this point, most of the activity has been in the mind of the planner(s). Now the game really starts. People in the organization must be motivated, persuaded, led, coordinated, encouraged, and so on. Involved here are concepts like teamwork, supervision, and productivity.

Leadership

Leadership involves interaction. It is a way of behaving—of persuading and inducing, of guiding and motivating. A totally rounded leadership form calls for a mastery of certain skill areas, the creation of the right climate within which the work group can function properly, and the direction and control of group activities.

Leadership style is often a reflection of personality; however, a single, consistent type of behavior may not always be applicable or desired. What works well with one person (or group) may not necessarily work at all with the next. Individuals, as well as groups, are extremely varied. Consequently, effective leadership requires an eclectic approach, taking into account the three-way match among leader, group members, and the situation at hand. Most people, over the long term, tend to rely on the style that yields the best results. Many of us are guilty of holding stereotypical notions about leaders. We tend to believe that a good leader is one who commands respect; who electrifies the atmosphere when entering a room; who is, without a doubt, aggressive, domineering, capable of manipulation, a skilled communicator, an extrovert. Our concepts even go beyond personality to physical attributes; we think that a good leader is usually taller and heavier (and more attractive) than the rest of us.

Oddly enough, some of the greatest leaders in world history, and many capable managers of major corporations, have been quiet, unassuming, introspective, short, and thin people. Management experts have often theorized about the kinds of personal traits necessary for effective performance in the role of leader. Studies have compared the qualities evinced by top executives with those demonstrated by unsuccessful leaders in order to uncover the characteristics that differentiate them. Several distinguishing attributes keep showing up; however, it must be kept in mind that leadership has three dimensions: the leader, those who are led, and the individual situation. Consequently, whether one rates high or low in these attributes does not necessarily make a person a good or bad leader.

A review of the following list of personal traits can be valuable in dealing with others:

adaptability	open-mindedness
alertness	optimism
communication skills	patience
confidence	persuasive powers
creativity	poise
curiosity	resourcefulness
dependability	sensitivity to others
drive	supportiveness
enthusiasm	teaching ability
evaluation skills	tolerance
flexibility	warmth
human relations skills	willingness to listen
maturity	willingness to take chances

Inasmuch as leadership activity also has a task-oriented, impersonal dimension, certain additional skills need to be developed. Among these are

1. the ability to establish priorities,
2. a capacity for giving credit when due,
3. skill at planning and scheduling,
4. proficiency in problem solving, and
5. a willingness to delegate responsibility to others.

Understanding Employees

Each individual within an organization is a complex, multifaceted person. Among his or her many sides are the intellectual, the physical, and the emotional, along with economic, social, political, and moral. So it is not surprising that people's behavior can be as complex and as difficult to interpret as people are themselves.

Personality is an amalgam of values, attitudes, and interpersonal response traits:

1. People hold values. Values are concepts we come to accept over the years as we interact with others and with our environment.
2. People form attitudes. Attitudes serve as vehicles for organizing knowledge, for adjusting to the world around us, for shielding us from confusion and pain, and for orienting us toward things that are pleasurable.
3. People develop response traits. We have habitual ways of responding to and dealing with others.

A review of any basic psychology text can provide many insights into human behavior. In turn, psychological understanding can enhance a manager's capability in motivating and directing employees.

Motives are the energizing forces that drive all of us and are behind most behavior. Many of our actions result from the interplay of several motives. Some motives are largely rational and based on logic; for example, filing an IFR flight plan under marginal weather conditions. The motives are quite clear and logical: (1) an accident could occur endangering life and property; and (2) violation of FAA regulations. On the other hand, many motives are of an emotional (or nonrational) nature.

The line of demarcation between rational and emotional motives is rather hazy. Not filing an IFR flight plan may be based on the emotional motive: fear of being cited by the FAA.

Furthermore, what motivates one person does not necessarily motivate the next. The same motive can lead to varied behaviors in different people. The same behavior in different people can result from different motives.

All of us are driven by many motives: economic, safety, social, or physiological ones like hunger, thirst, the need for sleep, and sex. The majority of our motives, however, are learned—those that we develop as we interact with our environment. One way to understand better the subject of human needs and wants is to review a notable theory proposed many years ago by the eminent psychologist Abraham Maslow. He suggested a hierarchy of human needs that can be arranged on different levels according to their "potency" for influencing behavior. He postulated that all of us are constantly struggling upwards to attain higher steps on this "pyramid of needs" until we reach its pinnacle. From time to time, most people are restrained from proceeding up the hierarchy or may be knocked down to lower levels by outside conditions (or, perhaps, by inner forces).

Translating Maslow's concepts into modern human resources thinking, we can expect employees to seek such things as the following:

1. *Level 1 (Physiological Needs):* a salary competitive with other firms with similar positions, adequate to provide the necessities of life.
2. *Level 2 (Safety Needs):* job security and safe working conditions. This need may lead to health and life-insurance coverage for spouse and children and a 401K program.
3. *Level 3 (Love and Belongingness Needs):* the feeling of being part of an organization and having a place in the group; acceptance by co-workers and employer; a friendly environment.
4. *Level 4 (Esteem Needs):* ego satisfaction, recognition (an occasional pat on the back), authority, and status within the group; the belief that the person's work is both responsible and respected.
5. *Level 5 (Need for Self-Actualization):* a chance for growth and the opportunity to demonstrate initiative; encouragement for the individual to participate and contribute to the fullest.

Several other well-known management concepts are worthwhile mentioning because of their relationship to businesses of all sizes.

Theories X and Y. More than 40 years ago, management theorist Douglas McGregor investigated the attitudes of supervisors toward their employees. His studies led him to conclude that most supervisors could be classified as belonging to one of two camps. Those who subscribe to what McGregor termed the *Theory X* approach are convinced that the average person doesn't like to work, has little if any ambition, and tries to avoid responsibility. Consequently, these supervisors feel that they need to watch workers closely and depend on the strategic application of both rewards and punishment in order to obtain satisfactory performance.

Other supervisors follow a different philosophy, the more positive *Theory Y* approach. They believe employees consider work to be as natural as play and rest, and that once committed to specific objectives, they will not only put out effort willingly but will also seek responsibility.

Theory Z. In recent years, much favorable publicity has appeared in the press with regard to Japanese management techniques. One popular book outlined the more salient attributes of the Japanese approach, dubbing the overall concept *Theory Z*—an obvious reference to McGregor's assessment of supervisory types. Substantial delegation of responsibility, trust in each individual, and decision by group consensus are characteristically seen in Japanese companies. Of course, some of their attributes (such as lifetime employment) cannot be incorporated easily into our own economy. Still, owners of small FBOs might well profit by modifying and applying other attributes to their own enterprises; for example, the participative approach to decision making and a genuine concern for one's employees.

Job Motivators and Hygiene Factors. In the 1960s, management theorist Frederick Herzberg researched the workplace to uncover those factors that appeared to exert some influence on the job satisfaction of employees or on worker motivation. He found two distinct sets of such factors: *motivators* (or satisfiers) and *hygiene factors* (dissatisfiers). Herzberg maintained that motivators appeal to higher level human needs and, therefore, not only motivate employees but can also increase the level of job satisfaction. Examples include recognition, responsibility, advancement, growth, and the work itself. On the other hand, some factors in the workplace that cater to people's lower needs (hygiene factors) apparently do little to encourage worker motivation. Nevertheless, they can, of course, contribute to employee dissatisfaction. Salary, working conditions, company policies, and relations with one's supervisor are hygiene factors.

Obviously, then, owners and managers of FBOs might do well to review Herzberg's findings. More highly motivated and satisfied employees might be developed through effective management policies that lead to (among other results):

1. top-quality working conditions,
2. catering to the worker's need for security,
3. delegating more responsibility,
4. encouraging group goal setting and decision making,
5. flexible scheduling,
6. job enhancement and/or redesign,
7. offering a promotional ladder with the company,
8. recognizing and rewarding the exceptional contribution.

EMPOWERING EMPLOYEES

Employees are responsible for making themselves perform well, but managers are responsible for creating an environment where that seems possible. Empowerment was one of the buzzwords of the 1990s. It means releasing an individual's power to succeed by removing the barriers that prevent it, such as lack of skills, not enough direction, or too little responsibility and authority. In order to empower employees, managers must create small successes and recognize the employee for the success. For these small successes to happen, managers must establish an environment where employees feel that they can succeed. This means encouraging creativity, setting goals, giving feedback, and recognizing performance.

Effective feedback needs to be timely, specific, and should focus on the behavior, not the individual. Positive feedback should be offered, and alternatives should be provided so employees can set measureable performance goals. Negative feedback should be depersonalized, while managers should personalize the positive.

Coaching is one method managers can use to give feedback. But it can also be used to teach, motivate, or challenge employees. There are seven basic steps in the coaching process:

1. Observing performance and recording observations.
2. Analyzing performance so it can be linked to behaviors.
3. Providing feedback that is timely and specific.
4. Interviewing by asking open- and closed-ended questions.
5. Setting goals and action plans for higher performance.
6. Following up on action plans to fine tune performance.
7. Reinforcing effective behaviors by complimenting efforts and results.

Although informal feedback is important, the need for a formal performance appraisal is necessary. It is important that managers and supervisors clearly outline expectations, observations, and evaluations in writing. Frequent and comprehensive work sampling, and written open-ended appraisals are necessary. If employees are surprised by information in their annual appraisals, they are not receiving enough informal feedback.

Decision Making

In business, most management decisions are made by intuition. Owners of small FBOs especially appear to fly by the seats of their pants in much the same way that Charles Lindbergh flew over the Atlantic many decades ago — without the benefit of the vast array of intricate instruments that decorate the cockpit of today's jet aircraft.

Intuitive decision making stems partially from a lack of familiarity with problem-solving techniques and partially from the realization that extensive resources — time, energy, and funds — should only be diverted to the most serious and complex problems. Happily, these major problems do not occur very often. When they do (for example, when one is contemplating a major building expansion or marketing campaign), the owner is often better off relying on the assistance of an experienced consultant.

Luckily, most problems in business repeat themselves, so once a satisfactory solution has been worked out (or accidentally hit upon), the entrepreneur knows how to solve the problem the next time it pops up. Only the new, infrequent, unique problems present a strong challenge.

Decision making is but one step in the problem-solving process. It is the last step in which the manager chooses the one alternative that seems best. The whole process is as follows:

1. *Diagnosing the problem.* On a sheet of paper, the manager writes a clear statement of the problem's "essence"; this will help pinpoint the problem clearly in mind as the manager works towards its solution. Many problems are quite complex; often there is a need to go further and break down the original problem statement into its major parts. Each part should then be summarized and written down as a "subproblem" statement. Another useful trick is to draw a simple diagram of the problem situation, making certain to put in all the elements involved.
2. *Gathering information.* Hunt for pertinent information to help solve the problem. (Facts are not only available from internal records, external sources of data, and primary research; they are also readily obtained from people.)
3. *Generate alternative solutions.* Develop a number of alternative solutions to the problem. (Creative thinking can help here.)
4. *Evaluate the alternatives.* Rate the alternatives according to each of several criteria; for example, cost, time, judged effectiveness or payoff, effect on management, and so on. Use a simple numerical rating scale, such as 0 = Poor, 1 = Fair, 2 = Good, 3 = Very Good, and 4 = Excellent. If some criteria are more important to the firm than others, then accord more weight to those in the analysis.
5. *Select the best alternative(s).* At this juncture, the manager makes his or her decision.
6. *Translate the decision into action.*

Of course, many more sophisticated techniques are currently in vogue for solving business problems. For the most part, these approaches are used by the larger companies and not by the small firm. There are methods that take into account chance or probability, those that use mathematics and statistics, those that require computer programming, and so on. These include game theory, decision theory, queuing theory, decision matrices, simulation, and linear programming. All of these methods (and others, too) lie well outside the scope of this chapter. A number of good books are available on the topic of decision making in business and industry.

CONTROLLING

There is a need to measure the results of the organizational plan while it is unfolding, as well as the necessity to make adjustments where and when needed. Logically, the control function cannot be separated from the planning function; they are interdependent, much like the two sides of the same coin.

Controlling is a process that includes analysis, setting standards, monitoring, securing feedback, and taking corrective action.

1. *Analysis:* Study and compare, for quantity and quality, the output of people and machines, the services provided, the systems employed, and so forth. Examine everything with a careful eye to standards and decision making.
2. *Setting Standards:* As a result of analysis, establish acceptable standards of performance in all areas. In turn, these standards become control valves, quantitative and qualitative measurements for future performance, guidelines for projecting cost, time, and sales.
3. *Monitoring:* The need for regular inspection and performance checks to note exceptions to the standards that have been set and possible reasons for the deviations.
4. *Securing Feedback:* A foolproof system for reporting deviations from standards must be established so that the proper people are notified regularly and promptly.
5. *Corrective Action:* Finally, all exceptions to the established standards must be acted on. Adjustments need to be made promptly so that contingent outcomes are brought back on target.

All areas of the business must be subject to this control function. Generally, managers think quite readily of inventory control, order processing, quality control, and production control. Yet controls are just as necessary in the personnel area (for example, in performance evaluation); in the financial end of things (where ratios can be used to investigate a variety of problems); in the long-term planning of projects; and so forth. For control is, in essence, self-discipline.

Communication

Service organizations such as FBOs run on communication. Prospective customers are located, contacted, and persuaded to buy products and services through communication. Similarly, employees are found, hired, trained, and directed; departments are managed; machines are manned and operated. Communication is the oil that lubricates the various gears and cogs in the free-enterprise system.

Let's examine the process of communication in business. There are a number of components involved. Indeed, communication in business appears to be a closed system with all parts interacting in synergistic fashion. The major elements which simplify a company's external communications with its customers are:

1. *Source:* the sender or originator of the messages.
2. *Messages:* information emitted by the source and directed to the receivers.
3. *Media:* the various carriers or transmitters of the messages (such as radio, newspapers, billboards, and so on).
4. *Receivers:* those for whom the messages are intended.
5. *Feedback:* customer reactions, demographic information, and other facts returned by or drawn back from customers to assist management in its decision making.

Improvements within any of these areas—for example, in the quality of messages sent or the refinement or elaboration of the feedback process—improve the productivity of the entire communication system.

Applied to a firm's internal organization, communication starts with verbal or written messages (orders, instructions, and the like) passed down from the top to lower levels. Feedback moves upward, completing the system. Of course, the effectiveness of this internal system also depends on unimpeded horizontal communication on each individual level.

Unfortunately, poor communication is commonly observed within organizations, perhaps due to the pressures of day-to-day details, which often make communicating on a face-to-face basis nearly impossible.

All messages to employees should be couched in terms that can be clearly understood and that convey the manager's exact meaning. To accomplish this objective, employers must understand the employees' point of view. Moreover, good listening skills constitute an important asset in communication; half-hearted listening interferes considerably with effective management. Encourage employees to listen, too. Employees should understand instructions and be encouraged to ask questions.

As a final point, all supervisory personnel should be effective in communications.

KEY TERMS

Planning
Long-term plans
Operational plans
Single-use plans
Standing plans
Budgets
Organization
Departments
Line-and-staff
Unity of command
Span of control
Operations manual

Staffing
Directing
Leadership
Personality
Motives
Theory X
Theory Y
Theory Z
Motivators
Hygiene factors
Controlling

REVIEW QUESTIONS

1. Identify and briefly describe the characteristics of successful FBOs. Why in planning considered to be the most important management function? What types of plans are there? Give several examples of each. List the step-by-step approach to planning.
2. Define organization. How can employee goals be at odds with company goals? What is the purpose of departmentalization? Describe the line-and-staff concept. What are some problems associated with flat and tall organizational structures? Explain the organizational principles of unity of command and span of control. What is the purpose of an operation manual? Briefly describe the sections normally included in an operations manual.
3. Describe the staffing process. List the most common recruiting sources. What is the purpose of interviewing? What are some advantages of having well-trained employees? Identify the major sections and items under those sections in an employee handbook. Describe the steps to be taken in establishing a training program. Why is employee turnover such a problem?
4. Why is it said that the game really begins with directing? Why is effective leadership so important in directing a company? Identify 10 personal traits that can be helpful in dealing with others. List five additional skills found in successful leaders. Define personality and motives. Discuss Maslow's levels of human needs and wants. Compare McGregor's Theory X and Theory Y approaches to supervision. What are the motivators and hygiene factors described by Herzberg? What is meant by empowering employees?
5. Describe the six steps in the decision-making process. Discuss the process of controlling. Give several examples of the control function in such areas as marketing, line service, and parts inventory. Why is communication the "oil that lubricates the various gears and cogs in the free-enterprise system"? Describe how communication is applied to a firm's internal organization.

REFERENCES

Boyd, Bradford B. *Management-Minded Supervision* (2nd ed.). New York: McGraw-Hill, 1984.
Brown, Deaver. *The Entrepreneur's Guide.* New York: Ballantine, 1980.

Burstiner, Irving. *The Small Business Handbook* (Rev. ed.). Englewood Cliffs, NJ: Prentice-Hall, 1989.

Donnelly, James H., Jr., James L. Gibson, and John M. Ivancevich. *Fundamentals of Management: Functions, Behaviors, Models* (5th ed.). Plano, TX: Business Publications, 1984.

Herzberg, Frederick. *Work and the Nature of Man.* New York: Thomas Y. Crowell, 1966.

Levinson, Robert E. *Problems in Managing a Family-Owned Business.* Washington, DC: SBA, Management Aids. #2.004, 1984.

Maslow, Abraham. *Motivation and Personality* (2nd ed.). New York: Harper & Row, 1970.

McGregor, Douglas. *The Human Side of Enterprise.* New York: McGraw-Hill, 1960.

Mescon, Michael H., Michael Albert, and Franklin Khedouri. *Individual and Organizational Effectiveness.* New York: Harper & Row, 1985.

Peters, Tom. *Thriving on Chaos: Handbook for a Management Revolution.* New York: Knopf, 1987.

Portnoy, Robert A. *Leadership: What Every Leader Should Know about People.* Englewood Cliffs, NJ: Prentice-Hall, 1986.

Reece, Barry L., and Rhonda B. Brandt. *Effective Human Relations in Organization* (2nd ed.). Boston: Houghton-Mifflin, 1984.

Richardson, J. D. and J. F. Rodwell. *Essentials of Aviation Management* (4th ed.). Dubuque, IA: Kendall/Hunt Publishing Company, 1990.

Stoner, James A. *Management* (3rd ed.). Englewood Cliffs, NJ: Prentice-Hall, 1986.

Chapter 5

Financial Planning and Control

OUTLINE

Financial Management
  The Balance Sheet
    Balance Sheet Categories
  The Statement of Income
    Statement of Income Categories
Financial Ratio Analysis
  Balance Sheet Ratio Analysis
  Income Statement Ratio Analysis
  Management Ratios
Forecasting Profits
  Factors Affecting Pro Forma Statements
  The Pro Forma Income Statement
  Break-Even Analysis
Budgeting and Cost Control
Types, Uses, and Sources of Capital
  Borrowing Working Capital
  Borrowing Growth Capital
  Borrowing Equity Capital
Financial Planning
  Long-Term Planning
Determining the Value of an Aviation Business
  EBITDA Analysis
  Discounted Cash Flow Analysis
  Interest, Taxes, Depreciation & Amortization
  Revenues, Cost of Sales, and Expenses
  Summary

OBJECTIVES

At the end of this chapter, you should be able to:

Describe the purpose and major categories of the Balance Sheet and Statement of Income.

Distinguish between Balance Sheet, Income Statement, and management ratio analysis and give examples of each.

Explain the purpose and factors affecting Pro Forma Statements.

List the steps in preparing a Pro Forma Statement.

Define Break-Even Analysis and summarize the steps in calculating the break-even point.

Discuss the importance of cash flow budgets and give several examples of typical budget reports.

Distinguish between equity capital, working capital, and growth capital and identify the major sources of loans for each.

Discuss the importance and process of short-term and long-term planning.

Compare and contrast EBITDA analysis and Discounted Cash Flow analysis in determining the value of an aviation business.

Financial planning affects how and on what terms an FBO will be able to attract the funding required to establish, maintain, and expand the business. Financial planning determines the number and type aircraft an FBO can afford to buy, the services provided, and whether or not the FBO will be able to market them efficiently. It affects the human and physical resources the FBO will be able to acquire to run the business. In short, it will be a major factor in determining the profitability of the firm. This chapter provides an overview of the essential components of financial planning and management.

FINANCIAL MANAGEMENT

Financial management is the use of financial statements that reflect the financial condition of a business to identify its relative strengths and weaknesses. It enables the firm to plan, using projections, future financial performance for capital, asset, and personnel requirements to maximize the return on shareholders investment.

Specifically, a financial management system enables the firm to

1. interpret past performance,
2. measure present progress,
3. anticipate and plan for the future,
4. control operations,
5. uncover significant trends,
6. compare results with similar firms within the particular industry,
7. make financial decisions, and
8. comply with government regulations.

The Balance Sheet

The *Balance Sheet* provides a picture of the financial health of a business at a given moment, usually at the close of an accounting period. It lists in detail those material and intangible items the business owns (known as its *assets*) and what money the business owes, either to its creditors (*liabilities*) or to its owners (*shareholders' equity* or *net worth* of the business).

Assets include not only cash, merchandise inventory, land, buildings, equipment, machinery, furniture, patents, trademarks, and the like, but also money due from individuals or other businesses (known as *accounts* or *notes receivable*).

Liabilities are funds acquired for a business through loans or the sale of property or services to the business on credit. Creditors do not acquire business ownership but promissory notes to be paid at a designated future date.

Shareholders' equity (*or* net worth *or* capital) is money put into a business by its owners for use by the business in acquiring assets.

At any given time, a business's assets equal the total contributions by the creditors and owners, as illustrated by the following formula for the Balance Sheet:

Assets	=	**Liabilities**	+	**Net Worth**
(total funds invested in assets of the business)		(Funds supplied to the business by its creditors)		(Funds supplied to the business by its owners)

This formula is a basic premise of accounting. If a business owes more money to creditors than it possesses in value of assets owned, the net worth or owner's equity of the business will be a negative number.

The Balance Sheet is designed to show how the assets, liabilities, and net worth of a business are distributed at any given time. It is usually prepared at regular intervals; for example, at each month's end, but especially at the end of each fiscal (accounting) year.

By regularly preparing this summary of what the business owns and owes (the Balance Sheet), the business owner/manager can identify and analyze trends in the financial strength of the business. It permits timely modifications, such as gradually decreasing the amount of money the business owes to creditors and increasing the amount the business owes its owners.

All balance sheets contain the same categories of assets, liabilities, and net worth. Assets are arranged in decreasing order of how quickly they can be turned into cash (*liquidity*). Liabilities are listed in order of how soon they must be repaid, followed by retained earnings (net worth or owner's equity), as illustrated in Figure 5–1, the sample Balance Sheet of XYZ Aviation Company.

Balance Sheet Categories

The categories and format of the Balance Sheet are established by a system known as Generally Accepted Accounting Principles (GAAP). The system is applied to all compa-

---

XYZ Aviation Company
Balance Sheet
December 31, 20___

ASSETS

Current Assets:

Cash	$ 52,500
Accounts receivable	40,000
Prepaid expenses, including insurance premiums	10,000
Inventory of aircraft	284,650
Parts	23,000
Total Current Assets	**$410,150**

Fixed Assets:

Shop equipment	21,500
Office equipment	7,000
Parts room	5,000
Improvements to leased facilities	100,000
	$133,500
Less depreciation and obsolescence	17,500
Net fixed assets	$116,000
Total Assets	**$526,150**

LIABILITIES AND NET WORTH

Liabilities:

Trade accounts payable	$ 21,700
Notes payable (aircraft)	220,500
Other payables	17,000
Accruals	10,000
Total Liabilities	**$269,200**

Net Worth:

Investors' contribution	$200,000
(Capital stock or capital loans)	
Add Surplus	56,950
	$256,950
Total Liabilities and Net Worth	**$526,150**

Figure 5–1. Balance Sheet for XYZ Aviation Company

nies, large or small, so anyone reading the Balance Sheet can readily understand the story it tells.

Assets and liabilities are broken down into the following categories:

Assets: An asset is anything the business owns that has monetary value.
- Current Assets include cash, government securities, marketable securities, accounts receivable, notes receivable (other than from officers or employees), inventories, prepaid expenses, and any other item that could be converted into cash within one year in the normal course of business.
- Fixed Assets are those acquired for long-term use in a business such as land, facilities, equipment, machinery, leasehold improvements, furniture, fixtures, and any other items with an expected useful business life measured in years (as opposed to items that will wear out or be used up in less than one year and are usually expensed when they are purchased). These assets are typically not for resale and are recorded in the Balance Sheet at their net cost less accumulated depreciation.
- Other Assets include intangible assets, such as patents, royalty arrangements, copyrights, exclusive-use contracts, and notes receivable from officers and employees.

Liabilities: Liabilities are the claims of creditors against the assets of the business (debts owed by the business).
- Current Liabilities are accounts payable, notes payable to banks, accrued expenses (wages, salaries), taxes payable, the current portion (due within one year) of long-term debt, and other obligations to creditors due within one year.
- Long-Term Liabilities are mortgages, intermediate and long-term bank loans, equipment loans, and any other obligation from money due to a creditor with a maturity longer than one year.
- Net Worth is the assets of the business minus its liabilities. Net worth equals the owner's equity. This equity is the investment by the owner plus any profits or minus any losses that have accumulated in the business.

The Statement of Income

The second primary report included in a business's financial management picture is the Statement of Income. The *Statement of Income* is a measure of a company's sales and expenses over a specific period of time. It is also prepared at regular intervals (again, each month and fiscal year end) to show the results of operating during those accounting periods. It too follows Generally Accepted Accounting Principles (GAAP) and contains specific revenue and expense categories regardless of the nature of the business. Figure 5–2 illustrates a sample Statement of Income for XYZ Aviation Company.

Statement of Income Categories

The Statement of Income categories can be summarized as follows:

- **Income** (gross sales less returns and allowances)
- Less **Cost of Goods** (costs charged directly against gross sales)
- Equals **Gross Profit** (gross income, minus direct costs before operating expenses)
- Less **Operating Expenses** (salaries, rent, heat, utilities, insurance, advertising and sales promotion, interest, office supplies, bad debt allowances, travel and entertainment, dues and subscriptions, depreciation, and miscellaneous expenses such as automobile expenses, legal fees, and so forth)
- Equals **Operating Profit** (profit before other nonoperating income or expense)
- Plus **Other Income** (income from dividends on investments, interest on bank accounts, customer charge accounts, and so forth)
- Less **Other Expenses** (interest expense)
- Equals **Net Income (or Loss) Before Taxes** (the figure on which taxes are calculated)
- Less **Income Taxes** (if any are due)
- Equals **Net Income (or Loss) After Taxes**

XYZ Aviation Company
Income Statement
December 31, 20____

Income:

Sale of aircraft	$130,000
Gross receipts from flight training, charter, and other flights	28,800
Receipts from sale of parts and accessories	48,000
Gross receipts for maintenance and repair of customers' aircraft	30,000
Gross receipts from line service (sale of fuel, cleaning, washing, and other services to customers' aircraft)	164,000
Payments received for storage of customers' aircraft	14,000
Gross Income	$414,800

Cost of Goods:

Cost of aircraft sold	102,000
Cost of fuel, spare parts, and other costs charged directly against receipts from flights and charters listed above (not including labor)	14,000
Cost of parts and accessories sold to customers	38,000
Cost of parts and accessories charged against receipts for maintenance and repair of customers' aircraft	10,000
Cost of line service to customers' aircraft (including cost of fuel sold, but not including labor)	89,000
Total direct costs (excluding labor)	$253,000
Gross Profit (on sales)	$161,800

Operating Expenses:

Salaries	$ 70,000
Rent, heat, and utilities	15,000
Insurance (on aircraft, structures, equipment, liability, and other insurance)	20,000
Advertising and sales promotion	2,000
Interest (on money borrowed to purchase aircraft and other equipment)	5,000
Office supplies	3,000
Bad debts allowances	1,500
Travel and entertainment	500
Dues and subscriptions	200
Depreciation (on buildings, equipment, and other fixed assets which are owned)	20,000
Miscellaneous expenses	5,000
Total Operating Expenses	$142,200
Operating Profit	19,600

Other Income:

Dividends	$ 700
Interest on bank accounts	400
Total Other Income	1,100
Total Income before taxes	20,700

Other Expenses:

Interest expense	$ 1,200
Net Income (or Loss) before taxes	19,500
Less provision for income taxes	1,600
Net Income (or Loss) after taxes	$ 17,900

Figure 5–2.   Income Statement for XYZ Aviation Company

Calculation of the Cost of Goods Sold category in the Statement of Income (or Profit-and-Loss Statement as it is sometimes called) varies depending on whether the business is primarily a service organization like an FBO or a manufacturer of aircraft components. The cost of goods sold during the accounting period involves beginning and ending inventories for an FBO. In manufacturing or a completion work shop (aircraft interior work), it involves not only finished-goods inventories, but also raw materials inventories, goods-in-process inventories, direct labor, and direct manufacturing overhead costs. *The Handbook of Small Business Finance,* U.S. Small Business Administration Small Business Management Series No. 15 has excellent illustrations of the different methods of calculation for Cost of Goods Sold for the various business types.

FINANCIAL RATIO ANALYSIS

The two major accounting statements—the balance sheet and the income statement—contain a great deal of information about the results of company operations and the current state of the firm's finances. Company management can manipulate this information in ways that yield meaningful insights for decision making. One of these ways is *Ratio Analysis.* Ratio Analysis enables management to spot trends in a business and to compare its performance and condition with the average performance of similar businesses in the aircraft service industry. An FBO can make comparisons of its ratios with other similar FBOs as well as its own ratios for several successive years. Unfavorable trends can be detected. Ratio Analysis may provide the all important early warning indications that allow a firm to solve business problems before they ruin the firm.

Balance Sheet Ratio Analysis

Important Balance sheet ratios measure liquidity and solvency (a business's ability to pay its bills as they come due) and leverage (the extent to which the business is dependent on creditors' funding). *Liquidity ratios* indicate the ease of turning assets into cash. They include the Current Ratio, Quick Ratio, and Working Capital.

Current Ratio. The *Current Ratio* is one of the best known measures of financial strength. It is figured as shown below:

$$\text{Current Ratio} = \frac{\text{Total Current Assets}}{\text{Total Current Liabilities}}$$

The main question this ratio addresses is: "Does the business have enough current assets to meet the payment schedule of its current debts with a margin of safety for possible losses in current assets, such as inventory shrinkage or collectable accounts?" A generally acceptable current ratio is 2 to 1. The minimum acceptable current ratio is obviously 1:1, but that relationship is usually playing too close for comfort.

If the business's current ratio is too low, a firm may be able to raise it by the following means:

1. Paying some debts.
2. Increasing the current assets from loans or other borrowings with a maturity of more than one year.
3. Converting noncurrent assets into current assets.
4. Increasing the current assets from new equity contributions.
5. Putting profits back into the business.

Quick Ratio. The *Quick Ratio* is sometimes called the "acid-test" ratio and is one of the best measures of liquidity. It is figured as shown below:

$$\text{Quick Ratio} = \frac{\text{Cash + Government Securities + Receivables}}{\text{Total Current Liabilities}}$$

The Quick Ratio is a much more exacting measure than the current Ratio. By excluding inventories, it concentrates on the really liquid assets, with value that is fairly certain. It helps answer the question: "If all sales revenues should disappear, could the business meet its current obligations with the readily convertible 'quick' funds on hand?"

An acid test of 1:1 is considered satisfactory unless the majority of the "quick assets" are in accounts receivable, and the pattern of accounts receivable collection lags behind the schedule for paying current liabilities.

Working Capital. *Working Capital* is more a measure of cash flow than a ratio. The result of this calculation must be a positive number. It is calculated as shown below:

$$\textbf{Working Capital} = \text{Total Current Assets} - \text{Total Current Liabilities}$$

Bankers look at Net Working Capital over time to determine a company's ability to weather financial crises. Loans are often tied to minimum working capital requirements.

A general observation about these three liquidity ratios is that the higher they are the better, especially if the firm is relying to any significant extent on creditor money to finance assets.

Leverage Ratio. The Debt/Worth or *Leverage Ratio* indicates the extent to which the firm is reliant on debt financing (creditor money versus owner's equity):

$$\textbf{Debt/Worth Ratio} = \frac{\text{Total Liabilities}}{\text{Net Worth}}$$

Usually, the higher this ratio, the more risky a creditor will perceive its exposure in the business, making it correspondingly harder to obtain credit.

Income Statement Ratio Analysis

The following Income Statement ratios measure a firm's profitability. *Profitability ratios* simply measure the profitability or unprofitability of a firm. Profits may be measured against a variety of data, such as sales, net worth, assets, and so forth. Generally, profitability ratios are expressed as percentages rather than proportions or fractions.

Gross Margin Ratio. The *Gross Margin Ratio* is the percentage of sales dollars left after subtracting the cost of goods sold from income. It measures the percentage of sales dollars remaining (after obtaining or manufacturing the goods sold) available to pay the overhead expenses of the company.

$$\textbf{Gross Margin Ratio} = \frac{\text{Gross Profit}}{\text{Income}}$$
$$(\text{Gross Profit} = \text{Income} - \text{Cost of Goods Sold})$$

Net Profit Margin Ratio. The *Net Profit Margin Ratio* is the percentage of sales dollars (Gross Income) left after subtracting the Cost of Goods Sold and all expenses, except income taxes. It provides a good opportunity to compare the company's "return on sales" with the performance of other companies in the industry. It is calculated before income tax because tax rates and tax liabilities vary from company to company for a wide variety of reasons, making comparisons after taxes much more difficult. The Net Profit Margin Ratio is calculated as follows:

$$\textbf{Net Profit margin Ratio} = \frac{\text{Net Profit Before Tax}}{\text{Gross Income}}$$

Management Ratios

Two additional *management ratios* derived from the Balance Sheet and Statement of Income are important for small businesses like FBOs.

Return on Assets Ratio. The *Return on Assets Ratio* measures how efficiently profits are being generated from the assets employed in the business when compared with the ratios of firms in a similar business. A low ratio in comparison with industry averages indicates an inefficient use of business assets. The Return on Assets Ratio is calculated as follows:

$$\textbf{Return on Assets} = \frac{\text{Net Profit Before Tax}}{\text{Total Assets}}$$

Return on Investment (ROI) Ratio. The *Return on Investment (ROI)* is perhaps the most important ratio of all. It is the percentage of return on funds invested in the business by its owners. In short, this ratio tells the owner whether or not all the effort put into the business has been worthwhile. If the ROI is less than the rate of return on an alternative, risk-free investment such as a bank savings account or certificate of deposit, the owner may be wiser to sell the company, put the money in such a savings instrument, and avoid the daily struggles of running a small FBO. The ROI is calculated as follows:

$$\textbf{Return on Investment} = \frac{\text{Net Profit before Tax}}{\text{Net Worth}}$$

These liquidity, leverage, profitability, and management ratios allow the business owner to identify trends in a business and to compare its progress with the performance of others through data published by various sources. The owner may thus determine the business's relative strengths and weaknesses. Sources of comparative financial information may be obtained from any public library or publishers listed under the references under this chapter.

FORECASTING PROFITS

Forecasting, particularly on a short-term basis (one year to three years), is essential to planning for business success. This process, estimating future business performance based on the actual results from prior periods, enables the FBO owner/manager to modify the operation of the business on a timely basis. This allows the business to avoid losses or major financial problems should some future results from operations not conform with reasonable expectations. Forecasts—or *Pro Forma Income Statements* as they are usually called—provide the most persuasive management tools to apply for loans or attract investor money. As a business expands, there will inevitably be a need for more money than can be internally generated from profits.

Factors Affecting Pro Forma Statements

Preparation of forecasts (Pro Forma Statements) requires assembling a wide array of pertinent, verifiable facts affecting the business and its past performance. These include the following:

1. Data from prior financial statements, particularly:
    a. previous sales levels and trends;
    b. past gross percentages;
    c. average past general, administrative, and selling expenses necessary to generate former sales volumes;
    d. trends in the company's need to borrow (supplier, trade credit, and bank credit) to support various levels of inventory and trends in accounts receivable required to achieve previous sales volumes.
2. Unique company data, particularly:
    a. facility capacity;
    b. competition;
    c. financial constraints;
    d. personnel availability.

3. Industry-wide factors, including:
   a. overall state of the economy;
   b. economic status of the FBO industry within the economy;
   c. population growth;
   d. elasticity of demand (responsiveness of customers to price changes) for product or service the business provides;
   e. availability of aircraft.

Once these factors are identified, they may be used in Pro Formas, which estimate the level of sales, expense, and profitability that seem possible in a future period of operations.

The Pro Forma Income Statement

In preparing the Pro Forma Income Statement, the estimate of total sales during a selected period is the most critical forecast. The owner/manager must employ business experience from past financial statements.

If, for example, a 10 percent increase in sales volume is a realistic and attainable goal, the first step is to multiply last year's gross income by 1.10 to get this year's estimate of total gross income. Next, this total has to be broken down by month, by looking at the historical monthly sales volume. From this it can be determined that the percentage of total annual sales fell on the average in each of those months over a minimum of the past three years. It might be determined that 75 percent of total annual sales volume was realized during the six months from July through December in each of those years and that the remaining 25 percent of sales was spread fairly evenly over the first six months of the year.

Next, is an estimate of the cost of goods sold by analyzing operating data to determine on a monthly basis what percentage of sales has gone into cost of goods sold in the past. This percentage can then be adjusted for expected variations in costs, price trends, and efficiency of operations.

Operating expenses (sales, general and administrative expenses, depreciation, and interest), other expenses, other income, and taxes can then be estimated through detailed analysis and adjustment of what they were in the past and what they are expected to be in the future. Putting together this information month by month for a year into the future will result in the firm's Pro Forma Statement of Income.

Preparation of the information is summarized below and in Figure 5–3.

1. **Income (Sales).** List the departments in the firm. A reasonable projection of the monthly sales for each department is entered in the "Estimate" columns. The actual sales are entered in the "Actual" columns for the month as they become available. Any revenue not strictly related to the business is excluded from the Income (Sales) column.
2. **Cost of Sales.** The cost of sales estimated for each month for each department is entered in the "Estimate" column. For product inventory, the cost of the goods sold for each department is calculated by subtracting the current inventory from beginning inventory plus purchases and transportation costs during the month. The "Actual" costs are entered each month as they accrue.
3. **Gross Profit.** Total cost of sales are subtracted from total sales.
4. **Expenses.** Total direct and indirect expenses for each department are entered in the "Estimate" columns. The "Actual" expenses are entered each month as they accrue. The advantage of departmentalizing expenses is that each segment of the business is held directly accountable. This often proves valuable when analyzing where cutbacks, expansion, or other actions might take place, and time is saved when reviewing specific numbers for segments of the operation. This system can also be useful for monitoring the performance of department managers. *Direct expenses* may be either fixed or variable in nature. Fixed expenses are those costs that remain fairly constant, regardless of business volume. For example, if a charter department is estab-

XYZ Aviation Company
Pro Forma Statement of Income
December 31, 20___

Departments	Sales		Cost of Sales		Gross Profit		Expenses						Net Profit	
							Direct				Overhead			
							Fixed		Variable		Indirect			
	Est.	Act.	Est.	Act.	Est.	Act.	Est.	Act.	Est.	Act.	Est.	Act.	Est.	Act.
Fueling														
Used Aircraft														
New Aircraft														
Charter/Air Taxi														
Rental														
Flight Training														
Hangar Mgmt.														
Aircraft Mgmt.														
Maintenance														
Parts														
Avionics Sales														
Paint Operations														
Display Case Sales														
Totals														

Figure 5–3. Pro Forma Statement of Income for XYZ Aviation Company

lished as a profit center, pilot salaries and aircraft lease payments are examples of direct fixed expenses. Variable expenses, on the other hand, vary directly with business volume. If using aircraft flight hours as the volume, then fuel and maintenance costs would be examples of direct variable costs. The more flying, the higher the expenses.

Overhead (Indirect) expenses are typically allocated costs and are fixed. Generally, they cannot be attributed to one particular department. Costs which may fit this description are administrative salaries, telephone, utilities, taxes, rent, advertising/promotion, office supplies, insurance, professional services, and interest. These indirect expenses must be allocated in an equitable, justifiable method to each department or profit center.

One accepted method is to allocate indirect expenses on a square footage basis. If the charter department occupies 20 percent of the total square footage of the facility, then 20 percent of the rent, utilities, administrative, and other indirect costs can be allocated to that profit center.

Another common allocation method that works in some situations is to allocate indirect costs as a percentage of sales for that profit center. If the profit center generates 15 percent of the firm's revenues, then 15 percent of the indirect costs are allocated to that profit center.

5. **Net Profit.** Total expenses are subtracted from gross profit to determine net profit. Because the individual departments have been divided into individual profit centers, management is now provided with a powerful financial decision-making tool. No longer will unprofitable or marginally profitable departments be hidden.

The Pro Forma Statement of Income, prepared on a monthly basis and culminating in an annual projection for the next business fiscal year, should be revised not less than quarterly. It must reflect the actual performance achieved in the immediately preceding three months to ensure its continuing usefulness as one of the two most valuable planning tools available to management.

Should the Pro Forma reveal that the business will likely not generate a profit from operations, plans must immediately be developed to identify what to do to at least break even — increase volume, decrease expenses, or put more owner capital in to pay some debts and reduce interest expenses.

Break-Even Analysis

Break-Even Analysis means a level of operations at which a business neither makes a profit nor sustains a loss. At this point, revenue is just enough to cover expenses. Break-Even Analysis enables the firm to study the relationship of volume, costs, and revenue.

Break-Even requires the FBO owner/manager to define a sales level in terms of revenue dollars to be earned within a given accounting period at which the business would earn a before-tax profit of zero. This may be done by employing one of various formula calculations to the business estimated sales volume, estimated fixed costs, and estimated variable costs.

Ordinarily, the volume and cost estimates assume the following conditions:

1. A change in sales volume will have no effect on selling prices.
2. Fixed expenses will remain the same at all volume levels.
3. Variable expenses will increase or decrease in direct proportion to any increase or decrease in sales volume.

The steps for calculating the break-even point are as follows:

1. Obtain a list of expenses incurred by the company during its past fiscal year.
2. Separate the expenses into either a variable or a fixed expense classification.
3. Express the variable expenses as a percentage of sales. For example, let's assume gross income (sales) was $1,200,000; fixed expenses, $400,000; variable expenses, $720,000; and net income, $80,000. Variable expenses are 60 percent of sales ($720,000 divided by $1,200,000). This would mean that 60 cents of every sales dollar is required to cover variable expenses. Only the remainder, 40 cents of every dollar, is available for fixed expenses and profit.
4. Substitute the information gathered in the preceding steps in the following basic break-even formula to calculate the break-even point.

$$S = F + V$$

Where: S = Sales at the break-even point
F = Fixed expenses
V = Variable expenses expressed as a percentage of sales

This formula means that when sales revenues equal the fixed expenses and variable expenses incurred in producing the sales revenues, there will be no profit or loss. At this point, revenue from sales is just sufficient to cover the fixed and the variable expenses. In this formula "S" is the break-even point.

Using the numbers in step 3, the break-even point may be calculated as follows:

$$
\begin{aligned}
S &= F + V \\
S &= \$400{,}000 + 0.60S \\
1.00S - 0.60S &= \$400{,}000 \\
0.40S &= \$400{,}000 \\
S &= \$1{,}000{,}000
\end{aligned}
$$

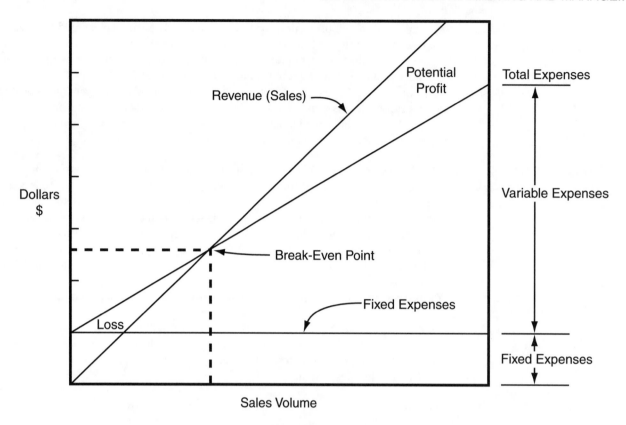

Figure 5–4. Break-Even Chart

The break-even formula can be modified to show the dollar sales required to obtain a certain amount of desired net income (or loss). To do this, let S equal the sales required to obtain a certain amount of net income (or loss), say $80,000. The formula then reads:

S = F + V + Desired Net Income	S = F + V − Desired Net Loss
S = $400,000 + .60S + $80,000	S = $400,000 + .60S − $80,000
1.00S − .60S = $480,000	1.00S + .60S = $320,000
.40S = $480,000	40S = $320,000
S = $1,200,000	S = $800,000

Break-even analysis may also be represented graphically by charting the sales dollars required to break even as shown in Figure 5–4.

BUDGETING AND COST CONTROL

Budgets are detailed plans that represent set objectives against which to measure results. They are valuable management tools. In effect, they are blueprints that enable the firm to anticipate what will be, establish specific objectives, and chart the right course to assist the business in attaining those objectives.

Additionally, by monitoring what happens as the firm passes through the budget period, management will be in a position to make necessary adjustments to keep the plan on target.

Cash Flow Budgets identify when cash is expected to be received and when it must be spent to pay bills and debts. It shows how much cash will be needed to pay expenses and when it will be needed. It also allows the manager to identify where the necessary cash will come from. For example, will it be internally generated from sales and the collection of accounts receivable — or must it be borrowed? (The Cash Flow Budget deals only with actual cash transactions; depreciation and amortization of good will or other noncash expense items are not considered.)

The Cash Flow Budget, based on management estimates of sales and obligations, identifies when money will be flowing into and out of the business. It enables management to plan for shortfalls in cash resources so short-term working capital loans may be arranged in advance. It allows management to schedule purchases and payments in a way that enables the business to borrow as little as possible. Because all sales are not cash sales, management must be able to forecast when accounts receivable will become "cash in the bank" and when expenses—whether regular or seasonal—must be paid so cash shortfalls will not interrupt normal business operations. The Cash Flow Budget enhances control by allowing management to continually compare actual receipts and disbursements against forecast amounts. This comparison helps management to identify areas for timely improvement in financial management.

By closely watching the timing of cash receipts and disbursements, cash balance on hand, and loan balances, management can readily identify such things as deficiencies in collecting receivables, unrealistic trade credit or loan repayment schedules. Surplus cash that may be invested on a short-term basis or used to reduce debt and interest expenses temporarily can be recognized. In short, it is the most valuable tool management has at its disposal to refine the day-to-day operation of a business. It is an important financial tool bank lenders evaluate when a business needs a loan, for it demonstrates not only how large a loan is required but also when and how it can be repaid.

The Cash Flow Budget can be prepared for any period of time. However, a one-year budget matching the fiscal year of the business is generally recommended. As in the preparation and use of the Pro Forma Statement of Income, the Cash Flow Budget should be prepared on a monthly basis for the next year. It should be revised not less than quarterly to reflect actual performance in the preceding three months of operations to check its projections.

In order to make the most effective use of Cash Flow Budgets to plan profits, reporting devices have to be established. These reports and reviews enable management to compare actual performance with budgeted projections and maintain control of the operations.

Cash Flow Budgets can be established for sales, cost of goods sold, selling expenses, administrative expenses, direct labor, and so forth.

Two typical budget reports are shown in Figures 5–5 and 5–6.

Cash Flow Budgets allow the owner/manager to anticipate problems rather than react to them after they occur. It permits comparison of actual receipts and disbursements against projections to identify errors in the forecast. If cash flow is analyzed monthly, the manager can correct the cause of the error before it harms profitability.

Report of Actual and Budgeted Fuel Sales
for the Year Ended December 31, 20___

Actual	Fuel Sales ($) Budgeted	Quarterly	Variations From Budget (Under) Cumulative
1st Quarter	$	$	$
2nd Quarter			
3rd Quarter			
4th Quarter			

Figure 5–5. Fuel Sales Budget

Budgeted Report on Administrative Expenses
For the Year Ended December 31, 20_____

Month of _____			Year to Date			
Budget	Actual	Variation	Budget	Actual	Variation	Remarks

Figure 5–6. Administrative Expenses Budget

TYPES, USES, AND SOURCES OF CAPITAL

The capital to finance a business has two major forms: debt and equity. Creditor money *debt* comes from trade credit, loans made by financial institutions, leasing companies, and customers who have made prepayments on orders.

Equity is money received by the company in exchange for some portion of ownership. Sources include the entrepreneur's own money; money from family, friends, or other nonprofessional investors; or money from venture capitalists, Small Business Investment Companies (SBICs), and Minority Enterprise Small Business Investment Companies (MESBICs) both funded by the SBA.

Debt capital, depending upon its sources (e.g., trade, bank, leasing company, mortgage company) comes into the business for short or intermediate periods. Owner or equity capital remains in the company for the life of the business (unless replaced by other equity) and is repaid only when and if there is surplus at liquidation of the business—after all creditors are repaid. Acquiring such funds depends entirely on the business's ability to repay with interest (debt) or appreciation (equity). Financial performance (reflected in the Financial Statements discussed earlier in the chapter) and realistic, thorough management planning and control (shown by Pro Forma statements and Cash Flow Budgets), are the determining factors in whether or not a business can attract the debt and equity funding it needs to operate and expand.

Business capital can be further classified as equity capital, working capital, and growth capital. *Equity capital* is the cornerstone of the financial structure of any company. Equity is technically the part of the Balance Sheet reflecting the ownership of the company. It represents the total value of the business, all other financing being debt that must be repaid. Usually, the firm cannot get equity capital—at least not during the early stages of business growth.

Working capital is required to meet the continuing operational needs of the business, such as "carrying" accounts receivable, purchasing inventory, and meeting the payroll. In most businesses, these needs vary during the year, depending on activities (flying hours, inventory build-up, seasonal hiring or layoffs, etc.) during the business cycle.

Growth capital is not directly related to cyclical aspects of the business. Growth capital is required when the business is expanding or being altered in some significant and costly way that is expected to result in higher and increased cash flow. Lenders of growth capital frequently depend on anticipated increase profit for repayment over an extended period of time, rather than expecting to be repaid from seasonal increases in liquidity as is the case of working capital lenders.

Every growing business needs all three types: equity, working, and growth capital. The firm should not expect a single financing program maintained for a short period of time to eliminate future needs for additional capital.

As lenders and investors analyze the requirements of the business, they will distinguish between the three types of capital in the following way: (1) fluctuating needs (working capital); (2) needs to be repaid with profits over a period of a few years (growth capital); and (3) permanent needs (equity capital).

If a firm is asking for a working capital loan, management will be expected to show how the loan can be repaid through cash (liquidity) during the business's next full operating cycle, usually a one-year cycle. If the firm is seeking growth capital, management will be expected to show how the capital will be used to increase the business enough to be able to repay the loan within several years (usually not more than seven). If the firm is seeking equity capital, it must be raised from investors who will take the risk for dividend returns or capital gains, or a specific share of the business.

Borrowing Working Capital

Working capital was defined earlier as the difference between current assets and current liabilities. To the extent that a business does not generate enough money to pay trade debt as it comes due, this cash must be borrowed.

Commercial banks obviously are the largest source of *working capital loans,* which have the following characteristics: (1) The loans are short term but renewable; (2) they may fluctuate according to seasonal needs or follow a fixed schedule of repayment (amortization); (3) they require periodic full repayment; (4) they are granted primarily only when the ratio of net current assets comfortably exceeds net current liabilities; and (5) they are sometimes unsecured but more often secured by current assets (e.g., accounts receivable and inventory). Advances can usually be obtained for as much as 70 to 80 percent of quality (likely to be paid) receivables and to 40 to 50 percent of inventory. Banks grant unsecured credit only when they feel the general liquidity and overall financial strength of a business provide assurance for repayment of the loan.

The firm may be able to predict a specific interval, say three to five months, for which it needs financing. A bank may then agree to issue credit for a specific term. Most likely, management will need working capital to finance outflow peaks in the business cycle. Working capital then supplements equity. Most working capital credits are established on a one-year basis.

Although most unsecured loans fall into the one-year line of credit category, another frequently used type, the amortizing loan, calls for a fixed program of reduction, usually on a monthly or quarterly basis. For such loans the bank is likely to agree to terms longer than a year, as long as the firm continues to meet the principal reduction schedule.

It is important to note that while a loan from a bank for working capital can be negotiated only for a relatively short term, satisfactory performance can allow the arrangement to be continued indefinitely.

Most banks will expect the firm to pay off loans once a year (particularly if they are unsecured) in perhaps 30 or 60 days. This is known as "the annual clean up," and it should occur when the business has the greatest liquidity. This debt reduction normally follows a seasonal sales peak, such as the summer or fall when flying weather is best, and most receivables have been collected.

Sometimes a firm finds that it is progressively more difficult to repay or "clean up" within the specified time. This difficulty usually occurs because (1) the business is growing and its current activity represents a considerable increase over the corresponding period of the previous year; (2) the firm has increased its short-term capital requirement because of new promotional programs or additional operations; or (3) the firm is experiencing a temporary reduction in profitability and cash flow.

Frequently, such a condition justifies obtaining both working capital and amortizing loans. For example, management might try to arrange a combination of a $15,000 open line of credit to handle peak financial requirements during the business cycle and $20,000 in amortizing loans to be repaid at, say $4,000 per quarter. In appraising such a request, a commercial bank will insist on justification based on past experience and future projections. The bank will want to know: how the $15,000 line of credit will be self-liquidating during the year (with ample room for the annual clean up); and how the business will produce increased profits and resulting cash flow to meet the schedule of amortization on the $20,000 portion in spite of increasing the business's interest expense.

Borrowing Growth Capital

Lenders expect working capital loans to be repaid through cash generated in the short-term operations of the business, such as selling goods or services and collecting receivables. Liquidity rather than overall profitability supports such borrowing programs. *Growth capital loans* are usually scheduled to be repaid over longer periods with profits from business activities extending several years into the future. Growth capital loans are, therefore, secured by collateral such as aircraft and other equipment, fixed assets which guarantee that lenders will recover their money should the business be unable to make repayment.

For a growth capital loan, management will need to demonstrate that the growth capital will be used to increase the cash flow through increased sales, cost savings, and/or more productivity. Although the building, equipment, or airplanes will probably be used as collateral for growth capital funds, management will also be able to use them for general business purposes. Even if the firm borrows only to acquire a new aircraft, the lender is likely to insist that all aircraft and equipment be pledged.

Instead of bank financing a particular aircraft, it may be possible to arrange a lease. The firm will not actually own the aircraft, but it will have exclusive use of it over a specified period. Such an arrangement usually has tax advantages. It lets the firm use funds that would be tied up in the aircraft, if the firm had purchased it. It also affords the opportunity to make sure the aircraft meets the FBO's needs before it is purchased.

Major equipment may also be purchased on a time payment plan, sometimes called a *Conditional Sales Purchase*. Ownership of the property is retained by the seller until the buyer has made all the payments required by the contract. (Remember, however, that time payment purchases usually require substantial down payments and even leases require cash advances for several months of lease payments.)

Long-term growth capital loans for more than five but less than fifteen years are also obtainable. Real estate financing with repayment over many years on an established schedule is the best example. The loan is secured by the land and/or buildings the money was used to buy. Most businesses are best financed by a combination of these various credit arrangements.

When an FBO goes to a bank to request a loan, it must be prepared to present the company's case persuasively. Management should bring its financial plan consisting of a Cash Budget for the next twelve months, Pro Forma Balance Sheets, and Income Statements for the next three to five years. Management should be able to explain and amplify these statements and the underlying assumptions on which the figures are based. Obviously, the assumptions must be convincing and the projections supportable. Finally, many banks prefer statements audited by an outside accountant with the accountant's signed opinion that the statements were prepared in accordance with generally accepted accounting principles and that they fairly present the financial condition of the business.

Borrowing Equity Capital

Equity capital sometimes comes from sources other than the business owner/manager or stockholders. *Venture capital* is one such source. Difficult to define, it is high risk capital offered with the principal objective of earning capital gains for the investor. While venture capitalists are usually prepared to wait longer than the average investor for a profitable return, they usually expect in excess of 15 percent return on their investment. Often they expect to take an active part in determining the objectives of the business. These investors may also assist the FBO owner/manager by providing experienced guidance in marketing, product ideas, and additional financing alternatives as the business develops. Even though turning to venture capital may create more bosses, their advice can be as valuable as the money they lend. However, venture capitalists are looking for businesses with real potential for growth and for future sales in the millions of dollars.

FINANCIAL PLANNING

Studies overwhelmingly identify bad management as the leading cause of business failure. Bad management translates to poor planning by management.

All too often, the owner/manager of an FBO is so caught up in the day-to-day tasks of managing the operation, seeing that aircraft are maintained, and struggling to collect receivables to meet the payroll that he or she does not plan. There never seems to be time to prepare Pro Formas or Budgets. Often FBO managers understand their business but not the financial statements or the records, which they feel are for the benefit of the IRS or the bank. Such overburdened owner/managers can scarcely identify what will affect their businesses next week, let alone over the coming months and years.

Success may be ensured only by focusing on all factors affecting a business's performance. Focusing on planning is essential to survival.

Short-term financial planning is generally concerned with profit planning or budgeting. *Long-term financial planning* is generally strategic, setting goals for sales growth and profitability over a minimum of three to five years.

The tools for short- and long-term plans have been discussed earlier in this chapter: Pro Forma Income Statements, Cash Flow Statements or Budgets, and Ratio Analysis. A business's short-term plan should be prepared on a monthly basis for a year into the future, employing Pro Forma Income Statement and the Cash Flow Budget.

Long-Term Planning

The long-term or strategic plan focuses on Pro Forma Statements of Income prepared for annual periods three to five years into the future. It is difficult imagining all the variables that will affect a business in one year, let alone the next three to five years. However, the key is control—controlling the firm's future course of expansion through the use of the financial tools discussed earlier in this chapter.

The first step is to determine a rate of growth that is desirable and reasonable. Using Pro Forma Statements and Cash Flow Budgets, the next step is to calculate the capital required to finance the inventory, aircraft, equipment, and personnel needs necessary to attain that growth in sales volume. The FBO owner/manager must anticipate capital needs in time to make satisfactory arrangements for outside funds if internally generated funds from retained earnings are insufficient.

Growth can be funded in only two ways: with profits or by borrowing. If expansion outstrips the capital available to support higher levels of accounts receivable, inventory, fixed assets, and operating expenses, a business's development will be slowed or stopped entirely by its failure to meet debts as they become payable. Such insolvency will result in the business's assets being liquidated to meet the demands of the creditors. The only way to avoid this "out-stripping of capital" is by planning to control growth. *Growth must be understood to be controlled.* This understanding requires knowledge of past financial performance and of the future requirements of the business.

These needs must be forecast in writing—using the Pro Forma Income Statement in particular—for three to five years in the future. After protecting reasonable sales volumes and profitability, the Cash Flow Budget must be used to determine (on a quarterly basis for the next three to five years) how these projected sales volumes translate into the flow of cash in and out of the business during normal operations. Where additional inventory, equipment, or other physical assets are necessary to support the sales forecast, management must determine whether or not the business will generate enough profit to sustain the growth forecast.

Often, businesses simply grow too rapidly for internally generated cash to sufficiently support the growth. If profits are inadequate to carry the growth forecast, the owner/manager must either make arrangements for working growth capital to borrow, on slow growth to allow internal cash to "catch up" and keep pace with the expansion. Because arranging financing and obtaining additional equity capital takes time, this need must be anticipated well in advance to avoid business interruption. Planning is a perpetual process. It is the key to prosperity for any company.

DETERMINING THE VALUE OF AN AVIATION BUSINESS

With an increasing number of ownership changes and mergers taking place in the industry, determining the value of airport-based businesses is on the rise. The concept of value is viewed in a variety of ways. Market value is generally defined as the most probable selling price of a property—assuming a willing and informed buyer and seller.

Although this may appear to be a simple concept, "willing and informed" are not always appropriate terms in the sale of a fixed base operation or other aviation business. Frequently, the owner/operator has reached a value conclusion based on various personal issues associated with the operation (time/money invested, years and effort devoted towards the business, loyalty to employees, retirement needs, and so forth), ignoring the actual foundations that create or diminish the business value.

The process of determining the value of a going-concern business must be based upon a more objective and substantial financial analysis. Business valuation is always a difficult task, but appraising a fixed base operation is typically even more complex. FBOs as ongoing business enterprises are typically valued by two methods:

- Multiples of Earnings Before Interest, Taxes, Depreciation, and Amortization (EBITDA); and/or a
- Discounted Cash Flow (DCF) analysis

Even though the multiple of *EBITDA analysis* is the most common in the aviation industry, the *Discounted Cash Flow Analysis* is often more appropriate in situations where an unstable market exists. An EBITDA analysis represents the conversion of one year's income into a value, while a DCF projects and evaluates an income stream over time. Both are appropriate means of valuation and use net income after the exclusion of certain noncash flow items.

EBITDA Analysis

This type of analysis is best suited for a stable operation that has experienced consistent revenue and expense trends historically, with similar trends expected over the next few years. This does not mean that the business has to have been stagnant, but that it has not shown significant fluctuations in either revenue sources or volumes in recent years.

This method analyzes one year's net income, converting it into a value estimate, using a "multiple" based upon the expected future stability of the business, overall economic climate, and financial risks associated with the business. The ability to project stabilized earnings is critical. An erratic revenue or expense history makes projecting future trends very difficult, in turn, reducing the reliability of the analysis.

Another difficult task in the EBITDA analysis is determining the appropriate multiple. Multiples represent the relationship between the selling price of an FBO or other aviation business, and its net earnings at the time of sale, or its pro forma earnings. The multiple is typically derived from sales of other FBOs or aviation businesses and, therefore, is only as good as the information that is available from either the buyer or the seller. Multiples are "all inclusive" of the buyer's perception of the stability of the business, anticipated growth trends, return on equity requirements, motivation of buyer and seller, and terms of sale. Without obtaining all of the details surrounding the transaction, multiples of EBITDA can be deceiving figures.

Discounted Cash Flow Analysis

DCF analysis is typically more appropriate in an unstable market, which probably describes most FBOs and specialized aviation businesses. An unstable market may be a situation where an operator is experiencing significant growth trends or is acquiring a competitor on the field whereby market share and margins are expected to change dramatically, or a scenario where a market is declining as the result of outside (or even internal) influences. In any case, this method works best when changes are occurring or are anticipated—either positively or negatively.

The DCF analysis projects revenues and expenses into the future based upon historic trends and prospective market and economic conditions. This projection is typically done on a departmental or classification basis, with each line item addressed individually. This allows for an analysis of specific revenue or expense items that may be expected to grow at a faster rate than others, as well as to account for those items that are fixed or will change as a percentage of another item.

The result is a more detailed "real world" assessment of an ongoing aviation business. As one might expect, an accurate and supportable projection of revenue and expense trends is the most significant factor in a DCF analysis.

The annual net income stream is converted into a present value by a discounting process. Each year's projected net income is "discounted" into a present value, using a rate of return consistent with the associated risk (based on the idea that revenues received in the future are worth less than the same revenues received now). Each year's discounted income is added to provide a current value estimate.

In some cases where a significant lease term remains after the selected discounting period (usually five to ten years), a reversionary value is added to reflect the fact that, if there is a continuing lease, the ability to generate income does not stop after the initial discounting period. The discount rate used in a DCF analysis is based upon investor return requirements given the risks associated with the future income stream. Depending upon the physical and economic characteristics of an FBO or aviation business, the existing lease agreement, the competitive environment, and overall stability of the business, discount rates may vary anywhere from 15 to 30 percent.

The complexity of the EBITDA or the DCF method lies in the evaluation and "recast" of financial information presented by the operator, with every operator offering his or her own method of bookkeeping. For instance, on the revenue side, many operators do not keep an accurate analysis of historical fuel volumes, types of fuel sales (retail, discounted retail, into-plane), or the historic margins associated with each. Such information is critical to the analysis of both past and future fuel revenues, which may significantly impact the profitability (and value) of the business. Expenses are also often inappropriately or incorrectly categorized. A misinterpretation of either revenue or expense items results in a skewing of the EBITDA, as well as the corresponding value conclusion.

Interest, Taxes, Depreciation and Amortization

Interest, income taxes, depreciation, and amortization are generally excluded from a business valuation. The result is that the firm is on a cash basis without consideration to the current owner's equity basis, financing terms, equipment basis, or competency of the accountant. All of the above items are a direct result of current owner investment and accounting procedures, not day-to-day cash flow, and differ from operator to operator, depending upon the desired taxation and yield results. By excluding these variable items, a business valuation can be done on a similar basis and a true value can be estimated.

Revenues, Cost of Sales, and Expenses

Revenues generated by an FBO or other aviation business are generally straightforward and typically reflect all income, excluding taxes. However, some forms of revenue warrant a greater risk than others, such as aircraft sales. Consequently, if significant, these revenues and corresponding expenses are typically extracted from overall revenues and analyzed separately, with alternative multiples or discount rates applied.

Cost of sales has a tendency to become a complex issue when evaluating an operating statement. In general, cost of sales represents the actual cost of the materials associated with the sale of specific items, such as fuel, catering, parts, pilot supplies, etc. In the case of fuel, both taxes and airport flowage fees are typically included, since each is part of the direct selling price, and may be reasonably calculated in the wholesale cost of the fuel.

Operating expenses generally create the greatest ambiguity during the valuation process. Every business operator handles the accounting function a little bit differently, with some creative accounting principles applied where appropriate. Although this is fine for the IRS, it is important to assess carefully all categories of expenses to ensure that they are applicable only to the day-to-day operations of the business. A frequent example relates to the owner's compensation package. In some cases, the owner's compensation is well beyond what is normally attributed to the day-to-day management of an operation.

Personal and auto expenses, special management perks, excessive travel budgets, or expenses related to the personal use of company aircraft are not typically included in a recast operating statement for the valuation process. This also goes for excessive legal or accounting expenses which may occur in a given year.

Typically, more normalized expense allocations are utilized in the valuation.

Another typical error found in many operating statements involves the repair and maintenance expense category. Improvements to facilities or acquisition of equipment are often deemed operating expenses, when it is more appropriate to recognize them as one-time capital improvements. Only the routine maintenance associated with the facilities and equipment are pertinent operating expenses. A good rule of thumb is that, if it is not a consistent annual expense, then it is probably better categorized as a capital expenditure.

Summary

The most important factor in determining the value of a going-concern business is simply the level of profitability that is currently presented and which can reasonably be expected to continue over time. Profitability is impacted by several significant components, including:

- Historic operating statistics
- Type and strength of the revenue stream
- Control of material costs
- Expenses associated with the operation of the business

Other significant factors that contribute to value are location (geographic area, size of airport, services offered); length of lease term and/or operating agreements; competition; and the conditions and terms of existing contracts (air carriers, cargo handling, and so forth).

While the influence of the emotional attachment to the business cannot be understated to a seller, the ability to generate a stable, consistent cash flow is the most significant factor in the creation of value.

KEY TERMS

Financial Management	Pro Forma Income Statements
Balance Sheet	Direct Expenses
Assets	Overhead Expenses
Liabilities	Break-Even Analysis
Shareholders' Equity (or net worth or capital)	Budgets
	Cash Flow Budgets
Statement of Income	Debt
Ratio Analysis	Equity
Liquidity Ratios	Equity Capital
Current Ratio	Working Capital
Quick Ratio	Growth Capital
Working Capital	Working Capital Loans
Leverage Ratio	Growth Capital Loans
Profitability Ratios	Conditional Sales Purchase
Gross Margin Ratio	Venture Capital
Net Profit Margin Ratio	Short-term Financial Planning
Management Ratios	Long-term Financial Planning
Return on Assets Ratio	EBITDA Analysis
Return on Investment (ROI)	Discounted Cash Flow Analysis

REVIEW QUESTIONS

1. What is the purpose of financial management? Describe the major categories of the Balance Sheet. Why must it balance? How does it differ from the Statement of Income? Summarize the categories under the Statement of Income.

2. What is the purpose of ratio analysis? Give several examples of Liquidity ratios. Define "working capital." What is the Leverage ratio? How does Income Statement ratio analysis differ from Balance Sheet ratio analysis? Distinguish between Gross Margin Ratio and Net Profit Margin Ratio. Why is the ROI ratio considered one of the most important ratios?

3. What are Pro Forma Income Statements? Discuss some of the factors affecting Pro Forma Statements. Describe the steps in preparing a Pro Forma Income Statement. Distinguish between direct expenses and overhead expenses. How can overhead expenses be allocated to individual profit centers?

4. What is the purpose of Break-Even Analysis? What are the basic assumptions in preparing a break-even chart? List the steps involved if preparing such a chart. What is the formula used?

5. Why are Cash Flow Budgets so important? What time frame are they normally prepared for? Give several examples of typical budget reports.

6. Distinguish between equity capital, working capital, and growth capital. What is the primary source for working capital loans? What is the time frame to "clean up" such loans? Why are growth capital loans generally secured by collateral assets? What is the advantage of leasing equipment?

7. What is a Conditional Sales Purchase? How does venture capital differ from other equity finance sources? Distinguish between short-term and long-term planning. Why is long-term planning so difficult for the small FBO? What is the difference between EBITDA analysis and Discounted Cash Flow analysis in determining the value of an aviation business. Summarize the important factors in determining the value of an aviation business.

REFERENCES

Annual Statement Studies. Philadelphia, PA: Robert Morris Associates, 1986.

Burstiner, Irving. *The Small Business Handbook* (Rev. ed.). Englewood Cliffs, NJ: Prentice-Hall, 1989.

Hartley, W.C., and Yale Meltzer. *Cash Management: Planning, Forecasting, and Control.* Englewood Cliffs, NJ: Prentice-Hall, 1979.

Hobbs, James B., and Carl L. Moore. *Financial Accounting* (3rd ed.). Cincinnati, OH: South-Western, 1984.

Horngren, Charles T. *Introduction to Management Accounting* (6th ed.). Englewood Cliffs, NJ: Prentice-Hall, 1984.

Keith, L., and R. Keith. *Accounting: A Management Perspective* (2nd ed.). Englewoods Cliffs, NJ: Prentice-Hall, 1985.

Key Business Ratios. New York: Dun & Bradstreet, Inc., 1990.

Kolb, Burton A. *Principles of Financial Management.* Plano, TX: Business Publications, 1983.

Lynch, Richard M., and Robert W. Williamson. *Accounting for Management: Planning and Control* (3rd ed.). New York: McGraw-Hill, 1983.

Neveu, Raymond. *Fundamentals of Managerial Finance* (2nd ed.). South-Western, Cincinnati, OH: 1985.

Troy, Leo. *Almanac of Business and Industrial Financial Ratios.* Englewood Cliffs, NJ: Prentice-Hall, 1986.

Richardson, J. D., and J. F. Rodwell. *Essentials of Aviation Management* (4th ed.). Dubuque, IA: Kendall/Hunt Publishing Co., 1990.

PART THREE
THE MARKETING PROCESS

Chapter 6

The Role of Marketing

OUTLINE

OBJECTIVES

At the end of this chapter, you should be able to:

Trace the evolution of marketing through three distinct periods of development.

Define the marketing concept and explain its importance to organizations success.

Define marketing.

Explain the importance of determining objectives in quantifiable terms.

Identify and highlight the steps in the process of segmenting the market.

Differentiate the three approaches to target marketing.

Describe each of the four Ps in the marketing mix.

Discuss the factors involved in implementing and controlling marketing plans.

Describe the uncontrollable variables that can affect a firms marketing efforts.

MARKETING DEFINED

Is marketing necessary? Many take for granted the products and services that are purchased and used every day. The many companies and individuals involved in expediting the flow of goods so that exchange can be made are not appreciated. Some even suggest that the price could be reduced by 30 percent to 50 percent if all marketing activities were eliminated. Is this elimination a viable alternative? Marketing is a powerful force in the world economy. Marketing is responsible for creating demand, goods and services, and jobs in many related fields like research, advertising, wholesaling, retailing, and transportation. Marketing has been a major factor in the increased quality of life enjoyed by developed countries throughout the world.

Marketing efforts observed today are far different from those used in the past. The evolution of marketing can be traced through three distinct periods of development. The first period is called the *production era* and covers the period of time from about 1870 to 1930. This era is characterized as a *seller's market*—demand for products exceeded the supply. Firms concentrated on efficient production to offer products that were well made. This production thinking worked due to limited competition and the imbalance between demand and supply. Marketing was not needed in this business environment. By 1930, technology had drastically changed that allowed manufacturers to produce more goods than they could sell. This condition is called a *buyers market*—supply exceeded demand. In this *sales era,* manufacturers focused on aggressively selling the oversupply of their products. Their philosophy was to "sell what the firm could efficiently make rather than making what the firm could sell." The initial marketing function that was introduced was one of aggressive sales tactics that often had the opposite of the desired effect because the customer was offended and refused to purchase the product. The sales era continued until the mid 1950s when customers became more selective and demanded products that better fit their needs. The third and current era is called the *marketing concept era* and emphasizes customer need fulfillment and customer satisfaction. The *marketing concept* is a customer-oriented, integrated, goal-oriented philosophy for the firm. It means that a firm aims all its efforts at satisfying its customers—at a profit. Instead of just trying to persuade customers to buy what the firm is selling, a firm implementing the marketing concept tries to produce what customers need and want. Market research plays an important role in assisting the firm to identify and monitor customer satisfaction. The three components of the marketing concept are (1) a customer orientation, (2) a total company effort, and (3) a profit—not just sales—as an objective.

Today, goods and services move through many different channels of distribution efficiently which allows consumers to satisfy their needs and wants on demand. The economic justification for a business firm today is that it has the ability to create utility or value for its customers. *Utility* is the want satisfying ability of a good or service. From a marketing perspective, there are three forms of utility: time, place, and possession. Time utility involves making the goods available when the customer wants them. Having line service available 24 hours each day is an example of time utility. Place utility involves making products available where the customer wants them. Place utility helps bring buyers and sellers closer together. General Motors creates place utility by transporting an executive to see an important client. Possession utility involves transferring of title for a product between the parties. The use of trade credit among marketing intermediaries and credit cards with consumers have greatly enhanced this utility.

This chapter views marketing from a microperspective and will investigate the role of marketing in a firm and demonstrate how essential marketing is to the long-term survival of an organization. What does the term "marketing" mean? Most people mistakenly equate the term with selling and promotion. *Marketing* is much more than selling and promotion and is more commonly defined as: *"The performance of business activities or functions that direct the flow of products and services from the seller to the buyer in order to satisfy customers and accomplish the company's objectives."*

Each part of the definition will be examined more closely. A variety of business activities must be performed to accomplish the over all objective which is to develop exchange relationships with customers. The three categories of marketing activities are exchange, physical distribution, and facilitating functions. Exchange or transactional functions involve buying and selling on the part of various channel members, like wholesalers and retailers, and the final customer. Logistical or physical distribution functions help satisfy time and place utilities by efficiently combining the components of warehouse locations, inventory strategies, material handling, and transportation modes that provide a satisfactory service level for the customer. Functions that facilitate exchange include financing, risk-taking, providing information through market research, and standardizing and grading products. It is important to note that each of these functions must be performed for exchange to take place. Who performs these functions and how they are performed depends on type of product, type of customer, geographical location, and urgency of the need.

The second part of the definition deals with satisfying customers; customer satisfaction is the ultimate objective of the marketing process. Marketing attempts to build stronger relationships with existing customers and to discover new target markets that fit well with the firm's expertise and objectives. Customers, not marketers, primarily determine what they need, want, and are willing to buy. It is the responsibility of marketing to identify and to satisfy customers' needs.

The final portion of the definition indicates that accomplishing the company's objective is an essential part of marketing. Just as the customers must be satisfied, the marketing plan must also achieve company objectives. The primary objective of the marketing plan is to make a satisfactory profit while meeting customers' expectations. Other objectives include increasing market share, expanding into the global market, introduction of new products, or increasing distribution efficiencies.

MARKETING MANAGEMENT

Marketing management is a three-phase process that includes planning marketing activities, directing the implementation of the plans, and controlling these plans. This process is so central to the activities of most organizations that they formalize it as a *marketing plan*, which is a road map to guide the marketing activities for a specified future period of time, such as one year.

PLANNING

Marketing planning involves making decisions that commit the firm to actions in order to reach organizational and marketing objectives effectively. Planning includes determining objectives, segmenting the market, selecting target markets, and establishing a unique marketing mix aimed at the particular audience. The *marketing mix* includes the product or service, price, channel of distribution (place), and promotion (advertising, sales promotion, personal selling, and publicity). These so-called controllable variables are referred to as the "four Ps" of marketing.

Determining Objectives

Marketing objectives should complement and be set within the framework of the larger company objectives. For example the firm's objectives might include increasing flight school revenues. A marketing objective would be to increase the number of students or to improve the student pilot retention rate. Because objectives are not equally important, a hierarchy of objectives should be specified for the marketing personnel.

Marketing objectives should be quantified and stated in understandable terms. Ideally, the attitudes of upper management toward the achievement of these objectives should also be ascertained. Top management must guide each department manager of a product-service area. For example, should a 20 percent increase in charter business be attained regardless of cost or only sought if return on investment is 18 percent or better? Even more important—but less quantifiable—should a 20 percent increase be obtained even if it requires high pressure selling, reduced availability or reliability, or other possibly unethical actions? (We hope not.)

Each department manager is responsible for generating a certain amount of revenue so that the profit objective can be reached. The sales force has the objective of achieving a designated sales quota. Advertising has the objective of creating a level of awareness of product-service areas within the target markets. Prices must be competitive and achieve a specific market share or target rate of return. Marketing research must be completed on time and within budget.

Objectives at all levels of the firm should be operationally specified. Each department manager should understand what activities must be undertaken, and what operations must be performed in order to accomplish the objectives. Quantification is usually helpful here; "increase sales by 10 percent" is more precise than asking the department manager to get "more sales than last year." Managers should not focus their efforts exclusively on objectives that can be quantified, however. It is fairly easy, for example, to measure the cost savings of holding parts inventory to a minimum, but it is very difficult to determine the degree of customer dissatisfaction which might be created when that minimum inventory results in being out of stock that delays repair of a customer's airplane.

Segmenting the Market

Market segmentation is the process of breaking down the total market into smaller, more homogeneous groups with similar needs that the firm can satisfy. A market-segmentation approach aims at a narrow, specific consumer group (market segment) through one specialized marketing plan that caters to the needs of that segment. Market segmentation has emerged as a popular technique for FBOs with highly specialized products and limited resources. Market segments should be as similar as possible with respect to needs. There also should be significant differences among segments and the segments should be large enough to be profitable.

Segmenting assists the firm in deciding which market to target and also to plan marketing mixes. Here is a look at an approach to segmenting.

1. *Identify the product-service areas to be segmented.* The first step involves identifying all of the product-service areas presently offered by the firm. This might include the following:

   Flight school   Hangar rental
   Airplane sales   Sale of gas and oil
   Rental: by Hour or by Trip   Accessories: for Plane or Pilot
   Charter: Scheduled   Services (weather, flight plans, charts, etc.)
             Non-scheduled
   Overhaul: Major
             Minor

2. *Identify all of the possible market segments.* This step includes an identification of all markets for the firms product-service areas. These might include the following:

   Pilots   Physicians
   Aircraft owners   Engineers
   High school students   Managers
   High school graduates   Professionals
   Community college flight   Proprietors
     program students   Salespeople
   Corporate fleet   Commuter airline

At this point, it is helpful to develop a matrix as shown in Table 6–1. This table shows the product-service areas on the left side and possible target markets across the top. The table includes evaluations of each product-service area against each market with a judgment of whether that will be of major or minor interest to the firm.

Another helpful analysis in determining possible market segments is to compare product-service areas with competitors. In this case, product-service areas would be shown across the top of a sheet of paper and on the left side, a listing of the firms chief competitors. Again, a matrix is formed in which the firm can rate competitors' strengths and weaknesses using a scale of one to five, with five being excellent and one being poor.

Table 6–1 Market Segmentation

Product-Service Areas		Pilots	Aircraft Owners	H.S. Students	H.S. Grads.	C.C. Flight Prog.	Corporate Fleet	Physicians	Engineers	Managers	Professionals	Proprietors	Salespeople	Commuter Airline
Flight School		O	O	X	X	X		X	X	X	X	X	X	
Airplane Sales		X	O		O		X	X	X	X	X	X	X	O
Rental:	Hour	X		X	X	X		X	X	O	X	O	O	
	Trip	X		O	X	X		X	X	X	X	X	X	
Charter:	Scheduled						X							O
	Non-Scheduled						X			X	X	X	X	
Overhaul:	Major		X				X							O
	Minor	O	X				O							
Hangar Rental		X				X								
Sale of Gas & Oil		X	X	X	X	X	X	X	X	X	X	X	X	X
Accessories:	Plane		X				X							O
	Pilot	X	X	X	X	X		X	X	X	X	X	X	X
Services		X	X	X	X	X	X	X	X	X	X	X	X	X

X = Major interest
O = Minor interest

The ratings reflect how well each competitor delivers that product-service. The firms can also rate themselves. In order to check their findings, some firms poll customers who are familiar with the competitive operations to evaluate both the firm and its competitors. Customers may come up with completely different perceptions of the firm and its competitors for the various product-service areas.

The objective of these exercises is to try to identify possible target markets and also point out a firm's strengths and weaknesses. Too many FBOs fall into the trap of trying to be all things to all markets with the result of not excelling at anything. The better approach is to do fewer things but to do them well.

> 3. *List all needs for the possible market segments that have been identified.* This is a "brain-storming" step. For each of the product-service areas, it is now important to identify the needs for all of the possible market segments. For example, using the flight school as the product-service area, what are the particular needs of high school students? Their needs include availability of an evening ground school, instructor availability from 3 p.m. to 6 p.m., competitive prices, installment payment plan, college credit for attainment of private pilots license, and counseling with parents.

The process of identifying segments and determining their accessibility necessitates focusing on customer needs. This, of course, is the essence of marketing management. It encourages the firm to track who buys its products—where, when, and how. Segmentation keeps the organization alert to changes in market conditions and competitors' actions. Competitive analysis may indicate which segments of the market are controlled by strong, entrenched competitors and which segments' needs are not fulfilled by present product-service areas.

Establishing Target Markets

Once the market segments are determined and the segmentation criteria are satisfied, the firm is ready to direct its effort toward one or more market segments. A *target market* is a segment that is the object of a firm's marketing mix. It is the opposite of *mass marketing* which does not attempt to differentiate between the market segments but instead, designs and aims its marketing mix at all segments.

A *single target market approach* means the selection of one primary market segment as the firm's target market. This concentrated marketing is a cost-effective way to market because there are no expensive variations of the marketing mix. Marketers narrow their sales potential by concentrating on a single market segment, but are exposed to more financial risk by not diversifying efforts into multiple target markets. A *multiple target market approach* means selecting two or more market segments — each will be treated as a separate target market — each will require a unique market mix. A *combined target market approach* means aggregating two or more similar market segments into one larger target market.

Most successful FBOs utilize the multiple and combined target market approaches. Mass marketing is not appropriate for the highly specialized product-service areas of the average FBO.

Establishing a Marketing Mix

Once the firm has determined its objectives and selected its target market(s), it is ready to begin planning the details of the marketing mix. The marketing mix was previously defined as the set of controllable marketing variables that the firm blends to produce the desired response in the target market. The marketing mix consists of everything the firm can do to influence the demand for its product. The many possibilities can be collected into four marketing mix variables: product, price, place and promotion.

The Product

A *product* is a combination of benefits, physical features, and services, designed to satisfy the needs/wants of identified target markets. This definition stresses that the word product includes both tangible products and intangible services. The ability of a firm's product to satisfy wants is the key to developing exchange relationships. Purchasers of aircraft are vitally concerned with parts and service availability, warranties, image of the brand name, and other intangible benefits that contribute to the total satisfaction of owning an aircraft. Flight students purchase an intangible service but are also concerned with other benefits such as quality, reputation of the school, and professionalism of the instructors.

There are four unique characteristics of services that offer marketers challenges different from marketing tangible products like airplanes. These four elements are referred to as the *four I's of services*. Services are intangible. The buyer must purchase on faith because it is often only after the sale that quality, benefits and dimensions can be evaluated. Service marketers should stress the benefits of the service instead of the service itself. Many aviation firms today are successful because they have differentiated their product by including key benefits that are sought out by their market. For example, an FBO builds line service business by including a free wash job with the purchase of 100 gallons of aircraft gas. The second characteristic is inconsistency. Since services depend on the people who provide them, their quality varies with each person's training, capabilities, and attitudes. A third characteristic of services, and related to the problems of consistency, is inseparability. In most cases the provider of the service cannot be separated from the service itself (A&P mechanic repairing an aircraft). The fourth characteristic identifies the inventory problems of services because many items are perishable and cannot be stored. Marketers must implement strategies that will assist in managing the level of demand for a service in line with the firm's ability to provide the service. FBOs have a continuing challenge in providing quality and timely maintenance while keeping overhead at profitable levels.

The Price

Price represents the exchange value of a good or service. Since customers perceive price as the sacrifice or cost they must pay, marketers must maintain the price level equal to or less than utility (satisfaction level). This cost-benefit relationship plays a major role in pricing strategies.

Price planning is systematic decision making by a firm regarding all aspects of pricing. A price contains all the terms of purchase: monetary and nonmonetary costs, discounts, handling and shipping fees, credit charges and other forms of interest, and late-payment penalties.

With price competition, sellers influence demand for their products primarily through changes in price levels. Non-price competition minimizes price as a factor in customer demand. This is accomplished by creating a distinctive product or service as expressed through promotion, customer service, availability, and other marketing factors. The more specialized a product or service offering is perceived to be by customers, the greater is the freedom of firm to set prices above competitors.

Price competition is a flexible marketing tool because prices can be adjusted quickly and easily to reflect demand, cost, or competitive factors. However, of all the controllable marketing variables, pricing strategy is the easiest for a competitor to duplicate.

Before a firm develops a pricing strategy, it must analyze the outside factors affecting price decisions. Price decisions depend heavily on elements external to the firm. This contrasts with product and promotion decisions, which are more directly controlled by the firm. The major factors affecting price decisions are customers, competition, costs, and products.

1. Customers. A firm must understand the relationship between price and customer purchases and perceptions. This relationship is explained by two economic principles—the law of demand and the price elasticity of demand. The *law of demand* states that customers usually purchase more units at a low price than at a high price. The *price elasticity of demand* defines the responsiveness of buyers to price changes in terms of the quantities they will purchase.

   Price elasticity is computed by dividing the percentage change in quantity demanded by the percentage change in price charged:

$$\text{Elasticity of Demand} = \frac{\text{Percentage change in quantity demanded}}{\text{Percentage change in price}}$$

   Elastic demand occurs if relatively small changes in price result in large changes in quantity demanded. Numerically, price elasticity is greater than one. With elastic demand, total revenue increases when prices are lowered and decreases when prices rise. For example, if flight instruction rates decreased by 10 percent and the number of students increased by 15 percent, then demand was elastic and total revenue would increase. *Inelastic demand* take place if price changes have little impact on quantity demanded. Price elasticity is less than one. With inelastic demand, total revenue increases when prices are raised and decreases when prices decline. If fuel prices increased by 5 percent and the quantity demanded decreased by 2 percent, demand is inelastic. Total revenue would increase in such a case. *Unitary demand* exists if changes in price are exactly offset by changes in quantity demanded, so that total revenue remains relatively constant. Price elasticity is one.

   Elasticity of demand depends primarily upon three criteria: the price, availability of substitutes, and urgency of need. In general, customers tend to be more responsive to price changes of high-ticket items, such as airplanes, than they are to low-priced items, such as pilot accessories sold over the counter. The more substitute products are available, the more responsive customers tend to be. Lack of substitutes is generally associated with inelastic demand. The more time customers have to shop around, the more elastic their demand. If a customer has an urgent need for a product, such as an aircraft part and cannot afford several days' delay, this customer will tend to be inelastic with regard to price.

2. Competition. Another element contributing to the degree of control a firm has over prices is the competitive environment within which it operates. An *oligopolistic market* has only a few firms that offer homogeneous products and have limited control over market pricing. Firms attempting to charge more than the current competitive price would attract few customers, because, demand for any particular firm's product is not strong enough to prevent customers from switching to competitors when prices are increased. Similarly, a firm would actually lose revenue by selling for less than the market price because competitors would immediately match any price reduction, thus establishing a lower market price.

A *monopolistic competitive market* contains many sellers and is characterized by, moderate level of competition, well-differentiated product-service areas, and strong control over price by individual firms. In this environment firms may succeed with higher prices because customers view their products as unique. Differentiation may be based on reputation, professionalism of personnel, newness of aircraft, attractiveness of facilities, services offered, or other factors. Marketers desiring to sell below market price can carve out a niche in this environment by attracting customers interested in the lowest price. The choice of price level depends on the firm's strategy, target market, and competitive environment.

3. Cost-oriented pricing. It is the most common method used because it has the advantage of simplicity. The price of a product must cover costs of manufacturing, promotion and distribution, plus a reasonable profit. There are at least three variations of this approach: mark-up pricing, cost-plus pricing, and rate of return pricing. *Markup pricing* is appropriate when the seller is not the manufacturer. A reseller will add a percentage of the invoice cost to determine the selling price. The size of the percentage markup will depend on such factors as inventory turnover rate, competition, and degree of elasticity.

Manufacturers of tangible products use *cost-plus* and *rate of return pricing* methods. Total unit costs are determined, and then a profit dollar amount or a desired rate of return percentage is added to arrive at the selling price. Cost-oriented approaches have a major disadvantage in that they give little or no consideration to customer demand. The price determined using this method only looks at internal factors (costs) rather than the market forces of supply and demand and the willingness of target markets to pay the asking price.

4. Products. There are numerous product characteristics which influence pricing. Three important ones are perishability, distinctiveness, and stage in the product life cycle.

- Perishability. Products that are perishable in a physical sense must be priced attractively to promote sales without costly delays. Intangible products, which cannot be stored, are also very sensitive to the right price level to assure a match between supply and demand. Perishability is also a concern as it applies to the consumption rate. Products that have a long life, like airplanes, tend to have an initial high cost because large amounts of services are purchased at one time. Second, owners of these types of products have a great deal of time to make replacement purchase decisions that reduces the persuasiveness of price.
- Distinctiveness. One of the major challenges facing marketing managers is to make their products different from their competitors'. If unsuccessful, pricing becomes a matter of meeting the market price. Distinctiveness can be achieved in many products through design changes, packaging, services provided, warranties, etc. Being able to charge higher prices for these differentiated products rewards the seller.
- Life cycle. The four stages of the product life cycle—introduction, growth, maturity, and decline—have an important impact on pricing decisions. During the introductory stage, a skimming policy or a penetrating policy is followed. *Skim-*

ming is particularly useful when introducing a unique product for which the initial price is very high and it appeals to the innovators. As competitors enter the market, price is reduced. *Penetrating* is setting a below-competition price in order to capture an immediate share of the market. Prices will be raised as some brand loyalty has been attained. Growth and maturity stage pricing is driven by the aggressiveness of competitors and a firms ability to remain distinctive in product lines. Decline stage pricing is usually geared to harvest the most revenue prior to the elimination of the product.

The Place

Place is concerned with delivering the product and services to customers in a timely manner. In addition to a convenient location on the airport the appropriate products and services must be available for each target market in the correct amount when customers need them. For example, aircraft used for flight instruction must be available when members of a target market need them—not off on a charter flight or in for maintenance. Place decisions are directly related to a firm's desired customer service level. *Customer service level* is a measure of how rapidly and dependably a firm can deliver what customers want. For the FBO it might mean having the appropriate parts inventory available. If a firm decides to lower overhead costs, it may also be settling for a lower customer service level by handicapping employee's ability to efficiently handle customer requests. On the other hand, obtaining a higher service level might increase sales that would in turn offset the increased costs. Clearly, a marketing manager has a decision to make about what service level to offer. Minimizing cost is not always the right answer.

The Promotion

Promotional planning is systematic decision making relating to all aspects of the development and management of a firm's promotional effort. *Promotion* is any form of communication used by a firm to inform, persuade, or remind people about its products, services, image, ideas, or community involvement.

The *promotional mix* consists of the following four major tools.

1. *Advertising.* Any paid form of nonpersonal presentation and promotion of ideas, products, or services by an identified sponsor.
2. *Sales promotion.* Short-term incentives to encourage purchase or sale of a product or service.
3. *Personal selling.* Oral presentation with one or more prospective purchasers for the purpose of making sales.
4. *Publicity.* Nonpersonal stimulation of demand for a product or service by placing commercially significant news about the firm in a publication like *Business and Commercial Aviation* or obtaining favorable presentation on radio or television that is not paid by the sponsor.

Within the advertising and sales promotion categories there are specific communication tools, such as mass media advertising, displays, print and specialty advertising, trade shows, brochures, literature, posters, contests, and flight training coupons. Many products, like airplanes, require the use of personal sales to first initiate contact and then to use sales skills to turn the prospect into a satisfied customer. Promotional activities such as these are often thought to be the major, if not the total, thrust of marketing in any FBO. Promotion is important, but no more important than the other three marketing mix variables. The firm's products and services, its prices and distribution strategies all communicate important information to buyers. The whole marketing mix, not just promotion, must be coordinated for the maximum communication impact.

IMPLEMENTATION OF PLANS

Marketing implementation is the process that turns the marketing plan into action assignments and ensures that such assignments are executed in a manner that accomplishes the plans' stated objectives. No matter how well the marketing program has been planned, nothing happens until a product has been sold or a service performed. All department managers must not only have input into the marketing plan, they also must enthusiastically endorse the plan and play an important role in its implementation. Specific skill areas required for successful marketing implementation include organization and execution.

Organizing for Implementation

An organization is a group of people with a common purpose or mission. This mission can best be achieved if each person has a specific responsibility, and all are joined in such a way as to facilitate and reinforce each other. All members of the organization must be guided by the marketing concept. This customer orientation requires a thorough understanding of customer needs, wants, and behavior. The focal point, then, is the customer. Ideally, all members of the organization should attempt to learn more about customers' needs and work to develop products and services to satisfy those needs.

Another important element is coordination. First, there should be coordination within the marketing mix variables. Second, marketing efforts must be coordinated within each department and among departments. Unless all departments see themselves working toward a common goal of satisfying customers, they will not be able to assist in adhering to the marketing concept.

Executing Marketing Plans

Another ingredient to successful implementation of the marketing plan is management of the execution phase by all members of the firm. Implementation responsibilities fall into three areas: delegation, communication, and motivation.

1. Delegation. It is necessary in organizations to delegate responsibilities to various people. Delegation is done both formally through organizational structure and informally. In addition to determining appropriate duties, delegation also means matching people's capabilities and preferences to those duties. In other words, delegation will not result in successful implementation unless (1) the duties to be performed have been clearly specified and (2) appropriate personnel have been assigned to perform those duties.

2. Communication. After responsibilities have been delegated, they must be coordinated to achieve the firm's objectives, and the information must be communicated. Communication involves shared understanding among individuals. Ideally, information should flow throughout the firm — not just down from the top — but up to the top as well as across the firm (among departments). Marketing plans are best implemented in a work environment that fosters complete and open information flow. Here are examples of several ways to improve communications:

   a. Information Dissemination: up-to-date organization charts, telephone directories; a company newsletter; an in-house library of industry material; a policy for releasing information as quickly as possible to avoid rumor.

   b. Instruction: training programs, formal performance appraisals, sessions with supervisors, and financial assistance for educational pursuits.

   c. Interaction: informal company gatherings and interdepartmental committees.

3. Motivation. Delegation and communication will be to no avail unless someone in a leadership position takes the responsibility to motivate people to perform the tasks expected of them. Perhaps the most succinct method of motivating people is to reward them for a job well done. The salesperson on commission, for example, will devote more time to making new sales than to handling old complaints. A flight instructor can be rewarded for a good student retention rate by giving the instructor the next charter flight. Prizes can be given to the line person of the month. All of these are motivating factors designed to reward exemplary performance in carrying out the marketing objectives of the firm.

CONTROL

Marketing control is the process of translating organizational objectives into quantifiable standards, periodically analyzing marketing results and taking actions that will correct the deficiencies affecting the FBO's ability to reach stated marketing objectives. It starts after the marketing program has been implemented and is monitored on a continuous basis. Generally speaking, control is the process that attempts to reconcile performance of the marketing plan with marketing objectives. The types of activities and standards differ across the four marketing mix variables. Thus, control is intertwined with planning. Some marketing authorities refuse to draw a precise distinction between planning and control, preferring instead to see them as two sides of the same coin.

Setting Standards and Measuring Results

The first step in marketing control is to translate organizational objectives into standards against which performance can be measured. In general, there are three bases for performance standards—industry norms, past performance, and managerial expectations.

Industry norms can be obtained from manufacturers, trade publications, and industry organizations. They can be quite useful as guidelines for marketing performance standards. Industry sales, pricing policies, and advertising strategies are examples of the types of information included. The underlying assumption of this kind of standard is that if the firm's performance is comparable to others in the industry, things "can't be too bad." This is not necessarily true. For example, an organization's market share may hold steady while the total market declines as in the case of single-engine aircraft sales in the '80s and '90s. On the other hand, the firm's market share may fall while the total market is expanding. In essence, industry norms provide comparisons with average performance.

A second basis for performance standards is past performance—how do this month's or year-to-date-sales compare to those of last month or last year? This information should be available from departments within the company. Past performance measures provide a minimum standard, a benchmark by which to measure subsequent efforts. Also, trends of performance over a period of time can be analyzed. However, the use of past performance assumes that historical patterns have relevance for future decisions. It may be misleading to measure current performance on the basis of these results.

The third basis for performance standards is managerial expectations. Forecasts, budgets schedules, and policy decisions become standards against which actual performance is measured. These standards may involve both industry norms and past performance, but they also take estimates of future conditions into account. To the extent that managerial expectations are realistic, they probably provide the most useful standards for measuring performance. Assessments of future conditions—based on the manager's intuition, experience, and information—provide perhaps the most feasible standards for the situation. Of course, compared with industry norms or past performance, managerial expectations are more subjective and uncertain. Consequently, they are more open to criticism.

Corrective Action

Efforts at marketing control will be to no avail if the actions necessary to bring actual performance into line with standards are not taken. The first problem facing a manager contemplating corrective action is identification of specific causes for the deviation from the standard. This is sometimes easier said than done. Another difficulty is one of time lags associated with the desired corrective action. Sometimes, a manager finds that because of the time lag between recognition of a problem and a decision about corrective action, the problem has changed before it has been addressed. Perhaps a salesperson's poor performance in a given period, for example, was the result of a personal problem that has now been resolved. There are no easy answers to guide corrective action.

Perhaps performance is not faulty. It may be that the objectives set by the plan were inappropriate due to totally unexpected competitive, economic, or governmental actions. If this is the case, the proper corrective action involves adjusting the plans rather than performance.

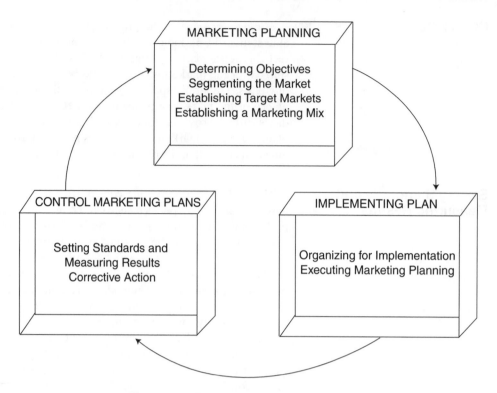

Figure 6–1. The Marketing Management Process

SUMMARY OF MARKETING MANAGEMENT

It is clear that the marketing management process is one of planning marketing activities, directing the implementation of the marketing plan, and controlling the plan (see Figure 6–1).

In Figure 6–1, all the steps are connected to show that the marketing management process is continuous. The planning job sets guidelines for implementation and specifies expected results that are compared in the control function to see if everything has worked out as projected. This feedback is especially important and can lead to changes. A manager should not only be concerned with the present plan, but must also be proactive by always looking for attractive new opportunities and creating new strategies.

UNCONTROLLABLE VARIABLES

The *uncontrollable variables* are those factors affecting a firm's performance that cannot be directed by marketing efforts. It must be recognized that any marketing plan, no matter how well conceived, might fail if adversely influenced by uncontrollable factors. Therefore, the external environment must be continually monitored and its effects incorporated into any marketing plan. The process of continually acquiring information about the trends occurring externally to the firm in order to be more efficient in planning as well as to be proactive is called *environmental scanning*. Uncontrollable variables that must be monitored and their trends analyzed are consumer demographics, competition, government regulations, the economy, technology, media, and public interest groups.

Consumer Demographics

Although a firm has control over the selection of a target market, it cannot control the characteristics of the population. Firms can react to but not control these consumer demographics: age, income levels, marital status, occupation, race, education, and place and type of residence. The U.S. population will continue to grow and there will be major changes in the country. On April 1, 2000, the population of the United States was 281,421,906 people that represented an increase of 13.1% over 1990. Because the U.S.

population is growing slowly, the average age is rising. In 1970, the average age of the population was 28—but the 2000 census shows that the average age jumped to 37. Since most marketers use age groups as one of the criteria in selecting homogeneous target markets, the change in the percentage of the population in different age groups will affect marketing strategies. For example, in the 18–24 age group, between 1980 and 1990, there was a 17.7 percent decrease, between 1990 and 2000, a 1.4 increase, and it is estimated that between 2000 and 2010 there will be a 14.8 increase. The major reason for the changing age distribution in different age groups is the U.S. birthrate. Expressed as the number of babies born per 1,000 people, the last 50 years indicates a major rise from 1935 of 18.7 to a high point of 25.0 in 1955. From this point forward the birth rate has declined to the current 2000 level of 14.0. The post-World War II baby boom (1947 to 1957) produced about 43 million babies. This is about one-sixth of the present U.S. population. This large group crowded into the schools in the 1950s and 1960s, and then entered the job market in the 1970s. Many of this group started to have children in the late 1970s and early 1980s that caused another ground swell at the elementary school level. In the 1980s and 1990s, the baby boomers were middle-aged. By the early twenty-first century, this group will reach retirement age. Because the baby boomers account for a large percentage of the population, they have been extremely important to marketers. This generation has a distinct profile compared with that of other age groups. Baby boomers have the highest education level, with one-fourth of those between the ages of 25 and 35 having college degrees; they have high incomes and during the 1990s they have been responsible for about half of all consumer expenditures. Many companies are designing products and developing marketing strategies to target this very important group.

Birth rates were very low during the 1960s and early 1970s causing a significant drop in the number of individuals entering college in the mid-1980s. This factor might be one of the major causes of the decline in student pilot starts in the early 1990s.

Another significant trend is the increasing number of women in the workforce and the types of jobs they are performing. In 1950, only 24 percent of wives worked outside the home. Now that figures is over 65 percent. Women are entering many nontraditional career paths and income levels for this target group is rising which gives them independence and purchasing power. In 1992 only 10 percent of the total number of pilots in the country were women, which should represent a significant potential in the years ahead.

Competition

A firm's competitors frequently affect its market planning and its success in attracting target market. There are three types of competition. The first is direct competition between companies offering similar products and services. Two charter companies on the same airport compete directly for that area's charter business.

The second type of competition occurs between companies that offer products or services that can be substituted for one another. Automobiles are competitors for general aviation aircraft as are commuter airlines because they both can be used to transport company personnel.

The third type of competition occurs because customers have limited financial resources. Marketers of dissimilar products and services are in competition with each other. The salesperson must help the customers prioritize their "wish" list to accomplish immediate sales. A business aircraft salesperson, for example, may have to persuade the prospect to defer the purchase of a new computer system so that credit resources will be available to secure an aircraft loan.

A firm must evaluate the marketing strategies of its competitors. Specifically, the firm must determine which markets are saturated and which are unfulfilled. The marketing plans and target markets of competitors, the images of competitors and their products, the strengths and weaknesses of competitors, and the extent to which consumers are content with the level of service provided by the competition must also be considered.

Government Regulations

A third uncontrollable variable affecting market planning is government regulation. In addition to the federal laws involving antitrust, discriminatory pricing, unfair trade practice, occupational health and safety, the aviation industry is faced with numerous regulations promulgated by the Federal Aviation Administration. The FAA is charged with the safe operation of aircraft in the airway system. In carrying out this responsibility, it develops many regulations, which can have an impact on a firm's marketing plans.

In addition to federal legislation and agencies, each state and local government has its own legal environment for firms operating within its boundaries.

The political climate also affects legislation. Consumerism, nationalism, foreign trade, zoning, wage rates, and other items are discussed and debated through the political process before legislation is enacted.

The Economy

Markets require purchasing power as well as people. Total purchasing power is related to current income, profits, prices, savings, and credit availability. An economic recession, high unemployment, and the rising cost of credit all affect purchasing power. A high rate of growth means the economy in the region or country is usually good and marketing potential large.

Of prime importance to firms are the perceptions of consumers regarding the economy. If consumers believe the economy will be favorable, they will increase spending. If they believe the economy will be poor, they will cut back on spending.

Some costs of doing business are often beyond the control of the firm. These include aircraft, parts and equipment, insurance, and interest rates. If costs rise substantially, marketing inflexibility is limited and lower profit margins may be necessary. When costs are stable, firms have greater opportunities to differentiate their strategies and expand sales.

When widespread cost increases, such as premiums for product liability insurance, drive the price of aircraft up, the result is a high rate of inflation; the prices of some products and services may go beyond the reach of many consumers, or consumers may be forced to alter their spending habits.

Of importance is what happens to consumers' real income, income adjusted for inflation, over time. The level of corporate profits after taxes can also affect the number and type of aircraft purchased by corporations. A high rate of unemployment adversely affects firms because people cut back on discretionary spending.

Technology

Our society is characterized as being in the age of technological change. Technology refers to the inventions or innovations from applied science or engineering research. The aviation industry has always been on the leading edge of technological change. Many technological advances are beyond the control of individual firms, especially smaller ones. However, unless they keep pace with improved technology, they will no longer remain competitive.

Media

The firm does not control the media yet they can influence the government's, consumers', and public's perceptions of an industry or a company's products and overall image. The media can provide positive or negative coverage of a company or an industry. Whenever an aircraft crashes or a drug smuggler using an aircraft is captured, the industry receive bad press. Companies should willingly distribute positive news releases.

Public Interest Groups

The number and power of public interest groups have increased during the past two decades and represent another uncontrollable variable. The most successful is Ralph Nader's Public Citizen group, which watchdog's consumer interests. Hundreds of other consumer interest groups — private and governmental — operate at the national, state, and local levels. Other groups to be considered are those seeking to protect the environment or advance the rights of minority groups.

CONCLUSION

An organization's level of success or failure in reaching its objectives depends on how well it directs and implements its controllable factors (marketing mix) and observes the impact of uncontrollable factors on the marketing plan. In order to improve the marketing effort and ensure long-run attainment of objectives, the firm needs feedback regarding the uncontrollable environment, the firm's performance, and how well the marketing plan is received. Feedback is obtained by measuring consumer satisfaction, looking at competitive trends, evaluating the relationship with government agencies, monitoring the economy, reading and reviewing the media, responding to public interest groups, analyzing sales and profit trends, talking with industry analysts, and employing other methods of gathering and assessing information.

After evaluating feedback, the firm needs to adapt its strategy to the business environment, while continuing to utilize its distinct advantages. To ensure long-term success, the firm must continually look for new opportunities that are attainable and fit into its overall corporate objectives, and respond to potential threats by revising marketing strategies.

KEY TERMS

Production era
Seller's market
Buyer's market
Sales era
Marketing concept era
Marketing concept
Utility
Marketing
Marketing plan
Marketing planning
Marketing mix
Market segmentation
Target market
Mass marketing
Single target market approach
Multiple target market approach
Combined target market approach
Product
Four I's of services
Price
Price planning
Law of demand
Price elasticity of demand

Elastic demand
Inelastic demand
Unitary demand
Oligopolistic market
Monopolistic competitive market
Markup pricing
Cost-plus pricing
Rate of return pricing
Skimming
Penetrating
Place
Customer service level
Promotion
Promotion mix
Advertising
Sales promotion
Personal selling
Publicity
Marketing implementation
Marketing control
Uncontrollable variables
Environmental scanning

REVIEW QUESTIONS

1. Define marketing and explain the three eras in the evolution of marketing.
2. Why is the ability to create utility the economic justification for a firm to be in business?
3. What is meant by segmenting the market? Why would it be helpful for a firm to compare its strengths and weaknesses against its immediate competitors? Do different target markets have different needs? Why is it preferable to express objectives in quantifiable terms?
4. A product may include more than a physical item. Explain.
5. Name and explain the four I's of services.
6. What are the major factors affecting price? Define elastic and inelastic demand. Differentiate between an oligolopolistic market and a monopolistic competitive mar-

ket. How do these competitive markets affect pricing strategies? Discuss the three types of cost-oriented pricing. What is meant by customer service level?

7. Define the four major tools in the promotional mix.

8. Implementing marketing plans involves delegation, communication and motivation. Describe the importance of these functions. How can workers be motivated? How does control differ from implementation? Describe several ways in which a firm can set standards.

9. What are the so-called uncontrollable variables that can affect a firm's marketing efforts? Why should a firm be aware of consumer demographics? Discuss several social trends that affect the marketing process. Explain the three types of competition faced by an FBO.

REFERENCES

Berkowitz, Eric N., and Roger A. Kerin, Steven W. Hartley, William Rudelius. *Marketing,* 6th Ed. Burr Ridge, IL. Irwin/McGraw-Hill, 2000.

Perreault, William D., Jr. and E. Jerome McCarthy, *Basic Marketing,* 13th Ed. Burr Ridge, IL. Irwin/McGraw-Hill, 1999.

Sandhusen, Richard L., *Marketing,* 32nd Ed. Hauppauge, New York. Barron's Educational Series, Inc., 2000.

Chapter 7

Marketing Research

OBJECTIVES

At the end of this chapter you should be able to:

Define marketing research and explain its purpose within an organization.

Give examples of different types of marketing research studies falling under market measurement, marketing mix, competitive situations, and the uncontrollable variables.

Describe the steps involved in the marketing research process.

Distinguish between primary and secondary data.

Identify five major sources of secondary data.

Describe research approaches, types of research instruments, sampling procedures, and methods of collecting data in a plan for collecting primary data.

MARKETING RESEARCH DEFINED

Marketing decisions are often complex ones that have major impact upon the firm's ability to reach its market share and profitability goals. Many factors in the external environment such as increasing competition, technology, governmental regulations, changes in the macroeconomy, and the constantly changing opinions, attitudes, and values of customers. The ultimate objective for engaging in marketing research is to assist managers in decision making, which is the essence of management; managers at all levels spend more time defining, making, and implementing decisions than in any other activity. It is essential; therefore, that systematic information gathering and analytical procedures contribute to effective an efficient decision making. Through research, management can reduce uncertainty in decision making.

Marketing research is also a vital business activity, providing a foundation for the planning, implementation, and control of marketing programs. It is an integral part of any management information system that provides a flow of inputs useful in marketing decision making.

Marketing research is the systematic process of gathering, recording, analyzing, and utilizing relevant information to aid in marketing decision making. Marketing managers today should understand that marketing research is an aid to decision making, not a substitute for it. Having the right kind of information available can greatly increase the probability that the best decision will be made.

SCOPE OF MARKETING RESEARCH

Marketing research has a broad scope including various types of studies (see Table 7–1). These studies can be grouped into four major categories: (1) market measurement studies, (2) marketing mix studies, (3) studies of the competitive situation, and (4) studies of the uncontrollables.

Market Measurement Studies

Market measurement studies are designed to obtain quantitative data on potential demand—how much of a particular product or service can be sold to various target markets over a future period, assuming the application of appropriate marketing methods.

Table 7–1   Types of Marketing Research Studies

1. Market Measurement
   a. Demand research
      (1). Determination of market characteristics
      (2). Measurement of market potential
      (3). Short-range forecasting (up to one year)
      (4). Long-range forecasting (over one year)
      (5). Buyer motivation
   b. Performance research
      (1). Market share analysis
      (2). Sales analysis
      (3). Establishment of sales quotas
      (4). Evaluation of test markets
      (5). Customer surveys
2. Marketing Mix Research-Controllable influences
   a. Product or service research
      (1). New product or service acceptance and potential
      (2). Existing products or service in new markets
      (3). Diversification of products
   b. Place research
      (1). Methods of delivering product or service to customers
      (2). Facility location
   c. Price research
   d. Promotion research
      (1). Studies of advertising effectiveness
      (2). Sales compensation studies
      (3). Media research
      (4). Studies of sales promotion effectiveness
3. Competition Research
   a. Competitive product or service studies
4. Uncontrollable Influences
   a. Studies of business trends
   b. Studies of legal constraints-rules and regulations
   c. Environmental impact studies
   d. Demographic studies

This data relates to market potential, sales potential, or both. *Market potential* is the maximum possible sales opportunity open to all sellers of a product or service during a stated future period to a target market. *Sales potential* is the maximum possible sales opportunity open to a particular company selling a product or service during a stated future period for a target market. For example, consider the business jet market. The market potential, macroperspective, for business jets over the next three years is 1,764 units. This represents total units all aircraft manufacturers participating in this market segment could sell over this time period. Cessna's sales potential, microperspective, would be approximately 756 units based upon their market share of 42.9 percent over the same stated three-year period.

Market measurement data is especially helpful in planning overall marketing strategy. In evaluating a proposed new twin-engine charter service, for example, management must estimate its probable marketing success. Analysis of market measurement data provides insights as to whether a potential market exists and, if so, its size. If management decides to add a new product, such as flight simulators, market measurement data is again helpful in determining target markets. In addition, breakdowns of potential sales by types of customers make it possible to ascertain which groups should be the targets for promotional efforts of varying amounts, and in what order they should be pursued. Management make similar use of market measurement data in resolving questions of whether to drop certain services, closing the avionics shop, for instance, or deemphasizing promotion to particular market segments.

Buyer motivation research studies probe the psychological, sociological, and economic variables affecting buyer behavior. These studies require trained psychologists, sociologists and economists to undertake them and interpret the resulting data. Few companies employ such people, and most motivation research is handled by outside consultants.

Marketing Mix Studies

Most marketing research studies focus on the elements of the marketing mix: product, place, price, and promotion. Management uses studies of these controllable variables to appraise the effectiveness of current product, service, pricing, and promotion policies, and to plan future policies and practices. Many firms make frequent studies of the effectiveness of advertising and other promotional devices, individual salespeople, existing sales methods, and sales compensation plans. Management can change the controllable variables with any formal study, but change is more effective with the added insight gained from research.

Studies of the Competitive Situation

More firms emphasize studies of the competitive position of their own products and services than they do studies of the nature and impact of their competitors' activities. Specifically, a study measuring the market share of a firm's products and services is more common than one which appraises the strengths and weaknesses of a competitor's products and services, evaluates the effects of a competitor's service improvement, measures the impact of a competitor's price change, or checks the effects of a competitor's revised advertising approach. Most companies could benefit by delving into competitors' marketing practices and policies. Management needs this information to understand how competitors' actions affect marketing strategy.

Studies of Influences of Uncontrollables

The studies of business trends, economic data, and industry statistics through the process of environmental scanning are the most widely used type of study in this category. Published information is available on such uncontrollables as interest rates, level of consumer credit, corporate profits, business expansion plans, and age and income distribution trends. Federal government publications such as the *Statistical Abstract of the United States,* the *County and City Data Book,* and *Survey of Current Business,* and the *Federal Reserve Bulletin* contain a great deal of information on the uncontrollables. The *U.S. Census of Manufacturers,* published about every five years, lists the number and size of manufacturing firms by industry group (Standard Industrial Classifications-SIC Codes). The *U.S. Census of Retail Trade,* also published about every five years, provides comparable detailed information on retailers. The U.S. Department of Commerce's Office of Business Economics gathers and publishes data on the national economic outlook. The Department of Commerce also maintains field offices to help firms looking for specific types of information. The *FAA Statistical Handbook,* and *Aerospace Facts and Figures,* an Aerospace Industries Association (AIA) databook, both provide statistical data on an annual basis. In addition, aviation trade associations such as General Aviation Manufacturers Association (GAMA) and National Business Aviation Association (NBAA), universities, and aviation and business periodicals provide detailed data of value to firms doing marketing research. *Business and Commercial Aviation, Air Transport World, Commuter Air, Business Week, The Wall Street Journal,* and *Sales and Marketing Management* are sources with considerable information on uncontrollables.

MARKETING RESEARCH PROCESS

The *marketing research process* consists of a series of activities: defining the problem and research objectives, designing the research, collecting the data, preparing and analyzing the data, and presenting the findings.

Defining the Problem and Research Objectives

The first step in research requires management to carefully define the problem and clearly state the research objectives. If the president of an FBO asks the flight department manager to "Go and develop data on the charter market or flight training market," the results will be disappointing. Hundreds of subjects can be researched about those two markets. If the research findings are to be useful, they must relate to a specific problem or opportunity facing the firm. The president and the researcher, in this case the flight department manager, must agree on the problem. "How can we attract more charter business or how can we improve the student pilot retention rate?" Collecting information is too costly to allow the problem to be defined vaguely or incorrectly.

At this point, management needs to set the research objectives. A well-defined problem statement gives direction to the research and assists in the formulation of research objectives. Some form of exploratory research is often needed to both refine and clearly state the problem and set research objectives. This informal investigation will attempt to uncover as much relevant information as possible. Sources for the investigation include knowledgeable employees who are directly involved in the situation, customers and current flight students who are directly affected by the problem, and internal sales and financial reports that pertain to the situation. Questions to be answered are: What is the frequency of use of our existing charter customers? What percentage of target businesses in the area is even aware of aircraft charter services? What is their perception regarding the cost of this service? At what stage in the flight-training program are students dropping out? What are their reasons? At the end of this first step, the researcher should know (1) the current situation; (2) the nature of the problem; and (3) the specific question or questions the research will be designed to answer.

Secondary Data

Secondary data consists of information that already exists, having been collected for another purpose. Researchers usually start investigation by collecting secondary data that can be obtained from internal or external sources. *Internal secondary data* is available within the company. *External secondary data* must be extracted from sources outside the firm. Table 7–2 shows many sources of secondary data.

Primary Data

Primary data is data collected from original sources for a particular study. Some researchers, unfortunately, collect primary data by developing a few questions and finding some businesses to interview. Data gathered this way might be useless or, even worse, misleading. Instead, a plan should be created for collecting primary data. Table 7–3 shows

---

Table 7–2   Sources of Secondary Data

---

1. Internal Sources

   Profit and loss statements, balance sheets, sales analysis, sales-call reports, inventory records, maintenance job orders, pilot training records, customer complaints, and previous research reports.

2. External Sources

   a. Government publications

   (1). *U.S. Industrial Outlook* provides information on industry segments including the costs of production, sales, and employment

   (2). *Statistical Abstract of the U.S.* provides summary data on demographic, economic, and social data in the United States

   (3). *County and City Data Book* presents statistical information on cities and counties on education, employment, income, housing, bank deposits, and retail sales.

   (4). Other government publications—Census *of Population, Census of Retail Trade, Wholesale Trade and Selected Services, Census of Transportation, Federal Reserve Bulletin, Monthly Labor Review, Survey of Current Business, Vital Statistics Report, FAA Statistical Handbook,* and the *FAA Forecasts of Aviation Activity.*

   b. Associations

   There are a wide variety of associations of manufacturers, distributors, and end users. The Encyclopedia of Associations lists every major trade and professional association. These associations often collect and distribute statistics and studies on their industry. Aviation associations such as ATA, RAA, NBAA, AOPA, GAMA, ADMA, NASAO and many others listed in the World Aviation Directory provide a wealth of information.

   c. Periodicals and books

   (1). General business—*Business Week, Forbes, Fortune,* and *Duns.* Business Periodicals Index lists business articles appearing in a wide variety of business publications. Standard and Poor's *Industry Surveys* provide updated statistics and analyses of industries. *Moody's Manuals* provide financial data and names of executives in major companies.

   (2). Marketing—*Journal of Marketing, Journal of Marketing Research, Journal of Personal Selling, and Sales Management, Industrial Marketing Management, Business Marketing,* and *Sales and Marketing Management.*

   (3). Aviation trade magazines—A wide variety of trade magazines exist which collect valuable statistics as well as provide surveys and reports. Some of these are *Business and Commercial Aviation, Air Transport World, Commuter Air, Aviation Week,* and *Space Technology, AOPA Magazine, Professional Pilot,* and *Aviation Equipment Maintenance.*

   d. The Internet

   Internet browsers like Netscape Navigator and Microsoft Internet Explorer have user-friendly menus to activate an Internet search. Popular search engines like Yahoo (*www.yahoo.com*) and AltaVista (*www.altavista.digital.com*) are especially efficient tools to use in researching on the Internet. Many computerized databases and index services are now available on the Internet by governmental agencies, libraries and public firms. For example, hundreds of publications, including newspapers from around the world are available for a small user fee from Dow Jones's interactive news retrieval system (*www.djnr.com*). Using the Internet to search for relevant secondary data does offer the researcher many advantages that result in reduced research time and costs. Areas that increase productivity include research staff who

Table 7–2 Continued

can work from their own desks rather than physically going to libraries and other research locations; Web-based information is already in digital form that allows convenient downloading into electronic spreadsheets. Most reports are either free or require a small user fee, and the information desired over the Internet is often more current and more focused because search engines allow time frames to be inserted and key words that provide very specialized information.

e. Consultants

There are a number of aviation and marketing consulting firms that have data on projects of a similar nature, broad experience in the area, and/or contacts that can provide useful information.

f. Nonprofit agencies

Educational institutions including those with aviation programs. Foundations like Ford and Carnegie, the Conference Board, and the Marketing Science Institute. Local chambers of commerce and the research section of the local library.

g. Commercial sources

A.C. Nielson provides data on television audiences and magazine circulation data. Simmons Market Research Bureau provides annual reports covering television markets for a wide variety of products, including demographic data by sex, income, age and brand preferences. Stock brokerage firms can provide annual reports on businesses. Local marketing research firms can provide surveys.

Table 7–3 Plans for Primary Data Collection

Research Designs
- Survey method
- Observation method
- Experiment method

Types of Research Instruments
- Questionnaire
- Mechanical instruments

Sampling Procedure
- Sampling unit
- Sample size
- Sample group

Method of Collecting Data
- Personal interview
- Telephone interview
- Mail questionnaire
- Electronic questionnaire
- Focus group interview

---

a plan that requires decisions on research designs, types of research instruments, sampling procedures, and methods of collection.

Designing the Research

Research Design

Once the research problem has been defined and objectives stated, the next step is to select a research design. A *research design* is a master plan that specifies the methods and procedures for collecting and analyzing the required information. It is a blueprint of the research plan of action. The stated objectives of the research are included in the design to ensure that information collected is germane to solving the problem. There are three basic design techniques for descriptive and causal research: survey, observation, and experiment. The most common is the survey. In the *survey method,* information is obtained directly from individual respondents through personal interviews, telephone interviews, mail questionnaires, electronic questionnaires, and focus groups. Questionnaires are used for specific responses to direct questions or for general responses to open-ended questions.

The survey method has two main uses: (1) to gather facts from respondents, and (2) to report their opinions. The survey method's accuracy and reliability varies in each application. Generally, it is most accurate and reliable when gathering facts and less so when recording opinion.

In the *factual survey,* respondents are asked to report actual facts such as, "Have you ever used a charter flight service? During an average month, how many times do three or more employees travel to a meeting location within 300 miles of your office? How often does your present travel mode or modes cause you to remain overnight or travel long hours?" Even the answers to factual questions are subject to error because some respondents have faulty memories, are unable to generalize about personal experiences, or may give answers they believe interviewers want.

The *opinion survey* is designed to gather expressions of personal opinion and record evaluations of air travel matters. "How do you feel about the quality of flight instruction received?" "What were your instructors strengths? weaknesses?" "What was the most difficult problem you encountered in using the self-paced learning materials?" Opinion surveys share the potential errors of factual surveys and, by forcing immediate answers to questions on subjects that the respondents have not thought about lately, may produce answers not accurately reflecting real opinions. In addition to response errors, survey results can be biased by excluding people who were not contacted (they were not at home) or who refused to cooperate. The statistical differences between a survey that includes only those people who responded and a survey that also includes those who failed to respond are referred to as nonresponse error. This problem is especially important in mail and telephone surveys because of the normally low response rate. To be able to use the survey results, the researcher must be sure that those who did respond were representative of those who did not. By selecting a group of nonrespondents and then contacting them, a researcher can determine the extent of the nonresponse error.

FBOs that rely on self-administered questionnaires must be aware of the *self-selection bias* that makes the survey results less useful. Surveys left for charter customers to fill out at the end of the trip fall into this category. A man who suffered minor injury due to turbulence or had coffee spilled on his suit is more likely to fill out the questionnaire than those passengers who were indifferent about the trip. Self-selection biases the survey because it tends to be overweighted by passengers with extreme positions and underweighted by those who were indifferent about the charter experience.

The second basic design technique is the *observation method* where marketing research data is gathered not through direct questioning of respondents but by observing and recording consumers' actions in a marketing situation. For example, line personnel are observed while they greet and service customers' aircraft. Students' questions and reactions are observed during preflight and postflight discussions with instructors.

The *experiment method* is the third technique and calls for selecting matched groups of subjects, giving them different treatments, and checking on whether observed differences are significant. An FBO, for example, may run two versions of a proposed advertisement (ad A and ad B) in a city newspaper, with half the circulation-carrying ad A and the other half carrying ad B. This experiment might be used to determine the more effective advertisement in different markets, which might then be placed in all newspapers and other direct mailings in the area.

Types of Research Instruments

Marketing researchers have a choice of two main research instruments in collecting primary data questionnaires and mechanical devices.

The *questionnaire* is by far the most common instrument used in collecting primary data. It consists of a set of questions presented to respondents for their answers. The questionnaire is very flexible in that there are many ways to ask questions. Questionnaires need to be carefully developed, tested, and debugged before they can be used on a large scale.

Prior to the actual start of constructing a questionnaire, the researcher must identify the questionnaire objectives, type, and method of collecting the data. Since the purpose of a questionnaire is to formulate questions to carry out the research objectives, it is imperative that these objectives be clearly understood. Questionnaires can be either highly structured, or unstructured that allow the interviewer to probe respondents and guide the interview according to answers received. Most questionnaires are highly structured so that responses can be summarized in numbers, like percentages, averages, or other statistics. The structured format provides fixed responses to questions that elicit uncomplicated answers that the respondent is both willing and able to provide. Five methods are used to collect data: personal interview, telephone, mail, Internet and focus groups. The method selected will have a major impact on the format of the questionnaire.

In constructing a questionnaire, the marketing researcher carefully chooses the questions to be asked, the form of the questions, the wording of the questions, and the sequencing of the questions. Common errors occur in questions by including those that cannot be answered, would not be answered, or need not be answered, and by omitting questions that should be answered. Each question should be checked to determine whether it contributes to the research objectives. Questions that are merely interesting should be dropped because they lengthen the time required and try the patience of respondents.

The form of the question can influence the response and there are four types of question formats available for communicating question content: open-end, multiple choice, dichotomous, and attitude rating scale questions.

Open-end questions allow respondents to answer in their own words. Open-end questions tend to reveal more because respondents are not limited in their answers. Open-end questions are especially useful in the exploratory stage of research where the researcher is trying to determine how people think and it is not measuring how many people think in a certain way. A major disadvantage of open-end questions is that the responses are difficult to record and tabulate which makes them very expensive to process.

Multiple-choice questions offer respondents a number of alternatives. Multiple-choice questions require less interviewer skill, take less time, and are easier for the respondent to answer. Four alternatives is the standard number of choices offered, and the respondent should be informed if more than one alternative can be selected. Researchers should rotate question sequence to help alleviate *position bias,* the tendency of respondents to select the first alternative in this type of question format.

Dichotomous questions require the respondents to choose one of two alternatives. The answer can be a simple "yes" or "no," and this is the most widely used of all question formats. Like multiple-choice questions, they eliminate interviewer bias and are easy and inexpensive to tabulate.

When the objective of the survey is to measure subjective variables like attitudes, motives, and perceptions, researchers use attitude-rating scales. The two most common rating scales are the Likert scale and the semantic differential scale. The *Likert scale* allows the respondents to indicate their attitude by checking how strongly they agree or disagree with statements about products or services that range from very positive to very negative. An FBO might use the following statements in a survey concerning the quality of their maintenance department.

The use of automated telephoning maintenance scheduling greatly speeds up the process.

Strongly Disagree (1)	Disagree (2)	Uncertain (3)	Agree (4)	Strongly Agree (5)

Researchers assign weights to the alternative responses to be able to quantify the measurement of the attitude. A weight of 5 is assigned to the very positive attitude, strongly agree. The weightings do not appear on the questionnaire itself.

The *semantic differential* is a popular attitude measuring scale and consists of a product or service question that allows the respondent to select on a seven-point scale one of two bipolar words that best represents the direction and intensity of their feelings. Bipolar adjectives such as inexpensive and expensive, good and bad, or clean and dirty are examples of words that are at opposite ends of the scale. An FBO attempting to measure prospective students' attitude about the price of a proposed new flight option might ask: Check the space below that describes how you feel about the cost of the new "Simulator Based" flight program.

Inexpensive	1	2	3	4	5	6	7	Expensive

Care must be given in the wording of questions. The respondent alone fills out most surveys so there is no opportunity to ask for clarification. The semantics problem in communication is always an area that needs attention. Words mean different things to different people depending on culture and geographical location. Words to avoid include often, frequently, many, some, rush, good, fair, and poor. The researcher should use simple, specific, unbiased wording, and the questions should be tested before they are widely used. Attention should also be given to sequencing. When lead questions are simple to comprehend, interesting, and easy to answer, respondents' cooperation can be maintained throughout the questionnaire. Respondents whose curiosity is not piqued early will get discouraged, and not complete the survey. Difficult or personal questions should be asked toward the end of the interview, and they should be presented in logical order.

Mechanical instruments include eye cameras, tachistoscopes, and galvanometers. An eye camera measures how long the eye lingers on a particular item in an advertisement. The tachistoscope flashes an advertisement to a subject with a predetermined interval, then the respondent describes what he or she remembers. A galvanometer measures a respondent's interest in or emotional reaction to a particular advertisement or picture based on body response.

Sampling Procedure

A sample is a portion or subset of the population from which it is drawn. A *population* or universe is any complete group of people or businesses that share some set of characteristics. Since only a small number of people in the population are surveyed, sampling cuts costs, reduces labor requirements, and gathers vital information quickly. Marketing researchers must develop a procedure that will help them find the appropriate sample for their research. First, who is to be surveyed? This is not always obvious. In the case of the charter services survey, should the sample be made up of businesses in any industry or businesses in selected industries with over 100 employees? In rating flight instructors, should only students who have dropped out of the program be surveyed? Should all students be surveyed at a certain stage in the flight program or only after completion? The researcher must decide what information is needed and who is most likely to have it.

Second, how many people or firms should be polled? Large samples are more reliable than small samples, but a researcher does not have to survey more than 5 percent of the actual or estimated population to get accurate answers.

Third, how should the people or firms in the sample be chosen? Sampling techniques fall into two categories: probability samples and nonprobability samples. The choice of sampling technique depends on the accuracy needed, cost, available information, research objectives, and other factors.

All samples observed or surveyed during marketing research studies are either probability or nonprobability samples. A *probability sample* is one in which every person or firm in the identified population being surveyed has a known chance of being sampled. An example of a probability sample is a *simple random sample* in which all members in the population have an equal probability of being chosen to participate in the sample. If you know, for example, that there are 500 Bonanza aircraft owners in your state, and you use a simple random sample, each owner is assigned a number from 1 to 500. Then you select, using a table of random numbers, the actual owners to be questioned. When the selected population contains disproportionate demographics like gender, researchers may choose to use a *stratified random sample* to eliminate the bias. The population is divided into two subgroups, males and females, and then a random sample is selected from each group. This method is an efficient procedure where subgroups hold divergent opinions. Probability sampling prevents the researcher's bias from influencing who is sampled, because the makeup of the sample is determined not by the researcher but by chance. The use of this technique allows the researcher to assign a statistical level of confidence. A 95 percent level of confidence means that the estimate will include the true value of what is being estimated 95 percent of the time.

Researchers using *nonprobability sampling* techniques arbitrarily select the sample according to their own convenience or judgment. Examples of nonprobability sampling include (1) *convenience samples* — any population member who is available; (2) *judgment samples* — individuals who are known to have a common interest in a type of product or service; and (3) *quota samples* — population is divided into subgroups and include a certain number of individuals from each subgroup. Savings in time and money are the major advantages of using this type of sampling. It is, however, inappropriate to apply standard statistical testing to nonprobability samples.

Methods of Collecting Data

Sampling is one of the most important aspects of marketing research because it involves identifying the respondents upon which conclusions will be based. Once the population to be surveyed has been identified, a researcher will select a representative (sample) group.

Personal interviewing is the most versatile of the five methods. The interviewer can ask more questions and can supplement the interview with personal observations. Generally, the interviewer follows a questionnaire and accurately records the responses. Personal interviewing is most expensive method and requires a great deal of planning, training of interviewers, and supervision. The face-to-face interview can be plagued with inaccurate responses because the respondent desires to please or impress the interviewer, or the respondent feels obligated to give an immediate estimate rather than a carefully thought out reply.

The *telephone interview* consists of an interviewer asking questions of a respondent over the telephone. Telephone interviewing is the most widely used method of collecting data. Its popularity derives from its low cost and rapid response. The telephone is less versatile than is face-to-face interviewing. The interviewer is less likely to be able to ask detailed open-ended questions on the telephone than in a face-to-face interview, but at the same time its anonymity allows the interviewer to ask questions that could not be asked face to face. A telephone interview is also limited because members of the sample may not have telephones, may have unlisted numbers, may not be available, or simply may not care to be interviewed.

The *mail questionnaire* may be the best method for reaching persons who will not give personal interviews or who may be biased by interviewers. It consists of a questionnaire sent to the respondent that is completed and returned by mail to the researcher. The primary problem with mail questionnaires is the low percentage of returns that result in a possibility of nonrespondent error. Nonrespondent error is the possibility that the people who did respond are different from the people who did not respond; therefore, the data would not represent the population.

With the growing number of available e-mail addresses, the *electronic questionnaire* is becoming more popular. Researchers can purchase a list of e-mail addresses of persons or businesses that fit the intended survey population and send them a questionnaire. Follow-up is inexpensive but researchers have found that many people do not have the technical skill to put the e-mail questionnaire into a "reply and edit" mode to type their answers in the appropriate places. Many companies use their home pages on the Web to post questions. Respondents can type their answers into drop-down menus or blank spaces.

Focus group interviewing consists of inviting from six to ten persons to gather for a few hours with a trained interviewer to discuss a product, service, organization, or other marketing topic. The qualified interviewer has objectivity, knowledge of the subject matter and general aviation industry, as well as understanding of group dynamics and consumer behavior. An unqualified interviewer's results can be worthless or misleading. The interviewer encourages free and easy discussion among the participants, hoping that the spontaneous discussion will disclose attitudes and opinions about a situation that would not be revealed by direct questioning. The comments are recorded through note taking or tape recording and are subsequently studied.

Analyzing the Information

After the information has been gathered, it must be analyzed. The purpose of this step is to extract the important information and findings from the data. A variety of analytical software programs are available ranging from simple descriptive statistics (means, medians, proportions) to complex multivariate analyses. Coverage of these topics is beyond the scope of this discussion. The researcher computes such statistics as frequency distribution and averages in preparing the findings. Tables, figures, and charts are often used to illustrate the findings.

Presenting the Findings

The last step in the marketing research process is presenting results, which are usually in the form of a written report, to management. It is recommended that the researcher not overwhelm management with numbers and sophisticated statistical techniques. The researcher should present relevant findings that are useful in major marketing decisions facing management.

KEY TERMS

Marketing research
Market measurement studies
Market potential
Sales potential
Marketing research process
Secondary data
Internal secondary data
External secondary data
Primary data
Research design
Survey method
Factual survey
Opinion survey
Self-selection bias
Observation method
Experiment method
Questionnaire
Open-end questions
Multiple-choice questions

Dichotomous questions
Likert scale
Semantic differential scale
Mechanical instruments
Sample
Population
Probability sample
Simple random sample
Stratified random sample
Nonprobability sample
Convenience samples
Judgment samples
Quota samples
Personal interviewing
Telephone interview
Mail questionnaire
Electronic questionnaire
Focus group interviewing

REVIEW QUESTIONS

1. What is the purpose of marketing research? Give several examples of market measurement studies. Distinguish between market potential and sales potential. Give an example of a market research study involving a competitive situation.
2. Why are defining the problem and determining the research objectives so critical for effective market research? Distinguish between primary and secondary data. Give four examples of external secondary data sources. Which is the most commonly used research design? Distinguish between a factual and an opinion survey. How does the observation method differ from the experiment method?
3. What is the most common instrument used in collecting primary data? In questionnaires, distinguish between open-end, multiple, and dichotomous questions. Give examples of a Likert and a semantic differential scale used to measure attitudes. What is a sample? What questions must be determined in developing an appropriate sample? Differentiate a simple random sample and a stratified random sample. Describe three methods of collecting primary data. Differentiate probability samples and nonprobability samples and give an example of each.

SUGGESTED READINGS

Evans, Joel R., and Barry Berman. *Marketing* (6th ed.). New York: Macmillan, 1994.

Perreault, William D., Jr. and E. Jerome McCarthy, *Basic Marketing* (13th ed.). Burr Ridge, IL, Irwin/McGraw-Hill, 1999.

Posner, Gerald, and Emil J. Walcek. "Implement Lead Follow-up System for More Business Marketing Sales," *Marketing News,* October 1985, p. 22.

Sandhusen, Richard L., *Marketing* (3rd ed). Hauppauge, New York, Barron's Educational Series, Inc., 2000.

Strauss, Judy and Raymond Frost. *E-Marketing* (2nd ed). Upper Saddle River, NJ. Prentice Hall, 2001.

Zikmund, William G. *Business Research Methods* (6th ed). Orlando, FL. Harcourt, 2000.

Chapter 8

Transportation Needs Assessment

OUTLINE

Business-to-Business Marketing
   Nature of Organizational Customers
   Unique Characteristics of Organizational Markets
   Buying Process
Travel Analysis
   Amount and Nature of Travel
   Travel Dispersion
   Type and Frequency of Airline Service
   Potential Aircraft Utilization
Types of Business Use Aircraft
   The Single-Engine Airplane
   The Light Twin
   The Medium Twin-Piston
   The Turboprop
   The Pure Jet
   The Helicopter
Equipment Selection Process
   Trip Distances and Number of Passengers
   Use and Users
   Environmental Aspects of Routes and Destinations
   Frequency of Trips
Performance and Financial Considerations
   Performance Analysis
   Financial Analysis
     Cost of Ownership
     Cost of Use
     Cash Flow Analysis
     Financing Aircraft
     Present Value
     Sales Application/Break-even Analysis
Summary

OBJECTIVES

At the end of this chapter you should be able to:

Explain the business-to-business market and give several examples.

Describe the following demand patterns in the organizational market: direct channels, derived demand, and inelastic demand.

Name and explain the three types of organizational purchase decisions.

Describe the buying center concept and identify and explain the traditional five roles of the members.

Describe the four major areas of investigation in a business aircraft travel analysis.

Distinguish between geographic, volume, and time dispersion.

Identify the three levels of airline service and how each relates to business aircraft use.

Describe five types of business aircraft use.

Highlight the five principal factors to consider in the equipment selection process.
Summarize the major considerations in the cost of owning an aircraft.
List the principal expenses under fixed and direct operating (variable) costs of use.
Explain the significance of a cash flow analysis.
Determine principal and interest payments using a loan amortization schedule.
Describe the use of present value in aircraft purchase decisions.
Explain break-even analysis as a sales tool for business aircraft.

BUSINESS-TO-BUSINESS MARKETING

The focus of this chapter is the travel analysis which is a powerful marketing tool used to assist nonusers of business aircraft to work through an in-depth transportation needs assessment. The prospect for this study is Champions Stores, Inc., a large sporting goods retailer, with its home office located in Montgomery, Alabama. To be effective in selling business aircraft, marketers must understand the nature of organizational markets, their unique demand, and purchasing characteristics.

Nature of Organizational Customers

Business-to-business marketing is a term that pertains to buying and selling goods and services between businesses. The products purchased are either for resale or for use by the purchasers in their day-to-day business operations. This type of marketing is far different from marketing products to household consumers. The term customer is used to describe business purchasers, whereas consumer commonly refers to purchases by individuals for their own or family needs. Business-to-business marketing is occurring when Cessna sells an aircraft to one of its dealers, and it also occurs when the dealer in turn sells the airplane to Southern Equipment & Supply Corporation for executive travel. When Office Depot sells office supplies to the local FBO, it is engaging in business marketing.

Unique Characteristics of Organizational Markets

When formulating strategies and developing marketing mixes, marketers will find that characteristics and demand patterns of the organizational market are different from the consumer market. Organizational markets tend to be more geographically concentrated than consumer markets. Many industries are located in specific areas of the country. Most aircraft manufacturers are located in Wichita, Kansas, and California's Silicon Valley is the home of the computer chip industry. This concentration of customers does offer marketers efficiency opportunities especially in promotion and distribution.

The potential number of customers in the organizational market is considerably less than in most consumer markets. Gulfstream Aerospace Corporation, a wholly owned subsidiary of General Dynamics, can sell its next-generation Gulfstream, the GV-SP to fewer than 1,500 organizations throughout the world. When segmenting this market, marketers must evaluate carefully whether there is a sufficient number of homogeneous businesses to make the target market a legitimate business opportunity. The small number of potential customers also stresses the need to develop strong customer relationships to ensure repeat business.

Demand patterns in the consumer market differ from demand patterns in the organizational market in the following areas:

1. *Direct channels* — Business buyers traditionally purchase directly from the manufacturer, rather than from a middleman as consumers do. This is especially true for products that are complex and expensive. Manufacturers will often use industrial distributors to sell and distribute products that are inexpensive and frequently purchased as accessories and supplies.
2. *Derived demand* — Manufacturers buy products to be used in the production of business-to-business goods and consumer goods. Thus, as the demand for these finished goods increases, the demand for components will also increase. For example, the need to purchase passenger seats by Raytheon Corporation is driven by the demand for their airplanes.

3. *Inelastic demand*—The demand for business goods tends to be inelastic, which means that the demand for a good or service is not sensitive to changes in price. This is opposite to elastic demand where there are significant changes in quantity demanded when there is a meaningful change in price. This inelastic demand characteristic occurs because the organizational product is often only a fraction of the total price of the final product of which it is part and will have little effect on the product's total price. Demand will not change with a change in price in the short run because it is difficult for manufacturers to modify production equipment that has been designed to handle specific component parts. The demand for corporate aircraft tends to be inelastic because the importance of purchase price is mitigated by the potential purchaser's need for speed, cabin configurations, capacity, avionics, and cost of use.

Buying Process

As businesses today strive for increasing productivity, the buying function in organizations has taken on added importance as a profit center. It is now viewed that investment in goods and services can be strategically managed and controlled to improve profitability and help maintain a competitive advantage. This changed perception of accountability of the purchasing function can spell opportunity for aircraft marketers who understand the change and are able to craft presentations to fit this new emphasis.

Organizational buying decisions are highly variable, ranging from routine decisions, which require little time and effort, to complex decisions entailing in-depth negotiations between the salesperson and the company. Organizational purchase decisions can be categorized into three types: straight rebuy, modified rebuy, and new buys. *Straight rebuys* are simply reorders. The products ordered are usually standard products that are routinely used and maintained in inventory. Straight rebuys would be similar to your purchasing bread and milk at the convenience store on your way home from school or work. *Modified rebuy* situations are essentially straight rebuy situations that require some additional information due to a change in price or specifications, or dissatisfaction with the present supplier. *New buys* involve products or services never considered before by the company. There is a high degree of risk and cost associated with this category of purchase decision. The investigation into the purchase of a business aircraft by Champions Stores fits into this category.

The increasing accountability and complexity of the purchasing function has led to the development of the *buying center concept* that pulls together key individuals who provide different expertise needed to make quality major purchases. The size of the group will vary from company to company and the membership will also change depending upon the product being purchased. In the business aircraft purchase decision, one of the members will certainly be the chief pilot. Different members in the buying center have different roles in the decision. The five traditional roles in the buying center are users, gatekeepers, influencers, deciders, and buyers. *Users* initiate the process by identifying the need, and generally will be users of the product or service. *Gatekeepers* have the responsibility and authority to control information, and the role is often played by the purchasing manager. Gatekeepers can determine which suppliers have access to the organization and its decision makers. *Influencers* are usually technical employees who have defined the criteria the purchase must meet. Sometimes the influencer is an outside consultant with expertise in the specific area under investigation. The *decider* is the executive who has the authority to select which product to purchase. Sometimes, the decision to purchase is not made by one individual, but by a group of individuals selected to participate as an executive committee. The *buyer* is the employee who actually has the authority to place the order with the selected vendor. It is usually an executive in the purchasing department. To be successful in selling to businesses, salespersons must be able to identify the various members of the buying center and understand their roles. This is oftentimes a challenge. The buying center concept emphasizes the importance of comprehending the corporate culture in marketing to organizational buyers.

With this overview of business-to-business marketing, the aircraft salesperson approaching Champions Stores will understand and appreciate the uniqueness of the market and the marketing strategies required to be successful.

TRAVEL ANALYSIS

The potential use of a business aircraft is based on its ability to make travel more efficient by either reducing travel time or increasing productivity for a given amount of time. *Travel analysis* is an evaluation of a firm's current travel modes and the amount and nature of travel presently undertaken. There are four major areas of investigation that guide an aircraft sales representative in attempting to determine if a business could use a company airplane. They are (1) amount and nature of travel; (2) travel dispersion; (3) type and frequency of airline service; and (4) potential aircraft utilization.

Knowing the *amount and nature of travel* is needed to determine whether there is enough travel to make a business aircraft feasible and if it is the kind of travel for which a private aircraft is suited. *Travel dispersion* categorizes the trips in terms of distance frequency, and volume of passengers. This information is useful in further defining a firm's travel patterns and determining whether these patterns are suitable for business aircraft use. The *type and frequency of airline service* is studied to determine the amount of time being spent traveling and whether a business airplane could reduce that time. The culmination of this study is to estimate the total annual utilization of a business aircraft for the firm.

Amount and Nature of Travel

Evaluating the possible use of a business aircraft begins with estimates about the overall amount of travel within the organization and the potential growth of such travel. However, this kind of evaluation can be more of a limiting factor than a justifying one. In other words, just proving the existence of a large quantity of travel is not necessarily sufficient evidence that the company could use an aircraft economically, as some trips may not be suited to business aircraft use.

The *amount and nature of travel* are determined by reviewing a prospective customer's past travel records. Depending upon the size of the firm and amount of travel, an average month or quarter is generally selected for analysis.

Take a hypothetical company called Champions Stores, Inc. based in Montgomery, Alabama, and look at its travel record for one month. Assume that the month selected is representative of travel throughout the year and therefore, will be used to make annual projections.

An analysis of the travel within this sample period made by a sales representative indicated that 19 individual round trips were made to 13 separate destinations (see Table 8–1). The trips were made by 16 employees including 4 executive officers, 3 department managers, 6 buyers, and 3 other administrative personnel. The information covers travel primarily by employees based at the company's home office in Montgomery.

Records indicate that the company's primary modes of travel are by automobile and scheduled airline. Costs of transportation were not provided. In addition, charter service has been utilized in the past. Poor airline service to company destinations and the emergency need to travel were listed as reasons for using charter service. The number of passengers on these charter flights was two to three people.

Approximately 50 percent of the Champions Stores' travel is scheduled (20 percent one to two weeks in advance and 30 percent scheduled two to five days in advance). Scheduled trips lend themselves to business aircraft usage due to the flexibility of scheduling thereby accommodating many more trips on the aircraft. The remaining 50 percent of travel, however, was listed as on-demand. For on-demand or emergency-type trips the availability of an immediate, fast transportation mode is an obvious necessity.

Travel Dispersion

An analysis of an organization's geographic time and volume dispersions of business travel is very important to a salesperson in determining the need for a corporate aircraft.

Table 8-1 Potential Aircraft Utilization—Champions Stores, Inc.

	Average No. of Passengers	Total Round Trips (1 Mo)	Total Annual Round Trips	Number One-Way Miles	Total Miles
From Montgomery, AL to:					
1. Atlanta, GA	2	2	24	160	7,680
2. New Orleans, LA	2	2	24	275	13,200
3. Greenville, SC	2	1	12	280	6,720
4. Charlotte, NC	4	1	12	330	7,920
5. Greensboro, NC	3	1	12	480	11,520
6. Mexia, TX	3	1	12	610	14,640
7. Fitzgerald, GA	3	1	12	180	4,320
8. Dallas, TX	2	1	12	600	14,400
9. London, KY	1	1	12	400	9,600
10. El Paso, TX	2	1	12	1200	28,800
11. Jacksonville, FL	2	2	24	325	15,600
12. Blount, TN	2	1	12	275	6,600
From New Orleans, LA to:					
Sherman, TX	2	1	12	475	11,400
13. Jackson, MS	2	2	24	180	8,640
Dallas, TX	2	1	12	450	10,800
TOTAL		19	228*		171,840*

*Since the potential total annual miles is likely to exceed any one aircraft's capabilities, this amount has been reduced by 25 percent to reflect trips which will probably be made by other travel modes due to scheduling conflicts, maintenance requirements, and so forth. This reduction results in a potential 171 round trips and 128,880 miles or 475 to 700 hours of flying time, depending on the aircraft selected.

The object of this analysis is to examine the environment within which a company plane would operate and includes the cities served, distances, and schedules to be maintained. Such an examination reveals valuable information regarding the efficiency of past travel and the probability of improving the efficiency.

Geographic dispersion of business destinations partially indicates whether or not a company aircraft can be effectively substituted for present travel (i.e., if present travel is primarily between large metropolitan cities with frequent and direct airline service, chances for substantial savings in productive man-hours may be minimized). *Volume dispersion* is the number of people traveling and indicates the relative importance of each destination. *Time dispersion* is the interval between trips taken by various individuals to the same destinations or destinations having proximity. This information helps determine the potential for combining company trips with the aircraft, which enables the aircraft to be used more efficiently. From this investigation of travel dispersion comes a clear picture of existing travel patterns, how a business aircraft could fit into these patterns, and how a company would benefit from using a company plane.

Champions Stores' travel destinations are located, for the most part, in the southeastern part of the United States, within the states of Texas, Georgia, Florida, Louisiana, Kentucky, North Carolina, Tennessee, Alabama, and Mississippi. The most distant destination within the company's primary marketing area is about 610 miles. Airline trip data shows the longest trip undertaken to be approximately 1,200 miles to El Paso, Texas.

An examination of the company's past business travel indicates that it is not seasonal.

Assume, for the example that travel will occur with equal frequency throughout the year. Checking the trips made by Champions Stores shows that the most frequently visited cities were Atlanta, New Orleans, Jacksonville, and Jackson, Mississippi. The frequency of air travel to other destinations will undoubtedly increase with the availability of a company aircraft. Most companies find that passenger load factors tend to grow as executives learn how to use the aircraft to their advantage.

Type and Frequency of Airline Service

Airline services provide a valuable business tool. However, these services have undergone considerable changes since deregulation in 1978. The trend has been for certified carriers to concentrate more on service to large hub cities and less to smaller cities. Conversely, business continues to expand from large metropolitan areas to smaller cities. When the present mode of travel is primarily scheduled airlines, the kind of airline service available to destinations determines the practicality of a business aircraft.

Three distinct classes of airline service exist: direct, indirect via connections, or none. The frequency of service will further modify the direct and indirect levels. If there are both frequent and direct airline flights to a company destination, a business aircraft's only measurable advantage may be its ability to transport company travelers at a savings in total direct costs. If service is infrequent and/or indirect, a company plane can significantly reduce travel time, airport layovers, and overnight stays, as well as take advantage of direct cost saving through group travel. If no airline service is available to a company destination, the alternative is usually either automobile travel or a combination of airline and rental car. An aircraft can generate substantial savings depending upon the proximity of the destination to one of 6,000 public airports not served by scheduled airlines.

An examination of Champions Stores' travel indicates that the majority of the company's travel is to cities with airline service. A significant portion of these cities, however, (50%) requires making connections due to lack of direct flights. Airline service is divided into the following classes:

1. Frequent Direct   6%
2. Frequent Indirect   25%
3. Infrequent Direct   13%
4. Infrequent Indirect   25%
5. No Airline Service   31%

Potential Aircraft Utilization

The projected use of a company airplane is an integrated function of all the elements discussed thus far. It is relevant to address both the amount of use the aircraft would receive and the ways in which it would be employed.

Measuring the potential for a company-owned aircraft requires some subjective analysis since the dates of individual trips are not known; potential grouping of such trips to estimate use of the aircraft involves an approximation of an average passenger load. Based on the data in the example, this average passenger load is estimated to be two to three people. In all probability, the passenger load will increase as the company finds new ways of using the aircraft to its advantage. Table 8–1 outlines the potential utilization for a company aircraft over a one-year period. As shown in this table, a conservative estimate indicates potential for 228 round trips covering approximately 171,840 miles. Although the aircraft will be based at the company headquarters in Montgomery, it would be used for several trips originating from the company's distribution warehouse in New Orleans. These figures have been included in the potential.

The amount of utilization indicated above is likely to be in excess of any single aircraft's capabilities. This is because of the large number of potential flying hours and round trips. With this type of utilization, conflicts will occur about availability of the aircraft for other business trips, necessary maintenance, and the like. For these reasons, Champions Stores may wish to consider a second aircraft at some time in the future after initial acquisition.

For this analysis, the annual potential has been reduced by 25 percent to more accurately reflect realistic figures for one aircraft. This reduction allows for such things as occasional maintenance and scheduling conflicts. The 25 percent reduction results in a more conservative potential for 171 round trips covering approximately 128,880 miles annually. Annual hours of utilization are determined by the following formula:

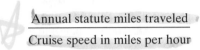

$$\frac{\text{Annual statute miles traveled}}{\text{Cruise speed in miles per hour}}$$

For a used twin-engine turboprop aircraft being considered by the management of Champions Stores, the annual hours of utilization would be 128,880/283 = 455 hours over approximately 200 flight days.

TYPES OF BUSINESS USE AIRCRAFT

Let the model fit the mission is the rule in selecting a business airplane. Recognizing this, manufacturers offer numerous models, including fixed-wing or helicopter, single-engine or multiengine, piston or pure jet, and each can be tailored to meet the specific requirements of a firm. "Tailored" is an appropriate word for the business airplane. Just as there are wardrobes for different occasions, there are airplanes for different uses. Like a wardrobe, once the proper airplane is selected, it can be "altered" to fit specific uses with the selection of avionics equipment, seating arrangements, wheels or floats, or both, in cargo or passenger configuration, or both.

The purpose of this section is briefly to review the categories of airplanes that a firm may consider. The next section will focus on the equipment selection process and how it relates to the hypothetical example of Champions Stores, Inc.

The Single-Engine Airplane

Most small businesses start with a single-engine airplane. Many times this beginning is because of an employee who uses an airplane the way other employees use their automobiles. From this use comes recognition of the benefits that are translated to other employees in similar situations.

The small business owner, the professional, or one of the key employees of a relatively small business usually flies an aircraft in this category personally. A single-engine airplane's range is utilized best in frequent trips in the 1,000 to 1,200 mile limit although it is capable of extended flight. A long flight requiring frequent business stops en route also can be handled well by the single-engine model. It has the capability to fly into and out of most airports, including grass strips. Since the traveler usually flies it, the cost of a professional pilot is saved.

Despite their relatively small size and low price tag, they are capable of carrying the most sophisticated instruments and communications equipment available, such as satellite-based Global Positioning Systems (GPS) and a variety of all-weather flight control and guidance equipment.

Since most of the flights are usually over short-stage lengths, the speed of one model over another frequently is not the most important consideration. Over a 300-mile distance, for instance, an airplane traveling at 150 miles an hour will take two hours to complete the trip, while one having a speed of 180 miles an hour will do it just 20 minutes faster.

Turbocharging in engines raises both speed of the airplane and its ability to operate at higher altitudes. This makes possible some "over-the-weather" flying and permits taking advantage of more favorable winds. These factors make longer distance travel more practical and begin to place a premium on speed when greater distances are a consideration. Convertibility of most single-engine models to cargo configuration enables carrying displays, samples, and similar equipment.

There are many modern piston-engine aircraft now in production to serve this entry-level business market. Cessna, New Piper, Raytheon, Mooney, and Commander all offer a number of different and well-proven single-engine aircraft for business use.

Cessna has reentered this market with an updated version of the 172 Skyhawk and the 182 Skylane. Piper's single-engine offerings include the Warrior III, Archer III, Arrow, and the high performance pressurized Malibu Mirage. Raytheon, which markets its aircraft under the Beech trade name, continues to offer the very popular Bonanza line.

A new single-engine piston aircraft will have a price tag of from around $160,000 to $850,000, depending on engine and avionics selected.

The Light Twin

More than an additional power plant is added on the twins. Utility increases many times over. In the twin field, night and weather travel takes on added meaning. While seating capacity and payload of the light twin does not vary much from the high performance single-engine models, the added power plant expands the use during darkness and adverse weather. De-icing equipment may be added for convenience and safety.

Seating capacity ranges from four to six. The light twin sometimes is flown by a professional pilot and sometimes by the individual businessperson who is making the trip. Since a flight over long distance is more likely to encounter varying weather conditions, the twin increases mobility for the company whose travel profile includes trips to different parts of the country.

Light twin-engine piston aircraft can range from about $450,000 to more than $850,000, depending on equipment installed. Piper's Seminole and Seneca V models and the popular Beech Baron 58 are excellent choices for economical acquisition and operating costs as compared to turbine aircraft.

The Medium Twin-Piston

When the company has a number of people traveling over the same routes, when in-flight conferences are required, or when all-weather operations are a routine matter, a medium twin is appropriate.

Customizing interiors to fit the specific needs and desires of the company begins in this range. High density seating in some models provides airline comfort for up to 10 or 12 passengers. Foldout tables, side facing seats or swivel seats make a mobile conference room. Divans offer seating for several, or bedroom comfort allows an executive to arrive at his destination thoroughly refreshed. A professional crew usually flies the medium twins. Their all-weather capability, range, and speed give great flexibility for short and long-distance flights.

The Turboprop

The turboprop provides the best of two worlds—the lower costs of propeller-driven airplanes with some advantages of the jet. Falling into the medium twin category, the turboprop usually is professionally flown. Its jet power and pressurization makes it well suited for medium and long trips at average speeds over 300 mph, yet it operates efficiently on short runs. This versatility is demonstrated by the Pilatus PC-12. With a 330 cubic foot pressurized cabin volume, the PC-12 can carry nine passengers over 1,600 nautical miles with VFR reserves and 1,400 nautical miles with IFR reserves.

While the cost of jet fuel is less per gallon than gasoline, consumption per hour of flying is more, but greater distances are covered. Initial purchase price is higher than for piston powered-twins but is still under the cost of a pure jet. The turboprop can fly into and out of smaller airports than the pure jet. As U.S. industry moves away from larger cities, the need to use smaller airports can be an important consideration. This is a major consideration for a company, like Champions Stores.

A number of foreign and domestic manufacturers offer turboprops designed for the business market. The leading twin-engine turboprop aircraft is Raytheon's Beech King Air Series with five different versions and the King Air's larger cousin, the 1900 Airliner.

The Pure Jet

At the top of the business fleet is the pure jet, with speeds well over 500 mph, it rivals the best of the airliners, and in flexibility, the best of the piston-powered aircraft. The mission of the business jet is to compress great distances into short expanses of time. Almost invariably professionally flown, the pure jet moves corporate executives to widely scattered points and returns them in a matter of hours. The environment of the jet is high altitude. For this reason it is most efficient for medium and long distance travel. Because of its speed, the jet, probably more than any other business airplane is used most frequently to drop off and pick up individuals over wide distances.

Business jets have been designed in a variety of sizes and capabilities to meet the needs of various target markets. The smallest, which carry from four to eight passengers, are certificated for single-pilot operation. These smaller jets can be purchased from $2–$4.5 million, again depending on the avionics and other equipment selected. The new VisionAire Vantage single-engine jet and the twin-engine Sino Swearingen SJ30-2 are examples of relatively new choices available in this entry jet market. The majority of business jets in operation today seats eight to ten passengers in a typical business configuration and operates efficiently over transcontinental or transatlantic distances. The largest market share in this niche is Cessna's Citation family. Other manufacturers offering models for this market segment include Raytheon's Beechjet 400A, Learjet's models 31, 60, and 45. Israel Aircraft Industries (IAI) produces the six-nine passenger Astra SPX and the Galaxy can be configured as a corporate shuttle and carry up to 18 passengers.

As more and more larger corporations turn to business aviation as a tool to increase productivity, a new class of business jet—the super midsize aircraft—is beginning to emerge. These aircraft are larger, but not as large as the so-called large class of jet. Their attractiveness is that they allow large teams of employees to be transported economically over longer ranges than standard midsize jets.

The IAI Galaxy, Raytheon Hawker Horizon, Cessna Citation X and the Dassault Falcon 2000 and Falcon 50EX are examples of this new class of jets. The Galaxy, for example, has a cabin that is 6 ft. 3 in. high and 7 ft. 2 in. wide. Powered by two Pratt & Whitney Canada PW306A engines, it has a range of 3,602 nautical miles at a Mach 0.82 cruise speed. The Falcon 2000 is powered by two CFM International CFE738-1-1B turbofans that produce 5,918 lb. thrust each. The cabin is 26 ft. 3 in. long, 6 ft. 2 in. high and 7 ft. 8 in. wide.

Large business jets are gaining popularity with global corporations that need intercontinental travel. Nonstop flights such as Chicago-Tokyo, New York-Abu Dhabi and London-Honolulu are now well within the capability of such aircraft as the Boeing Business Jet (BBJ), the Gulfstream V and GIV-SP, and the Bombardier Global Express.

The Boeing Business Jet is based on the popular 737-700 airliner fuselage joined to the 737-800 wings and landing gear. The BBJ cabin has 807 square feet of space and can accommodate about 20 people in a business setting.

The Gulfstream V has a modified and lengthened Gulfstream IV fuselage with a new and more efficient wing and larger tail surfaces. The 90,500-pound aircraft features a 50 foot 1 inch cabin that is 6 ft. 2 in. in height and 7 ft. 4 in. in width. The aircraft can maintain a 6,000 ft. cabin altitude up to an operating altitude of 51,000 ft.

The Bombardier Global Express carries up to 19 passengers and has a range in excess of 6,500 nautical miles. This range will give a company the ability to fly from New York to Tokyo nonstop. This range is due to Global Express' third-generation supercritical airfoil that gives it a Mach 0.88 cruise speed.

The Helicopter

Corporate use of helicopters is not new. The first civil helicopters were placed into use right after World War II. Corporate reliance on helicopters has expanded dramatically, growing with the machine itself. Today, Robinson, Bell, Sikorsky, Schweizer, Agusta, Eurocopter, and MD Helicopters produce highly efficient business helicopters.

The business applications of helicopters are almost endless, including herding livestock;

moving bank papers and checks; harvesting seed cones from the tops of coniferous trees for propagation of the best species without damage to the trees; timely movement of work crews and material for construction projects; and aerial survey/photography, to name just a few.

However, the most visible business application of helicopters is for the reliable, rapid transport of corporate executives. Many CEOs who regularly fly in helicopters refer to them as "time machines," because of the great savings in executive time made possible by the helicopters. The concept of "portal-to-portal" travel really pays off in convenience and time when one is able to eliminate ground travel by limo or taxi to and from the airport. Many firms have corporate helipads adjacent to their headquarters. The passengers walk to the helicopter and, ideally, fly directly to a heliport within walking distance of their destination.

When it is not practical to make the entire trip by helicopter, there is still a considerable advantage in using a corporate helicopter to shuttle passengers between the airport and their destination. There really aren't any typical business helicopters. They range from the compact but practical Robinson R-22, which is the world's smallest commercial helicopter, to the 44-passenger Boeing "Chinook." Some of the purely corporate machines are especially outfitted with plush upholstery, swivel chairs, and environmental control systems, and they are flown by a two-pilot crew. Others are much more austere, and some are flown by the CEO. However, the helicopters in use today are "third generation" helicopters which incorporate design feature that have been proven safe, reliable, and practical during many millions of hours of helicopter flight.

EQUIPMENT SELECTION PROCESS

The choice of a business aircraft must follow a detailed and comprehensive evaluation of a company's travel requirements, its current financial position, and intangible benefits which accrue through aircraft ownership. An aircraft's capability compared to the company's need must also be evaluated. The rule of thumb most commonly used is that the aircraft should be no more than is needed to satisfy most of the company's requirements. An aircraft with substantially greater capabilities than the company needs may have an adverse impact on long-term ownership.

As with any management decision, selecting suitable equipment is a matter of determining the relative importance of each of several factors, and then making a choice which best fits the resulting profile. There are normally five principal rational factors upon which to base an aircraft and equipment selection analysis. While all of these factors are important, the degree of importance of each factor rests with specific travel requirements.

1. *Trip Distances and Number of Passengers.* This information will help decide the size, range, and payload requirements that must be met. This factor is also important in selecting necessary or desirable equipment.
2. *Use and Users of the Aircraft.* Expected users of the airplane will affect type of aircraft, seating arrangements, performance requirements, and interior appointments. Special uses, such as cargo needs, will also affect the selection.
3. *Environmental Aspects of Route and Destinations.* The need for special systems, such as pressurization and turbo charging, runway performance requirements, and navigational package, is often predicted by these factors.
4. *Frequency of Trips.* This information helps qualify the relative importance of other factors. In addition, trip frequency requirements aid in equipment decisions, such as avionics and convenience options.
5. *Financial and Performance Considerations.* In any equipment selection decision, this information provides a rationale by properly balancing needs against costs.

The selection process is still subjective to a certain degree. Equipment such as cabin stereo systems, interior appointments, and convenience accessories remain largely a matter of personal taste.

Table 8–2 Frequency Distribution of Trip Distances

Distances	Number of Trip Legs* 100%	Number of Trip Legs* 75%	Percent	Cumulative Percent
0–100	0	0	0	0
101–200	120	90	26	26
201–300	96	72	21	47
301–400	96	72	21	68
401–500	72	54	16	84
501–600	24	18	5.3	89.3
601–700	24	18	5.3	94.7
701–800	0	0	0	94.7
801–900	0	0	0	94.7
901–1000	0	0	0	94.7
1000–1100	0	0	0	94.7
1101–1200	24	18	5.3	100
	456**	342**	100	

*Leg = Point A to Point B.
**The 342 annualized trip legs were determined by reducing the original 456 annualized total by 25 percent. (228 round trips × 2 = 456 trips legs × 75% = 342 trip legs.) The 342 legs would translate into 171 round trips.

Trip Distances and Number of Passengers

An examination of all potential trips likely to be undertaken by Champions Stores' aircraft indicates that the one-way distances range from approximately 160 to 1,200 miles. Table 8–2 is a frequency distribution of these one-way distances. As shown by this distribution, an aircraft capable of traveling 1,200 miles nonstop could meet 100 percent of the trip legs. However, 94.7 percent of all trip legs fell within the 101 to 700 mile range. Therefore, it would appear more realistic to give primary consideration to those trips falling within the 101 to 700 mile range. The company aircraft should have a nonstop range of at least 700 miles.

Based on examination of travel data, an average passenger load is two to three passengers. However, it is still necessary to establish what the maximum passenger density might be for Champion Stores. For example, assume that the salesperson in the interview with company personnel learned that the maximum number of people who have traveled together on past business trips was six. The company does not anticipate the maximum passenger requirement to increase with use of a business airplane. In aircraft selection, primary consideration should be given to aircraft with a maximum of eight seats (six passengers plus two pilots).

Use and Users

Champions Stores' airplane will be used primarily for transporting company executives and other personnel to various business destinations including company-owned stores and warehouses as well as to major cities such as Jacksonville, Dallas, New Orleans, and Atlanta where buyers make substantial purchases. The possibility of flying in manufacturers' representatives for meetings with company personnel also exists. Based on the number of potential hours of utilization and safety of corporate executives, the services of qualified, full-time pilot and copilot will be used in this case.

Environmental Aspects of Routes and Destinations

A review of the flight routes, which will be flown by the company, indicates the en route terrain, for the most part, is not mountainous. A flight altitude of 5,000 feet above mean sea level would be adequate to meet the minimum enroute IFR (Instrument Flight Rules) requirements for this area of the country.

Other types of terrain that will be encountered involve rough, densely wooded areas (North and South Carolina) and swampy areas (Florida and Louisiana). Additional flights over water may occur in the Gulf coast area. With the amount of travel that Champions Stores will be doing, low ceilings and fog, as well as icing conditions may be encountered occasionally by the aircraft. The information obtained indicated that a significant portion the company's travel (50%) is on an "on-demand" or emergency nature. This type of travel would probably require some night flying. In addition, speed in reaching the destination may be important.

Since an analysis of environmental conditions and seating requirements indicate the need for a twin-engine aircraft, for this example, only a twin-engine aircraft will be recommended. High altitudes en route on longer legs are anticipated, so a pressurized aircraft will be needed. Similarly, if high altitudes en route or landing at high elevation airports were anticipated, the airplane will have to have the additional power to operate in the rarefied air at high altitudes.

While our examination of the environmental aspects of routes and destinations does not necessarily indicate the need for pressurization or extra engine power, the company might prefer aircraft with these features because of concern for the comfort of its passengers.

Frequency of Trips

For this example, a potential for 171 round trips was demonstrated, accounting for approximately 455 hours of utilization annually. Since this indicates an above average utilization rate, it will be recommended that the aircraft selected have IFR capability, full de-icing equipment for all-weather capability, dual communications, navigational equipment, (including co-pilot instrument panel) and autopilot. The prevailing weather experienced in this part of the country would add validity to this recommendation.

Performance and Financial Considerations

To complete the equipment selection process, the performance characteristics of various aircraft under consideration must be examined in relation to costs. Within the criteria thus far established, a salesperson might now select three or four models that appear to meet the company's needs.

Performance Analysis

The technical performance capabilities of the aircraft under consideration must be fully evaluated. These include such factors as short runway performance, high temperature operating characteristics, payload-range capability, speed, and operational reliability.

Every aircraft has a given ability to land and take off on runways of varying lengths. This capability is certificated by the FAA and is shown in the flight manual for the aircraft. Normally, the shorter the runway, the smaller the load the aircraft can carry—either passengers or fuel. On extremely short runways, the load restriction may be so great as not to permit landing or takeoff at all. For example, small twin-engine propeller aircraft can operate on runways of 2,000 to 3,000 feet, whereas bigger and faster turbine (turboprop and jet) aircraft may require 5,000 to 7,000 feet, especially at higher temperatures.

An aircraft performance analysis must therefore take into consideration the length of runways offered at all airports that the company might wish to use. Then those lengths must be compared to the performance capabilities of the aircraft under consideration. This comparison would indicate what restrictions, if any, might affect the company's operations at particular airports.

Air temperature and airport altitude can also affect an aircraft's performance. The higher the temperature and the higher the altitude, the greater the runway length that is needed under specific payload (fuel and passenger) conditions. Conversely, with a constant runway length, higher temperatures or altitudes will tend to restrict the load the aircraft can carry. When an aircraft carries more fuel to travel longer distances, it invariably needs more runway space in which to take off.

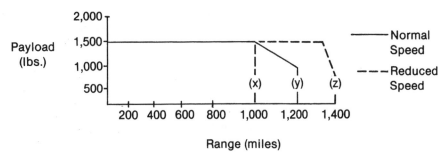

Figure 8–1. Payload Range Chart

Another performance consideration is the *payload range capability* of the aircraft. Each aircraft has, according to its particular weight, fuel capacity, engine type, and performance characteristics, a capability to carry a certain payload over a certain distance. A typical payload range chart is shown in Figure 8–1. This figure indicates that the aircraft can carry a maximum payload for a certain number of miles (point x). If additional range is desired, payload must be reduced to carry the necessary fuel load. The maximum range with a reduced payload would be represented by the point y. Some variation to this performance data would result from differing cruise speeds; an aircraft is normally able to fly farther if it travels at slower speeds, as indicated by the dashed line to point z.

When the payload-range capabilities of the different aircraft under consideration are known, the company is in a position to determine which aircraft will meet its earlier requirements, namely, the amount of fuel and the number of passengers to be carried.

The payload-range capabilities must also be compared to the runway lengths the company plans to use to determine what actual limitations may exist—either runway length restrictions or payload-range restrictions.

Financial Analysis

The final factor in the equipment selection process is the cost of the various aircraft under consideration. Normally, the costs arising from ownership of the aircraft are considered separately from those costs associated with its operation.

Cost of Ownership

Three principal things determine the *purchase price* of an aircraft: the base price, the price of the customized interior desired, and the avionics equipment (radios, navigational instruments, radar, and similar items) chosen. The costs associated with avionics equipment and customized interiors can add 30 percent or more to the base price of an aircraft. The prospective company may consider an outright purchase, a financial purchase or lease arrangement. These various options will be considered further in chapter 10.

Used aircraft may also be considered, often at prices substantially under a new aircraft cost. Of course, with a used aircraft, it is important to analyze the maintenance records of the aircraft and its engines. Total hours on the engines is also a major consideration if the number is high. However, a good used aircraft may be bought at a considerable price reduction over a new model without a substantial difference in performance or passenger convenience.

The *status of production* must be examined relative to cost. Each aircraft undergoes a significant evolutionary development after its initial design has been adopted. Thus, improvements to most operating criteria are made through increased engine power, increased weights, longer cabins, and increased speed and range. Prior improvements and the potential for additional improvements must be considered, recognizing that some of the future improvements may or may not be readily incorporated in an earlier model.

A forecast of the future disposal or trade-in value of the aircraft must be made to determine the net aircraft cost to the company (purchase price less disposal value). According to AIRCRAFT VALUE REFERENCE 2001, Volume 2, published by VREF

Publishing, Inc. in Shawnee Mission, Kansas, a five-year-old high performance single-engine aircraft had a disposal value of 90 percent, a five-year-old light twin, 86 percent, and a turboprop 73 percent.

Reliability and maintainability must be investigated with regard to cost. The broad spectrum of business aircraft includes a wide variety of technical and mechanical complexity in engines, avionics, and aircraft systems. Each step in overall complexity causes incremental changes in (1) amount of spare parts required, (2) technical proficiency of maintenance personnel, (3) cost of maintenance, (4) sophistication of test and maintenance equipment, and (5) overall thoroughness of the maintenance program.

Thus, maintainability is tied directly to the cost of ownership—what the company can support. A more sophisticated aircraft may require more attention for equal reliability. The local resources (either within the company or available at the airport) must be surveyed to determine if reliability might be compromised because of local inadequacies.

For smaller aircraft operation, maintenance can be accomplished almost entirely by a qualified maintenance repair station, where there would be little or no requirement for the company to keep facilities for its own mechanics. The larger and more sophisticated flight operation usually requires substantial maintenance manpower, many spare parts with room to store them, machine shop, testing facilities and perhaps an avionics shop. Also, there should normally be major hangar facilities, often an exclusively used hangar.

The cost of owning an aircraft affects the amount of income taxes paid. Airplanes are sold to individuals, sole proprietors, partnerships, and corporations. *Tax considerations* exist for all of these kinds of business enterprises even though the rate of taxation might differ. A business organized as a sole proprietorship or as a partnership does not pay taxes as such, but the individual proprietors or partners reflect their share of the profits or losses on personal income tax returns. Rates vary according to the individual's taxable income. A corporation is a legal entity that pays its own income taxes.

As Table 8–3 indicates, corporations today pay federal income taxes on a marginal rate basis starting at a minimum of 15 percent and with a maximum of 39 percent. Corporations are also liable for state income taxes and in Alabama, the rate is a flat 5 percent. To reflect these combined rates, all financial calculations and analysis in chapters 8 and 9 involved with the proposal for the purchase of a business aircraft by Champions Stores, a combined federal and state income tax of 39 percent will be used. Tax rates are an incentive for companies to purchase and operate aircraft. For example each dollar of deductible expense by Champions Stores will actually cost the corporation about 61 cents.

One of the more important features of the Tax Reform Act of 1986 was the improved depreciation allowance. Aircraft used by corporations and individuals for their own business transportation, are in the five-year class for determining the depreciation expense.

Table 8–3   Corporate Federal Income Tax Rates

Taxable income over	But not over	The tax is:			Of the amount over
$0	$50,000			15%	$0
$50,000	$75,000	$7,500	+	25%	$50,000
$75,000	$100,000	$13,750	+	34%	$75,000
$100,000	$335,000	$22,250	+	39%	$100,000
$335,000	$10,000,000	$113,900	+	34%	$335,000
$10,000,000	$15,000,000	$3,400,000	+	35%	$10,000,000
$15,000,000	$18,333,333	$5,150,000	+	38%	$15,000,000
$18,333,333				35%	0

Table 8–4   Depreciation and Book Value—$2,363,800 Business Aircraft—Six Years

End of Year	Depreciation Tax Basis***	Depreciation %	Depreciation Expense	Tax Savings (39%)	Book Value**
0					$2,363,800
1	$2,363,800	20%*	$ 472,760	$184,376	1,891,040
2	1,891,040	40%	756,416	295,002	1,134,624
3	1,134,624	40%	453,850	177,002	680,774
4	680,774	40%	272,310	106,201	408,464
5	680,774	40%	272,310	106,201	136,154
6	680,774	20%*	136,154	53,100	0
Totals			$2,363,800	$921,882	

*First and last mid-year averaging conventions apply
**Book Value equals cost of aircraft minus accumulated depreciation
***Depreciation tax basis equals aircraft cost plus State Sales tax

The allowable deductions will be computed using a 200 percent declining balance method. For five-year class property, this accelerated method doubles the straight-line rate (20 percent) thus providing additional tax savings during the early years. The depreciation schedule automatically switches from double declining to straight-line at the end of the third year. The depreciation calculations still include a half-year convention, which in effect treats the aircraft as if it were placed in service at mid-year. The new system extends the half-year convention to all dispositions of property. In other words, half a year depreciation will be allowed for the year in which the aircraft is sold. The effect of this is to spread the deduction for aircraft one year beyond the name of its class-six tax years for five-year property. Table 8–4 illustrates book value and depreciation for the proposed twin-engine turboprop aircraft for Champions Stores.

At the time of resale, the gain realized between the aircraft sales price and the current book value (called depreciation recapture) is treated as ordinary income.

The tax benefits of ownership directly reduce the actual cost of the aircraft. Table 8–5 *Capital Recovery Guide* illustrates how much capital Champions Stores will recover through tax savings and disposition of the aircraft after six years. The monthly net cost of ownership is only $6,613 over the 72-month period.

Cost of Use

The *cost of use* includes two types of expenses: fixed costs and direct operating expenses (variable costs). *Fixed costs* include those expense items which are incurred regardless of the amount of flying performed. Examples include crew salaries, recurrent training, insurance, and hangar rental or tie-down expense. *Direct operating expenses or variable costs* are the actual expenses of fuel, maintenance, and miscellaneous expenses that occur as a direct result of hours flown. Some aircraft components have predetermined or expected normal service lives that can be used to calculate an hourly cost of operation figure. For example, aircraft engines must be completely overhauled after say 2,100 to 3,600 hours depending on the engine. Other components like airframe, propeller and avionics are accounted for by conservative estimates of their maintenance requirements.

Tables 8–6, and 8–7 show the major items included under fixed and direct operating expenses for a twin-engine turboprop aircraft under consideration by Champions Stores. The figures are only illustrative. The actual costs would vary due to differences in accounting methods as well as differences in the cost of such items as fuel, labor services, engine overhaul, remanufactured engines, and avionics. In addition, the manner in which the aircraft is flown and used will have a direct effect on the actual hourly cost of use (number of hours flown annually, power settings used, type of airports encountered, environmental conditions, experience of the pilot.)

Table 8–5   Capital Recovery Guide

Twin-Engine Turboprop Aircraft—Six Year Analysis
Aircraft Acquisition Cost

Purchase Price		$2,230,000
State Sales Tax @ 6%		$133,800
Total		$2,363,800
Depreciation Expense		$2,363,800
Resale Value @ 71%		$1,583,300

Six Year Capital Recovery

Tax savings (39% corporate tax rate)

Depreciation	$921,882	
Total Tax Savings		$921,882
Disposal of Aircraft*		
Resale value	$1,583,300	
Less Taxes on Sale	$617,487	
Net Proceeds From Sale		$965,813
Total Capital Recovered		$1,887,695
Total Acquisition Cost		$2,363,800
Total Capital Recovered		$1,887,695
Net Cost of Ownership—Six years		$476,105
Per Year		$79,351
Per Month		$6,613

*If the aircraft is traded in, rather than sold outright, the taxes due on sale will be deferred. The depreciation basis on the new aircraft will be decreased by the trade-in value since the book value is zero.

Cash Flow Analysis

One the most frequently misunderstood and misused business terms is cash flow. It is often mistaken for operating income, revenue, or profit. A profitable FBO will need substantial inflows of cash from outside sources to keep it generating profit objectives. You can't spend profit — you only spend cash. Accurate cash management is as critical to a successful long-term business venture as accurate fuel management is for a long distance flight. Performing a cash-flow analysis by aircraft salespersons is essential for not only selling aircraft to corporations with in-house flight departments, but for all types of business aircraft acquisition. This includes company owned with operations contracted to another company, wet or dry lease, and fractional ownership. These variations will be discussed in detail in Chapter 10. Every prospect must understand thoroughly the impact the airplane will have on cash flows each year it is used.

When a company like Champions Stores is considering the purchase of a business aircraft, it is concerned with more than the initial purchase price and the amount of down payment. The net, after tax cost of operating the aircraft projected on a year-to-year basis for the entire period of ownership is of vital importance. This may turn out to be the key factor in the buy/not buy decision. The *cash flow analysis* example in Table 8–8 demonstrates this net after tax cost for Champions Stores.

Experience has demonstrated that the cash flow statement can accomplish the following benefits for the salesperson:

Table 8–6   Fixed Costs for a Twin-Engine Turboprop Business Aircraft

Expense Category		Estimated Cost Per year
Crew Salaries		
	Captain	$60,000
	Co-Pilot	$39,840
	Benefits	$29,952
Hangar Rental		$24,147
Insurance (1)		
	Hull (Physical Damage Coverage)	$8,920
	Single Limit Liability—25 Million Per Occurrence	$5,500
	Guest Voluntary Settlement Coverage	$1,000
Recurrent Training		$12,600
Computerized Maintenance Program		$1,850
Aircraft Modernization		$8,920
Refurbishing		$8,280
Weather Service		$2,235
	Total Annual Fixed Costs	$203,244

(1) Hull coverage rate 40 cents per $100 of value
    $500,000 GVS coverage
    $5,000 medical payments coverage at no charge

Table 8–7   Direct Operating Expenses (Variable Costs) for a Twin-Engine Turboprop Business Aircraft

Expense Category		Estimated Cost Per Hour
Fuel (1)		$259.00
Maintenance Labor (2)		$104.00
Parts—Airframe/Engine/Avionics (3)		$115.00
Engine Restoration (4)		$127.00
Propeller Overhaul		$3.00
Miscellaneous Expenses		
	Crew Expenses	$135.00
	Landing/Parking Fees	$6.00
	Supplies/Catering	$32.00
	Total Direct Operating Costs Per Hour	$781.00

(1) Fuel costs $2.29 per gallon
    Gallons per hour   113
(2) Maintenance labor costs per hour $69
    Maintenance hours per flight hour   1.5
(3) Engine Model PT6A-42
(4) 3600 hours

Table 8–8   Twin-Engine Business Aircraft Purchase Cash Flow Analysis

Input Data:

Aircraft Cost	$2,230,000	Federal Income Tax Rate: 39%		Monthly Payment: $29,697	
State Sales Tax @ 6%	133,800	Finance Rate: 9.25% APR	8 Years	Inflation Rate: 3%	
Total Acquisition Cost	$2,363,800	Money Value: 18%		Annual Hrs of Utilization: 455	

Expenditures	Year 0	Year 1	Year 2	Year 3	Year 4	Year 5	Year 6
Fixed Costs		$203,244	$209,341	$215,622	$222,090	$228,753	$235,615
Down Payment (15%)	$354,570						
Balance of Purchase	$2,009,230						
Principal Payment		$177,926	$195,101	$213,933	$234,582	$257,225	$282,053
Interest Payment		$178,436	$161,262	$142,430	$121,780	$99,137	$74,309
Loan Balance Payoff							$648,410
Taxes Due on Sale							$617,487
Operating Expenses		$355,355	$366,016	$376,996	$388,306	$399,955	$411,954
TOTAL EXPENDITURES	$2,363,800	$914,961	$931,720	$948,981	$966,758	$985,070	$2,269,828
CASH SOURCES							
Aircraft Loan	$2,009,230						
Disposal of Aircraft (71%)							$1,583,300
TOTAL SOURCES	$2,009,230						$1,583,300
TOTAL CHANGE (before taxes)	$(354,570)	$(914,961)	$(931,720)	$(948,981)	$(966,758)	$(985,070)	$(686,528)
TAX REDUCTIONS							
Fixed Cost		$79,265	$81,683	$84,093	$86,615	$89,214	$91,890
Depreciation		$184,376	$295,002	$177,002	$106,201	$106,201	$53,100
Interest		$69,590	$62,892	$55,548	$47,494	$38,663	$28,981
Operating Expenses		$138,588	$142,746	$147,029	$151,439	$155,982	$160,662
TOTAL TAX REDUCTION		$471,819	$582,283	$463,672	$391,749	$390,060	$334,633
CHANGE IN CASH FLOW	$(354,570)	$(443,142)	$(349,437)	$(485,309)	$(575,009)	$(595,010)	$(351,895)

TOTAL CASH FLOW	$(3,154,372)	Cost Per Mile (Average Annual Cost)	$525,729	$4.08
Cost Per Hour	$1,155	(Cruise Speed × Annual Hrs)	283 × 455
Net Present Value Cost	($1,963,285)	Cost/Seat Mile (Cost Per Mile)	$4.08	$0.68
		(Passenger seats)	6

1. Adds a professional touch to the sales presentation.
2. Assists the salesperson in dealing with the company's financial concern.
3. Satisfies the prospect's need for detailed cost information and net present value analysis; and
4. Helps move the sales process toward a favorable conclusion.

The significance of a cash flow analysis is that it shows the potential user an accurate estimate of the total after-tax cost of owning a business aircraft and projects the changes in the company's cash flow year by year. The following definitions are relevant:

1. *Fixed Cost* (Table 8–6) Annual fixed costs have been increased by an inflation factor of 3 percent.
2. *Loan Balance Payoff* = $648,410 because there are two years remaining on the loan contract.

3. *Taxes Due at Sale* are $617,487 that represents a corporate tax rate of 39 percent times the selling price in excess of book value.
4. *Depreciation Method* is double-declining balance.
5. *Operating Expenses* (Table 8–7) annual direct operating costs have been increased by an inflation factor of 3 percent.
6. *Disposal of Aircraft* is based on the present resale value of a similar six-year-old aircraft in relation to its original retail price. (71 percent).
7. *Total Cash Flow* indicates the total after tax cost of ownership over the six-year period.
8. *Cost Per Hour* is the average annual after-tax cost per hour of owning and operating the twin-engine turboprop aircraft. ($3,154,372)/2,730 hours.
9. *Net Present Value Cost* is derived from the money value rate of 18 percent. It represents the actual amount the aircraft will cost, based on borrowing money and keeping the company's funds free for reinvestment in the company at its average return on investment rate (Table 8–9).

Financing Aircraft

Attractive low-rate, long-term financing on up to 100 percent of an aircraft purchase price is essential in marketing aircraft. Some lending institutions have eliminated the down payment requirement, offer variable interest rates based on one or two percentage points over prime, and with terms of 12 years or more. A major general aviation manufacturer recently unveiled the following finance plan for several of its aircraft: Interest free for the first six months, 4.9 percent interest for the following year, interest at the prime rate for the succeeding year, and on the balance of the loan term, floating prime rate plus 2 percent. This type of creative financing illustrates that aircraft manufacturers generally play down lending activities and use incentive finance programs to stimulate sales.

The twin-engine turboprop aircraft being proposed to the management of Champions Stores is being financed over an eight-year period at 9.25 percent annual percentage rate (APR). After making a 15 percent down payment of $354,570, a fixed-rate loan for 8 years of $2,009,230 was arranged using Table 8–10, the following finance data for the cash flow analysis can be determined:

Monthly Payment	$1.478022 \times \$20,092.3 = \$ 29,697$
1st Year Annual Interest	$8.880811 \times \$20,092.3 = \$178,436$
1st Year Principal	$8.855453 \times \$20,092.3 = \$177,926$
Loan Balance Payoff	$32.271553 \times \$20,092.3 = \$648,410$

Table 8–9 Present Value Factor

Period	8%	10%	12%	14%	15%	16%	18%	20%
1	.926	.909	.893	.877	.870	.862	.847	.833
2	.857	.826	.797	.769	.756	.743	.718	.694
3	.794	.751	.712	.675	.658	.641	.609	.579
4	.735	.683	.636	.592	.572	.552	.516	.482
5	.681	.621	.567	.519	.497	.476	.437	.402
6	.630	.564	.507	.456	.432	.410	.370	.335
7	.583	.513	.452	.400	.376	.354	.314	.279
8	.540	.467	.404	.351	.327	.305	.266	.233
9	.500	.424	.361	.308	.284	.263	.226	.194
10	.463	.386	.322	.270	.247	.227	.191	.162

Note: These present value factors are rounded to a greater degree than is done by a computer; consequently, a calculation done manually may vary somewhat from the computer's result.

TABLE 8–10   Sample Loan Amortization Schedule 9.25% Monthly-Fixed Rate

Years 8   Monthly Payment 1.478022

Year	Annual Interest	Annual Principal	Year Ending Balance
1	8.880811	8.855453	91.144547
2	8.026046	9.710218	81.434329
3	7.088775	10.647489	70.786840
4	6.061036	11.675229	59.111611
5	4.934094	12.802170	46.309441
6	3.698376	14.037889	32.271553
7	2.343380	15.392884	16.878669
8	0.857595	16.878669	0

This Table shows how a $100 loan at 9.25 percent is paid off over an eight-year period by a level monthly payment. The Table also shows the total annual interest and principal payments and the year-end balance each year of the loan.

Present Value

The concept of present value is widely used by companies as they approach investment decisions. Financial comparisons among types of aircraft cannot be made accurately without it because this technique will tell the purchaser how much the aircraft will really cost over a predetermined period.

Money that will be received in the future is presently worth considerably less than its stated value. The promise of $10,000 twenty-five years from now sounds good, but if 10 percent per annum could be earned on the investment, then this promise is now worth less than $1,000. The present value of future payments is the reciprocal of compound interest.

This reciprocity of compound interest and present value is illustrated by the following example:

Today	5 Years Later
$1,000 Compounded @ 9%	=$1,538.62

$1,538.62 is the present value of $1,000 in five years

The present value of money due in the future will differ from company to company. It depends upon the rate of return (money value or discount rate) that is either available to the company or that the company has the ability to earn internally. This explains why a company can borrow for use in its business and still make money. The loan from the financial institution requires a lower rate of interest than can be achieved by the borrower.

Present value is used as the final step in the cash flow statement. This statement illustrates the net cash flow for each year Champions Stores owns and operates its aircraft. The present value of each of these net cash flows is determined and summarized; the resulting figure is the net present value (Table 8–11). This dollar figure tells the company how much money must be invested now at the company's stated money value to earn enough cash to meet all of the aircraft expenses as they come due each year. The net present value figure also brings six years of expenses to a single figure. Prospective aircraft purchasers can use net present value during the evaluation stage to compare the total expense of owning and operating comparable aircraft.

Sales Application/Break-even Analysis

The travel analysis is a powerful means of assisting a firm in analyzing the feasibility of purchasing an airplane for employee travel. In situations where the prospective firm is going to use the airplane to generate revenue, the break-even analysis is more appropriate. The aircraft salesperson will find it useful to calculate the prospective buyer's break-even point—that point at which the cost of operating the aircraft exactly matches the

Table 8–11 Net Present Value of Cash Flow Twin-Engine Turboprop Aircraft
Money Value Rate 18%

Year	Actual Cash Flow		Factor	Present Value
0	$(354,570)	×	$1.000	$(354,570)
1	$(443,142)	×	$0.847	$(375,341)
2	$(349,437)	×	$0.718	$(250,896)
3	$(485,309)	×	$0.609	$(295,553)
4	$(575,009)	×	$0.516	$(296,705)
5	$(595,010)	×	$0.437	$(260,019)
6	$(351,894)	×	$0.370	$(130,201)
Total Cash Flow	$(3,154,372)			$(1,963,285)

revenues generated through such activities as light instruction or charter. Since business firms must do better than just break-even, this analysis will help determine revenue levels sufficient to generate a predetermined profit objective.

To apply break-even analysis, two types of costs must be determined. Fixed costs are those whose level remains unchanged when hourly usage changes (monthly interest on aircraft loans, insurance, crew salaries, general overhead allocation). Direct operating expenses are those that do change in proportion to changes in aircraft use, and include gas, maintenance and hourly charges for maintenance reserves. To illustrate break-even analysis, a sales proposal based on a twin-engine aircraft used for charter purposes by a hypothetical company, Seacoast Charter, Inc., would be based on the following data:

Annual total fixed cost = $203,244
Charter revenue per hour = $1,200
Direct operating expenses per hour = $781

Mathematically, Seacoast Charter's total revenue hours required to break-even can be determined by using the following formula:

$$\text{BE (hrs)} = \frac{\text{Total Fixed Costs}}{\text{Charter Revenue Hr.} - \text{Direct Operating Expense Per Hr}}$$

$$= \frac{\$203,244}{\$1,200 - \$781}$$

$$= \quad 485 \text{ hours}$$

Break-even in hours is the point where total fixed and direct operating expenses equal total charter sales revenue. Either raising or lowering the hourly charter rate can change the break-even hours. If the competitive environment would allow an increase of $50.00 per hour to $1,250, the new break-even hours would be reduced by 52 hours to 433 hours.

The president of Seacoast Charter would also like to know how many charter hours the firm must sell to make $24,998 in the next 12 months. Using the following formula, the aircraft salesperson would be able to provide him with the answer.

$$\text{Hours required} = \frac{\text{Total Fixed Costs} + \text{Profit}}{\text{Charter Revenue Hr.} - \text{Direct Operating Expense Per Hr}}$$

$$= \frac{\$203,244 + 24,998}{\$1,200 - \$781}$$

$$= 545 \text{ hours}$$

To further assist Seacoast Charter in planning, the break-even concept can be used to determine the number of charter customers required over the next 12 months to meet the $24,998 profit objective. A review of past sales records indicates that the typical charter flight lasted 7.5 hours. Since 545 total hours were required, and the average hourly usage per charter flight was 7.5, then about 73 customers (545 hrs/7.5 hrs) must be sold during the next year.

In spite of some limitations, break-even analysis can be a powerful tool for aircraft salespersons to use in marketing business aircraft to corporations that will use the aircraft commercially to generate profits.

SUMMARY

At this point, it has been determined by performing a travel analysis that a need for a business aircraft exists. Costs have been examined as part of the selection process. The cost of ownership may be small or it may be so large as to make the aircraft prohibitive. A decision is required by management, but first, other elements must be added. The problem facing the purchaser of a business aircraft is how to relate the "What does it do for me?" or worth of the aircraft to its cost. This relationship between product worth and product cost is known as the value analysis or costs versus benefits analysis. This subject will be taken up in the next chapter.

Break-even analysis was presented to convince those prospects that are purchasing an aircraft, not for employee travel, but a capital asset that will provide them an adequate return on the investment by using the airplane for revenue generation.

KEY TERMS

Business-to-business marketing	Environmental aspects of routes and
Direct channels	destinations
Derived demand	Frequency of trips
Inelastic demand	Financial and performance considerations
Straight rebuys	Payload-range capability
Modified rebuy	Cost of ownership
New buys	Purchase price
Buying center concept	Status of production
Users	Trade-in value
Gatekeeperes	Reliability and maintainability
Influencers	Tax considerations
Decider	Depreciation
Buyer	Capital Recovery Guide
Travel analysis	Cost of use
Amount and nature of travel	Fixed costs
Travel dispersion	Direct operating costs
Type and frequency of airline service	Compound interest
Geographic dispersion	Present value
Time dispersion	Break-even
Trip distances and number of passengers	Cost per mile
Use and users of the aircraft	Cost per seat mile

REVIEW QUESTIONS

1. Describe business-to-business marketing.
2. Identify and explain three business market characteristics and demand patterns that are different from the consumer market.
3. Differentiate the three types of buying decisions made by organizations and explain the buying center concept.
4. What is the purpose of a travel analysis? How can the amount and nature of a firm's

travel be determined? What is the object of the travel dispersion analysis? Distinguish between geographic, volume, and time dispersion. Describe the general trend of airline services since deregulation. What are the three levels of airline service and how do they relate to business aircraft use?

5. What is meant by the statement "let the model fit the mission?" Distinguish between the single-engine and light twin-engine aircraft in terms of performance. What are the major criteria for stepping up to a medium twin? When would the use of a corporate helicopter be prudent?

6. Trip distances and number of passengers help determine aircraft requirements? What is the significance of determining the use and users of the aircraft? Describe what is meant by the environmental aspects of routes and destinations. Why is it important to determine the frequency of trips?

7. What are the major factors to consider in a performance analysis? What is a pay-load-range chart? Discussion the importance of status of production, trade-in value and reliability and maintainability in selecting an aircraft. Describe the significance of depreciation expense to a corporation.

8. Distinguish between cost of ownership and cost of use. Give some examples of fixed costs of use and direct operating costs. Determine the cost per mile for an aircraft whose annual cost is estimated to be $50,000; cruise speed 200 mph; and estimated 500 annual flying hours. If this aircraft has five passenger seats, what is the cost per seat mile?

9. What are the major factors to consider in a performance analysis? What is a pay-load-range chart? Discuss the importance of status of production, trade-in value and reliability and maintainability in selecting an aircraft. Describe the significance of depreciation expense to a corporation

10. Identify three benefits of a cash flow analysis to the sales process.

11. Use the Sample Loan Amortization Schedule to determine the monthly interest on an eight-year 9.25 percent loan for $450,000.

12. Compound interest is the reciprocal of present value. Explain how prospective aircraft purchasers use net present value analysis in their decision making process?

13. Describe how break-even analysis can be used as a sales tool.

Chapter 9

Value Analysis: Costs versus Benefits

OUTLINE

OBJECTIVES

At the end of this chapter you should be able to:

Describe the purpose of the value analysis in the evaluation of business aircraft.

Distinguish between tangible and intangible benefits.

Compare the use of a business aircraft flown by a hypothetical company over a route with direct and nondirect airline service.

Explain the importance of load factor when comparing the use of a business aircraft with the airlines.

Define value per man-hour (VMH) and describe two ways it can be determined.

Explain the "en route productivity" factor.

List five intangible benefits of business aircraft use.

INTRODUCTION

Before getting into the specifics of value analysis, which is the major focus of this chapter, it might be valid to draw the following analogy between the purchase of a business aircraft and a computer. If a company uses a computer for payroll accounting or inventory control, it will be difficult to make its substantial investment in the equipment payoff. The computer can handle such routine tasks more quickly, possibly more accurately and with fewer people, but the direct savings or benefits are not likely to be considerable. On the other hand, if the company uses the computer creatively, it can uncover the new world of e-business that would allow them to continuously optimize business activities through digital technology. E-business involves attracting and retaining the right customers and business partners along with digital communication, e-commerce, and online research. A computer might completely streamline supply chain management, business intelligence, customer relationship management, and the everyday tasks of order entry, purchasing, invoicing, and inventory control. This could not only allow the company to handle and retain present customers more efficiently, but also to capture new ones. Without belaboring the point, the computer, when used imaginatively, can completely revamp a company's traditional ways of doing business and open up numerous new opportunities for economic growth.

So it might be with a business aircraft. It would be short sighted to use a plane simply to do what a company is now doing, only in a faster and cheaper manner. If a plane is to justify itself as a worthwhile investment, it must also make a major contribution to the firm's economic growth and profitability.

VALUE ANALYSIS

Value analysis is a quantitative comparison of actual business trips taken by company personnel, selected from the sample travel data developed by the sales representative. The comparison depicts the differences in travel costs, travel time, overnight stays, and value per man-hour required between present travel modes and the business aircraft under consideration. In the form presented, this comparison will substantiate the relative equivalence of the airplane's direct costs versus present travel costs. It will, in addition, provide a clear indication of the level of manpower savings that are likely to result through the utilization of a business airplane on these trips. This quantitative comparison is commonly referred to as the *tangible benefits* because they determine fairly accurate revenue producing values.

Looking at these tangible benefits first, it is not too difficult for an experienced sales representative or analyst to demonstrate the savings, if any, that can be made over airline and automobile expenses when a company uses its own aircraft. It is considerably more difficult to compute the dollars gained as a result of saving the time of key personnel.

There are several factors to consider when determining just what "saved time" is worth. One is comfort and its relationship to morale and productivity. The frustration involved in fighting heavy automobile traffic, plus standing in line at check-in counters or gates, or waiting to make connecting flights can substantially reduce a person's energy and morale. The more discomfort and inconvenience that is eliminated, the better a person is apt to perform.

Saving time for key personnel is not only important from a pure clock-time standpoint. Just one trip a week that saves five hours adds up to a saving of 22 hours a month, 264 hours a year. This is the equivalent of 33 additional working days a year. Whether the individual is a salesperson or chairman of the board, these four and one half additional weeks of productive time can be calculated to illustrate dollar savings to the company.

The value of the savings, together with the accompanying intangible benefits, should in theory, offset the annual cost in order to justify acquisition of a company aircraft. *Intangible benefits* are those that cannot be wholly quantified in terms of dollars saved or revenue produced. For example, more contacts with the firm's customers and improved morale are intangible benefits. Simply stated, business aviation helps a company obtain maximum productivity from its two most important assets—people and time. See Table 9–1.

Sample Trips

For this analysis, three round trips typical of those that might be taken by the hypothetical company, Champions Stores, Inc. have been chosen for comparison. For example, Table 8–2 in Chapter 8 shows a total of 342 trip legs including 90 in the 101 to 200 mile range in the 75% column. It is assumed that most of these trips were made by automobile. Trip A is representative of this group. Trips B and C represent distances of 401 to 500 miles, and 601 to 700 miles. Other trips could have been selected, but these are considered to be typical for this analysis. Trip B includes indirect airline service with a connecting flight in Atlanta and Trip C includes indirect airline service with a connecting flight in Dallas/Ft. Worth to Waco, TX. A rental car will be used to travel the 40 miles to Mexia, TX.

Trip A—Montgomery, AL to Fitzgerald, GA and Return
Trip B—Montgomery, AL to Greensboro, NC and Return
Trip C—Montgomery, AL to Mexia, TX and Return

Basic Assumptions

The following assumptions have been made for the sample trips:

1. All cost comparisons assume a passenger load of three key persons traveling together.

Table 9–1 Time and Cost Comparison for Trip A—Montgomery, AL to Fitzgerald, GA and Return (Hypothetical)

	Time Comparison	
	Elapsed Time (Round Trip)	
	Automobile	**Business Aircraft**
Office to Airport.	—	:30
Terminal Boarding	—	:30
En Route Time (1)	9:00	1:16
Deplaning Time	—	:30
Airport to Office		:30
Total	9:00	3:16

(1) The use of two lane highways is required between Columbus, GA and Fitzgerald, GA.

Cost Comparison—Round Trip			
		Automobile	**Business Aircraft**
Travel—En Route	(1)	$76.86	$1,466.85
RONs	(2)	256.20	—
Rental Car	(3)	—	31.72
Value per Man-Hour (VMH)	(4)	2,639.25	799.54
Total Cost		$2,972.31	$2,298.11

(1) Automobile—360 miles @$.35 per mile (Less 39% tax savings).
   Business aircraft—1.27 hrs. @ $1,155/hr.
(2) RONs—$140/person × 3 persons (Less 39% tax savings).
(3) Rental car—$52/day—unlimited mileage (Less 39% tax savings).
(4) (4) VMH = $\dfrac{2.5 \times \$92,000}{2,000 \text{ hrs.}}$ (av. salary) = $115.00/hr.

VMH Summary

Automobile

Total Time: $115.00 × 9 hrs. × 3 persons		$3,105.00
En Route Time: 9 hrs.—15% productivity credit (3,105.00 × .15)		−465.75
		$2,639.25

Business Aircraft

Total Time: $115.00 × 3.27 hrs. × 3 persons		$1,128.15
En Route Time: $115.00 × 1.27 hrs. × 3 persons	$438.15	
Less 75% productivity credit	.75	−328.61
		$799.54

2. Airline schedules and fares are obtained from www.travelocity.com.

3. Time allowed for enplaning and deplaning airline flights is 30 minutes and for the business aircraft, 15 minutes. Airline enplaning and deplaning time can vary considerably depending upon the size of the airport and whether or not baggage was checked.

4. Time required for scheduling connecting flights is 50 minutes between flights.

5. The business aircraft has a cruising speed of 283 mph and an operating cost of $1,155 per hour (from the cash flow statement, Table 8–8).

6. Hotel/motel expenses are $95 per night per person and meals and tips for those individuals remaining overnight (RONs) are $45 per person.
7. Rental car expenses are based on $52 per day with unlimited mileage.
8. Costs associated with company automobiles have been set at $.35 per mile.

Trip A—Montgomery, AL to Fitzgerald, GA and Return

A time and cost comparison for Trip A is shown in Table 9–1. On a pure direct cost comparison, (automobile $333.06 vs. business airplane $1,466.85) such a trip would probably not justify a business aircraft, except for the substantial savings in time that results in less fatigue for the travelers. However, when comparing the value of each person's time, the importance of business aircraft is clearly demonstrated. The emphasis here is on value, not simply what a person earns per hour. Several formulas have been developed to evaluate the worth of executive time. The most commonly used is the *Value per Man-Hour* (*VMH*) which is determined by dividing the average salary of the travelers multiplied by a constant productivity factor by annual work hours (i.e., average salary $\times$ 2.5/2,000). The 2,000 annual work hours number is obtained by multiplying 40 hours per week times 50 weeks per year. In practice, only 1,500 hours per year are actually productive hours and might be a more realistic denominator in the formula. The standard 40-hour work week assumption is modified by some who feel that highly placed executives/managers are more apt to work 50–55 hour weeks which produce 2,500 to 2,750 annual hours.

A second method of determining the value of executive time increases the productivity factor as annual salary increases. It is generally accepted that raises in salary are justified by considerably greater increases in the individuals contribution. This method assumes that most salaried employees spend about 2,000 hours per year on the job of which about 1,500 hours per year are truly productive to the company's profitability. As Table 9–2 indicates, employees in the $100,000 salary range have a value per hour of $1,250.

The National Business Aviation Association, Inc. in its Management Aids article "The Management Accountability Factor" introduced the *en route productivity* factor. This interesting concept addresses the question: "How much can executives accomplish while traveling in a commercial airliner or a business aircraft?" The productivity of a group of executives abroad a commercial airline is extremely low due to (1) lack of work facilities; (2) hesitancy to discuss sensitive corporate matters; (3) distractions resulting from the mass handling of passengers; and (4) impossibility of conducting a meeting with two or more persons. Because of these reasons, the estimated value of the time on an airline trip or automobile trip is only 15 percent. This credit of 15 percent will be used in determining the VMH in the three selected trips for Champions Stores.

The "en route productivity" credit for time spent aboard a corporate aircraft is esti-

Table 9–2 The Value of Executive Time*

Yearly Salary	Hourly Pay	Productivity Factor	Value/Hour	Annual Contribution
$ 10k	$ 5.00	2.50	$ 12.50	$ 18,750
20k	10.00	5.00	50.00	75,000
30k	15.00	7.50	112.50	168,750
40k	20.00	10.00	200.00	300,000
50k	25.00	12.50	312.50	468,750
75k	37.50	18.75	703.13	914,695
100k	50.00	25.00	1,250.00	1,875,000
150k	75.00	37.50	2,812.50	4,218,875
200k	100.00	50.00	5,000.00	7,500,000
250k	125.00	62.50	7,812.50	11,718,875
500k	250.00	125.00	31,125.00	46,687,500

*Source: Business & Commercial Aviation magazine

mated at 75 percent. The justification for the much higher percentage is based upon the following reasons:

1. Full privacy allows open reference to and use of proprietary information and materials.
2. Cabin configurations are conducive for meetings and open discussions among members of a firm or with clients without risk of being overheard or compromising proprietary information.
3. Modern aircraft cabins can be equipped with computers, fax machines, photocopiers and phones that enable executives to work as though in their offices.
4. Improved opportunity for air to ground communications.
5. More available time to devote to working, not waiting after take off and less time to clean up before landing.

Another feature of the business aircraft compared to automobile travel on business trips such as this one is load factor. Four or five executives including assistants could make the trip and return the same day. Not only would this be uncomfortable in an automobile, the expense involved in remaining overnight would be costly. In addition, the aircraft enables junior members of management to gain valuable experience by making such business trips.

Trip B—Montgomery, AL to Greensboro, NC and Return

Time and cost comparisons for Trip B are shown in Tables 9–3 and 9–4. The best airline routing for this trip includes a connecting flight in Atlanta. There is very little difference in cost on this selected business trip but there is a five hour and 30 minute difference in time. The use of the business aircraft reduces the delay and fatigue associated with travel to and from the airline terminal, check-in, baggage claims, and the time to change planes in Atlanta.

The importance of load factor is clearly demonstrated in Figure 9–1. After a load factor of three, additional passengers can be transported on the business aircraft at no added "out-of-pocket" costs while travel by airline increases arithmetically with the load factor.

Trip C—Montgomery, AL to Mexia, TX and Return

Time and cost comparisons for Trip C are shown in Tables 9–5 and 9–6. Champions Stores wanted to diversify its business model and decided to purchase a sporting goods manufacturer in Mexia, Texas. The lack of direct commercial service again demonstrates the time saved by flying on a business aircraft. The timesaving from this one trip,

Table 9–3 Time Comparison for Trip B—Montgomery, AL to Greensboro, NC and Return (Hypothetical)

		Elapsed Time (Round Trip)	
		Airline	**Business Aircraft**
Office to Airport	(1)	:45	:30
Terminal Boarding	(2)	1:00	:30
En Route Time	(3)	7:23	3:23
Deplaning Time	(4)	1:00	:30
Airport to Office	(5)	:45	:30
Total		10:53	5:23

(1) General aviation terminal facility is usually easier to reach, with less traffic than on the vehicular circular drive serving the airline terminal and easier parking.
(2) Airline terminal boarding includes baggage check-in, security screening, walk to gate position, waiting, and loading. This can add considerable time depending upon the time of day.
(3) Includes time required to change planes in Atlanta going and return.
(4) Includes walk to airline baggage claim area, the typical wait, and walk to ground transportation.
(5) Leaving the airport from the general aviation terminal facility is generally much quicker.

Table 9–4   Cost Comparison for Trip B—Montgomery, AL to Greensboro, NC and Return (Hypothetical)

		Total Cost (Round Trip)	
		Airline	**Business Aircraft**
Travel—En Route	(1)	$1,722.03	$3,903.90
Rental Car	(2)	31.72	31.72
Value per Man-Hour (VMH)	(3)	3,371.68	981.52
Total Cost		$5,125.43	$4,917.14

(1) Airline Ticket—$941 round trip × 3 persons (Less 39% tax savings).
    Business Aircraft—3.38 hrs @ $1,155/hr.
(2) Rental car—$52 per day, unlimited mileage (Less 39% tax savings).
(3) (3) VMH $\frac{2.5 \times \$92,000}{2,000 \text{ hrs.}}$ (av. salary) = $115.00/hr.

VMH Summary

Airline

Total Time: $115.00 × 10.88 hrs. × 3 persons		$3,753.60
En Route Time: $115.00 × 7.38 hrs. × 3 persons	$2,546.10	
Less 15% Productivity Credit.	.15	−381.92
		$3,371.68

Business Aircraft

Total Time: $115.00 × 5.38 hrs. × 3 persons		$1,856.10
En Route Time: $115.00 × 3.38 hrs. × 3 persons	$1,166.10	
Less 75% Productivity Credit	.75	−874.58
		$981.52

when annualized, will add several more productive days for the three busy executives. In addition, the elimination of overnight stays will certainly have a positive impact on employee morale and family relationships.

Again, on this trip, the importance of load factor is illustrated. Additional passengers can be taken on the business aircraft at no additional expense while the airline/charter combination would increase time and cost arithmetically. This is an important consideration for companies wishing to expose junior personnel to business situations in the field, such as having junior sales representatives accompany a senior staff member to a customer's site.

Summary

Table 9–7 provides an annualized summary of the three trips. Based on only 27 trips per year or slightly less than 16 percent of the annual estimate of 171 (see Table 8–2), Champions Stores could save 474 man-hours (based on three passengers) and a cost savings of $8,501.

As previously stated, the trips selected were representative of this company's travel pattern. For example, 26 percent of this company's current travel (45 trips—from Table

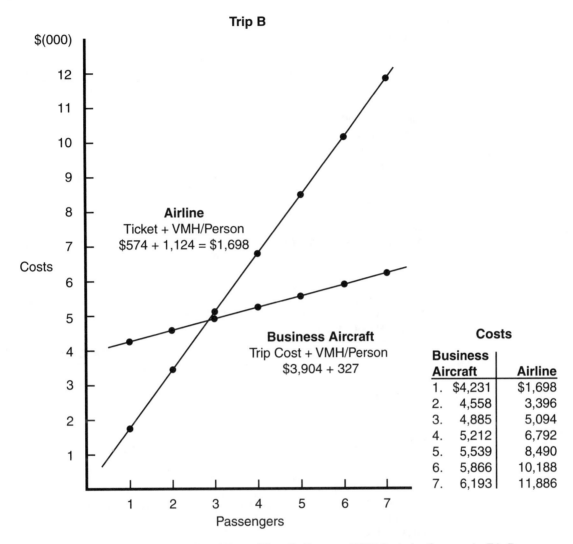

Figure 9–1. Relationship of Load Factor When En Route and VMH Costs Are Compared—Trip B

8–2) were made by automobile at a distance under 200 miles. The Fitzgerald, GA trip was representative of this group.

It also must be remembered that this saving was based on three passengers using each mode of transportation. Whenever load factor increases, travel costs by airline increase arithmetically where there is no additional expense, other than value per man-hour for the business aircraft.

Another value of a business aircraft lies not only in the time and cost savings involved in unproductive travel time, but in *morale costs* as well. Morale costs is another element in total savings. It includes both the off-hours travel (before 8:00 a.m. and after 5:00 p.m.) and the time spent away from home overnight. On an annualized basis this can result in a considerable savings.

INTANGIBLE BENEFITS

Business aircraft have been referred to as time machines. Speed in transportation is synonymous with time and the business aircraft of today is a time machine that compresses distances into minutes and hours. In the world of business and commerce, time means money. Wages are paid by the hour, salaries by the week, profits by the quarter and taxes by the year. Business people sitting in airline terminals, driving on highways for

Table 9–5 Time Comparison for Trip C—Montgomery, AL to Mexia, TX and Return (Hypothetical)

	Elapsed Time (Round Trip)	
	Airline	**Business Aircraft**
Office to Airport	:45	:30
Terminal Boarding	1:00	:30
En Route Time (1)	7:08	4:19
Deplaning Time	1:00	:30
Airport to Plant (2)	2:00	—
Airport to Office	:45	:30
Total	12:38	6:19

(1) Connecting flight in Dallas/Ft. Worth to Waco, TX includes time required to change planes.
(2) Time required to drive from the Waco airport to the plant in Mexia

Table 9–6 Cost Comparison for Trip C—Montgomery, AL to Mexia, TX and Return (Hypothetical)

		Total Cost (Round Trip)	
		Airline	**Business Aircraft**
Travel—En Route	(1)	$1,806.21	$4,989.60
Rental Car	(2)	63.44	—
RONs	(3)	256.20	—
Value per Man-Hour (VMH)	(4)	3,988.37	1,062.60
		$6,114.22	$6,052.20

(1) Airline Ticket—$987 round trip × 3 persons (Less 39% tax savings).
  Business Aircraft—4.32 hrs @ $1,155/hr.
(2) Rental Car—$52 per day, unlimited mileage (Less 39% tax savings).
(3) RONs $140/person × 3 persons (Less 39% tax savings).
(4) (4) VMH $\dfrac{2.5 \times \$92,000}{2.000 \text{ hrs.}}$ (av. salary) = $115.00/hr.

VMH Summary

Airline

Total Time: $115.00 × 12.63hrs. × 3 persons		$4,357.35
En Route Time: $115.00 × 7.13 hrs. × 3 persons	$2,459.85	
Less 15% Productivity Credit	.15	−368.98
		$3,988.37

Business Aircraft

Total Time: $115.00 × 6.32hrs. × 3 persons		$2,180.40
En Route Time: $115.00 × 4.32 hrs. × 3 persons	$1,490.40	
Less 75% Productivity Credit	.75	−1,117.80
		$1,062.60

Table 9–7   Summary of Tangible Benefits Trips A, B, and C Based on 3 Passengers

Sample Trips	Trips Per Year	TIME COMPARISON (Hours)				Tangible Benefit (Savings)	
		Automobile/Airline		Business Aircraft			
		Each Trip	Year	Each Trip	Year	Per Trip	Year
A	9	27:00	243:00	9:48	88:12	17:12	154:48
B	9	32:39	293:51	16:09	145:21	16:30	148:30
C	9	37:54	341:06	18:57	170:33	18:57	170:33
Annual Totals: 27			877:57		404:06		473:51

Sample Trips	Trips Per Year	COST COMPARISON				Tangible Benefit (Savings)	
		Automobile/Airline		Business Aircraft			
		Each Trip	Year	Each Trip	Year	Per Trip	Year
A	9	$2,972.31	$26,750.79	$2,298.11	$20,682.99	$674.20	$6,067.80
B	9	5,125.43	46,128.87	4,917.14	44,254.26	208.29	1,874.61
C	9	6,114.22	55,027.98	6,052.20	54,469.80	62.02	558.18
Annual Totals: 27			$127,907.64		$119,407.05		$8,500.59

hours and spending nights in motels are throwing away time and money. As more and more organizations manage "rightsizing" initiatives, they are discovering the need to maximize the productivity of the same or fewer employees to accomplish equal or greater amounts of work and ensure their competitive position and long-term success. As business aircraft improve employee time management and efficiency, they can help eliminate the need for additional personnel, reducing payroll costs, and help maximize a company's competitive marketing advantage.

Table 9–8 gives an insight into the perceptions of senior executives of the intangible benefits derived from the use of a business aircraft.

No matter what the particular mission of the business aircraft, the ultimate reasons for its use are the same: save time otherwise lost by inflexible schedules; compress time so that an

Table 9–8   Corporate Aircraft Benefits as Reported by Senior Executives of a Major Corporation

1. Time Savings
2. Operational Reliability
3. Lessened Fatigue
4. Efficiency of Personal En Route Work
5. Avoidance of Overnight Stops
6. Ability to Visit Multiple Destinations Within Limited Time
7. Schedule Flexibility
8. Customer Contact and Support
9. Ability to Respond Promptly to Customers and Associates
10. En Route Conferences and Briefings (Group Travel)
11. En Route Rehearsals and Program Finalizations
12. Ability to Conduct Classified Meetings
13. Carriage of Parts and Displays
14. Departmental/Interdepartmental Communication and Coordination
15. Security (Cabin)
16. Security (Personnel)

hour-long transaction out of town does not require an overnight stay, and expand time so that productivity is greater.

It is generally agreed that a company's top decision-makers are in a position to weigh the relative importance of intangible benefits such as convenience, comfort, or even prestige. The reason for this is that the decision-makers are also usually the users of the aircraft. They recognize that the intangible, rather than the tangible factors, often provides the margin of profit in business aircraft use. Accountants and comptrollers may wish to be shown the tangible benefits of cost savings in dollars as well as increased productivity that can be measured. Their evaluations will eventually become major determinants in all major aircraft purchase decisions. There still remain the areas of subjectivity and judgment, especially in regard to the worth of an employee's time to his company and the values placed on the intangible benefits.

No universal means have been devised, as yet, to measure the benefits of these intangibles that are so readily and universally accepted as existing. These intangibles are, however, becoming major determining factors in aircraft decisions. Cost-savings analysis should not outweigh astute business judgment that considers all factors, including those that cannot be determined in the usual cost-savings analysis. David Lyall, EMJ Corporation's chief pilot states,

> Airlines are often the cheapest way to go between Boston and Chattanooga, but, often, the cheapest option can be the most costly one if you miss a meeting. Airline flights from Boston to Atlanta were delayed so often that our people would miss their airline connections to Chattanooga and would have to drive there, getting in at 2 a.m. When you have a meeting the next day at 7 a.m., that's totally unacceptable. If you can leave Boston at 7 a.m. on a business aircraft and be in Chattanooga at 9:30 a.m., that's not a bad deal.

The business aircraft's efficiency depends on the wisdom with which it is employed. The aircraft can range from a valuable cost-saving and profit-making piece of equipment, to a pure cost center incapable of revenue or profits, depending upon its utilization. With modern business methods, under utilization rarely occurs. Utilization of an aircraft is the basis for productivity.

Where cost is a trade-off against time, several factors must be considered: the intrinsic value of the person or cargo to be moved; the emergency need for travel to be accomplished; the perishable nature or deterioration rate of a situation; and, any seasonable peak demand requirement.

Convenience and comfort are other major intangible benefits closely related to timesavings. Convenience is more than just another amenity. It means flexibility — the ability to go when and where needed with little or no notice. It results in simplification of travel from point to point. The meaningfulness of comfort stems from the relationship of comfort to fatigue and the effects fatigue has on productivity. Intangible benefits fall into seven broad areas:

1. *Recruiting and retaining key personnel.* The right person in the right place at the right time can change everything. West coast venture capitalist Neal Dempsey said, "There's nothing more impressive to people you're trying to hire than to tell them you'll send the plane for them. Flying a candidate into our headquarters on a business aircraft lets them know we're serious." Business aircraft do provide additional comfort and convenience for busy executives who travel frequently. The use of a business aircraft can result in:
   a. Increased ability to attract and employ key personnel in competition with other companies in the industry.
   b. Improved morale factor by not being on the road constantly.

c. Reduced travel fatigue and its effect on productivity. When employees are subjected to stress and abnormal schedules, their effectiveness begins to decline. Although the degree may vary, it is significant enough to be a factor. The following elements of mental and physical performance that contribute to overall effectiveness of employees can be adversely affected by consistent commercial air travel:

(1). Utilization of intellect in evolving answers and arriving at solutions to objectives of meeting.

(2). Exercise of initiative involving and expressing viewpoints that are pertinent to objectives of the meeting.

(3). Maintenance of patience.

(4). Alertness to opportunities that develop during the meeting discussions.

(5). Ability to maintain stamina so that objectives are not compromised.

d. Minimizing nonbusiness hours away from home. Family time before and after traditional business hours is critical to most key employees. Because a stable, supportive family can have a strong effect on employee morale and productivity, scheduling which minimizes time away from home can be a major benefit.

2. *Increased management mobility.* Competition among companies is, in the final analysis, competition among managements. Competition is not between business products or the efficiency of facilities. Over a period of time, these factors can be changed by the quality and effectiveness of the management group. Management's real value to the company, its employees, and stockholders lies in its ability to use time effectively. The quantity of executive talent needed to manage a major corporation is not limited. However, the demand for such talent is growing. The solution is to make the best use of the talents available. The near total scheduling flexibility inherent in business aircraft — even changing itineraries en route can be a powerful asset. As aircraft can arrive and depart on the executives' schedule, typically waiting for them in the ordinary course of business, meetings can be moved up, back or extended without penalty, risk, or unnecessary scheduling pressures. Overnight trips also can be avoided. If managed proactively, this benefit can improve business results. Thus, a business aircraft can minimize additional personnel requirements by increasing an executive's area of control.

3. *Increase sales.* By minimizing or eliminating many of the barriers to travel, business aircraft allow business opportunities to be more readily considered and acted upon. Business aircraft users frequently form profitable new relationships in the aviation and aerospace industries, and customers in other, often-rural areas of the country — once practically unreachable and thus unconsidered — are newly accessible. The use of a business aircraft conveys the image of an efficient, well-run company committed to fast action and service.

Aviation has not lost its glamour, and there are distinctive uses of business aircraft that can and do provide the marginal edge that often can make the difference between completing a transaction and just missing one. Aaron Henschel, President, Henschel — Steinau Incorporated, Englewood, New Jersey, speaks to the potential of business aircraft assistance to increasing sales when he was interviewed by *Flying Magazine.* He says:

General aviation is the best investment I've made. We're a medium size company in our industry, but I wouldn't have some of my top clients if it weren't for my decision to take up flying. My company designs and markets point-of-purchase advertising displays for clients such as Hershey Chocolate Company, Upjohn Company, General Foods, Philip Morris, and Burroughs-Wellcome Company. We employ twenty people including a sales staff of eight who call on accounts from Kalamazoo to Buffalo. People are impressed by the fact that our company can react quickly and airplanes give us a tremendous competitive advantage in many areas. For example, we flew one customer into Marsh Field — the small airport close to Boston — to see our supermarket displays in that region. We had him back at Teterboro Airport near New York by 10:45 a.m. and, by 11:30 a.m., he was in his mid-town Manhattan office.

A business aircraft provides shorter reaction time to new business opportunities.

4. *Outpace competition.* As our industrial, computerized society becomes progressively more advanced and sophisticated, the pace of doing business increases commensurately. Add to this trend the growing decentralization of business, and it is easy to see that fast transportation is one of management's major requirements in the battle for competitive supremacy. The flexibility of scheduling and the ability to get to out-of-the-way places, provide management with an increased ability to stay even with or ahead of competition. Nick A. Caporella, chairman and CEO of National Beverage Corp. of Fort Lauderdale illustrates the competitive advantage when he said,

> Today, not only do you have to have the right price, programs, brands and ingredients, but you also need a rapport with retailers. And there's no better way to build that rapport than to personally pick up a CEO in your Falcon 2000. That's the best way in the world to do business — people like to do business with people they like.

5. *Business entertainment.* It is quite common for businesses to entertain customers or potential customers. A business aircraft can be a viable piece of equipment in this regard. Many companies use their aircraft to fly employees and customers to hunting, fishing, sightseeing, or other recreational areas. Although considered as nonbusiness, these trips often have a very direct return by serving to enhance company-customer relationships.

6. *More contacts with present customers.* It is a marketing adage that a company's present customers are the best prospects for additional sales. The more attention a company can give them, the better its chances to convert those customers into repeat orders. Spotting a customer problem and the ability to solve it by getting personnel to the customer's facility might save an existing account.

Frequently, customers are so widespread that management cannot afford to contact more than one or two on a given trip. A company aircraft can give management (as well as sales, service, and technical personnel) the chance to maintain closer contact with key accounts.

Sheldon Coleman, former Chief Executive Officer of the Coleman Company, stated in an interview with *Business and Commercial Aviation,*

> . . . We also use our airplanes to fly our executives out into the field to talk with, and listen to, the dealers and customers. We call that "brainstorming." In our business it is essential for us to stay close to our customers, to detect any significant problems, or to spot a trend. We go where the action is. That's the firing line and that's where we have to be.

7. *Serving companies that demand fast action.* An increasingly greater number of companies are engaged in business that is time sensitive to high-speed transportation; for example, they may need the capability of flying in personnel or equipment to keep a customer's production line from shutting down.

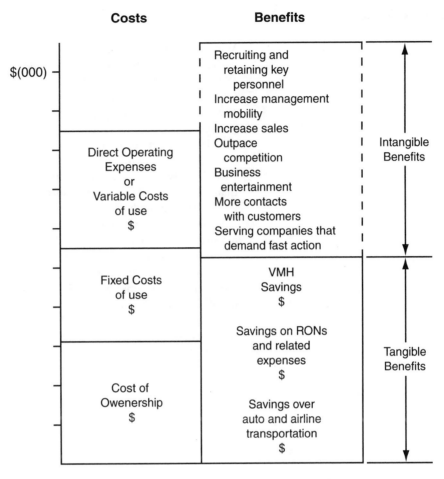

Figure 9–2. Value Analysis: Cost Versus Benefits

CONCLUSION

This chapter opened by drawing an analogy between the business aircraft and a computer. The evaluation or value analysis of a proposed capital investment is essentially a matter of logic. It is the process of weighing the benefits to be derived from the investment against the cost of making the investment (see Figure 9–2).

Use of a business aircraft avoids airline ticketing, security clearances, missed connections, late flights, luggage lines, and highway delays in getting to and from major airports. Many companies utilize their own aircraft as an en route conference room thus reducing unproductive travel time to a minimum.

Some of these benefits can be tangible and readily quantified in terms of dollars and cents. Others may be quite intangible and difficult to quantify. Whether the benefits are tangible or intangible, management must, in considering the wisdom of a capital investment, formulate an opinion of the beneficial effects which the proposed investment will have on the income statement, in terms of increased revenues or reduced expenses, or both. Against these, it must weigh the cost of the capital investment.

KEY TERMS

Value analysis   Value per Man-Hour (VMH)
Tangible benefits   En route productivity factor
Intangible benefits   Morale costs

REVIEW QUESTIONS

1. Why is the purchase of a business aircraft similar to the purchase of a computer? What is the difference between tangible and intangible benefits of business aircraft use? Why are business aircraft referred to as "time machines?"

2. Quarterly airline travel by employees of Modern Day Furniture Company between cites A and B (round trip) has been one person 8 times; two persons 5 times; three persons 2 times; and four persons once. Each of the eight employees named on the airline ticket stubs are in the $70,000/year salary bracket. Round trip airfare for one person between cities A and B is $450. It takes an employee 4 hours to go from City A to B by airline (also 4 hours for the return trip). Determine the (1) total quarterly fares; (2) average load factor; (3) VHM; and, (4) total quarterly airline travel expenses including VMH.

   Using a high performance single-engine aircraft and flying into a general aviation airport closer to City B takes 2.5 hours from City A. (5 hours for the round trip) Aircraft operating expense is $200 per hour. Assuming the same number of legs flown as the airline (32) and the same load factor, the total hours flown will be _____ and the total flying expense will be $_____. Determine the total quarterly expenses including VMH using the business aircraft.

   Assuming the trips can be made in a total of 24 legs through better scheduling using the business aircraft, what would the load factor have to be _____? What would the total flight expense be? Using the previously determined VMH and flying 24 legs, what are the total quarterly expenses including VMH _____?

Chapter 10

Methods of Acquiring a Business Aircraft

OUTLINE

Introduction
Company-Owned Aircraft
    Company-Owned — Management Company Operated
    Joint Ownership — In House Flight Department
    Co-ownership — Management Company
    New versus Used Aircraft
    Maintenance
    Financing the Aircraft Purchase
Buying and Selling Used Aircraft
    The Market
    Purchasing Used Aircraft
    Pre-purchase Inspection
    Negotiating the Purchase
    Aircraft Registration
Financing
Retailing Aircraft
Leasing
    Advantages and Disadvantages of Leasing
    Types of Leases
Fractional Ownership
    Fractional Ownership Programs
    Advantages of Fractional Ownership
Charter
    Contract Flight Services
    Comparison of Methods
Conclusion

OBJECTIVES

At the end of this chapter you should be able to:

Compare and contrast the purchase of new versus used aircraft.

Give several reasons for the company owned — management company operated method of acquiring a business aircraft.

List the primary factors on which finance charges on an aircraft loan are based.

Describe the four methods available to owners desiring to sell their aircraft.

Discuss some of the factors to consider in purchasing a used aircraft.

List several of the major points included in an aircraft sales contract.

Distinguish between simple interest and add-on interest.

Describe floor planning as a financial technique.

Determine the retail price of an aircraft using the markup formula.

Discuss the advantages and disadvantages of leasing.

Compare the capital lease with the operating lease.

Discuss the major elements in fractional ownership programs.

Identify some of the advantages of fractional ownership.

Explain how a firm might use charter aircraft for business purposes.

Distinguish between chartering and contract flight service.

Summarize the four major methods of acquiring business aircraft discussed in this chapter.

INTRODUCTION

The decision to acquire a business aircraft is a major step. A company that has never owned or operated an aircraft must first determine that an airplane is a worthwhile acquisition. Companies that already operate planes and want to expand or upgrade their fleets, have the aviation experience to guide them in evaluating new equipment.

Once there is agreement that an airplane is desirable, management can select a particular make and model, properly equipped, from the great variety available.

Need and cost, as previously discussed, are the basic considerations, but potential users of business aircraft also must weigh many other factors to determine whether an airplane has a valid place in their organizations. Many companies seek outside advice in making their business aviation decisions. Sales representatives from the aircraft dealers and distributors, as well as specialized aviation consulting firms, offer advice and counsel. Assistance from other companies, including members of NBAA who operate aircraft, is often available.

Chapters 8 and 9 demonstrated that weighing potential need for an aircraft usually involves detailed examination of company travel records covering a representative time period, to measure total volume and to identify travel patterns. This examination should reveal how many employees travel regularly, which ones do the most traveling, where they go, at what times of the day or week, typical length of trips, extent of group travel, and the proximity of frequently visited destinations to airports. Total annual cost of travel and the value per man-hour (VMH) of those traveling are usually considered in making comparisons between airline and automobile with a business aircraft.

Because of the wide range of aircraft available, it is important to identify company travel characteristics and requirements as clearly as possible in order to match them with aircraft capabilities. Some companies that have experience with business aircraft have developed internal checklists to help management evaluate and select aircraft.

A great majority of planes operated by business firms are owned or leased by the companies that use them, but a growing number of users are choosing fractional ownership. The point is that a company seeking private air transportation can obtain it in a variety of different ways. Although there are many variations and combinations among the methods of acquiring use of a business aircraft, they can be reduced to four basic ones:

1. Company-owned — new or used
   a. Company-owned aircraft — in-house flight department
   b. Company-owned aircraft — management company
   c. Joint ownership — in-house flight department
   d. Co-ownership — management company
2. Leasing — wet or dry
   a. Capital lease
   b. Operating lease
3. Fractional ownership
4. Charter — individual or contract

What might be an appropriate method for one company may be completely inappropriate for another. Like a suit of clothes, the method has to fit the company's needs to wear well. This chapter will discuss the four basic methods, along with slight variations.

COMPANY-OWNED AIRCRAFT

The principal advantages of ownership are optimum utility, convenience, and safety. Consequently, corporate aviation departments get maximum use from their aircraft. All business owners carry on their flight operations in accordance with FAA regulations.

Many also have developed additional corporate procedures that have resulted in safety records comparable to those of the scheduled airlines.

Usually, one company-owned airplane, efficiently used, can satisfy 75 percent of the air transportation needs of the people it is intended to serve. Anything over 75 percent will usually necessitate special charter or lease arrangements. Many companies have different types of aircraft in their fleets to meet various needs.

A whole aircraft in-house flight department affords the highest possible levels of control, service, and security/confidentiality. Sans intercompany scheduling conflicts or maintenance downtime, the aircraft is always available. If the aircraft is not available, the owner can use charter, airlines, timeshare, or interchange to meet flight demands.

A *time-sharing agreement* involves the lease of an airplane with flight crew to another party, and no charge is made for the flights conducted under that arrangement other than the following:

1. Fuel, oil, lubricants, and other additives.
2. Travel expenses of the crew, including food, lodging, and ground transportation.
3. Hangar and tie-down costs away from the aircraft's base of operations.
4. Insurance obtained for the specific flight.
5. Landing fees, airport taxes, and similar assessments.
6. Customs, foreign permits, and similar fees directly related to the flight.
7. In-flight food and beverages.
8. Passenger ground transportation.
9. Flight planning and weather contract services.
10. An additional charge equal to 100 percent of the expenses listed under number one.

Under an *interchange agreement,* one company leases its airplane to another company in exchange for equal time, when needed, on the other company's airplane, and no charge, assessment, or fee is made, except that a charge may be made not to exceed the difference between the cost of owning, operating, and maintaining the two airplanes.

A company-owned aircraft is the most flexible method of business flying. As owner, the company is not subject to restrictions imposed by charterers or lessors with regard to insurance requirements, operating restrictions, and other contractual provisions. On the other hand, having an owned aircraft can be inflexible if the company is not getting the hourly utilization expected, or if it has purchased the wrong aircraft and must dispose of it.

The owner maintains total control over and manages aircraft operations. As such, the owner is completely liable for all operations. All flight department personnel are on the owner's payroll, and the owner must deal with in-house personnel issues. Crew quality is consistent and owner controlled, and the owner is directly in charge of training crew and maintenance personnel.

Productivity, in terms of cost per hour flown, is the lowest of any of the methods of operation as long as the annual hourly utilization is achieved. Ideally, a company should use its own aircraft as extensively as possible to derive the greatest productivity from business flying.

Operating costs vary depending on aircraft use, and the lowest cost of operations is realized at reasonable utilization levels (above 400 flight hours per year), although deadheading or positioning costs can play a factor. To help offset costs, a flight department can opt to charter out its aircraft, but only after receiving Part 135 approval to do so.

Since the department operates under Part 91, the federal excise tax (FET) does not apply; instead, the noncommercial fuel tax is applied. The aircraft may be fully depreciated over a six-year period, realizing the maximum tax benefit for the company. However, state sales tax must be paid on the acquisition cost.

This option requires a higher capital investment of the negotiated acquisition cost, but the owner has the freedom to purchase any aircraft at any price. The owner also has complete control over how the aircraft is outfitted. In addition, the aircraft can be sold, upgraded, or downgraded at any time.

Company Owned— Management Company Operated

Operation of a company-owned aircraft by a *management company* is attractive to firms not wanting to take on the responsibility of operating their own aircraft. Under contract, the management company provides crew, maintenance, and all administrative responsibilities. Because of this arrangement, the owner shares liability with the management company. Flight department personnel are not on the owner's payroll.

This method can provide excellent, customized service. Like a company-owned in-house flight department, the aircraft is nearly always available. If the aircraft is not available due to maintenance or scheduling conflicts, the owner can use charter, airlines, timeshare, or interchange to meet flight demands.

The level of safety can vary widely, depending on the competence and operating philosophy of the particular management company. Nearly all management companies that offer this type of service operate under Part 135 of the Federal Aviation Regulations, which is designed for commercial operators and requires higher minimum safety standards than Part 91, which is the part most company-owned and operated aircraft are operated under. However, these are minimum regulations and not closely scrutinized by the FAA. As a result, there is considerable variance in the safety standards adhered to by individual management companies.

As a rule, the company-owned, management company-operated method is expensive simply because the company has to pay for the services provided. One of the major selling points for using management company services is that the company owning the aircraft will be able to save some fixed costs by selling time on the aircraft when the owning company is not using it. In some cases, selling time is valid and workable.

Operating costs vary depending on aircraft use, and the lowest cost of operation is realized at reasonable utilization levels, but deadheading or positioning costs can increase these costs.

Simply stated, aircraft management firms offer the one- and two-aircraft operator the economies of scale generally available only to large fleet operators. The scope of services differs widely among the many aircraft management firms. Most of the larger firms provide flight planning, 24-hour central dispatch and flight following, storage, insurance, training, backup pilots, and most maintenance. Some firms have set up agreements with their customers whereby each customer has an entire fleet of aircraft at its call, if necessary. For example, if a company owns one aircraft but needs four others for some special purpose one day, it can borrow time, in effect, on these other aircraft, with the stipulation that it will repay this borrowed time by permitting other companies to use its aircraft.

In addition to timesharing agreements, virtually all aircraft management firms can charter a customer's aircraft under a commercial certificate, which also improves utilization while helping to offset some of the client's operating costs.

The owners pay the noncommercial fuel tax as long as they maintain possession of and control over the aircraft. The aircraft may be fully depreciated over a six-year period, realizing the maximum tax benefit for the company. However, state sales tax must be paid on the acquisition cost.

This option requires higher capital investment of the negotiated acquisition cost, but the owner has the freedom to purchase any aircraft at any price. The owner has complete say in how the aircraft is outfitted, the aircraft can be sold, upgraded, or downgraded at any time.

In summary, there are five distinct advantages of a management operation:

- It maintains an "arm's-length" arrangement with the owner in which all the aircraft-related administrative functions are performed outside the owner's company, thus relieving the need to commit internal resources.

- It can deliver Part 135 charter revenues back to the owner to help defray costs.
- It removes from the company any politically or employee-sensitive aircraft-related cost accounting.
- It provides anonymity and security because an owner's aircraft becomes part of a fleet of many owners, and those who might be trying to use Internet tracking programs to identify a particular aircraft user find it extremely difficult.
- It maintains a pragmatic perspective toward the owner's aircraft. The aircraft is looked upon as a business asset detached from personal involvement, perhaps unlike a flight department.

Joint Ownership— In-House Flight Department

Joint ownership is an arrangement whereby one of the registered joint owners of an airplane employs and furnishes the flight crew for that airplane and each of the registered joint owners pays a share of the charges specified in the agreement.

A joint-ownership in-house flight department can also provide excellent and customized service. However, aircraft availability requires coordination with the joint owners and advance planning. If the aircraft is not available, either owner can use charter, airlines, timeshare, or interchange to meet flight demands.

Owners maintain control over and manage aircraft operations, and the liability for these operations is shared by both owners. Flight department personnel are on the owners' payroll, and the owners must jointly address any in-house personnel issues. Crew quality is consistent and controlled by the owners, who are responsible for crew and maintenance personnel training.

Operating costs vary, depending on aircraft use (again, the lowest cost of operations is realized at reasonable utilization levels), and deadheading or positioning costs increase these costs. To help offset operating costs, the owners can opt to charter out their aircraft, but this may put more of a squeeze on aircraft availability.

Owners pay the noncommercial fuel tax since they operate the aircraft under Part 91. However, FET charges could apply if an owner's aircraft share does not closely match the percentage of use. For example, Company A owns 90 percent of the aircraft, while Company B owns 10 percent, but each uses the aircraft equally. Because Company B's share is not proportional to its aircraft use, the IRS deems this to be a commercial operation (FET applies), even though operations are conducted under Part 91. Aircraft depreciation is shared by the owners and they must pay state sales tax on their share of the aircraft acquisition fee.

This option requires a higher capital investment for the negotiated acquisition cost on the part of the owners. They must also agree on what aircraft to purchase and how to outfit it. Either owner can sell its share in the aircraft at any time, and the aircraft can be sold, upgraded, or downgraded as needed.

Co-Ownership— Management Company

A *co-ownership management company* also provides customizable service, but aircraft availability requires coordination and planning. If the aircraft is not available, either owner can use charter, airlines, timeshare, or interchange to meet flight demands.

Owners maintain control over but delegate the management of aircraft operations. Liability for these operations is shared by the owners and the management company. Flight department personnel are not on the owners' payroll, and crew quality is consistent. The owners also delegate control of crew and maintenance personnel training to the management company.

Operating costs are inversely proportional to aircraft use, and deadheading or positioning costs will increase these costs. Annual operating costs may be higher than joint ownership due to management fees. To help offset operating costs, the owners can opt to charter out the aircraft, but this could adversely affect availability.

Owners pay the noncommercial fuel tax as long as they maintain possession of and control over the aircraft. However, the aforementioned share/use percentage rule applies, as well. Aircraft depreciation is shared by the owners, and they must pay state sales tax on their share of the aircraft acquisition price.

This option requires the owners to ante up a high capital investment of the negotiated acquisition cost. They must also agree on what aircraft to purchase and how to outfit it. Either owner can sell its share in the aircraft at any time, and the aircraft can be sold, upgraded, or downgraded as needed.

New versus Used Aircraft

The demand for new and used business aircraft has been strong since the mid-1990s. Although many companies have considered fractional ownership or charter, others have realized that a company-owned plane is an excellent choice. It will remain the prime source of large and small business aircraft. Used aircraft are generally less expensive to purchase; however, prices have drifted upward in recent years reflecting scarcity of certain models, particularly trainers. However, an intelligent decision about buying new or used should draw on all aspects of expense not simply the purchasing price.

Many new aircraft dealers and distributors are active in the used aircraft market because they frequently take older planes in trade against the sale of new aircraft. Also, some firms specialize in handling used planes. These firms, operating similarly to used automobile wholesalers, usually sell in large numbers, often to dealers and distributors overseas; they are also active in the reconditioning of individual aircraft for sale at retail. Then, too, there are brokers for the sale of used aircraft.

Although the used aircraft market can be compared to the used automobile market in some respects, it is very different in at least one critical aspect. While the buyer of a used automobile may buy a "lemon," this is definitely not the case with used airplanes. Aircraft must be licensed by the FAA when put into service initially, then must be relicensed annually therefore. The licensing procedure requires the plane to be subjected to periodic inspections to ensure that it is being maintained in airworthy condition. Records of inspection, along with records of maintenance and repair activities, are a permanent part of each airplane's records and are passed along from one owner to another. Thus, it is possible to get a good picture of a used airplane's current condition by studying the records of its usage, maintenance, and repair. This requirement for regular inspections of airplanes and written records of repairs and overhauls, may also partially explain why an active used aircraft market exists today and why there is ready acceptance on the part of buyers of well-maintained used aircraft. In addition, many used aircraft have enjoyed stable market values at a high percentage of their original purchase prices. The AOPA puts out an excellent booklet entitled "How to Buy a Used Aircraft" which includes a checklist of special precautions for prospective used aircraft purchasers.

Good pre-owned airplanes represent substantial value. Over 80 percent of all corporate aircraft sold in the United States are pre-owned. A company can buy a five-year-old aircraft, reconfigure the interior to its specific requirements, upgrade the avionics with the latest safety enhancements, and have the equivalent of a brand-new airplane at a fraction of the cost. The company's financial exposure is minimal because, historically, used airplanes hold their values over time. They are very liquid assets. A five-year-old airplane can retain 80 to 90 percent of its original value, and many aircraft, such as King Airs, have actually appreciated beyond their original cost.

Despite the active sales in used aircraft in recent years, new airplanes still offer some very sound advantages.

Financing is apt to be more liberal on a new airplane, with lower interest rates and longer repayment terms. Lending institutions tend to feel that their investments are better secured with new rather than used equipment and will make some financial concessions to encourage new purchases.

Similarly, insurance companies are generally more eager to insure new rather than used airplanes, and their rates reflect that attitude. A new aircraft has no wear on the components, so there is a greater statistical probability that everything will function normally for a longer period of time than on a used airplane.

A new aircraft warranty can also be an advantage particularly if a firm is considering buying a sophisticated single- or twin-engine aircraft with complex systems. Though most modern airplanes are reasonably trouble-free, there is definitely a correlation between maintenance cost and systems complexity; the more complex an airplane, the more it will cost to maintain.

Another consideration is the fact that a new airplane has no maintenance or operation history. The first buyer has the opportunity to control the break-in and day-to-day flight record of the aircraft. A firm can strictly regulate operating practices and make certain the aircraft is properly treated to maximize utility and efficiency. Though logbooks can give some indications of how well or poorly a used airplane was treated, there is no way to know for sure.

High among the benefits of buying a new aircraft are the advantages that go with better performance, greater comfort, improved efficiency, and personalized appearance. Innovations in the aerodynamic and powerplant art often allow new aircraft to realize better speed and efficiency than older models. State-of-the-art avionics are part of the newer equipment. While it is true that new communication radios and navigation equipment may be fitted to older airplanes, avionics installations typically will be simpler and cleaner if done at the factory when the aircraft is built. Also, a buyer may realize a lower price purchasing new radios with the aircraft, because the manufacturer can benefit from volume discounts not always available to outside vendors.

Cabin comfort is a subjective judgment, but there is little doubt that interior appointments and even cabin size improve with newer models. Today's airplanes often offer more luxurious and durable fabrics and leathers than older models. Buying new also offers a firm the option of personalizing the paint and interior to its individual taste. How important these latter items are to a firm in evaluating a new versus used aircraft, is really a management decision.

Maintenance

Whether purchasing a new or used airplane, maintenance is a major factor that prospective owners need to study carefully. Aircraft must be maintained according to strict FAA rules and regulations. Good maintenance can be costly, but it is infinitely less expensive than having an engine quit somewhere between airports. Also, a well-maintained aircraft will bring a higher price when it is time to trade it in.

There are hundreds of FBOs located on virtually every sizable airport in the country, as well as around the world, that provide maintenance. These businesses must meet stringent FAA requirements. Many FBOs are also the authorized service centers for the major airframe and engine manufacturers.

Larger corporate operators of business aircraft have their own in-house maintenance organization, or possibly they share a maintenance operation with two or three partners. This concept is generally only viable with companies operating a fleet of aircraft.

Financing the Aircraft Purchase

Most companies have lines of credit available through their banks. However, it is often preferable to keep this credit available for other needs such as short-term borrowings, working capital requirements or capital improvements. There are a number of aircraft financing specialists, including banks, finance companies and the manufacturer's finance organizations. The majority of these institutions finance nationwide and are able to handle most transactions by telephone, e-mail, fax or mail. Once a call is received from an aircraft dealer or purchaser, preliminary financial information is taken over the phone along with a complete description of the aircraft. Financial statements are usually forwarded by mail. Credit investigation is often handled by phone. In many instances, a decision is made on the loan within hours of receipt of the financial statements.

Most finance charges on aircraft loans are based primarily on four factors:

1. *Amount of the loan.* A larger loan may warrant a lower rate than a small loan.
2. *Amount of the down payment.* Greater equity in the aircraft results in less risk, thus a lower rate.
3. *Terms of the loan.* Lenders tend to look for a higher rate over a long term as a hedge against inflation.
4. *Credit strength of the borrower.* The most credit-worthy customers will enjoy the best rates.

Most financial institutions will require a down-payment of 20 percent on used aircraft and 25 percent on a new aircraft. The additional amount for new aircraft is because of increased depreciation which occurs during the first year. Lenders experienced in aircraft finance keep abreast of the total aircraft market and consider this in setting downpayment rules on specific aircraft. If a company can purchase an aircraft at an exceptionally good price, a smaller down payment would be requested. Once again, terms of the loan and credit of the borrower are factors in determining the necessary amount of cash required on the purchase.

The majority of aircraft loans are repaid in monthly installments. Aircraft loan specialists know that some borrowers have specific needs. Repayment plans have been set up quarterly, semiannually or on annual schedules. Occasionally, fixed-principal payments plus interest are arranged. Under this plan, each payment is smaller than the one before it since interest is less as the principal balance declines. Once in a while a company may desire smaller monthly payments than would normally be necessary to repay the loan. The lender may be able to arrange such a loan with a balloon payment at the end which would be paid in a lump sum or would be refinanced. These basic plans vary among aircraft lending institutions.

Lending institutions specializing in aircraft financing are equipped to handle the paperwork involved with aircraft purchase and financing in an orderly and rapid manner. They have direct connections with the FAA in Oklahoma City and can obtain a title search on an aircraft in a matter of hours. There are often documents pertaining to the aircraft which may cloud the title, such as forms unrecorded for some reason or old liens which have not been released. The lender can usually clear up these problems in a short time. The registration of an aircraft is also handled by the lender. This is an area where the financial institution can be of considerable assistance to the borrower.

Strong economic growth in recent years and unprecedented demand for business aircraft have created a favorable climate for financing aircraft. First, banks and financial institutions that have not previously been willing to fund business aircraft purchases have overcome their preconceptions about the market in a bid to share in this period of strong demand. Second, relatively low interest rates and abundant capital markets have combined to make borrowing an attractive and feasible proposition.

The latter 1990s have brought in a number of new capital sources looking for a piece of the business aviation loan market. The residual values of business aircraft have proven themselves to be stronger than those of commercial aircraft. To aircraft finance consumers, more financial sources mean more choice and more competitive deals.

For customers with good credit histories, the range tends to be both lower and narrower. Specialist business finance sources generally focus on expertise and flexibility as ways to set themselves apart from opportunistic rate cutters in the marketplace.

The options available to business aircraft purchasers are set to be further expanded by the emerging Internet-based finance tools. Following the trend in retail banking, these sources will likely make their way into the market with highly competitive interest rates made possible by pared administrative costs. However, the newcomers' lack of specialist knowledge could further obfuscate an already complex choice for would-be loan and lease customers.

Manufacturers play a vital role in securing funding for sales of both new and used aircraft in their broad portfolio of products. However, manufacturers tend to push their own finance facilities first.

BUYING AND SELLING USED AIRCRAFT

The Market

Used aircraft come from many sources. Aircraft manufacturers estimate that one out of every four new airplanes go to first-time owners, while three out of four new airplanes go to individuals and businesses trading in an older aircraft. This chain reaction provides a constant supply of pre-owned aircraft, and puts the fixed based operator actively in the used aircraft business. Often the profit on the transaction is not fully realized until the trade-in is successfully sold. Other major sources for used aircraft are (1) businesses in distressed industries; (2) individual owners; (3) repossessions from banks, leasing companies and finance companies; (4) foreign sellers; and (5) corporate owners who desire to replace their aircraft.

Owners desiring to sell their aircraft can approach the disposal in one of four ways. The best approach will depend upon the owners' desire to receive "top" dollar for their airplanes, the owners' know-how in handling the details of the transfers, and their ability to expose the airplanes to a sufficient number of qualified prospects. The advantages and disadvantages of the four approaches are as follows:

1. Sale by owner. If a buyer can be found quickly, this approach has the potential to generate the highest profit. The owner must have tracked the market well enough to know precisely what the aircraft was worth. Owners have difficulty in getting adequate exposure for their aircraft, and they lack the expertise to handle the many details required to complete the exchange.
2. Sale by a broker. A broker acts as an agent to bring a buyer and a seller together. This method involves listing the aircraft with an established broker who will then represent the owner in the sale of the aircraft. When the sale has been consummated, the broker will deduct five percent from the selling price for the commission. For their 5 percent commission, brokers bring exposure, know-how, and prompt action. The broker will handle all details in the transfer, saving the owner considerable time.
3. Sale to a dealer. From an economic standpoint, selling or trading an aircraft to a dealer is like selling it wholesale. The dealer must buy the airplane at a price which allows a markup sufficient to cover expenses on the transaction and make an appropriate profit. A dealer takes physical possession of the aircraft for resale, often upgrading the interior or avionics before it goes on the market. This method is the quickest and simplest of the approaches, but with an obvious cost.
4. Sale to an original equipment manufacturer (OEM). An OEM's resale group normally offers good after-sales support, pilot training, and referrals to insurance agencies, FBOs, and maintenance shops that have experience with the particular aircraft. At the same time, OEMs usually carry out an extensive inspection of any trade-in or resale aircraft in their own shops before it goes on the market. This can mitigate a substantial amount of risk to the pre-owned aircraft customer, but also adds to the cost.

Currently, about 80 percent of used business aircraft transactions worldwide are done through independent dealers and brokers. The choice between a dealer, broker, or OEM is often not clear cut, since each sector has its advantages. OEMs are a particularly good source for higher valued business aircraft because of their quality business practices. By the same token, there are many ethical brokers and dealers. The dealer/broker industry has tried to police itself, and people generally know who they are.

Although many late-model aircraft changing hands are normally still under a manufacturer's warranty, which will transfer to the new owner, most dealers and brokers sell older aircraft on an as-is basis without warranties. For this reason, buying an aircraft from a dealer with an extensive maintenance capability is often advisable, especially if that dealer is situated near where the individual or company plans to base the aircraft. However, that is often not possible.

While most independent dealers do not offer warranties on used aircraft, those with in-house maintenance capability are more receptive to negotiating special after-sale customer-support programs. But even without on-site maintenance, independent dealers offer some advantages not always available from the manufacturers that sell the aircraft they have taken in trade for new equipment. The dealers tend to be smaller and more streamlined, and, for this reason, decisions as to what will be included in the price of an aircraft can be done more rapidly because there is no large bureaucracy to deal with. Arrangements include upgrades, modifications, and maintenance that need be done on the aircraft before it is delivered to the buyer. The important thing is that a reputable dealer is always trying to build a special relationship with customers so that they will want to come back to buy their next airplane.

It is important in dealing with dealers or OEMs that the company or individual stick to aircraft that they have determined will meet their needs. Often dealers or OEMs are more concerned with selling what they have in inventory to make their commission, rather than selling an aircraft that will really meet the customer's needs.

Prices for a quality used aircraft depend on recent market trends for the specific model being considered. The best benchmark for appraisal is what the prices have been for the past six months. This information can be obtained from dealers or brokers, who can research this through the four recognized database sources: the Aircraft Blue Book, Vref, Jetnet, and Amstat.

Although prices of late-model used aircraft tend to be high, some buyers are willing to spend the money, since the wait for delivery of new aircraft can average one to two years from the time they are ordered. Although a used aircraft may cost less, many older aircraft require significant upgrades or refurbishment that can be time consuming, particularly in a tight market.

Purchasing Used Aircraft

It is important to examine the history of the aircraft, regardless of its age, by making a comprehensive inspection of all records pertaining to the aircraft's operation and maintenance. Buyers are encouraged to have the aircraft inspected by a qualified mechanic and a pilot in the case of higher valued business aircraft. In the case of incomplete maintenance logbooks, the buyer should initiate an in-depth research effort to fill in any gaps in the aircraft's maintenance history.

Some manufacturers who accept trade-in aircraft actually interview past owners and talk with the managers of facilities that have maintained the aircraft. The company will also contact the FAA to find out if any Form 337s have been filed for the aircraft. An *FAA Form 337* must be filled out in the event of a major alteration or repair of the aircraft. The forms are available at the FAA's Oklahoma City facility. Form 337s are examined because the information they provide may have a bearing on any work that the buyer might want to have done on the aircraft. If the buyer is considering a significant upgrade of the avionics or a completely new interior, the Form 337 will indicate what weight-and-balance changes have been made as a result of the alterations.

In addition to the maintenance log, the prospective buyer should review the airframe log, which deals with hours flown and cycles, as well as incidents and accidents. A complete airframe log should also indicate compliance with past airworthiness directives, as well as the manufacturer's recommended inspection schedules. *Airworthiness directives* are used to notify aircraft owners of unsafe conditions about their aircraft and to prescribe the conditions under which the airplane may continue to be flown. "The Airworthiness

Directives Summary," published by the Superintendent of Documents, should be consulted by the prospective purchaser to confirm that all applicable ADs have been complied with.

Airworthiness certificates are issued by a representative of the FAA after the aircraft has been inspected, is found to meet the requirements of the Federal Aviation Regulation (FAR), and is in a condition for safe operation. This certificate is displayed in the aircraft and is transferred when the aircraft is sold. It is important to note that the Standard Airworthiness Certificate remains in effect as long as the aircraft receives the required maintenance and is properly registered in the United States. It does not assure that the aircraft is currently in a safe operating condition. A general guideline when looking at logbooks is to note the ratio of flight hours to cycles. Fewer cycles (takeoffs and landings) normally mean that less stress has been put on the airframe. As a rule of thumb, buyers should not consider an aircraft that has less than two flight hours per cycle, because the aircraft will probably require some near-term heavy maintenance.

Once the logbooks have been inspected, a demonstration flight that allows the buyer to make a trial run may be in order. Most OEMs and dealers will permit this. However, unlike a short flight in the vicinity of the airport in a small aircraft in which the seller usually bears the cost, the buyer will have to pay the seller for any expenses incurred on a long demonstration flight.

For most heavy turbo-prop and jet equipment, a demonstration flight over a planned route is very desirable. If there is going to be a problem with the pressurization system, it is going to occur when the aircraft reaches flight altitude. For those companies that do not want to make a demonstration flight in the form of an actual point-to-point trip, a test flight of at least one hour at different altitudes is recommended.

In addition, any squawks revealed in the demonstration or short test flight allow the buyer to go into the all-important pre-purchase inspection with at least some knowledge of what should be looked at more closely. The former owner's maintenance facility is likely to be aware of something that perhaps was not entered into the logbook by a previous owner, since the authorized service center or OEM may have done the repairs. This is especially true if the airplane has been maintained under some type of factory maintenance plan, which is always a good reference when considering a pre-owned aircraft.

The buyer should ask if the engines are on a recognized engine management program, because those that are will have a complete set of maintenance records.

Pre-Purchase Inspection

The aircraft buyer should approach a *pre-purchase inspection* in a proactive fashion. The first thing to look for is any sign of corrosion and cracking. Corrosion is irreversible in its deteriorating effects on the airframe, and it is important to know whether damage has been done to the aircraft. It is also important to know if maintenance squawks have been addressed to assure that there are absolutely no hidden problems waiting to appear.

Technicians should perform a thorough engine inspection. They should check compression, examine the insides with a borescope, and do an oil analysis. If there is a problem with the engine, that should be factored into the purchase price. Technicians should check the mechanical components, the pulleys, linkages, and other mechanical parts. These are readily replaced, if necessary, but needed repairs are identified before purchase, not after. It is important for the buyer to look for functional avionics. If the airframe and engine are acceptable but avionics equipment needs upgrading, it should be installed at the time of purchase so that it can be included in the financing package, and possible dealer discounts on avionics at time of purchase can be used. This is also the time to upgrade the interior if it needs work.

A complete pre-purchase inspection can take from several hours for a light single-engine aircraft to seven or eight days for a typical business jet. With the advice of the person who has reviewed the logbooks, the buyer should go to the shop with a complete written description of the specific items the pre-purchase inspection is to cover. This is important because the OEMs and most service centers will offer a pre-packaged type of pre-purchase inspection. It is important to make sure that the inspection covers anything not included in the package that the adviser recommends.

If the aircraft under consideration is about due for a major inspection, the buyer may want to use that event as the basis for any pre-purchase inspection. The major inspection that would have to be done anyway could be the foundation for the inspection.

Pre-purchase inspections are not free. Sellers are not obligated to cover the pre-purchase inspection costs. An inspection on a light single-engine aircraft can cost several hundred dollars and from eight thousand to thirty thousand dollars for a corporate aircraft, depending on its size and complexity.

Although the buyer normally pays for the inspection, the buyer can negotiate with the seller to pay for repairs that might be needed as a result of what turns up. Most reputable sellers will agree to do that, even though the buyer might not always get dollar for dollar.

The bottom line for every pre-purchase inspection is to find what needs to be fixed so that the airplane will be ready to fly upon acceptance. The buyer may have decided beforehand that he or she wanted to have the aircraft repainted, the avionics suite upgraded, or a new interior installed; but these items would have been something the buyer would have done after accepting the aircraft. The important thing is that the aircraft is flyable with no problems upon acceptance.

The following list includes the major items to be considered in evaluating a used aircraft:

1. General:
   a. Total hours airframe? _____
   b. Hours flown while seller had it? _____
   c. Date of latest annual inspection? _____
   d. Latest 100-hour inspection? _____
   e. Number of hours since latest annual or 100-hour inspection? _____
      _____
   f. Have you checked carefully for metal corrosion inside wings and tail? _____
      _____
   g. Any sign of touch-up painting? _____ Aircraft in any accidents? _____
      _____
   h. Are all parts readily available? _____
   i. How many gallons of gas used per hour? _____
   j. How many quarts of oil? _____
   k. Does the plane look clean and well-cared for? _____
2. Engine:
   a. Total time? _____ Engine ever been overhauled? _____
   b. Top or major? _____ When? _____
   c. Total time since overhaul? _____
   d. Engine clean? _____ Free of rust, corrosion? _____
   e. Evidence of oil leaks? _____ Checking on hose? _____
   f. Clamps cutting? _____ Copper lines cutting? _____
   g. Chafing? _____ Sharp bends? _____
   h. Metal particles in the oil screen? _____
   i. Does the engine turn up maximum rated rpm on the ground? _____
      _____
   j. Have you checked the cylinders for compression? _____
   k. How much will a new or exchange engine cost? _____
3. Propeller:
   a. Finish in good condition? _____ Blade sheath in good condition? _____
      _____

   b. Any looseness in prop? _____ Free travel? _____
   c. Have all propeller bulletins been complied with? _____
   d. Any evidence of oil leaks? _____
   e. Spinner in good condition and secure? _____
4. Wings:
   a. Cuts in leading edge? _____ Inspection plates present? _____
   _____
   b. Any wrinkles in the skin? _____ Loose tape on fabric-covered plane? _____
   _____
   c. Sprung rivets on metal airplane? _____
   d. Loose bolts or struts? (Rock ship vigorously at wing tips) _____
   _____
   e. Any fuel stains indicating fuel tank or fuel system leaks? _____
   _____

5. Controls:
   a. Do all surfaces move freely and evenly? _____
   b. Hinges in good shape? _____
   c. Control cables have proper tension? _____
       Securely attached? _____
   d. Are cables rusty or worn looking? _____
   e. Everything properly secured? _____
6. Landing gear:
   a. Tires worn or cracked? _____ Struts properly inflated? _____
   _____
   b. Shock absorbers or bungees in good shape? _____
   c. Any nosewheel shimmy? _____ Do brakes hold properly? _____
   d. Brake fluid leaking? _____ All brake clips in place? _____
   _____

7. Doors and windows:
   a. Open easily? _____ Latch securely? _____
   b. Loose or twisted hinges? _____ Any cracks? _____
8. Cabin interior:
   a. Upholstery clean? _____ In good condition? _____
   b. Condition of windshield? _____
   c. Seats move easily, lock securely? _____
   d. Heater works? _____
9. Radios and instruments:
   a. Have you checked all radios and instruments? _____
   b. Are all installations neat? _____ Do all radio crystals work? _____
   _____
   c. VOR equipment meet accuracy tolerances? _____
   d. Record of VOR equipment checks for IFR operation? _____
   e. Are transmitters FCC type-accepted? _____
   f. Are they listed on FCC license? _____
   g. All instruments properly calibrated? _____
   h. Do gyros process excessively? _____
   i. Altimeter/static system inspection for IFR within last 24 months? _____
   _____

Negotiating the Purchase

   When all inspections and evaluations are satisfactory, it is time to make the owner an offer. The offer should allow for an adequate markup. This format will allow the dealer to put money into the aircraft to make it attractive to a prospective buyer. A dealer attempting to build a sound aircraft sales business will not follow the principal: "Buy the airplane for as little as possible, put as little money as possible in the clean-up phase, and then sell the airplane at the highest price possible."

When the offer has been accepted, a binder is given along with the signing of a simple sales agreement. The sales agreement identifies the parties, the specific airplane by "N" number, price, date of closing, and any other terms or conditions of the sale.

This is the definitive purchase agreement spelling out all of the criteria that must be met before the aircraft is accepted. As examples, sales contracts generally state that the aircraft will be delivered to the buyer in airworthy condition as a baseline, but they can also include all of the conditions agreed to. They could include repairs, refurbishment, the completion of a successful test flight, and/or the delivery time and date. If a certain component the buyer wants installed is not available, by the time the airplane is scheduled for delivery, it is important that the buyer and seller have an understanding that the component will be installed by a specific date.

With all the points to be covered in buying a used aircraft, the final responsibility for what is ultimately delivered comes down to the buyer. The buyer must beware.

The following sample sales contract covers many points aimed at protecting the interests of the buyer and seller. Obviously, the particular points in an agreement of this type are open to negotiations originating from either side.

(Buyer's name) hereby formally offers to Purchase one (manufacturer) (model) bearing manufacturer's Serial No. _____ and FAA Registration No. _____ from (Seller's name) for an agreed-upon price of $ _____ USD subject to the following terms and conditions:

1. Receipt by (Seller) within _____ hours of a deposit in the amount of $ _____ USD from (Buyer), which shall be refundable to (Buyer) in whole or in part as specified herein.

2. (Seller) has made representations to (Buyer) that the subject aircraft, with the specifications as presented to (Buyer) on (date), is in good working order and properly maintained, that the paint and interior as (representative condition), and that it will be delivered to (Buyer) in an airworthy condition with no fuel, oil, or hydraulic leaks, and with all integral components and systems in normal operating order.

3. (Seller) represents that it is the legal owner of the aircraft, holding good and beneficial title thereof, and at the time of delivery will be able to transfer free and clear title to the aircraft to (Buyer) on or before (date).

4. (Seller) shall make the aircraft available to (Buyer) at (location) no later than (date) to allow (Buyer) to perform a prepurchase inspection, which inspection shall be completed no later than (date), for purposes of verification of specifications and representations as to appearance and condition. The cost of performing this inspection shall be borne by (Buyer); the cost of positioning the Aircraft shall be borne by (Seller).

5. Upon completion of the above inspection, (Buyer) may, at it's sole and absolute discretion, elect not to proceed with the purchase, such decision to be made within _____ hours of completion of the inspection. In that event, (Seller) shall immediately refund to (Buyer) the deposit monies previously tendered, less (Seller's) direct expenses for moving the aircraft to and from (location of inspection). However, if the inspection reveals the representations of the condition of the aircraft were knowingly or significantly inaccurate, and (Buyer's) election not to purchase is based on these revelations, then the deposit monies held by (Seller) shall be immediately returned to (Buyer) in full, and (Buyer) shall not be liable or responsible to (Seller) for any costs incurred by (Seller) whatsoever.

6. If, after completion of the inspection, (Buyer) wishes to proceed with the purchase, (Buyer) will notify (Seller) within _____ hours of such intent, and (Seller)

hereby agrees to rectify, at (Seller's) expense, any discrepancies revealed by the inspection.

7. Upon such notification to proceed, (Buyer's) deposit shall become binding and nonrefundable pending structure and execution of a contract of sale to be finalized within _____ days, and delivery of the Aircraft on or before (date). Both parties agree to exercise their respective best efforts to formulate and finalize this contract.
8. (Seller), upon receipt of this offer to purchase, will immediately notify (Buyer) in writing by letter, e-mail, or fax of (Seller's) understanding, acceptance, and agreement with the terms and conditions herein.

Before the closing date, the buyer should make, or have made, a search of the records and encumbrances affecting ownership at the Aircraft Registration Branch, FAA Aviation Records Building, Aeronautical Center, 6400 South MacArthur Boulevard, Oklahoma City, Oklahoma 73125. A list of title search companies will be furnished upon request. When the title search is received, it will show the present owner, the lien-holder if any, and the dollar amount of the lien.

Aircraft Registration

After purchasing the used aircraft, a *Certificate of Aircraft Registration* must be secured from the FAA Aircraft Registry. An aircraft is eligible for registration only if it is owned by a citizen of the United States or a governmental unit and is not registered under the laws of any foreign country. An Aircraft Registration Application, AC Form 8050–1, consisting of an original (white) and two copies (green and pink) can be obtained from any FAA General Aviation District Office.

When applying for a Certificate of Aircraft Registration, an Aircraft Bill of Sale, AC Form 8050–2, must also be submitted. Until the permanent Certificate of Aircraft Registration is received, the pink copy of the application serves as a temporary certificate for 90 days and must be carried in the aircraft.

Financing

An aircraft dealer has three basic financing alternatives: cash, installment loans, and floor planning contracts.

Paying cash for expensive inventory, like aircraft, is generally considered unwise. Most managers of FBOs need capital for operating expenses and therefore must look to outside sources for funds to purchase used aircraft. Paying cash is the simplest of the three methods, but usually not practical.

To build adequate levels of inventory, newer aircraft dealers will turn to installment loans for their source of funds. These types of loans are available from banks and finance companies like Cessna Finance Corporation and CIT Corporation. Financing aircraft inventory by this method requires equal monthly payments over a period of six months or more. The payments include an interest charge and a partial principal payment. Financial institutions offer loans on either a simple interest basis or on an add-on interest basis.

Simple interest is charged only on the outstanding balance of the loan. The required monthly payment can be determined from financial tables or by multiplying the stated interest rate by the outstanding balance at the end of each month. A $50,000.00 one-year loan at 12 percent APR (annual percentage rate) would require monthly payments of $4,442.50. Since the interest is charged only on the outstanding balance of the loan, the annual percentage rate under this method of financing equals the stated rate.

The *add-on interest* method of determining monthly payments is commonly used in aircraft financing and results in a much higher APR than does the simple interest method. The one-year $50,000 loan with a stated interest rate of 12 percent used in the above example would require monthly payments of $4,666.50 with the add-on method. Aircraft dealers need to understand the difference between simple and add-on interest methods of computing finance changes to efficiently finance their aircraft inventory.

Established aircraft dealers will employ the use of floor planning to assist them in maintaining a good selection of aircraft. *Floor planning* is a financial arrangement whereby the bank, or other financial institution, will provide the dealer with short-term financing at moderate interest rates.

Floor plan programs vary depending on competition, economic conditions, and geographical location. A typical program will charge the dealer 1 percent per month on the wholesale value of the aircraft. The bank will either take title to the aircraft or place a lien on the title as its protection in the event of default by the dealer. The dealer will have from four to six months to sell the aircraft. If the aircraft is still in inventory at the end of this time, the aircraft will be placed on an installment loan basis, and the dealer will be required to make monthly principal and interest payments.

Floor planning is the preferred method of financing inventory. It allows the dealer to carry an adequate inventory of used aircraft while conserving capital. Since only interest is being paid on the wholesale value of inventory, the monthly cost is much less than the installment loan method where both principal and interest must be paid. The major disadvantage of floor planning is the tendency to carry too many or too expensive aircraft in inventory because of the minimum cost associated with this method.

Retailing Aircraft

Since the objective of pricing is both sales and profit, the dealer must be very careful to select the right price. In pricing, a number of issues must be considered. Some of the more important ones are the following:

1. Price competition from competitors.
2. Effects on exchange. Price is simply value expressed in terms of dollars. Potential buyers will equate the price of the aircraft with the perceived quality.
3. Influence on profits. The selling price must generate sufficient revenue to cover expenses and to provide an acceptable profit.

The pricing technique traditionally used in aircraft sales is markup pricing. *Markup* is the dollar amount added to the cost of the aircraft to determine the selling price. The size of the markup is the result of two factors:

1. Expenses to prepare the aircraft for resale, marketing, financing, general overhead allocation, and a target profit.
2. Inventory turnover rate. Usually, the greater the turnover rate, the smaller the markup required to accomplish the FBO's objective.

Markup is expressed as a percentage of selling price, and the formula used to determine the retail selling price of the aircraft is:

$$\text{Selling price} = \frac{\text{Cost}}{100\% - \text{Markup }\%}$$

The following example illustrates how Ace Aviation Inc. determined the retail price for the used aircraft which cost $90,000, and the profit on the completed transaction which took three months to close.

Price Determination — Used Aircraft

Retail price ($90,000/100% − 38%)	$145,161
Purchase price	90,000
Gross margin or gross profit (38%)*	———
	55,161

Expenses

Floor plan (1%) ($90,000 × .01 × 3 months)	$2,700
Insurance	
Hull coverage — $1.00 per $100 of aircraft value. ($900 × $1.00/4)	225
Liability — $1,000,000 single limit. $800 per year. ($800/4)	200
Minor repairs and detailing the aircraft	1,450
Selling costs	
Advertising — newspaper, handbills, etc.	1,350
Sales commission — 10% of gross profit (.10 × $55,161)	5,516
General overhead	2,500

Total expenses	13,941
Net profit before taxes	$41,220

*The 38% markup was determined from past sales experience to be adequate for target profit objectives.

LEASING

Leasing is another way of acquiring the use of a business aircraft. Business aircraft can be leased from professional leasing companies; some banks; aircraft manufacturers, either directly or through their finance subsidiaries; and even through some larger aircraft dealers, distributors and fixed base operators.

Leasing is typically done for a first aircraft or if the company has been downsizing, because then it will only show up on the books as an operating expense. Leasing is not as common today in corporate aviation as it was a decade ago. People often leased then because they were afraid that the aircraft would become obsolete, but, in fact, several used aircraft types have since become more valuable than they were new. With interest rates having been relatively low, it has been easier to offset the expense through finance rather than a lease.

Other financiers take the view that leases are still in vogue in the right circumstances, such as for customers who want lower debt loads and a higher return on the asset base of the company. Apart from keeping the aircraft off the balance sheet, other features include a lower annual cash outflow and a slower amortization of the cost, which is more evenly spread and never taken down to zero. In these days of long production backlogs for new business jets, for example, leases also allow companies to take advantage of an interim aircraft while waiting for their new model to be delivered.

Essentially, the lease versus loan equation comes down to an individual customer's propensity for risk — his experience as an aircraft operator and level of confidence about reselling the asset. With a lease, a customer is taking no risk on how the aircraft will hold its value since the asset is entirely owned by the lessor. The client basically forfeits the tax benefits associated with aircraft ownership in favor of a reduced rental rate, with the lessor taking the fiscal breaks.

Leases will routinely specify detailed maintenance requirements for the aircraft and specifications for the condition in which it must be returned at the end of the lease term. The assumption is generally made that all parts will be in their mid-time-between-overhaul condition, and it will normally be a requirement that the next major checks have been completed. Insurance also has to be maintained, with specified coverage.

Some manufacturers of large corporate aircraft are willing to tie guaranteed maintenance costs per flight hour programs to a lease. GE Capital has included crew-training credits in some deals, and it is understood that this sort of add-on cover could be extended to powerplant maintenance cover in the wake of the purchase of Garrett Aviation Services by parent group General Electric.

A lease may be either short-term — a few months or a few years, or long-term — as many as 15 or 20 years. The maximum length of the lease is determined mostly by the type of aircraft. Average lease terms are 8 to 10 years, but it is common for these to be terminated early as the customer's needs change. It is not uncommon in the United States for operators to break their original lease before the 5-year mark. This trend has underscored the importance of ensuring that sufficiently flexible cancellation terms are written into a lease.

There are two basic methods of leasing an aircraft, wet or dry. A *wet lease* is a contract whereby the owner of the aircraft (the lessor) makes an aircraft available for the user (the lessee), and also provides everything needed to operate the airplane: fuel and oil, maintenance, insurance, and storage. A flight crew may also be provided. The lessee's rental payment includes a fee that usually covers the cost of ownership, fixed and variable operating costs, and reserves, plus a profit to the lessor. In many ways the wet lease is similar to a charter except that the wet lease is usually made for a longer period of time. Depending on whether the lessor can provide these services more efficiently than the lessee, the rental payment for a wet lease may or may not be less expensive for a company. A *dry lease* or net lease is the more common type of lease arrangement. Here the lessor supplies only the airplane for a fee and the lessee is obligated for all fixed and variable operating expenses.

Advantages and Disadvantages of Leasing

Some of the advantages of leasing are summarized below:

1. *Conservation of capital.* One of the major advantages of leasing is that it conserves working capital. Generally, firms engaged in leasing do not require a substantial down payment at the beginning of the lease. Depending on the credit worthiness of the lessee only one or two months' advance payment may be required. Whereas the down payment required on the purchase of an aircraft using loan financing can be 15 percent of the purchase price or more, like the purchase example in Chapter 8. This saving can be substantial, assuming the lessee earns more on its working capital than the effective interest rate of the lease.

2. *Tax savings.* There are two ways a company can benefit from the tax savings of leasing. First, the full amount of each monthly lease payment of a properly structured lease is a deductible business expense for federal income tax purposes. Under the purchase scenario, a company is entitled to depreciation deductions, but only the interest portion of their loan payment is deductible. Second, if a company can not take full advantage of its depreciation deductions, a leasing company can generally take full advantage of the tax benefits of depreciation and pass the benefit of these deduction to the lessee in the form of a lower monthly lease payment.

3. *Preservation of credit lines.* A lease is generally not considered debt and, in most instances, does not restrict a company's borrowing capacity or reduce the amount of funds available under existing credit lines.

4. *Flexibility.* No assets are required to refinance or to liquidate before upgrading equipment. Leasing makes it easier to upgrade and time acquisitions with changing market conditions and company growth.

5. *Extends length of financing.* This is an important subcategory of the preceding benefit. In contrast to typical loans, leases may be obtained for nearly the entire length of the economic life of the aircraft.

6. *Reduces the risk of technological and physical obsolescence.* The risk associated with the expected value of an aircraft at the end of the lease term is placed on the lessor. If the company purchased the aircraft and the expected value of the aircraft declines the overall cost of ownership to the company would increase.

There are several disadvantages in leasing. During the lease term, the lessee usually cannot own the airplane or have an equity interest in it. Should the airplane have a residual value higher than the amount used to determine the lease rental payments, the lessor would receive this gain as owner, not the lessee. An improperly structured lease could be determined to be a purchase agreement or fail to meet the Internal Revenue Service (IRS) guidelines for a lease and the lessee would lose the tax and accounting benefits of leasing. Depending on the specific terms and conditions, a lease may cost the lessee more than a purchase. For instance, if the lessor requires additional insurance coverage or maintenance to be performed by the lessee.

Types of Leases

Leasing companies offer many different types of leases with different term lengths and various options. Within the leasing industry, the accounting profession, and under the Internal Revenue Code there are numerous names or titles for leases. As a consequence, sometimes there is a great deal of overlap and confusion, since the same type of lease may be known to the lessee, lessor, tax accountant, and financial analyst by a different name. However, from a lessee perspective, there are two basic types of leases; a *capital lease,* and an *operating lease.*

A *capital lease* resembles the acquisition of a business aircraft with the use of debt financing, and for income tax and financial accounting it is treated exactly like a loan. The aircraft is included as an asset and the lease obligation (payments) is recorded as a liability on the lessee's balance sheet. The lessee is allowed to include only the imputed interest portion of the lease payment and the applicable depreciation amounts for the period as expenses and as a tax deduction. Under this form of lease the company's monthly rental payment will amortize the entire cost of the aircraft plus a fair return (interest) for the lessor. At the termination of the lease term, the lessee has the option to purchase the aircraft for a $1.00 or some other nominal amount.

The lessor may offer various options, such as an early termination based on a formula similar to paying off a loan early. For example, assume that a company has a seven year capital lease for a $100,000.00 aircraft with the option to terminate the lease and purchase the aircraft at the end of five years. The lease contract calls for monthly payments of $1,634.40 for a total of $37,289.60 plus a $1.00 purchase option. At the conclusion of the 84-month period, the lessee would have paid the entire cost of the aircraft plus an effective rate of interest of 9.5 percent per year over the term and can acquire the aircraft for $1.00. If the lessee wishes to terminate the lease early, the payoff or purchase price to the lessee would be $33,660.46 plus the $1.00 purchase option. This amount is equal to the amount necessary to pay off a 9.5 percent $100,000.00 loan at the end of five years.

In recent years, increased tolerance of so-called *synthetic leases* on the part of the IRS has offered a way for U.S. corporate operators to have their cake and eat it, too. These leases allow customers to keep the aircraft on their books for tax purposes, while allowing them to keep the asset out of the company's annual report. This sounds-too-good-to-be-true proposition will work only for firms and individuals with the right tax and accounting profiles.

The more traditional operating lease, which has become a standard feature of the commercial airliner finance market, is suitable for those who cannot enjoy further tax benefits and who want to get their aircraft completely off the books.

An *operating lease* which is known as a "*true lease*" according to IRS regulations, provides the lessee with the use of the aircraft for a fixed period of time in exchange for rental payments. At the conclusion of the lease term the lessee returns the airplane to the lessor. Alternatively, the lessor may offer a purchase option, but the amount of this purchase option must be for the fair market value of the aircraft. Usually, this type of lease is recognized by the accounting profession in accordance with Generally Accepted Accounting Principles (GAAP) and by the IRS as a lease and not a purchase, and the company receives the accounting and tax benefits of leasing. Neither the aircraft nor the lease obligation is recorded on the company's balance sheet, and the rental payments are fully deductible for federal income tax purposes. The guidelines established by the IRS and GAAP specify the accounting and tax treatment of leases based on the specifics of the lease agreement. These guidelines should be consulted to be sure the lease agreement being proposed will be treated as a lease.

The structuring of *operating lease* payments is one of the more complicated aspects of leasing. Payments can be structured using; pre-tax, after-tax, return on investment (ROI), or return on equity (ROE) structuring methodologies. Ordinarily, a lessor estimates the residual value of the aircraft at the termination of the lease contract. They then calculate the rental amount required to achieve its required rate of return taking into consideration the tax benefits (e.g., depreciation deductions) available to it as the owner of the aircraft.

FRACTIONAL OWNERSHIP

The concept of fractional ownership was started by Executive Jets' NetJets program with four fractional jet owners in 1986. It evolved from a program that began in 1964 when the Pennsylvania Railroad provided the start-up capital for Executive Jet Airways. The new company ordered ten of the then brand new Learjet 23s, and the mission was to provide a service where people would buy blocks of usage and jets would be dispatched with efficiency to take customers wherever they wanted to go. The company went international in 1965 and changed its name to Executive Jet Aviation. By 1974 Executive Jet, or EJA as it was widely known, had expanded its fleet to include airplanes other than Learjets, up to and including a Boeing 707, until it was bought in 1986 by RTS Capital Services, a New York firm engaged in equipment financing through leveraged leasing. This gave EJA additional capital and airplanes for its charter fleet and provided RTS with operational and technical support for its fleet of leased aircraft.

The name was changed to Executive Jet, Incorporated, which became the parent company of the NetJets' fractional ownership program. The basis of the fractional ownership concept was to combine the flexibility of chartering with the advantages of ownership. This concept is not new, however. The genius of fractional ownership came in the form of a "core fleet" of aircraft. The *core fleet* is a group of airplanes owned by the fractional ownership provided directly and not resold to users. This fleet is used to supply transportation to shareowners when the inevitable scheduling conflicts occur. The application of the core fleet concept has proven to be the basis of fractional ownership success.

Fractional Ownership Programs

Fractional ownership programs are multiyear programs covering a pool of aircraft, each of which is owned by more than one party and all of which are placed in a dry lease exchange pool to be available to any program participant when the aircraft in which such participant owns an interest is not available. As an integral part of these multiyear programs, a single company provides the management services to support the operation of the aircraft by the owners and administers the aircraft exchange program on behalf of all participants. By purchasing an interest in an aircraft that is part of the program, an owner gains round-the-clock access to a private jet at a fraction of the cost. In addition to access to the aircraft in which it owns an interest, it also has access to all other aircraft in the program, as well as the support of a management company that will handle all arrangements relating to maintenance, crew, hiring, and all administrative details relating to the operation of a private aircraft.

Share size determines the amount of the down payment, the monthly management fee, and the annual flight hour allocation. For example, a one-quarter share will require a down payment equal to one-quarter of the manufacturer's suggested retail price. The down payment secures the one-quarter share access to the aircraft, or through the interchange agreement, another aircraft in the program, 24 hours a day, 7 days a week, for up to 200 hours of occupied flight time per year. The monthly management fee is also related to the share size and covers all operational costs of the aircraft. This fee takes care of pilots, maintenance, catering, and all other operational aspects of owning a private jet.

Share sizes are typically available incrementally from one-sixteenth or 50 flight hours per year; one-eighth or 100 flight hours per year; one-quarter or 200 flight hours per year, to one-half, 400 flight hours per year. Shareowners may "upgrade" to a larger aircraft, or "downgrade" to a smaller aircraft, trading flight hours based upon a predetermined exchange rate. Share size also determines simultaneous availability of multiple aircraft; the larger the share, the more likely multiple aircraft are available. There is also a fee charged for occupied hours flown.

Owners share tax liabilities and benefits as a percentage of the share owned. Even though all operations are conducted under Part 91, the IRS deems it to be a commercial operation, meaning FET applies. In the future, fractionals will operate under *FAR Part 91 Subpart K,* if the FAA adopts a proposed rule. Primary among the changes from current regulations are stricter weather-reporting and runway-length requirements, leveling the playing field between Part 135 operators and fracitonal providers.

A lower capital outlay equal to the share bought must be paid up front, and this acquisition cost may or may not be negotiable depending on the provider. Owners can lease or purchase their shares, but they are limited to selecting an aircraft available via the provider. Fractional aircraft of a given program generally have standard interiors and exteriors, and the shareowners usually have no say in how the aircraft are outfitted.

Owners can upgrade or downgrade their aircraft at any time (hourly rates for upgrades/ downgrades are charged via a predetermined sliding scale). In addition, owners may liquidate their shares after meeting a minimum time requirement or paying an early withdrawal penalty. In any case, share sellers must pay a *"remarketing fee"* to the fractional provider, which ranges anywhere from four to ten percent of the aircraft's "selling price." Furthermore, the airplane's residual value may be lower due to higher cycles and airframe hours (fractional aircraft each average more than 1,100 flight hours per year).

In 1986, when NetJets began, there were four fractional jet owners; by 1993, there were 89 and the number was growing fast. Over the next seven years the total number of shareowners by the four leading providers reached 3,596 with NetJets capturing close to half of the market (see Figure 10–1).

In July 1998, Berkshire Hathaway, Inc., acquired Executive Jet, adding strong confirmation to the considerable value in fractional ownership. The Berkshire Hathaway acquisition also added financial resources and strength, ensuring Executive Jet's continued growth around the world.

NetJets aircraft range from light jets like the Cessna Citation SII, Citation V-Ultra, and Citation Excel to the midsize Citation VII, Hawker 800XP, and Hawker 1000. The newest additions are the super-midsize Dassault Falcon 2000, the Citation X, which is the world's fastest business jet, and the Boeing Business jet.

Bombardier entered the fractional ownership market in May 1995 with its Dallas-based Flexjet program. The Flexjet program began with 22 owners and grew to 683 by 2000. At a portion of the full-ownership cost, a company can purchase shares in Bombardier Learjet 31A, Learjet 45, and midsize, transcontinental Learjet 60 aircraft. Flexjet owners can also gain global flight capability with shares in a wide-body Challenger 604. The new world-spanning Bombardier Global Express is also available.

Raytheon launched its Travel Air fractional ownership company in August 1997 with one customer, and by 2000 it had 683 shareholders. Although the vast majority of its fractional ownership shares are bought outright, in 1999, Wichita-based Travel Air made the process even easier by introducing a leasing program in addition to the customary options of paying cash or financing. The leasing option is offered by Travel Air through Fleet Capital Leasing's Corporate Aircraft Finance Division. This five-year leasing program requires no money down, and payments are made monthly at a rate that will be fixed for a period. At the end of five years, owners may walk away from the lease without further obligation.

Raytheon Travel Air is unique in that it is the only fractional-ownership program

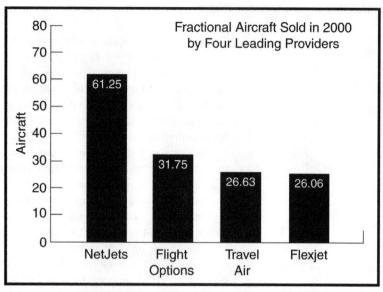

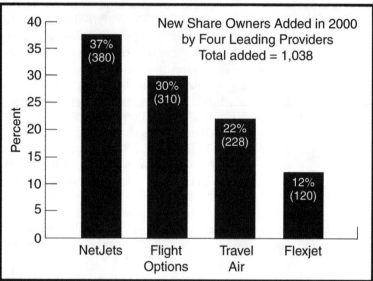

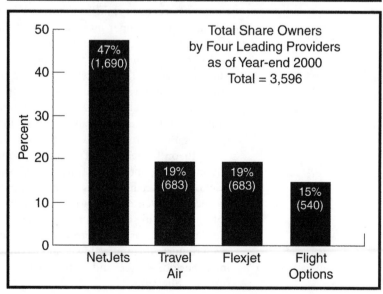

Figure 10-1. Fractional ownership—2000. Source: *Aviation International News,* April 2001

offering shares of a turboprop aircraft in addition to a complete line of business jets. Currently, the turboprop Raytheon King Air, the Raytheon Beechjet and the midsize, transcontinental Hawker 800XP are available.

Flight Options, which operates out of Cuyahoga County Airport in Cleveland is the newest and fastest growing provider selling 31.75 fractional aircraft and adding 310 new shareowners in 2000 (see Figure 10–1). Flight Options operates Beechjet 400As, Challenger 601s, Citation IIs, and Hawker 800s.

Other competitors have joined the market in recent years, including United Bizjet, a subsidiary of UAL Corporation, whose principal subsidiary is United Air Lines. United Bizjet plans to start operations in the fractional ownership market by 2002 with additional plans to provide corporate shuttle and charter services. Firm orders have been placed for Gulfstream IV-SPs, Gulfstream Vs, and Dassault Falcon Jets. The company decided to develop a fractional program in the late 1990s when management identified the growing business aviation market as a core area for expansion.

Advantages of Fractional Ownership

Fractional ownership offers many unique advantages over full ownership. Aircraft availability is guaranteed at any time with as little as four hours' notice, and all aspects of the aircraft's operation are managed by a provider. All of the leading providers, and most of the new entrants, do not charge for "deadhead" flight segments. A *deadhead leg* is one in which the aircraft is positioned for subsequent use. In a fractional ownership, deadhead legs are required to position aircraft for a shareowner's use, position the aircraft for one of the other aircraft shareowner's use, or return the aircraft to its base of operations. If a fractional owner operates to and from the same point of origin, the benefits of a fractional share can be substantially diminished. However, *positioning flights* are common, and more frequent deadhead legs further justify fractional ownership.

It has been estimated that roughly 80 percent of fractional owners are new to business aviation, and many of the other 20 percent use fractional participation to supplement their own in-house business flight capability. The advantages of fractional ownership regarding the deadhead segments and the availability of multiple aircraft have enabled the traditional flight department to become more efficient through the use of "supplemented lift." The term *supplemented lift* describes the use of a fractional share to supplement an existing corporate fleet. Supplemental lift is used to reduce the costs of deadheading, to facilitate maintenance schedules, and as a fleet multiplier when the demand for aircraft exceeds the flight department's existing fleet. This provides a flight department additional aircraft types. For example, a Challenger 604 or Global Express may be a perfect fleet complement for an intercontinental flight with 10 passengers aboard, while an economical Learjet 31A may be just right when two passengers are flying a short distance.

Aircraft availability is essential to the success of a fractional ownership program. Aircraft availability is enabled by the core fleet by limiting the number of shares sold per aircraft, and by drawing upon charter aircraft. The core fleet, as previously mentioned, is a number of aircraft that are held in reserve and in which shares are not sold.

Fractional ownership offers all the usual financial advantages of owning capital equipment, plus the unique advantage in that the terms of the fractional agreement typically guarantee the liquidity of the investment. A fractional share offers an effective means of air transportation, with costs directly proportionate to utilization.

CHARTER

Charter service companies provide aircraft and crew to the general public for hire. It offers the ultimate in air-travel flexibility. Chartering an airplane is similar to hiring a taxi for a single trip. The charter company provides the aircraft, flight crew, fuel, and all other services for each trip. The charterer pays a fee, usually based on mileage or time, plus extras such as waiting time and crew expenses. Chartering aircraft is particularly attractive for a firm that does not frequently require an airplane or does not often need a supplement to its aircraft.

Chartering can also be cost effective for a group of executives traveling together or for an emergency. When the individual businessman is traveling alone, the airlines, including regional carriers, would be more cost efficient, especially if the trip were between two cities well served by scheduled carriers.

Charter costs can range from as little as a couple hundred dollars per hour for a four-place single-engine piston aircraft to as much as five or six thousand dollars per hour for a corporate jet. In addition, there may be extra fees for position, waiting, catering, airport use, crew overnights, and so forth. Charges vary from region to region, with the highest rates being levied in the northeastern United States and southern California.

One of the most comprehensive resources available for charter customers is *The Air Charter Guide,* a compendium of more than 3,000 charter operators worldwide, including 1,800 in the United States. It is available in print or on CD-ROM.

Most of the revenue gained from the charter flight goes to the aircraft owner (charter companies seldom own more than a couple of aircraft—most of their fleets are on leaseback or other agreements with the actual owners or lessors) with the charter operator receiving a commission, usually between 10 and 15 percent of the cost of the entire trip. The charter rate can be "wet," meaning the costs for fuel, on-board catering, landing and positioning fees, crew expenses, and other charges are included in the cost. A "dry" rate means that these and other charges are added onto the hourly rate. Most charter firms also charge a two-hour-per-day minimum rate on their jet-powered aircraft and a one-hour minimum on their turboprops.

The weak economy during the early 1990s, along with a rash of company acquisitions, forced a number of companies to reduce the size of their fleets or eliminate them entirely. Many of these companies turned to chartering aircraft as an alternative. Some corporations opted for the least costly havens of aircraft management firms, while others simply appended their planes onto a convenient FAR 135 charter certificate to defray the costs of ownership.

Since the mid 1990s and the growth of fractional ownership, many of the better charter operators are busy supporting the fractional companies. Backup lift provided to fractional ownership companies provides the nation's charter services with substantial revenue. Backup lift support is not the only form of flight services that charter operators offer to fractional providers. When faced with the inevitable grounded aircraft, a fractional provider must respond quickly. Response to a grounded aircraft is frequently more readily facilitated by a charter organization. Getting flight crews, technicians, tools, and parts to the disabled aircraft as quickly as possible is essential to the fractional provider. Consequently, fractional ownership has stimulated significant air charter business in recent years.

Many corporate aircraft operators charter aircraft for the following reasons:

1. To keep flying when its own aircraft are down. When company airplanes are in for maintenance, repair, outfitting, or refurbishment, chartering allows employees to continue to fly as usual.
2. Supplement its airlift capability. A flight department can offer broader services by chartering aircraft of similar capacity to their own, or those with different mission capabilities (helicopters or corporate aircraft, for example).
3. Avoid overequipping. Generally, it is more cost efficient to charter occasionally than it is to underutilize a larger aircraft.
4. Have a less expensive alternative to airline travel. If a company needs to transport a large number of people to a single location at one time, it may be cheaper and more convenient to charter a large airplane that it would be to send the group on the airlines.
5. Test the business aviation waters. Chartering may be the safe method for a company to become involved with business aviation. The classic way in which companies get

their own aircraft is through an evolutionary process that begins with spot chartering and leads to contract chartering, leasing, participation in an aircraft management program and, finally, establishment of a corporate flight department.

6. Reenter the field of business aviation. Many companies gave up their aircraft during the last recession and have now found chartering a good way to enjoy once again the benefits of business aviation without making a capital commitment.

7. Fly before buying. For those companies that are contemplating upgrading to a new class of aircraft or adding equipment, chartering is a good way to conduct an in-depth operational evaluation of additional capability.

As commercial operators, charter firms must conform to more stringent operating and maintenance requirements called for in Federal Aviation Regulations. In addition, each charter operator, regardless of the types of airplanes used, must have an air taxi certificate on file with the FAA. This certificate is issued by the FAA after proper application and local inspection. It also evidences minimum insurance coverages and limits.

A review of any local listing in the yellow pages of the telephone directory will reveal no lack of charter operators. Local FBOs chartering single-engine aircraft to large operations chartering jumbo jets can be found.

The following checklist includes the major factors to be considered in evaluating a charter operator's performance. Many companies also use the services of a consultant to perform an impartial safety audit of charter operators or contract flight departments that have used specific operators in the past.

1. Operations:
   a. Pilot qualifications and records: total hours, time in type and ratings.
   b. Pilot training: source, flight training, ground school, and continuing proficiency training.
   c. Pilot turnover: average length of employment.
   d. Flight crew knowledge of the operations manual.
   e. Schedule, average weekly flight time, and working conditions.
2. Maintenance:
   a. Number of personnel, regular and temporary.
   b. Staff qualifications: records and experience, school training, and average number of years' experience.
   c. Staff turnover: average length of employment.
   d. Supervision and sign-off authority.
   e. List of factory approvals for service work, including rebuilding.
   f. Equipment and shop facilities: airframe, powerplant, and avionics.
   g. Record keeping: computer, staff, and facilities.
   h. Company maintenance manual evaluation.
   i. Program for timed removal of key aircraft components.
   j. Airworthiness Directives compliance.
   k. Ground safety, including fueling, servicing, and fire and crash facilities, if any.
   l. FAA repair station approval?
   m. Engine overhaul in house? If not, where?
   n. Premature failures of engines and major components.
   o. Spare parts stock.
3. Fleet Equipment:
   a. Type and number of aircraft, including year of manufacture.
   b. General condition of aircraft.
   c. Survival equipment, including over-water flights.
   d. Weight and balance records, including staff responsibility.
   e. Instruments: avionics for IFR flights, and international flights over water.

      f. Cabin equipment: catering service, phones, seating, lighting, and air condition-
         ing.
    4. Fitness:
      a. Financial condition and credit rating.
      b. Insurance coverage, including copy of certificate.
      c. Owner and length of time in business.
    5. Safety:
      a. Total hours flown during the past five years.
      b. Number and type of incidents.
      c. Accidents: minor, major, and fatal.
      d. Ratio of hours flown to accidents.
    6. Morale:
      a. Responsiveness of staff.
      b. Flight crew professionalism, general appearance, and courtesy.
      c. Evaluation of management.

Service can vary widely among charter companies, ranging anywhere from poor to excellent. Aircraft availability depends on market demand, and there is no guarantee of aircraft availability from any one charter operator. If a particular charter aircraft is not available, another vendor or the airlines must be used to meet travel demands.

Crew and mechanics are employed by the charter provider, which also controls personnel training. Crew changes are likely as they rotate from a pool. The charter firm is fully liable for the flight.

This option typically provides the lowest cost at lower usage levels, and reduced hourly charges may be negotiated at higher utilization rates (commonly referred to as block charter). Charter customers must pay for all ancillary charges, including deadheading and positioning costs, catering bills, landing fees, taxes (FET applies), and so on. No depreciation tax benefits are available to charter customers, but they may write off charter costs as a business expense.

Contract Flight Service

Contract Flight Service is the same as chartering an aircraft except that the customer buys a block of airplane time, mileage, or trips, usually over a certain period. Contract flight service is particularly suited to a company that has frequent and predictable need for business aircraft which is not enough to justify owning or leasing an airplane. This method also is used by companies who operate aircraft but need to supplement their own service.

Contract flight service can be very effective for a company which requires frequent travel that can be planned well in advance, and for companies scheduling many simultaneous trips in different directions.

Almost all charter operators will negotiate flight service contracts over a specified time period based on aircraft miles, hours, or trips. In terms of cost this arrangement can be more attractive than individual charter flights. However, similar to charter flights, beyond 200 hours of annual use the company will probably find it less costly to consider leasing or owning.

COMPARISON OF METHODS

As a general guideline, charter service is best when annual utilization is less than 100 hours. Fractional ownership is the preferred approach when utilization is between 100 and 400 hours, and total ownership is best when annual utilization is above 400 hours.

Any one of these estimates is not a precise indictor of which type of service is best in all cases. The choice is not based solely upon annual utilization rates. The best method is affected by a number of factors. Included are:

1. Route structure
2. Daily round trips

3. Extended-stay one-way trips
4. Fixed or variable passenger capacity
5. Demand for multiple aircraft
6. New or used aircraft
7. Positioning or deadhead legs
8. Owner status (no flight department or an existing flight department)
9. Service quality
10. Cost
11. Liability
12. Capital commitment
13. Tax consequences

Another underlying factor is level of control. A business must consider who they want to control such factors as aircraft availability, type, and quality, as well as liability and crew qualifications and training.

The dilemma is that in business aviation "one size does not fit all." What may work for one company is not necessarily the right move for another, and a choice made today may not meet next year's travel needs. The stakes are quite high. Business aviation is a complex field where the wrong choice can cost a lot of money.

To justify establishing a new flight department to support a corporate aircraft, the annual utilization rate should be forecast between 350 and 400 hours at a minimum. An existing flight department, one with operational and support resources already established, should have a forecast annual utilization rate around 250 hours. In either case, however, purchase of a used aircraft instead of a new aircraft can reduce the annual utilization rate estimate by as much as 100 hours.

The used aircraft purchase evaluation must also take into consideration the costs associated with maintaining aging airframes, powerplans, associated systems, and noise abatement.

One reason for the interest in fractional ownership in recent years is the increased residual value of business aircraft, particularly business jets.

Leasing aircraft reached its peak during the mid 1990s. It kept the aircraft off the company's balance sheet. This changed during the late 1990s when a company could buy an aircraft, operate it for two or three years, and sell it at well above what it cost. Consequently, leasing has lost its popularity.

Whether buying, leasing, fractional ownership, or charter, the same rule still applies—the company must know what its travel requirements are before utilizing business aviation. Its needs must be determined, not its wants.

Tables 10–1, 10–2, and 10–3 provide a summary of the methods discussed in this chapter.

CONCLUSION

Although many companies have acquired the use of business aircraft through various methods, few suddenly have purchased or leased their own airplanes without having had some previous experience that helped identify their needs. The normal introduction into business aviation is through a process that allows adjustment to one level before ascending further. Sales representatives use their own aircraft or rent them for business purposes or may begin by chartering. If the demand is great enough, contracting for a block of time is the next logical step. If the amount of chartering indicates that a firm would be better off with an airplane of its own, wet leasing might be considered. While wet leasing, the company has the opportunity to evaluate whether or not it should progress up the ladder to dry leasing. Here a company might want to enter first into a short-term dry lease as trial. After this, the company should have enough experience in business aviation and sufficient knowledge of its needs to determine whether or not to enter a fractional ownership program or to purchase an airplane outright, enter into a long-term dry lease or to step back to one of the previous rungs on the ladder more appropriate to its requirements.

Table 10–1   Company-Owned or Leased Aircraft—New or Used. Adapted from NBAA material

	In-House Flight Department	**Management Company**
Definition	• An entity is the only registered owner of an aircraft and uses an in-house flight department.	• An entity is the only registered owner of an aircraft and a management company operates the aircraft.
Service Quality	• Highest level of control/service possible • Immediate availability likely • If aircraft not available, must use charter, airlines, timeshare, or interchange • Best possible confidentiality/security	• Potentially excellent; customizable • Immediate availablity likely • If aircraft not available, must use charter, airlines, timeshare, or interchange • Pax can leave personal items on aircraft
Aircraft Administration	• Owner/lessee maintains total control over and manages aircraft operations • Personnel on owner's payroll; must deal with in-house personnel issues.	• Owner/lessee maintains control over, but delegates management of aircraft operations to management company • Personnel not on owner's payroll
Crew Quality	• Consistent; owner-controlled • Owner controls training of crew and mechanics	• Consistent, owner input, crews possibly assignable • Owner delegates control of pilot and mechanic training
Operating Costs	• Variable; utilization-dependent, lowest cost of operation at reasonable utilization levels • Subject to deadhead/positioning expense	• Variable; utilization-dependent • Annual costs may be higher than an in-house flight department (because of management fee) • Subject to deadhead/positioning expense
Cost Offsets	• There may be a charter option to help offset costs	• There may be a charter option to help offset costs • Possible availability of fleet discounts for fuel, insurance, and crew training
Liability	• Completely liable	• Shares liability with management company
Tax Consequences	• No commercial federal excise tax applicable • Noncommercial fuel tax applies • Maximum depreciation benefit	• No commercial federal excise tax (owners pay noncommercial fuel tax instead) as long as owner maintains possession, command, and control of the aircraft • Maximum depreciation benefit
Capital Commitment	• Higher capital investment of negotiated acquisition cost	• Higher capital investment of negotiated acquisition cost
Aircraft Acquisition and Disposition	• Can lease or purchase any aircraft at any price • Can select aircraft make/model, interior and exterior • Can choose when to upgrade, downgrade or sell	• Can lease or purchase any aircraft at any price • Can select aircraft make/model, interior and exterior • Can choose when to upgrade, downgrade, or sell

Table 10–2 Joint Ownership/Co-Ownership. Adapted from NBAA material

	In-House Flight Department	Management Company
Definition	• Two or more entities are registered owners of an aircraft, and one of the owners operates the aircraft for both owners	• Two or more entities are registered owners of an aircraft and use a management company to manage the aircraft for both.
Service Quality	• Potentially excellent; customizable • Availability requires coordination and planning • If aircraft is not available, must use charter, airlines, timeshare, or interchange	• Potentially excellent; customizable • Availability requires coordination and planning • If aircraft not available, must use charter or airlines
Aircraft Administration	• Owners/lessees maintain total control over and manage aircraft operations • Personnel on owner's payroll; owner must deal with in-house personnel issues	• Owners/lessees maintain control over, but delegate management of aircraft operations to management company • Personnel not on owner's payroll
Crew Quality	• Consistent; owner-controlled • Owner controls training of crew and maintenance personnel	• Consistent, owner input, crews possibly assignable • Owners delegate control of pilot and mechanic training
Operating Costs	• Variable; utilization-dependent • Subject to deadhead/positioning expense	• Variable; utilization-dependent • Annual costs may be higher than joint ownership (because of management fee) • Subject to deadhead/positioning expense
Cost Offsets	• There may be a charter option to help offset costs	• There may be a charter option to help offset costs • Possible availability of fleet discounts for fuel, insurance, and crew training
Liability Tax Consequences	• Completely liable • Owners share tax liabilities and benefits • No commercial federal excise tax applicable • Noncommercial fuel tax applies • Owners share depreciation benefit	• Shares liability with management company • Owners share liabilities and benefits • No commercial federal excise tax (owners pay noncommercial fuel tax instead), as long as owners maintain possession, command, and control of the aircraft • Owners share depreciation benefit to the share owned
Capital Commitment	• Owners share higher capital investment of negotiated acquisition cost	• Owners share higher capital investment of negotiated acquisition cost
Aircraft Acquisition and Disposition	• Can lease or purchase any aircraft at any price • Can jointly select aircraft make/model, interior and exterior • Can jointly choose when to upgrade, downgrade or sell	• Can lease or purchase any aircraft at any price • Can jointly select aircraft make/model, interior and exterior • Can jointly choose when to upgrade, downgrade or sell

Table 10–3   Fractional Ownership and Charter. Adapted from NBAA material

	Fractional Ownership	**Charter**
Definition	• Several entities are registered owners of an aircraft and hire a management company to manage the aircraft and allow the management company to exchange this aircraft among their fleet of aircraft.	A company that provides aircraft and crew to the general public for compensation or hire (profit)
Service Quality	• Potentially excellent; more generic • Aircraft availability guaranteed at all times, sourced via owned, fleet or charter aircraft • Advance notice required (4–8 hours) • More than one aircraft may be available at the same time, depending on contract terms and/or subject to availability • Charter aircraft may be substituted for program aircraft • Unable to leave equipment and/or personal belongings on board aircraft	• Potentially excellent; more generic • Possible inconsistent service from vendor to vendor • Availability depends on market demand; no guarantee of aircraft availability from any one vendor • If aircraft not available, must use other charter vendor or airlines
Aircraft Administration	• Owners maintain control over but delegate management of aircraft operations to fractional provider (management company) • Personnel not on owner's payroll	• None, not applicable • Personnel not on owner's payroll
Crew Quality	• Crew changes likely, rotating from pool • May be able to request specific crew or use own crew • Owners delegate control of pilot and mechanic training	• Crew changes likely, rotating from pool • No control of pilot or mechanic training
Operating Costs	• Fixed on a per-hour basis, based upon flight time, plus set ground time per operation used to calculate billed usage charges • All fees (including deadhead and positioning charges), except international handling and customs charges included in overall fee structure • Higher costs when compared to other forms of ownership at higher utilization levels, or charter at lower utilization levels.	• Lowest overall cost at minimum usage levels • Consistent charges at low utilization rates, subject to negotiated reductions at higher usage levels • Subject to ancillary charges such as catering, landing • Subject to deadhead/positioning expense
Cost Offsets	• None applicable	• None applicable
Liability	• Shared liability with fractional provider	• Not necessarily immune from liability
Tax Consequences	• Owners share tax liabilities and benefits • Federal excise tax imposed on direct operating costs • Owners share depreciation benefits to the share owned	• Federal excise tax imposed on charter rate • No depreciation benefit available as no aircraft are owned
Capital Commitment	• Lower capital outlay equal to a percentage of an aircraft share which may or may not be negotiated	• None
Aircraft Acquisition and Disposition	• Can lease or purchase • Limited to aircraft available via provider • No aircraft customization • Can choose to upgrade at any time; can choose to downgrade or sell after meeting minimum time requirement or pay penalty • A remarketing fee is charged for aircraft disposition. • There may be penalties for early withdrawal from the program • Lower residual value because of higher hours/ cycles; known at purchase	• None; no ownership

KEY TERMS

Timesharing agreement
Interchange agreement
Management company
Joint ownership
Co-ownership management company
FAA Form 337
Airworthiness directives
Airworthiness certificates
Pre-purchase inspection
Certificate of aircraft registration
Simple interest
Add-on interest
Floor planning
Markup
Wet lease

Dry lease
Capital lease
Synthetic leases
Operating lease
Core fleet
Fractional ownership
FAR Part 91, Subpart K
Remarketing fee
Deadhead leg
Positioning flights
Supplemental lift
Charter services
The Air Charter Guide
Contract flight service

REVIEW QUESTIONS

1. Why is a company-owned aircraft the most flexible method of business aviation? What are timesharing and interchange agreements? List some of the advantages of company-owned aircraft operated by a management company. What are some of the pros and cons of joint ownership?

2. Finance charges on aircraft loans are primarily based on four factors. What are they? What is the reason for the strong competition in the field of aircraft finance in recent years? Describe four methods owners may use in selling their aircraft. What are some of the areas to be considered in evaluating the purchase of a used aircraft? Define: FAA Form 337; airworthiness directives, and airworthiness certificates.

3. What are the major points covered in an aircraft sales contract? Distinguish between simple and add-on interest. What is floor planning? Give an example of the retail price of an aircraft including all of the items in the markup formula.

4. Why is leasing an aircraft not as popular as it was in the early 1990s? Distinguish between a dry and a wet lease. List four distinct advantages in leasing an aircraft. What is the primary disadvantage of leasing? What is a capital lease? How does this differ from an operating lease? What are synthetic leases?

5. How was the concept of fractional ownership started? What are fractional ownership programs? Who are the major fractional providers? What is the function of FAR Part 91, Subpart K? Discuss some of the reasons for the tremendous growth in fractional owners during the late 1990s. What is meant by the term "supplemental lift"?

6. When might chartering an aircraft be considered the most effective method of acquiring the use of a business aircraft? List some of the reasons why corporate aircraft operators may charter aircraft. What are the major factors to be considered in evaluating a charter operator's performance? How does a straight charter differ from contract flight service?

7. What are the general guidelines, in terms of annual hourly utilization, when considering charter, fractional ownership, company ownership, or leasing? What are some other factors that may be considered? Compare and contrast fractional ownership with a company-owned aircraft in terms of service quality, aircraft administration, crew quality, operating costs, liability, tax consequences, capital commitment and aircraft acquisition and disposition.

Chapter 11

Promotion and Sales

OBJECTIVES

At the end of this chapter, you should be able to:

Name and describe the four components in the promotion mix.

Discuss the objectives of advertising.

Distinguish between the following types of advertising: product, institutional, pioneering, competitive, comparative, and reminder.

Explain the importance of an advertising budget and message.

Summarize the advantages and disadvantages of the leading advertising media.

Describe several methods of measuring advertising effectiveness.

Give four examples and describe the purpose of sales promotion.

Describe several publicity techniques that may be used by an FBO.

Define prospecting.

List five aircraft prospecting sources and describe the type of information given.

Highlight some of the basic business information needed by an aircraft salesperson to qualify a prospect.

Discuss the approach, presentation, handling objections, close, and follow-up steps in the selling process.

THE PROMOTIONAL MIX

In order to communicate the availability of its products a firm can use one or more of four promotional activities: advertising, sales promotions, publicity, and personal selling. The *promotional mix* is the combination of one or more of these activities.

Advertising is any paid form of nonpersonal communication about an organization, product, or service by an identified sponsor. The paid aspect of this definition is important because advertising normally must be purchased. The nonpersonal component of advertising is also important. Advertising involves mass media that are many and varied, including magazine and newspaper space, outdoor posters, signs, banner towing, direct mail, radio, television, catalogs, directories, and circulars.

Although advertising lacks the immediate feedback of personal selling, it can reach large numbers of potential customers at relatively low cost. By using advertising in a promotional mix, a company can control what it wants to say and, to some extent, to whom the message is sent. If an FBO wants college students to receive its message on flight training, advertising space can be purchased in a college campus newspaper.

Sales Promotion involves marketing activities other than advertising, publicity, or personal selling, that stimulates customer purchases and company effectiveness. Sales promotion activities include trade shows, coupons, contests, premiums, and free samples that are basically aimed at increasing sales. A $35 coupon appearing under an FBO's advertisement in a local newspaper to be used for an introductory flight is an example.

Publicity is an unpaid form of nonpersonal communication about any organization, product, or service by an identified sponsor, which can take the form of a news story, editorial, or product announcement. An announcement in the local activities section of the newspaper, informing the public that the area aircraft model builders club meets in the conference room of Ace Flying Service at 7:00 p.m. on the last Thursday of the month, is a form of publicity. Publicity is generally thought of as favorable and is planted by the firm or its advertising agency to promote the company by informing or reminding the public about its products and/or services. Negative publicity can occur, however, such as when an airplane crashes, or local citizens complain about noise created by airplanes taking off and landing at the local airport. Publicity can happen without the urging of a firm, just for its news value.

Personal selling is a two-way flow of communication between a representative of the firm and a customer for the purpose of making a sale. The two-way flow of communication distinguishes personal selling from other forms of promotion.

Costs associated with personal selling are high, but there are distinct advantages. A representative can control to whom the presentation is made and can also see or hear the potential buyer's reaction to the message. If the reaction is unfavorable or not completely understood, the salesperson can modify the message. The flexibility of personal selling also can be a disadvantage because different salespeople can change the message regarding the product or service so that no consistent communication is given to all customers.

In putting together the promotional mix, a firm must consider the balance of elements to use. There is no one right promotion blend. Each must be developed as part of a unique marketing mix (four Ps) for each target market.

ADVERTISING

Advertising can play an important role in the promotion blend. In contrast to personal selling, advertising is a form of mass selling that attempts to make potential buyers aware of and interested in a firm's products and services. In other words, it takes a "shotgun" approach, whereas personal selling "zeroes in" on individuals with a "riflelike" approach.

While the level of advertising as a percentage of sales varies among industries, U.S. corporations average about 3 percent of their sales dollar on advertising. Unfortunately, many smaller firms such as FBOs pay very little attention to this important ingredient in the marketing mix.

Few companies, big or small, have the in-house expertise to develop their own advertising programs. Consequently, they turn to advertising agencies who are specialists in planning and handling mass selling details. Some agencies are one-person operations. At the other extreme, an agency may have as many as 8,000 employees. Some agencies specialize in business advertising and others in retail advertising. Basically, an advertising agency carries out the following functions:

1. Plans advertising.
2. Selects media and contracts for space and time.
3. Prepares the advertising, including copy, layouts, and other creative work.
4. Produces finished advertisements in the physical form required by different media.
5. Creates and produces direct-mail pieces and other collateral material.
6. Checks invoices and evidence that advertising has been run as scheduled (such as tear sheets from publications and affidavits from broadcasting stations). The bills from vendors who supplied materials and services for preparing the advertising are reviewed by the agency.

An advertising agency begins by becoming familiar with the company and what it sells. Perhaps the agency's members already have a background of experience with similar businesses. If so, they concentrate on learning about the specific operation. They study promotional objectives and determine the role advertising can play in helping accomplish the objectives. Then the agency recommends what approach the advertising message should take and the specific media to use. Perhaps the question is whether to use newspapers or radio or a combination of the two, or how much of the advertising should be in trade publications and how much in the form of direct mail and other sales literature.

Agencies are paid in four ways: (1) commissions allowed by media; (2) fees paid by the firm; (3) service charges on materials and services purchased for preparation of advertising; and (4) charges for advertising not involving commissions, such as direct mail.

Commissions allowed by media to advertising agencies are usually 15 percent of the cost of advertising space or time purchased. Most media have two rate schedules, national and local. National rates are higher and include agency commissions. When the lower local rates apply, with a few exceptions agencies are not allowed to deduct commissions. The commissions included in the national rates are allowed only to agencies. Commissions received from media are the major source of income for most agencies.

When an advertising agency is used, an individual from the firm, working along with the agency account executive, is responsible for coordinating the agency's activities with related company activities. This individual participates in the agency's planning and conduct of advertising campaigns; thus ensuring that they are consistent with the firm's overall marketing strategy.

Advertising Objectives

Every advertising campaign should have clearly defined objectives that must flow from prior decisions on the market to be targeted and the marketing mix. Accurate measurement of stated objectives such as sales, market share, and profits should be taken before and after the campaign. Firms who fail to do this will only have an intuitive feeling about the effectiveness of their campaigns.

Advertising objectives should specify:

1. What is to be accomplished and the target market. Some examples are:
    To increase line service business — NBAA members
    To increase the number of flight students — College students
    To develop charter business — Local businesses with over 100 employees
    To increase maintenance business — Local, single-engine aircraft owners.
2. The time period for accomplishing the objectives.

The objectives listed above are not as specific as they could be. A firm may want to sharpen them for its own purposes. For example, a general objective: "To increase the number of flight students," could be rephrased more specifically: "To increase the number of student pilots by 20 percent during the next three months."

Setting reasonable advertising objectives is part of the art of marketing. The first time a manager sets objectives, they will probably be based on an educated guess, despite the logical analysis that may have gone into the choice. In time, however, experience in setting objectives and observing the actual results of particular advertising campaigns will allow the manager to select more realistic objectives.

The advertising objectives largely determine which of two basic types of advertising to use: product or institutional. *Product advertising* takes three forms: (1) pioneering, (2) competitive or comparative, and (3) reminder. Product advertising tries to sell a product or service to final users or middlemen. *Institutional* advertising attempts to develop good will for the company and enhance its image, instead of promoting a specific product or service. In practice, a firm may employ both of these two basic types of advertising simultaneously.

Pioneering advertising tries to develop demand for a product or service category rather than for a specific company. It informs the target market what the product or service is, what it can do, and where it can be found. FBOs placing an ad describing charter services in the local chamber of commerce newsletter is an example.

Advertising that promotes a specific company's products or service is *competitive advertising*. The objective of this advertising is to persuade the target market to select the firm's offerings rather than those of a competitor. An increasingly common form of competitive advertising used by the airlines and other segments of the aviation industry is *comparative advertising*. This form of advertising shows one firm's strengths relative to competitors.

Reminder advertising is used to reinforce prior knowledge about the product or service such as a brochure sent to a business aircraft owner who recently had aircraft serviced at the local FBO. "The next time you are in Fort Lauderdale, drop by and see us. It was a pleasure serving you."

Establishing an Advertising Budget

Once the advertising objectives have been determined, a budget must be established for each product or service. Deciding on the ideal amount is a difficult task because there is no precise method to measure the results of advertising spending. There are five traditional approaches to deciding how much to spend for advertising: (1) spending all the firm can afford; (2) allotting a certain percentage of net sales; (3) matching the advertising expensitures of competitors; (4) investing for future profits; and (5) the objective-and-task method.

The all-we-can-afford approach treats advertising as a luxury. This is a financial rather than a marketing approach. It does not consider what advertising can or should accomplish.

A percentage of sales approach is popular because it provides a formula—for instance, a certain percent of past sales—and it is simple and easy to use. Using the previous year's sales as the base seems to assume that advertising is the result of sales rather than sales the resulting of advertising. Furthermore, it makes no provision for increasing business and may not even allow enough money to maintain the current level of advertising. A variation of the percentage approach is the unit-of-sales method. This method establishes the amount of advertising on the basis of unit quantities of goods instead of dollar sales. This method is suitable for a firm with a narrow product line.

Trying to match the advertising of competitors is a defensive rather than an aggressive approach. It tends to produce advertising programs that are not tied to stated objectives and result in inefficient expenditures.

Advertising is considered an investment for future profit. It is primarily for introducing new products or services where extensive advertising dollars are required to get the product adopted. Any possible profits are plowed back into advertising and other promotional and sales activities.

The last of the five methods for creating advertising budgets is regarded by many as the best. The objective-and-task method builds a budget by first deciding what type of advertising is needed to accomplish the stated objectives. The principal problem with this method is the danger of being too ambitious. When the budget is totaled, the cost of the campaign may be more than the firm can possibly afford. The solution is usually to revise the objectives and/or modify the time for reaching them.

Recent research conducted by the Strategic Planning Institute for Cahners Publishing Co. identified the following decision rules that can be used to determine the size and focus of a firm's ad budget.

- Market share—A company that has a higher market share must generally spend more on advertising to maintain its share.
- Sales from new products—If a company has a high percentage of its sales resulting from new products, it must spend more on advertising compared to companies that have well-established products.
- Market growth—Companies competing in fast-growing markets should spend comparatively more on advertising.
- Unit price (per sales transaction)—The lower the unit price of a company's products, the more it should spend on advertising because of the greater likelihood of brand switching.
- Product price—Both very high-priced (or premium) products and very low-priced (or discount) products require higher ad expenditures because, in both cases, price is an important factor in the buying decision and the buyer must be convinced (through advertising) that the product is a good value.
- Product quality—Higher-quality products require a greater advertising effort because of the need to convince the customer that the product is unique.
- Degree of standardization—Standardized products produced in large quantities should be backed by higher advertising outlays because they are likely to have more competition in the market.

Most FBOs are small and have limited resources for advertising. Repeating advertisements can stretch advertising dollars. Savings occur through reduced preparation costs, both creative and mechanical. A number of studies have shown that advertisements repeated as many as four times do not lose their effectiveness. A later insertion attracts about the same number of readers as the first one.

Another way to get extra mileage from the advertising budget is to convert newspaper and magazine advertisements to direct mail. This is especially helpful when expensive color plates have been produced. The FBO already has an investment in copy, layout, art, and mechanical preparation. With little revision, a direct mail piece can be created. Another suggestion is to use a reprint of the advertisement as an attachment to a letter or as a self-mailer.

Advertising Message

Next, the firm develops its *advertising message,* the overall appeal for its campaign. The message in an advertisement is often called the copy. Copy results from a combination of analytical thinking based upon a clear understanding of the firm's products and services with a liberal use of imagination. The actual advertisements are produced by creative individuals at the advertising agency—the copywriters and artists—but the overall evaluation and approval of copy is the responsibility of marketing management.

The copy must fit both company and advertising objectives; it must be consistent with the target audience and the product or service itself. Generally, an early step is to develop a campaign theme—a keynote idea or unique selling proposition—as some marketing people refer to it. This keynote idea should provide continuity and have significant impact upon target market segments. For example, business aircraft have frequently been referred to as time machines—the theme being saving time and increasing productivity.

Language or visual messages projecting the central theme must be created; most advertisements use both. An effective message (1) attracts the market's attention, (2) is understandable, and (3) is believable.

Media Selection

The firm's next step is choosing the advertising media to carry the message. There is a wide variety of media from which to choose and this decision is primarily related to the target audience, the product or service, available budget, and campaign objectives.

Table 11–1 summarizes the advantages and disadvantages of the leading media. Newspapers are an important local medium with an excellent potential for reaching a large audience. They also allow great flexibility in the size of ads that may be a few lines or a complete page. Very little lead-time is needed to place or change an ad and it can be tailored to current developments. The short life of a newspaper ad is a drawback along with the inability to tailor the message to a specific target market.

Magazines and trade journals are certainly some of the fastest growing media. Color is used most effectively in magazines, and the big advantage of this medium is the great number of special interest publications that appeal to target markets. The long lead-time required for magazine ads results in more general and less timely information. The cost of magazine and trade journal advertisements compared with other media is another disadvantage.

Direct mail advertisements can reach a very homogeneous market and convey a great deal of information. Mailing lists can be obtained for specific aircraft owners in a particu-

Table 11–1   Advertising Media

Medium	Advantages	Disadvantages
Newspapers	Short lead time needed, flexible, good local market coverage, inexpensive	Short life, poor reproduction quality, general audience, limited creativity, heavy ad competition
Magazines and Trade Journals	High geographic selectivity, long life, high quality reproduction, good pass-along readership	Long lead time, poor frequency, ad clutter, expensive
Direct Mail	Audience selectivity, no ad competition, personal approach, inexpensive	High throwaway rate, receipt by wrong person, low credibility
Radio	Selective market, high frequency, low cost	No visual contact, customer distractions
Television	Combines sight, sound and motion, high attention, persuasive	General audience, relatively expensive, lead-time, short message
Billboard	High repeat exposure, low cost, low competition, color creative options	General audience, legal restrictions, inflexible
Telephone/Business Directory	Low cost, coverage of market, specialized listings	Clutter of ads, limited creativity, long lead-time
Internet	High degree of selectivity, interactive	Large competition

lar geographic area. Direct mail advertising is a relatively inexpensive form of advertising although many people view direct mail as junk. The challenge is to get the recipient to open the letter or brochure.

Radio advertisements are fairly inexpensive and are particularly effective for local messages. Radio stations can be valuable in target marketing because of the different listening audiences. Lead-time for developing radio ads is short. The main disadvantage of radio is the inability of the prospective customer to review the message. Another problem is the ease with which customers can switch stations and tune out a commercial. Radio also competes with people's attention as they do other activities, like driving or working.

Television has a major advantage over all of the other media in that it combines sight and sound. Its primary disadvantage is cost. The combination of a general audience and cost are sufficient detriments to eliminate this medium from most FBOs' promotion mix.

An effective medium for reaching a general audience in a specific locale is billboard advertising. The drawback in billboards is the inability to present lengthy advertising copy. Also, in many areas, laws have been passed to restrict the use of this medium.

Advertising in telephones and business directories is used by all firms and can be very effective because prospective customers seek out the firm. The cost is rather inexpensive but its weakness is that directory ads compete with so many other similar ones. This medium is often called *directional advertising*. The prospect has already established the need, and is looking for the best alternative to satisfy the need.

An emerging medium, Internet advertising is booming. The overall Web population is reaching critical mass. Recent surveys show there are 25 to 40 million adult Web users in the United States—between one-eighth and one-fifth of the population. Twenty-five million Americans use the Web at least one a week, and 8.4 million are daily users. Internet advertising offers a variety of advantages. It offers an exceptional ability to target specific customers, has the ability to be interactive, and can be customized to unique target markets. Rates on the Net are typically $10 to $40 per 1,000 viewers, which is in line with the cost of national magazine rates.

Measuring Effectiveness

The final element in the advertising campaign is measuring its effectiveness, which should be measured in terms of criteria derived from the firm's overall advertising and marketing objectives.

If advertising objectives are sales related (e.g., to increase sales or improve market share) then it is possible to determine whether the advertising has been effective in reaching customers. However, advertising is only one cause of sales. Other aspects of marketing, including improved product or service, other forms of promotion such as personal selling and pricing, all contribute to sales performance.

Some firms pretest advertising effectiveness before starting the campaign. A panel of customers or knowledgeable individuals might be asked to rate which ad would most influence them. Customers might be asked to evaluate several ads and then recall the source and as much of the content of the message as they can. The uniqueness of an ad can be best measured by this method. Post testing an advertisement can also be used. For example, results can be measured by orders mailed back; coupons brought in, or number of customers who respond to an ad for a sale. Recall tests can be used in which customers are asked to recall everything about an ad in a trade magazine or newspaper to which they subscribe. This test measures an ad's ability to be noticed and remembered.

SALES PROMOTION

Sales promotion activities supplement both advertising and personal selling. It is usually not directed at as large an audience as advertising, but is directed at much larger groups than a typical personal selling effort. Included are such activities as trade shows, exhibits, coupons, trade allowances, demonstrations, and dealer incentives.

Given the diversity of sales promotion activities, it is apparent that they are designed to reach many target markets and to achieve a variety of objectives, such as the following:

1. Identifying sales leads (trade shows)
2. Inducing prospective customers to try a new service (flight instruction coupons)
3. Increasing the share of an established market (price breaks on a block of charter hours)
4. Improving name recognition (calendars, matchbooks, T-shirts, pens, and posters with the firm's name)

Sales promotion has several distinct advantages. First, it involves the prospective customer. Customers must return the flight coupons to receive instruction, or they must use free samples or throw them away. Additionally, sales promotion activities can offer true value to the user; money can actually be saved. Finally, sales promotions can be directed to narrowly defined market segments. For example, flight coupons can be mailed to prospective users in high-income areas, or a brochure announcing a specially priced maintenance package can be directed to particular aircraft owners.

The following sales promotion activities are typically used by FBOs:

1. *Coupons.* Coupons are certificates entitling the bearer to a stated saving on the purchase of a specific product or service. Coupons can be mailed, enclosed with other products, or inserted in ads. They can be effective in stimulating sales and getting a customer to try a new product or service.

2. *Price incentives or deals.* Short-term price reductions are commonly used to increase trial among potential customers or to retaliate a competitor's actions. These special deals generally work best when they are used infrequently or when the product or service being offered is relatively new.

3. *Promotional contests and sweepstakes.* Promotional activities that involve customers in games of skill are called contests, while those involving customers in games of chance are called sweepstakes. For example, in the case of a contest, customers (present or prospective) may be required to complete a puzzle, identify a vintage aircraft, or complete a sentence for a prize. Sweepstakes are often used to increase fuel sales or to sell aircraft. The aircraft manufacturers have sponsored a number of sweepstakes over the years with the winner receiving a new aircraft.

4. *Premiums.* Premiums are offerings of merchandise at a low cost or free as an incentive to purchase those products or services or suggestions to visit the locations where the products or services can be obtained. Premiums serve as reminders and include such items as calendars, miniature flashlights, key chains, business card holders, T-shirts, pens, posters, and a host of other promotional items with the firm's name displayed.

5. *Demonstrations.* Demonstrations are sometimes used by FBOs selling aircraft or charter services. A price break may be given to a prospective customer on a demonstration flight of an actual trip. Demonstrations involve a personal presentation of how the service works. It is often effective but is an expensive technique and has limited application.

6. *Point-of-purchase promotions.* Point-of-purchase promotions are special displays, signs, banners, and exhibits that are set up in schools, stores, mall entrances, and the like to promote a product or service. These promotions serve to remind customers that a product or service is available at a given location (a sign at the local flight shop next to the cash register advertising an FBO).

7. *Trade shows.* Many firms use trade shows such as the annual NBAA convention to advertise their products and services. Participating companies expect several benefits, including generating new sales leads, maintaining customer contacts, introducing new products and services, meeting new customers, and selling more to present customers.

Another form of sales promotion is *cooperative advertising.* This is an agreement in which a manufacturer, like Cessna, pays a portion of an FBO's local advertising costs. These costs are shared on a fifty-fifty basis up to a specified limit. Sales promotion efforts can also be directed at a firm's employees. Awards or gifts might be given to employees for exemplary service. Many firms pick up the cost of uniforms and jackets with the company logo. Line personnel, pilots, instructors, mechanics, salespeople, and office personnel, all could be considered for appropriate apparel. These items not only add to the professional image the company hopes to project but also create a feeling among employees that they are part of a team.

PUBLICITY

Publicity is the last component of the promotion mix and is another means firms can use to promote their products and services to mass audiences. It involves free promotion about the product, service, or organization in the media. Publicity is generally considered to be a part of a larger concept, that of *public relations.* Company public relations has several objectives, including obtaining favorable publicity for the firm, building a good image in the community, and handling adverse rumors and stories that circulate.

FBOs generally have many topics available to them with potential for publicity. Some of them are listed below:

1. New products or services
2. Product donations
3. Special events such as air shows, open houses, construction, and expansion plans
4. Airport planning activities
5. Athletic sponsorships
6. Charitable activities such as providing an aircraft for emergency purposes
7. Personnel news such as promotions, service anniversaries, retirements, student solos and licenses, contest winners, and management participation in local service clubs

Several *publicity techniques* are available. These include the following:

1. *News releases.* News releases are short statements about the firm's products, services, or organization released to the news media.
2. *Feature articles.* Feature articles, usually containing up to 3,000 words are prepared for a specific publication such as a trade journal.
3. *Press conferences.* Press conferences involve inviting news people to hear a specific announcement and ask questions.
4. *Records and films.* Canned speeches, records, and films are available from organizations such as GAMA and NBAA for radio and television stations, to be shown in schools, or to social or civic groups.

Publicity needs to be managed carefully and to be effective; it must be integrated into the total promotional campaign. In this way the full force of advertising, sales promotion, publicity, and personal selling can complement one another.

THE PERSONAL SELLING PROCESS

Unlike the other promotional activities, personal selling is a distinctive communication form because it is two-way rather than one-way communication. Personal selling involves social interaction with the prospect and salesperson influencing each other by what they say and do. The outcome of each sales situation depends upon the success of both parties in communicating with each other and reaching a common understanding of goals and objectives. A salesperson should tailor the communication to fit the prospect's needs.

Many titles are used to identify people in the field of sales. The titles indicate the amount of selling done and the amount of creativity required to perform the sales task. Three types of personal selling exist: inside sales, executive sales, and sales support activities. Typically, *inside salespersons* process routine orders, engage in telemarketing, and facilitate the exchange of products between face-to-face customers. *Executive salespersons* operate outside in assigned territories, when appropriate, and identify prospective customers, provide these prospects information, influence prospects to purchase products, close sales, and follow-up after the sale to build lasting customer relationships. *Sales support salespersons* assist executive salespersons by performing promotional activities and providing technical expertise.

As products and services become more complex and expensive, personal selling becomes more important in the promotional mix. Highly technical products such as aircraft require greater emphasis on personal selling than other less sophisticated products. The task of an aircraft salesperson best fits the executive sales category and the seven-step selling process will illustrate the format used to create sales by these salespersons.

Personal selling can be represented as a seven-step sequence that must be accomplished for success.

1. *Prospecting.* Searching for and identifying potential customers. Identifying primary and secondary sources.
2. *Preapproach.* Qualifying the prospects.
3. *Approach.* Securing an interview to perform a travel analysis.
4. *Presentation.* Developing additional information. Performing a value analysis (see Chapters 8 and 9). Making a formal presentation to the prospective firm's decision-makers.
5. *Handling objectives.* Anticipating buyer resistance and developing effective responses.
6. *Closing.* Finalizing the details of the transaction and asking for the order.
7. *Follow-up.* Establishing a good relationship, reassuring the customer, and handling questions. Setting the stage for repeat sales.

Prospecting

Just as firms analyze markets seeking opportunities for their products and services, sales-people seek potential customers. *Prospecting* is the first step in the selling process, and it involves the continuing search for potential buyers. This search for prospects is generally the sole responsibility of the salesperson. Firms may assist by engaging in direct mail or print advertising, which invites readers to inquire about the firm's products and services. These leads would then be turned over to the sales force for follow-up. Qualified prospects are the raw material for future sales. Salespersons must develop skills in this area to assure that presentations are only made to those prospects that have an unfilled need and the financial ability to satisfy that need. The process begins with an in depth macro view of the total potential markets and then refined to organizations that fit the following profile:

- The company's operations require frequent trips beyond a 300-mile radius to destinations not well served by commercial aviation.
- These frequent trips require two or more persons to travel together.
- The financial health of the company would allow the purchase or lease of an aircraft.
- Their business operations presently require the use of air transportation to accomplish sales and marketing objectives.

Size and Scope of Markets

Most of the resources and reasons to buy general aviation airplanes lie within the business and government sectors of the economy. The best prospects for aircraft and

Table 11–2 Business and Government Markets

Industry	Number of Private Businesses	
	Thousands	Percent
Agricultural, forestry, and fisheries	855	4
Mining	185	1
Construction	2,443	11
Manufacturing	845	4
Transportation, communications, and public utilities	993	4
Wholesale and retail trade	4,455	19
Finance, insurance, and real estate	3,033	13
Services	10,312	44
	23,121	100
Government market		
Government units	88	
Total	23,209	

Source: Statistical Abstract of the United States, 2000, page 299 and 535.

associated services are organizations that can use them to make their own business efforts more productive and more profitable.

Businesses and governmental units include all the buyers in the nation except the final consumers. These buyers purchase and lease tremendous volumes of capital equipment, raw materials, manufactured parts, supplies, and business services. The aggregate purchases of business and government buyers in a year are far greater than those by final consumers. There are more than 23 million businesses in the United States (see Table 11–2). The first four categories of businesses (agricultural, forestry and fishing, mining, construction and manufacturing) sell tangible products and represent 20 percent of the firms. Transportation, communications, and public businesses represent 4 percent of the total businesses. Resellers (wholesalers and retailers) account for 19 percent of the firms, and the service industry (finance, insurance, real estate, and services) complete the types of businesses and represent 57 percent. Governmental units are the federal, state, and local agencies that buy goods and services for the constituents they serve. About 88,000 of these government units exist in the United States.

Measuring Business and Government Markets

Measuring the business and government markets is an important first step for an aircraft salesperson interested in gauging the size of these markets. Fortunately, information is readily available from the federal government to do this. The federal government regularly collects, tabulates, and publishes data on these markets using its *Standard Industrial Classification (SIC) System.* The SIC system groups organizations on the basis of major activity or the major product or service provided, which enables the federal government to list the number of establishments, number of employees, and sales volumes for each group, designated by a numerical code. Geographic breakdowns are also provided where possible.

The SIC system begins with broad, two-digit categories such as food (SIC code 20), tobacco (SIC code 21), and apparel (SIC code 23). Often each of these two-digit categories is further divided into three-digit and four-digit categories, which represent sub industries within the broader two-digit category. The SIC system permits a firm to find the SIC codes of its present customers and then obtain SIC-coded lists for similar firms that may want the same type of products and services. Also, SIC categories can be monitored to determine the growth in the number of firms, number of employees, and sales volumes to identify promising market opportunities.

Prospecting Sources

The total prospective business aircraft market can be thought of as an iceberg. Above the waterline are the highly visible corporations appearing in *Fortune's* top 500 or top 1,000 lists. These include such companies as General Motors, ExxonMobil, IBM, Procter and Gamble, and General Electric. Over one-half of the *Fortune* top 1,000 firms own or operate aircraft for business purposes. Each year *Business and Commercial Aviation Magazine,* using data supplied by Aviation Data Service, Inc. breaks down the *Fortune* top 1,000 firms by SIC code and compares the number of aircraft operators and nonoperators for each category. There is no problem compiling information on these publicly owned firms or for that matter, on the next 25,000 leading U.S. corporations. Detailed information concerning these firms can be found in business directories such as *Dun & Bradstreet,* and *Standard & Poor's,* which are in most public libraries (see Table 11–3).

There is still another layer of businesses, not listed in any national business directory, representing the balance of the 23 million companies. It is the upper one million companies of this business stratum that represents about 80 percent of the owners of general aviation aircraft. These businesses form part of the iceberg market profile that is immediately below the waterline. These are the companies listed in the telephone book, chamber of commerce directories, civil club rosters, state chamber of commerce directory, individual industry directories, medical society directories, and professional society rosters. They are companies, associations, and partnerships run by successful businesspeople in any city or area. Some major categories include the following:

General contractors	Utility companies
Machinery manufacturers	Food product manufacturers and distributors
Wholesalers	Printers and lithographers
Retailers	Banks
Petroleum and natural gas companies	Insurance agents, brokers and companies
Pharmaceutical companies	Transportation equipment manufacturers
Automobile dealers	

Under each business type, there are hundreds of subcategories and many companies listed. The objective is to prepare the most thorough list of business prospects who logically could use private air transportation to do one or all of the following things:

1. Expand sales territory
2. Make faster on-the-spot management decisions at remote branches
3. Expedite service to customers
4. Use a faster mode of travel without being subject to airline routes and schedules
5. Utilize a quicker way to get raw materials
6. Expedite shipment of parts
7. Expand medical service to outlying areas
8. Bring customers to the plant
9. Go to buying markets
10. Develop far-reaching real estate prospects
11. Manage big farms and ranches
12. Put new marketing plans into action

With this understanding of the various types and sizes of business prospects and the answers to the above specific operational needs that air transportation can efficiently satisfy, the sales person can employ the traditional prospecting tools to build an inventory of company names. These "suspects" would then be qualified prior to actually attempting to make an appointment. Traditional sources of prospects would include the following:

Table 11–3 Resources Used for Identifying and Qualifying Prospects

Publication	Type of Information
STANDARD & POOR'S Stock Reports	Companies with stock listed on the New York Stock Exchange, the American Stock Exchange, over the counter and regional stock exchanges. Provides company history with recent financial developments and prospects for the future.
STANDARD & POOR'S Corporation Records	Corporation history, financial status and personnel of major corporations.
STANDARD & POOR'S Register of Corporations, Directors & Executives	Provides information on moderate to large size corporations. List company officers, type of business, sales volume, number of employees, etc. Also contains cross reference of directors and executives.
STANDARD & POOR'S Industry Survey	Provides history and status of basic industry.
MOODY'S Industrial Manual	Provides information on company history, financial data, subsidiaries, officers and directors, and corporate financial information.
MOODY's Public Utility Manual	Information similar to above.
MOODY'S Bank & Finance Manual	Information similar to above.
MOODY'S Handbook of Common Stocks	Provides information on company history, recent developments, and future prospects for the company. Large U.S. corporations.
THOMAS REGISTER	Product information and profiles on more than 123,000 U.S. companies. Includes asset ratings, company executives, location of sales offices, distributors, plants, service/engineering offices.
DUN & BRADSTREET'S Million Dollar Directory	Provides sales volume, names of officers and key people of major corporations to include telephone numbers, number of employees, type of business (minimum net worth $1,000,000).
DUN & BRADSTREET'S Middle Market Directory	Provides sales volume, names of officers and key people of major corporations to include telephone numbers, number of employees, type of business (net worth $500,000 to $999,999).
BEST'S Insurance Reports	Provides information on company history, management personnel, operations and financial structure of all major U.S. life and casualty insurance companies.
WHO'S WHO	There are many *Who's Whos* such as *Who's Who in America, Who's Who in Commerce and Industry, Who's Who in Science, Who's Who in Insurance, Who's Who in American Women.* An ideal source for personal information on prominent persons.
NEWSFRONT'S 25,000 Leading U.S. Corporations	25,000 leading corporations grouped by state and city. Provides names of chief executive officer and financial size.
STATE INDUSTRIAL DIRECTORIES	Published by each state. Provides basic information on the state's major industries, type and size of company, chief executive officer, and sales volume is typical of the information listed.
ANNUAL REPORTS	Many libraries contain recent annual reports of companies listed on the New York and American Stock Exchanges. Local brokerage houses will usually have annual reports for local industries.
TRADE DIRECTORIES	These directories contain information on many industries such as grocery, lumber, food stuffs, manufacturing, etc. Ideal for vertical prospecting within industries already favorable to aircraft utilization.

1. Existing customers — A salesperson's customer base is an excellent source of leads. Frequent contacts with customers will not only provide new additional sales but if the customer is pleased with the product and service, referrals will be gladly given.
2. Interview replacement — This technique is often referred to as the "Endless Chain Method" because if it is worked correctly, it becomes the primary source of leads. Prior to leaving the closing interview, successful or unsuccessful, the salesperson attempts to secure the names of three or four individuals or businesses that could benefit from the use of their own aircraft. Experience shows that out of these leads, one interview will be secured. The interview to leads ratio will be greatly enhanced if the salesperson obtains permission to use the name of the person who gave them the lead.
3. Acquaintances and friends — Salespersons usually enjoy being with others socially and in church and community activities. These contacts often result in good leads.
4. Direct mail — This technique is used to supplement the methods identified above. Lists of names, which meet predetermined criteria, are purchased and processed either internally or by a company specializing in direct marketing. Leads are generated whenever a prospect requests additional information as a result of a direct marketing communication. A study by Posner and Walcek indicates that for every 100 responses
   - 3 will purchase the advertised product within 3 months
   - 20 have a legitimate need, authority, and intention to buy within 12 months.
   - 37 are gathering information to support a future purchase decision.
   - 40 are collecting information or are simply curious.

Preapproach

The qualifying stage of prospecting, known as the *preapproach* in the selling process, is extremely important. The preapproach step involves the selection of prospects who warrant further attention. It is this smaller group that becomes the "prospect" group because the salesperson determines that each company needs the product or service, can finance the purchase, and has the authority to buy. In qualifying prospects, a sales representative will attempt to develop information regarding the following questions:

1. Who are the decision-makers and what are their hobbies?
2. Are these individuals involved in the ownership or management of any other businesses? Are they located in one area or decentralized?
3. If they are involved in other businesses, what are they and what is their size?
4. What has the company's sales performance been in recent years? Growing? Diminishing? Same?
5. What is the company's competitive position? (Number one, trying to be number one, smallest, newest, and oldest?)
6. Do other firms in their industry use business aircraft? (Get examples)
7. What is the company's financial position and what is the outlook for growth in its business?
8. Describe the marketing, distribution, and field sales organizations.
9. Who are some of the company's major customers?
10. Do customers have branch offices that need to be contacted regularly? Where are they and how many?
11. Does the company ever use scheduled airlines for executive and sales travel? Shipping goods and equipment? Receiving raw materials? Moving parts and service personnel?
12. Does it ever use air charter service?
13. Which department or division of the company utilizes scheduled air transportation the most?

14. Do any employees in the company fly themselves? How many? What kind of aircraft do they fly?
15. Have they ever rented aircraft? For what purposes?
16. In the operation of the business, do they travel primarily to large metropolitan areas or to rural or outlying areas? Get examples of some of these places.
17. Do they transport major customers to their plants and offices? Would an aircraft do this job better?
18. What length trip does the company make?
19. What is the average number of people who travel together?
20. If the prospect is a manufacturing company, what raw materials does it use? Where do they come from?

From this information, the sales representative attempts to determine the following:

1. Any possible direct relationship between an airplane and increased sales territory or sales volume. Could the prospect quickly and efficiently, reach otherwise inaccessible customers, with a private airplane?
2. How will the use of aircraft relate to overall expansion and growth for the prospect?
3. How will the aircraft increase the performance of the salesmen? Management personnel? Outline some examples.
4. Considering the company's financial strength and profitability, how important are tax and depreciation considerations to the prospect in the purchase of an aircraft?
5. Would a finance or lease plan be of benefit to the prospect?
6. Would the "prestige" factor of aircraft ownership be of any value to the business?
7. What additional use might there be for aircraft in the prospect's business?
8. Is there a flying group or association this company could belong to that might help it decide to fly its own aircraft? Flying Physicians, National Real Estate Fliers Association, Flying Adjusters, Lawyer-Pilots, Flying Funeral Directors, or Flying Veterinarians are some of the specialized groups.

Qualifying information is necessary before detailed plans for visiting the prospect can be formulated. Such knowledge permits the customization of selling strategy. The sources of qualifying information are for the most part the same as the sources already mentioned for identifying prospects and developing basic information. Qualifying, however, involves deeper research and indicates more detailed questioning of sources who know more than just basic information. Chambers of commerce personnel may have particular knowledge about operations of important area businesses. Trade association secretaries often keep clippings with details about successes and problems of industry firms. Certainly, employees of the prospective firm may be in a position to give information about who makes buying decisions and how they are made. Secretaries of prospective companies may be in a position to reveal strategic facts. They are also in an excellent position to know about a buyer's problems and competitive activity. Analysis of credit ratings and annual reports show financial strength, company plans, and buying-power information.

Sometimes it is necessary to call on prospects to gain qualifying information before setting up a formal interview. Prospects themselves are usually the best sources of information about their companies. In these cases, the salesperson must first sell the need for qualifying information or fact-finding interview because asking for management time is like asking for money. Some prospects resist preliminary surveys, feeling that they may disrupt normal activities, constitute a threat to the firm's right to privacy, or create an obligation for a detailed survey or even a purchase. Most potential aircraft users, however, realize that a sales representative selling major capital goods is unable to analyze their problems and serve their needs without detailed operational information.

Approach

The strategies used by the salesperson to secure an interview and establish rapport with the prospect is called the *approach.* The use of the Travel Analysis in aircraft sales necessitates that the first interview be a fact-finding one where data is gathered in order to perform an analysis of the prospect's air transportation needs. One of the following three approach strategies are used to secure this first fact-finding interview:

1. Direct personal contact. In making a personal visit, the salesperson has the opportunity to evaluate the business premises, talk to company personnel, and to become better prepared for the prospect. The advantage of this strategy is that if the prospect is available, the interview can take place immediately. The major disadvantage is the time wasted by either having to wait to see the prospect, or finding that the prospect is out or too busy to be seen that day.

2. Telephone call. Using the telephone has many advantages over the direct personal contact. By calling ahead, the prospect will be available at the appointed time, thus no waste of the salesperson's time. This method allows the salesperson to efficiently schedule appointments so that daily and weekly activity quotas can be met. The major disadvantage of telephoning is that it is easy to be turned down over the telephone. Success with this approach requires skillful telephone techniques to be able to navigate through the "screeners" and to persuade the prospect to grant an interview.

3. Personal letter. Personal letters, individually signed by the salesperson, may be the best and most professional method to use to secure an interview. Letters introduce the salesperson and the selling company, the product, or service being offered, and specifically states that a telephone call will be made in a few days to arrange a convenient time for an interview. Colorful brochures may be included that describe the product or service in more detail. During this promised telephone call, the salesperson suggests alternative times for the interview. In doing so, the prospect's attention is focused on the issue of when to meet not whether to meet.

Presentation

Prior to the first face-to-face meeting with the prospect, the salesperson should understand that the success of that interview will depend upon understanding the following assumptions concerning the prospect and his or her environment:

1. The salesperson is interrupting the prospect. The salesperson must redirect the prospect's attention from what that person was doing immediately prior to the interview to the salesperson's objective of the meeting.

2. The salesperson must use the prospect's time wisely. The interview format must be carefully organized and well prepared.

3. If the salesperson is talking to the right person in the company, that person's perception of the worth or value of the interview will probably determine future success or failure.

4. Generally, since the salesperson initiated the interview, the prospect is satisfied with the company's current usage of air transportation.

5. The prospect wants to purchase profitability.

The type of presentation used by the salesperson depends upon the nature of the product or service. If the needs of the prospect are obvious, the product offered is standardized, and the salespersons are new and not well trained, then the *organized approach* is recommended. With this method, the salesperson follows a company-prepared outline — a canned sales presentation. This approach has the weakness that all potential customers are treated alike so whether successful or not, the salesperson probably won't know why or learn from the experience. The organized approach may be suitable for simple selling tasks, but for complicated situations like selling business aircraft, it is not a satisfactory strategy.

The *unstructured approach* is a problem-solving one in which the salesperson and the prospect define needs and problems and then collect supporting data. The exploration of needs using the fact-finding interview technique is the first of a two-interview system used by aircraft salespersons. After the data has been analyzed to determine the best fit between prospect's requirements and selling company's product, a second interview is requested to make a presentation of recommendations.

The format for the organized approach and the second interview of the unstructured approach is centered around the following five steps:

1. Gaining the prospect's *attention.* Talk to prospects about something that interests them.
2. Arousing the prospect's *interest.* Tell the prospects what the product will do to benefit or serve them.
3. *Convincing* the prospect that it is an intelligent action to purchase the product. Give the prospect sufficient information about the product to prove that purchasing the product is justifiable.
4. Arousing the prospect's *desire* to purchase. Determine the prospect's primary buying motive and then explain how the product will satisfy the unfilled need. Finally, paint a word picture of the satisfaction to be derived from the purchase.
5. *Closing* the sale successfully. Get a positive decision by weighing the advantages against the disadvantages.

Sales presentations can be enhanced with various aids such as booklets (business aircraft feasibility studies), flip charts, slides and films, computer software demonstrations, and product brochures. Often a demonstration trip is arranged so that the prospect can learn first hand how the use of a business aircraft can fulfill the company's transportation needs. These types of demonstrations are particularly effective in showing what the aircraft will do for the prospect and proving that the business aircraft is truly a business tool that will help solve problems and open many opportunities not presently available to the prospective company.

Handling Objections

Objections by the prospect are a natural occurrence during any sales presentation and should be welcomed as a chance to get the prospect involved and to expand the discussion into areas of concern. An objection does not mean that the prospect does not want the product. In the majority of cases, prospects object because they lack information.

The best way to handle objections is to minimize them by covering the common questions adequately in the sales presentation. The answers to the most common objections, complaints, and criticisms, should be in the form of positive selling points. When objections are anticipated and minimized, it is more difficult for the prospect to form negative opinions about the proposal that might result in a fixed position or issue.

Experienced salespersons realize that selling is made easier when objections surface because it is much easier to deal with a prospect who talks than with one who doesn't. Objections throw light on the prospect's thinking and tell the salesperson what subjects need amplification before attempting to close the sale.

Successful salespersons use the basic principles of handling objections skillfully during the sales presentation. Many prospects offer excuses that are not real obstacles to buying. When the objection is identified as an excuse, the actual reason why the prospect is unwilling to buy must be established. Tactful questions can penetrate the excuse "smoke screen" and probe for valid objections which the prospect may have concealed. Another technique to deal with objections is called the boomerang. This technique turns an objection into a reason for buying. A prospect states: "Your organization is entirely too small to provide the service we will require." The response by the salesperson might be, "Our small size is one of our assets — it permits us to give personalized service." The skillful use of these techniques will keep the presentation positive and moving toward a successful conclusion.

Closing

The *closing step* is the logical conclusion to a well-organized sales presentation and involves obtaining a purchase commitment from the prospect. This step is the most important and the most difficult because it is often unclear when the prospect is ready to buy. Closing clues are signals that indicate that a close should be attempted. Closing clues can be either physical or verbal. Physical signals are actions by the prospect such as nodding or smiling in agreement to the proposal. Verbal closing clues may be questions or comments such as: "What kinds of financing are available?" or "That aircraft is certainly modern looking." A number of different closing techniques can be employed. Salespersons can simply ask for the order or go over the points of agreement and offer to clarify any questions the buyer may have. Another closing approach assumes that the prospect is ready to buy and the salesperson asks, "Did you decide on the special avionics package or do you prefer the standard equipment?" This technique is called the alternative choice method.

By asking the prospect "which paint scheme did you decide upon?" the salesperson is using the decision on minor points method. This technique is used when the prospect is reluctant to make the big decision, which is to buy or not buy, but is comfortable in making a series of minor ones. Offering the prospect specific inducements, such as attractive interest rates, special price on a particular item of equipment, or a one-year extension on the new warranty can be effective in getting immediate positive results.

Follow-up

The last and very important step in the selling process is the *follow-up* after the sale. Salespersons depend upon repeat sales that are enhanced by post-sales activities. Making sure that promises made at the time of the sale concerning delivery, equipment packages, training for employees, and others, are met to the customer's satisfaction. Continuing to stay in contact with the customer will usually pay dividends in the form of referrals and additional sales.

KEY TERMS

Promotional mix	Publicity techniques
Advertising	Inside salespersons
Sales promotion	Executive salespersons
Publicity	Sales support salespersons
Personal selling	Seven step selling process
Product advertising	Prospecting
Institutional advertising	Standard Industrial Classification (SIC)
Pioneering advertising	system
Competitive advertising	Preapproach
Comparative advertising	Approach
Reminder advertising	Organized approach
Advertising message	Unstructured approach
Directional advertising	Objectives
Cooperative advertising	Closing step
Public relations	Follow-up

REVIEW QUESTIONS

1. What is the promotional mix? Distinguish between advertising and sales promotion. Why do firms use advertising agencies? Give some examples of advertising objectives. Distinguish between product and institutional advertising.
2. Explain several methods of establishing an advertising budget. What is the advertising

message and how is it developed? Summarize the advantages and disadvantages of the following media: newspapers, magazines and trade journals, direct mail, and radio. Give several examples of how the effectiveness of advertising can be measured.

3. What is the purpose of a firm's sales promotion activities? Identify and briefly describe five sales promotion activities used by FBOs. What is cooperative advertising?

4. How does publicity differ from public relations? Identify some of the topics available to an FBO that have potential for publicity. Describe several publicity techniques.

5. Name and describe the three types of sales positions.

6. Define prospecting. What is the Standard Industrial Classification (SIC) system? Name seven aircraft prospecting sources.

7. What is the objective of qualifying the prospect? What is the objective of the approach stage? Discuss some of the techniques used by sales representatives in presenting a product or service to a prospective buyer. Describe several closing techniques. What is the importance of the follow-up stage?

REFERENCES

Berkowitz, Eric N., Roger A. Kerin, Steven W. Hartley, and William Rudelius. *Marketing,* (6th ed.). Burr Ridge, IL: Irwin/McGraw-Hill, 2000.

Jain, Subhash C., *Marketing Planning & Strategy* (6th ed.) Cincinnati, Ohio: South-Western College Publishing, 2000.

Kotler, Philip, and Gary Armstrong. *Marketing, An Introduction* (3rd ed.). Englewood Cliffs, NJ.: Prentice Hall, 1992.

Perreault, William D. and E. Jerome McCarthy. *Basic Marketing* (13th ed.). Burr Ridge, IL: Irwin/McGraw-Hill, 1999.

Chapter 12

Sales Management

OUTLINE

Introduction
Establishment of a Strategic Sales Program
    Sales Objectives
    Determining Manpower Requirements
Implementation of the Sales Program
    Recruiting
        Qualifications
        Job Analysis
    Recruiting Sources
    Selection
    Training
    Compensation
Evaluation and Control
    Supervision
    Evaluation

OBJECTIVES

At the end of this chapter, you should be able to:

Define sales management.

Distinguish between sales management and other management functions within an organization.

Explain the purpose of establishing sales objectives.

Describe the process of determining manpower requirements.

List some of the questions that must be answered in developing a job analysis.

List the elements that must be included in preparing a job description.

Describe three potential sources in recruiting sales personnel.

Discuss ten characteristics that must be evaluated in selecting a salesperson.

Summarize some of the major areas to be considered in a typical on-site training program for a new aircraft salesperson.

Describe the three basic methods of compensating salespersons.

Discuss the five primary areas of salesperson's activities that require supervision.

Describe the two basic methods of evaluating a salesperson's performance.

INTRODUCTION

Personal selling is a basic component of the marketing program of almost every firm and a critical component in the promotion mix for FBOs. The importance of personal selling relative to the other components depends on various characteristics of the marketing strategy. Among the major characteristics to consider are the size and nature of the target market, the complexity and service requirements of the products, and the other components of the marketing mix for each particular product. It is not unusual for an FBO's expenditures on the personal selling component to be greater than those on all other promotional mix components combined. Even when the cost of the personal selling function is not great, it is important that it be integrated with the other components of the marketing mix to assure accomplishment of marketing objectives.

If the sales force is going to be successful in helping the organization reach corporate goals, their activities must be managed. The individual in the firm who is responsible for this function is called a sales manager. *Sales management* is the management of the personal selling component of the FBO's marketing program. During the early stages in the evolution of marketing management, the role of the sales manager was viewed very narrowly. The responsibilities usually were limited to such tasks as recruiting and selecting a sales force, and their training, supervising, and motivating these salespeople. Today, sales management has taken on an expanded role. In addition to the above-mentioned responsibilities, the sales manager is involved in recruiting and selecting salespersons, setting sales goals, planning a program to reach these goals, and evaluating the results. This chapter will look at the sales manager's role as three integrative processes: the establishment of a strategic sales program, the implementation of the sales program and the evaluation and control of the sales force performance.

The personal selling process discussed in the last chapter is a marketing activity that requires particular skills and abilities. Aircraft sales representatives play many roles — information gatherer, service technician, pilot, persuader, customer-ego-builder, problem solver and coordinator of other promotional mix decisions to name a few. Salespersons often operate independently of direct supervision, so they must handle the ambiguities and role conflicts of their positions with relatively little help and guidance from management. Salespersons play the primary roles in many marketing situations.

Sales management is just one of several managerial tasks in an organization. A typical FBO employs managers of line operations, maintenance, flight operations and so on. However, sales management may be the most difficult type of management for several reasons. In addition to line responsibilities like flight operations and maintenance, sales management activities are watched closely by top management and performance is measured. Upper management can specify objectives and translate them in quantifiable standards: ten new charter accounts opened by each sales representative this year; or, ten new and eighteen used aircraft sold by the aircraft sales department. It is not difficult to determine, therefore whether sales managers, like their counterparts in the maintenance shops or flight schools, are doing their jobs.

On the other hand, sales management is unlike flight operations, maintenance, or financial management in that it primarily involves the management of human, rather than physical or capital assets. Flight operations and maintenance managers do have personnel problems but people are the most important responsibility of sales managers.

Salespersons consider themselves professionals whose work requires a high degree of independent judgment and individual initiative. Yet, among other professionals, salespeople are judged by precisely formulated and measured standards of performance. It is much more difficult to accurately assess performance of a charter pilot or a company accountant.

ESTABLISHMENT OF A STRATEGIC SALES PROGRAM

Sales Objectives

Strategic planning is done at many levels in an organization. The sequence of strategic planning usually follows this pattern: total company planning, which includes a mission statement; strategic business unit planning; marketing planning; and sales force planning. The sales manager has some input into the overall strategic planning process, but has direct responsibility for the sales force planning portion.

At the heart of strategic planning are the concepts of objectives, strategies, and tactics. Sales force objectives are goal statements. Goals establish direction and provide benchmarks that can be measured to determine degree of success. They must be specific, written with clarity, and aligned with organizational objectives.

The sales manager must establish the sales volume and activity objectives and the sales productivity objectives. The sales volume objectives can be output related by focusing on dollar or unit volume. The activity objectives relate to the number of sales calls, prospects found, demonstrations conducted, or other measurable activities by salespersons. Productivity implies a relationship between costs and expenses and volume of sales. A frequently used index to express productivity is the formula of sales expenses divided by dollar sales volume.

Determining Manpower Requirements

Once the objectives are in place, the sales manager formulates the strategy that is the plan of action—the blueprint to accomplish the objectives. More detailed programs, called tactics, are then developed to spell out how resources are to be allocated and what actions are to be taken, by whom, and over what time frame.

Second, the issue of sales force size must be addressed. If the firm has too few salespersons, then opportunities for sales and profits will be lost, or if there are too many salespersons, turnover will be excessive, sales costs will be out of line, resulting in reduced profits. Management's decision on the size of the sales force reduces down to estimating the total number of salespersons that will be needed to achieve the company's sales and marketing objectives. One method used by aircraft sales managers is to set up a matrix as shown in Table 12–1.

The sales manager will attempt to estimate future sales volume over a particular time period, perhaps three years. Here are some of the factors to be considered:

1. How many salespersons have left the company during the past three years?
2. How many salespersons can we expect to lose in the next three years? (expected attrition)
3. How many of the present salespersons will be replaced?
4. What annual sales volume do we want to reach three years from now?
5. What is the average annual sales volume produced by the present sales force?
6. Based on the above average, how many salespersons will be needed to produce the sales volume listed in Question 4 above?

Using this information, the sales manager will determine:

1. The number of salespeople needed during the next three years
2. Less the number of salespeople presently employed
3. Plus the number of salespeople expected to be lost through attrition and turnover
4. Total new salespeople required

IMPLEMENTATION OF THE SALES PROGRAM

Recruiting

Recruiting is the process of seeking out, interviewing, and inducing qualified persons to apply for open sales positions. It is an ongoing activity due to personnel turnover and company growth. Turnover is inevitable, and sometimes beneficial when either unmotivated or uncontrollable salespersons terminate their employment. High salesperson turnover contributes to higher marketing costs and lower profits because of

1. increased recruiting and selection costs,
2. increased training costs, and
3. lost sales because of lack of continuity of the sales effort.

Qualifications

The first step in recruiting is to determine the qualifications and abilities needed. There is little evidence today that any common traits are always present in successful salesper-

Table 12–1   Personnel Requirements

1. During the last full sales year how did the firm's sales performance measure up to its objectives?

Past Year's Sales Quota by Model	Actual Sales by Model	Salesperson Responsible for Making the Sale	In the Future, Can This Salesperson Be Expected to Produce:		
			More	**Same**	**Less**

2. During the next full sales year what sales objectives does the firm expect to reach and who will do the actual selling?

Next Year's Sales Quota by Model	Name of Salesperson Who Will Be Assigned Sales Responsibility	Does the Assigned Salesperson's Record and Potential Justify the Assignment?		
		Yes	**No**	**Unknown**

sons and always absent in unsuccessful salespersons. A major aircraft organization has a list of five traits considered important for success that are ranked as follows: (1) character, (2) industry, (3) ability, (4) courage, and (5) personality. The specific type of salesperson needed depends entirely on the nature of the job. To fully understand the type of person required, it is necessary for the sales manager to perform a job analysis. This task not only assists the sales manager, but also is an invaluable resource for the prospective salesperson to gain complete understanding of the position and its expectations. A *job analysis* involves finding, studying, and summarizing the information that serves as the basis for the *job description* and the job specifications. These can be two separate instruments, or they can be combined into one document.

Job Analysis

The following is a checklist commonly used by sales managers in developing a job description:

1. *What is the exact job title?* A title provides recognition for the individual and helps the person understand the responsibilities and objectives.
2. *What is the salesperson's job?*
   a. Selling new and/or used airplanes?
   b. Substitute as a charter pilot?
   c. Other specific duties?
3. *How will the salesperson be paid?*
   a. Salary and/or commission amounts?
   b. Payment or settlement frequency?
   c. Handling of expenses?
      1) Traveling
      2) Entertainment
      3) Other
4. *What are the educational requirements?*
5. *What prior experience is required?*
   a. Flying experience and ratings?
   b. Sales experience?
   c. Other experience?
6. *How much traveling will the salesperson do?*
   a. Evenings away from home?
   b. Weekly or monthly flying time?
7. *What type prospects will the salesperson contact?* The type of prospects called upon will help decide the proper personal, educational and experience background for a salesperson.
8. *What are the salesperson's area and product assignments?*
   a. Product assignment?
   b. Area assignment?
   c. Owner or nonowner prospects?
9. *How much supervision will the salesperson receive?*
   a. Scheduled meetings with management?
   b. Daily report requirements?
   c. Sales records?
   d. Other requirements?
10. *What job pattern will the salesperson follow?*
    a. Working hours?
    b. Demonstrations?
    c. Authority to accept or reject orders?
11. *What advancement opportunities will the salesperson have?*
    a. As a salesperson?
    b. In other advanced positions?

After completing this checklist the sales manager will have the basic elements of the salesperson's job analysis. The next step is the preparation of a *job description*. The following is an example for an aircraft salesperson.

1. *Job Title.* "Aircraft Sales Representative"
2. *Basic Job.* The salesperson will be primarily concerned with the sale of new aircraft and used aircraft in the company inventory. Although special assignments such as charter flying may be made by management, these "additional assignments" will be limited to less than _____% of the salesperson's working hours.

The salesperson will be responsible for locating new prospects, initiating contacts, and "follow-through" activities until the sale is consummated. The salesperson will also work on specific prospects assigned by company management.

During the workweek the sales representative will be expected to spend assigned *on duty* time in the sales office to handle walk-in prospects and telephone inquiries.

3. *Reimbursement.* Commissions will be based on the adjusted gross profit of each individual sale. Methods of computing this adjusted gross profit will be described in a separate document. The salesperson will have a drawing account of $ _____. Sales commissions will be computed and totaled each month; the drawing account will be subtracted and the credit balance will be paid to the sales representative. By special arrangement, a portion of this drawing account may be considered as salary and not deducted from the commissions.

Entertainment and traveling expenses incurred by the sales representative in connection with sales activities will be the responsibility of the salesperson. Special cases where the management is expected to absorb travel or entertainment expenses must be authorized in advance.

Inexperienced salespersons will be granted a probation and training period for orientation and development of prospect clientele. A review of their progress will be made at the end of the first 60-day probation period, during which a flat salary plus expenses may be substituted for the normal commission arrangement.

4. *Education.* The sales representative must have two years of college. Preference will be given to individuals with a four-year bachelor's degree and courses in aviation management, finance, marketing, and sales.

The salesperson will be required to make both verbal and written presentations, perform flight demonstrations, and close the sale. These duties require education in the technical aspects of different model aircraft. Other helpful education will include knowledge of aircraft financing, leasing, insurance, and taxes.

5. *Experience.* Flight experience and some degree of pilot proficiency are a prerequisite. In order to qualify as a salesperson the applicant should have a minimum of _____ hours first pilot experience and a minimum of a commercial pilot license. Twin-engine and instructor ratings are desirable.

Any sales experience, particularly where contact with top executives and/or large dollar amounts are involved, will count most favorably. Experience in composing sales letters, speaking before large groups, or serving as an officer in civic organizations is particularly valuable.

6. *Travel Requirements.* The salesperson may expect frequent business-use demonstration trips requiring one or more nights away from home. On an average, one or two nights a week away from home will be required. Anticipated flying time will average _____ to _____ hours each week.

7. *Type of Prospects.* The salesperson's prospects will be presidents and executives of corporations, partners, individual proprietors, and other company officers. Thus the salesperson must be able to speak fluently and convincingly with people of this caliber and discuss large dollar amounts without hesitation. Since corporate pilots are often involved in the sale, the salesperson must be equally at ease and convincing with professional pilots in order to consummate the sale.

8. *Product-area Assignments.* The salesperson will responsible for the sale of (type) _____ aircraft in the _____ territory. In addition to calling on aircraft owners, salespersons must schedule at least _____ % of their time calling on non-owners in order to develop new prospects.

9. *Supervision.* The salesperson will be responsible for the maintenance of a prospect desk file and for following all reporting procedures prescribed in the company sales control system. The salesperson will report directly to the sales manager for advice, counseling, and assistance in closing.

The sales representative will attend the regular 8 A.M. Monday sales meeting to receive instructions and exchange information with the other salespersons on current sales problems.

10. *Job Pattern.* The salesperson will be expected to work a minimum of _____ hours per week reporting each weekday morning at 8 o'clock.

The salesperson may use any and all company demonstrators and the matter of local demonstration is subject only to individual judgment and the availability of the airplane.

Nonlocal demonstrations must be prearranged with the sales manager. No charge will be made against the salesperson for local demonstrations or approved nonlocal demonstrations.

The salesperson may accept aircraft and equipment orders at the published list price, but the sales manager must approve all other offers. When trade-ins are involved, the salesperson will fill out an appraisal sheet for the trade-in and analyze the condition and equipment concerned. The salesperson will then recommend a trade-in allowance that must be approved by the sales manager.

11. *Advancement Opportunity.* Since the salesperson's compensation is directly related to actual volume of sales, chances to increase earning power are virtually unlimited. Possibilities for advancement would naturally be first to the position of sales manager and then to a position of general managerial responsibility. Such advancement will be dependent on the proven performance of the individual salesperson and opportunities that may develop within the company.

Recruiting Sources

The next step is to seek applicants who qualify for, and aspire to, the position of an aircraft sales representative. This search is also a marketing activity. The company is seeking "customers" who are willing to exchange their time, energy, education, and experiences for the rewards offered by the position. There are a number of potential sources of sales personnel:

1. Those individuals with knowledge of the organization and its products, like present employees who want to move into sales. Sales managers often consider the advancement and training of people within their company. A mechanic who knows airplanes inside and out, an accountant who understands aviation tax advantages and write-offs, a line chief who understands owner problems and needs, might prove to be a find salesperson with a little training and guidance.

2. Those with experience selling high-priced products. Sales managers can develop contacts for sales representative positions through such local sources as bankers, chamber of commerce personnel, aviation editors of newspapers, teachers of self-development courses, sales and advertising clubs, and fraternal and civic groups.

Private employment agencies and college placement offices can also be utilized. The college alumni office can often identify individuals who might have the qualifications for a sales position.

3. Other prospects include an experienced aircraft salesperson employed with a competing firm or a licensed flight instructor who flies on weekends and holds a sales job during the week. However, it is important that individuals falling into the latter category are interested in being a salesperson first and a pilot second. Sales motivation must be dominant and flying incidental.

Recruiting methods vary with the source. *Direct recruiting* by executives is used to reach identified candidates including those from inside the company and from schools. *Indirect recruiting* methods, such as placing classified advertisements in newspapers or trade journals are used for attracting experienced salespeople.

Advertisements generally produce a large number of applicants, but their quality is often questionable. The cost of reaching potential salespersons through advertise-

---

Table 12–2   Sample Classified Advertisements for an Aircraft Salesperson

---

1. Salesperson, with flying background, will be chosen to present and demonstrate airplanes to local businessmen and corporations.

The person chosen will receive up to $ _____ starting monthly income.

Thorough school and field training.

Proven potential up to $100,000 per year.

If you have proven sales background, can show ability to deal with top business executives, have enough flying ability to handle single and multi-engine airplanes, we would like to talk to you.

Interview by appointment only. Call today,

or

2.a Up to $3,000 monthly income to start.

  b. $100,000 potential.

  c. Lifetime opportunity—no age limitation.

  d. Thorough sales training.

  e. A nationally adertised product.

  f. Flying ability necessary.

  g. Perhaps you have never thought of changing jobs, but no one should close the door on an opportunity.

Replies strictly confidential. Write Box _____ . We will contact you for an appointment.

or

3. WANTED SALESPERSON FOR A MAJOR AIRCRAFT DISTRIBUTOR IN NEW ENGLAND AREA

Sales experience and pilot's license desirable. Salary and commission. Interesting and challenging position. Reply by letter, including resume to: Box E693, Herald.

---

ments is low, but the poor quality puts an additional burden on the selection process. The quality of the applicants can be improved by careful selection of the media and the wording in the ad. The use of specialty magazines like *Professional Pilot* will improve the quality of the applicants. More detailed information given in the ad concerning job description and job specifications will reduce the number of unqualified applicants. To be effective, recruiting ads must attract attention and have credibility. Table 12–2 gives several examples of classified recruiting advertisements.

Selection

Systems for selecting salespersons range from simple one-step procedures, consisting merely of an informal personal interview, to complex multiple-step systems, using numerous and varied devices and techniques for gathering information and evaluating prospective sale representatives. A selection system should be a set of successive "screens." After any one of these screens, job candidates may be dropped from further consideration. The number and relative sophistication of the screens depend upon the resources that management invests in its selection process. Among commonly used selection screens or steps are interviews, application forms, references and recommendations, physical examination, credit reports, and psychological tests (aptitude, intelligence, personality, and others).

Determining what makes a good sales representative is difficult and the list of characteristics is endless. However, some obvious things, which an experienced interviewer will attempt to evaluate during a personal interview are:

- Appearance
- Mannerisms
- Enthusiasm

- Voice
- Ability to communicate
- Education

Successive hurdles

- Personal character
- Ambition
- Willingness to work
- Dependability
- Health
- Intelligence
- Mental attitude

- Employment history
- Aviation knowledge
- Flight experience and ratings
- Leadership
- Sales ability
- Other observed factors

The interviewer will normally write a brief summary about the applicant including overall impression and any areas of deficiencies about the individual.

Training

Newly hired salespersons are seldom prepared to immediately become productive, regardless of their background and ability. Even the smallest FBO should have a sales training program to supply salespersons with proper attitudes, knowledge of industry, company, products, and selling skills. Larger firms with sizable sales staffs often have organized programs, some of which involve classroom and seminar sessions. Smaller firms are more apt to have informal, flexible methods of training. Initial training will vary from three weeks to several months depending upon the experience of the new salesperson and the nature of the sales task. Content of the initial training program includes the following subjects: product information, promotional activities, pricing practices, territory management, sales techniques, market trends, major competitors and their products, and company policies and procedures. Although initial training is often conducted in group sessions, or self-paced tutorials, most sales training is provided on-the-job with personal instruction and supervision. Some beginning salespersons need constant attention, coaching, refresher training, and careful supervision during the first year or more.

An example of a typical on-site training program for a new aircraft salesperson covering a three-week period is included in Appendix D.

Who should do the training? This question is faced by both small and large FBOs. Preparing and conducting formal training sessions with company personnel is time consuming and reduces their availability for other duties. Sales managers do not always possess skills required to be effective in the training environment. Many FBOs have chosen to supplement their training programs by either bringing people on the premises to conduct training sessions, or send salespersons to seminars and schools sponsored by trade associations, distributors and manufacturers, independent training companies, and colleges and universities. Successful training programs are conducted by persons who understand that *learning* is the acquiring or transfer of skills, facts, or attitudes to one person from another. Sales training is more productive when these principles of learning are followed:

1. We learn best by doing—"experience is the best teacher"—certainly where selling skills are concerned.
2. Oral instruction is probably the least effective teaching method unless followed by or interspersed with trainee discussion.
3. Discussion by trainees causes thought about the subject and helps change or modify attitudes and facts.
4. Demonstration is quite effective in teaching facts or skills, particularly if followed by the learner's own participation.

A psychologist has stated that trainees learn 10 percent of what they hear, 30 percent of what they see, 50 percent of what they hear and see, but 90 percent of what they hear, see, and do.

Compensation

Designing a compensation plan that motivates salespersons and also achieves company goals is indeed a difficult task. The first step is to establish a level of annual earnings that will attract, retain, and develop a competent sales force. The size of the company, sales task performed, and compensation programs of competitive companies influence the level of earnings. Paying the sales force either too much or too little is unsatisfactory. Overpaying salespersons relative to other employees can cause serious morale problems, and underpaying salespersons can actually increase costs by causing high turnover which results in lost sales and more recruiting and training expenses.

The second step involves the selection of one of the following three compensation plans: (1) straight salary, (2) straight commission, or (3) a combination of salary and an incentive in the form of commissions, bonuses, or both.

A *salary* is a fixed amount, paid at regular intervals, for time expended, rather than for specific performance. The strengths of this plan are (1) regularity of income provides some element of security; (2) tends to reduce turnover during the development stage; and (3) sales management can more easily direct salespersons in such nonsales activities as survey taking and public relations. The major limitation is that income is not directly related to sales results. However, this weakness can be partially overcome by frequent salary reviews and rewarding better performance with greater percentage salary increases.

The *straight commission* plan compensates the salesperson in direct proportion to sales achievements. The strong motivating influence is the major strength of this system. The obvious weakness is uncertainty about total income and its unevenness. To assist salespersons under this plan, a *draw* is used to allow the payment of a predetermined dollar advance against future commissions. The draw is especially beneficial for newer salespersons and in companies with major seasonal swings in sales.

Combination plans are by far the most popular because they incorporate the strengths from the two previously discussed plans. These plans provide salary for security, stabilization and sales manager control, and commissions or bonuses for motivation. Today, the base salary will account for approximately 70 percent of total compensation under a typical combination plan.

In the case of *new aircraft sales,* defined as either a current model demonstrator or stock aircraft, or one undelivered from the manufacturer which has never been sold, the typical 20 to 30 percent commission rate applies to the adjusted gross profit on each new aircraft sold. The *adjusted gross profit for a new aircraft sale* is determined as follows:

Sale price of the aircraft before applicable taxes if no trade-in is involved or
Sale price of the aircraft before applicable taxes, plus an amount equal to the
wholesale value of the trade, or trades as established by the sales manager
less
Dealer cost of the new aircraft
plus
Warranty and free service expenses
plus
Additional selling expenses — such as additional equipment installed, painting, flight or ground instruction (other than normal checkout of pilot or owner), and storage.

A *used aircraft sale* is generally defined as any aircraft not meeting the definition of a new airplane above. In addition, aircraft which were purchased new are considered "used" if they have been owned by the dealership for 12 months, or more, or when 90 days have elapsed since the first delivery of a succeeding model. In the case of used airplane sales, the sales representative typically receives a commission (20 to 30 percent) on the adjusted gross profit for a used airplane sale. The *adjusted gross profit for a used airplane sale* is determined as follows:

Sale price of the aircraft before applicable taxes if no trade-in is involved or
Sale price of the aircraft before applicable taxes, plus an amount equal to the
wholesale value of the trade or trades, as established by the sales manager

less

Inventory value of the used aircraft

plus

Additional equipment installed, painting, flight or ground instruction (other than normal checkout of pilot or owner), storage, inspection, relicense or maintenance and

delivery expense, if out of the area.

All firms have additional forms of financial incentives. Bonuses, which are one-time payments for exceptional performance, are used throughout the year to emphasize certain products, or activities. Various sales contests also offer mechanisms through which salespersons are stimulated not only to increase profitable sales volume, but also to achieve specific marketing objectives.

Obviously, income is critically important, but reliance upon the basic compensation plan as the sole motivator is shortsighted. Nonfinancial incentives are also important; praise and recognition, autonomy, and freedom from fear and worry will build morale and encourage salespersons to be self-motivated.

EVALUATION AND CONTROL

Supervision

Supervision refers to the direct working relationships between the sales manager and the sales force. The supervisory style used by the sale manager will be tailored to fit the needs of the salespersons and the nature of the sales task. If individual salespersons are successful, then the company will be successful.

The amount of supervision required is important for the sales manager to determine. Oversupervision wastes time and hampers performance, while undersupervision affects morale and decreases productivity. One of the major factors influencing the amount of supervision is the quality of the sales force. If the recruiting and selecting process has resulted in top-notch salespersons joining the company, supervision time will be minimized. Other factors, which impact this decision, are size of the sales territory, size and concentration of the sales force, and the method of compensation. In general, salespersons paid on salary will require more supervision than those who receive a major portion of their income from incentive plans.

Sales quotas serve as an effective supervisory tool in addition to being a method of motivating salespersons. The annual sales forecast provides the primary basis for establishing sales quotas. By breaking the forecast down into parts, that is, into quotas for individual persons, sales managers define the results expected from each salesperson. A good quota system will have the following characteristics:

- Fair — Accurately reflect the potential and the constraints of the specific territory assigned to the salesperson.
- Challenging — Sufficiently high to make the salesperson reach, but not so high that it is perceived unattainable.
- Understandable
- Flexible — Should flow with the need to change.
- Geared with the attainment of corporate objectives

Involving the sales force in the quota setting process will help assure acceptance and raise the probability of attainment.

Most salespersons need supervision and direction to help them channel their efforts along the paths that will achieve their goals. Organization and control of the aircraft selling function illustrates one of the important areas of required supervision. The sales manager should help salespersons properly organize their selling day to utilize their time more effectively. Daily attention is required in five types of the salespersons' activities: (1) prospecting, (2) selling, (3) demonstrating (4) closing and (5) sales control.

1. *Prospecting.* Good sales management allows sales representatives to develop their own prospects. This practice, however, does not relieve the sales manager from the responsibility of reviewing the qualified prospects with the sales representative.
2. *Selling.* Sales managers insist on daily contact with their salespersons. In addition, they constantly remind the salespersons that they have a minimum number of calls to make each day. Eventually this becomes an accepted habit rather than a requirement. Normally a sales manager will make at least one call per week with the salesperson. It is important that the sales manager recognize the status, problems, and objectives of the call. After the interview the sales manager should review the presentation with the salesperson, pointing out strengths and weaknesses. If this is a second or third call, the presence of two people will often apply psychological pressure that can result in a sales commitment.
3. *Demonstrating.* It is important for the sales manager to know each salesperson's flying ability. Sales managers normally review a salesperson's presentation and demonstration techniques at least once a month. Telling the same story over and over has caused some salespersons to become bored with their own product. Salespersons should know which demonstrators are available and company policy regarding use of the aircraft and demonstration charges.
4. *Closing.* Sales managers are often available when closing the sale. Most sales close more expeditiously by using a third party expert. The sales manager should have prior knowledge on any finance or lease proposals and be prepared to support the salesperson's recommendations. The sales manager should be aware of the prospect's major and minor objections and the answers the sales representative has given.
5. *Sales control.* Organization and control of the aircraft selling function is a major responsibility of the sales manager. Through improved organization and more efficient planning the sales manager can more effectively coordinate sales and sales management functions. One of the common sales control tools is the *Daily Sales Call Planning Chart* (see Table 12–3). The purpose of this chart is to assist sales representatives in organizing their daily work plan. The sales representative at the start of each business day prepares it so that both the sales representative and sales manager know which prospects are to be contacted and what the sales representative plans to accomplish during the day. It also enables the sales manager to check the sales representative's organization and provide assistance based on detailed knowledge of daily activities.

Evaluation

Successful implementation of the personal selling strategy depends on the performance of the salespersons, individually and as a group. Consequently, sales management needs ways in which to appraise performance. The job can be judgmental as decisions are made about whether salespersons have met their predetermined quotas, and it is also developmental, because the future growth of the sales force depends on performance evaluation and feedback.

Salespersons are evaluated on their quantitative and qualitative performances. *Quantitative performance* may include dollar sales volume, direct contribution to profit, number of single and multiengine aircraft sold, and number of new prospect visits per month. A salesperson's batting average is a popular evaluation tool. The average is calculated by dividing the number of sales by the number of presentations. This performance index is a measure of productivity, and it encourages better prospecting and strengthens closing techniques. *Qualitative performance* includes more general items such as the salesperson's knowledge of the company, aircraft, customers, and competitors, as well as sincerity, flying ability, attitude, appearance, temperament, and motivation.

Table 12–3 Items Included on Daily Sales Planning Chart

Date: _____   Salesperson: _____

TELEPHONE CONTACTS

Individual's Name and Company   Specific Objective

1.
2.
3.

E-MAIL/FAX/LETTER CONTACTS

1.
2.
3.

PERSONAL CONTACTS

1. Company _____ Individuals _____
   Specific Call Objective _____
   Visual Aids _____ Aircraft Model _____
   Sales Steps to Be Accomplished:

1. Prospecting _____	2. Contacting _____	3. Interest _____
4. Preference _____	5. Proposal _____	6. Close _____
7. Follow-up _____	8. Expanding the fleet _____	

Remarks: _____
_____
_____
_____

Three common methods used to evaluate sales performance are (1) achievement of quotas, (2) comparison with other salespersons, and (3) comparison with last year's performance. *Quotas* are the expected performance of the overall sales task assigned to an individual. Salespersons who meet or exceed their quotas are rewarded and those who fall short should be give additional support and direction.

Comparing salespersons with their peers can also help a sales manager decide which salespersons need additional assistance. This method of evaluating performance can be misleading since variations in territory potential, competition, and type of accounts handled can affect performance, regardless of the skill level of the salesperson. Comparing prior performance with current results is another way of measuring a salesperson's contribution. If, for example, a salesperson's sales increased 10 percent over last year, despite a decline in industry sales, this record demonstrates solid progress.

KEY TERMS

Sales management	New aircraft sales
Recruiting	Adjusted gross profit for a new aircraft sale
Job analysis	
Job description	Used aircraft sales
Direct recruiting	Adjusted gross profit for a used aircraft sale
Indirect recruiting	
Learning	Daily sales call planning chart
Salary	Quantitative performance
Straight commission	Qualitative performance
Draw	Quotas

REVIEW QUESTIONS

1. What is sales management? How does it differ from flight or maintenance management? Discuss the importance of establishing sales objectives.

2. How is the size of the sales force determined? What are some of the questions a sales manager must answer in determining manpower requirements?

3. What is a job analysis? Describe some of the questions that must be answered in preparing a job analysis. How does a job description differ from a job analysis? What are some of the considerations that must be addressed in preparing a job description?

4. Discuss several potential sources of salespersons. Design a classified advertisement for a junior salesperson. Describe some of the common steps in the selection process for new salespersons. In interviewing a potential candidate for a sales position, what are some of the characteristics an interviewer would attempt to evaluate?

5. Give some of the major topics covered in a typical three-week on-site training program for a new aircraft sales representative. What are the three basic ways of compensating salespersons? What is the adjusted gross profit for a new airplane sale? A used airplane sale? What are some other important motivators for salespersons besides basic compensation plans?

6. Sales managers supervise their personnel in five primary areas. What are they? What is the daily sales call planning chart? Distinguish between evaluation of quantitative and qualitative performance of sales representatives. What are quotas? What are some other methods used in appraising sales performance?

REFERENCES

Churchill, Gilbert A., Niel M. Ford, and Orville C. Walker, Jr. *Sales Force Management.* (6th ed.). New York: Irwin/McGraw-Hill, 1999.

McCarthy, E. Jerome, and William D. Pereault, Jr., *Basic Marketing* (13th ed.). New York: Irwin/McGraw-Hill, 1999.

Stanton, William J. and Richard H. Buskirk. *Management of the Salesforce* (8th ed.). Home wood, Illinois: Richard D. Irwin, 1991.

APPENDIXES

Appendix A

Study Guide

This Study Guide is designed to assist you in learning the material covered in the text and during class sessions. It contains objective questions, including multiple choice, true-false, matching and fill-in. Answers to all of these questions are located at the end of each chapter. Following the objective questions in each chapter are Questions to Think About and Exercises. These provide over 70 real-world, applications-oriented questions, which allow you to work out in a practical way the marketing and management principles that you have been studying.

STUDY GUIDE—CHAPTER 1
General Aviation: A Historical Perspective

A. *MULTIPLE CHOICE:* Circle the letter that corresponds to the best answer.

1. In October 1910, the first international air meet was held in the U.S. at
   - a. Dominguez Field, CA.
   - b. Belmont Park, NY.
   - c. Polo Grounds, Washington, DC.
   - d. College Park, MD.
2. The first aircraft sold commercially was a
   - a. Curtiss Jenny.
   - b. Curtiss June Bug.
   - c. Laird Swallow.
   - d. Wright Flyer.
3. Prior to World War I the largest aircraft manufacturing company in the United States was the
   - a. Wright Aeronautical Corporation.
   - b. Weaver Aircraft Company.
   - c. Travel Air Manufacturing Company.
   - d. Curtiss Aeroplane and Motor Company.
4. The Kelly Air Mail Act of 1925
   - a. provided the establishment of airports, airways, and navaids.
   - b. created the first licensing of planes and pilots.
   - c. turned over the carriage of mail to private carriers.
   - d. outlawed barnstorming.
5. The first Beech aircraft was the
   - a. Bonanza.
   - b. Staggerwing.
   - c. Twin Beech Model 18.
   - d. Queen Air.
6. Cessna's first independent production model airplane, built in 1927, was the
   - a. C-34.
   - b. 120.
   - c. Comet.
   - d. Crane.
7. Cessna's entry into the jet market came in
   - a. 1953.
   - b. 1961.
   - c. 1968.
   - d. 1974.
8. William Piper acquired the following company in 1931
   - a. Taylor Brothers Aircraft Company.
   - b. Weaver Aircraft Company.
   - c. E. M. Laird Company.
   - d. Travel Air Manufacturing Co.
9. The general aviation community felt that private flying after World War II would
   - a. primarily be restricted to business use.
   - b. greatly expand.
   - c. be cut back significantly.
   - d. grow modestly.

10. Beginning in the 1950s the general aviation aircraft manufacturers directed their marketing efforts towards the _____ market.
    a. mass
    b. business
    c. commercial
    d. airline

11. Which of the following statements concerning the immediate post-World War II period is *not* true?
    a. Beech introduced the Bonanza for $7,435.
    b. Many VA students dropped out of flying after receiving their private pilot's license.
    c. General aviation aircraft were restricted to non-air carrier airports.
    d. Ex-military pilots were not satisfied with the slow speed offered by many of the light aircraft.

12. Cessna and Piper introduced their first four-place light twins aimed at the business market during the
    a. early 1950s.
    b. mid 1950s.
    c. early 1960s.
    d. mid 1960s.

13. General aviation experienced tremendous growth during the
    a. early 1950s.
    b. late 1950s.
    c. early 1960s.
    d. late 1960s.

14. General aviation aircraft sales hit an all-time high in
    a. 1966.
    b. 1973.
    c. 1978.
    d. 1981.

15. Beech Aircraft Corporation was acquired in 1980 by
    a. Raytheon Corp.
    b. Lear-Siegler.
    c. General Dynamics.
    d. Lockheed Aircraft Corp.

16. Many of the early barnstormers
    a. were in favor of the Air Commerce Act of 1926.
    b. were ex–World War I pilots.
    c. held licenses issued by Bureau of Air Commerce.
    d. were ex–Post Office Department pilots.

17. Travel Air Manufacturing Company was formed by
    a. the Stearman brothers, Burke, and Cessna.
    b. Moellendick, Laird, Douglas, and Bellanca.
    c. Beech, the Lockheed brothers, and Ryan.
    d. Cessna, the Stearman brothers, and Beech.

18. Which of the following statements concerning the immediate post–World War II period is correct?
    a. Piper developed the first J-3 Cub.
    b. Beech came out with the 120/140 series.
    c. Airline service contracted because of the widespread use of general aviation aircraft.
    d. Hundreds of civilian flight training schools started all over the country.

19. Which of the following was *not* a problem for the industry immediately after World War II?
    a. Most of the less expensive aircraft were prewar models.
    b. The availability of war surplus aircraft.
    c. Much tougher FAA regulations regarding licensing private pilots.
    d. A high percentage of VA students dropping out of flying after receiving their private pilot licenses.

20. All of the following navaids appeared during the 1950s *except*
    a. VORs.
    b. TCAs.
    c. unicom.
    d. three-axis autopilot.

21. Many new aircraft were certificated during the 1960s including all of the following *except*
    a. Piper Cherokee.
    b. Piper Tri-Pacer.
    c. Cessna Skyhawk.
    d. Mooney Mustang.

22. The _____ was the first jet designed specifically for the general aviation market.
    a. Cessna Citation
    b. Lockheed Jetstar
    c. Learjet
    d. North American Sabreliner

23. The 1970s could be described as a decade of
    a. tremendous production.
    b. declining sales as a result of the oil embargo.
    c. foreign competition.
    d. consolidation and contraction in light aircraft manufacturing.
24. The Piper Tomahawk was designed during the 1970s to compete with the
    a. Cessna 150.
    b. Beech Bonanza.
    c. Mooney Mustang.
    d. Lear 23.
25. One of the most successful light-twins produced during the 1970s was the
    a. Grumman-American Cougar.
    b. Cessna Cardinal.
    c. Piper Seminole.
    d. Beech Duchess.
26. All of the following events took place during the 1980s *except*
    a. escalating product liability insurance costs.
    b. Beech and Cessna were acquired by large conglomerates.
    c. GAMA developed into a strong and effective lobbying and public relations organization.
    d. the Investment Tax Credit was eliminated.
27. The growth in the small-package delivery industry in the 1980s provided a big boost in _____ sales.
    a. Piper Warrior
    b. Cessna Caravan
    c. Beech Baron
    d. Gulfstream IV
28. One of the major factors causing the decline in new general aviation aircraft sales during the 1980s was
    a. foreign competition.
    b. competition among the major air carriers.
    c. sharply rising acquisition and operating costs.
    d. tightening of FAA certification standards.
29. All of the following have been cited as reasons for the decline in general aviation aircraft sales *except*
    a. the level of professionalism required to fly in today's air traffic environment.
    b. changing tastes and preferences among traditional business and pleasure users.
    c. lowering of tariffs causing a flood of foreign models to enter the market.
    d. used aircraft were readily available.
30. All of the following factors have been cited as causes for the decline in general aviation aircraft sales during the 1980s, *except*
    a. airline deregulation
    b. the Tax Reform Act
    c. the Clean Air Act
    d. product liability claims
31. Which of the following factors caused the decline in the number of student starts from the late 1970s through the early 1990s?
    a. Two major economic recessions.
    b. Repeal of the GI Bill of Rights.
    c. Airline hiring decreased significantly.
    d. Greatly expanded military flight training in response to the cold war.
32. All of the following represented challenges to the GA industry during the 1980s, *except:*
    a. decline in the number of manufacturers and FBOs.
    b. product liability.
    c. decline in the number of students and private pilots.
    d. decline in the number of airports.
33. The FAA's "General Aviation Action Plan"
    a. streamlined its certification of new aircraft.
    b. included cutting red tape.
    c. sponsored a general aviation design competition.
    d. improved navigation through satellite-based systems.

34. WAAS
    a. supports navigation in all phases of flight.
    b. is used in aircraft and other vehicles on the airport surface.
    c. puts real-time weather information in the cockpit.
    d. is a worldwide effort to develop common aviation standards.
35. The goal of AGATE was to
    a. improve navigation through satellite-based systems.
    b. decentralize the FAA decision-making process.
    c. utilize new technology to produce safer, more efficient aircraft.
    d. None of the above.
36. The "No Plane, No Gain" Campaign was sponsored by
    a. FAA and NASA
    b. AOPA and NATA
    c. ATA and RAA
    d. GAMA and NBAA
37. The goals of "GA Team 2000" included
    a. securing additional funding.
    b. the improvement of flight school marketing.
    c. generating flight training leads.
    d. All of the above.
38. The EAA sponsored the following program:
    a. Young Eagles
    b. AvKids
    c. Project Pilot
    d. Be A Pilot
39. Which of the following statements is correct regarding the 1990s?
    a. The number of fractional ownership programs leveled off.
    b. Cessna resumed production of selected single-engine piston aircraft.
    c. GA Team 2000 was a direct result of the work performed by NASA.
    d. The goal of PEARC was to sponsor general aviation design competition for aeronautical engineering students.
40. General aviation aircraft shipments continued to decline into the 1990s, reaching a low of 928 units in
    a. 1991
    b. 1994
    c. 1996
    d. 1999
41. The general Aviation Revitalization Act (GARA) of 1994
    a. was designed to secure additional funding to expand the GA Team 2000 effort.
    b. sponsored a General Aviation Design Competition for aeronautical engineering students.
    c. imposed an 18-year statute of repose, limiting products liability suits.
    d. provided funding to design a revolutionary combustion aircraft engine.
42. During the 1990s, _____ became the leading fractional ownership program.
    a. NetJets
    b. Flexjet
    c. Travel Air
    d. Flight Options
43. General aviation experienced a revitalization of the industry during the
    a. early 1980s
    b. late 1980s
    c. early 1990s
    d. late 1990s
44. The decade of the 1990s closed with
    a. a feeling of optimism for the GA industry.
    b. a decline in sales of single-engine piston aircraft.
    c. repeal of the Clean Air Act of 1991.
    d. a significant increase in the number of FBOs from the 1970s

B. *TRUE/FALSE:* Circle "T" if the statement is true, "F" if it is false.

T   F   1. The first commercial sale of an airplane took place in August 1908.

T   F   2. The first Gordon Bennet Speed Trophy race was won by Claud Graham-White.

T   F   3. The organization which licensed pilots to fly in air meets prior to World War I was the Aero Club of New York.

T   F   4. Over 95 percent of the U.S. Army pilots trained during World War I flew the Curtiss JN-4 Jenny.

T   F   5. The Air Commerce Act of 1926 marked the beginning of the end of barnstorming in the United States.

T   F   6. One of the biggest and best known barnstorming groups was the Gates Flying Circus.

T   F   7. The Laird Swallow was primarily designed to carry mail.

T   F   8. Travel Air Manufacturing Company was formed by Jake Moellendick and Buck Weaver.

T   F   9. Beech Aircraft Corporation was founded during the depths of the depression in April 1932.

T   F   10. The Beech Bonanza has been in continuous production longer than any other general aviation aircraft.

T   F   11. The C-34, high-wing, four-place aircraft was largely the creation of Duane Wallace.

T   F   12. Eighty percent of the military pilots during World War II received their initial flight training in a J-3 Cub.

T   F   13. Most marketing studies indicated a greatly depressed general aviation aircraft industry in the immediate post-World War II period.

T   F   14. Some of the manufacturers of combat aircraft during World War II developed general aviation aircraft in the postwar period.

T   F   15. Over 30,000 light aircraft were sold in 1946.

T   F   16. The airlines and the general aviation community started their long fight over the use of airspace and airports in the postwar period.

T   F   17. General aviation aircraft sales grew steadily during the period from 1946 to 1949.

T   F   18. The need for IFR capability became apparent during the mid-1950s.

T   F   19. The use of turbine power for general aviation aircraft was introduced in the late 1950s.

T   F   20. GAMA was formed in 1960.

T   F   21. The Curtiss Aeroplane and Motor Company was the successor to the Aerial Experimental Association.

T   F   22. Wamego, Kansas, became the early home of general aviation.

T   F   23. William T. Piper was a barnstormer during the early 1920s.

T   F   24. Many World War II pilots were dissatisfied with the general aviation aircraft available in the 1940s.

T   F   25. Static free VHF radios became factory options on many aircraft during the 1950s.

T   F   26. By 1965, the general aviation aircraft fleet had grown to 95,000 airplanes.

T   F   27. The Learjet had its roots in a European private-venture military jet that never went into full production.

T   F   28. The Mooney Mustang proved to be one of the most successful aircraft of the 1960s.

T   F   29. More general aviation aircraft were sold during the 1970s than any decade before or after.

T   F   30. During the 1980s, there was a steady decline in new general aviation aircraft sales.

T   F   31. The manufacturers focused their efforts on turboprops and jets during the 1980s.

T   F   32. The Tax Reform Act of 1986 was designed to promote sales by offering tax credits to business aircraft purchasers.

T   F   33. Changing tastes and preferences has been cited as a reason for the decline in general aviation aircraft sales.

T F 34. General aviation has always been a cyclical industry, and the decline in new aircraft sales mirrored the recession-ary economy during the 1980s.

T F 35. Historically, the general aviation industry has paralleled the economic cycle of the national economy until the 1980s.

T F 36. Foreign-manufactured business jets declined as a percentage of total business jet sales in the 1990s.

T F 37. The number of flight schools increased during the 1980s in response to the increase in airline hiring.

T F 38. The Aviation Weather Information (AWIN) program was an effort by the FAA to put real-time weather information in the cockpit.

T F 39. The purpose of AGATE is to make learning to fly less time consuming and less costly.

T F 40. Because GPS has become so widely used, the Department of Transportation decided to discontinue LORAN C.

T F 41. Project Pilot was co-sponsored by the FAA and GAMA.

T F 42. The EAA sponsored "GA Team 2000."

T F 43. GAMA offers publications, awards, and scholarships to bring aviation education into the classroom.

T F 44. Amateur-built aircraft showed steady growth during the early 1990s.

T F 45. In January 1997, Cessna delivered its first new single-engine piston aircraft since 1986.

T F 46. In 1995, general aviation aircraft shipments increased after a 17-year decline.

T F 47. Most fractional owners have owned or operated corporate aircraft in the past.

T F 48. Fitted with auxiliary fuel tanks, winglets, and upgraded engines, the Boeing Business Jet 2 can fly from Los Angeles to London.

T F 49. Total turbine shipments more than doubled between 1994 and 2000.

T F 50. General aviation aircraft shipments are expected to surpass production totals during the 1970s by 2010.

C. *MATCHING:* Select the letter on the right which corresponds to the description on the left.

_____ 1. the first aircraft sold commercially.   a. Twin Beech Model 18

_____ 2. a general aviation aircraft which entered the market in 1946 and is still being produced.   b. Cessna 172

_____ 3. most WWII military pilots received their first instruction in this aircraft.   c. Piper Apache

_____ 4. first built in 1937, this aircraft saw service during WWII as a transport and trainer for bombardiers. d. Curtiss June Bug

_____ 5. an aircraft flow by the barnstormers after WWI.   e. Laird Swallow

_____ 6. the world's most successful lightplane in terms of number sold.   f. Cessna C-34

_____ 7. a popular, light twin-engine aircraft introduced in the mid-1950s.   g. Beech Staggerwing 17

_____ 8. winner of the 1935 Detroit News trophy race.   h. Piper J-3 Cub

_____ 9. the first aircraft produced by Beech.   i. Curtiss Jenny

_____ 10. one of the first aircraft built in Wichita by a group of general aviation pioneers.   j. Beech Bonanza

D. *QUESTIONS TO THINK ABOUT AND EXERCISES:*

1. What factors led to the strong growth of general aviation aircraft sales during the late 1960s and late 1970s? Why didn't these trends continue into the 1980s? How did the industry address the factors that caused the decline in aircraft sales?
2. What can be learned from history as the industry enters the twenty-first century? How do you foresee the industry by the year 2010?

ANSWERS TO OBJECTIVE QUESTIONS:

A. *Multiple Choice*

1. b	6. c	11. c	16. b	21. b	26. c	31. b	36. d	41. c
2. b	7. c	12. b	17. d	22. c	27. b	32. d	37. d	42. a
3. d	8. a	13. d	18. d	23. a	28. c	33. b	38. a	43. d
4. c	9. b	14. c	19. c	24. a	29. c	34. a	39. b	44. a
5. b	10. b	15. a	20. b	25. c	30. c	35. c	40. b	

B. *True/False*

1. F	6. T	11. T	16. T	21. T	26. T	31. T	36. F	41. F	46. T
2. F	7. F	12. T	17. F	22. F	27. T	32. F	37. F	42. F	47. F
3. T	8. F	13. F	18. T	23. F	28. F	33. T	38. T	43. T	48. T
4. T	9. T	14. T	19. F	24. T	29. T	34. F	39. T	44. T	49. T
5. T	10. T	15. T	20. F	25. T	30. T	35. T	40. F	45. T	50. F

C. *Matching*

1. d	6. b
2. j	7. c
3. h	8. f
4. a	9. g
5. i	10. e

STUDY GUIDE—CHAPTER 2
The Scope of General Aviation

A. *MULTIPLE CHOICE:* Circle the letter that corresponds to the best answer.

1. The general aviation fleet includes all civil
   a. aviation aircraft excluding certificated airlines.
   b. aviation aircraft including certificated and noncertificated airlines.
   c. and military aircraft.
   d. aviation aircraft used for business and pleasure purposes only.
2. Of the total number of registered civil aircraft on record with the FAA at the end of the century, general aviation accounted for over _____ percent.
   a. 68
   b. 75
   c. 86
   d. 96
3. At the end of the century, there were approximately how many active general aviation aircraft on record with the FAA?
   a. 171,000
   b. 196,000
   c. 220,000
   d. 238,000
4. The largest category of flying in terms of primary use is
   a. business.
   b. instructional.
   c. personal.
   d. rental.
5. "Executive/corporate" aircraft are distinguished from "business" aircraft according to primary use because the
   a. former category includes aircraft used by corporate executives only.
   b. latter category includes aircraft used by corporate executives only.
   c. former category includes aircraft used for transporting employees and/or property and flown by professional pilots.
   d. latter category includes aircraft used for transporting employees and/or property and flown by professional pilots.

6. "Instructional" flying includes all of the following *except*
   a. formal instruction with an instructor aboard.
   b. formal instruction specified by a flight instructor who is not aboard the aircraft.
   c. proficiency flying.
   d. a licensed private pilot working on an instrument rating.

7. Fish spotting by aircraft would be considered
   a. aerial application.   c. business
   b. aerial observation.   d. other use.

8. At the end of the century, there were over _____ aircraft landing facilities reported by the FAA.
   a. 12,000   c. 19,000
   b. 17,000   d. 21,000

9. The type of airports of particular concern to the FAA and the general aviation community because of their vulnerability to sale are
   a. public-use, privately owned airports.   c. private-use airports.
   b. public-use, publicly owned airports.   d. heliports.

10. As of December 31, 1999, the number of active *private* pilots in the United States was approximately:
   a. 115,000   c. 340,000
   b. 259,000   d. 423,000

11. All of the following would be considered public use of aircraft, *except:*
   a. drug interdiction   c. law enforcement
   b. transport of government personnel   d. real estate developers.

12. Which of the following statements concerning the post-deregulation period is *not* true?
   a. Many smaller cities have lost airline service from the major and national air carriers.
   b. Scheduled air carrier service has become more concentrated at major hubs.
   c. The number of middle and top management personnel has increased.
   d. Air carriers have scheduled more service around the popular traveling times.

13. _____ represents approximately 70 percent of the active general aviation fleet.
   a. Single-engine piston aircraft.   c. Turbine aircraft.
   b. Multiengine piston aircraft.   d. Rotorcraft.

14. Which of the following is not a key factor in using business aircraft?
   a. saving time   c. avoiding the hassle of airline terminals
   b. prestige   d. saving money

15. Which of the following factors could *not* be considered a major reason for the reliability and capability of general aviation aircraft?
   a. federal aviation regulations
   b. foreign competition
   c. network of FBOs in the United States
   d. research and development by the airframe and engine manufacturers

16. Use of aircraft for drug interdiction would fall under the following primary use category:
   a. Aerial observation.   c. Aerial other
   b. Public use.   d. Medical

17. The following primary use categories are dominated by rotorcraft *except:*
   a. Medical   c. Air Tours
   b. External load   d. Aerial other

18. The aerial other primary use category includes aircraft for:
   a. weather modification.
   b. search and rescue.
   c. mapping and photography
   d. crop spraying.

19. In 1999 the corporate and business fleet represented about _____ percent of the total active general aircraft.
   a. 10   c. 22
   b. 16   d. 34

20. The most widely used type of aircraft operated by NBAA companies is the
    a. ME Piston.
    b. Turboprop
    c. Turbojet.
    d. Rotorcraft.
21. Aerial observation includes all of the following uses *except*
    a. hunting.
    b. mosquito control.
    c. search and rescue.
    d. mapping/photography.
22. This organization represents over one-half of the pilots in the United States.
    a. AOPA
    b. AAAE
    c. ATA
    d. ADMA
23. General Aviation airports:
    a. offer flexibility to business flyers.
    b. attract industry
    c. stimulate economic growth.
    d. do all of the above.
24. Which of the following categories of airports are most subject to sale because of economic, political, or personal reasons?
    a. Publicly Owned/Publicly Used
    b. Privately Owned/Publicly Used
    c. Privately Owned/Privately Used
    d. Heliports
25. All of the following active pilot categories showed a decrease in certificates held during the period from 1980 to 1999 *except*
    a. Airline Transport
    b. Commercial
    c. Private
    d. Student
26. The most widely used equipment in the world for making safe runway approaches under marginal weather conditions best describes the
    a. VOR.
    b. TCA.
    c. FSS.
    d. ILS.
27. Dollars that are channeled throughout the community from aviation businesses is called:
    a. deposit expansion
    b. yield spreads
    c. multiplier effect
    d. velocity growth
28. Of the approximately 5,000 publicly owned airports in the United States, the schedule airlines only serve about:
    a. 250
    b. 480
    c. 600
    d. 820
29. The aerial application primary use category would include all of the following uses, *except:*
    a. insect control.
    b. reforestation.
    c. chemicals in agriculture.
    d. seeds in agriculture.
30. Aircraft used for racing, towing gliders, and aerial advertising would be examples of which of the following uses:
    a. personal
    b. aerial other
    c. public use
    d. other flying
31. From the mid 1980s through the mid 1990s, major U.S. manufacturers shifted almost entirely to:
    a. single-engine piston aircraft
    b. multi-engine piston aircraft
    c. turbine aircraft
    d. rotorcraft

32. Websites can be particularly helpful to manufacturers:
    a. by providing contact phone numbers and e-mail addresses.
    b. by allowing customers to download technical information.
    c. by enabling customers to order parts.
    d. by all of the above.
33. Which of the following statements concerning the Web is *not* correct?
    a. Sales of pre-owned aircraft over the Web may soon threaten traditional aircraft selling.
    b. There are a number of excellent sites for professional online assistance with every facet of trip planning.
    c. The Web has become the preferred tool for an array of online charter reservations services.
    d. Customers of airframe manufacturers can use websites to order parts or download technical information.
34. In the world of Web classifieds, the dominant source is:
    a. Aircraftbuyer.com
    b. Aircraftdealers.net
    c. Trade-a-plane.com
    d. Aircraftdealer.com
35. The main reason(s) for conducting business online is to:
    a. generate inquiries from the general public.
    b. increase revenues and reduce transaction costs.
    c. reduce advertising costs.
    d. All of the above.

B. *TRUE/FALSE:* Circle "T" if the statement is true, "F" if it is false.

T   F   1. Today's general aviation airplane is a business tool much the same as a computer.

T   F   2. Ever since the early 1960s, general aviation aircraft have represented at least 96 percent of the total U.S. civil aircraft fleet.

T   F   3. There are 10 primary use categories.

T   F   4. The executive/corporate transportation primary use category only includes aircraft operated by professional pilots.

T   F   5. Over two-thirds of the "*Fortune* 500" companies operate business aircraft.

T   F   6. Personal flying includes business and pleasure use of aircraft.

T   F   7. The majority of pilots flying today's executive/corporate aircraft received their first instruction in the military.

T   F   8. An air taxi operates under Part 91 of the Federal Aviation Regulations (FARs).

T   F   9. Proficiency flying is considered a part of instructional use of an aircraft.

T   F   10. Use of an aircraft for aerial observation would fall under FAR Part 135.

T   F   11. Aerial firefighting is included under aerial application.

T   F   12. At the end of 1999, approximately 35,000 aircraft were being flow for executive and business use in the United States.

T   F   13. Business aircraft can include everything from a Cessna 172 to a Boeing 737.

T   F   14. There are over 5,000 publicly owned airports in the United States.

T   F   15. The airframe and engine manufacturers usually exceed FAA minimums in designing and building general aviation aircraft.

T   F   16. The National Business Aviation Association (NBAA) represents more than 30,000 members who own or fly general aviation aircraft.

T   F   17. Two-thirds of NBAA members operate turbojets.

T   F   18. A number of organizations represent the interests of the business and pleasure flier; by far the most important is the ALPA.

T   F   19. Charter companies operate under FAR Part 91.

T   F   20. Aerial advertising aircraft fall under the Other Flying primary-use category.

T   F   21. The number of active private pilots in the United States stayed around the same during the 1980s and 1990s.

T   F   22. The number of student pilot certificates has decreased significantly between 1980 and 1999.

T   F   23. VORs were developed during the 1960s.

T   F   24. Air route traffic control centers (ARTCCs) collect and disseminate weather information, file flight plans, and provide in-flight assistance and aviation advisory services.

T   F   25. Approximately 70 percent of all the hours flown by general aviation aircraft are for business and commercial purposes.

T   F   26. In recent years kit aircraft have been very popular.

T   F   27. The number of FBOs actually increased during the 1990s despite the decline in aircraft sales.

T   F   28. The importance of new pilots is a key factor in expanding aircraft sales.

T   F   29. More than one-half of the sightseeing flights are made in lighter-than-air aircraft.

T   F   30. Between 1994 and 2000 general aviation shipments and billings more than tripled.

T   F   31. In the FAA's annual survey of owners, an active aircraft is an aircraft flown at least 50 hours during the survey calendar year.

T   F   32. Air taxi firms operate under FAR Part 135.

T   F   33. Repeal of the GI Bill of Rights in 1979 had a significant effect on flight training for years afterward.

T   F   34. The medical category is dominated by helicopters.

T   F   35. The "multiplier effect" refers to the number of general aviation airports within 50 miles of a major hub airport.

T   F   36. The decline in the number of active student pilots and student starts began in 1980 following the repeal of the GI Bill of Rights in 1979.

T   F   37. The most useful purpose of an airframe manufacturer's website is handling inquiries from the general public.

T   F   38. Retrieval of weather information online has become the most popular use of the Web among pilots.

T   F   39. One of the best known parts distributors is Aviall.

T   F   40. Because the Web is a rather expensive communication medium, few publications have chosen to establish sites.

C.   *MATCHING:* Select the letter on the right which corresponds to the description on the left.

_____ 1. represents more than 360,000 members who fly general aviation aircraft.   a. NBAA

_____ 2. includes 50 U.S. companies that produce general aviation aircraft, components, and   b. AOPA
supplies.

_____ 3. serves as a lobbyist and chief spokesperson for FBOs and air taxi operators.   c. ADMA

_____ 4. represents over 6,000 businesses that operate corporate aircraft.   d. GAMA

_____ 5. represents companies that manufacture and distribute aircraft parts, supplies, and   e. NATA
equipment.

D.   *FILL-IN:* Complete the following sentences.

1. Three examples of aerial application are

a. _____

b. _____

c. _____

2. Three examples of aerial observation are

   a. _____

   b. _____

   c. _____

3. Give two economic benefits of general aviation airports.

   a. _____

   b. _____

E.   *QUESTIONS TO THINK ABOUT AND EXERCISES:*

1. The role of the general aviation industry in the overall air transportation picture has received little attention compared with the publicity garnered by scheduled airlines. In fact, the scheduled airlines would like to see much of the light aircraft activity at the major hubs curtailed. Discuss the relative importance of general aviation as a partner with the scheduled airlines in the air transportation system.

2. What economic factors do you foresee as being important to the continued growth of each primary use category discussed in this chapter. Which categories will show the greatest growth into the new century? the slowest growth or decline? why?

3. What are some of the reasons people want to learn how to fly? How does this explain the ups and downs in the number of student starts over the years? What can the general aviation aircraft manufacturers do to increase the number of student starts, and the number completing their private pilot's certificate? What relationship is there between the number of student starts and the sale of new aircraft? Why have the foreign aircraft manufacturers had such success in the American market? Do you foresee continual growth in the kit aircraft market? why?

4. What can the FAA and general aviation community do to stem the demise of privately owned general aviation airports around metropolitan areas?

5. Select a website and write a critique based upon the following characteristics: content, graphics, interactivity, readability, navigation, customer orientation, purpose, and updating.

ANSWERS:

A.   *Multiple Choice*

1. a	6. c	11. d	16. b	21. b	26. d	31. c
2. d	7. b	12. c	17. d	22. a	27. c	32. d
3. c	8. c	13. a	18. a	23. d	28. c	33. a
4. c	9. a	14. b	19. b	24. c	29. a	34. c
5. c	10. b	15. b	20. c	25. a	30. d	35. b

B.   *True/False*

1. T	6. T	11. F	16. F	21. F	26. T	31. F	36. T
2. T	7. F	12. T	17. T	22. T	27. F	32. T	37. F
3. F	8. F	13. T	18. F	23. F	28. T	33. T	38. T
4. T	9. F	14. T	19. F	24. F	29. T	34. T	39. T
5. T	10. F	15. T	20. T	25. T	30. T	35. F	40. F

C.   *Matching*

   1. b

   2. d

   3. e

   4. a

   5. c

D.   *Fill-in*

1. a. distribution of chemicals in agriculture

   b. distribution of seeds in agriculture

   c. fish stocking and reforestation

2. a. aerial mapping/photography and surveillance
   b. pipeline and powerline patrol
   c. fish spotting, search and rescue, traffic advisory, oil and mineral exploration
3. a. attracting industry
   b. stimulating economic growth

STUDY GUIDE—CHAPTER 3
The Fixed Base Operator: Backbone of General Aviation

A. *MULTIPLE CHOICE:* Circle the letter that corresponds to the best answer.

1. The primary business of virtually all FBOs is
   a. flight instruction.
   b. aircraft sales.
   c. maintenance.
   d. line service.
2. Avionics sales and service would normally fall under
   a. aircraft sales.
   b. maintenance and repair.
   c. line service.
   d. corporate flight service.
3. Maintenance and repair service include
   a. cleaning a transient aircraft's windshield and vacuuming the cabin.
   b. sale of parts and accessories.
   c. turbine starting and de-icing equipment.
   d. exterior cleaning of aircraft.
4. Under a corporate flight service arrangement
   a. the aircraft must be owned by the FBO.
   b. the billing is normally a flat annual fee.
   c. maintenance is provided by the FBO but pilots are employed by the corporation.
   d. the FBO is responsible for flight operations, maintenance, and administrative support.
5. Which of the following FBO nonincome services would be considered an absolute necessity?
   a. pilot or crew sleeping quarters
   b. pilot ready room or area
   c. recreational facilities
   d. a conference room for visitors
   e. all of these
6. Small fixed base operators
   a. all provide flight instruction.
   b. frequently begin as generalists and develop into specialists.
   c. normally begin as specialists and develop into generalists.
   d. have made above normal profits in recent years.
7. Since the early 1980s, the number of FBOs has
   a. stayed about the same.
   b. increased
   c. decreased.
   d. risen in the late 1970s and then fallen during the early 1980s.
8. Large FBOs
   a. generally use modern management techniques.
   b. have better access to financial sources.
   c. have investments running into millions of dollars.
   d. all of these.
9. The first step in establishing an FBO is
   a. determining the characteristics of the community.
   b. selecting a site.
   c. preparing a market analysis.
   d. getting assistance from the FAA.

10. Site selection for a fixed base operator
    a. is no more difficult than any other business.
    b. can have a significant effect on future business.
    c. is easier on larger airports with established facilities.
    d. is almost entirely at the discretion of the FAA.

11. Information concerning a particular airport, such as plans for future expansion, number of based aircraft, and aircraft movements, can be obtained from the
    a. airport management.   c. FAA District Airport Engineer.
    b. local chamber of commerce.   d. state aviation bureau.

12. Customer (or public) facilities
    a. are generally the same areas used by employees at an FBO.
    b. must be completely equipped and functional from a pilot's standpoint.
    c. include the outdoor tie-down area.
    d. must include a visitors' conference room.

13. Which of the following would not normally be a responsibility of the chief pilot?
    a. hearing student and instructor complaints
    b. maintaining a close liaison with local FAA personnel
    c. developing a system to alert line personnel of incoming transient aircraft
    d. conducting introductory flights and tours of the facility

14. Standardization is needed in all but one of the following areas. Which one?
    a. flight procedures and maneuvers   c. customer relations
    b. flight and ground curriculum   d. student evaluation

15. Good ramp planning calls for
    a. two-way taxi routes.
    b. availability of rental cars.
    c. training aircraft parked away from the flight office so as not to interfere with transient aircraft.
    d. A designated refueling parking spot for fuel truck operations.

16. NATA estimates that there are somewhere between _____ FBOs in the United States.
    a. 3,000 and 3,500   c. 4,000 and 4,500
    b. 3,500 and 4,000   d. 4,500 and 5,000

17. Which of the following statements regarding trends in the FBO industry is not correct?
    a. Airframe manufacturers are directly competing in a number of traditional FBO service areas.
    b. Conforming to governmental regulations for such things as underground fuel storage tanks is a lesser problem today than it was during the 1980s.
    c. Insurance premiums have risen since the early 1990s.
    d. Corporate self-fueling has been on the increase at many airports.

18. The concept of an FBO as a business center means it
    a. will turn over the responsibility of dispensing fuels to a single tank farm.
    b. may be acquired by or become partners with established hotel chains.
    c. will offer conference rooms, food services, personal computers with modem, and other types of business services.
    d. will increase sales of nonaviation products.

19. A market analysis includes
    a. the number of potential customers.
    b. community income levels.
    c. weather conditions.
    d. all of the above.

20. All of the following are advantages in joining an FBO chain except
    a. economies of scale.
    b. assured profitability.
    c. national identity.
    d. no exceptions, all of the above are advantages.

21. An FBO might consider joining a chain if it
    a. has a sound reputation for quality services and support.
    b. operates in a strong geographical location.
    c. is located in an underexposed geographical area.
    d. is well established and profitable.
22. By joining an FBO chain
    a. an operator loses all personal identity.
    b. there is a large pool of ideas from which to draw.
    c. management decision making is limited.
    d. higher profits are assured.
23. Dispatcher and/or receptionist personnel should be
    a. in uniform or dress that is immediately identifiable to transient pilots.
    b. able to explain company insurance policies.
    c. familiar with ramp safety procedures.
    d. in close liaison with local FAA personnel.
24. Mobile fueling equipment
    a. is more flexible.
    b. is less costly.
    c. is safer.
    d. results in less evaporation.
25. All of the following are responsibilities of the chief pilot *except* to:
    a. establish a program to recruit new students and improve attrition.
    b. make regular checks on student attitudes.
    c. conduct introductory flights and tours of the facility.
    d. call customers who have become inactive.
26. The most common line service provided by FBOs is:
    a. storing planes
    b. minor maintenance
    c. fueling
    d. aircraft cleaning
27. Completion work includes the:
    a. financing of aircraft sales.
    b. design and installation of interiors.
    c. sale of parts and accessories in addition to minor maintenance.
    d. management and operation of corporate-owned aircraft.
28. Avionics and instrument work can only be performed under a FAR _____ repair station certificate.
    a. Part 61
    b. Part 65
    c. Part 145
    d. Part 147
29. Rates for chartered planes depend upon all of the following factors, *except* the:
    a. length of time the plane will be used.
    b. size and type of plane.
    c. need for a pilot or crew.
    d. time of day or night.
30. All charter operators are regulated under FAR _____.
    a. Part 91
    b. Part 121
    c. Part 135
    d. Part 145
31. All of the following FBO nonincome services would be considered necessary, *except:*
    a. private meeting rooms
    b. preflight planning rooms
    c. in-flight catering
    d. pilot supplies

32. Which of the following trends in the FBO business is correct?
    a. Shorter-term contracts between aircraft operators.
    b. Consolidation.
    c. More local and regional charter services.
    d. Less difficulty in keeping pilots and maintenance personnel.

B. *TRUE/FALSE:* Circle "T" if the statement is true, "F" if it is false.

T   F   1. The term "Fixed Base Operator," or simply FBO, was derived from the barnstormer era of the 1920s.

T   F   2. Exterior custom painting is considered a part of "completion" work.

T   F   3. The FBO normally handles the assignment of pilots under a corporate flight service arrangement.

T   F   4. All FBOs provide primary, advanced, and recurrent flight training.

T   F   5. It is normal for an FBO to provide at least four of the six services discussed in this chapter.

T   F   6. If an FBO caters to corporate aircraft operators with professional crews, it is desirable to have sleeping quarters available.

T   F   7. It is estimated that there are over 6,000 FBOs at the 5,000 publicly owned airports in the contiguous United States.

T   F   8. The major difference between major and medium-sized FBOs is the type of services provided.

T   F   9. Most FBOs fall into the medium-size category.

T   F   10. Small FBOs typically lack formal management training.

T   F   11. An operator who only engages in flight training would be considered a specialized aviation operation and not an FBO in the true sense of the term.

T   F   12. The bankruptcy of an FBO has about the same effect on the financial community as any other business enterprise.

T   F   13. The actual site location of an FBO on an airport is really insignificant because all facilities can generally be reached with equal ease in an airplane.

T   F   14. Acquiring an existing facility on the airport is always preferred to building a new one.

T   F   15. Customer recreational facilities are just as important as a comfortable waiting lounge for a medium-sized FBO.

T   F   16. A display case or room devoted to pilot supplies and accessories is nice to have, but is generally an unprofitable area.

T   F   17. Employee showers and locker rooms are desirable, but not really needed because they have little effect on employee relations.

T   F   18. Some FBOs pay a bonus to instructors whose students complete an entire course.

T   F   19. Flight instructors should concentrate on their skills as pilots and not be distracted by salesmanship.

T   F   20. Dispatcher and/or receptionist personnel should be trained to call customers who have become inactive.

T   F   21. Under a corporate flight service arrangement, insurance coverages will often be provided under the FBO's policy.

T   F   22. Airframe manufacturers are now competing with FBOs in such areas as maintenance, painting, interior, and avionics work.

T   F   23. Some manufacturers now offer inclusive long-term maintenance and parts packages with the purchase of an aircraft.

T   F   24. FAR Part 61 flight schools allow more flexibility to rearrange lesson content.

T   F   25. The concept of the FBO as a business center will diminish as operators concentrate on aviation-related services in the new century.

T F 26. It is expected that an upturn in the economy during the new century will increase the number of FBOs.

T F 27. The characteristics of the community will greatly affect an FBO's operations.

T F 28. The cost/benefit relationship for joining an FBO chain is particularly viable for smaller FBOs.

T F 29. Belonging to a national or international chain is beneficial to virtually all FBOs.

T F 30. Flight personnel should have an understanding of sales and customer relations.

T F 31. The sale of fuel and lubricants is typically the leading revenue generator for an FBO.

T F 32. One of the advantages of completion work is that it does not have to be performed in accordance with manufacturers' specifications.

T F 33. Used parts and accessories are not subject to FAA standards.

T F 34. Some of the larger FBOs handle the financing of aircraft sales and long-term leases.

T F 35. An FAR Part 61 flight school must have a detailed, FAA-approved course curriculum.

T F 36. Virtually all FBOs can now service turbine-powered business aircraft and their passengers.

T F 37. When the upturn in aircraft sales began in 1995, the average single-engine, piston-powered aircraft was 27 years old.

T F 38. There has been a trend towards fewer FBO chains in recent years.

C. *FILL-IN:* Complete the following.

1. FBO services fall into six areas. They include
   a. _____
   b. _____
   c. _____
   d. _____
   e. _____
   f. _____

2. List five nonrevenue customer service areas available for transient pilots.
   a. _____
   b. _____
   c. _____
   d. _____
   e. _____

D. *QUESTIONS TO THINK ABOUT AND EXERCISES:*

1. Why are the reception and ramp areas so important from a marketing standpoint? Include in your answer the major activities which are carried out in these areas.
2. Develop all of the particulars in establishing a new aircraft dealership and sales department.
3. Prepare a market analysis in your county to determine if there is a need for a new FBO.
4. Develop a matrix of typical rates for all income services (flight training, charter, maintenance, etc.) provided by FBOs in your area.
5. Develop an employee training program for new line service personnel and flight instructors. This would consist of a training manual and checklist including all items necessary to orient a new employee to policies, procedures, and job responsibilities.
6. Using FBO Customer Services Checklist as a guide, ask a local FBO if you can prepare an inspection of his operation.
7. Some FBOs pay a bonus to instructors whose students complete an entire course. Discuss the pros and cons of such an arrangement. How do you feel about instructors receiving a finder's fee for recruiting students? a commission for developing charter accounts?

ANSWERS:

A. *Multiple Choice*

1. d	6. c	11. a	16. c	21. c	26. c	31. d
2. b	7. c	12. b	17. b	22. b	27. b	32. b
3. b	8. d	13. c	18. c	23. b	28. c	
4. d	9. c	14. c	19. d	24. a	29. d	
5. b	10. b	15. d	20. b	25. d	30. c	

B. *True/False*

1. T	6. T	11. T	16. F	21. T	26. F	31. T	36. F
2. T	7. F	12. F	17. F	22. T	27. T	32. F	37. T
3. T	8. F	13. F	18. T	23. T	28. F	33. F	38. F
4. F	9. F	14. F	19. F	24. T	29. F	34. T	
5. T	10. T	15. F	20. T	25. F	30. T	35. F	

C. *Fill-In*

1. a. line services
    b. maintenance
    c. aircraft sales
    d. charter and rental
    e. corporate flight service
    f. flight training
2. a. attrractive lounge area
    b. clean rest rooms
    c. pilot ready room or area
    d. pilot or crew sleeping quarters
    e. a conference room for visitors and recreational facilities

STUDY GUIDE—CHAPTER 4
Managing a Fixed Base Operation

A. *MULTIPLE CHOICE:* Circle the letter that corresponds to the best answer.

1. Successful FBOs:
    a. engender an "espirit-de-corps" among all employees.
    b. thrive on change.
    c. maintain organizational fluidity.
    d. all of the above.
2. Long-term productivity at an FBO
    a. cannot be achieved because of low wages paid to hourly employees.
    b. requires a concern on the part of management for people and production.
    c. can only be achieved by having superior management.
    d. is directly related to monetary incentives.
3. All of the following are characteristics of well managed FBOs *except*
    a. quality conscientiousness.   c. tight supervision.
    b. marketing orientation.   d. technological awareness.
4. Being marketing oriented means
    a. knowing your own strengths and weaknesses and those of the competition.
    b. offering the lowest prices and the best service.
    c. becoming active in community and trade associations.
    d. all of the above.

5. Which of the following statements is *not* correct?
   a. Excellence is a journey, not a destination.
   b. Well-managed FBOs can literally manage by report.
   c. Price consciousness is of paramount importance on the road to profitability.
   d. Well-managed FBOs use positive reinforcement with employees.

6. Effective management begins with
   a. directing.
   b. organizing.
   c. planning.
   d. staffing.

7. Company policies regarding customer service, pricing, and personnel are examples of _____ plans.
   a. single-use
   b. operational
   c. short-term
   d. standing

8. An example of a line worker in a line and staff organization would be a(n)
   a. pilot
   b. accountant.
   c. receptionist/dispatcher.
   d. avionics technical advisor.

9. The number of people a supervisor can oversee depends on a number of factors, including all of the following *except* the
   a. supervisor's capabilities.
   b. abilities of the subordinates.
   c. authority given to the supervisor by top management.
   d. nature of the work to be performed.

10. Which of the following statements is *not* correct regarding the operations manual?
    a. Relieves management from making the most difficult decisions.
    b. Promotes continuity in management style throughout the organization.
    c. Defines authority clearly and distributes responsibility.
    d. Becomes a training tool for employees.

11. Training employees falls under
    a. organizing.
    b. staffing.
    c. directing.
    d. controlling.

12. The purpose of the employment interview is
    a. to supplement information on the application form.
    b. to gain an insight into the prospective employee's appearance and personality.
    c. to encourage the interviewee to talk about themselves and how they might contribute to the organization.
    d. all of the above.

13. A probationary period
    a. should last at least one year.
    b. is not necessary for hourly workers.
    c. should include frequent observation and rating of the new employee.
    d. is optional at most smaller FBOs because the worker can easily be observed.

14. Which of the following statements concerning training is not true?
    a. Training should be a continuous process.
    b. Training lowers the turnover rate.
    c. Training increases operational costs.
    d. Training improves employee morale.

15. The most common training method is
    a. lecture.
    b. seminars and conferences.
    c. role playing.
    d. on-the-job.

16. The first step in establishing a training program is
    a. selecting the training methods to be used.
    b. preparing a needs assessment.
    c. determining the curriculum.
    d. selecting the instructor(s).

17. Which of the following statements is correct regarding the employee turnover problem?
    a. Most turnover is caused by poor supervisory practices.
    b. All employee turnover is expensive for the company.
    c. An exit interview should be conducted.
    d. Answers b and c are true statements.
18. Persuading, guiding, and motivating employees best describes
    a. controlling.   c. unity-of-command.
    b. Theory X.   d. leadership.
19. All of the following are accepted personal traits of good leaders *except*
    a. extroverted.   c. persuasive.
    b. creative.   d. adaptable.
20. Good leadership demonstrates
    a. the ability to establish priorities.
    b. skill at planning and scheduling.
    c. a willingness to delegate responsibility to others.
    d. all of the above.
21. An amalgam of values, attitudes, and interpersonal response traits best describes
    a. motivators.   c. hygiene factors.
    b. personality.   d. motives.
22. Motives are the
    a. concepts we come to accept over the years as we interact with others.
    b. habitual ways of responding to and dealing with others.
    c. attitudes formed over years.
    d. energizing forces that drive all of us.
23. Maslow's highest level of needs were described as
    a. esteem.   c. self-actualization.
    b. safety.   d. physiological.
24. Job security and safe working conditions would be included under Maslow's _____ needs.
    a. Safety   c. Esteem
    b. Physiological   d. Security
25. The belief that employees consider work to be as natural as play and rest, and that once committed to specific objectives, they will not only put out effort willingly but will also seek responsibility, best describes Theory
    a. W.   c. Y.
    b. X.   d. Z.
26. Theory Z includes
    a. the participative approach to decision making.
    b. rewards and punishment in order to obtain satisfactory performance.
    c. work is natural as play and rest, and that once workers are committed to specific objectives, they will seek out responsibility.
    d. none of the above.
27. The second step in the problem-solving process, after diagnosing the problem, is
    a. generating alternative solutions.
    b. gathering information.
    c. determining the origin of the problem.
    d. solving the problem.
28. Most creative thinking takes place in which of the following steps in the problem-solving process?
    a. diagnosing the problem
    b. gathering information
    c. generating alternative solutions
    d. evaluating the alternatives
29. The management function of controlling includes
    a. forecasting methods.   c. leadership styles.
    b. motivating employees.   d. setting standards.

30. Which of the following statements concerning communications is not correct?
    a. Communications start with messages.
    b. Feedback moves upward, completing the communication system.
    c. Good listening skills constitute an important asset in communication.
    d. Communications should be clear enough so that employees will not have to ask questions.
31. Giving employees positive reinforcement means:
    a. demanding quick action.
    b. people are encouraged to achieve their full potential.
    c. expecting quality conscientiousness.
    d. paying employees competitive wages and benefits.
32. Planning for the annual fly-in and open house at a local airport would be an example of:
    a. long-term plans.
    b. operational plans.
    c. single-use plans.
    d. standing plans.
33. Each new position within the company should include all of the following, *except:*
    a. the specific job title.
    b. the duties and responsibilities
    c. promotion criteria.
    d. reporting relationships.
34. Leadership depends upon:
    a. the qualities of the leader.
    b. those who are led.
    c. the individual situation.
    d. All of the above.
35. A competitive salary would be an example of Maslow's:
    a. physiological needs.
    b. safety needs.
    c. esteem needs.
    d. self-actualization needs.
36. The first step in the decision-making process is:
    a. gathering information.
    b. diagnosing the problem.
    c. determining the facts.
    d. determining alternatives.
37. Setting standards means:
    a. taking corrective actions.
    b. decision making.
    c. acceptable performance.
    d. securing feedback.
38. Which of the following statements concerning feedback is not true?
    a. Both positive and constructive feedback should be offered.
    b. Measurable performance goals should be established.
    c. Negative feedback should be personalized to be effective.
    d. It should be timely, specific, and focus on the behavior.

B. *TRUE/FALSE:* Circle "T" if the statement is true, "F" if it is false.

T F   1. FBOs that encourage the entrepreneurial concept are likely to be the most profitable in the future.

T F   2. Getting things done on time and at a reasonable price means employees' attitudes are of secondary importance.

T F   3. One of the primary roles of management is to shape and manage the values of the company.

T F   4. Well-managed FBOs expect employees to be highly motivated on their own.

T   F   5. Management information systems do not necessarily have to be understood by operations personnel.

T   F   6. All of the concepts of a well-managed FBO are basic and can be easily achieved.

T   F   7. Setting objectives, considering alternatives, and making choices are all part of the planning process.

T   F   8. Most small FBOs have more problem directing their company's operations than planning.

T   F   9. Budgets are the end-product of forecasts and plans.

T   F   10. Departmentalization generally increases as a firm grows because of the greater specialization of tasks to be performed.

T   F   11. An effective supervisor can literally manage any number of subordinates.

T   F   12. An operations manual helps identify problems before they arise, minimizing "crisis management."

T   F   13. All operations manuals should have a "miscellaneous" section for those areas not easily categorized.

T   F   14. Staffing includes recruiting, selection, training, and directing employees.

T   F   15. It is best for the owner/manager to personally check all references offered by job applicants.

T   F   16. Most small FBOs cannot afford the time or spare personnel for training.

T   F   17. Setting up a timetable and schedule is the first step in establishing a training program.

T   F   18. A good leader can be quiet, unassuming, and introspective.

T   F   19. Effective leadership depends upon the leader, the group members, and the situation at hand.

T   F   20. Good leaders demonstrate a proficiency in problem solving.

T   F   21. The energizing forces that drive all of us and are behind most behavior are physiological needs.

T   F   22. The same motive can lead to varied behaviors in different people.

T   F   23. Ego satisfaction, recognition, authority, and status within a group best describes Maslow's need for self-actualization.

T   F   24. Supervisors who feel that workers must be watched closely and given rewards and punishment in order to obtain satisfactory performance describes McGregor's Theory X.

T   F   25. Working conditions, company policies, and relations with one's supervisor are hygiene factors according to Herzberg.

T   F   26. Encouraging group goal setting and decision making leads to more highly motivated and satisfied employees.

T   F   27. Doing nothing is an alternative in the problem-solving process.

T   F   28. Planning is the process that includes analysis, setting standards, monitoring, securing feedback, and taking corrective action.

T   F   29. All areas of a business must be subject to the control function.

T   F   30. Good listening skills constitute an important asset in communication.

T   F   31. Well-managed FBOs can literally manage by report.

T   F   32. Planning a new row of "T" hangars to be built during the next year would be an example of operational plans.

T   F   33. Tests are inexpensive and a good way to evaluate potential employees.

T   F   34. Unexplained gaps in the employment record of an individual can be sufficient cause for turning down an applicant.

T   F   35. Often a new employee receives adequate initial training but is thereafter expected to "go it alone."

T F 36. Motives can be rational or emotional.

T F 37. Participative management would be associated with Theory Y.

T F 38. The management function of controlling means supervising employees.

T F 39. If employees are surprised by information in their annual appraisals, they are not receiving enough informal feedback.

T F 40. Reinforcing effective behaviors by complimenting efforts and results will generally lead to less productive workers.

C. *FILL-IN:* Complete the following.

1. The five functions of management are
   a. _____
   b. _____
   c. _____
   d. _____
   e. _____

2. List five management policies that can lead to more highly motivated and satisfied employees other than a competitive salary.
   a. _____
   b. _____
   c. _____
   d. _____
   e. _____

3. List the six steps in the problem-solving process.
   a. _____
   b. _____
   c. _____
   d. _____
   e. _____
   f. _____

D. *QUESTIONS TO THINK ABOUT AND EXERCISES:*

1. Assume that you are managing an FBO during the twenty-first century. What is your prescription for survival?
2. Why is it so common that an owner/manager of a small FBO will thoroughly plan a cross-country flight, but when it comes to business planning, very little time or thought is put into the process?
3. Is leadership an innate ability or can it be learned?
4. Herzberg maintained that certain factors influence job satisfaction and performance. Give some examples of how these factors apply to flight instructors, maintenance technicians, and office personnel at an FBO.
5. Why is doing nothing an alternative in the problem-solving process? Can doing nothing be a viable solution?

ANSWERS:

A. *Multiple Choice*

1. d	6. c	11. b	16. b	21. b	26. a	31. b	36. b
2. b	7. d	12. d	17. c	22. d	27. b	32. d	37. c
3. c	8. a	13. c	18. d	23. c	28. c	33. c	38. c
4. a	9. c	14. c	19. a	24. a	29. d	34. d	
5. c	10. a	15. d	20. d	25. c	30. d	35. a	

B.   *True/False*

1. T	6. F	11. F	16. F	21. F	26. T	31. T	36. T
2. F	7. T	12. T	17. T	22. T	27. T	32. F	37. F
3. T	8. F	13. F	18. T	23. F	28. F	33. F	38. F
4. F	9. T	14. F	19. T	24. T	29. T	34. T	39. T
5. F	10. T	15. T	20. T	25. T	30. T	35. T	40. F

C.   *Fill-In*

1. a. planning
    b. organizing
    c. staffing
    d. directing
    e. controlling
2. a. top-quality working conditions
    b. catering to the worker's need for security
    c. delegating more responsibility
    d. encouraging group goal setting and decision making
    e. flexible scheduling
       Also including: job enhancement and/or redesign; offering a promotional ladder with the company; and recognizing and rewarding the exceptional contribution.
3. a. diagnose the problem
    b. gather information
    c. generate alternative solutions
    d. evaluate the alternatives
    e. select the best alternative(s)
    f. translate the decision into action

STUDY GUIDE—CHAPTER 5
Financial Planning and Control

A.   *MULTIPLE CHOICE: Circle the letter that corresponds to the best answer.*

1. Financial planning affects the
    a. number and type of aircraft an FBO can afford to buy.
    b. services provided.
    c. profitability of the firm.
    d. all of the above.
2. A financial management system enables a firm to do all of the following *except*
    a. interpret past performance.
    b. make a profit.
    c. make decisions.
    d. uncover significant trends.
3. The _____ provides a picture of the financial health of a business at a given moment, usually at the close of an accounting period.
    a. shareholders' equity   c. Balance Sheet
    b. Statement of Income   d. net worth
4. The most liquid asset is:
    a. accounts receivable.   c. land.
    b. inventories.   d. none of the above.

5. Current assets include all of the following *except*
   a. government securities.
   b. prepaid expenses.
   c. accrued expenses.
   d. accounts receivable.
6. Equipment loans are
   a. current assets.
   b. fixed assets.
   c. current liabilities.
   d. long-term liabilities.
7. The Statement of Income:
   a. measures a company's sales and expenses over a specific period of time.
   b. is the assets of the firm minus its liabilities.
   c. is the gross profit of the business less cost of goods.
   d. measures current assets over a specific period of time.
8. Balance Sheet ratios measure
   a. a firm's profitability.
   b. return on assets.
   c. liquidity, solvency, and leverage.
   d. return on investment.
9. All of the following are liquidity ratios *except*
   a. current ratio.
   b. gross margin ratio.
   c. quick ratio.
   d. working capital.
10. If a business's current ratio is too low, it may be able to raise it by
    a. paying some debts.
    b. converting current assets into noncurrent assets.
    c. increasing short-term borrowing.
    d. none of the above.
11. Working capital
    a. indicates the extent to which the firm is reliant on debt financing.
    b. is a measure of cash flow.
    c. measures how efficiently profits are being generated.
    d. is the percentage of sales dollars (gross income) left after subtracting the cost of goods sold.
12. The percentage of sales dollars left after subtracting the cost of goods sold from income is the
    a. net profit margin ratio.
    b. gross margin ratio.
    c. return of assets ratio.
    d. leverage ratio.
13. The return on assets ratio measures the
    a. percentage of return on funds invested in the business by its owners.
    b. percentage of sales dollars (gross income) left after subtracting the cost of goods sold and all expenses, except income taxes.
    c. efficiency of profits generated from the assets employed in the business.
    d. extent to which the firm is reliant on debt financing.
14. The return on investment is calculated as follows:
    a. $\dfrac{\text{Net Profit Before Tax}}{\text{Net Worth}}$
    b. $\dfrac{\text{Net Profit Before Tax}}{\text{Total Assets}}$
    c. $\dfrac{\text{Net Profit Before Tax}}{\text{Gross Income}}$
    d. $\dfrac{\text{Gross Profit}}{\text{Income}}$
15. Income (Sales) minus cost of sales equals
    a. net profit.
    b. gross profit.
    c. net income.
    d. gross return after costs.
16. Aircraft lease payments would be an example of a (an)
    a. direct fixed cost.
    b. direct variable cost.
    c. overhead cost.
    d. indirect operating expense.

17. All of the following are accepted methods of allocating indirect expenses to a particular department *except*
    a. square footage basis.
    b. percentage of sales.
    c. number of employees.
    d. no exceptions; all of the above are accepted methods.

18. Under break-even analysis, volume and cost estimates assume
    a. a change in sales volume will have no effect on selling price.
    b. fixed expenses will remain the same at all volume levels.
    c. variable expenses will increase or decrease in direct proportion to any increase or decrease in sales volume.
    d. all of the above.

19. Which of the following statements concerning cash flow budgets is *not* correct?
    a. The cash flow budget only deals with actual cash transactions.
    b. Cash flow budgets can be established for sales, cost of goods sold, selling expenses, and so forth.
    c. Cash flow budgets have little effect on a business's decision to borrow money because it primarily measures cash needed to pay current expenses.
    d. The cash flow budget can be prepared for any period of time.

20. _____ is required to meet operational needs of a firm such as purchasing inventory or meeting the payroll.
    a. Equity capital   c. Growth capital
    b. Working capital   d. Operating capital

21. Growth capital
    a. is required to meet the operational needs of a business.
    b. is directly related to the cyclical aspects of the industry or economy.
    c. would be needed to build twenty new "T" hangars.
    d. would be needed to increase parts inventory during the busy season.

22. Equity capital can be obtained from
    a. venture capitalists.   c. banks.
    b. leasing companies.   d. mortgage companies.

23. Debt capital can be obtained from
    a. venture capitalists.
    b. nonprofessional investors.
    c. leasing companies.
    d. Small Business Investment Companies (SBIC's).

24. Which of the following statements is *not* correct?
    a. Lenders of growth capital depend on anticipated profitability for repayment over an extended period of time.
    b. Every business needs equity, working, and growth capital.
    c. Equity capital is generally repaid within one year.
    d. Debt capital is primarily obtained from financial institutions.

25. The largest source of working capital loans are
    a. savings and loan associations.   c. investment banks.
    b. commercial banks.   d. credit unions.

26. Lenders and investors will distinguish between the three types of capital, (1) working, (2) growth, and (3) equity in the following way:
    a. fluctuating needs—(1) and (2) only.
    b. needs to be repaid with profits over a period of years—(1), (2), and (3).
    c. permanent needs—(3) only.
    d. limited needs—(2) and (3) only.

27. Working capital loans have the following characteristics:
    a. They are short term but renewable.
    b. They may fluctuate according to seasonal needs or follow a fixed schedule of repayment (amortization).
    c. They are granted primarily only when the ratio of net current assets exceeds net current liabilities.
    d. All of the above.

28. Most banks will require a firm to pay off working capital loans
    a. within 30 or 60 days.   c. within 180 days.
    b. within one year.   d. within five years.

29. Ownership of the property is retained by the seller until the buyer has made all the payments required by the contract under a
    a. venture capital loan.
    b. conditional sales purchase.
    c. working capital loan.
    d. none of the above.
30. In acquiring an aircraft there are usually tax advantages
    a. by leasing.
    b. under a conditional sales purchase.
    c. by paying cash.
    d. under a venture capital arrangement.
31. When an FBO goes to a bank to request a loan, it should bring its financial plan including
    a. cash budget for the next twelve months.
    b. pro forma balance sheets.
    c. income statements.
    d. all of the above.
32. Venture capital
    a. comes from sources other than the business owner/manager or stockholders.
    b. requires a substantial down payment and security in the form of capital assets.
    c. is often provided with the stipulation that the investor take an active role in the management of the company.
    d. a and c are correct.
33. A firm's short-term financial planning
    a. is generally concerned with profit planning or budgeting.
    b. focuses on pro forma statements of income prepared for annual periods up to three years.
    c. involves capital funding projects presently under way.
    d. is concerned with short-term borrowing primarily from commercial banks.
34. One of the best measures of liquidity is the:
    a. Current Ratio
    b. Leverage Ratio
    c. Quick Ratio
    d. Debt/Worth Ratio
35. The percentage of sales dollars left after subtracting the cost of goods sold from income is the:
    a. Net Profit Margin Ratio
    b. Gross Margin Ratio
    c. Return on Assets Ratio
    d. Return on Investment Ratio
36. All of the following factors can affect forecasts (Pro Forma Statements), *except:*
    a. quality and number of employees.
    b. previous sales levels and trends.
    c. competition.
    d. overall state of the economy.
37. If fixed costs are $500,000 and variable costs equal .60 (Sales), determine the sales needed to earn a profit of $60,000.
    a. $1,200,000
    b. $1,400,000
    c. $1,600,000
    d. $1,800,000
38. Building a new hangar to accommodate growth and to be repaid over five years would be an example of a firm seeking:
    a. equity capital
    b. working capital
    c. growth capital
    d. short-term capital

39. EBITA analysis:
    a. is more appropriate in situations where an unstable market exists.
    b. is more appropriate for a stable operation that has experienced consistent revenue and expense trends historically.
    c. discounts the annual net income stream into a present value.
    d. works best when changes are occurring or are anticipated to occur—either positively or negatively.

40. _____ generally create the greatest ambiguity during the valuation process.
    a. Revenues
    b. Taxes
    c. Cost of sales
    d. Operating expenses

B. *TRUE/FALSE:* Circle "T" if the statement is true, "F" if it is false.

T F 1. A financial management system enables a firm to compare results with similar firms and within the particular industry.

T F 2. Assets are funds acquired for a business through loans or the sale of property or services to the business on credit.

T F 3. Fixed assets are typically not for resale and are recorded in the balance sheet at their net cost less accumulated depreciation.

T F 4. Exclusive-use contracts are considered to be a current asset because their termination could be at any time.

T F 5. Notes payable to banks would be considered a long-term liability.

T F 6. Net worth equals the owner's equity.

T F 7. Gross profit equals income less operating expenses.

T F 8. The Statement of Income is also called the P and L Statement.

T F 9. Ratio analysis enables management to spot trends in a business and to compare its performance and condition with the average performance of similar businesses in the industry.

T F 10. Liquidity ratios measure profitability or unprofitability of a firm.

T F 11. A firm may raise its current ratio by increasing the current assets from new equity contributions.

T F 12. The quick ratio is a much more exacting measure than current ratio.

T F 13. The percentage of sales dollars (gross income) left after subtracting the cost of goods sold and all expenses, except income taxes is called gross margin ratio.

T F 14. Management ratios are derived from the Balance Sheet and Statement of Income.

T F 15. Pro forma income statements are forecasts.

T F 16. Expenses should be departmentalized whenever possible.

T F 17. Taxes, rent, advertising, office supplies, and professional services would be considered direct fixed expenses.

T F 18. Overhead (indirect) expenses are often allocated to a particular department based on a percentage of sales for that profit center.

T F 19. The pro forma statement of income is generally prepared on a weekly basis.

T F 20. Total expenses are subtracted from gross profit to determine net profit.

T F 21. Break-even analysis means a level of operations at which revenue is just enough to cover expenses.

T F 22. The cash flow budget enables management to plan for shortfalls in cash resources so short-term working capital loans may be arranged in advance.

T F 23. One source of debt capital is venture capitalists.

T   F   24. Equity capital remains in the company for the life of the business.

T   F   25. Working capital is required to meet operational needs such as an inventory buildup.

T   F   26. If a firm is seeking equity capital, management will have to demonstrate how the equity will be repaid.

T   F   27. Working capital loans are always secured by capital assets.

T   F   28. Banks only grant unsecured credit when they feel the general liquidity and overall financial strength of a business provide assurance for repayment of the loan.

T   F   29. The difficulty in paying off a working capital loan often occurs because the firm is growing and its current activity represents a considerable increase over the corresponding period of the previous year.

T   F   30. For a growth capital loan, management must demonstrate that the growth capital will be used to increase the cash flow through increased sales, cost savings, and/or more productivity.

T   F   31. Long-term capital loans generally do not exceed five years.

T   F   32. Venture capitalists often take an active role in the management for the firm.

T   F   33. Poor management of the firm is often the result of lack of financing.

T   F   34. Planning generally comes easy to FBO managers because they are experienced in dealing with FAA requirements.

T   F   35. Businesses often grow too rapidly for internally generated cash to sufficiently support the growth.

T   F   36. Working capital equals total current assets minus total current liabilities.

T   F   37. The Return on Investment (ROI) indicates the extent to which the firm is reliant on debt financing.

T   F   38. Actual expenditures may not exceed budgeted amounts.

T   F   39. Under a conditional sales purchase, ownership of the property transfers to the buyer at inception.

T   F   40. Venture capitalists are usually prepared to wait longer than the average investor for a profitable return.

T   F   41. The Discounted Cash Flow Analysis results in a more detailed "real world" assessment of an ongoing aviation business.

T   F   42. Interest, income taxes, depreciation, and amortization are generally excluded from a business valuation.

C.   QUESTIONS TO THINK ABOUT AND EXERCISES:

1. Why are so many small FBO managers adverse to financial planning and management?
2. Ratio analysis can be used to compare a firm over a period of several years or with its competitors' performance. When might one approach be better than the other?
3. Discuss the various methods of allocating overhead expenses. Under what circumstances would one method be better than another? Put yourself in the position of a department manager supporting one method over another.
4. How should a department operating and capital budget be established? Should budgets be amended when the forecasts upon which they were made also change?
5. Why is good banking relationships so important? When might it be appropriate to seek venture capital?

ANSWERS:

A.   *Multiple Choice*

1. d	7. a	13. c	19. c	25. b	31. d	37. b
2. b	8. c	14. a	20. b	26. c	32. d	38. c
3. c	9. b	15. b	21. c	27. d	33. a	39. b
4. d	10. a	16. a	22. a	28. b	34. c	40. d
5. c	11. b	17. c	23. c	29. b	35. b	
6. d	12. b	18. d	24. c	30. a	36. a	

B.   *True/False*

1. T	7. F	13. F	19. F	25. T	31. F	37. F
2. F	8. T	14. T	20. T	26. F	32. T	38. F
3. T	9. T	15. T	21. T	27. F	33. F	39. F
4. F	10. F	16. T	22. T	28. T	34. F	40. T
5. F	11. T	17. F	23. F	29. T	35. T	41. T
6. T	12. T	18. T	24. T	30. T	36. T	42. T

STUDY GUIDE—CHAPTER 6
The Role of Marketing

A.   *MULTIPLE CHOICE:* Circle the letter that corresponds to the best answer.

1. Marketing
   a. strictly includes selling and promotion.
   b. is concerned with how society uses its limited resources to satisfy unlimited wants.
   c. includes those business activities which direct the flow of products and services from seller to buyer in order to satisfy customers' needs and accomplish a firm's objectives.
   d. includes both b and c.

2. The philosophy to "sell what the firm could efficiently make rather than making what the firm could sell" describes the
   a. production era
   b. marketing concept
   c. sales era
   d. creation of utility

3. Sellers' market occurs when
   a. demand for products exceeds the supply
   b. a few buyers are very disappointed with the quality of their purchase
   c. supply of goods exceeds the demand
   d. a new department store has a grand opening.

4. Accomplishing a company's objectives means
   a. earning a reasonable profit.
   b. increasing market share.
   c. broadening the product line.
   d. all of these.

5. The marketing management process includes all of the following *except*
   a. planning.
   b. competition.
   c. implementation.
   d. control.

6. A firm's "marketing mix" would *not* include
   a. place.
   b. promotion.
   c. product.
   d. potential customers.

7. The first step in market segmentation is identifying
   a. all of the possible market segments.
   b. all needs for the possible market segments.
   c. the product-service areas to be segmented.
   d. a marketing mix for each segment.

8. The three-step approach to segmenting markets
   a. applies to both individuals and businesses.
   b. minimizes the need for management judgment and intuition.
   c. requires extensive market research and computer analysis.
   d. none of these.

9. After markets have been segmented, the next step includes
   a. establishing target markets.
   b. determining objectives.
   c. establishing a marketing mix.
   d. organizing for implementation.

10. Marketing objectives
    a. may be quite different from a firm's overall objectives.
    b. should be quantifiable if possible.
    c. include establishing a marketing mix.
    d. are normally established by top management without consultation of the sales force.
11. A "marketing mix" includes
    a. the customer and the "four Ps."
    b. all controllable and uncontrollable marketing variables.
    c. product, place, price, and personnel.
    d. only those variables which a marketing manager can control.
12. The concept of a "product"
    a. includes goods but not services.
    b. includes potential customer satisfactions or benefits.
    c. includes all elements in the marketing mix.
    d. means a physical item with its related functional and aesthetic features.
13. Which of the following is NOT one of the four I's of services?
    a. inventory
    b. intangible
    c. inseparability
    d. incompatible
14. The "price" variable is
    a. the most important part of the marketing mix.
    b. an uncontrollable variable for most marketing managers.
    c. independent of the nature of competition.
    d. none of these.
15. When demand is elastic and price _____, then total revenue _____.
    a. increases, increases
    b. decreases, increases
    c. decreases, decreases
    d. decreases, stays the same
16. The elasticity of demand for a product depends upon the
    a. availability of substitutes.
    b. importance of the item in the customer's budget.
    c. urgency of the customer's need.
    d. all of these.
17. The "place" variable is *not* concerned with
    a. the customer service level.
    b. when and where products and services are wanted.
    c. communicating which products and services are offered for sale, and where and when.
    d. channels of distribution.
18. Promotion is concerned with
    a. how appropriate messages are communicated to target customers.
    b. informing customers that the right product or service is available at the right place at the right price.
    c. blending personal selling, mass selling, and sales promotion.
    d. all of these.
19. Advertising
    a. is another name for sales promotion.
    b. involves direct face-to-face relationships between sellers and potential customers.
    c. is any paid form of nonpersonal presentation of ideas, products, or services by an identified sponsor.
    d. is the only form of promotion which must be paid for.
20. A firm's promotion should seek to _____ target customers about the company and its marketing mix.
    a. inform
    b. persuade
    c. remind
    d. all of these
    e. both a and b

21. Implementing the "marketing concept" includes
    a. customer orientation, resource utilization, and sales maximization.
    b. resource utilization, sales growth, and profit maximization.
    c. customer orientation, total company effort, and profit.
    d. customer orientation, total company effort, and sales growth.

22. Executing the marketing plan includes
    a. planning, implementing, and feedback.
    b. delegation, communication, and motivation.
    c. hiring, training, and planning.
    d. marketing, feedback, and control.

23. Marketing "control" does *not* include
    a. setting standards.
    b. implementing marketing strategies.
    c. measuring performance.
    d. taking corrective action.

24. Which of the following variables is *within* the control of marketing managers?
    a. consumer demographics
    b. public interest groups
    c. selection of a target market.
    d. level of technology

25. Which of the following uncontrollable variables probably had the greatest effect on the number of student pilot starts in recent years?
    a. low birth rates in the 1960s and early 1970s
    b. availability of training aircraft
    c. decline in the number of flight instructors
    d. increased government regulations

26. Which of the following trends is *not* an example of changes in consumer demographics?
    a. the declining birth rate in the United States
    b. a growing number of women in the work force
    c. a decline in interest rates
    d. a rise in population in the "sunbelt" states

27. Which of the following should *not* be classified as government regulations and the political environment?
    a. consumerism
    b. inflation
    c. nationalism
    d. FAA legislation

28. The marketing concept includes all of the following concepts *except*
    a. producing those products with the largest production efficiency
    b. customer orientation
    c. integrated organization effort
    d. long term success

29. Marketing of services is different from marketing tangible products in all of the following ways except
    a. provider of service cannot be separated from the service itself
    b. service is perishable
    c. difficult to maintain consistent quality
    d. services are easily differentiated

30. In an oligopolistic market, if one firm raises its price, that firm's total revenue for that product will
    a. remain the same because the other firms will lower their prices also
    b. go down
    c. go up
    d. remain the same for a while and then go up

31. A new product which would appeal to innovators and those with large discretionary incomes should use the _____ pricing policy.
    a. penetrating
    b. skimming
    c. rate of return
    d. status quo

32. The promotion mix variable designed to provide incentives to purchase a product or service is
    a. sales promotion
    b. advertising media
    c. public relations
    d. publicity

33. Customer service level is mainly concerned with which marketing mix variable?
    a. product
    b. price
    c. promotion
    d. place (distribution)
34. The responsibility of _____ marketing plans fall into three areas: delegation, communication and motivation.
    a. planning
    b. implementing
    c. executing
    d. both b and c

B. *TRUE/FALSE:* Circle "T" if the statement is true, "F" if it is false.

T   F   1. Satisfying customers' needs is the ultimate objective of the marketing process.

T   F   2. Marketing planning is the process of analyzing marketing results and correcting decisions that are affecting a firm in the present.

T   F   3. Segmenting assists a firm in selecting target markets.

T   F   4. Establishing a marketing mix is part of implementing the plans.

T   F   5. A target market is a segment at which a firm aims its marketing mix.

T   F   6. Mass marketing is essentially the same as a multiple target market approach.

T   F   7. A combined target market approach means choosing two or more market segments—each of which will be treated as a separate target market—needing a different marketing mix.

T   F   8. Marketing objectives derive directly from a firm's overall objectives.

T   F   9. A "marketing mix" includes all external variables affecting marketing management.

T   F   10. The product of flight training includes the quality and professionalism of the instructors.

T   F   11. Price elasticity is computed by dividing the percentage change in price by the percentage change in quantity.

T   F   12. Costs always have less effect on prices than consumers and competition.

T   F   13. Some FBOs rely almost exclusively on costs in establishing prices.

T   F   14. Promotion includes personal selling.

T   F   15. In contrast to personal selling, mass selling is more flexible in adapting to customer needs and attitudes.

T   F   16. Publicity is always less effective than advertising.

T   F   17. Acceptance of the "marketing concept" requires that all departments focus their efforts on satisfying customer needs.

T   F   18. Ideally, information should flow throughout the firm from the top down to avoid confusion.

T   F   19. The best way to motivate employees is through monetary awards.

T   F   20. Marketing "control" is the process that attempts to reconcile performance of the marketing plan with marketing objectives.

T   F   21. The first step in the marketing control process is setting standards.

T   F   22. Managerial expectations of company performance is more subjective than comparisons with industry norms.

T   F   23. Taking corrective action is probably the easiest step in the marketing control process.

T   F   24. Any marketing plan, no matter how well conceived, may fail if adversely influenced by uncontrollable factors.

T F 25. A good marketing strategy will disregard the strategies of competitors.

T F 26. The major factors affecting price decisions are customers, competition, costs, and products.

T F 27. The more substitutes there are for a product, the more responsive buyers will be to price reduction.

T F 28. Markup pricing is appropriate when the seller is the manufacturer of the product.

T F 29. Cost-oriented approaches to price determination give little or no consideration to customer demand.

T F 30. The price of a product stays level throughout its life cycle.

T F 31. Specific skill areas required for successful marketing implementation include organization and execution.

T F 32. The first step in marketing control is to take corrective action.

T F 33. Marketers must understand that a major source of competition is from suppliers of dissimilar products and services.

T F 34. Utility is the want satisfying ability of a good or service.

T F 35. Environmental scanning is a technique used to monitor controllable variables.

T F 36. A significant trend that affects marketing is the increasing number of wives working outside the home. That number today is approximately 65 percent.

C. *FILL-IN:*

1. Marketing management is a three-phase process which includes planning, implementing, and control. List the specific steps under each phase.

   Planning
   a. _____
   b. _____
   c. _____
   d. _____

   Implementation
   a. _____
   b. _____

   Control
   a. _____
   b. _____

2. List seven of the so called uncontrollable variables of marketing management.
   a. _____
   b. _____
   c. _____
   d. _____
   e. _____
   f. _____
   g. _____

D. *QUESTIONS TO THINK ABOUT AND EXERCISES:*

1. Establish criteria for identifying small businesses in your area which may have a need for a company airplane (e.g., number of employees, total sales, area of operation, etc.)

2. Assume that you have identified the following two target markets for flight training: professional women and students. What are the particular needs of these markets? List three specific objectives for each market. Design a marketing mix for each market.

3. Select two FBOs in your area and compare at least four similar product-service areas offered by them in terms of the four p's.
4. Define the marketing concept in your own words and then suggest how acceptance of this concept might affect the organization and operation of a local FBO.
5. Discuss ways in which employees of a large aircraft service facility can be motivated other than by direct monetary remuneration.
6. Our charter and rental aircraft business is down compared to last year and short of management's expectations. From this we can conclude that our marketing plan was poorly conceived. Do you agree?
7. Identify three uncontrollable variables of marketing management and discuss their impact on used and new aircraft sales.
8. Discuss how the marketing of services like maintenance is different from the marketing of a tangible product.
9. Explain the following equation: Price = Utility.
10. If charter prices increased by 10% and demand decreased by 4%, demand is considered unitary/elastic/inelastic. Select one of the three degrees of elasticity and explain why the market reacted to the change in price in that relationship.
11. Take a service like aircraft maintenance and illustrate the four I's of services.

ANSWERS:

A. *Multiple Choice*

1. c	6. d	11. d	16. d	21. c	26. c	31. b
2. c	7. c	12. b	17. c	22. b	27. b	32. a
3. a	8. a	13. d	18. d	23. b	28. a	33. d
4. d	9. a	14. d	19. c	24. c	29. d	34. d
5. b	10. b	15. b	20. d	25. a	30. b	

B.   *True/False*

1. T	6. F	11. F	16. F	21. T	26. T	31. T	36. T
2. F	7. F	12. F	17. T	22. T	27. T	32. F	
3. T	8. T	13. T	18. F	23. F	28. F	33. T	
4. F	9. F	14. T	19. F	24. T	29. T	34. T	
5. T	10. T	15. F	20. T	25. F	30. F	35. F	

C.   *Fill-in*

1. *Planning*
   a. segmenting the market
   b. establishing target markets
   c. determining objectives
   d. establishing a marketing mix

   Implementation
   a. organizing for implementation
   b. executing marketing planning

   Control
   a. setting standards
   b. corrective action
2. a. consumer demographics
   b. competition
   c. government regulations
   d. the economy
   e. technology
   f. media
   g. public interest groups

STUDY GUIDE—CHAPTER 7
Marketing Research

A. *MULTIPLE CHOICE:* Circle the letter that corresponds to the best answer.

1. Marketing research can assist management
   a. by supplying information for planning, implementing, and controlling marketing strategies.
   b. in studying competitive situations.
   c. in developing marketing mix strategies
   d. all of these

2. A market research study designed to determine the potential charter business in a particular area would be an example of a
   a. market measurement study.
   b. marketing mix study.
   c. competitive study.
   d. study of uncontrollable influences.

3. Information contained in sources such as the *Statistical Abstract of the United States* are useful in studies concerning
   a. competition.
   b. uncontrollables.
   c. market measurement.
   d. marketing mix research.

4. The best source for a marketing manager researching information on education, employment, income, and retail sales in a particular area is the
   a. County and City Data Book.
   b. Census of Retail Trade.
   c. Statistical Abstract of the U.S.
   d. local telephone directory.

5. The first step in the marketing research process is
   a. conducting a formal research project.
   b. defining the problem and research objectives.
   c. conducting an informal investigation.
   d. selecting a competent marketing researcher.

6. Secondary data is readily available from
   a. government sources.
   b. trade associations.
   c. consultants.
   d. all of these.

7. Which of the following is *not* a part of the four-step marketing research process?
   a. developing primary and secondary data
   b. defining the problem and research objectives
   c. analyzing the information
   d. selection of a marketing research specialist

8. Which of the following research methods would *not* be used by a marketing manager when gathering primary data?
   a. personal interviews
   b. observation
   c. mail survey
   d. literature search

9. In developing a sampling procedure, marketing researchers must determine:
   a. who is to be surveyed.
   b. how many people or firms should be surveyed.
   c. how should the people or firms in the sample be chosen.
   d. all of these.

10. A low percentage of responses is one of the problems of
    a. personal interviews.
    b. telephone interviews.
    c. mail questionnaires.
    d. group interviews.

11. The method of collecting data generally depends upon all of the following, *except:*
    a. cost.
    b. time constraints.
    c. type of firm conducting the research.
    d. availability of respondents.

12. Maximum possible sales opportunities open to all sellers of a product or service during a stated future period for a particular target market is called
    a. sales potential
    b. market potential
    c. sales forecast
    d. market forecast

13. At the end of the first step in the marketing research process a researcher should know all of the following *except*
    a. the current situation
    b. the nature of the problem
    c. the specific question or questions the research is to find the answer to
    d. the type of data the research process calls for

14. The most common instrument used in collecting primary data is the
    a. personal interview
    b. questionnaire
    c. mechanical electric eyes
    d. responses received from satisfied customers

15. A sample in which every person or firm in the identified population being sampled has a known chance of being sampled describes a
    a. probability type sample
    b. nonprobability sample
    c. simple random sample
    d. both a and c

16. All of the following are examples of nonprobability sampling techniques *except*
    a. quota sample
    b. random sample
    c. convenience sample
    d. judgment sample

17. Standard statistical testing can only be used with which one of the following types of samples?
    a. quota sample
    b. convenience sample
    c. judgment sample
    d. random sample

18. _____ is the most widely used method of collecting primary data.
    a. Telephone interview
    b. Use of data bases
    c. Personal interview
    d. Mail questionnaire

19. Sources of secondary data include all of the following *except*
    a. private databases
    b. government statistics
    c. A. C. Nielsen
    d. data from opinion surveys

20. All of the following statements about buyer motivational research studies are true *except*
    a. probing the psychological, sociological, and economic variables affecting buyer behavior
    b. require trained personnel to conduct the study
    c. cannot be done by most large firms internally
    d. are an example of price research

21. Determine the sales potential for Sunshine FBO flight training program using the following data: 5-year market potential = 3,500; Sunshine's market share = 32 per cent.
    a. 224
    b. 700
    c. 1,120
    d. 3,500

22. All of the following are widely used in studies of influences of uncontrollables *except*
    a. existing products or services in new markets
    b. business trends
    c. economic data
    d. industry statistics

23. Asking business executives if they have ever used a charter flight service illustrates which type of survey?
    a. statistical
    b. factual
    c. descriptive
    d. opinion
24. Selecting matched groups of subjects illustrates which research design?
    a. experimental
    b. observation
    c. survey
    d. focus group
25. Requiring the respondent to choose one of two alternatives on a survey questionnaire illustrates a/an
    a. open-end question
    b. dichotomous question
    c. multiple choice question
    d. true-false question
26. A _____ is a portion or subset of the population to be surveyed.
    a. universe
    b. group
    c. census
    d. sample
27. When the population contains disproportionate demographics like gender, researchers use a
    a. simple random sample
    b. convenience sample
    c. stratified sample
    d. nonprobability sample

B. *TRUE/FALSE* Circle "T" if the statement is true, "F" if it is false.

T F   1. Sales potential and market potential are basically the same thing.

T F   2. Research designed to determine the effectiveness of advertising would be considered a market measurement study.

T F   3. The U.S. Census of Manufacturers lists the number and size of manufacturing firms according to its SIC code.

T F   4. Published information and statistics on the state of the economy is readily available from a number of sources.

T F   5. If you want to find detailed secondary data concerning consumers living in a particular city during a recent year, you would be most likely to find this data in the County and City Data Book.

T F   6. Secondary data can be obtained within the firm and from external sources.

T F   7. The most commonly used method of acquiring primary data is the observation method.

T F   8. Use of questionnaires, focus groups, or telephone interviews is common in the experiment method.

T F   9. An opinion survey is designed to gather actual facts from respondents.

T F 10. An open-ended question in a survey form permits respondents to formulate their own answers.

T F 11. Personal Interviewing is the most versatile method of collecting primary data.

T F 12. The big advantage of telephone interviewing is its low cost and rapid response.

T F 13. A sample is a portion of the population surveyed.

T F 14. It is generally recommended that marketing researchers use the most sophisticated statistical techniques available.

T F 15. FBOs that use self-administered questions must be aware of the self-selection bias that makes the survey results less useful.

T F 16. A major disadvantage of multiple-choice questions is that the responses are difficult to record and tabulate.

T F 17. The semantic-differential type question is a popular attitude measuring scale.

T F 18. A major advantage of electronic questionnaires is their low cost.

T F 19. Convenience sampling is an example of probability sampling.

T F 20. The problem of self-selection bias is primarily associated with surveys located in areas, like the seat pocket on a charter flight.

T F 21. Use of the telephone is the most versatile of the four methods of collecting primary data.

T F 22. Quota samples are probability samples because a certain percentage of each group is represented.

T F 23. One of the major concerns about face-to-face interview technique is that the interview can be plagued with inaccurate responses.

T F 24. Market measurement studies are designed to obtain qualitative data on potential demand.

T F 25. Sales potential is a microperspective.

T F 26. Most marketing research studies focus on the elements of the marketing mix.

T F 27. A study measuring the market share of a firm's products and services is an example of competition research.

T F 28. Secondary data consists of information that already exists.

T F 29. Nonprofit agencies and aviation consultants are excellent sources of primary data.

T F 30. Open-end questions include all the possible answers, and respondents make a choice among them.

T F 31. Good questionnaire construction will put personal questions toward the front.

C. *FILL-IN:* Complete the following sentences.

1. The marketing research process involves four steps. They are:
   a. _____
   b. _____
   c. _____
   d. _____
2. List five methods of collecting primary data.
   a. _____
   b. _____
   c. _____
   d. _____
   e. _____

D. *QUESTIONS TO THINK ABOUT AND EXERCISES:*

1. Why is marketing research necessary? What may result if managers rely exclusively on intuition? How could an FBO use the marketing research process to determine customer attitudes towards its line service?
2. Develop a ten-question survey that includes open-end, multiple-choice questions, and Likert and semantic differential scales to determine the attitude of the following customers of an FBO: (a) students who have dropped out of flight training, (b) students who have recently received their Private Pilot's Certificate, (c) maintenance customers, and (d) charter customers.
3. Describe an experiment to evaluate the effectiveness of a new brochure which has been developed to stimulate your aircraft rental business. What are your target markets?

4. A flight school is interested in learning what special concerns young women have about flight training. The chief instructor found an article in an aviation trade publication which highlighted the careers of a number of women flying commercially and in the military. Many of these women received their first flight training at local FBOs. Evaluate the possibilities for relevance, credibility, and accuracy of this potential secondary source of information for the flight school.
5. Describe how you would conduct a random sample of aircraft owners in your state to ensure reliability of the data.

ANSWERS:

A. *Multiple Choice*

1. d	6. d	11. c	16. b	21. c	26. d
2. a	7. d	12. b	17. d	22. a	27. c
3. b	8. d	13. d	18. a	23. b	
4. a	9. d	14. b	19. d	24. a	
5. b	10. c	15. d	20. d	25. b	

B. *True/False*

1. F	6. T	11. T	16. F	21. F	26. T	31. F
2. F	7. F	12. T	17. T	22. F	27. T	
3. T	8. F	13. T	18. T	23. T	28. T	
4. T	9. F	14. F	19. F	24. F	29. F	
5. T	10. T	15. T	20. T	25. T	30. F	

C. *Fill-In*

1. a. defining the problem and research objectives
   b. plan and conduct the research
   c. analyzing the information
   d. presenting the findings
2. a. personal interview
   b. telephone interview
   c. mail questionnaire
   d. electronic questionnaire
   e. focus group interviewing

STUDY GUIDE—CHAPTER 8
Transportation Needs Assessment

A. *MULTIPLE CHOICE:* Circle the letter that corresponds to the best answer.

1. Which of the following is *not* one of the 4 major areas of evaluation in a travel analysis?
   a. amount and nature of travel   c. travel dispersion
   b. amount of travel expenses   d. type and frequency of airline service
2. Which of the following identifies the three distinct levels of airline service?
   a. direct, indirect via connections, none   c. direct, layovers, indirect via connections
   b. direct, trunk lines, none   d. direct, infrequent, none
3. Turbocharging an aircraft engine
   a. reduces the problems of icing.
   b. increases runway length requirements for take-off.
   c. raises speed and higher altitude capabilities.
   d. reduces aircraft range due to additional fuel consumption.
4. Seating capacity for light twins ranges from
   a. up to 4 seats.   c. 4 to 7 seats.
   b. 4 to 6 seats.   d 4 to 8 seats.

5. The three principal components used in determining the purchase price of the airplane are
   a. base price, avionics, and engine package.
   b. base price, customized interior, and avionics.
   c. base price, financing costs, and avionics.
   d. none of the above is correct.

6. Which one of the following is not evaluated in determining cost of ownership of a corporate aircraft?
   a. status of production
   b. purchase price
   c. reliability and maintainability
   d. all of the above should be evaluated

7. Which of the following business enterprises pay income taxes?
   a. corporations
   b. sole proprietorships
   c. partnerships
   d. both b and c

8. Cost of use expenses include
   a. fixed costs
   b. direct operating expenses
   c. finance expenses
   d. both a and b

9. A cash flow statement shows the prospective purchaser
   a. tax savings from deductible items.
   b. annual interest charges on the aircraft loan.
   c. net present value cost for the 6 year period.
   d. all of the above are correct.

10. An amortized loan is one that requires the borrower to
    a. make monthly principal and interest payments.
    b. pay off the balance of the loan early.
    c. make at least a 20 percent down payment.
    d. pay interest rates which are 2 percentage points over the prime interest rate.

11. Present value of future payments is
    a. the same as compound interest.
    b. the rate of return expressed in dollars.
    c. the reciprocal of compound interest.
    d. usually greater than the future value.

12. Break-even analysis is the relationship between
    a. revenue, total costs, and reserves.
    b. cost of use, variable costs, fixed costs.
    c. revenue, hourly cost of use and fixed costs.
    d. cost of use, maintenance costs, fixed costs, and revenue.

13. Break-even analysis will show the prospective purchaser
    a. total hours of charter required to earn a predetermined profit.
    b. the marginal profit for each revenue hour.
    c. when the aircraft should be traded in.
    d. the best hourly rate to charge for charter in relation to competition.

14. The four areas considered by the aircraft salesperson when determining if a business needs an airplane include all of the following *except*
    a. financial health of the company
    b. amount and nature of travel
    c. travel dispersion
    d. frequency of airline service

15. The objective of conducting a travel analysis is to
    a. determine the financial capacity of the prospect firm
    b. estimate the total annual utilization of a business aircraft
    c. provide a master plan for executive travel
    d. determine the total cost of transportation for the firm

16. Determine the annual hours of utilization for a business aircraft using the following data: 230 round trips; leg distance 330 miles; average cruise speed is 260 mph.
    a. 292 hours
    b. 373 hours
    c. 584 hours
    d. 858 hours

17. Which of the following aircraft would be considered at the top of the business fleet?
    a. turboprop
    b. pure jet
    c. medium twin
    d. light twin
18. Advantages of a light twin over a single-engine airplane include
    a. more economical to operate
    b. increased utility
    c. six foot headroom
    d. comfort for up to 10 to 12 passengers
19. Business applications of helicopters include all of the following *except*
    a. timely movement of work crews
    b. herding of livestock
    c. international executive travel
    d. shuttle executives between airport and their destination.
20. The concept of "portal to portal" travel is best exemplified by using
    a. jet aircraft
    b. business aircraft and then taxi
    c. helicopters
    d. commercial aircraft to a hub, and then using a commuter
21. Select the one factor which is not included in the purchase of a business aircraft.
    a. base price
    b. price of maintenance contract
    c. price of interiors
    d. price of avionics
22. Forecasting the future resale or trade-in value of the aircraft is *not* associated with
    a. purchase price of the airplane
    b. performance analysis
    c. reliability and maintainability
    d. status of production
23. Which of the following types of organizations do *not* pay income tax on their earnings?
    a. partnerships
    b. corporations
    c. sole proprietorships
    d. both a and c do not directly pay income tax on their earnings
24. Double declining depreciation will
    a. allow corporations to deduct the expense in equal annual installments
    b. change to straight-line depreciation after the third year
    c. allow the corporation to change the annual depreciation percentage to better fit their financial situation
    d. depreciates the acquisition cost down to a 10% salvage value
25. Cash flow statements accomplish all of the following benefits for the salesperson *except*
    a. adds a professional touch to the sales presentation
    b. demonstrates the value of executive time lost using commercial air travel
    c. assists the salesperson in dealing with financial concerns
    d. provides detailed cost information and net present value analysis
26. The actual amount the aircraft will cost, based on borrowing money and keeping the corporation's funds free for reinvestment in the corporation at its average return on investment rate is called
    a. total cost of the aircraft
    b. net present value cost
    c. return on investment
    d. purchase price

27. Using the break-even formula, determine the number of hours required to break even: annual fixed costs $62,000; charter revenue per hour $275; and operating costs per hour $189.
    a. 225
    b. 328
    c. 500
    d. 721

28. Direct operating expenses would include all of the following *except*
    a. cost for insurance
    b. gas and oil expense
    c. routine maintenance
    d. hourly charges for maintenance reserves

29. Which of the following is considered a fixed cost?
    a. hangar rental fee
    b. annual inspections
    c. routine airframe maintenance
    d. both a and b are fixed costs

30. Physical damage insurance in aircraft insurance is usually called:
    a. collision insurance
    b. comprehensive insurance
    c. hull insurance
    d. property damage coverage

B. *TRUE/FALSE:* Circle "T" if the statement is true, "F" if it is false.

T F 1. Travel dispersion analysis helps determine whether there is enough hourly utilization to make a business aircraft feasible.

T F 2. Certificated carriers are concentrating more of their service to hub cities.

T F 3. The annual hours of aircraft utilization is determined by multiplying miles flown by cruise speed in miles per hour.

T F 4. A turboprop aircraft requires less runway for take-off and landings than do pure jets.

T F 5. A trip leg is point A to point B.

T F 6. An important consideration in the aircraft purchase decision is the future resale or trade-in value of the aircraft.

T F 7. The Tax Reform Act of 1986 greatly improved the depreciation allowance.

T F 8. When a corporation sells its aircraft for more than the current book value, the gain is taxed as a capital gain, not ordinary income.

T F 9. Direct operating expenses are actually variable costs.

T F 10. Aircraft can be 100 percent depreciated over a 6 year period.

T F 11. Book value and current market value are usually equal.

T F 12. Insurance is considered a fixed cost.

T F 13. Money received in the future is presently worth considerably less than its stated value.

T F 14. Type and frequency of airline service is one of the four areas investigated to help determine the need for a corporate aircraft.

T F 15. Proving the existence of a large quantity of travel is not necessarily sufficient evidence that a corporation could economically use an aircraft.

T F 16. The type and frequency of airline service is studied by the salesperson to determine the total cost of commercial travel.

T F   17. To be more accurate, a full year of past travel records is used to determine the amount and nature of business travel.

T F   18. Charter service is often used because of poor airline service to desired destinations and the emergency need to travel.

T F   19. Volume dispersion is the number of people traveling and indicates the relative importance of each destination.

T F   20. Turbocharging in aircraft engines raises both speed and the aircrafts ability to operate at higher altitudes.

T F   21. Helicopters in use today are "third generation" helicopters which incorporate design features that have been proven safe, reliable, and practical.

T F   22. Air temperature and airport altitude basically have no affect on aircraft performance.

T F   23. Normally, the shorter the runway, the smaller the load the aircraft can carry.

T F   24. One of the major factors to consider when purchasing an aircraft is reliability and maintainability.

T F   25. Cost of use is the same as variable cost.

T F   26. Book value of an airplane is the same as replacement value.

T F   27. When a business aircraft is sold, the gain realized between the aircraft sales price and the current book value is treated as capital gains.

T F   28. For depreciation purposes, airplanes are considered five-year class property.

T F   29. Direct operating expenses of an airplane include future costs of engine overhaul.

T F   30. Present value is actually the reciprocal of compound interest.

T F   31. Break-even analysis is a very useful tool to help convince a company to purchase its own aircraft for executive travel.

C. *QUESTIONS TO THINK ABOUT AND EXERCISES:*

1. Business aircraft are promoted as productivity tools not business toys. What are the major factors which support this statement?
2. Identify four specific qualifications a business should possess to be a legitimate prospect for a business aircraft.
3. There appears to be a direct relationship between the speed of an aircraft and its price. What are some business factors which might justify a faster aircraft?
4. Using the Capital Recovery Guide format, determine the net *annual* cost of ownership for the following corporation:
   Purchase Price: $750,000
   Sales Tax: 6%
   Disposal Price: 82% of purchase price
   Tax Rate: 39%
5. What is the impact on hourly cost of use when the annual hours of utilization are overstated and do not materialize?
6. Use a present value factor table to answer the following question: Would you rather have $5,000 today or $18,000 in 10 years? (Money value = 14%)
7. Prepare a proposal for a new trainer aircraft which would show a local flight school the number of training hours required to make $15,000 profit before taxes.

ANSWERS

A. *Multiple Choice*

1. b	5. b	9. d	13. a	17. b	21. b	25. b	29. d
2. a	6. d	10. a	14. a	18. b	22. b	26. b	30. c
3. c	7. a	11. c	15. b	19. c	23. d	27. d	
4. b	8. d	12. c	16. c	20. c	24. b	28. a	

B.   True/False

1. F	5. T	9. T	13. T	17. F	21. T	25. F	29. T
2. T	6. T	10. T	14. T	18. T	22. F	26. F	30. T
3. F	7. T	11. F	15. T	19. T	23. T	27. F	31. F
4. T	8. F	12. T	16. F	20. T	24. T	28. T	

STUDY GUIDE—CHAPTER 9
Value Analysis: Costs versus Benefits

A.   *MULTIPLE CHOICE:* Circle the letter that corresponds to the best answer.

1. A value analysis
    a. substantiates the relative equivalence of the business aircraft's direct costs versus present travel costs.
    b. only looks at intangible benefits of aircraft ownership.
    c. provides a clear indication of the amount of manpower time saved.
    d. both a and c are correct.

2. The most commonly used value per man-hour formula is
    a. $\dfrac{\text{Average Salary} \times 3}{2{,}500 \text{ hours}}$

    c. $\dfrac{\text{Average Salary} \times 2.5}{2{,}000 \text{ hours}}$

    b. $\dfrac{\text{Average Salary} \times 2.5}{2{,}500 \text{ hours}}$

    d. $\dfrac{\text{Average Salary} \times 2}{2{,}000 \text{ hours}}$

3. The "En Route Productivity" factor
    a. develops a higher dollar credit for airline travel than for business aircraft travel.
    b. is concerned with time savings due to shorter flights.
    c. recognizes that corporate aircraft are an extension of the executive's office.
    d. is just theory and has no real-world applicability.

4. When corporate aircraft are used on business flights, time savings result from
    a. using general aviation terminals in hub areas.
    b. ability to land at smaller airports closer to final destination.
    c. faster air speed than air carriers.
    d. both a and b are correct.

5. The break-even load factor shows
    a. a comparison between airline ticket cost and hourly cost of use for an aircraft for a specific trip.
    b. a comparison between maximum passengers compared with maximum cargo.
    c. number of passengers required for a charter operation to break-even.
    d. none of the above.

6. _____ of an aircraft is the basis for productivity.
    a. Fuel efficiency
    b. Purchase price
    c. Utilization
    d. Comfort

7. Intangible benefits of business aircraft ownership include
    a. increased management mobility.
    b. recruiting tool for management personnel.
    c. public relations tool.
    d. all of the above.

8. For a corporation to justify the purchase of a business aircraft the aircraft
    a. must do what a company is now doing, only faster and cheaper.
    b. ownership costs must be lower than current ticket costs.
    c. all management must have equal access to the aircraft.
    d. the aircraft must make a major contribution to growth.

9. Factors to consider when determining just what "saved time" is worth include
    a. comfort.
    b. effect on energy and morale.
    c. additional productive business hours.
    d. all of the above.

10. A value analysis is a powerful sales tool because it convincingly demonstrates
    a. the dollar savings derived from tax savings.
    b. time savings due to the faster airspeed of the business aircraft.
    c. the ability of a business aircraft to deliver a management team to its destination with a minimum of unproductive time.
    d. the dollar value of intangible benefits.

11. _____ is a quantitative comparison of actual business trips taken by company personnel.
    a. Value analysis
    b. Productivity analysis
    c. Time savings analysis
    d. Value per man hour analysis

12. The traditional formula used in determining the value per man hour figure uses _____ hours in the formula.
    a. 1,500
    b. 2,000
    c. 2,500
    d. hours are not used in the formula

13. The "en route productivity" credit for time spent aboard a corporate aircraft is estimated at _____ percent.
    a. 15
    b. 25
    c. 65
    d. 75

14. The "en route productivity" credit for time spent aboard a commercial airliner is estimated at _____ percent.
    a. 15
    b. 25
    c. 65
    d. 75

15. All of the following are intangible benefits categories of using business aircraft *except*
    a. increased management mobility
    b. outpace competition
    c. reduction of total transportation costs
    d. more contacts with present customers

16. When there is a cost trade-off against time, the following factors must be considered *except*
    a. seasonal peak demand requirement
    b. emergency need for travel to be accomplished
    c. perishable nature of a situation
    d. convenience and comfort of the travelers

17. Value analysis is a quantitative comparison between
    a. two business trips using competitive business aircraft
    b. two business trips using different routes
    c. two business trips using a business aircraft in comparison with the scheduled airlines
    d. two business trips using a business aircraft compared with a charter flight

18. When the salesperson selects the business trip to use in the value analysis, he/she should
    a. select one going to a busy hub city
    b. always make it the longest in terms of miles
    c. select one that is not well served by scheduled airlines
    d. select one that is infrequently used by the prospect

19. The following factors contribute to low productivity of executives aboard a commercial airliner *except*
    a. lack of work facilities
    b. noise level of the engines
    c. hesitancy to discuss sensitive corporate matters
    d. distractions resulting from mass handling of passengers.

20. The justification for a much higher productivity credit for travel aboard a business aircraft include all of the following *except*
    a. cabin configuration
    b. ability to use smaller landing fields
    c. privacy
    d. improved opportunity for air to ground communications

B. *TRUE/FALSE:* Circle "T" if the statement is true, "F" if it is false.

T F 1. Value analysis is a quantitative cost comparison between two business aircraft.

T F 2. En route time in a corporate aircraft receives a 75% productivity credit.

T F 3. The standard 40-hour work week is often modified to a 50–55 hourly week in determining the value per man hour.

T F 4. The hourly cost of use of a business aircraft does not change with the passenger density.

T F 5. Morale costs are important considerations and they include off-hour travel time.

T F 6. Executives recognize that tangible, rather than intangible factors usually provide the margin of profit in business aircraft use.

T F 7. The ultimate reason for using business aircraft is to save time.

T F 8. Flexibility of use is an important intangible benefit of business aircraft ownership.

T F 9. Underutilization of the business aircraft is not a concern because all costs of ownership are directly related to hours of use.

T F 10. Intangible benefits can be quantified to assist in justifying the purchase of a business aircraft.

T F 11. The "en route productivity" factor used in the value analysis was first introduced by Cessna Corporation.

T F 12. Speed of the corporate aircraft is one of the justifications used in the "en route productivity" analysis.

T F 13. It would be short sighted to use an aircraft only to do what a company is currently doing, only in a faster and cheaper manner.

T F 14. Saving clock time through the use of a business aircraft will also often increase morale and an executive's energy level.

T F 15. Recruiting and retaining key personnel are important intangible benefits of business aircraft ownership.

T F 16. Intangible benefits are those that cannot be wholly quantified in terms of dollars saved or revenue produced.

T F 17. Saving time for key personnel is only important from a pure clock-time standpoint.

T F 18. The higher the load factor, the more advantageous the business aircraft travel costs become.

T F 19. Business aircraft have been referred to as time machines.

T F 20. Comfort is a major intangible item when executives are the principal users of the aircraft.

C. *QUESTIONS TO THINK ABOUT AND EXERCISES:*

1. From a sales and marketing standpoint, what kind of destination should be selected to be included in the value analysis?
2. The traditional productivity factor used in determining value per man-hour is 2.5. Should a corporation expect greater productivity factor from its middle and upper management?
3. A corporate airplane is a time machine. Identify five specific areas where time can be saved when the business airplane replaces the airline.
4. "En Route Productivity" credit is only allowed on the actual flight time in the Value Analysis. Why is it inappropriate for the credit to be applied to the total time of the trip?
5. When a large percentage of a corporation's business travel is between hub cities, it is quite difficult to justify the purchase of a business aircraft. Why? What role would intangible benefits play in this situation?

6. Using the Official Airline Guide, or a web based reservation system, and a business aircraft which has an airspeed of 250 mph, and hourly cost of use of $413, perform a value analysis for a round trip from Orlando, Florida, to Paris, Tennessee, with a passenger density of 4 persons. (39% tax). Be sure to include "en route productivity credits.

ANSWERS

A. *Multiple Choice*

1. d	4. d	7. d	10. c	13. d	16. d	19. b
2. c	5. a	8. d	11. a	14. a	17. c	20. b
3. c	6. c	9. d	12. b	15. c	18. c	

B. *True/False*

1. F	4. T	7. T	10. F	13. T	16. T	19. T
2. T	5. T	8. T	11. F	14. T	17. F	20. T
3. T	6. F	9. F	12. F	15. F	18. T	

STUDY GUIDE—CHAPTER 10
Methods of Acquiring a Business Aircraft

A. *MULTIPLE CHOICE:* Circle the letter that corresponds to the best answer.

1. Which of the following statements concerning a company-owned aircraft is *not* true?
    a. It offers the least amount of restrictions.
    b. It provides the lowest cost per hour if the aircraft is flown extensively.
    c. Efficiently used, it can satisfy 100 percent of a company's air transportation needs.
    d. None of these are true.

2. Compared to used aircraft, new aircraft purchases
    a. generally include lower interest rates and longer repayment terms.
    b. usually entail higher insurance costs on comparably valued aircraft.
    c. require more maintenance because there is no operation history.
    d. normally suffer poorer performance until the aircraft is flown for several hundred hours.

3. Which of the following statements concerning a used aircraft is *not* true?
    a. Cost of a 3-year-old model can be as much as 30 percent lower than a new model.
    b. They are subject to less stringent, airworthy licensing requirements.
    c. Interest rates charged by financial institutions are generally higher.
    d. Insurance rates are generally higher on comparably valued aircraft.

4. A new aircraft
    a. can generally be fitted with avionics equipment more easily and at less cost than a used aircraft.
    b. does not perform as efficiently as a used aircraft.
    c. is more costly to maintain than a used aircraft.
    d. cannot include selected interior appointments because these are standardized at the factory.

5. The big advantage of having an FBO operate a company's aircraft is
    a. better safety.   c. lower cost.
    b. no need to have an aviation department.   d. tax advantages.

6. Finance charges on aircraft loans are lower
    a. on small loans.   c. the higher the equity.
    b. for long-term loans.   d. the lower the credit rating.

7. The increase in used aircraft sales in recent years can be attributable to all of the following, *except*
    a. lack of new aircraft technology.
    b. high price of new aircraft resulting from higher production and marketing costs.
    c. products liability.
    d. government regulations imposed on newer aircraft.

8. Sources of used general aviation aircraft include all of the following, *except*
   a. businesses in distressed industries.
   b. the military.
   c. individuals and businesses upgrading their aircraft.
   d. bank repossessions.

9. Sale of an aircraft through a broker
   a. is the least costly method.
   b. requires the broker to purchase the aircraft.
   c. gives the owner broad exposure and generally prompter action.
   d. is the simplest method.

10. Airworthiness directives are
    a. used to notify aircraft owners of unsafe conditions about their aircraft.
    b. issued by a representative of the FAA after the aircraft has been inspected.
    c. issued after every 100-hour inspection.
    d. published by the National Transportation Safety Board.

11. Which of the following is probably least important to check when considering the purchase of a used aircraft?
    a. Airworthiness Directives Summary
    b. aircraft logbook
    c. date of last 100-hour inspection
    d. FBO who performed the regular maintenance

12. A sales agreement
    a. identifies all of the pilots who will fly the aircraft.
    b. indicates the price and date of closing.
    c. lists all applicable AD notices.
    d. all of these.

13. The Aircraft Registration Branch of the FAA is located in
    a. Atlantic City, New Jersey.
    b. Wichita, Kansas.
    c. Oklahoma City, Oklahoma.
    d. Washington, District of Columbia.

14. Generally, the most expensive way for an aircraft dealer to acquire aircraft is
    a. floor planning.
    b. paying cash.
    c. securing an installment loan.
    d. manufacturer financing.

15. Charging interest only on the outstanding balance of the loan is referred to as
    a. installment purchasing.
    b. simple interest.
    c. add-on interest.
    d. floor planning.

16. Under a floor planning arrangement the financial institution will
    a. only charge interest on the outstanding balance of the loan.
    b. use an add-on interest method.
    c. provide the dealer with short-term financing at moderate interest rates.
    d. only charge interest while the aircraft is being flown.

17. The pricing technique traditionally used in aircraft sales is
    a. markup pricing.
    b. competitive pricing.
    c. profit margin.
    d. demand potential.

18. The following formula is used to determine the retail selling price of an aircraft.

    a. $\dfrac{\text{cost}}{\text{markup \%}}$

    b. $\dfrac{\text{cost}}{\text{markup \% + 100\%}}$

    c. $\dfrac{\text{cost}}{100\% - \text{markup \%}}$

    d. $\dfrac{\text{markup \%}}{100\% - \text{cost}}$

19. If an aircraft dealer established a retail selling price of $130,000 for a used aircraft with a markup of 35 percent, the cost of the aircraft must have been approximately
    a. $96,300
    b. $84,500.
    c. $78,200.
    d. none of these.

20. Which of the following is *not* an advantage of leasing?
    a. conservation of working capital
    b. easier to upgrade equipment
    c. preservation of credit lines
    d. lowest cost

21. Under which of the following types of leases could the leasee purchase the aircraft for $1.00 or nominal amount at the end of the term?
    a. wet lease
    b. dry lease
    c. capital lease
    d. operating lease

22. Chartering aircraft is particularly attractive for a firm which
    a. uses aircraft infrequently.
    b. needs a special purpose aircraft.
    c. is considering purchasing an aircraft.
    d. all of these.

23. Contract flight service is
    a. quite different from chartering aircraft.
    b. very attractive for firms using aircraft more than 200 hours a year.
    c. used by companies needing to supplement their own aircraft.
    d. only done on an hourly basis.

24. These leases allow customers to keep an aircraft on their books for tax purposes, while allowing them to keep the asset out of the company's annual report.
    a. synthetic leases
    b. capital leases
    c. operating leases
    d. wet leases

25. Aircraft management firms are particularly attractive for
    a. operators with a large fleet of aircraft.
    b. operators with one or two aircraft.
    c. operators who fly in excess of 500 hours per year.
    d. charter operators.

26. Aircraft management firms can provide all of the following services *except*
    a. timesharing agreements.
    b. insurance.
    c. chartering a customer's aircraft.
    d. no exceptions, all of the above can be provided.

27. Finance charges on aircraft loans depend upon all of the following factors *except*
    a. length of the loan.
    b. amount of the down payment.
    c. the company's experience in operating aircraft.
    d. amount of the loan.

28. Which of the following statements concerning leasing is not correct?
    a. Should the airplane have a residual value higher than the amount used to determine the lease payments, the lessor would receive this gain as owner, not the lessee.
    b. An improperly structured lease could be determined to be a purchase agreement under IRS guidelines.
    c. A lease is considered debt under a company's balance sheet and, consequently, may restrict the firm's borrowing capacity.
    d. Leasing makes it easier to upgrade equipment.

29. A corporate aircraft operator might charter aircraft
    a. to supplement its airlift capability.
    b. because it is less expensive than ownership if estimated annual flying hours exceed 500.
    c. because it is less costly than using the airlines.
    d. all of the above.

30. All of the following are major operational factors to be considered in evaluating a charter operator *except*
    a. geographical area of operations.
    b. flight crew knowledge of the operations manual.
    c. pilot qualifications and records.
    d. pilot training and turnover.

31. All of the following would be considered no charge under a time-sharing agreement, *except:*
    a. fuel and oil
    b. wages and travel expenses of the crew
    c. in-flight food and beverages
    d. passenger ground transportation

32. A company-owned aircraft:
    a. is the least flexible method of business flying.
    b. is the most productive regardless of the hours flown.
    c. operates under FAR Part 91 and, as such, the federal excise tax does not apply.
    d. may be fully depreciated over a seven-year period.

33. Which of the following statements regarding a company-owned-management company-operated aircraft operation is not true?
    a. Nearly all management companies who offer this type of service operate under FAR Part 135.
    b. The company owning the aircraft may be able to save some fixed costs by selling time on its aircraft.
    c. The company may have access to other aircraft in the management company's fleet.
    d. All of the above statements are true.

34. Which of the following is not a problem under the co-ownership-management company-operated arrangement?
    a. Aircraft availability
    b. Chartering the aircraft
    c. Type of aircraft to purchase
    d. Selection of crew

35. During the late 1990s and early twenty-first century:
    a. fewer financial institutions were willing to finance aircraft purchases.
    b. interest rates rose sharply.
    c. manufacturers became more active in securing funding for sales of new and used aircraft.
    d. the residual value of new business aircraft declined.

36. Which of the following methods of selling an aircraft offers the least exposure?
    a. Sale by owner
    b. Sale by a broker
    c. Sale to a dealer
    d. Sale to an OEM

37. Which of the following methods of selling an aircraft requires the most extensive inspection?
    a. Sale by owner
    b. Sale by a broker
    c. Sale to a dealer
    d. Sale to an OEM

38. Which of the following methods of selling an aircraft can be the most flexible in terms of providing upgrades, modifications, and maintenance to be performed to enhance the sale?
    a. Sale by owner
    b. Sale by a broker
    c. Sale to a dealer
    d. Sale to an OEM

39. An FAA Form 337 must be completed:
    a. upon the sale of every aircraft.
    b. in the event of a major alteration or repair of an aircraft.
    c. prior to the issuance of an airworthiness certificate.
    d. for all turbo-prop and jet equipment.

40. A(an) _____ is used to notify an aircraft owner of unsafe conditions about their particular aircraft.
    a. FAA Form 337
    b. Pre-Purchase Inspection Form
    c. Airworthiness directive
    d. Airworthiness certificate

41. Which of the following statements regarding a pre-purchase inspection is not correct?
    a. The first thing to look for is any sign of corrosion and cracking.
    b. If avionics equipment needs upgrading, it should be installed at the time of purchase.
    c. Pre-purchase inspections are generally free.
    d. Technicians should perform a thorough engine inspection.

42. Which of the following statements concerning fractional ownership is not correct?
    a. Share size determines the amount of the down payment, the monthly management fee, and the annual flight hour allocation.
    b. Share sizes typically start from one-sixteenth or 50 flight hours per year.
    c. Owners share tax liabilities and benefits as a percentage of the share owned.
    d. Operations are conducted under FAR Part 135 so there is no question regarding the commercial nature of any flight.

43. The leading fractional aircraft provider in 2000 in terms of total share owners was:
    a. Flexjet
    b. NetJets
    c. Travel Air
    d. Flight Options

44. The first airline to join the fractional market was:
    a. American
    b. Delta
    c. Northwest
    d. United

45. All of the following are advantages of fractional ownership, *except:*
    a. All aspects of the aircraft's operation are managed by a provider.
    b. Minimal charges for deadhead legs by all of the leading providers.
    c. Aircraft availability is guaranteed at any time with as little as four hours' notice.
    d. The terms of most fractional agreements guarantee the liquidity of the investment.

46. As a general guideline, charter service is best when annual utilization is less than _____ hours annually.
    a. 100
    b. 150
    c. 200
    d. 250

B. *TRUE/FALSE:* Circle "T" if the statement is true, "F" if it is false.

T F   1. Companies will often seek outside assistance when considering the acquisition of business aircraft.

T F   2. Companies that own or lease aircraft would never need to charter.

T F   3. Generally one aircraft, if it is selected correctly, can meet 90 percent of a company's air transportation needs.

T F   4. The used aircraft market has experienced the same downturn in activity as the new aircraft market.

T F   5. A used aircraft is similar to a used automobile in that an individual or business could buy a definite "lemon."

T F   6. There is a definite correlation between maintenance cost and systems complexity.

T F   7. A new aircraft warranty covers the life of an aircraft so there is really no advantage in this regard in purchasing a new aircraft versus a used one.

T F   8. It is possible to get a fairly good picture of a used airplane's current condition by studying the records of its usage, maintenance, and repair.

T F   9. Two or more companies jointly purchasing an aircraft is a very effective way of increasing utilization with very few disadvantages.

T F 10. Very few financial institutions are engaged in corporate aircraft loans because of the specialized nature of the business.

T F 11. The down payment for used aircraft is the same as for new aircraft.

T F 12. The longer the term of an aircraft loan, the lower the interest rate.

T F 13. Most used aircraft are sold directly by the owner.

T F 14. The principal buyers of used aircraft today are end users—those who will actually operate the aircraft.

T F 15. The *Aircraft Bluebook* assists owners, brokers, and dealers in establishing current market value of used aircraft.

T F 16. Airworthiness certificates are used to notify aircraft owners of unsafe conditions about their aircraft.

T F 17. Most aircraft dealers buy the aircraft for as little as possible, put as little money as possible into the clean-up phase, and then try to sell the airplane at the highest price possible.

T F 18. A sales agreement always identifies the specific airplane by "N" number.

T F 19. A Certificate of Aircraft Registration must be secured from the FAA upon purchasing a used aircraft.

T F 20. Aircraft dealers can obtain installment loans for the purchase of aircraft from the manufacturers' own finance companies.

T F 21. Floor planning is the preferred method of financing dealer aircraft inventory.

T F 22. If a used aircraft cost the dealer $60,000 and markup percentage was estimated to be 40 percent, the retail price would be $84,000.

T F 23. Under the wet lease, the lessor only provides the aircraft and fuel.

T F 24. Conservation of working capital is a big advantage of leasing aircraft.

T F 25. Under an operating lease, the lessor places an estimated value on the aircraft at the termination of the contract.

T F 26. Financing is apt to be more liberal on a used airplane, with lower interest rates because of the operating history.

T F 27. One disadvantage for an operator using an aircraft management firm is the lack of opportunity to charter its aircraft.

T F 28. Sale of an aircraft by a broker is generally the quickest and simplest method.

T F 29. A lease is generally not considered debt.

T F 30. For income tax purposes, the capital lease is treated exactly like a loan.

T F 31. Most firms own or lease aircraft before getting involved with chartering aircraft.

T F 32. It is more cost efficient to charter occasionally than it is to underutilize a larger aircraft.

T F 33. Hangar and tie-down costs away from the aircraft's base of operations would not be considered a charge under a time-sharing agreement.

T F 34. Under an interchange agreement, a charge may be made not to exceed the difference between the cost of owning, operating, and maintaining the two airplanes.

T F 35. Because a company-owned aircraft operates under FAR Part 91, the noncommercial fuel tax does not apply.

T F 36. Aircraft management firms offer the one- and two-aircraft operator economies of scale generally available only to large fleet operators.

T F 37. Under a joint ownership arrangement, aircraft depreciation is shared by the owners.

T F 38. Pre-owned aircraft represent under one-third of all corporate aircraft sold in the United States.

T F 39. Manufacturers have played a lesser role in securing funding for sales of new and used aircraft in recent years.

T F 40. Selling an aircraft to a dealer is probably the quickest and simplest approach for an owner to use in disposing an aircraft.

T F 41. Most used business aircraft transactions worldwide are done through original equipment manufacturers.

T F 42. Airworthiness certificates are issued by the aircraft manufacturer after the aircraft has received a major modification.

T F 43. A pre-purchase inspection can take from several hours to seven or eight days.

T F 44. Leasing actually decreased in popularity during the late 1990s.

T F 45. Fractional aircraft owners may liquidate their shares at any time after 30 days and face no withdrawal penalty.

T F 46. Virtually all of the fractional aircraft providers offer shares of turboprop aircraft in addition to a complete line of business jets.

T F 47. Supplemental lift is used to reduce the costs of deadheading, to facilitate maintenance schedules, and as a fleet multiplier.

T F 48. Charter services have declined in recent years with the growth in fractional ownership.

C. *QUESTIONS TO THINK ABOUT AND EXERCISES:*

1. Determine the price of a new, fully equipped, multi-engine aircraft, then compare its price with the same model used aircraft using the Aircraft Bluebook, Trade-a-Plane, local newspapers, or similar source.
2. Request copies of sample aircraft leases from several sources and compare the terms under each example. Select a new aircraft and compare the cost of ownership versus leasing for your hypothetical example.
3. Develop a chart which clearly demonstrates the advantages and disadvantages of ownership, leasing, and charter. Also include the circumstances under which each method would be most appropriate (e.g., hourly utilization needed, flexibility, safety, costs, etc.).
4. Compare the charter and contract flight service rates for several FBOs in your area. Develop a list of prospects for these services. What criteria did you establish for inclusion on your list (e.g., annual sales, profitability, number of employees, marketing area served, type and amount of traveling by employees, etc.)?
5. Discuss with a local financial institution the criteria it uses to evaluate a retail dealer for its floor planning programs and the key components of its current plan.
6. Request copies of sales material from two or three of the leading fractional providers and compare features and costs.

ANSWERS:

A. *Multiple Choice*

1. c	7. d	13. c	19. b	25. b	31. b	37. d	43. b
2. a	8. b	14. b	20. d	26. d	32. c	38. c	44. d
3. b	9. c	15. b	21. c	27. c	33. d	39. b	45. b
4. a	10. a	16. c	22. d	28. c	34. d	40. c	46. a
5. b	11. d	17. a	23. c	29. a	35. c	41. c	
6. c	12. b	18. c	24. a	30. a	36. a	42. d	

B. *True/False*

1. T	6. T	11. F	16. F	21. T	26. F	31. F	36. T	41. F	46. F
2. F	7. F	12. F	17. F	22. F	27. F	32. T	37. T	42. F	47. T
3. F	8. T	13. F	18. T	23. F	28. F	33. T	38. F	43. T	48. F
4. F	9. F	14. T	19. T	24. T	29. T	34. T	39. F	44. T	
5. F	10. F	15. T	20. T	25. T	30. T	35. F	40. T	45. F	

STUDY GUIDE—CHAPTER 11
Promotion and Sales

A. *MULTIPLE CHOICE:* Circle the letter that corresponds to the best answer.

1. The promotion mix
   a. consists totally of advertising and personal selling.
   b. is highly standardized by industry.
   c. is comparatively easy to design once the total promotional budget is established.
   d. is a highly individualized decision area.

2. Ace Aviation is quite adept to planting commercially significant news items in the mass media. This firm is employing
   a. advertising.
   b. sales promotion.
   c. publicity.
   d. creative advertising.

3. Any paid form of nonpersonal communication about an organization, product or service by an identified sponsor is called:
   a. advertising.
   b. sales promotion.
   c. publicity.
   d. public relations.

4. U.S. corporations annually spend an average of _____ percent of each sales dollar on advertising.
   a. 1
   b. 3
   c. 6
   d. 10

5. Focusing an aircraft firm's advertising on the name and prestige of the company is called _____ advertising.
   a. pioneering
   b. competitive
   c. institutional
   d. product

6. An aircraft manufacturer's magazine ad stressing its aircraft advantages is an example of
   a. competitive.
   b. pioneering.
   c. primary.
   d. institutional.

7. The best approach to determining the advertising budget is
   a. setting the budget as a percentage of annual sales.
   b. setting the budget at a level comparative with competition.
   c. the amount necessary to meet the proposed objectives.
   d. to wait and see how much profit the firm will make.

8. Advertising agencies
   a. are specialists in planning and handling mass selling details.
   b. are the advertising departments of large corporations.
   c. are specialists in publicity.
   d. are generally not needed by large corporations since large corporations have in-house expertise.

9. The effectiveness of an advertising message can be measured by how well it
   a. is believable.
   b. attracts the identified target markets' attention.
   c. is related to the long lead time required of television copy.
   d. both a and b are correct.

10. The primary advantage of newspaper advertising is
    a. its good reproduction quality.
    b. the long lead time required to change copy.
    c. its good local market coverage.
    d. the lack of competition with other ads.

11. Which of the following groups contain the largest number of business firms in the United States?
    a. manufacturing
    b. services
    c. retailers
    d. construction

12. The letters SIC stand for
    a. Service Industry Classification.
    b. Selected Intermediate Customers.
    c. Standard Industrial Classification.
    d. Selected Industrial Characteristics.

13. Simmons Flight School is offering a trial flight as an inducement for enrolling in its flight program. This is an example of
    a. sales promotion.
    b. publicity.
    c. advertising.
    d. seeking potential customers.

14. Which of the following steps in the selling process should come first?
    a. qualifying prospects
    b. preapproach
    c. approach
    d. seek potential customers

15. Anticipating buyer resistance and developing effective responses defines
    a. closing.
    b. handling objections.
    c. follow-up.
    d. approach.

16. Criteria used in seeking prospective corporations for the business aircraft include
    a. two or more persons traveling together.
    b. trips in excess of 150 miles one-way.
    c. financially stable.
    d. all of these statements are criteria.

17. Probably the best and most professional method for an aircraft salesperson to use in securing an interview is
    a. personal letter followed by a telephone call.
    b. telephone call.
    c. direct personal contact.
    d. none of these methods.

18. The unstructured approach to a sales presentation is
    a. not generally used by business aircraft salespersons.
    b. used when the needs of the prospect are obvious.
    c. actually a canned sales presentation.
    d. a problem solving approach.

19. The format for the organized approach to a sales presentation is best represented by which of the following?
    a. attention, interest, desire, and closing
    b. attention, desire, interest, and closing
    c. attention, interest, convincing, desire, and closing
    d. attention, convincing, interest, desire, and closing

20. Which of the seven steps in the selling process is considered the *most* important and the *most* difficult?
    a. follow-up
    b. closing
    c. handling objections
    d. approach

21. Which of the following two methods of determining the promotional budget are the *most* popular?
    a. percentage of net sales/objective-and-task approach
    b. investing for future profits/percentage of net sales
    c. percentage of net sales/units-of-sales method
    d. matching competitors/objective-and-task approach

22. All of the following are closing techniques *except*
    a. alternate choice
    b. decision on minor point
    c. answering sincere objections
    d. assume the prospect is ready to buy

23. All of the following will help small FBOs stretch their promotional budget *except*
    a. reducing fuel prices by 8 cents per gallon
    b. use reprints of a print advertisement as a direct mail piece
    c. repeating the same ads at predetermined intervals
    d. use only media which give almost 100% geographical coverage

24. An effective message accomplishes all the following *except*
    a. presented in an understandable way
    b. is believable
    c. attracts the target markets attention
    d. identifies those markets with insufficient potential

25. A marketing manager should recognize that
    a. business firms outnumber individual customers for general aviation aircraft.
    b. retailers make up the largest number of business firms.
    c. there are about 88,000 government units in the United States.
    d. both b and c are true statements.

26. Measuring the effectiveness of advertising is difficult because of all the following factors *except*
    a. other aspects of marketing influencing sales
    b. competitive advertising
    c. delay in response
    d. limited advertising budget

27. A sales promotion activity which generates new leads, maintains customer contacts, and helps introduce new products and services describes
    a. demonstrations
    b. point-of-purchase promotions
    c. trade shows
    d. follow-up after the sale

28. Establishing a good relationship, reassuring customers, and handling questions describes which step in the selling process?
    a. approach
    b. close
    c. preapproach
    d. follow-up

29. Which of the following statements about answering objections to buy is false?
    a. objections throw light on the prospects thinking
    b. objections should be welcomed by the salesperson
    c. most objections by prospects are really excuses and are best dealt with in that light
    d. objections can be answered in a way that will help turn it into a reason for buying
30. Advantages of using the telephone to initially contact the prospect include all of the following *except*
    a. saves time over direct personal contact
    b. is more professional
    c. will assure the salesperson an interview
    d. increases productivity of the salesperson
31. Which of the following media is often called directional advertising?
    a. directory ads
    b. direct mail
    c. internet advertising
    d. outdoor billboards
32. Which of the following types of salespersons is most appropriate for the person selling business aircraft?
    a. order taker
    b. sales support
    c. inside salesperson
    d. executive salesperson
33. Greater success will come when an aircraft salesperson understands all of the following statements prior to the initial sales interview *except*
    a. salesperson must use the prospects time wisely
    b. salesperson is interrupting the prospect
    c. most corporations operate on a fiscal year accounting basis
    d. prospect wants to purchase profitability
34. A marketing manager could turn to SIC data published by the federal government to find
    a. the sales volumes of various industry groups.
    b. the number of employees for various industry groupings.
    c. the number of firms for various industry groupings.
    d. all of these.
35. Detailed information concerning the top 25,000 U.S. corporations can be found in
    a. Dun and Bradstreet's directories.   c. Best's Insurance Reports.
    b. state industrial directories.   d. chamber of commerce directories.
36. What business information is probably the *least* important to an aircraft salesperson?
    a. location of home office and all branches   c. credit rating
    b. number of production workers   d. markets served
37. In the qualifying stage of prospecting, an aircraft salesperson will attempt to:
    a. prepare a thorough list of prospects.
    b. select prospects who warrant further attention.
    c. call on hot prospects.
    d. prepare a formal presentation.
38. Which of the following sources is probably *least* appropriate in developing qualifying information?
    a. chamber of commerce   c. the company under consideration
    b. annual reports   d. a competing firm

B. *TRUE/FALSE* Circle "T" if the statement is True, "F" if it is False.

T F   1. The promotion mix includes two components: advertising and sales promotion.

T F   2. A major disadvantage of advertising is the lack of immediate feedback.

T F   3. Publicity is any unpaid form of nonpersonal communication about a product or service.

T F   4. In contrast to personal selling, advertising takes a "rifle-like" approach rather than a "shotgun" approach.

T F   5. Advertising agencies sometimes handle the overall marketing planning for a small FBO.

T F   6. The objective of institutional advertising is to sell a product or service to a final user.

T F   7. A brochure sent to a business aircraft owner who recently had its aircraft serviced is an example of reminder advertising.

T F   8. A common approach to setting an advertising budget is to base the budget as a percentage of last year's sales.

T F   9. The message in a flight school's advertisement is called the copy.

T F   10. Magazines and trade journals are some of the fastest growing media.

T F   11. Most advertisements use both language and visual messages.

T F   12. Special interest magazines like *Flying* are useful to "zero-in" on target markets.

T F   13. The big disadvantage of billboards is their extremely high cost per location.

T F   14. Pretesting advertising effectiveness can be useful in determining recall, and uniqueness of an advertisement.

T F   15. Improving name recognition through imprinting T-shirts is an example of publicity.

T F   16. The objective of the preapproach stage in the selling process is to search for potential customers.

T F   17. The endless-chain method of prospecting is used at the end of an unsuccessful sales interview to secure the names of potential prospects.

T F   18. A fact finding interview is a major characteristic of the organized approach to a sales presentation.

T F   19. Determining the prospects primary buying motive arouses *desire* to purchase.

T F   20. Objections should be welcomed as a chance to get the prospect involved in the interview.

T F   21. Spending all the firm can afford is the most logical approach to determining the size of the promotional budget.

T F   22. The principal problem of using the objective-and-task approach to determining promotional budgets is the danger of being too ambitious.

T F   23. Sales promotion activities include the use of mass media like radio.

T F   24. Publicity like advertising is a nonpersonal presentation of an idea or product.

T F   25. Commissions allowed by media to advertising agencies are usually 15% of the cost of advertising.

T F   26. One of the functions of advertising agencies is to create and produce direct mail pieces and other collateral material.

T F   27. Pioneering advertising tries to promote a specific company's product or service.

T F   28. In practice, firms usually do pioneering or competitive advertising and institutional advertising simultaneously.

T F   29. Trying to match the advertising dollar expenditures of your competition is a defensive rather than an aggressive approach.

T F   30. Advertising in telephone directories is used by practically all firms.

T F   31. Prospecting is the first step in the selling process.

T F   32. Thomas's Register provides product information and profiles on more than 123,000 U.S. companies.

T F   33. Personal information which would be helpful to an aircraft salesperson during the qualifying stage might include organization memberships.

T F   34. The qualifying stage involves the selection of prospects who warrant further attention.

T F   35. Sometimes it is necessary to call on prospects to obtain qualifying information before setting up a formal interview.

T F 36. From the qualifying information, a salesperson might determine that an aircraft would be a decided asset to a firm.

T F 37. "Endless Chain Method" is a useful tool to qualify prospects.

T F 38. A study by Posner and Waleck indicated that for every 100 direct mail responses, 3 persons will purchase the advertised product within 3 months.

T F 39. Corporate aircraft salespersons need two types of information about prospects—personal information on key decision makers and business information.

T F 40. An effective technique is to qualify the prospect on the first interview.

C. *QUESTIONS TO THINK ABOUT AND EXERCISES:*

1. The promotion mix consists of (1) advertising, (2) sales promotion, (3) publicity, and (4) personal selling. Indicate which component of the promotion mix is being illustrated by the following activities.
   a. An announcement in the local activities section of the newspaper informing the public that the local aircraft model builders club will meet next Tuesday evening.
   b. Seacoast Airlines, a local commuter, offered children between 10 and 16 years of age airline tickets in exchange for five proofs-of-purchase seals from Kellogg cereals.
2. In allocating the promotional budget, which time frame should receive emphasis: When business is good, or when business is declining?
3. Look through one special-interest magazine, like *Flying,* and find ads which illustrate each of the three product advertising objectives: pioneering, competitive or comparative, and reminder.
4. Television has the big advantage over all of the other media in that it combines both sight and sound. Why is it generally not cost effective for a local FBO to use this medium extensively in communicating with its target markets?
5. Interview a professional salesperson and ask the following questions:
   a. Why did he or she enter the selling field?
   b. What does he or she like most about the career?
   c. What does he or she dislike most about the career?
   d. What special preparation did he or she make prior to entering the field?
   e. What advice does he or she have for a person considering the selling field as a career?
6. Assume you are a business aircraft salesperson and are employed by Hangar Four. What information should you research before you make your first call on a prospect, and what information would you seek on the first sales interview.
7. React to this statement: "Sales presentations should always be prepared in such a way as to anticipate all major objections before they occur."
8. Using the library and local chamber of commerce, develop a list of prospects for your charter or leasing service. Develop three marketing-oriented personal and business facts about your prospects.
9. Develop a newspaper advertisement designed to attract prospects. How might an aircraft salesperson prospect for new or used aircraft owners?

ANSWERS

A. *Multiple Choice*

1. d	5. c	9. d	13. a	17. a	21. c	25. c	29. c	33. c	37. b
2. c	6. a	10. c	14. d	18. d	22. c	26. d	30. c	34. d	38. d
3. a	7. c	11. b	15. b	19. c	23. a	27. c	31. a	35. a	
4. b	8. a	12. c	16. d	20. b	24. d	28. d	32. d	36. b	

B. *True/False*

1. F	5. T	9. T	13. F	17. T	21. F	25. T	29. T	33. T	37. F
2. T	6. F	10. T	14. T	18. F	22. F	26. T	30. T	34. T	38. T
3. T	7. T	11. T	15. F	19. T	23. F	27. F	31. T	35. T	39. T
4. F	8. T	12. T	16. F	20. T	24. T	28. T	32. T	36. T	40. F

STUDY GUIDE—CHAPTER 12
Sales Management

A. *MULTIPLE CHOICE:* Circle the letter that corresponds to the best answer.

1. It is important to have a good program for selecting salespersons because
    a. there is a limited number of sales positions.
    b. job descriptions are then easier to prepare.
    c. a good selection program makes it easier to train, supervise, and motivate salespersons.
    d. a lot of qualified people are seeking sales jobs.

2. A good job description is *least* likely to include information about
    a. the names of the newspapers where recruiting ads are generally run.
    b. the specific title of the position.
    c. educational requirements.
    d. amount of supervision the salesperson will receive.

3. Recruiting methods vary with the source. Direct recruiting by salesmanagers is used
    a. by placing ads in trade journals.
    b. to reach identified candidates inside the company.
    c. to reach identified candidates from schools.
    d. both b and c are correct.

4. Sales training program content includes
    a. product information.
    b. territory management.
    c. major competitors and their products.
    d. all of the above.

5. Training programs
    a. are all formalized and very structured.
    b. usually last only 1 month.
    c. vary from company to company.
    d. are usually not necessary because the new salespersons already possess the required knowledge and skills.

6. Recruiting is
    a. an ongoing activity.
    b. an activity required only at the beginning of each year.
    c. the process of selecting qualified applicants.
    d. determining the number of salespersons required during a specific time frame.

7. The role of an aircraft salesperson would include which of the following:
    a. pilot.
    b. customer-ego builder.
    c. service technician.
    d. all of the above.

8. The three key characteristics good sales volume and activity objectives should possess are
    a. precise, measurable, and specified time period.
    b. measurable, affordable, and specified time period.
    c. precise, easily attainable, and covering a two-year period.
    d. affordable, attainable, and presented to salespersons for their approval.

9. The first step in recruiting is to
    a. determine the qualifications and abilities needed.
    b. determine manpower needs.
    c. select the proper recruiting sources.
    d. determine the expected turnover and attrition rate.

10. Which of the following selection screens or steps is generally first?
    a. physical exam
    b. credit report
    c. interview
    d. aptitude test

11. When designing a compensation plan, the first step is to
    a. determine the total sales for the year.
    b. determine the impact of turnover.
    c. establish the level of earnings required to support an adequate salesforce.
    d. select the proper compensation method.

12. Which one of the following methods of compensating aircraft salespersons is the most popular?
    a. salary 100%
    b. salary 70%, commission 30%
    c. salary 30%, commission 70%
    d. commission 100%
13. The major strengths of a 100% salary compensation plan are
    a. some element of security.
    b. income is directly related to sales.
    c. greater sales manager control over salespersons activities.
    d. both a and c.
14. The major *advantage* of the straight commission compensation method is
    a. certainty of income.
    b. rewards in direct relationship to accomplishments.
    c. fixed cost to the employing organization.
    d. to assist newer salespersons until they become established.
15. The 20 to 30% commission rate is applied to the _____ on a new aircraft sold.
    a. gross profit
    b. net profit
    c. adjusted gross profit
    d. selling price
16. In addition to formalized compensation plans, many firms use some of the following except _____ to provide additional motivation.
    a. sales contests
    b. bonuses
    c. praise and recognition
    d. reduction in commission rate
17. Supervisory style used by the sales manager should be
    a. consistent to all his salespersons.
    b. tailored to fit individual needs of the salespersons.
    c. authoritarian to maintain control.
    d. based upon size of the salesforce.
18. Sales quotas
    a. serve as an effective supervisory tool.
    b. are usually developed from the bottom up.
    c. should not involve input from the salesforce.
    d. are not useful when salespersons are paid 100% salary.
19. A salesperson's batting average is a popular evaluation tool. The average is calculated by
    a. $\dfrac{\text{Number of Sales}}{\text{Number of Presentations}}$
    b. Number of sales $\times$ Number of presentations
    c. $\dfrac{\text{Dollar Value of Sales}}{\text{Number of Sales}}$
    d. Dollar Value of Sales $\times$ Number of Sales
20. Three common methods used to evaluate sales performance include all of the following *except*
    a. achievement of quotas.
    b. direct comparison with other salespersons.
    c. ratio of sales to sales expenses.
    d. comparison with an individuals last years performance.
21. The importance of personal selling relative to the other promotion mix components depends on all of the following characteristics *except*
    a. size and nature of the target market
    b. the price of the product
    c. service requirement
    d. emergency of the need
22. Sales managers usually have direct responsibility for
    a. salesforce planning
    b. mission statements
    c. marketing planning
    d. promotional budgeting

23. All of the following factors influence the size of the salesforce *except*
    a. turnover
    b. company growth
    c. sales objectives
    d. annual sales volume of your major competitor

24. A recruiting tool which produces a large number of poor quality applicants is
    a. attending a career day at a university
    b. employment agencies
    c. advertisements in a local newspaper
    d. advertisements in a trade journal

25. Screens used in the selection process for aircraft salespersons include all the following *except*
    a. trial job performance
    b. psychological tests
    c. application form
    d. physical examination

26. The acquiring or transferring of skills, facts, or attitudes by one person from another is called
    a. job enrichment
    b. productivity
    c. learning
    d. job enlargement

27. In sales training, the technique which is *least* effective is
    a. discussion between trainee and instructor
    b. oral instruction alone
    c. showing audio visuals
    d. using demonstrations where appropriate

28. Combination compensation plans are popular because
    a. they are least expensive to the company
    b. they provide security and motivation
    c. they weed out the poor salespersons
    d. they reward the exceptional salesperson the most

29. The major factor influencing the amount of supervision required by the sales manager is
    a. quality of the salesforce
    b. compensation plan
    c. size of the sales quota
    d. geographical scope of the company

30. Daily attention is required in all of the following salesperson's activities by the sales manager *except*
    a. follow-up techniques
    b. prospecting
    c. sales control
    d. selling techniques

B. *TRUE/FALSE:* Circle "T" if the statement is True, "F" if it is False.

T   F   1. A frequently used index to express productivity is the ratio of sales expenses divided by dollar sales volume.

T   F   2. Sales management is the accomplishment of sales objectives through the effective and efficient performance of the selling process.

T   F   3. Two skills that are essential for sales manager success are outstanding selling ability and leadership.

T   F   4. Sales volume objectives and activity objectives serve as performance standards in evaluating the sales force.

T   F   5. Recruiting primarily involves selecting from a pool of applicants.

T   F   6. A job analysis and a job description are actually used interchangeably.

T F 7. It is not uncommon to require at least two years of college to be selected as an aircraft salesperson.

T F 8. Present employees who desire to move into sales are a good recruiting source.

T F 9. Overpaying salespersons relative to other employees can cause serious problems.

T F 10. The major disadvantage of 100% salary compensation plan is its inability to motivate.

T F 11. A draw is nothing but a guaranteed salary.

T F 12. The commission rate for selling a new aircraft generally runs from 5 to 10% of the adjusted gross profit of the aircraft being sold.

T F 13. Sales contests are fun, but really do not stimulate increased profitable sales.

T F 14. In general, salespersons on salary require more supervision than do salespersons paid on a combination plan.

T F 15. Straight commission is the most popular form of compensation.

T F 16. Sales quotas are usually derived by breaking the sales forecast down into parts.

T F 17. Time utilization is an important supervisory area for the sales manager.

T F 18. Good sales management requires that salespersons develop their own prospects.

T F 19. Salespersons should be evaluated on their quantitative as well as their qualitative performances.

T F 20. Comparing salespersons with their peers is a reliable method of evaluating performance.

T F 21. It is important for the sales manager to know each salesperson's flying ability.

T F 22. In general, salespersons paid by 100% commission require the most supervision.

T F 23. Involving the salesforce in its own quota setting will raise the probability of success.

T F 24. The highest amount of learning takes place when a trainee hears, sees, and participates.

T F 25. Advertisements for new salespersons develop greater responses when the copy is not very specific.

T F 26. A job analysis is just another term for job description.

T F 27. Recruiting is an ongoing activity of sales management.

T F 28. Tactics, in strategy formulation, spell out how resources are to be allocated.

T F 29. Personal selling is a critical component in the promotion mix for most FBOs.

T F 30. Most sales managers would agree that some salesperson turnover is constructive.

C. QUESTIONS TO THINK ABOUT AND EXERCISES:

1. Why do outstanding salespersons frequently make poor sales managers?
2. React to the following statement: "The major disadvantage of using the 100% salary plan for compensating aircraft salespersons is that it fails to provide motivation to excel."
3. It is more desirable to select aircraft salespersons who already possess selling skills over persons who are new to the selling field and train them through company programs. Comment.
4. Assume that you are now in the job market and are seriously considering a sales position. Describe what skills and personality you think it takes to be a good aircraft salesperson.
5. Which compensation plan would you prefer to work under—salary, commission, combination? Why?
6. Generally speaking, salespersons want the most money possible for performing their tasks, while sales managers try to keep payroll expenses down. What goals do both parties share in regard to the compensation method used?
7. Is some turnover in sales force membership healthy? Explain.

ANSWERS

A. *Multiple Choice*

1. c	6. a	11. c	16. d	21. d	26. c
2. a	7. d	12. b	17. b	22. a	27. b
3. d	8. a	13. d	18. a	23. d	28. b
4. d	9. a	14. b	19. a	24. c	29. a
5. c	10. c	15. c	20. c	25. a	30. c

B. *True/False*

1. T	6. F	11. F	16. T	21. T	26. F
2. T	7. T	12. F	17. T	22. F	27. T
3. F	8. T	13. F	18. T	23. T	28. T
4. T	9. T	14. T	19. T	24. T	29. T
5. F	10. T	15. F	20. F	25. F	30. T

Appendix B

Corporate Aircraft Sales Presentation

Appendix B is included to provide an example of a typical transportation analysis presentation. This marketing proposal is completed after extensive fact finding interviews with the prospect. The proposal includes the following essential components: introduction, aircraft selection rationale, financial analysis, and a value analysis. The business aircraft salesperson would present this proposal to the executives of the prospect corporation.

AVIATION SUPPLY, INC.

TRAVEL DATA AND FINANCIAL ANALYSIS FOR MANAGEMENT CONSULTANTS

By

William E. Pulling
and Aviation Supply Staff

To

Dr. Bruce Chadbourne
President of Management Consultants, Inc.

AVIATION SUPPLY, INC.

One Aviation Drive
Daytona Beach, Florida 32014

November 20, 200X

Dr. Bruce Chadbourne, President
Management Consultants, Inc.
2000 Prestige Drive
Tampa, Florida 32777

Dear Dr. Chadbourne:

We met on September 29, 200X to discuss your company's new transportation needs and the contracting of my firm, Aviation Supply. As you requested, my team has analyzed Management Consultants' annual transportation data; our findings and recommendations are illustrated in this report.

This report will clearly show and justify the corporate aircraft that best meets your transportation needs. Along with our recommendations, we will present a detailed analysis of the financial impact of operating a corporate aircraft. This financial analysis is composed of the Capital Recovery Guide, Fixed and Direct Operating Expenses and a Cash Flow Analysis (present value) with the effect of the depreciation and taxes. One very important section of this report will be the comparison of the scheduled air carrier to the corporate operated aircraft, in both cost and time. From this report, you will gain a stronger understanding of the positive impact a corporate aircraft presents, as well as the relevant costs associated with its operations.

If I can provide additional information, or if you still have any unanswered questions, please feel free to contact me at work (904) 253–5561, extension 1284, or at my home (904) 788–0396.

Aviation Supply and I would like to thank you for the opportunity of presenting this report to you. I am looking forward to helping in the implementation of the new corporate aircraft into your company's operational system. We are also hopeful that this report will answer all your questions and meet with your approval.

Very truly yours,
AVIATION SUPPLY, INC.

William E. Pulling
President

INTRODUCTION

In this world of high technology and multi-million-dollar deals, companies must stay competitive and in tune with changing times. Just as the computer became a vital tool for business in achieving a higher level of efficiency, the corporate aircraft can also increase productivity for the company. Operating a corporate aircraft will not only increase productivity, but will also provide many other positive benefits.

These positive benefits can be subdivided into two main categories: Tangible and Intangible factors. It is essential to discuss the intangible factors at this point, although it is very difficult to assign a dollar and cents value to the direct costs and benefits. They must be evaluated and considered in any study which examines the real costs and benefits of the

1. Less executive fatigue—lower stress
2. The competitive advantage of getting there first.
3. Effortless travel versus crowded terminals, inconvenient flights and waiting at luggage lines.
4. Fewer husbandless/wifeless nights for the executives' families.
5. The availability of a superior travel service for use by customers.
6. Insuring the security of corporate executives.
7. The aircraft is a symbol of success—customers want to deal with successful companies.
8. Face-to-face communication—closing deals.

Figure B-1. Intangible Benefits

corporate aircraft. To illustrate these factors, Figure B-1 is used to make the company aware of the scope and nature of these intangible benefits. It is important that top management review this list and realize that there are many more benefits than just these eight.

As mentioned before, the other category is the tangible factors. These factors can be illustrated in a dollar value. The remaining portion of this report is dedicated to these cost/benefits which will be completely and clearly discussed. With both the tangible and intangible factors displayed, this feasibility study will furnish the foundation to fully realize the vital potential of a corporate aircraft in aiding a successful organization.

AIRCRAFT SELECTION

By fully reviewing the transportation data provided from Management Consultants, we had originally selected the Beechcraft Super King Air 300. This aircraft is a highly dependable twin-engine turboprop (a propeller driven by a jet engine) and can be purchased for $2,475,000. However, we have reevaluated the data given, and have chosen the Cessna Citation S/II as the best aircraft to meet the needs of Management Consultants. This small business jet is one of the most popular and reliable aircraft on the market today. The purchase price of this aircraft is $3,450,000.

Time/Aircraft Comparison

Both aircraft are excellent modes of transportation in the different categories that they represent. However, when considering the critical aspect of time, the Super King Air 300 would spend too much of it in the air. To illustrate this point, we have calculated the time to and from Pawhuska, Oklahoma (Management Consultants' longest leg at 1030 miles). In this mock situation, we have preset the departure time (7:00 a.m.) and the time allotted for the meeting (6 hours) to be the same in both cases. This will help highlight the flight time of both aircraft. As shown in Figure B-2, the result is the Cessna Citation S/II saved one hour and forty minutes of valuable flight time, over the Super King Air 300, and allows the executives to be home by 5:26 p.m. the same night.

Although one hour and forty minutes may not seem like a significant amount of time, this will become relevant if expressed over a one-year period. In this case, 50 hours are saved per year on this trip alone.

Total Picture

Based predominantly on the Cessna Citation S/II's timesaving ability, this report would not be complete unless we compared the total time savings on all destinations. The following figures (B-3 and B-4) show the flight time needed by the Citation S/II in comparison to the Super King Air 300, to reach all five of Management Consultants' destinations from Tampa, Florida. Calculations were made using the average cruise speed of 403 knots (463 mph) for the Citation and 290 knots (334 mph) for the Super King Air 300. As illustrated in Figure B-3, the destination ranging between 410–485 miles will save 20–23 minutes when using the Citation. In addition, the farther the destination, the more signifi-

	Citation S/II	Super King Air 300
Departure time (Tampa)	7:00 a.m.	7:00 a.m.
En route	2 hrs. 13 min.	3 hrs. 3 min.
Arrival Time (Pawhuska)	9:13 a.m.	10:03 a.m.
Allotted Meeting Time	6 hrs.	6 hrs.
Departure Time (Pawhuska)	3:13 p.m.	4:03 p.m.
En route	2 hrs. 13 min.	3 hrs. 3 min.
Arrival Time (Tampa)	5:26 p.m.	7:06 p.m.

Total Time Saved Per Trip . . . . 1.0 hrs. 40 min.
Number of Trips (Annual) 30
Total Time Saved Per Year . . . . 50.0 hrs.

Figure B-2. Time Comparison

cant the amount of time saved, as Pawhuska (Bartlesville) shows. Total time savings annually for all five destinations is shown in Figure B-4. As a result, even the small amount of time savings will frequently add up to a significant amount. Your company will save 174 hours per year by operating the citation S/II. A special note, the Citation S/II cannot operate out of Pawhuska due to the length of the runway. The closest airport that can support the operations of the Citation S/II is Bartlesville. Executives who fly into this airport will have a 30-minute drive to Pawhuska, which will reduce the total time savings to 144 hours annually. Even this amount of time saving is meaningful and can be reallocated to an efficient maintenance program for the Citation S/II. This should reduce downtime for the aircraft that causes interference to Management Consultants' flight schedules.

Locations and Operations

It is important to know the destinations where Management Consultants needs to travel. As shown in Figure B-5, a summary of these locations and significant information for operations into these destinations is provided. Further illustrated in Figure B-5, Pawhuska, Oklahoma, is not large enough to support the operation of the Citation S/II.

Destination	Statute Miles	Citation S/II Flight Time	Super King Air 300 Flight Time
Gainesville, GA	470	1:02	1:25
Montgomery, AL	410	0:54	1:14
*Bartlesville, OK	1030	2:13	3:03
Anderson, SC	430	0:56	1:18
Bessemer, AL	485	1:04	1:28

*Pawkuska's runway is too short for the Citation, so Bartlesville was chosen as the closest airport.

Figure B-3. Time/Speed Saving Comparison

Destination	Annual Legs	Citation Time Saving/Leg	Total Time Savings (Hours)
Gainesville, GA	80	0:23	30.67
Montgomery, AL	104	0:20	34.67
Bartlesville, OK	60	1:10	70.00
Anderson, SC	78	0:22	28.60
Bessemer, AL	24	0:24	9.60
Total Time Saved Per Year			173.56

Figure B-4. Total Annual Time Savings

As expressed before, a 30-minute drive from Bartlesville is required. The meaning of VFR (visual flight rules) and IFR (instrument flight rules) are associated in the aircraft operations and in this report for the purpose of illustrating the availability of the airport. Those indicating IFR will allow aircraft to land and take off in minimum weather conditions with a higher degree of safety. In this case, all of the destinations, except Pawhuska and Bessemer, are available during minimum weather conditions. Bessemer is available only during good weather. As the weather affects the landings, the runway length is another characteristic that determines if an aircraft can land and take off safely. The Citation S/II requires 3,430 feet to take off and 3,140 feet to land. As shown in Figure B-5, all destinations, except Pawhuska, are within the minimum standards demanded for the Citation S/II operations. The other information provided in the Destination Summary is background data which is a small factor in determining operations into and out of these

Destination	VFR/ IFR	Longest Runway	Fuel Jet A	Distance from City	Arpt Hrs.	Car Hotel
Gainesville, GA	IFR	5,000' × 100'	Yes	0 mi S	daylt	both
Montgomery, AL	IFR	9,001' × 150'	Yes	6 mi SW	24 hrs	both
*Pawhuska, OK	VFR	3,200' × 100'	No	4 mi W	daylt	both
Bartlesville, OK	IFR	6,200' × 100'	Yes	1 mi NW	5a-6p	both
Anderson, SC	IFR	5,000' × 150'	Yes	3 mi SW	daylt	both
**Bessemer, AL	VFR	3,800' × 100'	Yes	4 mi SE	daylt	both
Birmingham, AL	IFR	10,000' × 150'	Yes	5 mi NE	24 hrs	both

*Citation cannot operate into Pawhuska because of the length of runway.
 Bartlesville is the alternative airport.
**Birmingham is Bessemer alternative if poor weather around Bessemer.

Figure B-5. Destination Summary

Destination	Number Traveler	Number Legs	Number Trips	%	Cum %
*Gainesville, GA	5	80	400	29	29
*Montgomery, AL	3	104	312	23	52
Pawhuska, OK	4	60	240	18	70
*Anderson, SC	4	78	312	23	93
Bessemer, AL	4	24	96	7	100

*Most traveled destinations.

Figure B-6. Sample Passenger Density

Range	Number Legs	%	Cum %
<410	104	30	30
410–480	158	46	76
>485	84	24	100

Figure B-7. Trip Density

airports. In Figure B-6, the places where Management Consultants has the highest passenger density are indicated by an asterisk (Gainesville, Montgomery and Anderson). These locations show a passenger density of greater than 20 percent. Trip density illustrated in Figure B-7 shows the average range that is being traveled by Management Consultants personnel. In this case, the range being traveled the most is between 420–480 miles.

FINANCIAL ANALYSIS

In this portion of the report, we have enclosed all the financial information, and we have also calculated the impact associated with ownership/operations of the Citation S/II. The following list illustrates the financial information provided:

Figure B-8:   Capital Recovery Guide
Figure B-9:   Fixed Costs
Figure B-10:   Estimated Direct Operating Expenses

From the Capital Recovery Guide, you can see that despite the acquisition price of $3,622,500.00, the Citation S/II will only cost $10,230.00 per month. This amount was derived from 100 percent depreciation of the aircraft and 70 percent return on the purchase price to indicate disposal price in six years. In addition, the benefits of tax savings were also calculated.

As to the disposal price, we at Aviation Supply, are estimating all Cessna Citations at 70 percent of acquisition price. We feel with the combination of today's strong used aircraft market, the issue over manufacturing products liability, and the popularity of the Cessna Citation S/II, that 70 percent is a realistic calculation.

At this time, we would like to address the low utilization in the first year. With present transportation data, Management Consultants' planned utilization is only 404 hours. According to the National Business Aviation Association (NBAA), the Cessna Citation should have an annual utilization of 312 hours on the low side, 955 hours on the high side

Citation S/II—Six Year Analysis

Aircraft Acquisition Cost
Purchase Price			$3,450,000.00
State Sales Tax @	5%		$ 172,500.00
Total			$3,622,500.00

Depreciation Expense			$3,622,500.00
Resale Value @	70%		$2,415,000.00

Six-Year Capital Recovery

Tax Savings (39% corporate tax rate)
Depreciation	$ 1,412,755	
Total Tax Savings		$1,412,775.00

Disposal of Aircraft
Resale Value	$ 2,415,000	
Less Taxes on Sale	$ 941,850	
Net Proceeds From Sale		$1,473,150.00
Total Capital Recovered		$2,885,925.00

Total Acquisition Cost		$3,622,500.00
Total Capital Recovered		$2,885,925.00
Net Cost of Ownership	Six Years	$ 736,575.00
	Per Year	$ 122,763.00
	Per Month	$ 10,230.00

Figure B-8. Capital Recovery Guide

Expense Category	Estimated Cost Per Year
Crew Salaries	
Captain	$ 67,425
Co-Pilot	$ 47,352
Benefits	$ 34,433
Hangar Rental	$ 20,913
Insurance	
Hull (Physical Damage Coverage @ .28 per $100	$ 9,660
Single Limit Liability—100 M Per Occurrence	$ 14,000
Admitted Liability—$500,000/seat	$ 2,250
Recurrent Training	$ 13,400
Navigation Chart Service	$ 3,061
Computer Mx. Program	$ 1,850
Aircraft Modernization plus Uninsured Damage	$ 13,800
Refurbishing	$ 15,540
Weather Service	$ 2,300
Total Annual Fixed Costs	$ 245,984

Figure B-9. Fixed Costs

Expense Category	Estimated Cost Per Hour
Fuel (1)	$ 509.96
Fuel Additives—2% of fuel	$ 4.18
Mature Level Maintenance (2)	
Labor at $74.00 per hour	$ 168.72
Parts-Airframe, Avionics and Engine Consumables	$ 137.28
Engine Restoration (3)	$ 176.54
Miscellaneous Expenses	
Crew Expenses	$ 135.00
Landing/Parking Fees	$ 11.33
Supplies/Catering	$ 36.00
Total Direct Operating Expenses Per Hour	$ 1,179.01

NOTES:

(1) 209 gallons per hour
(2) 2.28 labor hours per flight hour
(3) 2000 Jet Support Services "Complete" for (2) Pratt & Whitney Canada JT15D-4B.

Figure B-10. Estimated Direct Operating Expenses

and 619 hours on the average. As you can see, Management Consultants will be within the lower limit by 92 hours (404 hours–312 hours). We at Aviation Supply feel in order to receive a proper hourly utilization from this aircraft, it should be flown around the 600 hours per year. Considering that this is Management Consultants' first year to operate a corporate aircraft, we are confident that utilization will increase. It is well-known in corporate aviation that once a company exposes its personnel to an aircraft, more personnel on the average, will want to use it. However, if the utilization does not increase, there are several options open to your company, ranging from leaseback to chartering.

In preparing this report, we tried to provide vital information for the present, as well as the future. In addition, we wanted to illustrate a detailed analysis of the cost associated with the operation and ownership of a Cessna Citation S/II.

CASH FLOW/ PRESENT ANALYSIS

Review the following items to ensure an understanding of the variables in the cash flow analysis.

Cash Flow Analysis Assumption

Finance Rate	10% APR
Years Financed	9 (108 months)
Acquisition Price	$ 3,622,500
Downpayment (20%)	$ 724,500
Amount Financed	$ 2,898,000
Inflation Factor	3.1%
Federal Income Tax Rate	39%
Sales Tax Rate	5%
Monthly Payment	$ 40,800
Depreciation	Double Declining

Input Data:

Aircraft Cost	$3,450,000	Federal Income Tax Rate: 39%		Monthly Payment: $40,800	
State Sales Tax @ 5%	$ 172,500	Finance Rate: 10% APR 9 Years		Inflation Rate: 3.1%	
Total Acquisition Cost	$3,622,500	Money Value Rate: 15%		Annual Hrs of Utilization: 404	

Expenditures	Year 0	Year 1	Year 2	Year 3	Year 4	Year 5	Year 6
Fixed Costs		$ 245,984	$ 253,610	$ 261,471	$ 269,577	$ 277,934	$ 286,500
Down Payment (20%)	$ 724,500						
Balance of Purchase	$ 2,898,000						
Principal Payment		$ 209,217	$ 231,125	$ 255,327	$ 282,063	$ 311,598	$ 344,227
Interest Payment		$ 280,383	$ 258,476	$ 234,274	$ 207,538	$ 178,002	$ 145,374
Loan Balance Payoff							$ 1,264,443
Taxes Due on Sale							$ 941,850
Operating Expenses		$ 476,320	$ 491,086	$ 506,310	$ 522,005	$ 538,187	$ 554,871
TOTAL EXPENDITURES	$ 3,622,500	$ 1,211,904	$ 1,234,297	$ 1,257,382	$ 1,281,183	$ 1,305,721	$ 3,537,315
CASH SOURCES							
Aircraft Loan	$ 2,898,000						
Disposal of Aircraft (70%)							$ 2,415,000
TOTAL SOURCES	$ 2,898,000						$ 2,415,000
TOTAL CHANGE (before taxes)	$ (724,500)	$ (1,211,904)	$ (1,234,297)	$ (1,257,382)	$ (1,281,183)	$ (1,305,721)	$ (1,122,315)
TAX REDUCTIONS							
Fixed Cost		$ 95,934	$ 98,908	$ 101,974	$ 105,135	$ 108,394	$ 111,755
Depreciation		$ 282,555	$ 452,088	$ 271,253	$ 162,752	$ 162,752	$ 81,376
Interest		$ 109,349	$ 100,806	$ 91,367	$ 80,940	$ 69,421	$ 56,696
Operating Expenses		$ 185,765	$ 191,524	$ 197,461	$ 203,582	$ 209,893	$ 216,400
TOTAL TAX REDUCTION		$ 673,603	$ 843,326	$ 662,055	$ 552,409	$ 550,460	$ 466,277
CHANGE IN CASH FLOW	$ (724,500)	$ (538,301)	$ (609,029)	$ (595,327)	$ (728,744)	$ (755,261)	$ (656,088)

TOTAL CASH FLOW	$ (4,607,280)	Cost Per Mile	(Average Annual Cost)	$ 767,800	$4.11
Cost Per Hour	$ 1,901		(Cruise Speed × Annual Hrs)	463 × 404	
Net Present Value Cost	$ (3,120,627)	Cost/Seat Mile	(Cost Per Mile)	$ 4.11	$0.59
			(Passenger seats)	7	

Explanatory Notes for Purchase Analysis
1) Loan balance payoff is $1,264,443 because three years remain on the financing period.
2) Depreciation method is double declining balance method. Basis is equal to 100% of $3,622,500.00 (acquisition cost).
3) Deductible expenses includes fixed cost, depreciation, interest, and operating expenses. All of these items have had a 3.1% inflation factor calculated in.
4) Cash received at sale is Aviation Supply's estimate that the Citation S/II sale value after six years will be 70%. This is $2,415,000.00 minus taxes of $941,850.
5) Total Cash Flow indicates the total after-tax cost of ownership for the Cessna Citation S/II over six years.
6) Cost Per Hour is the average annual after-tax cost per hour of owning and operating the Citation S/II over the six year period.
7) Present Value Cost is derived from the discount rate of 15%. It shows the actual cash amount (in today's dollars) of the total net cash flow.

Figure B-11. Citation S/II Cash Flow Analysis

The following cash flow analysis (shown under Figure B-11) is simply a breakdown of cost over the next six years. Starting with Total Expenditures, these represent all the costs to support the aircraft and are before the effects of taxes. The tax effect on Total Expenditures is shown under Total Tax Reduction. The change in Cash Flow represents the difference between Total Change (before taxes) and Total Tax Reduction. Finally, Total Cash Flow is the sum of all the Cash Flows over the six-year period. If you take this amount and divide it by the total six-year utilization, (2424 hrs.) you determine the Cost Per Hour. In this case, the Cessna Citation S/II will cost $1,901 per hour of use, over the next six years of operation.

VALUE ANALYSIS

In this section, we will show how the corporate aircraft can be a time machine. This is best illustrated when the corporate aircraft is compared to scheduled air carriers. The airlines operate on the basis of moving groups of people, on their timetable, and to predetermined locations. However, the principle behind a corporate aircraft is the flexibility to move individuals, or small groups, when and where they want to go.

In this comparison between the corporate aircraft and the scheduled air carriers, we have selected the trip between Tampa, Florida, and Bessemer, Alabama. Management Consultants has indicated that its personnel must travel 12 times a year into Bessemer, with an average of four persons per trip. Bessemer is located 15 miles southwest of Birmingham, the largest city that can support air carrier operations. As mentioned before, Bessemer can handle the Citation S/II during good weather only; during poor weather, Birmingham would be used. For this comparison, we are operating the corporate aircraft into Bessemer.

At the present, Delta Airlines cannot efficiently meet Management Consultants' requirements. Delta can have your four (4) executives in Burmingham by 8:23 a.m. by departing Tampa at 6:15 a.m. and having an unproductive one-hour layover in Atlanta. After arriving in Birmingham, your executives would hve to rent a car from Budget, Hertz, or National and drive to Bessemer for their 10:00 a.m. meeting. The driving time one way will be approximately 15 to 20 minutes under normal driving conditions. By our calculation, your executives would arrive one hour before the appointed time. We must also state that all our calculations are dependent upon the ability of the airline to provide an on-time schedule, which is not always the case.

According to Delta, on the return trip, the flight would depart at 7:50 p.m. This would give the executives two hours and fifty minutes waiting for the flight, boarding and flying to Atlanta for a one-hour and seven-minute wasteful layover, and finally arriving at Tampa around midnight. So, the total time of this trip would be 18 hours. We at Aviation Supply feel that this is too long a day to ask employees to work. We would recommend the executives stay overnight and fly back the next morning. However, by doing so, you would increase the cost for the trip. In this scenario, you can clearly see that the airline wastes your executives valuable time and also increases the cost of travel.

On the other side of the coin, the corporate aircraft can provide your company with a means of travel that would work to your schedule. With the same destination illustrated in the airline scenario, the Citation S/II can fly direct/non-stop to Bessemer. The airport at Bessemer is only four miles southeast of the city, a short taxi cab ride to the meeting place. After the meeting, the aircraft will leave once all four executives are onboard and will have them back in Tampa by 4:38 p.m. The total time involved in this trip is 9 hours and 38 minutes. This would be a reasonable amount of time for an executive to work. Plus you would not have the additional cost of hotel and car rental. The corporate aircraft can save your company time and this is illustrated in Figure B-12, Time Comparison (one leg).

As can be seen, the time saved by using the Citation S/II is a significant amount. More important than the time savings are the intangible factors. By using the Citation S/II, your executives, can fly in comfort, are productive while en route, avoid airline layovers, and can return to their families within the same day. The latter two reasons may very well influence the length of time these executives will stay at Management Consultants, Inc.

The Bessemer illustration is just one location Management Consultants must travel to. The same time saving can be found when comparing the other five cities your company executives must visit. The location of some of the other cities may lead one to believe that the airlines are not servicing the business people.

In addition to the time saving and the intangible benefits, you will find an analysis of the cost associated with flying the corporate aircraft versus the airline. Figures B-13 and B-14 will illustrate the true benefits of the corporate aircraft.

SUMMARY

In this report, we have shown you all of the considerations involved with the acquisition of a Cessna Citation S/II. We at Aviation Supply Inc. fully recommend this aircraft because the Cessna Citation S/II will meet the needs of your transportation requirements at the present time and also in the future. As explained, the Cessna Citation's hourly utilization for the first year is low (but within the limitations), however, it will increase with exposure.

Again, my team and I would like to thank you for allowing us to bring this important information to you. I am hopeful that the information will enable you to understand the positive benefits and the total impact of the Citation S/II to Management Consultants. I have enjoyed preparing this report for you and look forward to hearing from you soon.

	Tampa to Bessemer	
	Airline (Delta)	**Corporate Aircraft Citation S/II (6)**
1. Office to Airport	:20	:20
2. Terminal Boarding Checkin—Atlanta	1:30	:10
3. En route Time	1:38	1:04
4. Deplaning Time	:15	:10
5. Airport to Meeting	:26	:20
	4:09	2:04

NOTES:
1. Office to Airline (Delta)/Airport is the same.
2. :30 boarding time (require by airline per regulation) plus 1:00 layover at Atlanta.
5. Deplaning, check-out rent-a-car, and the drive to Bessemer from Birmingham.
6. No notes for the corporate aircraft side.

Figure B-12. Time Comparison (one leg)

AIRLINE (Delta)

1. *Ticket Cost*
   $499.00 × 96 Trips $47,904.00
   Less 39% Tax Savings   −18,682.56

   Total Cost of Airline Tickets $29,221.44

2. *Value Per Man Hour*

   $$VMH = \frac{\$120,000 \times 3.1}{2100} = \qquad \$ \quad 177.14$$

3. *Cost of Executive Time*
   4.15 hrs. × 96 trips × $177.14   70,572.58

4. *Productivity Credit (15%)*
   1.63 hrs. × 96 trips × 177.14 = $27,718.87
   Less 15% Productivity Factor =   −4,157.83

   Total Cost of Executive Time $66,414.75

5. *Other Business Expenses*
   Hotel (4 rooms × $95.00 × 12 times) $4,560.00
   Food ($45/man per day for 1.5 days × 12 times)   3,240.00
   Car (2 days @ $52/day × 12 times)   1,248.00

   Business Expenses   9,048.00
   Less 39% Tax Savings   −3,528.72

   Total Business Expenses $5,519.28

Airline Cost Summary:
   Total Ticket Costs $29,221.44
   Total Executive Time Cost $66,414.75
   Total Business Expenses $5,519.28

Total Cost for Airline $101,155.47

NOTES:
1. 96 Trips = 24 legs/year × 4 executives
2. $VMH = \dfrac{\text{Annual Salary} \times 3.1 \text{ (Support Factor)}}{42 \text{ hrs./week} \times 50 \text{ weeks/year}}$
3. 4.15 hours represents Total Trip Time.
4. 1.63 hours represents Actual Flight Time.
5. 12 times = 12 times/year to Bessemer.

Figure B-13. Tampa—Atlanta—Bessemer

CORPORATE AIRCRAFT (CITATION S/II)

1. *Aircraft Costs*
   $1,901.00/hr × 1.07 hrs. × 24 legs $48,817.68

2. *Cost of Executive Time*
   2.07 hrs. × 96 trips × $177.14 $35,201.26

3. *Productivity Credit (75%)*
   1.07 hrs. × 96 trips × $177.14 = $18,195.82
   Less 75% Productivity Factor =   −13,646.87

   Total Cost of Executive Time $21,554.40
   Corporate Aircraft (Citation S/II):

   Total Aircraft Cost $48,817.68
   Total Executive Time Cost   21,554.40

   Total Cost for Aircraft $70,372.08

Total Comparison
   Total Airline Cost $101,155.47
   Total Corporate Aircraft   70,372.08

   Savings/Year $30,783.39

   $1,282.64 Saved by Citation per Leg

NOTES:

1. $1,901.00 is the operating cost per hour.
2. 1.07 is the En Route Time.
3. 2.07 hours is the Total Trip Time.

Figure B-14. Tampa—Bessemer

Appendix C

FBO Marketing and Management Cases

PREPARING FOR CASE DISCUSSION

Appendix C includes 21 marketing and management related cases. They are intended to build on the material in the text, improve reasoning skills, and stimulate class discussions. The questions following each case are not intended to direct the discussion. They are there to help you analyze the case in advance and prepare for the discussion of it. There is no one "right" answer to a case problem. You should look for all possible solutions and select the one—or ones—most likely to succeed under existing conditions.

The marketing and management principles involved in a case are not limited to the suggested chapters in which they might be used. Job problems—and the cases describing them—are seldom limited to a single issue. The cases represent a wide variety of business situations and problems which required someone to make a decision. "Facts" of a case include opinions and inferences; they must be lined up and evaluated in a thorough and orderly manner. Don't jump to conclusions without digging deeply enough beneath the surface, without weighing the circumstances, or thinking through the results of proposed actions. If you want more data in the framework of a case, the thing to do is to make assumptions and evaluate their reasonableness.

Approach to be Used
1. Read the material carefully. Underline important data and statements.
2. In a sentence or two *identify the major problem* or key issue facing the individual or organization.
3. *List the most important facts* that relate to the problem or issue.
4. Read each question following the case.
5. Review the text. In particular, look for information pertaining to the case questions.
6. *Write up answers* to the questions *based on your analysis of the case.* Be sure your answers are not a summary of the case, but are analyses and recommendations.

Suggested Case(s) for Chapters

Case	Chapter
1. Marketing General Aviation Aircraft	1
2. Nationwide Air	3
3. Building Teamwork Among Management	4
4. Skyways, Inc.	4
5. Flightline Aviation School	4
6. AVMARK, Inc.	4
7. Crescent Air Center, Inc.	5
8. Proaero Interiors, Inc.	5
9. Harrison Flying Service	6
10. George's Aero Maintenance Service	6
11. FBO Marketing Promotions	6
12. Adams Aviation	7
13. Carolina Aero, Inc.	7
14. Pacific Jet Sales	7

1. CASE ANALYSIS—MARKETING GENERAL AVIATION AIRCRAFT

Howard Sellinger, senior vice president of marketing for one of the large general aviation aircraft manufacturers, had just delivered a speech before a convention of pilots. Sellinger's speech, to a group of nearly 200 people, was "The Bright Side of the Marketplace for General Aviation Aircraft" and dealt with the economy in the next several years and things the light aircraft manufacturers were doing to provide better aircraft to meet the needs of the business community.

During the question-and-answer session that followed the 45-minute talk, one gentleman impatiently called out for the mobile microphone. He commended Sellinger for the job his company was doing and for the interesting speech. "However," he said, "you have not been objective in your presentation because never once did you talk about the personal or fun-to-fly market. You marketers are forgetting the person who brought you to the dance. It was the weekend pilot who flew for business and pleasure purposes that bought thousands of your aircraft and represented your bread and butter market for a number of years. Now you have literally abandoned us by producing a few single-engine aircraft models and making them so expensive that many of us old timers have been priced out of the market. You have opened the door to foreign competition. As the man spoke, a number of affirmative nods indicated to Sellinger that the speaker was saying something the others believed. The gentleman continued.

"When are you going to give us what we want in product quality, service, warranties, truthful advertising, more reasonable prices, and more value? Now you force on us what you think is best. Well, how about making available for us what we really want? And, you know, you just might come out a lot better for it. Your products liability problem would not be as bad if you were selling 15,000 aircraft a year instead of 3,000. I understand that manufacturers have received little or no relief in product liability insurance premiums since the August 1994 enactment of the General Aviation Revitalization Act. Perhaps the real reason for the decline of the general aviation industry is the overpricing and overproduction of general aviation aircraft in the mid-1970s and 1980s, leaving an oversupply of suitable used aircraft."

"You marketers, and I am calling you one of them, Sellinger, only because it's every marketer's responsibility and not because I'm accusing you personally, but you marketers are all alike. Your main goals are to sell your product and make money. It doesn't really matter how you do it as long as the bottom line is acceptable, because that's how you measure success."

"I might be getting carried away, but between you people and the FAA, the private pilot like myself is either being expensed or legislated out of the skies. FAA rules, regulations, or avionics equipment required is forcing many business and pleasure pilots to curtail their flying or join the growing inactive ranks. As if you marketers and the FAA weren't enough, there are the small FBOs who are trying to stay alive in today's environment by gouging us with ever-rising prices. Mr. Sellinger! Do you know what some of us are paying to have our aircraft serviced and maintained at our local GA (general aviation) airport? Hangar and tie-down rates have become outrageous!

"Ah, well, I could go on and on. I've only hit on a few of the problems affecting the personal aircraft market. Where is the future of general aviation, Mr. Sellinger, if you abandon this market? What are you doing to increase the number of student starts? They are the very lifeblood of the industry. The bright side of the marketplace for general aviation aircraft. Bosh! C'mon, Mr. Sellinger, let's get with it and be more realistic instead of your dream world. You marketers are eternal optimists."

Sellinger, completely silent during the 5-minute oration, sensed he was on the spot and he knew he had to come up with a solid answer to the critic's attack on marketing general aviation aircraft.

QUESTIONS:
1. Do you agree with the critic's appraisal of the personal market? Why or why not?
2. What should Sellinger say in his rebuttal to the critic's charges?

2. CASE ANALYSIS—NATIONWIDE AIR

Jim Young had nursed his Personal Aviation Services, Inc. to a healthy fifth birthday at a large midwest airport, and was expanding into a full-service FBO. But to continue growing, he needed to stand out more—to be a place that people would recognize and go to instantly. He was seriously considering the possibility of acquiring a franchise with one of the new national aviation service chains.

Nationwide Air was formed in 1998 by a group of Texas oilmen at an FBO in the Houston area. By 2001, franchises were sold to 23 independently owned and operated FBOs in the United States and one in London and one in Frankfurt. The company plans to have a chain of 60 to 70 FBOs worldwide by 2005. The current franchised operators have a total of close to 100 airplanes, from single-engine and light twins to Lear jets and G-2s available for charter.

Nationwide Air projects itself as a chain of luxury FBOs aggressively marketed to charter customers and corporate operators of medium to large turbine aircraft. To retain that image, the company franchises only operations that meet specific standards. It must operate turbine equipment and meet certain other equipment and operating standards. The FBO has to be on a field with at least a 5,000-foot runway, it must have assets in excess of $2.5 million, and it must be in the top class of FBOs on the airport. Amenities must include a customer lounge, a pilot lounge, catering service, jet fuel, air charter, at least minor maintenance capability, and rental car or limousine service.

Standardization is enforced throughout the chain. FBOs not only must offer certain levels of service to join, but must conform to Nationwide Air's procedures for line service and maintenance operations and even policies on how much staffing the operation should have at any one time. Nationwide Air's staff of specialists visit each FBO periodically and conduct inspections and audits, making recommendations and offering job-specific training programs for everyone from line-service personnel and mechanics to pilots, accountants, and managers. All FBOs are provided a comprehensive operations manual that includes virtually every aspect of the operation, from pilot training records to customer service procedures.

The current franchise fee is about $60,000 and a prospective FBO must sign a contract agreeing to remain a Nationwide Air facility for at least 10 years. In addition to the franchise price, there is a $3,000 per month advertising/training fee that each facility pays. Nationwide Air also gets a percentage (from 10 to 15 percent) of the price of each charter it refers to them.

Young tried to sum up all of his positive and negative feelings concerning a franchise operation. On the positive side, he would acquire the advantages of a national chain while remaining independently owned and operated. Nationwide Air is a nationally recognized name that is advertised monthly in national corporate aviation magazines and other promotions. "There are thousands of no-name, unrecognizable facilities," Jim was quoted as saying. "When you are talking about the name Nationwide Air, you are talking about a full-service FBO, and that would enable me to maximize my market share on the airport."

Other advantages in becoming a Nationwide Air franchise include the economies of scale in buying everything from office supplies and insurance to fuel and aircraft parts, and customer referrals from Nationwide Air and other operators in the chain.

On the negative side, Jim Young is concerned about the franchise fee and particularly the $3,000 per month advertising/training fee. Virtually all of the advertising is national in scope with very little earmarked to promote individual local operators. Young also fears that in meeting the chain's standards, he may have to develop his facilities beyond what the business can support. He also feels that the 10 to 15 percent commission on referral character business may make his prices uncompetitive with other operators in the area.

QUESTIONS:
1. Do you foresee the continued growth of franchise FBOs? Why?
2. What recommendation would you give to Jim Young?

3. CASE ANALYSIS—BUILDING TEAMWORK AMONG MANAGEMENT

It is 9 a.m. and Bob is sitting at his desk staring out at the flight line over a stack of papers that represent last week's "to do" file. The receptionist is holding his calls, and he has postponed two afternoon appointments. He is wondering when and where his career took a wrong turn. He remembers the first day he started as a flight instructor. Although inexperienced and nervous, he survived those early years and worked his way up to flight department manager. A glance at Bob's office reveals impressive training certificates, several complimentary letters from customers, and commendations from FAA and NATA. More recently,

Bob won the company "Excellence in Management" award. Bob has always been a team player, and is becoming increasingly frustrated because the other managers are not.

Now, just minutes before he must attend the monthly department heads' meeting, he questions his career decision to become a manager. It isn't what he expected, and he feels unappreciated by the other managers. They have their own agendas and are very protective of their problem-solving ideas. Furthermore, their overall perception of the flight department is one of a "necessary evil." After all, their departments—not flight—rake in the profit. Bob remembers how much fun he had as a professional pilot and wonders why the relationship-building skills he developed as a professional pilot have been less than effective with his fellow department managers. Well, it's time to make that long walk down the hall to the conference room and endure another meaningless meeting. Maybe things will change!

John is located across the hangar and is the line services department manager. Unlike Bob, John is confident that he has found his career niche as a manager and has great expectations for the future of his department. This confidence is due in part to his ability to recognize and solve operational problems before they become exaggerated and uncontrollable. His dominant style keeps his peers and subordinates on their toes. It is not unusual for John to have one or two emotional explosions during meetings or problem-solving sessions with his line crew. He seems to enjoy the fear that he contributes to the work environment and views it as his protective mechanism. He often jokes with his peers about his management style. He boasts that this "style" has not been invented, and yet, he continues to operate a productive "taut ship." It is not his fault that one out of three people hired leaves his department before their fifth month. He just can't compete in such a tight labor market!

Bob and John have distinct management styles that are driven by different motives and career goals. Their management careers seem to be headed in separate directions that could leave the company and its employees in their wake. Bob and John represent a "snapshot" of the "management team" that consists of three additional department heads and a general manager. Is this company doomed? Will Bob find happiness? Will John shed his "Darth Vader" style? Will the other managers overcompensate for Bob's and John's deficiencies? How can this company continue to operate at historical levels of efficiency?

Their company, Blue Sky Flyers, has experienced a recent business downturn which has motivated senior management to review the company's management system and develop cost-containment strategies where necessary. To their surprise, they learned that their management team was actually poisoning their own and their subordinates' attitudes, motivation, and initiative. This was eating away at the company's "team spirit" and dragging productivity down. In summary, the operation was headed for a collision with unwanted problems and eroding profitability.

Blue Sky's situation is not uncommon among aviation retailers. Most operations have effective department managers who are skillful at producing a profit but may be less skilled at working with their peers and subordinates. The managers may have a tendency to "do it themselves" versus getting results through their staff or may have a tendency to reject peer group recommendations. In short, the manager may be too ego-involved. This type of ineffective teamwork exacts an indirect cost to the corporation. A company that is confronted with these critical issues should begin a comprehensive management development program that would improve interdepartmental cooperation, reduce employee turnover, and incorporate proven "team building" techniques.

Here are some reasons why a manager may not want to be a team player:

1. His or her basic behavioral predisposition may not require or desire constant interaction with a peer.
2. Positional and career insecurity—the individual may feel that "unshared knowledge" of his or her specific department creates job security.
3. May not understand his or her own goals and cannot relate to others who establish and attain goals.
4. May not have the ability to "hold on" to a goal, changing goals and directions numerous times during the year. This tendency preempts the desire to make group or team commitments.
5. He or she does not trust peers or senior management.
6. Fear of failing a team assignment.
7. Planning to resign.

QUESTIONS:

1. Why does Bob feel unappreciated by the other managers? If Bob's personal goal is to improve his relationship-building skills within his peer group, how can John adjust his dominant style and accommodate Bob's need to grow?
2. How can both managers work on joint projects and be productive while accommodating each other's career needs.
3. Effective "team building" requires each team participant to accept the teams' goals and objectives and take ownership for the results—good, bad, or indifferent. Do you agree? Why?
4. Why is it necessary for the general manager to perform a comprehensive review of the motives and goals of each

manager? Can senior management tolerate different management styles (like those of Bob and John) and still meet department and company goals?

4. CASE ANALYSIS—SKYWAYS, INC.

Skyways, Inc. recently celebrated its 40th year at Mid-America Regional Airport. Although the company is basically a fixed base operation, its main source of revenue has been aircraft sales and support to commuter, regional, and small overseas airlines. During its earlier years the company concentrated on purchasing packages of phased-out U.S. airline aircraft, and found secondary markets for them overseas.

In 1976, the company was appointed the North American distributor for a foreign manufacturer and support of its turboprop and jet aircraft.

Many owners, some traveling across the world, employ Skyways to update, standardize, or overhaul their aircraft. Recently two aircraft from Arabian American Oil Company in Saudi Arabia and one from Mobile Oil in Nigeria were overhauled. Skyways maintains a large inventory of parts. Some are purchased direct from the factory; others have been obtained through the purchase of airline inventories as they change equipment. The company is an official service center and the exclusive parts distribution center in the midwestern United States for a large U.S. aircraft manufacturer. There are over 30 mechanics and parts department staff to support these services.

Bryan Burns, manager of the line service department for Skyways, has 14 employees reporting to him. Servicing corporate and business and pleasure aircraft, Skyways pumps approximately two million gallons of fuel annually to a wide range of aircraft including jets.

There has been an increase in the amount of air carrier activity at Mid-America Regional Airport during the past year, and Burns has learned that two regional air carriers and one major carrier will be offering competitive bids for a fueling contract at the airport. He is quite excited about the prospect of servicing airliners and feels that it would be an excellent source of revenue at a time when aircraft sales are down and maintenance has leveled off.

Airlines typically purchase fuel directly from the oil companies and then negotiate a contract with an FBO for storage, inventory, and pumping into the aircraft. Fueling isn't the only on-ground airline business which may be available. Cleaning of aircraft and deicing services may also be contracted.

Only one other FBO on the airport is considering offering a bid, but it is a much smaller operation than Skyways. Burns has learned from airline fuel procurement personnel that the pumping fees generally run no higher than 25 cents per gallon, with hook-up fees ranging from $25–$50. Prices can vary, depending on whether fuel is pumped from a truck or hydrant, and price breaks are sometimes negotiated for volume service.

Burns estimates the cost of a used stainless steel, jet fuel truck at between $80,000 and $125,000, with new ones going as high as $300,000. Used deicing trucks can be bought for $50,000 and up, but an operator can expect to pay as much as $170,000 for a new unit. Trucks can also be leased from the fuel companies at significantly lower costs. Underground fuel tank costs are running up to $3.50 per gallon capacity (a 20,000 gallon storage tank capacity would cost about $70,000).

Besides expenditures for fuel storage facilities and ground handling equipment, servicing larger commercial aircraft requires an investment in line-worker training in accordance with FAA regulations. Once airlines award a contract, they generally provide additional training for FBO employees servicing their aircraft.

Servicing airlines would also mean hiring additional personnel. Another consideration would be the higher liability insurance costs as a result of working on larger, more expensive commercial aircraft. The possibility of getting the air carriers to assume part of the liability exists, but this would be subject to negotiation. However, some carriers require that the FBO provide its own coverage and limits of liability, sometimes with assistance from its fuel suppliers.

Burns has another concern regarding the financial stability of one of the regional carriers. He has heard of several situations where a carrier went bankrupt and the FBO was left in line with a considerable number of creditors. Despite the risks, he has also learned that servicing air carriers can provide a good source of revenue for FBOs. "It can provide a needed service for the airlines, plus it can help strengthen Skyways financially and our position within the community," Burns concluded.

QUESTIONS:
1. Do you think Skyways, Inc. should seriously consider entertaining an airline servicing contract at this time? Why?
2. In his meeting with air carrier personnel, what are some of the discussion items Burns should bring up before the bids are let?
3. How should Burns present his proposal to Skyways' management? Should he wait until the bids are let?

5. CASE ANALYSIS—FLIGHTLINE AVIATION SCHOOL

During general aviation's boom days of the 1960s and the 1970s, flight schools prospered, helped by the Veterans Administration's encouragement of aviation careers for vets and a growing economy. Affordable two- and four-place GA aircraft were being built and sold in record numbers, and the number of student pilots closely followed changes in the level of economic activity.

Things altered significantly during the 1980s. Student starts and the level of most flying activity plummeted in the early 1980s as the economy went into a recession. Despite an improving economy in recent years, many flight schools realize that a strong economy alone did not bring them students. Joanne Calabrese found herself in that position in early 2001 as manager of Flightline Aviation School, a flight training facility located at a small GA airport outside of a major southeastern metropolitan area. In her early thirties, Joanne made a career change four years ago after working for a management consulting firm for five years after college. Working as a flight instructor and charter pilot for Flightline and several other firms in the area, she was a highly motivated, hard working individual.

Flightline operates all current model aircraft, none more than twenty-five years old, with a total of 13 aircraft available for training. These range from Cessna 152 to 421 aircraft. All but the 414 and the 421 are used exclusively for training. Those larger twins also are used for charter and Part 135 operations. The flight school operates 24 hours a day, 7 days a week. There are five full-time CFIs reporting to Calabrese, including chief instructor, Tom Correa, a young, personable, and aggressive CFI with three years' experience. These individuals are augmented by two part-time instructors who work on weekends. There are presently around 100 active students including 35 or so working for private licenses. Most of the others are pursuing commercial licenses and instrument ratings. Only six or seven are going for an ATP rating.

Calabrese feels very strongly that if you are going to sell anything, including flight training, you have to develop a professional marketing campaign and hire a professional to direct it. Nine months ago she hired Lori Kligfeld, a person with a number of years of marketing and sales experience for a major business machine manufacturer.

"Lori knew nothing about aviation when I took her on," explained Calabrese, "but she knew sales and marketing, and being a quick study, got a handle on aviation in record time. She came aboard full-time and in addition to salary gets a commission on sales-flight training as well as aircraft."

One of Kligfeld's first projects was to develop a very attractive brochure-mailer which provided basic information on what Flightline offers and a brief questionnaire on the back of a postage-paid business reply card. This was used in a mail campaign directed at 1,500 area pilots holding a wide variety of licenses and ratings. No effort was made to reach and attract new pilots. The list represented, in Kligfeld's view, "people who already had decided they could afford to learn to fly or upgrade their licenses." The response was very good and resulted in a number of sales.

Next came a continuing newspaper/magazine advertising campaign. The major daily newspaper in the area topped the media list. Beyond that, media were very carefully selected on the theory that the advertising message should be exposed to "people who can afford to fly." For example, advertising was placed in particular affluent community newspapers. The local chamber of commerce magazine drew a good response. It was also at Kligfeld's suggestion that Flightline initiate a $35 demonstration lesson for prospective students which includes a thorough half-hour of ground indoctrination, student participation in the preflight inspection, and a 30- to 40-minute flight with the prospect in the left seat. This has been very successful and the school now gives these demo lessons at the rate of almost one a day. The program resulted in six new students the first month. To sustain a prospect's interest in lessons after the introductory flight, Flightline offers a book of $575 worth of coupons that can be used for flight training for only $500 which represents a 15 percent discount. Kligfeld also uses the monthly billing statements to notify customers of promotional activities, such as upcoming ground schools or special discount plane rental rates.

In a recent meeting with Calabrese and Correa, Kligfeld outlined some of her plans for the next year which include the following:

1. Four jointly sponsored aviation seminars aimed at promoting safety. Manufacturers representatives, FAA personnel, and local aviation organizations (such as the 99s, Civil Air Patrol, or pilots association) would participate.
2. Conducting a series of guided tours of the facility and airport for various nonaviation groups. (She feels this can intensify the interest in someone who has always had a desire to fly but has never followed up on it.)
3. Providing guest speakers for area high school career days.
4. Sponsoring a youth aviation program. Flightline could either assume responsibility for an already developed program (such as Explorer Scouts, Experimental Aircraft Association, or Civil Air Patrol Cadets), or create a new program for one of these or other local youth groups.

5. Sponsoring a flying club to promote flight training and aircraft rental.
6. Encouraging flight instructors to become active members of local business, and fraternal and aviation organizations.
7. Working with airport officials to hold an air show during the summer.
8. Maintaining a close relationship with a nearby community college's flight department—either by providing adjunct instructors or serving in an advisory capacity.

Lori Kligfeld would like to see Tom Correa and the other full-time flight instructors take a much more active role in the marketing game plan. Although Calabrese is in favor of it, Correa has some reservations and has already received some negative feedback from two of his instructors. "I was hired as a flight instructor, not a sales representative," one was overheard to say. Another expressed his concern to Correa regarding the time commitment to participate in the activities which Kligfeld has outlined. "It sounds like she wants us to work harder to increase her commission. Frankly, I'd rather fly airplanes than attend business luncheons, give speeches to high school students, or conduct tours."

Tom Correa is now faced with the task of formulating a response to Joanne Calabrese regarding Lori Kligfeld's plans. He knows Joanne is in favor of the program and Lori has done an exceptional job in generating new business during the past year. On the other hand, he can appreciate some of the concerns expressed by his instructors and wonders if Lori, with her limited aviation background, really understands their role as flight instructors.

QUESTIONS:

1. Why do you think the flight instructors feel the way they do? What might be done to activate their interest and get them involved in Kligfeld's plans?
2. Formulate a response for Tom Correa to Joanne Calabrese regarding the participation of his instructors in the marketing game plan.
3. Is a separate marketing person really needed or could this function be handled by Calabrese or Correa?

6. CASE ANALYSIS—AVMARK, INC.

Al Rott is a supervisor in the engine overhaul department of a large FBO in the Midwest. Al's particular unit of 15 maintenance technicians is responsible for repairing and overhauling turbine engines primarily for corporate operators.

At almost 6:30 p.m. on a Friday night, over two hours past his usual time to leave for home, Al was in his office, looking out the window with a very concerned expression on his face, trying to remember and understand what happened over the last two months. His first thoughts recall the three-day supervisory training program he attended some eight weeks ago at a nearby university management-development center. The program covered many topics, from communications to understanding motivation.

The most vivid experience was a session on leadership, when he completed a questionnaire that was supposed to measure his style of leadership on two dimensions: task orientation and employee orientation. The results, which showed him to be very high on task orientation but very low on employee orientation, were a surprise to him because he always thought of himself as being pretty much people centered on the job. He also recalled the seminar leader suggesting that the most effective leadership style was one that was high on both task orientation and employee orientation.

This leadership session was of particular importance to Al because of the problems he was having in his department. The busy spring season was just around the corner, which meant a big productivity push by management to handle the increased flow of business experienced at that time of year. His technicians could be divided almost equally into two groups: those who performed at 100 percent of hourly standards or above as set by the engine manufacturers, and those who rarely exceeded 85 percent of standards.

Two technicians were key examples of these two groups. First, there was Ralph Hansen, who worked as a lead technician and inspector for the last four years. Ralph was dependable, quality conscious, and always performed between 100 percent and 110 percent of standards. On the other hand, there was George Mehallis, another lead technician, who had been employed at Avmark for almost three years. In Al's opinion, George spent too much time socializing with other technicians and being the first one out the door at 4:00 p.m. each day. His performance rarely exceeded 80 percent of standards. Several times, Al had strongly warned George about his lack of attention to his work and his performance. These warnings usually had an effect for a few days, but then his old ways returned. George was not the only one who received these warnings from Al.

The supervisory training program convinced Al that what he needed to do to improve the performance of his technicians was to increase his employee-oriented behavior and attempt to be high on each style dimension. He made a special point to be more open and friendly to George and other low performers, to take more interest in George's personal life, and try to be more sympathetic about the increased emphasis on performance.

As Al sat looking out the window, he was both dismayed and puzzled. His attempt at being more employee oriented was a flop. Not only had George's performance not changed, but many technicians, including Ralph Hansen, were performing under 90 percent of standards. With the busy season just beginning, his supervisor, the department manager, and even the general manager were on his back to improve his department's performance. He sat there wondering what to do next.

QUESTIONS:
1. Evaluate Al's experience at the supervisory training program.
2. Why was his attempt to be more "employee oriented" a failure?
3. What change in Al's leadership behavior is needed to improve the performance of his department?

7. CASE ANALYSIS—CRESCENT AIR CENTER, INC.

Tim Gauntt is working as a charter pilot and aircraft sales representative for a large FBO located at a very active general aviation airport, which is also served by several regional air carriers. A college graduate with a flight and aviation management background, Tim has been with this firm for four years and has developed a good rapport with the local business community. Last year's salary and commission came to a little over $38,000. He expects a slight increase this year but doesn't see much long-run opportunity with this company. As a result, he is seriously considering changing jobs and investing $45,000 in Crescent Air Center, Inc.—an established FBO located at a similar GA airport in the next county. There is no carrier activity at this airport, but this county's population and business development is expanding faster than any of the neighboring counties. Sam DeGrego, the present owner, is nearing retirement and has not developed anyone to run the business. He has agreed to sell the business to Jim Rice, a lawyer-entrepreneur, who has invited Tim to invest and become general manager. Mr. Rice has agreed to give Tim his current salary plus a company car and 1 percent of profits. However, Tim must invest to become part of the new company. He will obtain a 5 percent interest in the business for this $45,000 investment.

Crescent Air Center's sales last year amounted to a little over $1.7 million, broken down as follows: aircraft sales, $755,000; maintenance and parts, $380,000; line service (primarily fuel sales), $315,000; flight training, $205,000; and charter and rental, $75,000. The company bearly broke even (after paying Mr. DeGrego a salary of $60,000). The company has not made a profit for several years, but has continually upgraded its facilities and training aircraft which are relatively new.

Financially, the company seems to be in fairly good condition—at least as far as book value is concerned. The $45,000 investment would buy approximately $60,000 in assets, and ongoing operations should pay off the seven-year note. The balance sheet as of December 31, 200X was as follows:

Assets (thousands)			Liabilities and Net Worth (thousands)		
Cash		$ 33	Liabilities:		
Accounts Receivable		80	Accounts Payable		$ 94
Hangar and Office	$155		Notes Payable—		
less depreciation	80		7 years (aircraft)		265
		75			
Aircraft	$1,500		Net Worth:		
less depreciation	510		Capital Stock		810
		990	Retained Earnings		9
Total assets		$1,178	Total Liabilities and Net Worth		$1,178

Mr. Rice feels that—with younger, aggressive new management—the company has a real opportunity for profit. He has no plans to make any staff changes at this time but will await Tim's recommendations in this regard. The major thrust will be to develop the new and used aircraft sales business. He would also like to build up the company's charter business and attract more maintenance work, particularly corporate multiengine accounts. There is tough competition in these markets from other FBOs in the area.

QUESTIONS:

1. Considering the status of the general aviation industry today, evaluate Jim Rice's marketing strategy.
2. How would you advise Tim Gauntt? Explain your reasoning.

8. CASE ANALYSIS—PROAERO INTERIORS, INC.

Proaero Interiors, Inc., a small aircraft refurbishing company located at Klingman Field on the east coast of Georgia, was organized by Bill Nason in 1985. Nason managed the firm until 1995, at which time he found that other business matters required most of his time. In March 1995, Bob Schuster, vice president of one of Proaero's competitors, was brought in as president and given complete responsibility for the operations of Proaero Interiors. Proaero's work included cabinet modifications and installations, upholstering, carpet work, aircraft painting, avionics upgrading, and light maintenance.

Since almost 60 percent of Proaero's sales were generated during the fall and winter seasons because of the decreased flying activity, the company had been following a similar pattern incurring costs for supplies. One of Schuster's first decisions was to change this practice by attempting to increase sales during the spring and summer months so that Proaero serviced customers at an even rate throughout the year. A second decision Schuster made was to change Nason's banking connections to Security National Bank. Primarily because Nason frequently carried large cash balances, Security National had actively sought the account for two years prior to 1995. Although Schuster agreed to move Proaero's account to Security National, he was able to reduce the size of Proaero's cash balances significantly without adversely affecting operations.

One result of these changes was that Schuster found it necessary to borrow from Security National Bank prior to each of the big selling seasons. The loans were on a short-term basis, with the proceeds being used to increase inventory in anticipation of increased sales. The loans were made under a line of credit arrangement whereby the bank agreed to lend Proaero funds as they were needed up to a total of $110,000. The loan agreement stated, however, that total borrowing under the credit line must be retired after each selling season before Proaero started borrowing to build up inventory for the next selling season. Proaero had been taking full advantage of this line of credit, and until recently, the company had been able to repay the loan in full before the next inventory buildup.

In late July 2001, Proaero began building up inventory for the 2001 fall and winter season. On August 5, Proaero used the first $30,000 of its line of credit to buy raw materials. By November 1, 2001, the company had borrowed a total of $108,000, and it was completing its fall season and making plans for the late winter season. Schuster knew that if Proaero wanted to borrow again for the next inventory buildup, it would have to repay this $108,000. Before 2000, Proaero had been able to convert its inventory and accounts receivable into enough cash rapidly enough so that by November 30 the short-term loan was completely paid off. Since Proaero used a fiscal year that ended on November 30 rather than a calendar year, the bank loans did not normally appear on any of the company's annual financial statements. This, of course, made the company's ratios look better than would have been the case had the books been closed on December 31. However, in the years ending November 30, 2000, and November 30, 2001, Proaero was not able to repay the entire amount by November 30 (see Figure C-1).

Following the 2001 fall season, Proaero found itself with a relatively large unsold inventory. Because of this, the company was only able to repay $10,000 of its $108,000 loan by November 30. It was also having difficulty meeting its accounts payable obligations. Schuster believed these problems stemmed from the fact that, for the first time in Proaero's history, the company had failed to adjust rapidly enough to the decline in business aircraft sales. As a result, Proaero's fall-winter sales were significantly below previous levels for this season.

Schuster decided that because sales in the next month and a half would not generate enough cash to repay the loan, some additional equity capital was needed. The Nason family agreed to supply this capital, and Schuster used part of the funds to repay the entire loan by January 5, 2002. Although the accounts payable balance remained higher than usual, it was reduced by $22,000.

In early February of every year, Schuster renewed with the bank the $110,000 line of credit for the coming fiscal year. Renewal was usually automatic. On February 2, 2002, Schuster made an appointment to see Ursula Davidson, who has handled the Proaero account at Security since 1998. Schuster was interested in increasing the credit line to $150,000, with the additional $40,000 to be used to reduce past-due accounts payable.

In the year since Schuster last visited the bank, the Federal Reserve System, in an effort to keep inflation under control, had tightened credit conditions. This tight money situation prompted Security National Bank to review critically all existing loans and to grant credit increases only on an exception basis.

Before the February 2nd meeting, Davidson examined Proaero's operating statements for the last three years (see Figures C-1 and C-2). She noted that Proaero's profits had declined while total assets had increased. She also noted that Proaero had

PROAERO INTERIORS, INC.
Balance Sheet
November 30, 2001[a]

	1999	2000	2001
Cash	$ 22,000	$ 14,000	$ 12,000
Accounts receivable	90,000	100,000	130,000
Inventory	105,000	180,000	300,000
Total current assets	$217,000	$294,000	$442,000
Land and building	24,000	40,000	70,000
Equipment	54,000	59,000	77,000
Other asset	1,500	800	100
Total assets	$296,500	$393,800	$589,100
Notes payable, bank	—	$ 39,000	$ 98,000
Accounts payable	$ 60,000	90,000	185,000
Accruals	18,000	22,300	31,600
Total current liabilities	$ 78,000	$151,300	$314,600
Mortgage	17,000	16,000	15,000
Common stock	75,000	75,000	75,000
Paid-in surplus	60,000	60,000	60,000
Retained earnings	66,500	91,500	124,500
Total liability and equity	$296,500	$393,800	$589,100

[a] Proaero follows a December 1 to November 30 fiscal year.

Figure C-1. Balance Sheet for Proaero Interiors, Inc.

PROAERO INTERIORS, INC.
Income Statement (in thousands)
November 30, 2001

	1999	2000	2001
Income	$975	$1,013	$1,020
Cost of goods sold	794	815	824
Gross profit	$181	$ 198	$ 197
General and selling expenses	75	80	83
Depreciation	8	9	13
Interest	8	8	9
Other	15	20	24
Income before taxes	$ 75	81	$ 67
Taxes (34%)	26	27	23
Net income	$ 49	$ 54	$ 44

Figure C-2. Income Statement for Proaero Interiors, Inc.

become a slow-paying account. Most of Proaero's suppliers offered a 2 percent cash discount on all bills paid within 10 days, but Proaero was unable to take advantage of this discount.

At the meeting with Davidson on February 2, 2002, Schuster explained that Proaero had misjudged the market that fall and that the resulting sales decrease was the cause of the company's problems. He also mentioned that personnel changes had been made to ensure that such misjudgments would not occur again.

Davidson told Schuster that although this sales decline might be causing some of Proaero's working capital problems, she believed that the major problem was that Proaero was expanding its investment in assets too quickly. As Davidson saw it, the crisis following the fall season—the one that Schuster had solved by increasing paid-in equity capital—was the inevitable result of too rapid an expansion over the last few years. The recent purchase of new equipment worth $25,000 and the purchase of one of the buildings which Proaero had been renting were given as two examples of actions that were creating an excessive cash drain on the firm. Davidson told Schuster that, considering tight credit conditions and her feeling about Proaero's recent troubles, she would have to consider carefully both the $110,000 credit line and the request to increase the line by $40,000. She said that more analysis would be necessary and that she would inform Schuster of Security National's final decision within the next two weeks.

QUESTIONS:

1. Calculate the key financial ratios for Proaero and, based on these ratios, give a brief summary of Proaero's financial condition.
2. What factors have caused the firm's declining liquidity?
3. What factors have caused the declining return on total assets?
4. What action should Davidson take concerning Proaero's request for a $150,000 line of unsecured credit?
5. Assuming the bank turned down the application to increase the credit line, what adjustments, if any, could you suggest that might make the new loan acceptable?

9. CASE ANALYSIS—HARRISON FLYING SERVICE

Harrison Flying Service was the oldest flight school in Midland County which was served by three general aviation airports. Located at the most active of the three fields, the company had an established reputation for having quality instructors, well-maintained aircraft, and personal attention. Wayne Harrison, the president and owner, his chief pilot, Jan Bussel, and the three instructors knew most customers by name and relied on personal contacts to maintain a steady growing business. New housing and apartment developments led to a rapid expansion in population in the last five years, and new businesses were moving into the growing market. Within the past six months, Arrow Air, formerly based at the major air carrier airport serving the area, has moved to the GA airport where Harrison is located. For the first time, Harrison found himself faced with a tough competitor for new accounts.

Arrow air launched a strong marketing campaign that offered newer aircraft, ATC single-engine simulators, and a comprehensive self-paced ground school learning program. Flying hour rates for comparable aircraft were slightly higher than Harrison's. Harrison was convinced that he had to develop some new services and then launch an advertising campaign to convince potential customers that his flying school could meet their particular needs with a convenient package of services.

What little advertising Harrison Flying Service had done in the past had been a combined effort with the local radio station or newspaper. No advertising agency had been used, and no thought was being given to using one this time. Harrison decided on a campaign with the theme "Whatever your flying goals—Harrison Flying Service will help you achieve them." He thought the ads should feature brief descriptions of individuals with goals and how they achieved them by taking flight training at Harrison Flying Service. He believed that by treating each customer as an individual with an individualized goal, he could attract new customers on the basis of a more personal approach. It would be a way, he reasoned, of showing that Harrison recognized that not all people come to a flight school for the same reasons.

QUESTIONS:

1. Identify the different market segments that Harrison might serve.
2. List several different types of individuals whose "goals" could be featured in the advertisement.
3. What appeals should be used?
4. Does it make sense to segment the market for flying services?

10. CASE ANALYSIS—GEORGE'S AERO MAINTENANCE SERVICE

Two years ago, Bill George bought the inventory, equipment, and business of Central Florida Aircraft Maintenance Company and moved into an old hangar located at Wilton Beach Airport, an active GA field on the southeast coast of Florida. A 28-year-old former navy mechanic, Bill had earned his Airframe and Powerplant (A & P) license and an Associate Degree in Aviation Maintenance Technology while in the service.

One of the reasons Bill wanted to establish an aircraft maintenance facility was his past work experience. From the time he was 17, Bill had worked for Al Hraba either part-time or full-time except for his four years in the navy. Mr. Hraba operated Wilton Beach Aviation, a very successful facility, offering maintenance and line service including fueling to a wide range of corporate and individual customers operating all types of aircraft including jets. There are two other full-service FBOs located at Wilton Beach Airport and it is rumored that one is near bankruptcy. Both of these companies have small maintenance departments which primarily concentrate on their own aircraft and a few single and light multiengine aircraft operated by their customers. Neither company has been very aggressive in seeking new business, and as a result, Mr. Hraba's has been the dominant facility at the airport.

Mr. Hraba prides himself on quality service and has a loyal clientele. Specializing in corporate and business aircraft, Hraba has built a strong customer following. For 35 years, Hraba's major source of new business has been satisfied customers who tell others about his quality service. Wilton Beach Aviation is so highly thought of that it is listed on the NBAA's list of recommended facilities in the area.

Bill George felt that he knew the maintenance business as well as Mr. Hraba, having worked for him many years. Bill was anxious to reach his $250,000 per year sales objective because he thought this would provide him a comfortable living in Wilton Beach. As he saw it, his only opportunity was direct competition with Hraba. In addition to an advertisement in the yellow pages, Bill had done some advertising in the local newspapers.

Bill had developed a small clientele and was now grossing about $3,000 a week. He had, of course, expected that the business would grow much more and that he would be able to hire additional personnel after a year or so. Some of Bill's customers were Hraba's regulars who, for one reason or another, needed immediate work done which Hraba couldn't handle. While these people knew Bill and had confidence in his work, they preferred Hraba's "quality-care" image and experience. Bill had also picked up some work from several local flying clubs, a banner towing service, and a new flight training school with no maintenance facility. Sometimes, Bill did get more work than he could manage. This happened during the winter months when there was considerable corporate activity at Wilton Beach Aviation, and Bill received the overflow business which was primarily single and light multiengine aircraft.

After about a year and a half in business, Bill began to think about quitting. While he hated to think about losing his investment and leaving Wilton Beach, he couldn't see any way of competing against Al Hraba.

QUESTIONS:
1. Why wasn't Bill able to reach his objective of $250,000?
2. Do you think Bill should continue to stay in business at Wilton Beach airport?

11. CASE ANALYSIS—FBO MARKETING PROMOTIONS

Intelligent, innovative marketing is often the difference between succeeding as a fixed base operator and merely struggling each day to exist.

Successful marketers do much more than advertise. They create impressions. Good ones. They use every means at their disposal—from the neatness of their shops to the quality of their services, from the appearance of the mechanics to the display of their merchandise—to lure customers into their business establishment and keep them coming back. In many ways, they may be exactly like their less successful counterparts, but they *seem* different.

Shortly after I graduated from Hempstead High School in Hempstead, New York, in 1953, I made the decision I wanted to fly, so I went to a fixed base operator at Zahn's airport in Amityville, New York.

When I arrived at the FBO, I was somewhat surprised to find a guy sitting behind the counter wearing a baseball cap with a pair of wings stuck through the bill, a dirty sweat shirt, and a dirty pair of khaki trousers. He had at least a one-day growth of beard.

Without leaving his chair, he looked up at me and asked, "What do you want?"

I told him I wanted to learn to fly, and he said, "Why?" So I told him. He listed to my youthful reasons—I was full of excitement and a sense of adventure—and he finally agreed to teach me.

He did, in fact, teach me to fly, though it seemed to cause him a great deal of pain and anguish. I remember vividly his shouting from the back seat of his Piper J-3 Cub that my mother and father were never married, along with a number of other unsavory comments.

Today, fortunately, we've grown a long way from that style of doing business. In 1953, marketing in aviation practically was nonexistent. Marketing, back them, was an approach of *ready, fire, . . . aim.*

The marketing we talk about today is really an umbrella word. It includes not only advertising, but public relations, sales promotions, and merchandising concepts.

In effect, marketing is everything you do up to, but not including, making the sale. Many fixed base operators do an excellent job of marketing their services. Some examples are as follows:

Merchandising

A Columbus, Ohio, dealer has turned a large lobby into a merchandising area. When walk-in trade comes through the lobby, they see on display spark plugs, oil filters, vacuum pumps, batteries, tires—all virtually stacked to the ceiling. This FBO relies on the premise that if someone comes in to buy a couple of sick sacks, he or she also will have the opportunity to buy a couple of new tires, a box of spark plugs, or maybe even a new engine. This is, of course, exaggerated, but the FBO's merchandising concept has improved parts sales dramatically. The FBO operates under the correct supposition that if a product is out of sight, it is out of mind.

The Giveaway

Another fixed base operator in South Dakota wanted to improve and increase shop work. The operator had an oil change promotion in which a customer who bought an oil change received a free videotape on World War II fighter aircraft. Shell Oil Co. sold the FBO the oil and provided the tapes, so all the FBO had to do was come up with a creative brochure to mail to his customer base.

The object was to bring more customers in, which the promotion did. But, more important, the operator had the opportunity to talk to these new customers about additional maintenance, such as annual inspection, adding more avionics to their radio package, or replacing a tire that looked worn.

The Cooperative Arrangement

Another FBO, this one in Michigan, decided to improve parts sales through a sales promotion program. The parts manager made a spark plug, oil filter, and igniter program his first promotion. He contacted distributors, explained what he wanted to do, and told them he would be buying a large quantity of these products. He wanted the best price available and asked if they would accept returned unused inventory without the customary restocking charge.

It wasn't hard for the parts manager to find a distributor willing to work with him and help him in developing the specifics of a sales promotion program. The promotion was something to the effect of "Buy a box of spark plugs and receive a free buck knife, or buy two boxes and receive a winter vest, etc."

The outcome of the promotion was phenomenal. The operator had an 80 percent increase in spark plug sales, a 79 percent increase in oil filter sales, and a 60 percent increase in igniter sales. The company ended up having to buy additional merchandising aids and products for the sales promotion.

The FBO wanted to advertise its parts department with its excellent inventory of general aviation parts and products. This company now has a walk-in trade it never had before, and all its competitors know it is in business.

Video Promotion

Another FBO in West Virginia conquered the problem of advertising by deciding to have a first-class engine overhaul shop. The FBO had a flight school, a charter service, a maintenance facility, line service, etc., but recognized it had to have something different to attract business into the shop.

Along with advertising, the FBO decided to develop a videotape. The FBO went to the local television station and explained its objectives and limited budget. It just so happened the station had an instructional program with a local college. The FBO was able to tie the two programs together to produce the tape—a step-by-step presentation on how the company's technicians overhaul the engine, what it looks like inside and what it will look like on the outside when it's done. The FBO sent the tape free to any prospective customer considering an overhaul.

And did the program work! Many customers told the company they'd never seen the inside of an engine and had no idea what went on in an engine overhaul. The videotape not only vividly described an overhaul, but it detailed other facets of the FBO's operation, including its charter, flight training, and maintenance services.

QUESTIONS:

1. There are a tremendous number of things an operator can do to help develop and support a broader customer base without spending a lot of money. Put on your marketing hat and see how many innovative promotions you can come up with for a medium-sized FBO with a limited budget.

12. CASE ANALYSIS—ADAMS AVIATION

Hugh Adams has been operating Adams Aviation, a full-service FBO for 15 years and has slowly built revenues to $4 million a year. Operating from a busy GA airport located about 40 miles from a midwestern metropolitan area with over 2 million people, Adams serves a wide variety of individuals and businesses.

During the past two years, flight school enrollments have leveled off even though the number of new students continues to increase. The reason lies in the fact that an equal number of students are dropping out of the flight training program. Virtually all of the individuals who dropped out were working towards their private pilot's license. Some of them eventually come back but most do not. Adams feels that his prices are competitive with other operators in the area, and all of his equipment flown by students is under 15 years old. His facilities are considered to be the best in the area and while there has been a greater than normal attrition in flight instructors as a result of airline hiring, the quality has not diminished in recent years. In fact, Adams Aviation instructors are considered to be very professional by most people in the local aviation community.

Because of the student dropout problem, Adams recently conducted a telephone survey of 131 former students (those who had received at least 5 hours of dual instruction) and obtained responses from 60 as to why they dropped out (see Table C-1).

Responses were categorized into five areas: (1) too expensive, (2) lost interest, (3) too much work, (4) another operator, and (5) personal. Typical responses under each category were as follows:

1. *Too expensive*—"More expensive than I anticipated," "I ran out of money," "Other commitments took priority money-wise."
2. *Lost interest*—"It wasn't as exciting after a while," "I realized that it was not for me," "My instructor suggested that I fly more regularly to maintain proficiency."
3. *Too much work*—"The ground instruction was too difficult," "It was more work than I expected," "I could not devote the time that was necessary."
4. *Another operator*—"Flying Hours were less at _____ Flying Service," "My friend is giving me instructions in his aircraft," "I liked the instructors better at _____ Flying Service."
5. *Personal*—"My career plans changed," "I am planning to move from the area," "The timing was wrong but I expect to come back in the future."

Table C-1 Responses from Student Pilots Who Dropped Flight Training after 5 Hours of Dual Instruction in 20XX

Age:	Under 25		25-to-40		Over 40		Total	
Total Number:	67		36		28		131	
Number Responding:	31		14		15		60	
Percentage:	46.3%		38.9%		53.6%		45.8%	
Dropped Out:	BS*	AS*	BS	AS	BS	AS	BS	AS
Responses								
1. Too expensive	4	7	2	2	0	1	6	10
2. Lost interest	1	3	1	2	2	3	4	8
3. Too much work	3	6	2	4	3	4	8	14
4. Another operator	1	3	0	0	1	0	2	3
5. Personal	1	2	0	1	1	0	2	3
Total:	10	21	5	9	7	8	22	38

*BS—Before solo
*AS—After solo

Hugh Adams planned to meet with his flight instructors on Saturday morning to discuss the results of the survey and to get their ideas as to what might be done to improve the situation. One thing he intended to suggest is the acquisition of some self-paced learning aids to address the problem of ground training. Until now the only formalized ground training was a series of 10-week evening courses which were held periodically throughout the year. He was also aware that the instructors would probably bring up the idea of obtaining a flight simulator which they had discussed quite frequently.

QUESTIONS:

1. Evaluate Mr. Adams's thinking. What would you advise him to do based on the results of the survey?
2. Is this a good way to determine why students have dropped out of training? Can you think of any alternative methods?

13. CASE ANALYSIS—CAROLINA AERO, INC.

Carolina Aero is a full-service FBO with more than 100 employees, a large flight department, line service, and airframe and engine repair shop. It services everything from Cessna 172s to Piper Malibus and Cessna Citations. The repair facility, with 16,000 square feet of floor space, is a Pratt & Whitney and Caravan service center.

The company is a departmentalized operation, and each sector of the business gets a written summary of income and expenses, broken down by month and year-to-date. The responsibility for turning a profit in the service department rests on the shoulders of Jim Louganis, maintenance director.

"We operate on the premise that if you don't know your costs, there is no way you can control them," says the 43-year-old department head. "Right now, maintenance yields one of the company's best profit margins figured as a percentage of gross income."

Repair business is growing. Only seven years ago, Louganis's department grossed about $800,000. This year it should land close to $1.45 million, a commendable 80 percent growth rate. Repair billings now contribute about 25 percent of Carolina Aero's total gross sales.

"I used to work for an FBO that believed the only department that mattered was sales," explained Louganis. "The rest of us were there just to support sales. Today, new airplanes are not selling and flight school activity is down. However, people are still out there flying, and as airplanes get older, they need more repairs."

Carolina's hourly charges are very competitive with other FBOs in the area. Larger airplanes appear to net more repair dollars for the FBO, in part because Louganis demands the same quality work on a 172 as he does on a Citation. No corners are cut, and a perfect safety record of no injury accidents due to accountable mechanical failures is evident. Employee costs are held to about one-third of billable shop charges. This doesn't include fringe benefits, which add about 25 percent to employee costs. Experience has also proven that a one-to-three ratio of supervisors to mechanics is ideal.

Louganis is also very particular about the individuals he hires and their appearance in the hangar. Tough standards have created difficult times for the department head. "We operate the shop 16 hours a day and keep it plenty busy," he points out, "but we used to run three shifts and still have considerable overtime. The problem is finding qualified people, particularly supervisory personnel, to staff a third shift. We've found running extra shifts helps reduce expensive overtime and can be quite profitable since most of our overhead is already covered by the first shift."

Louganis prefers hiring airframe and power plant licensed mechanics (A&Ps) with some general aviation experience because inexperienced personnel are not especially productive during their first two years. During that time, he has them move airplanes, care for shop equipment, and assist mechanics when practical. Recently, Carolina Aero has lost some of the newer mechanics to the major air carriers which offer an attractive wage and fringe benefit package. "I haven't lost any of my experienced people to the airlines," he states. "Several have been here more than 10 years, and overall, our experience level is between six and seven years." Louganis himself joined Carolina Aero as a mechanic in 1984, one year after the business was founded.

With two shifts and 16 mechanics, the maintenance department handles between 200 and 300 work orders per month. The first shift ends at 4:30 p.m. and the second one begins at 4 p.m., permitting an orderly transition for unfinished jobs. A shop foreman is assigned to each shift, who schedules work, orders parts, and troubleshoots for the staff. Carolina Aero owns most test equipment, which Louganis figures is valued at more than $350,000. Mechanics largely furnish their own hand tools, and the more experienced ones also start buying some of their test gear as well.

Most of Carolina Aero's business comes from corporate customers rather than business and pleasure aircraft owners. "Image" is an important attraction to the corporate clientele. "Image means a neat, well-organized shop, and professional-looking technicians. We have lots of competition in this area," Louganis points out. "Our company sends out a newsletter (called 'Carolina Calling') promoting business, and we do place some ads in trade magazines, but most of our new business comes from word of mouth. Satisfied customers have been our best advertisement."

Mr. George Stephano, president of Carolina Aero, is on the aviation advisory committee of a nearby community college which offers an A&P program. Louganis has hired a number of their graduates over the years and presently has four students working part-time in a cooperative education program.

During the past year, Carolina Aero has developed a number of systems training boards, engine cut-a-ways, and several other training aids for the school on a cost plus labor basis. Word has gotten out and Carolina Aero has received inquiries from several other schools offering flight and maintenance programs regarding the possibility of developing training aids for them. Stephano is quite excited about the idea and is thinking about developing a separate company called Carolina Tech-Aids. In a memo to Louganis, the president described the tremendous market potential that has relatively little competiton.

Recognizing the president's enthusiasm, Jim Louganis wants to develop a well thought-out explanation of why he cannot get very excited about the proposal. He knows he and his mechanics are already overworked and could not possibly redirect personnel and resources at this time. Furthermore, there has been no mention of how Carolina Tech-Aids would be promoted, exactly which training aids are in demand and by whom.

QUESTION:

1. Evaluate this situation. What would you advise Jim Louganis to say and do?

14. CASE ANALYSIS—PACIFIC JET SALES

Pacific Jet Sales is a large distributor of corporate jet aircraft with facilities at five major airports in the western United States. It is attempting to increase its market penetration for a particular model. The company enlisted a marketing research firm to conduct focus group interviews with several corporate jet owners and a number of potential owners. A focus group interview involves interviewing 6 to 10 people in an informal group setting. When open-ended questions are used, the interviewer attempts to get group interaction to stimulate thinking and get immediate reactions. The results of these qualitative studies were reported to Pacific's management in late 2001. Pacific intended to use this information to devise marketing plans and strategy for 2002 and 2003.

The focus group found that with corporate jet owners, the purchase process is often begun by the CEO, a board member, or a pilot. Some respondents reported that a salesperson for an aircraft manufacturer was the stimulus for action.

Most owners and potential owners of corporate jets indicated that the CEO is central in the decision on whether to buy a jet or not. Other very important people in this decision are the chief financial officer of the company and sometimes certain members of the board of directors.

Several members of the focus groups were corporate pilots. They wanted to know not only about certain features of the equipment, but also operating characteristics such as range with various loads, minimum runway requirements, and fuel burn rates. Training capability was also important to these individuals. They stated that the pilot often has veto power over purchase decisions and may have a strong influence on which model is chosen. If the pilot does not like one model of airplane, this individual can stop the purchase. It appears from the focus group results that the pilot often controls the flow of information about corporate jets within the organization.

The corporate legal staff is usually involved in formulating the purchase agreement. The actual acquisition of the jet is done by the purchasing department. However, these departments have little to say about whether the plane will be purchased or what type of plane is actually bought.

The respondents in the focus group indicated that middle and upper management are the ones who most often use the plane. Sometimes important customers and board members also make use of the plane. The general advice of these individuals is sought at some point in the purchase decision process. The actual decision making on the part of the companies takes between three and six months. They usually do not come to a purchase decision in fewer than three months. The nonowners in the focus group generally thought they would follow the pattern of those who had purchased in the past. However, they were not really sure how the decision making would occur within their organizations.

Pacific sold 8 corporate jets during the first 10 months of 2001 and expects at least 2 more sales by year-end. It hopes to sell at least 12 during 2002 and 16 in 2003. Management was scheduled for a major meeting to discuss the results of the marketing research study.

QUESTIONS:

1. How does the "buying center" (people who participate in or influence a purchase) and the various roles relate to the purchase of a corporate jet?
2. What type of decision process is used for corporations in buying an airplane such as this?
3. How should Pacific Jet Sales segment the market?
4. What general advice would you give for developing a marketing strategy based on the focus group results?

15. CASE ANALYSIS—ONE-STOP SHOPPING AT SEMINOLE AVIATION

One-stop shopping has come to Seminole Aviation at Executive Airport in Fort Lauderdale. Through the Seminole Preferred program, customers at Seminole can get their rental cars and their hotel keys by simply stopping at the FBO's flight desk.

"They (customers) do not have to wait in lines," says Pete Rotavonni, sales manager for Seminole.

"They have one contact point; that's our flight desk." A lot of FBOs have preferred hotels but nobody had one-stop check-in.

"The last thing they want to do is wait in three or four lines: our desk, the car rental desk, and the front desk of the hotel. With our program, they've only had to sign two forms at our desk and they're gone. They can go right to their rooms."

The Seminole Preferred program invites flight crews to sign up by supplying their credit card information, driver's license data, telephone number, and mailing address. This information is entered into the computer so that when the individual calls ahead, Seminol's customer service people can call up the information and make the necessary arrangements for a car rental and hotel check-in.

Through a previous arrangement, the hotels have agreed to supply Seminole with room keys, and the on-site car rental agency supplies the cars.

"The hotels initially had problems with giving us hotel keys, from a security point of view," Rotavonni says. "But we made them realize that if people can trust us with their $20 million airplanes, we can certainly be trusted with their hotel rooms. Once that hurdle was cleared, the program has been working fantastically."

"It's one of those programs in which we really have something to sell to people rather than just giving discounts on gas," Ratavonni says. "We say this as a value-added service because we didn't have to lower our yields to attract people. It increased the value of our FBO and, really, it doesn't cost us any money."

QUESTIONS:

1. Seminole now wants to broaden the program beyond rental cars and hotel rooms. Can you think of additional products and/ or services that a flight crew and its passengers might need while visiting the Fort Lauderdale area?
2. After you have identified additional vendors in the area and evaluated their product and service, what might they offer to attract Seminole's customers?
3. How should Seminole market its one-stop shopping program to existing and potential customers?
4. What are the advantages of one-stop shopping for Seminole's customers?

16. CASE ANALYSIS—QUALITY CHEMICAL—FROM FLIGHT DEPARTMENT TO CHARTER

Bill Smith, director of flight operations for Quality Chemical (formerly American Distillers and Chemical Corp.), has seen corporate aviation from both sides—first from his decades as pilot, chief pilot, and aviation manager of a blue-chip flight department, and now as a coordinator of its air transport charters.

Since 1998, when American Distillers elected to terminate its 36-year term as a corporate airplane operator, Smith has been running its planeless aviation department as its charter manager, serving as the company's agent for booking aircraft charter flights.

Of course he misses running a sizeable flight department with 18 employees, and he misses flying the Gulfstream IIs and IIIs the company used to have—but he doesn't miss all the headaches. "I don't have to worry whether the grass around the hangar is mowed, if the ramp is plowed, or if the roof leaks." Smith and Quality's board of directors also no longer need worry about the costs of running a flight department, one of the first areas board members and company stockholders tend to scrutinize when cutting back on company expenses.

The decision by Quality's chairman, John Rodriquez, to sell its aircraft and hangar was based on economics, Smith said, and coincided with the company's change of business strategy. The company was also divested of all of its beverage line—which included Grapeland Wines, Gloster's Gin, and Old Southern Bourbon—that accounted for its name. "When Mr. Rodriquez made the decision to close the flight department, he called me into his office and said, 'We've run a world-class operation for 36 years. Now we are going to run a world-class aviation department without airplanes,' " Smith recalled.

Although Quality's business direction has changed, its travel requirements have not gone away. Quality is broken into two operations—the executive offices located in New York City and the chemical group based in Cincinnati, Ohio—and corporate executives constantly travel between the two. In addition, the Cincinnati-based chemists usually visit Quality plants located throughout the United States. Smith coordinates the charter flights for both the New York and Cincinnati operations. "Charter is the only way to go," he said. "There are too many delays with the airlines. Time is extremely valuable to our employees. We need them."

As an example, Smith recalled a recent early morning chemical spill from a railroad tank car in Maryland. The spill threatened a nearby stream. "Our crisis management team in Houston called me at 1 a.m. and told me that people were needed on the spot quickly," he said. "Within three hours we had someone on the scene coordinating the clean-up efforts. That would not have been possible had I relied on the airlines."

At the beginning of this year, Smith projected that Quality's managers and executives would fly an average of 60 hours per month on charter aircraft. His prediction was wrong. "For the first four months of 2002, we have been averaging 86 hours per month," he said. Because of the number of hours, Quality may soon decide to lease an airplane, Smith said. "When you lease an airplane, you can identify with it. You have your choice of interior decor and paint, scheme, and a dedicated crew. That would be ideal." But rather than reorganizing a flight department, Quality will go the management route. "It would be the best of both worlds for the corporation to have its own airplane and have a charter/management group take charge of it," he said.

Smith sees more businesses turning to charter/management operators to act as their flight departments over the next decade. "It's becoming more and more the corporate way," he explained. "Operating a full-blown flight department has always been a concern of a company's stockholders because of the costs involved." But he conceded large, established corporate flight departments will remain.

Smith, who holds several aviation safety records, does not fly as much as he did when he was Quality's chief pilot and flight department manager. However, he stays current in the Gulfstream. "Quality has allowed me to be a standby pilot for another major corporation [in its Gulfstream]," he said. He added that all training costs are picked up by Quality.

While Smith cites the advantages of chartering as opposed to running a flight department or using the airlines, a second blue chip corporation's pilot, Bob Williams, had opposite feelings. "When you're a 135 operator, you're a mini-airline," said the pilot, whose company maintains a flight department and also charters out its aircraft through a charter/management firm. "There is an enormous number of rules and regulations regarding charter. Part 91 flight planning is easier. No flight releases need to be obtained."

Also, Williams indicated, "there is more time to prepare for a Part 91 flight," unlike the "spur-of-the-moment" preparation for a charter trip. "We usually get a day or two's notice for a domestic Part 91 trip," he said, "and international trips are known weeks in advance. This makes it easier to get visas."

The company for whom the pilot works owns and operates the aircraft and flies some 250 hours a year under Part 91. Over the past two years, the aircraft has averaged some 450 hours per year flying under Part 135 operations. The aircraft has a dedicated crew with the same pilots flying for both Part 91 and 135 operations. Maintenance, he said, is handled by mechanics employed by the corporation.

The company, he said, has run its own flight department for a number of years but could no longer justify the expense, hence the decision to add extra revenue through charter. The aircraft, in order to comply with Part 135 regulations, needed to be fire blocked, but, Williams said the company is not apprehensive about doing it. "It was something that had to be done in order for us to stay in business."

There have been times, Williams said, when a company trip conflicted with a charter flight. "The boss then has to make a decision," he said. "Does he tell the charter people 'no' or does he cancel his own trip?"

Keeping control of the company aircraft is important to him, Williams said. "As the sole pilot [in command] of the aircraft, I have a vested interest in it and in the company. Our mechanics maintain the aircraft. I shop around for discounts and the mechanics look for the best prices on parts and equipment. Anything I can do to save money for the company, I'll do."

QUESTIONS:

1. Discuss the advantages and disadvantages of chartering aircraft. Should Quality consider leasing an aircraft at this time? Explain. What are some of the reasons why Quality might choose an aircraft management firm?
2. Mr. Williams's firm decided to charter its aircraft in order to supplement the number of flying hours and justify ownership of the aircraft. What are the advantages and disadvantages of this arrangement?

17. CASE ANALYSIS—AERO FUELING SERVICES CO., INC.

The Aero Fueling Services Company is a large, well-known corporate aircraft fueling operation with facilities at nine major airports across the United States. The company is recognized throughout the GA industry for its outstanding service and excellent facilities for corporate customers including lounges, meeting rooms, and accommodations for crew members during layovers. Aero's fuel prices tended to be on the high side which was justified by management because of the high costs associated with providing above average products, services, and personnel. Unfortunately, their prices had not reflected the downward trend in prices during recent years, and as a result the company lost an alarming amount of business, particularly single-engine and light-twin business aircraft, to a number of aggressive FBOs who competed largely on price.

Bob Hagelberger, director of marketing for Aero, decided to initiate a sales promotion campaign for six months in which pilots would receive a certificate for 35 cents a gallon off their next fuel purchase. Each certificate indicated how many gallons of fuel were purchased and the dollar amount to be applied to the next purchase. Every time the aircraft was refueled at an Aero facility, the pilot would redeem the certificate and be issued a new one for the subsequent purchase. Aero would keep a record of the transactions on its computer, and at the end of each month during the six-month period, pilots reaching a certain minimum gallonage, which varied by type of aircraft, would receive a notice in the mail advising that they were eligible for various gifts which included pilot supplies, pen and pencil sets, TVs, radios, VCRs, and airline tickets. Pilots could claim a gift which represented a certain number of points or let their point total accumulate for a more expensive gift.

Hagelberger expected to launch a national advertising campaign in selected aviation trade magazines which would highlight his campaign. In addition, an extensive list of former, present, and potential customers from each location would be developed for a mailing campaign.

One reason why Hagelberger wanted to initiate this sales promotion campaign was to test the price elasticity of demand (consumer responsiveness to price changes) in various markets. Results of the six-month campaign would also determine whether or not it was worth continuing. To make such a decision, Hagelberger felt that a study at the end of six months would have to gather the following two types of information.

1. The study should measure the awareness of and trial of the sales promotion campaign. It should also measure the price elasticity of demand before and after the campaign.
2. The study should measure the extent to which different market segments (single-engine and multiengine aircraft owners, turbine aircraft operators, etc.) were influenced by the sales promotion campaign.

QUESTION:
1. Design a personal interview questionnaire for use in the study to measure the effectiveness of the campaign. Explain how the use of your questionnaire will obtain the information requested by Hagelberger.

18. CASE ANALYSIS—EXECUTIVE CHARTER SERVICE

The Executive Charter Service had been operating for 10 years, offering transportation services from a very active general aviation airport located in the suburbs of a large southeastern metropolitan area. The company has managed a modest profit every year in spite of the existence of two major competitors, both larger than Executive Charter. The current year's record, however, showed not only a decline in rates and a 10 percent drop in the number of hours flown, but also an increasing number of complaints by customers.

Last year, John Archibald, president of Executive Charter, and Gerry Pucci, his marketing manager, launched an advertising campaign for "Buy-a-block of hours" designed to increase their charter business. The Buy-a-block theme promised fast, dependable service at sliding scale discounts for firms buying 50 or more charter hours in advance. The campaign caught on and in the first two months, many new customers called Executive Charter for service. Management was pleased with initial results, but because of the sudden strain on a barely adequate fleet of aircraft, service proved quite unreliable. Half of Executive Charter's aircraft were over eight years old and subject to maintenance problems. The company simply did not have enough aircraft in operation to meet the sudden demand yet maintain good service to regular customers and on-demand service.

Archibald had approved the Buy-a-block campaign concept and the funds requested by the marketing manager for use on radio and newspaper advertising. It was by far the largest advertising expenditure ever undertaken by Executive Charter, although the company had rarely advertised in the past except in the telephone yellow pages. Little thought, however, had been given to anticipating the effects of a successful advertising campaign.

The maintenance manager had not been consulted or advised of a possible increase in the maintenance work and was short two mechanics during the first month of the new service. The flight department had hired only one new part-time pilot for the campaign. The resulting service to customers was poor. Quite frequently aircraft were late or not available, resulting in complaints and loss of some old customers. With the increased flying hours, maintenance work increased, and the mechanics could not handle it, despite additional overtime.

Archibald was puzzled by the fact that an advertising campaign with such great initial response had fizzled into a loss as year's end approached. After charter hours had increased 20 percent during the first three months of the campaign, they declined 10 percent the last three months of the year. Archibald was also besieged by more problems and bickering from his various departments than he had ever experienced in his 10 years of running the charter company. Life had become one crisis after another, with constant equipment problems resulting in disgruntled employees and angry customers. In the past, his management philosophy had been characterized by delegating most of the operating decisions to the department heads. "I don't tell Pucci about marketing, Benson about flight operations, or Grumbach about maintenance. My role is to formulate policy and handle problems as they arise."

Chaos had developed from what had first appeared to be a highly effective advertising campaign that seemed sure to elevate Executive Charter's position in the local charter market. Archibald knew things just could not be allowed to continue this way. Something had to be done.

QUESTIONS:
1. What problems face Executive Charter Service?
2. Identify the major facts and evaluate the alternatives.
3. Recommend an appropriate course of action for Archibald.

19. CASE ANALYSIS—AEROSTAR MANUFACTURING COMPANY

In 2002 Aerostar Manufacturing Company, a U.S. manufacturer of the popular Twin-Engine Airwagon, was planning a four-pronged segmented advertising approach to reach the various market groups influential in the purchase of its aircraft. The Airwagon is powered by two Pratt & Whitney PT6A-112 engines that develop 500 mhp each. It has a useful load of 4,400 lbs., a payload of 2,800 lbs. in cargo or passengers. The aircraft has a quick change capability for all-cargo or a passenger configuration offering 14 seats. A four-foot by four-foot cargo door expedites loading of bulk packages. Maximum range at 280 mph cruise, with fuel reserves, is 1,000 miles. The unit price is approximately $1 million.

Mr. Jack Bowater, account executive for the Aerostar account at the Sullivan Advertising Agency, commented on the segmented approach as follows:

"This segmented idea evolved for two reasons. First, we're trying to service the specific needs of each specific market by directing each program straight at the heart of the market. This means a carefully thought out copy approach and media selection for each market. Secondly, as Aerostar introduces new products over time, we find ourselves in new markets with new needs which we haven't had to hit previously. For example, the commuter market is quite new for us and it dictates an approach completely different from anything we've ever used to sell executive aircraft."

The 2002 Aerostar advertising budget of $900,000 was devoted entirely to national print media. In addition, the company spent approximately 10 percent of this sum to produce sales promotion aids and literature, along with another 15 percent for various trade shows, exhibits, and sales promotion meetings.

The 2003 segmented advertising program was presented to Aerostar management in october 2002 by Mr. Bowater. The following comments were made regarding each of the segmented markets:

1. Corporate/Executive Market

Since 95 percent of Aerostar sales went to corporations rather than individuals, this was regarded as the single most important market segment. Mr. Bowater stated: "This is the audience that represents the greatest sales potential. These are the corporate executives—the company presidents and administrative officers—the top-income people who guide the affairs and destinies of their companies. These people have varied experience, and some are very sophisticated about airplanes, having owned and used them in their business. Many even have fleets of corporate aircraft, but others have never owned airplanes and know very little about them." He went on to point out that "our advertising must talk to both groups . . . telling them how the Airwagon will solve their own particular problems." Magazines that are synonymous with quality and success have been used in the past. "What better place for airplanes that also stand for quality and success," he told the Aerostar management team in attendance.

2. Commuter Airline Market

Aerostar has sold some aircraft to this growing market. Bowater pointed out that "we've had to learn a brand new language to properly address this market. Aerostar has literally entered the airline business—impressively—with a brand new model that solves commuter airline problems as they have never been solved before. The Airwagon is designed to meet the unique demand of commuter airlines."

Our audience for this new product includes air taxi operators, commuter and regional air carriers, and cargo and mail carriers, as well as investors and business people who are considering the purchase of aircraft for leasing to the aforementioned carriers.

3. Aerospace and Military Market

This campaign began several years ago to convince the defense/aerospace market of Aerostar's technical competence. "In the past, we have used a variety of publications to reach this very sophisticated and diversified audience," Bowater stated. "The combination of these publications blankets all of the military services . . . the scientists . . . engineers and technicians of the vast NASA complexes . . . the Department of Defense, and the key corporations that are suppliers to both military and aerospace services."

4. International Business Market

Overseas, Aerostar uses a simplified segmentation approach similar to its domestic market segmentation. The major difference of course is in language. Bowater pointed out that "we approach each international audience in its native tongue and select publications which are directed at the business community."

QUESTIONS:

1. Please assist Mr. Bowater and the Aerostar marketing staff in identifying publications to be used for each of the four segmented markets.
2. Indicate the primary copy thrust (product features, corporate image, etc.) which you would use in each of the markets.
3. How would you establish a budget for each of the markets?

20. CASE ANALYSIS—PAYTON AVIATION, INC.

Payton Aviation is a successful and innovative FBO located at one of the busiest GA airports in the Los Angeles area. Founded by Ken Payton in the 1960s, it has grown into a full service operation including aircraft sales and service, parts for Piper and Cessna products, a busy charter department with everything from 172s to Lear jets on the flight line, ground and flight training from Private to the ATP (and Lear Type ratings), and aircraft rental of some 30 aircraft.

One of the most profitable and fastest growing areas in recent years has been the sale of pilot supplies and other aviation related paraphernalia. In addition to two display cases in the main lobby, Payton has set up an aviation store, called "Plane Things," with two separate entrances, one off the lobby and the other directly from the parking lot. The store includes another three cases plus book racks, wall displays, and clothing racks.

As assistant manager of Payton's flight school, Linda Inciardi is charged with a variety of responsibilities, one of which is to manage the flight desk and Plane Things. The firm recently installed a computerized system of sales tracking, making it easy to determine what is selling and what is not. Inciardi says the computer allows Payton to track sales of each item, helping determine which products to buy and how many of each to stock.

Payton's counter displays are fairly aggressive in that they offer more than the usual array of charts, plotters, and manuals. Under Inciardi's direction, Payton stocks a little of everything from earplugs, computers, and sunglasses, to headsets, flight jackets, and even full Jeppesen pilot navaid subscriptions. As a long-time Cessna dealer, Payton carries a fairly complete selection of flight manuals to cover its most popular brands of aircraft rentals.

There is also an assortment of vanity items: wearing apparel, such as sweaters, T-shirts, jump suits, jackets, and shirts. Prominently displayed in Plane Things are a wide variety of aviation books, airplane models, brief cases, wall clocks, pictures, desk sets, and other gift items.

The company normally has two special seasonal promotions. One is a summer clearance sale and the other is a Christmas promotion. At Christmas, the company not only adds to its inventory but also exhibits many gift items. These include glassware, Christmas tree ornaments, calendars, watches, pen and pencil sets, and similar items.

Payton diminishes its tracking problems by ordering the bulk of its items from central distribution houses, rather than from many individual manufacturers. The houses can supply several different companies' products with one order.

Originally designed for rental and training customers, the store now caters to outside customers from surrounding communities and airline passengers who see Payton's advertisement in the terminal building. There are two commuter air carriers which operate from this field and the terminal building is only a short walk from the entrance to Plane Things.

Linda Inciardi is in the process of developing the store's first catalog which she plans to send to present and former customers of Payton Aviation. Catalogs will also be available in the terminal area for interested airline passengers.

QUESTIONS:
1. Can you think of any specific target markets which might be appropriate for Payton's catalog?
2. Which publications might be used for advertising the catalog's availability?
3. How might the catalog be used to advertise the flight school?

21. CASE ANALYSIS—QUALITY AIRCRAFT SALES AND LEASING CO.

Paul Rose, vice president of marketing for the Quality Aircraft Sales and Leasing Company of Chicago, Illinois, knew he had to make a decision to select a sales manager for the company's 16-person sales force. Seven months previously, the former sales manager had resigned to accept a vice presidency of sales for a smaller competitor. During the last few months, Rose had assumed direct control of the sales forces, but he clearly saw that in doing so he was not only neglecting his other responsibilities, but also was doing a poor job of managing the sales force.

Quality Aircraft Sales and Leasing Company conducted a worldwide operation from its Chicago headquarters and two regional offices, one in New York City and the other in Los Angeles. Serving primarily as an aircraft broker, Quality was also a major engine and parts supplier to a variety of clients including airlines, corporate operators, and foreign governments. The sales manager worked out of the Chicago office, which included five representatives, and primarily concentrated on the domestic market, Canada, and the Caribbean. The Los Angeles office was base for seven representatives including one individual who was located in Tokyo. This office handled the Pacific basin and Central and South America. It was also the fastest growing and most profitable office. Four representatives reported to the New York office, although one was based in Frankfurt and another in London.

The sales manager was charged with the full responsibility for maintaining an effective field sales force. This included hiring, firing, training, supervising, compensating, controlling, and evaluating the sales force. Moreover, he was responsible for all the paper work connected with the sales department. At times he had to work closely with the sales reps in handling special accounts or particularly important deals. There was a senior representative in each of the offices to assist the sales reps in particular business situations, but they had no organizational authority over these individuals. The sales manager spent about half of his time away from the Chicago office. The job required an extensive amount of traveling. He reported directly to Rose.

Rose's search for a new manager had narrowed down to two men, Russ Sheldon and Jim Woida, both of whom were seemingly well qualified for the job. Rose had taken the files on the two prospective managers home for the weekend to contemplate his decision. He had decided to announce his selection Monday morning.

As he reviewed Russ Sheldon's file, he fully realized that if Sheldon was not made sales manager, some repercussions might be felt. Russ was not only one of the best sales representatives, but also was well regarded throughout the organization. Sheldon, now 39 years old, had been with the company for close to 20 years, having started as a line boy in their FBO division located at a major eastern airport. He had attended a community college for about a year but directed most of his time, money, and attention to acquiring various pilot licenses and ratings and accumulating hours. He was subsequently hired by the corporate flight department and spent close to eight years flying various types of equipment for several corporations which had a contract with Quality for flight service. He transferred to the New York City sales division where he worked for the previous sales manager for four years before moving to Chicago as senior representative when his boss was promoted to sales manager for the company. He had been in the Chicago office for close to six years, except for a nine-month period when he opened the company's Los Angeles office. Russ had hired several of the representatives for that office including the present senior representative. Since the sales force was paid on a salary plus commission basis, Russ had become moderately wealthy. His annual earnings had been about $85,000 over the past several years. In fact, the sales manager position paid a flat salary which was negotiable but probably would be from $75,000 to $80,000.

Sheldon was married to an understanding woman of considerable charm. Their two children were in high school and, to Rose's knowledge, were outstanding youngsters. The Sheldons were extremely adept at entertaining and socializing. Hardly a week passed that they did not have some type of social event in their home.

Although Sheldon had very little college background, Rose knew he was intelligent, motivated, and had acquired considerable business know-how. Upon learning of the previous sales manager's resignation, Sheldon had come directly to Rose and requested the position. He outlined his achievements for the company and then gave a brief account of the goals that he would work toward as manager. Rose recalled acknowledging at the time that Sheldon was certainly a prime candidate for the job and that he could be assured he would be given every consideration. However, Rose had told Sheldon that the decision was not entirely his (Rose's) to make. The president had suggested that a thorough search be made in order to assure that the best person available was placed in the position.

Privately, Rose had some reservations about making Sheldon sales manager, but he was hesitant to bring his thoughts into the open for fear of engendering animosities that would later haunt him. First, he was fearful that if he promoted Sheldon he would lose a good salesman and might get a poor manager. He had seen it happen in other companies, and sales management literature was full of warnings that top salesmen might not make good sales managers. The two jobs required different skills. Second, Rose was worried that Sheldon would find the sales manager's salary inadequate, despite his insistence that he would be more than happy with it. Third, he was afraid that because Sheldon enjoyed customer contact, he would not like the paper work and personnel problems associated with the sales manager position. Finally, Rose was a little concerned by Sheldon's relationships with the other representatives; he was well liked by everyone and was known as "a guy who would give you the shirt off his back." Would Sheldon be able to maintain discipline among the sales force?

Rose proceeded to review his other leading candidate, Jim Woida, with whom he had been acquainted for more than four years. They were both members of the Chicago Sales Executives Club, the Glen Ridge Country Club, and were very active in the Greater Chicago Aviation Association. Woida was a sales manager for a larger midwest aircraft distributor and had developed an enviable reputation in the industry for building an outstanding sales force. Woida was 33 years old, married with three young children, had a college degree in aviation management, and had an extensive flight background. He had taken several graduate courses in management over the years. While he had a most agreeable disposition, all evidence indicated that he ran a tight ship. He demanded high performance and got it. Rose had casually mentioned the job opening to Woida one day at the club, on the off chance that he might know some outstanding person he could recommend for the job. Woida had hesitated for a moment, then replied, "Let's have a drink. I think we should talk."

He then confided that his firm was about to be sold, and from what he had learned about it, he was somewhat less enthralled about his potential bosses. "They are not my kind of people," he went on to say. "From what I know of you and your operation, I think I would like very much to be considered for the job."

Rose sat for two hours contemplating the pros and cons for each man. He was still undecided.

QUESTION:

1. Which person would you select as sales manager? Why?

Appendix D

Three Week On-site Training Program for a New Aircraft Salesperson

FIRST WEEK

Date Complete

Monday

1. Tour the facilities, which includes an introduction of the sales representative to key _____
   personnel. Salesperson should learn:
   a. Who does what.
   b. Where it is done.
   c. Where to get answers to questions.
   d. Where help is available when it's needed.

2. Review company organization, rules, and regulations: _____
   a. Who reports to whom?
   b. What authority do they have over the salesperson?
   c. What's expected from the salesperson?
   d. What the salesperson can expect from the company.

3. Study salesperson's job description and compensation plan: _____
   a. Salesperson's responsibilities and authority.
   b. Compensation plan.
      1. How commissions are computed.
      2. When and how commissions are paid.

4. Review opportunities for advancement and/or personal and financial growth. _____

5. Conduct an open discussion period to answer salesperson's questions. _____

Tuesday

1. Discuss company's short- and long-term objectives. _____

2. Study company's "area of responsibility." _____
   a. Distributor's retail area.
   b. Dealer areas and responsibilities.
   c. Area and product assignments of other salespersons.

3. Tour the nearest dealer facility. _____
   a. Become acquainted with dealer personnel.
   b. Understand how distributor and dealer coordinate retail sales activities.

Wednesday

1. Study product brochures and underline important product benefits. _____

2. Study the Sales Data Handbook: _____
   a. Demonstrate ability to answer technical questions using the handbook as an aid.
   b. Demonstrate ability to compute operating costs using the computation guides in
      the handbook.

3. Make a sales call (as observer only) with an experienced aircraft salesperson. _____

4. Critique the sales call with the experienced salesperson and the sales manager: _____
   a. What was the sales call objective?
   b. Was that objective achieved?
   c. Identify problems encountered in the call.
   d. Explain attempted method of solving the problems.

Thursday 1. Study Pilots' Handbooks. _____

2. Study Performance & Specifications data. _____

3. Observe walk-around ground presentation by experienced salesperson. _____

4. Prepare personal checklist for walk-around ground presentations of aircraft. _____

5. Practice the walk-around ground presentation of aircraft. _____

6. Make a ground walk-around presentation of aircraft to the sales manager or sales trainer. _____

Friday *1. Study flight demonstration manual. _____

*2. Receive a flight demonstration by an experienced demonstration pilot. _____

*3. Restudy flight demonstration techniques manual and prepare notes for personal flight demonstration regimen. _____

Saturday *1. Give flight demonstration of aircraft to sales manager. _____

*2. Critique flight demonstration with sales manager. _____

*The training schedule can be interrupted at any convenient point to provide necessary flight proficiency training for the new salesperson.

SECOND WEEK

Monday 1. Study local prospect control system. Salesperson should know: _____
   a. How prospect records are maintained:
      1. By the company.
      2. By the salesperson.
   b. Sales call reporting procedures.
   c. How sales activities are coordinated.

2. Become familiar with on-site prospect reference and qualifying materials: _____
   a. Records of aircraft owners.
   b. Standard reference materials.

3. Learn how to qualify prospects for: _____
   a. Need for an airplane.
   b. Ability to buy an airplane.
   c. Desire for an airplane.

4. After a study period, provide the sales manager with: _____
   a. A walk-around ground presentation of the airplane.
   b. A flight demonstration of the airplane.

5. Critique the above presentations with the sales manager. _____

Tuesday

1. Practice walk-around demonstration and flight demonstration of the airplane. _____

2. Select five good prospects from records of current aircraft owners and explain your choice to the sales manager. _____

3. Visit the main local library and research the "five good prospects" to obtain precall information. Salesperson should know: _____
   a. The names and titles of key company officials.
   b. The type of business activity.
   c. The ability of the company to buy a business airplane.
   d. The company's probable travel patterns as indicated by:
      1. Branch offices.
      2. Geographical areas covered.
      3. Industry distribution methods and patterns.

Wednesday

1. Make a sales call (as observer only) with an experienced aircraft salesperson. This sales call should be a first-time call on an aircraft owner. _____

2. Critique sales call with the experienced aircraft salesperson and the sales manager. _____

3. Use the study period to outline presentation intended for the salesperson's first call on an aircraft owner. _____

4. Observe experienced salesperson making telephone calls for appointments. _____

5. Outline telephone presentation to be made when asking for appointments. _____

6. Set up first sales call appointment by telephoning one or more of the selected "five best prospects." _____

Thursday

1. Practice walk-around and flight demonstration procedures. _____

2. Make first "solo" sales call on one of the "five best prospects." _____

3. Critique sales call with the sales manager. _____

4. Study procedures used to write up an aircraft sales order. _____

Friday

1. Study aircraft leasing and financing procedures: _____
   a. Complete dummy lease agreement form.
   b. Complete dummy finance agreement form.

2. Accompany an experienced salesperson (as an observer only) on a "second or third-time sales call." _____

3. Critique the above sales call with the experienced salesperson and the sales manager. _____

Saturday	1. Review week's activities with the sales manager. _____
	2. Research and select "five nonowner prospects" at the public library. _____

THIRD WEEK

Monday	1. Discuss the "five nonowner prospects" with the sales manager and defend their selection. _____

	2. Attempt to make telephone appointments with: _____
	    a. Five nonowner prospects.
	    b. Or five best owner prospects.

	3. Make sales calls and/or demonstrations. _____

Tuesday	1. Study used aircraft market: _____
	    a. Blue books.
	    b. Company appraising techniques and procedures.
	    c. Company policies on trade-ins.

	2. Accompany an experienced salesperson (as an observer only) on a used-aircraft sales call. _____
	3. Critique the above sales call with the experienced salesperson and the sales manager. _____
	4. Make sales calls and/or demonstrations. _____
Wednesday	1. Continue prospecting activities. _____
	2. Make sales calls and/or demonstrations. _____
	3. Study the preparation of a written proposal and prepare a sample proposal. _____
Thursday	1. Practice demonstration techniques . . . ground and flight. _____
	2. Study comparative merits of own and competitive aircraft. _____
	3. Make sales call with the sales manager as an observer. _____
Friday	1. Build a qualified prospect list of 20 aircraft owners and 5 nonowners. Defend selections with the sales manager. _____
Saturday	1. Review entire training schedule with sales manager and identify areas that need further study and practice. _____

Normally a sales manager will conduct in-depth interviews with the new salesperson at least once each week during the three-week training program. After several months on the job new salespersons are generally sent to one of the manufacturers' schools for one of the many professional sales techniques courses.

Index